To Kim and Robbie

Contents

ATTITUDES

ATTITUDES

SECOND EDITION

D. W. Rajecki
Indiana University–Purdue University at Indianapolis

SINAUER ASSOCIATES, INC. PUBLISHERS
Sunderland, Massachusetts

Library of Congress Cataloging-in-Publication Data

Rajecki, D. W., 1939–
    Attitudes / D. W. Rajecki.—2nd ed.
       p. cm.
    Rev. ed. of: Attitudes, themes and advances. c1982.
    Includes bibliographical references.
    ISBN 0-87893-786-2 : $24.95
    1. Public opinion.   2. Attitude (Psychology) I. Rajecki, D. W.,
1939–   Attitudes, themes and advances. II. Title.
HM261.R36   1990
303.3′8—dc20   89-38465
                                                     CIP

Printed in U.S.A.

9 8 7 6 5 4 3 2

Preface

Different social scientists study different attitudes for different reasons. Moreover, they bring to their endeavors a wide variety of theories and methods. Because the concept of attitude is important to many disciplines, a large number of energetic workers are involved. Science on such a scale can be gratifying, but it can also be overwhelming and confusing.

My own way of sorting things out is to see various approaches to the field of attitudes as ranging from the narrow to the broad. That is, I try to identify and keep in mind the level of analysis of a particular study or theory. An allusion to biology will help clarify my meaning. Some biologists work at the level of the cell. Others work with more complicated, multicellular entities called tissues. Still others study interrelated structures of tissues called organs. Finally some biologists deal with total assemblages of organs called organisms. All of these people are concerned with the same thing—biology—but each has her or his preferred level of analysis. Some look at things from a presumably narrow (cellular) and some from a presumably broad (organismic) perspective.

By analogy, one can view particular areas of theory and research on attitudes as falling at a certain level of analysis, or at least at some point on a narrow-to-broad dimension. This assumption is the basis for the organization of the five units within this book. Briefly, Unit 1 (Chapters 1 and 2) is concerned with the functions, structures, and measurement of attitudes per se, and the focus there is necessarily narrow. Next, Unit 2 (Chapters 3 and 4) takes up the somewhat broader matter of the relationship of attitudes to behavior. Following that, Unit 3 (Chapters 5, 6, and 7) deals with medium-range theories about three fairly specific attitudinal phenomena: the effects of repeated exposure to an attitudinal object, the influence of group discussion, and a phenomenon called cognitive dissonance. In turn, Unit 4 (Chapters 8, 9, and 10) speaks to quite broad attitudinal matters that impinge on us frequently in our daily social lives: intergroup biases, persuasive communications, and attitudes toward the self. Finally, Unit 5 (Chapters 11 and 12) presents the widest vista of all, with an analysis of the influence of mass media and an examination of public opinion about national matters.

Now, no one would claim that the structure I have placed on this book's contents in any way approaches the elegance found in biology.

However, that parallel is still useful. Consider a laboratory biologist studying the internal mechanisms of a cell. For all I know, it may not matter to that scientist whether the cell came from a cat or a mouse. On the other hand, a field biologist studying a cat stalking a mouse is doubtless oblivious to any given cell in either animal. The importance of their respective areas notwithstanding, these two biologists may have very little to say to one another regarding their work.

The reader will discover a similar irony at places in this text. On the one hand, a social scientist who is interested in the internal (intrapsychic) dynamics of attitudes may not care what the attitudinal object is—it might just as easily be abortion or anchovy pizza. On the other hand, some other social scientist who is concerned with the success and failure of American presidents might be utterly indifferent to intrapsychic processes and concentrate exclusively on the opinions of large aggregates of the population. As in the case of the two biologists, these two social scientists may have little to say to one another, scientifically speaking.

The object lesson to be learned here is that the units of this book are not interchangeable, and no given unit necessarily reduces to some other unit. Given the state of the art, the units are perhaps best thought of as free-standing. However, I am sure that both of the hypothetical biologists in the example above were contributing to our understanding of life on earth, and I am equally sure that all of the researchers represented in this book have made significant contributions to our understanding of attitudes.

Acknowledgments

I am indebted to many people for their help in the preparation of this text. First and foremost I wish to acknowledge the book's reviewers: Icek Ajzen, Steven J. Breckler, John F. Dovidio, and John B. McConahay. The special assistance of Drew C. Appleby, Robert F. Bornstein, and Paula M. Niedenthal is also appreciated.

Research for the volume was made easier and more pleasurable by the significant contribution of the staff of the IUPUI Science and Engineering Library, especially Jean Gnat, William F. Mayles, Lynn Carson, Randi L. Stocker, Ann Koopman, Kari Berger Jahr, Rachel Cleveland, Margaret Vollmer, and Antoinette O'Connor. I am also grateful for the support of Barbara B. Fischler, Director of the IUPUI University Libraries.

Finally, I thank the editorial and production staff of Sinauer Associates, Inc., for their hard work and patience—especially their patience.

THE CONCEPTUALIZATION OF PSYCHOLOGICAL ATTITUDES

What is an apple and why is it not an orange? An apple has a certain shape, color, density, acidity, weight, and other features, all of which can be expressed in numerical terms. The values of these qualities for an apple differ from the respective dimensions of an orange, and it is on this basis that apples and oranges are scientifically discriminated. That is, we cannot really know apples from oranges until we measure them.

Measurement is one of the prime problems in the study of attitudes. A number of solutions to this problem have been offered, and a discussion of these methods is presented in Chapter 1. Areas to be covered include scaling techniques, field-experimental methods, and polls and survey sampling, among others.

The first chapter also includes a traditional definition of attitudes and an outline of their psychological functions. However, definitions and lists of functions do not tell us everything. For instance, a definition of *automobile* is useful in increasing our understanding, but does not tell us much about how the thing actually works. To fully appreciate the nature of an automobile it is necessary to get down to the level of nuts and bolts. The purpose of Chapter 2 is to reach just such a nuts-and-bolts level. The conceptual components of attitudes are introduced, and structural aspects of attitudes are considered.

CHAPTER ONE

OVERVIEW AND METHODS OF ATTITUDE RESEARCH

Consider certain statistics from *The Harper's Index Book* (Lapham, Pollan, and Etheridge, 1987).

- Percentage of Iowans who think music videos are among the "least useful changes" in modern life: 67
- Percentage of Americans who rank Detroit as the nation's worst city: 64
- Percentage of Midwesterners who judge their chances of going to heaven as good to excellent: 69
- Percentage of Americans who say that being single today is "not a fully acceptable life-style": 38
- Percentage of Americans who say the wheel is the greatest invention of all time: 11
- Percentage of Americans who say the United States has never used nuclear weapons in a war: 11
- Percentage of Americans who never read books: 45

What on earth do these wildly disparate (if fascinating) facts have in common? The answer is that they all are expressions or reflections of what are known as social-psychological attitudes.

Why study attitudes? The domain of attitudinal research and theory is so large as to defy an easy answer to this question. One could say that interest in the topic is widespread because so much of our personal and social lives are touched by psychological attitudes. The English language has many words that label and describe such phenomena—like *beliefs, convictions, desires, feelings, hopes, judg-*

3

ments, opinions, sentiments, and *wishes.* It seems that just about everything we experience or do is somehow related to one or another of the words in this list. Why do we sense that we should go to work, brush our teeth, raise a family, save money, be a good neighbor, be kind to animals, dress properly, aspire to an education, or whatever, if it were not for our attitudes?

Another compelling reason for the broad interest in attitudes is implied in the preceding paragraph. There is a pervasive impression in the layperson and the scientist alike that our behavior is influenced by our attitudes, whereby attitude is seen as the cause and behavior is seen as the effect. Because it is the business of psychology to analyze behavior—whether for purposes of understanding or modification—psychological attitudes as causative agents become extremely important elements for study. Of course, it is a matter for research to determine just how closely attitudes and behavior are related, but even if the relationship turns out to be weak under some circumstances, that too would be a matter of considerable interest in understanding our behavior.

Therefore, there is no shortage of reasons for the study of attitudes, and the literature in this area is huge. By way of bringing order to such an immense undertaking, this chapter and the next provide an introduction to some of the basics in the field. The chapter at hand has several parts. To begin, there is a section that attempts to provide a comprehensive working definition of a psychological attitude. Next, there is a section on attitudes and their functions; this unit elaborates how attitudes may serve our psychological needs. Further along, a section on measuring attitudes considers the serious issue of how to quantify and compare (scale) attitudes. Since scientific measurement is at the heart of the issue, several methodologies are discussed, and these are accompanied where appropriate by examples of the types of data each produces. Finally, field-experimental techniques, polls and surveys, and special methods for attitude research are discussed.

Defining Attitudes

Gordon W. Allport, an eminent social psychologist, provided an early and comprehensive definition of attitudes.

An attitude is a mental and neural state of readiness, organized through experience, exerting a directive or dynamic influence upon the individual's response to all objects and situations with which it is related (Allport, 1935).

What follows is a point-by-point look at Allport's definition.

AN ATTITUDE IS A MENTAL AND NEURAL STATE OF READINESS

Attitudes, in this context, are psychological entities. They reside in the private experience of the individual; therefore, we cannot directly experience one another's attitudes. However, if these attitudes truly exist, then it follows that they can be measured. As is the case with other psychological states or variables (fear, anger, joy), this measurement will have to be indirect. A student of these mental entities needs some type of method or procedure to allow the expression and recording of attitudes. One such method is quite straightforward. We can simply ask an individual to report her or his attitude and write down what is reported. But it turns out that this particular approach has severe limitations for a rigorous assessment of attitudes, so alternative methods are necessary. The issue of measurement is taken up in detail in subsequent sections.

AN ATTITUDE IS . . . ORGANIZED THROUGH EXPERIENCE

It is unlikely that people were born with their current attitudes toward this, that, and the other. It is far more likely that they acquired these attitudes along the way. Attitudes can arise from single and multiple experiences, both direct and indirect. For example, people in many countries are required to register for the military draft or to pay high taxes. These demands can be more or less *personally* upsetting or comforting, depending on the citizen's circumstances, and one's reaction to one's government depends in some degree on the direct experience of the impact of its policies. On the other hand, some of our experiences with governmental policies are relatively *indirect*. The government's stance on an outer space program or its choice of colors for the president's office probably have little direct impact on the daily lives of most of its citizens. Has that stance or choice altered what one plans to do for recreation tonight or what one will have for lunch tomorrow? Probably not. Yet positions on these matters would enter into our evaluation of our government. Finally, some of our attitudes are gained from experiences with other people. We are inclined to share the attitudes of our associates and sometimes even seek the attitudes of others so that we can form our own. An attitude on whether or not there is a God no doubt was shaped by the attitudes of one's parents, friends, and teachers.

AN ATTITUDE . . . EXERT[S] A DIRECTIVE OR DYNAMIC INFLUENCE

Attitudes prompt us to do things. One supposes that this is all to the good, because people need strong motivation to act in certain ways or both the individual and the species would perish. To illustrate this point, consider for the moment some obvious examples outside the domain of attitudes. Nutrients for our bodies must be replenished regularly for our health and normal functioning, so someone (Mother Nature?) or something (evolutionary selection?) provided us with a reminder to eat: hunger pangs. To take a second biological example, members of the species must reproduce themselves or the species would disappear, so we are endowed with intense sexual stirrings that are difficult to ignore. In this vein, attitudes can be viewed as another—if very different—psychologically based form of motivation. These psychological entities are as important for the organization of human behavior as are the biological factors of hunger and reproductive drive. (What are *your* attitudes toward eating and sex?) But this is not to say that motivational systems never result in ill effects. Our appetite for food can lead to obesity and our sexual urges can lead to exploitation and victimization, not to mention neuroses. Attitudes, for their part, can and do lead to social problems such as unfair discrimination, oppression, and even genocide. But, for better or worse, they get us to act in certain ways. The relation of attitudes to behavior is taken up in later chapters.

An Attitude Is . . . [an] Influence upon the Individual's Response to All Objects and Situations with Which It Is Related

Attitudes not only influence us to do things but also direct us to do them in an orderly and coherent fashion. Generally, we are consistent because of our attitudes. Imagine observing someone placing a political candidate's bumper sticker on his or her car. It is not hard to further imagine that person making a campaign contribution to that candidate, advocating that candidate to associates, and perhaps even volunteering to canvass or make phone calls on behalf of that candidate. These very different responses in separate situations make sense collectively, because if that person has a positive attitude toward a particular candidate, this attitude tends to govern all of her or his different responses. For example, it would be strange if on election day our imaginary person voted for some other candidate! In fact, this inconsistency would make no sense at all, and we would look for the set of attitudes that prompted our fictional person to act in such a bizarre and inconsistent way. Obviously, such gross inconsistencies are relatively rare. Knowing a person's attitudes gives us confidence that we can predict or anticipate his or her actions in general.

SUMMARY

If it is really the case that psychological attitudes have the properties listed in the preceding outline, then their importance in our social lives cannot be overestimated. Indeed, Allport, in his seminal chapter in 1935, argued as follows:

> The concept of attitude is probably the most distinctive and indispensable concept in contemporary American social psychology. No other term appears more frequently in experimental and theoretical literature. Its popularity is not difficult to explain. It has come into favor, first of all, because it is not the property of any one psychological school of thought, and therefore serves admirably the purposes of eclectic writers . . . The term likewise is elastic enough to apply either to the dispositions of single, isolated individuals or to broad patterns of culture. Psychologists and sociologists therefore find in it a meeting point for discussion and research. This useful, one might almost say peaceful, concept has been so widely adopted that it has virtually established itself as the keystone in the edifice of American social psychology (Allport, 1935).

Allport was probably correct in his estimate then, and he would still be fairly accurate if his assessment were applied to the social-psychological theorizing and research of the 1970s and the 1980s. Although mainstream social psychology is more diversified than it was 50-odd years ago, and although the concept has not remained peaceful (noncontroversial), the study of attitudes continues to occupy a central place in the discipline. By one estimate, in the *Psychological Abstracts* from 1970 to 1979 there were 20,209 books and articles listed under the heading of "attitude" (Dawes and Smith, 1985). From another perspective, I am lucky to have access to the PsycLIT Database via the SilverPlatter Information System, which is basically a computer-based version of the more familiar *Psychological Abstracts*. Out of curiosity, I "asked" PsycLIT how many articles it had listed from 1974 to 1982 and from 1983 to 1988 on seven social-psychological topics. As can be seen in Table I, articles on attitudes are far and away the most numerous. There is little doubt that the study of attitudes is, and will remain, an important focus in the social sciences.

Attitudes and Their Functions

It was noted that attitudes are a source of behavioral motivation and organization. A way to understand how attitudes relate to psychological motivation and organization is to inquire into what purpose they serve. For example, the reader has an attitude toward her or his national government for a reason. What is that reason? Why does

TABLE I
Reference articles on various topics available from the PsycLIT database

	TIME PERIOD	
Topic	1/74–12/82	1/83–6/88
Attitudes	15,446	14,120
Aggression	2,730	2,102
Attribution/social cognition	2,168	2,036
Individual differences	2,065	1,828
Group dynamics	1,124	866
Altruism	380	239
Social influence	196	180

Note. The search that revealed these figures was conducted in June, 1988.

one bother to concern oneself with the government when ignoring it completely might very well make life easier or more comfortable? Do people have political awareness because they desire to be good citizens? On the other hand, they may also have attitudes about jogging, sailing, biking, or other leisure activities. But certainly people's feelings about these sporting activities can have little to do with their obligations as citizens. Citizens are free to engage in personal exercise as they wish, so they probably have the latter attitudes for reasons different from the reason for their attitude toward the government. McGuire (1969) has summarized four reasons why attitudes exist. To put it another way, he has outlined four functions attitudes may serve (see also Katz, 1960). His list is not exhaustive (there could be other functions), and the functions themselves are not to be thought of as mutually exclusive (a given attitude could serve more than one function). To consider an attitude as serving a function not only gives us a clue to its origin (if understanding is the goal), but also instructs us how to proceed with developing methods of attitude change (if modification is the goal). Imagine that one wanted to change a person's attitude toward smoking cigarettes. To do so, it would be wise to find out not only the current attitude but also the reason the person holds the attitude at all. Let us look at McGuire's four functions of attitudes.

UTILITARIAN OR ADAPTIVE FUNCTION

We like things that lead us to our goals and dislike other things that lead to failures. This idea makes a certain amount of sense. If we are attracted to effective persons, methods, or policies, then we will be in a position to employ those things. From another perspective, if we shun the things that frustrate us, we avoid further frustrations. Along these same lines, attitudes themselves can serve utilitarian functions. Members of groups expect one another to conform to group standards or rules, and deviants and nonconformists run the risk of rejection. In this regard it may be wise or even necessary to adopt the group's consensus on an issue as one's own to ensure one's continuing membership. This possibility sounds like conformity, but conformity to some degree is the price we pay for existing in groups.

Changing this kind of rational attitude is a straightforward matter, at least theoretically. All one need do is change the utility of the attitudinal object. The efficiency of the object in reaching a certain goal can be modified or the goal itself might be changed. For example, if a person liked to drive a large car because it was comfortable, gasoline prices could be raised to a level that would make driving such a car psychologically uncomfortable. That is, pinch the driver in the wallet. This possibility was dramatized in recent history. In 1980 there were news reports that sales of large U.S. cars were down 43% from 1979, a decline that was attributed to soaring fuel prices over the same period. Apparently, people's preferences (attitudes) shifted to smaller, more economical vehicles. Finally, to change attitudes that are based on social pressure, one could modify the person's pattern of group membership.

ECONOMY OR KNOWLEDGE FUNCTION

No one can possibly deal with every detail in his or her social life. For the sake of manageability, some details are lumped together in broad categories and others are ignored altogether. Consider how we deal with large blocks of people. Although no two people are completely alike, we have a tendency to assign people to categories and then react to these individuals in terms of what we assume about the category. If a professor considers all students to be lazy by virtue of their being students, then it is an easy matter to deal with bothersome requests to extend deadlines for assignments or to take makeup examinations for missed tests. A student asking for such a grace period might receive an automatic denial because of that attitude. This action might make the professor look unsympathetic and callous, but it would avoid the bother of pondering the merits of individual cases. Further, humans seem to have a need for real or illusory control over things in their lives (Lefcourt, 1973). An attitude toward something suggests some control over that thing; at least you have the impression that you know what it is and how you feel about it.

To change an attitude having an economy function requires the presentation of more information. The person could be shown how the economy of an attitude is actually a false economy (uneconomical). That is, he could be shown that the error of his ways may result in small short-term gains, but large long-term losses. For example, the professor may gain a few minutes by being unrelenting, but most of those disappointed students are going to be alumni someday and may carry a grudge. Moreover, the person could be given new information or new experiences with the attitudinal object. In this sense, the knowledge function and the utilitarian function have something in common.

EXPRESSIVE, SELF-REALIZING FUNCTION

People desire a suitable social image and a degree of assertiveness. Expressing an attitude can serve both of these ends. For instance, a woman in a U.S. television commercial for the Orkin pest control company stated quite emphatically that she never has and never will tolerate cockroaches and that she certainly would not think of having them in her kitchen. Accordingly, in expressing this sentiment, she came across as a very determined and conscientious person. Anyone, for that matter, could use a similar expression of attitudes as a method of creating an impression. At other times our attitudes can help us protect our own self-image. We occasionally do things we regret. You may regret the last time you walked past a Salvation Army kettle and failed to make a contribution; this action would seem to make you a stingy, uncaring person. But if you can convince yourself that most destitute people really do not want to work and therefore do not deserve your sympathy, your regret will fade.

Changing an expressive attitude might require providing the person with an alternative way of projecting a desirable image. Further, it might be pointed out to him or her that such attitudes might backfire or boomerang if they come to be viewed as an attempt at ingratiation or an attempt to manipulate others. Finally, where protection of self-image is concerned, it might be shown to her or him that such attitudes are actually rationalizations and that rationalized views or positions can be more unflattering than flattering.

EGO-DEFENSIVE FUNCTION

People sometimes have experiences, thoughts, and urges that they find intolerable. McGuire suggests the example of a child who forms a burning hatred for her or his father. Because of the danger of overt aggression against the parent, the child might deal with this problematic hostility via the classic defense mechanism of reaction-formation. The child may begin to idealize the father to overcome the maladaptive aggressive urges. Further, a person who judges, for example, that he or she has improper sexual appetites or experiences may project these feelings on others. That is, he may see himself living in a lascivious or perverted community against which standards his own sexual proclivities are seen as harmless. To put it another way, if you have shoplifted and are bothered by it, you may see yourself as living in a den of thieves.

The connection between the persons who are the object of the ego-defensive attitudes and the function of those attitudes is almost arbitrary. That is, the child idealizes the father because he or she happens to hate the father; if the mother were hated, she would be idealized. In the case of projection, almost anyone could serve as the screen on which to project. Therefore, providing the holder of such an attitude with objective evidence that her or his attitude is simply wrong should have little impact on that attitude. For a person who is projecting his or her sexual anxiety on society, statistics on real people's actual sexual behavior is irrelevant. What is needed in these cases is insight, catharsis, or cognitive reorganization.

In sum, there are a variety of reasons why one might hold a given attitude. The attitude might serve one or more of these four functions. For example, a person who holds an intense racial bias may be using it to serve all four of the functions. Prejudice can be utilitarian, because directly or indirectly the ingroup (my group) will benefit and the outgroup (other group) will suffer. Prejudice can also serve the economy function, because reactions based on stereotypes do not require reflection or deliberation and the stereotype itself is a way of sorting out the social environment. Bias can also serve one's public or private image as a way to account for one's prejudicial behavior. Finally, a prejudiced attitude may be used to expiate one's guilt over the mistreatment of the victimized group or individual. And there are other attitudes that serve multiple functions. I am thinking of professional attitudes such as those of medical doctors toward their patients and those of professors toward their students, and I am sure that the reader can think of more examples in his or her own life. Thus, anyone who goes into the business of persuasion or attitude change is faced with a distinct challenge because of the functions of attitudes.

Currently, there is definitely a renaissance of research and writing on the functional perspective. Evidence for this assertion comes from a recent volume edited by Pratkanis, Breckler, and Greenwald (1989), *Attitude Structure and Function*. Their book contains many chapters about research and theorizing on the functions of attitudes. For me, perhaps the most generally useful paper was written by Sharon Shavitt. In her chapter, Shavitt (1989) provides (1) an overview of theory in the area; (2) a history of early (it must be admitted) failed researches; (3) a précis of contemporary, successful research trends on selected functions; (4) a set of procedures for the operationalization of functional theories of attitudes; and (5) a set of suggestions for future directions in functional research. It seems that the functional approach to the study of attitudes is "alive and well."

Measuring Attitudes

Before we can discuss substantive matters in subsequent chapters, we must establish some groundwork so that there is an understanding of just what a researcher means by saying that he or she measured someone's attitude. Because governments were mentioned in preceding illustrations, let us continue with a consideration of politicians' attitudes and of attitudes toward politicians. The President of the United States might serve our purpose well, because that office is highly visible both at home and abroad. These types of attitudes will illustrate issues connected with measurement.

A president's career usually begins with a series of successful election campaigns. Campaigns themselves are interesting because they are enormous and expensive programs aimed at attitude formation and change. Although a candidate's experience, record, and overall political philosophy are important, what characterizes a United States presidential campaign is that everyone involved does a lot of talking. The challengers especially have the freedom and opportunity to say just about anything they choose, and most of what these aspirants say expresses their attitudes. Some of the campaign talk is generated not only to prompt a positive reaction on the part of the voters but also to correct (change) preexisting negative attitudes. It seems all candidates have some problems with their "image."

As an exercise, let me make up some fictional candidates and sets of issues from some hypothetical late-twentieth-century presidential campaign. Consider certain fictive candidates' attitudes:

- Candidate Joe Blowe is on record as stating that, rather than fearing that Russian leaders are planning world conquest, we should view them as being very insecure.

- In contrast, Republican John Dough asserts that the Soviet Union is not seeking equality in world relations but is after superiority.
- Somewhat in line with Dough's view is Democrat Rocky Rhodes's position that, whereas America had recently suffered a series of international political setbacks, this country could still show the Soviets its strength.
- Finally, Republican candidate John "Jack" Armstrong takes the most extreme position by stating that the recent Russian military output has produced one of the largest arms buildups of all time.

Now, consider certain fictive attitudes toward the candidates:

- Blowe, struggling with the decision to run as an Independent, is concerned that he might be viewed as overambitious or as having a messiah complex.
- Dough, for his part, is working to overcome the idea that he is simply a nice guy who jogs, and that, in fact, he may be something of a wimp.
- Different still are the problems of Rhodes, whose staff members are concerned that the press coverage of a recent lark on the pleasure boat *Monkey Morals* has hurt him badly in the voters' eyes.
- Finally, Armstrong is faced with the problem that people might assume that he is too young and has yet to develop a rationale for his candidacy.

The point of displaying this mass of attitudinal information is this: How could one *express* the differences in attitudes seen in the preceding examples? Referring to the matter of foreign policy, one can see that Blowe and Armstrong are very far apart on attitudes toward the Soviet Union, but just *how far* apart are they? Dough and Rhodes seem to be somewhere between the more extreme reactions to the Russians, but are these intermediate positions *nearer* to that of Blowe or to that of Armstrong? Further, is it possible to compare in a meaningful way the candidates' potentially negative images? Which is worse, to be seen as overambitious, or as a wimp, or as too young? If one image is worse than the others, *how much* worse is it? Finally, let us turn for a moment to your reaction to the current president. I would wager that if I asked a group of students for their opinions of the president, I would end up with the following sorts of replies: "He's .O.K., I guess."; "I think he's a jerk."; "He's trying to do the best under the circumstances."; "He's a great man!"; or "I just don't care one way or the other." The problem remains that, although these all may be genuine and legitimate sentiments, putting them in some kind of *order* or estimating their *magnitude* would be difficult.

The terms emphasized in the foregoing passage—*express, how far, nearer, how much, order,* and *magnitude*—all have a quantitative connotation. They reveal an inclination to convert our real-life, flesh-and-blood attitudinal experiences into mathematical terms such as "amount" or "distance." This problem has faced social scientists from the beginning. Obviously, measurement is a prerequisite to comparison and analysis, but just how does one *measure* attitudes? One part of the problem is that units of measurement that are useful elsewhere (for instance, inches, pounds, gallons, volts, or decibels) do not appear to be suitable or even applicable. Second, we are not usually aware of our attitudes quantitatively; instead, we experience them in our gut, heart, soul, mind, or wherever. Even so, the task of measurement is not impossible. In fact, even the layperson quantifies her or his attitudes occasionally, and this quantification is both meaningful and interpretable. Consider the title of the film comedy *10* and the implication of the advertisement seen in Figure 1. If we can meaningfully quantify our reaction to someone's appearance, there is hope for quantification in other areas.

Social psychologists have developed a variety of measurement devices. There are good reasons for the existence of more than a single index. Not all investigators could use the approaches developed by fellow social scientists. Different workers wanted to ask different research questions, so they devised methods suitable for their own tasks. To borrow an example of the usefulness of a variety of tools from physical measurement, while one can easily convert inches into miles, one would not want to use a 12-inch ruler to measure the actual distance between Cleveland and Chicago. Neither would one want to use a yardstick to determine the size of a blood cell. Similarly, since we have different types of attitudes (as was seen in the above section on functions), the best methods for measuring these may also be different. Further, some researchers study attitude formation and change on an individual-by-individual basis, whereas others prefer to capture current, specific attitudes of whole populations.

Clearly, these aims call for quite different techniques. Presented in the following sections are several forms of attitude measures. We begin with a discussion of scales of various kinds, methods that have been widely used in the laboratory and beyond. Next, techniques for field studies are taken up, followed by a discussion of sociological polls and surveys. Finally, certain special techniques for special purposes are presented. Where appropriate, we examine some data (results) that illustrate the applications and products of these approaches.

SCALING TECHNIQUES

Attitude scales are not completely unlike the weighing scales used in the supermarket, and they also resemble scales like rulers and

Did you say a 10, boys?
Keep counting.

Diamonds.
And suddenly you feel irresistible.   De Beers

FIGURE 1
QUANTIFICATION OF AN ATTITUDINAL REACTION to the physical appearance of a person. The woman in the advertisement is said to deserve a score of 10, or more.

yardsticks. If you happened to catch a fish, you could put it on a market scale to record its weight as a number and you could lay it alongside a ruler to record its length as a number. Should someone else have caught and measured a fish, you could compare one with the other. In fact, you could meaningfully compare the two fish in a long-distance telephone call even after the fish had been eaten or discarded. Such is the power of scales to capture and represent reality. The measured object need no longer exist, yet it can still be studied. This capability motivates the student of attitudes. He or she wants to measure my attitude and yours so that the two can be meaningfully compared. Or the scientist may want to measure our attitudes over time or after certain events to check for stability and change.

Attitudes are not nearly as accessible as fish are. I pointed out in an early part of this chapter that attitudes are psychological entities that can be detected or reflected only indirectly. By tradition, the methods for analyzing our psychology are termed OPERATIONAL DEF-INITIONS. An operational definition of stage fright might be sweaty palms or stuttering speech. One may never directly experience some-one else's stage fright, but everybody can hear the stuttering and see the sweat. The idea of operational definitions sounds like a good one, but there is no automatic guarantee that a given definition is the ideal one for the job it is supposed to serve, or whether it is indeed measuring anything at all. Therefore, we will always have to be alert for invalid measures. Still, these tools are the best we have for the moment, so let us examine some scales as operational defi-nitions of attitudes.

Semantic differential scales. One of the simplest scales to describe is the semantic differential. This type of scale was developed by Osgood, Suci, and Tannenbaum (1957) in their research on the con-notative meaning of words. Most words have two meanings, DENO-TATIVE and CONNOTATIVE. The denotative meaning is basically the dictionary definition of the word. For example, "mother" denotes the female biological parent of a child. But if you were a child, "mother" might have much more meaning. The word might connote warmth, nurturance, protection, and love. However, for some other child, the same word might connote indifference, neglect, and cruelty.

The semantic differential approximates one's connotation of a word in a straightforward fashion. The "semantic" in the title is represented by pairs of everyday adjectives; the "differential" part means that the members of each pair are opposite or contrary (for example: hard, soft). A pair of such adjectives is a bipolar (two-ended) relationship. If one obtained an ordinary ruler and wrote one of the adjectives on one end, then wrote the remaining adjective on the other end, he or she would have constructed a BIPOLAR ADJECTIVE SCALE. One can then construct as many different bipolar adjective scales as desired as long as the supply of adjectives holds out. A collection of bipolar adjective scales constitutes a semantic differential scale. Here are some examples of such bipolar scales.

GOOD .____.____.____.____.____.____.____. BAD
STRONG .____.____.____.____.____.____.____. WEAK
FAST .____.____.____.____.____.____.____. SLOW

The use and interpretation of the semantic differential is also quite straightforward. The first scale in the example represents an evaluative judgment; the remaining two represent estimates of potency and activity. (The evaluative scale is the most widely used in attitudinal research.) Consider your mother (or some other person) for a minute, and then consider these three scales. What about your mom? Is she good or bad, strong or weak, fast or slow? Put an imaginary mark on each of the scales that represents your estimates. If you feel that she is very good, put the mark near that end of the scale. If she is neither good nor bad, put the mark near the middle of the scale. Complete this exercise for the remaining scales. Now, if we asked all the members of the class to do this, we could compare the various pictures of mothers that would emerge. Or we could calculate your group's average impression of their mothers. The important thing to recognize, though, is that we have *measured* your attitude toward your mother. By systematically assigning values to the points on each scale, or by viewing the scale as some kind of ruler, we can *quantify* your reaction.

The semantic differential may seem straightforward to the point of being simpleminded. However, it is a powerful tool that can produce impressive results if used creatively. An illustration of this measure's power comes from a study by Osgood and Luria (1954). These researchers learned of a woman who, under the care of clinical psychologists, was diagnosed as having multiple personalities, one of which had the name Eve White and another of which had the name Eve Black. Osgood and Luria arranged to have Eve White and Eve Black (at different times) complete a semantic differential having good–bad, active–passive, and strong–weak scales. The woman's two personalities both rated fifteen concepts: LOVE, CHILD, MY DOCTOR, ME, MY JOB, MENTAL SICKNESS, MY MOTHER, PEACE OF MIND, FRAUD, MY SPOUSE, SELF-CONTROL, HATRED, MY FATHER, CONFUSION, and SEX.

The ratings of the concepts by Eve White and Eve Black were plotted in three-dimensional space with good (up) and bad (down) on the vertical axis, active (left) and passive (right) on the horizontal axis, and strong (far) and weak (near) on the depth axis (Figure 2).

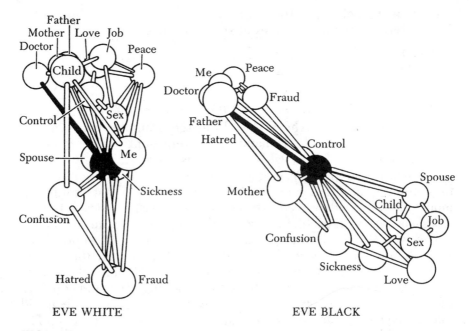

EVE WHITE   EVE BLACK

FIGURE 2
THREE-DIMENSIONAL DISPLAYS of the self-evaluations of Eve White and
Eve Black, using the semantic differential. (After Osgood and Luria, 1954.)

Osgood and Luria (1954) described these two personalities, beginning
with Eve White:

*Eve White perceives "the world" in essentially normal fashion, is well socialized,
but has an unsatisfactory attitude toward herself* [all italics in the original].
Here the usual societal "goods" are seen favorably—MY DOCTOR, MY FA-
THER, LOVE, SELF-CONTROL, PEACE OF MIND, and MY MOTHER are
all *good* and *strong* whereas FRAUD, HATRED, and to some extent CON-
FUSION are *bad*. Chief evidence of disturbance in the personality is the fact
that ME (the self-concept) is considered a little *bad*, a little *passive*, and
definitely *weak*. Substantiating evidence is the *weakness* of her CHILD as she
sees him (or her), and the essential meaninglessness to her of MY SPOUSE and
SEX. Note also the wide evaluative separation between LOVE and SEX.

How very much different is Eve Black:

*Eve Black has achieved a violent kind of adjustment in which she perceives
herself as literally perfect, but, to accomplish this break, her way of perceiving
"the world" becomes completely disoriented from the norm.* The only exceptions
to this dictum are MY DOCTOR and PEACE OF MIND, which maintain their
good and *strong* characteristics . . . But if Eve Black perceives herself as being

good, then she also has to accept HATRED and FRAUD as positive values, since (we assume) she has strong hatreds and is socially fraudulent. So we find a tight, but very un-normal, favorable cluster of ME, MY DOCTOR, PEACE OF MIND, HATRED, and FRAUD. What are positive values for most people—CHILD, MY SPOUSE, MY JOB, LOVE, and SEX—are completely rejected as *bad* and *passive*, and all these except CHILD are also *weak . . .* Note also that in this personality LOVE and SEX are closely identified, both as *bad, weak, passive* things (Osgood and Luria, 1954).

Used in this way, the semantic differential is evidently sensitive to the respondent's personal judgments, however many separable personalities that respondent has.

Intuitive interval scales. The only assumption underlying the use of semantic differential rating scales is that people can make meaningful judgments about anything. However, the creators of other scales wish to study a particular trait, dimension, or attitude. For instance, clinicians want to make more or less specific diagnoses, so they may employ scales that presumably detect particular maladies and that give an indication of the severity of the malady. Examples of such tests are the widely known Minnesota Multiphasic Personality Inventory and the Manifest Anxiety Scale. The implication is that if one wants particular kinds of answers, he or she had better ask particular kinds of questions. Asking a patient how tall he is will probably reveal very little about his anxiety in general. Furthermore, if the test is to measure degree or amount of the condition, then the items on the scale have to be sensitive to the magnitude or extent of the thing being measured. That is, different items should represent different points on the scale, and there should be a known or estimated interval between the items.

A number of social psychologists have also wished to measure particular dimensions and the degree to which a dimension was represented in certain people. Therefore, they set out to construct specific interval scales. To create such a scale successfully, the test-maker must rely on some standard for the selection or construction of scale items. One such standard is the researcher's own professional judgment or intuition. Briefly, in this approach the tester selects items he or she thinks will do the job. One example of this approach is the social distance scale developed by E. S. Bogardus.

Bogardus (1925) was interested in studying people's racial, ethnic, and national prejudices. He reasoned that, if a person was prejudiced against someone, then that person would try to maintain some social distance between himself and the target of his prejudice. That is, undesirables end up "on the wrong side of the tracks." To measure such feelings, Bogardus put together the following set of items, ranging in intimacy from 1 (low) to 7 (high).

    1. Would exclude from my country
    2. [Would admit] as visitors only to my country
    3. To citizenship in my country
    4. To employment in my occupation in my country
    5. To my street as neighbors
    6. To my club as personal chums
    7. To close kinship by marriage

This is a nice-looking scale. It certainly seems to be singleminded in nature; there definitely is some sort of social-psychological interval between any two adjacent items.

Indeed, when Bogardus applied his scale to a sample of Americans (U.S.) described as "mature persons of experience, being of two groups, either young businessmen, or public-school teachers," he obtained striking results. He asked these upstanding citizens to consider foreigners of various nationalities (Canadians, English, Germans, Poles, Turks, and several others) and to specify the minimum distance allowable for each, in terms of the scale. The results indicated that Canadian and English foreigners would be received, literally with open arms. These groups were welcome to become kin. To the contrary, Germans could only get as far as one's club, and Poles and Turks were barely admissible, being allowed citizenship at best.

But there are two fundamental problems with intuitive interval scales. The first is the order of the items. Can we trust the tester's judgment (or our own) about what items go where on the scale? This problem was "discovered" by Brewer and Campbell (1976), who, in doing survey work among natives in East African countries, simply assumed that a workable social distance scale would be: (a) willing to work with a person, (b) willing to have a person as a neighbor, (c) willing to share a meal with a person, or (d) willing to become related to a person by marriage. Obviously, they based the order—a, b, c, d—on Western customs. However, when they examined their data, they found clear internal evidence that the order of intimacy in that culture was actually c, a, b, d. Our intuition or assumptions can fail us where order is concerned. The second problem with intuitively selected items has to do with the intervals between the points they are supposed to represent. It seems that there is no safe, a priori way of intuitively estimating the size of those intervals with any accuracy. There are, happily, ways of empirically estimating the scale values of scale items.

Empirically determined scales. I. Thurstone's equal-appearing interval scale. Thurstone (1928) offered a method for building attitude scales with items spaced at known and equal-appearing intervals. In using the Thurstone procedure, one first obtains a large number of various scale items that have the potential to measure the dimension of interest. This initial selection must be based on someone's intuition or judgment, but we will not leave it at that, for, beginning with new steps, we will formally sort things out. Allport (1935) has summarized all the steps in the procedure, so we might as well follow his cookbook outline:

1. Specify the attitude variable to be measured.
2. Collect a wide variety of opinions relating to it from newspapers, books, or individuals.
3. Assemble on cards approximately 100 such typical opinions.
4. Require at least 200 to 300 judges to sort these cards into piles (eleven being the convenient and commonly used number), each pile representing *equidistant degrees of the attitude according to each judge's estimation* [emphasis added].
5. Calculate the scale value of each of the items by computing the median of the scale assigned to it by the judges and the dispersion of judgments around the median.
6. Retain such statements that have small dispersions and are on the whole equally spaced. Give approximately equal representation to each of the intervals secured. Clarity and brevity of wording may furnish additional bases for selection.
7. In applying the scale, the subject checks every statement with which he or she agrees; the score is the mean scale value for all the endorsed statements.

As suggested by the added emphasis, the heart of the Thurstone method is found in Allport's step 4. The researcher relies on the judgments of a large number of people to sort out the items for the scale. Steps 5 and 6 then indicate that if these judges (who worked individually, of course) cannot agree on which pile to place an item, throw the item out! That item does not reflect the dimension of interest (or some point on that dimension) because different people react to it in different ways and its exclusion will help purify the scale. Picking the final items is easy. The researcher chooses items most consistently assigned to one or another pile. The relative position of the pile is also used in calculating the item's scale value.

Empirically determined scales. II. Likert's summated rating scale.
To use Likert's (1932) method to arrive at a purified scale, one would
again start with some arbitrarily large number of items that had the
potential to measure the dimension of interest. Assume that we want
to measure people's attitudes toward nuclear power plants. One
statement that might reflect a person's attitude on the issue of nuclear
power might be, "I think nuclear power plants are a great benefit to
the people in this country." On this and other items the respondent
has a chance to react by choosing one of perhaps five response
categories.

1. _____ Strongly agree
2. _____ Agree
3. _____ Undecided
4. _____ Disagree
5. _____ Strongly disagree

The subject's score for that item is shown on the left and depends
on her or his choice. In this case, a high score would indicate an
unfavorable attitude toward the issue, whereas a low score would
indicate a positive attitude.

Once we have a collection of such items, we will give them, not
to judges, but to the sample of subjects whose attitude we really
want to measure. When they complete the entire scale, the sums
for all items for all subjects are calculated; and on the basis of her or
his score, each subject is assigned to one of three categories: (a) the
25% of the sample who were the *most* favorable toward that issue,
(b) the 25% of the sample who were the *least* favorable toward the
issue, and (c) the 50% who were neither the most nor the least
favorable.

The point here is that the people in the two extreme groups have
the strongest feelings about the issue, and it is likely that they are
the clearest or most knowledgeable about the area. This consideration
brings us to the heart of the Likert technique. If a scale item really
reflects one's attitude toward an issue, then that item ought to discriminate between the extreme groups. That is, if most persons in
the favorable group agreed with the item, most persons in the unfavorable group should disagree with that item. An item that is
endorsed (agreed with) by both groups is not sensitive to the differences between those groups. It then becomes a mechanical matter
to find those items that are endorsed by both extreme groups and
throw them out. The items that do discriminate between the ex-

tremes are retained, and everybody's attitude is recalculated on the basis of the purified scale.

Empirically determined scales. III. Guttman's interlocking scaling technique. Finally, a third empirical scaling technique will be illustrated. Guttman (as elaborated by Dawes and Smith, 1985) offered a way to select scale items that was based on an assumption that sets of interlocking entities exist. In this context the entities that interlock are (a) people's attitudes and (b) items on an attitude scale. For an example of the principle of interlocking, let us start with a simple situation. Suppose we have five math students we want to evaluate (order from best to worst) and five math problems we want to scale (order from hardest to easiest). Short of any other information, we could accomplish both objectives by finding the interlocking order of these two sets of entities. That is, the students can be ordered with respect to the problems, and the problems can be ordered with respect to the students. Thus, they interlock.

To find the interlocking order, we will test all five students with all five problems. If a student masters a particular problem, he or she is assigned a score of 1 for it; if not, a score of 0 is assigned. When all the scores are in, matrices like that shown in Figure 3 are constructed. The matrix on the left contains a record of the students' successes on the problems (the 1s), but it does not seem to tell us much until it is transposed in an attempt to create a perfect, inverted triangle of 1s, as shown in the matrix on the right. The triangle on the right side of Figure 3 reveals both the order of the students and the order of the problems. In our terms, the technique has scaled (ordered) the problems for us. The resulting interlocking order of students and problems is shown in Figure 4.

The use of Guttman's interlocking technique for the construction of an attitude scale is similar to the preceding math problem example. As noted, it is assumed that people's attitudes interlock with items on an attitude scale, and to find that interlocking order, it is a straightforward matter to administer the test and then look for the triangle of responses, as we did in Figure 3. Of course, if a triangle does not emerge, the items cannot be said to be ordered on a Guttman scale.

Since the Thurstone, Likert, and Guttman empirical scaling methods are something of a set, only one of these—Guttman's—will be illustrated. An issue to which the technique has been applied is physicians' attitudes toward abortion. The researchers Koslowsky, Pratt, and Wintrob (1976) judged that a sample of physicians consti-

Problems

Students	A	B	C	D	E			C	D	A	B	E
Dan	0	0	1	1	0		Sue	1	1	1	1	1
Joe	1	0	1	1	0		Pam	1	1	1	1	0
Pam	1	1	1	1	0		Joe	1	1	1	0	0
Pat	0	0	1	0	0		Dan	1	1	0	0	0
Sue	1	1	1	1	1		Pat	1	0	0	0	0

FIGURE 3
MATRICES USED IN GUTTMAN SCALING to establish the interlocking orders of students and problems.

tuted one set in an interlocking order and that the conditions under which they would approve of the performance of an abortion was another. The doctors were interviewed and were asked under which of eleven different circumstances they would approve of an abortion for a woman. Those circumstances (scale items in our parlance) and the proportion of physicians giving their approval under each are listed in Table II. One's feelings about the ethical and moral aspects of abortion aside, the interlocking technique yielded the scale point (circumstance) order shown in Table II. In this case, the items were ordered with respect to the doctors, and the doctors were ordered (implicitly) with respect to the items.

OTHER SCALES

The scaling techniques outlined in the preceding sections are of long standing in social-psychological research. However, it should not be thought that these are the only methods for building scales; the interested student or instructor should see Dawes (1972) and Dawes and Smith (1985) for a fuller and more technical treatment of measurement issues. On the basis of these techniques a great many specific scales have been constructed and published, and these are

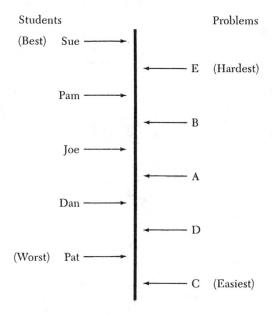

FIGURE 4
INTERLOCKING ORDERS of students and problems based on the Guttman
scaling technique.

in more or less active use. A complete listing and description of such
scales would require a book very much larger than this one. Indeed,
Robinson (Robinson, Rusk, and Head, 1968; Robinson, Athanasiou,
and Head, 1969; Robinson and Shaver, 1973) made such a compilation several years ago, and the resulting stack of published pages is
many inches thick! A sampler of various scales described by Robinson
and his coauthors is presented in Table III. Therefore, before the
prospective scale-maker spends time developing his or her own scale,
I recommend that he or she first consult the Robinson volumes or
one of the several abstracting services. It might be that the desired
scale already exists.

Field-Experimental Techniques

So far, we have discussed paper-and-pencil measurement devices
useful in the laboratory, but there are other ways of experimentally
measuring people's attitudes, even outside the laboratory. Two that
will be presented here are the WRONG NUMBER TECHNIQUE and the
LOST LETTER TECHNIQUE.

TABLE II
A Guttman scale of circumstances under which physicians would not approve
an abortion

Circumstance	Percent not approving abortion
Career or education would be disrupted	60
Too young to have the child	57
Financially unable to support the child	55
Too old to have the child	55
Does not want the child	54
Being unmarried would be a problem	48
Pregnancy or childbirth is a threat to mental health	32
Pregnancy or childbirth is a threat to physical health	28
Pregnancy is a result of rape or incest	28
Risk of congenital abnormality	25
Pregnancy or childbirth is a threat to life	23

After Koslowsky et al. (1976).

WRONG NUMBER TECHNIQUE

Gaertner and Bickman (1971) used this technique to study racial attitudes in Brooklyn, New York. The subjects were residents living in what were known to be predominantly black or white neighborhoods. The questions were whether a black person would be more willing to help a black or a white victim and whether a white person would be more willing to help a black or a white victim. The "victims" (actually actors in the employ of the researchers) revealed their alleged plight by phoning (between 6:30 and 9:30 P.M.) the subjects in the following manner:

CALLER: Hello . . . Ralph's garage? This is George Williams . . . Listen, I'm stuck out here on the parkway, and I'm wondering if you'd be able to come out here and take a look at my car?
SUBJECT'S EXPECTED RESPONSE: This isn't Ralph's garage. You have the wrong number.
CALLER: This isn't Ralph's garage! Listen, I'm terribly sorry to have disturbed you, but listen . . . I'm stuck out here on the highway, and that was the last dime I had! I have bills in my pocket, but no more change to make another phone call. Now I'm *really* stuck out here. What am I going to do now?
SUBJECT: (The subject might volunteer to call the garage. If he or she does not, the caller goes on.)

TABLE III
A sampler of scale titles compiled by Robinson and coauthors

Volume	Scale
Measures of political attitudes	Political–economic conservatism scale Willingness to tolerate nonconformists Attitude toward communists Domestic social welfare scale Big business–minded scale Attitude toward socialized medicine Pro-integration scale Foreign policy goals and personal values Isolationism scale Attitudes toward world affairs International hostility inventory Attitudes toward war
Measures of occupational attitudes and occupational characteristics	Job satisfaction scale Managerial job attitudes Job attitudes and job satisfaction of scientists Attitude toward the supervisor Group morale scale Meaning of work scales A proverbs test for supervisor selection Attitudes toward labor and management Attitudes toward working for the government Attitude toward automation Attitude toward employment of older persons Opinions about work of the mentally ill
Measures of social-psychological attitudes	Self-concept semantic differential Purpose-in-life test Alienation scale Fascist attitudes scale Dogmatism scale Social values questionnaire Faith in people Inventory of religious belief Adjective ratings of God Repression–sensitization scale Body cathexis scale Twenty statements (Who am I? Who are you?) test

After Robinson, et al. (see text).

CALLER: Listen . . . do you think you could do me the favor of calling the garage and letting them know where I am? I'll give you the number. They know me over there.

Like the subjects, the callers were either black or white, or at least they seemed to be. The "black" caller used a "modified 'Southern Negro'" dialect;* the white caller used a speech style "typical of whites in New York." Having made the call to the subject, the caller, who was at the fictional Ralph's garage, waited to see who called in to help the victim. The result of the study was that the black residents were less prejudiced (by this measure) than white residents. Blacks were equally likely to assist both black and white callers, but whites were more likely to help whites than to help blacks.

Lost Letter Technique

Milgram (1972) proposed this technique for measuring the prevailing attitudes in a community. Like the preceding wrong number technique, it is an unobtrusive measure. That is, given the procedure involved, a subject need not realize that he or she is involved in a research project. Although such procedures raise certain ethical questions (Dawes and Smith, 1985), their advantage is that they might elicit more honest or true responses than would more intrusive measures such as the scales that were discussed above.

To see how the technique is supposed to work, let us make up an example. Suppose we had formed the hypothesis that people in the South were more antiabortion than people in the North. The first step in using the lost letter technique to test this hypothesis would be to prepare a large number of ambiguous, noncontroversial letters, all of which are identical and made to look like originals. Next, we would seal these letters in stamped envelopes, half of which were addressed to a proabortion (actually, fictitious) organization and half of which are addressed to an antiabortion (actually, fictitious) organization. In reality, we would address these envelopes to our own post office box or building. Researchers would take these "letters" to certain target cities in the North and South and conveniently "lose" them. By that I mean that they would plant the letters in places where they could be easily found by passersby.

Having planted the letters, we need only wait to see which letters come back from which cities. The rationale is that if people in a

---

*By current American convention, the terms *black* or *African-American* are used to refer to persons of African descent; however, if some previous investigator used the term *Negro* for this purpose, her or his terminology will be used below (in quotes) when necessary.

certain region are generally proabortion, they would be more likely to mail that version of the letter, presumably in an effort to further the cause of that kind of organization. On the other hand, these proabortion citizens would not return the antiabortion letter, perhaps in an effort to frustrate that type of organization. The opposite pattern should hold if people in a given region were generally antiabortion.

Variations on the lost letter technique are the MISDIRECTED LETTER TECHNIQUE and the QUASI-QUESTIONNAIRE TECHNIQUE. In the former, a subject would find in her or his mailbox a letter addressed to someone else with a particular kind of name. In the latter, a phony questionnaire would be sent to a subject (occupant) to be returned to someone with a particular kind of name. In both cases, the idea is that if something in that particular kind of name served to identify the race, or religious or political affiliation, of the intended recipient, subjects with certain prejudices would be more or less likely to put the article back in the mail.

Kremer, Barry, and McNally (1986) used both of these variations in a study of religious prejudice in Northern Ireland. It happens that "Patrick Connoly" would be taken for a Catholic and "William Scott" would be assumed to be a Protestant by residents of that part of Ireland. By using the quasi-questionnaire technique, Kremer et al. sent "transportation" questionnaires to residents of Catholic and Protestant districts in a town with a known history of sectarian conflict. Half the households in each district received surveys to be sent to "Patrick Connoly" and half received surveys to be returned to "William Scott." When the returns were in, the pattern of prejudice in this town was clear. Protestant households did not discriminate and returned an equal number of questionnaires to each name. On the contrary, Catholic households did show bias: twice as many letters were returned to "Patrick Connoly" as were returned to "William Scott."

Polls and Surveys

The techniques we have seen thus far have their respective uses in estimating the attitudes of relatively small, specific sets of people. How could one go beyond limited designs to find out about broader patterns of attitudes in, say, all of America? For example, just what proportion of Americans strongly self-identify themselves as being anticommunist, religious, supporters of the National Rifle Association, or supporters of the gay rights movement? The answer to this type of question is the practice of polling or SURVEY RESEARCH.

In the treatment that follows I have relied principally on Kish's 1965 book, *Survey Sampling*. By now, however, there are a number of general treatises on survey research, and the interested reader will benefit from consulting any of these (cf. Asher, 1988; Fowler, 1984; Kalton, 1983; Schuman and Kalton, 1985). Further, my exposition concentrates on sampling techniques, because in my view that is the unique contribution from this domain. But since we have been sensitized to the issues of measurement and scaling, it is important to point out that survey researchers have also paid a great deal of attention to the designing of questionnaires and the construction of survey questions. Readers with an interest in this aspect of polling are referred to Converse and Presser (1986), Fink and Kosecoff (1985), Fox and Tracy (1986), and Labaw (1980).

My expressed interest was about the attitudes of "Americans." That is a pretty big group of people, but if I am determined to stick with this set, it is defined as the POPULATION I wish to study. Kish (1965) defines the population in terms of (a) content, (b) units, (c) extent, and (d) time. If I more specifically wanted to learn how Americans might vote in the 1996 presidential primary elections, these elements might be (a) all persons, (b) who were eligible and willing to vote, (c) and who resided in states that hold presidential primaries (d) during the first 6 months of 1996. If we were to decide to question every last member of this population, we would conduct a CENSUS, such as previous decennial censuses carried out by the federal government. Unfortunately, because of its scope, any census is bound to be expensive, and as individual researchers we do not have the resources that are at the disposal of the federal government. Therefore, we would do better to turn to survey sampling rather than to a complete census.

SURVEY SAMPLING refers to theories, procedures, and standards for selecting and measuring only a part of a population (hence the term *sample*) in order to make estimates about the population in general. To appreciate the relationship of the SAMPLE to the population, Kish (1965) describes the members of the population as a deck or file of index cards upon which is written the desired information. In our case the information is the person's attitude. He says that "sampling would consist of selecting a fraction of the cards, then computing statistics from the sample to estimate the population values. For example, the sample mean $\bar{y}$ can be computed for estimating the population mean $\bar{Y}$." The trick is in picking the fraction of the cards and computing the sample results so that they truly approximate the characteristics of the population.

Elaborate and highly quantified procedures for picking and analyzing a sample have been devised, but a detailed consideration of these technicalities is beyond the scope of this chapter. These methods can be found in references cited above. However, it is possible to outline here several sampling procedures and to recommend for some and against others.

MODEL SAMPLING

MODEL SAMPLING methods are based on broad assumptions about the population in question. That is, the researcher who uses any of these methods assumes that on the basis of chance or on the basis of intuition, he or she will be able to obtain a meaningful sample. One set of model samples are those that are HAPHAZARD. Here the researcher draws conclusions from whatever persons come to hand. The casual "man-on-the-street" interview is a haphazard sample. Another kind of model sample is based on EXPERT CHOICE, wherein one relies on some authority to define the sample. For instance, we might decide to limit our political poll to the state of Maine if we seriously subscribe to the pundit's claim that "as goes Maine, so goes the nation." A final form of model sampling to be considered is the QUOTA SAMPLE. In quota sampling, the interviewers (called enumerators in the polling industry) are instructed to contact certain kinds of people in certain proportions. For example, in a survey of social attitudes in East Africa, Brewer and Campbell (1976) did *not* wish to interview a representative sample of the population; rather, they chose to concentrate on individuals who they assumed would have social influence—young, literate males.

PROBABILITY SAMPLING

The representative results of model sampling are open to serious error because the assumptions or intuitions of the practitioner may simply be incorrect or, as in quota sampling, results are intentionally unrepresentative. There are other forms available that are not susceptible to these problems; these are called PROBABILITY SAMPLES. "In probability sampling, every element in the population has a known nonzero probability of being selected" (Kish, 1965). That is, probability sampling matches the sample to the population. Because we already know something about the characteristics of the population from the most recent census, we will base our sample on what is known. If we know that 50% of the voters are women, then 50% of the people in our sample should be women. If 10% of all voters are black, then black persons should make up 10% of the sample, and so on. The sample of actual people can then be selected on some truly random basis or in some unbiased systematic way in which we might pick every other, or every tenth, of every thousandth person in our pool.

Standard dwelling unit procedure. A variant on probability sampling involves the selection of dwelling units on an equally probable basis. Why would a researcher want to select dwelling units? If we choose a person's name based on some selection process, it might nevertheless be difficult to locate that person. However, if we locate a STANDARD DWELLING UNIT, it is very likely that someone lives in that unit. If we visit enough units, we are bound to come up with a representative sample of people, but more efficiently than if we had started out looking for particular individuals. For example, Blumenthal, Kahn, Andrews, and Head (1972) wanted to interview approximately 1,400 men representative of the American adult male population. On the basis of information in the files at the Survey Research Center at the University of Michigan, they sent their enumerators to 1 dwelling out of 25,850 such units on their list. Similarly, Campbell, Converse, and Rodgers (1976) desired a representative sample of 2,164 adult Americans, so they picked 1 out of every 22,500 dwellings in the list. To show how close this procedure approximates the total population, Campbell et al. compared the characteristics of their sample with the characteristics of Americans as revealed by the 1970 decennial census. Table IV shows that their sampling procedure resulted in a very close approximation to the census figures.

Stratified sampling procedures. Related to dwelling sampling are procedures known as STRATIFIED RANDOM SAMPLING or STRATIFIED SYSTEMATIC SAMPLING. These procedures are used when the researchers are interested in surveying large but delimited areas, such as people in all the major cities in the United States. This huge domain can be broken down to more manageable levels or strata. To begin, cities themselves could be the first stratum; a relatively small number of cities would be chosen (randomly or on the basis of some unbiased system). The next stratum might be residential blocks within chosen cities; only certain blocks need be designated to form the sample. Finally, within a designated block, a third stratum might be dwelling units; only a few of the units would be required to complete the sample. The actual respondent might then be any competent adult female or male living in the unit.

Well, what are the answers to the questions about Americans'

TABLE IV
Respondent characteristics in the Campbell survey sample and the 1970 American population

| Characteristic | SOURCE | |
	Survey[a]	Census[b]
Region of residence		
Northeast	22.0	24.3
North Central	27.9	28.0
South	33.8	31.0
West	16.3	16.7
Sex		
Male	44.4	48.7
Female	55.6	51.3
Race		
White	87.2	87.5
Black	10.1	11.1
Other	2.7	1.4
Age		
18–24	18.6	17.7
25–34	19.7	18.7
35–44	17.4	17.4
45–54	17.8	17.4
55–64	12.7	13.9
65–74	9.0	9.3
75 and over	4.9	5.8
Education		
Eighth grade or less	23.2	27.8
Some high school	18.6	17.1
High school graduate	34.1	34.0
Some college	12.1	10.2
College degree	11.9	11.0
Median income	$8400	$8335

After Campbell et. al. (1976)
[a] The survey was conducted in July and August of 1971.
[b] Census figures for 1970 for the American population.

stands on the issues of communism, religion, the National Rifle Association, gay rights, and others? The Times Mirror Center for the People and the Press was also interested in these matters and in 1987 commissioned the Gallup Organization—a prominent polling agency—to do a survey of the American electorate. Using sampling techniques described earlier, the Gallup people conducted face-to-face interviews with 4,244 people (Ornstein, Kohut, and McCarthy, 1988). Part of the results of that survey are shown in Table V. Clearly, more Americans are against communism than are for gay rights. You may have guessed that, but now we know it.

TELEPHONE SURVEYS

In their review, Schuman and Kalton (1985) identified TELEPHONE SURVEYS as the most widely used method in the field today. This recent development has brought mixed blessings, though. On the positive side, telephone surveys cost half as much as the more traditional sort, phone polls can be completed quickly and, with a feature called random-digit-dialing, samples can be obtained that compare favorably with those from the earlier sampling techniques. On the negative side, nonresponse rates (failure to obtain or complete an interview) for telephone surveys are even a bit higher than for face-to-face contacts, questions and responses are restricted to those

TABLE V
Percentages of the American electorate that strongly identify themselves with certain terms

Term	Percentage of respondents
Anticommunist	70
A religious person	49
A supporter of the civil rights movement	47
A supporter of the peace movement	46
An environmentalist	39
A supporter of the anti-abortion movement	32
A Democrat	31
A supporter of the women's movement	29
A supporter of business interests	28
A conservative	27
A supporter of the National Rifle Association	27
A union supporter	27
Pro-Israel	25
A Republican	20
A liberal	19
A supporter of the gay rights movement	8

After Ornstein et al. (1988).

that can be communicated orally, and both enumerators and respondents report less enjoyment with the phone surveys than the other sort of interview. Still, because of the pressures of limited time and money facing researchers, Schuman and Kalton (1985) predicted that the telephone survey will prevail in the future. Readers interested in more detail concerning telephone surveying should refer to Frey (1983) and Guenzel, Berkmans, and Cannell (1983).

Special Methods

Up to this point we have encountered a wide variety of techniques for the measurement of attitudes, and surely these would serve the career of the busiest researcher or student. Still, there are several more methods that deserve to be mentioned, for these have special, and in some cases indispensable, advantages.

THE BOGUS PIPELINE

Social science researchers are sometimes in the position of asking questions about sensitive matters, and casual answers to these questions cannot always be trusted. People (including myself) have a tendency to provide answers that flatter them, or that protect them from criticism or blame, or that simply provide a response they think the questioner wants to hear. These are generally referred to as "socially desirable answers," and efforts have been made to find means to get through them to the truth. One such laboratory technique is known as THE BOGUS PIPELINE (Sigall and Page, 1971).

In using the bogus pipeline, the experimenter, in effect, convinces the subject that "I can read your mind." The subject is first asked for some trivial information concerning her or his mundane likes and dislikes for music, sports, and films. A paper-and-pencil semantic differential, ranging perhaps from −3 (bad) to +3 (good), is used to record these reactions. The subject is then taken to a fabulous-looking device and is told that this brand-new invention can infallibly detect a person's true feelings through "implicit muscle movements." One uses the machine, it is explained, by manually turning a wheel that moves a pointer on a dial that ranges from −3 to + 3. The subject is asked to indicate mundane likes and dislikes again, this time by using the machine. By now the experimenter has sneaked a look at the original questionnaire answers, and the marvelous machine provides output (generated by the experimenter) that exactly matches the subject's original answers. If this were not enough, the subject is instructed to try to lie—that is, to aim the pointer at an incorrect expression of liking for something. But the machine cannot be beaten and the correct (original) answer is again produced.

In a test of the validity of the bogus pipeline procedure, Quigley-Fernandez and Tedeschi (1978) practiced two deceptions on their subjects. First, they convinced people that the bogus pipeline really did work and then "accidentally" gave the subjects answers to a test they were about to take. In short, subjects were in a position to cheat on the test if they wanted to, because it appeared to them that nobody connected with the research knew that they had discovered the answers. Most people used the "leaked" answers. The heart of the experiment was at a later point when the experimenter asked each subject if he or she had found out any specific information on how to answer the test. Half the subjects were asked the question in a typical face-to-face interview; the other half had to reply using the bogus pipeline method. The results of this last step were perfectly clear. Of the 20 subjects in the usual face-to-face interview, only one confessed, whereas in the pipeline condition, 13 of 20 told the truth. This difference indicates the validity of the procedure as a means for promoting truthful answers.

ARCHIVAL SOURCES

Brief mention will be made of ARCHIVAL SOURCES in attitudinal research. Much can be learned—at a certain level of understanding—from information found in many sources in print and in other forms of media. For instance, a partial history of racial attitudes in America could be gleaned from an analysis of the rosters of major league baseball teams from the 1900s to date. In other words, "baseball reflects America's history" (Mazer, 1987). To take another example, the so-called sexual revolution of the 1960s and 1970s could be documented in part by a compilation of the sales records of sexually oriented popular magazines such as *Playboy* and *Playgirl*. The list of possible archives is very long, and use of these sources is limited only by common sense.

For a final example, there is considerable evidence for sexism in many cultures. One aspect of this bias is found in the depiction of women in the media as seen in the second-rate social roles they are often assigned in ads, commercials, and dramas. A subtle expression of this sexist bias is the phenomenon of "face-ism" (Archer, Iritani, Kimes, and Barrios, 1983). In three separate studies, Archer et al. combed American periodicals, publications from 11 cultures, and artwork over 6 centuries. A consistent finding in these archives was that men's pictures usually involved mostly the head and that pictures of women more often included the full figure. In subsequent tests the authors found that facial prominence had an impact on ratings of the intelligence of those so depicted; thus, face-ism is a subtle but important feature of sexism, and its discovery in archival sources points up their usefulness. (The issue of sexism will be taken up in more detail in a later chapter on media.)

META-ANALYSIS

Finally, an important and useful source of data on attitudes is simply other people's published data. When a number of research papers on a given topic accumulate, this is known as a literature. Traditionally, a literature is "reviewed" in a narrative, qualitative fashion, such as that seen in the reviews in many of the chapters in this book. However, there is another way to evaluate a literature, and this involves a quantitative technique known as META-ANALYSIS. In a meta-analysis, the very numbers (data) reported by various authors are combined into a new global analysis, hence the term "meta." By using this procedure it is possible to discover overall patterns of relationships not necessarily evident in individual publications (see Hunter, Schmidt, and Jackson, 1982; Wolf, 1986). By now a number of areas of research on the social psychology of attitudes have been subjected to meta-analysis, and where applicable these will be discussed.

Validity

It is obvious by now that social scientists have developed a lot of different ways to study attitudes, and, of these, rating scales are apparently in heaviest use (Dawes, 1972). What do these scales measure? Do they measure anything at all? I think the answer is that, yes, they can measure attitudes in a meaningful way. Part of my confidence comes from a clever study conducted by Dawes (1977). He had his departmental colleagues rate each other's height, not with rulers, but with rating scales. Dawes converted five attitude scales to height scales: for example, a semantic differential was expressed as short–tall, and a Likert-like scale was expressed as extremely tall, very tall, fairly tall, neither tall nor short, fairly short, very short, and extremely short. *All* of the separate scale results correlated very well with the staff members' actual heights in inches, and when Dawes combined them into a single index, the correlation (r) was an impressive .98. Clearly these sorts of scales have the potential to measure something—and apparently in a meaningful way.

CHAPTER TWO

COMPONENTS AND STRUCTURE OF
ATTITUDES

Early researchers tended to concentrate on single, fairly narrow definitions of an attitude, as exemplified by the work on social distance (see Bogardus, 1925) discussed in Chapter 1. Currently, the focus is not exclusively on the content of a given attitude, but also on internal components and dynamics of attitudes and on the relationships among attitudes and other phenomena such as overt behavior. We consider these topics separately. In this chapter we cover work on the internal components of attitudes and interattitude relations; subsequent chapters deal with the issue of attitude–behavior consistency.

In the pages to follow, the basic components of attitudes—the A-B-Cs, so to speak—are identified and defined. Next, the very validity of these components is scrutinized, and their possible role in persuasive processes discussed. Finally, the relationship of attitudes to one another are treated in two sections on the structure of attitudes.

The Components of Attitudes

Consider any psychological attitude. What exactly is involved when a person experiences that attitude toward its object? Let us dissect an attitude and examine its COMPONENTS. Generally, writers have conceived that there are perhaps three attitudinal components; by way of a handy mnemonic (memory aid), these have been termed the A-B-Cs of attitudes. For convenience, we can examine the components of an attitude toward some visible and important individual in a person's life. Just about everyone has, or has had, a supervisor of some sort, whether that supervisor was in the role of boss, teacher, or guardian. As our hypothetical person reflects on such a supervisor, what is going through her or his head?

A: THE AFFECTIVE COMPONENT

One of the things we experience when we think of a figure like a boss is an affective, or emotional, reaction. Typically, we *feel* a certain way when we consider the figure. If that figure were to walk into the room, what would one's gut reaction be? Would there be a sense that he or she was likable, or would the figure engender a feeling of dislike? Is the person's accent pleasant? What sort of emotive reaction is there to the color of his or her skin or style of clothes? As the reader can imagine, there is a wide variety or range of possible feelings of this sort. Our language is replete with labels for such affective reactions, and for purposes of illustration a small sampler of these is provided in Table I. In short, the affective component is essentially the *evaluative* element in an attitude, on the

TABLE I
Terms that illustrate the A-B-C components of attitudes

Component	Terms	
A: affect	liking	loathing
	disliking	angriness
	loving	happiness
	hating	sadness
	fearing	pride
	wanting	boredom
B: behavior	buy	destroy
	hit	endorse
	kiss	hire
	rent to	fire
	vote for	choose
	donate to	reject
C: cognition	will lead to	causes
	goes with	yields
	has/have	produces
	are	costs
	comes from	prevents
	results in	mediates

basis of which the attitude holder judges the object to be good or
bad.

B: THE BEHAVIORAL COMPONENT

Another thing likely to enter into one's awareness as the boss
comes to mind is a *consideration* of past, present, or future *behavior*
regarding him or her. Has one criticized or praised the boss lately?
If possible, would one switch jobs or supervisors to get away from
this boss? Thus, the B component (behavior) represents an *intentional* or action element in attitudes. Examples of other forms of
behavioral inclinations (or histories) regarding attitudinal objects are
presented in Table I.

However, a caveat is useful here. In later chapters the issue of
attitude–behavior consistency will be taken up. Therefore, the behavioral component of attitudes should not be confused with behavior
per se. Certain writers have been sensitive to this distinction and
have taken care that their readers distinguish between these two
considerations. For example, Bagozzi (1978) called the B dimension
the "conative" or "action tendenc[y]" component, and Ajzen and
Fishbein (1970) named such a dimension "behavioral intentions
which are assumed to mediate overt behavior." Keep these distinctions in mind.

C: THE COGNITIVE COMPONENT

The term *cognition* covers a variety of things, but here it means
any bit of information, fact, or knowledge relevant to the attitudinal
object. That is, cognitions tell us about the functions, implications,
or consequences of the object of the attitude. Certain types of cognitions seem to be indisputably true: fire is hot, ice is cold, and the
earth rotates around the sun. Further, certain things cause other
things or influence outcomes: eating too much food and a lack of
exercise can cause obesity. On the other hand, there are other types
of cognitions that are less obviously true, and one may possess information that is more or less valid. For instance, is it really true that
smoking can cause lung cancer and other maladies? Do blondes really
have more fun? In the United States, is the Democratic party really
the war party and do Republican leaders actually favor big business
interests over the common man? Considering our hypothetical boss,
is he or she delivering the rewards that we were promised at the
time we were hired? Are the boss' instructions really the best way
to get things done? Convictions about these debatable possibilities
represent cognitions insofar as one *believes* his or her opinions to be

correct. In sum, cognitions are basically *beliefs* about the attitudinal object; further examples of typical cognitions are offered in Table I.

CONSISTENCY ACROSS THE A-B-C COMPONENTS

Although conceptually distinct, the three components of attitudes are at least intuitively related. Reference to Allport's 1935 definition of an attitude as seen earlier reveals an implicit statement of CONSISTENCY. It seems to make sense that if our cognitions about an object change, our affect for the thing would be revised accordingly. Schematically, this consistency relationship could be diagrammed thusly: C → A. For example, if a person bought a new car for its appearance and performance and subsequently discovered that it also got good gas mileage (cognition = this car saves me money, too), the person would probably be that much more pleased with the purchase (affect = now I *really* like this car). If, on the other hand, the car proved to be an unbearable expense, one would doubtlessly end up disliking the thing intensely. Again, C → A. To extend the example, if your cognitions and affect for the car were positive, then your intentions or behavior toward the car would probably also be positive. One would be more likely to utilize and maintain the vehicle than to sell it, neglect it, or junk it. Here, the diagram would be A + C → B.

The two examples just discussed were diagrammed C → A and A + C → B. In the first case, new or changed cognitions would probably lead to new or changed affective states; in the second case, affect and cognition might well have an impact on behavior. But whereas these examples are intuitively obvious, what about somewhat less straightforward predictions? Would it be possible to have an instance where A → C? That is, would a new or changed affective state produce or lead to changes in cognitions? Moreover, if there truly were a mechanism for ensuring consistency across the three components, would it be possible to demonstrate a pattern of B → A + C? Could a new or changed behavior toward an object result in a modification of the affect and cognitions associated with that attitudinal object? Answers to these queries are available in the literature, and it is to this evidence that we now turn.

C → A consistency? Although we have tentatively accepted the C → A proposition, it will not do any harm to check it out with some data. An interesting, large-scale "field experiment" will serve. In November of 1986 the American public received some unwelcome and disturbing news. The Reagan administration, whose leader had insisted on an unwavering policy of no concessions to terrorists or political kidnappers, had apparently become involved in an arms-for-hostages deal with Iran. This bad news was compounded by further information that some of the money involved was covertly sent to aid the Contras in Nicaragua. What came to be known as the Iran-Contra Affair (a.k.a. "Iranscam" and "Iranamok"; Greenfield, 1987) provided Americans with what can be considered a host of new cognitions about their federal government and its chief executive. How might these cognitions have influenced citizens' affect toward the President?

For many years, pollsters have been taking standard measures of such affective reactions to the President. These are the well-known "Approve" and "Disapprove" ratings. For example, the question asked of respondents by the Gallup Organization is, "Do you approve or disapprove of the way _____ is handling his job as president?" The respondent has the options of selecting Approve, Disapprove, or No Opinion. These results are usually reported in terms of proportions: either the raw proportion of those respondents approving or disapproving in an entire sample or the relative rate of approval among only those who had some opinion. In any event, the cognitions that stemmed from the Iran-Contra Affair had a quick and profound impact on Mr. Reagan's job approval ratings.

Up to a point, 1986 had been a good year for President Reagan. Gallup polls (and other sources) showed a rock-steady raw approval rating in the sixties (61–68%) from January to October, and an even better relative approval rating ("Reagan's Job Performance—Overall," 1987). Unfortunately, when Iranamok came along, the bottom dropped out. Figure 1 traces shifts in Approve and Disapprove ratings in the period from about mid-1986 to mid-1987. As noted, the picture looked rosy up until October, 1986, and then changed drastically. At first, Mr. Reagan denied everything, and that did not help his cause. In January the House and Senate formed committees to begin to investigate the affair, and the administration had been more or less forced to form its own investigative committee, the Tower Commission. These developments did not sit well with the public, and by February of 1987 Reagan's Approve and Disapprove ratings had made a massive flip-flop. This unaccustomed disapproval persisted until about the time of the Tower Commission report that only certain administration officials were involved in the scandal. President Reagan was made to look a little foolish about his ignorance of his administration's actions, but it seemed to be clear that he had not figured centrally in the mess.

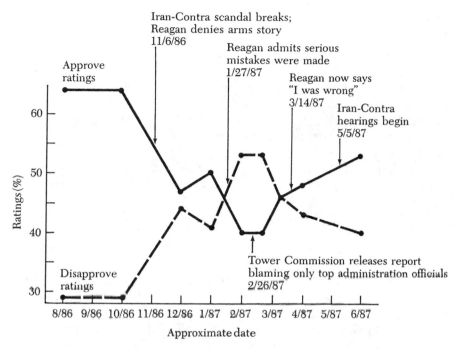

FIGURE 1
PERCENTAGE OF RESPONDENTS INDICATING APPROVAL OR DIS-
APPROVAL of President Reagan's job performance over the period of the
Iranamok incident in 1986 and 1987.

As Mr. Reagan's apparent noninvolvement became more obvious,
his approval ratings rapidly improved. The Approve and Disapprove
indexes again flip-flopped by April, 1987, and by June of that year
they had reached stable and, I am sure, welcome levels. Mr. Reagan
was always a hard man to keep down. No doubt part of his resilience
as an executive is attributable to his *personal* popularity. Keep in
mind that what are plotted in Figure 1 are his *job* approval ratings.
When the Gallup people inquired about respondents' feelings about
"Reagan as a person," his personal approval ratings never slipped
below 71% in the period covered in Figure 1 and did not even *budge*
as a consequence of Iranscam ("Reagan, the Man," 1987).

In sum, as contrasting patterns of cognitions were made available
to the American public in 1986 and 1987, its affect toward President
Reagan's job performance changed accordingly. When the relatively
bad news came in during November and December of 1986, there

were huge negative shifts in affect to match. Then, with the relatively good news available in the early spring of 1987, people again changed their evaluations of this personally popular man. To put it another way, C → A.

A → C consistency? An experimental investigation of the A → C link poses a special problem. Specifically, how might the researcher manipulate affect directly? One possible solution to this problem was offered by Rosenberg (1960). He hypnotized subjects and gave them posthypnotic suggestions that they would have strong positive or negative affective reactions to certain topics of that day. Sure enough, when subjects "woke up" they somehow brought their cognitions in line with their new affective reactions to the issues.

A more recent, and perhaps less exotic, method of directly evoking affective responses in people was offered by Niedenthal and Cantor (1986). Their approach relied on a large literature that showed that subjects' favorability reactions to photographs of faces were very much determined by the amount of pupil dilation of the eyes of the models. A very consistent finding is that subjects react much more favorably to photos of persons with dilated pupils than to photos of persons with constricted pupils. In this context, what is most interesting is that this influence can occur outside the awareness of the subject.

Niedenthal and Cantor took advantage of this automatic, stimulus-based affective reaction to test some ideas of how people categorize one another. For them, "it seems plausible to suspect that an initial nonconscious affective reaction to a person can guide a perceiver's selection from among available descriptive categories with which to organize his or her cognitive representation of the person" (Niedenthal and Cantor, 1986). In other words, for them it was plausible that A → C.

To check out this possibility, the researchers needed two sets of materials: some pictures of men and women with variations in pupil dilation, and some descriptions with which the people in the pictures could be characterized. Having obtained the photos, they created through pretests a large sample of positive or negative descriptions that were applicable to men or women, respectively. For example, here are one positive and one negative description for both male and female models:

Positive, female   She does charity work, is inventive, has warm, soft hands, and supports social programs.

Negative, female	She easily avoids noticing people, has a domineering personality, rarely shows emotions, and likes wealthy people.
Positive, male	He spends a lot of time with his wife and kids, is humorous, never frowns, and likes to drink beer.
Negative, male	He is driven by a desire for money, is paranoid, is unhealthy, and is unconcerned about the future.

The procedure for using these materials was fairly straightforward. A subject was shown a picture of a person with either dilated or constricted pupils and then was read a certain description of that person like those in the examples above. The subject's task was to indicate on a scale from 1 to 7 whether the description was not at all likely (1) to very likely (7) to fit the person in the picture. And it can be seen in Table II that the automatic, stimulus-based affective reactions to the size of the pupils in the pictures did influence subjects' cognitive categorizations of those models. Subjects felt more strongly that favorable descriptions applied to models whose pupils were dilated rather than constricted and that unfavorable descriptions applied more strongly to people with constricted pupils. In short, A → C.

B → A + C consistency? Can one's sheer behavior toward an object influence cognitions and affect regarding that object? Could this occur in the absence of new, external information? This proposition might first strike the reader as odd; we usually think about the reverse process, whereby beliefs and feelings influence behavior (A + C → B). However, the B → A + C link is plausible, and as a matter of fact, the bulk of Chapter 7 is devoted to this issue. For now, let us examine one of the earliest experiments devoted to this

TABLE II
Ratings of the likelihood that favorable or unfavorable descriptions were true of persons in pictures with dilated or constricted pupils

	PUPIL CONDITION	
Description	Dilated	Constricted
Favorable	4.33	4.08
Unfavorable	3.61	4.17

After Niedenthal and Cantor (1986).
Note. Ratings of the likelihood that a description was true of a person with dilated or constricted pupils ranged from 1 (not at all likely) to 7 (very likely).

topic. In a classic study, Brehm (1956) measured women's cognitions and affect regarding particular consumer products and then induced them to behave in a certain way toward those products. After the behavior occurred, Brehm checked for changes in subjects' affective and cognitive reactions.

The women (college students) were told that they were involved in consumer research and that their task was to evaluate products such as a toaster, a sandwich grill, a watch, and others. To get an idea of their combined affective–cognitive response, they were asked to rate each item for its desirability, where desirability meant the object's net usefulness in terms of its attractiveness and quality and how much it was needed. Following the initial ratings, the women were told that they could choose one of the objects as payment for their services, but that for various reasons their choices would be limited. Surreptitiously, the experimenter checked to see what two items were very desirable to a subject and then forced her to choose between those two things. For our purposes, it can be said that the chooser's behavior toward the chosen item was different from her behavior toward the item that was rejected. In a control condition, some other women were simply given a gift and thus did not choose (i.e., did not behave differentially toward one thing or another).

When the choice had been made or the gift had been accepted (depending on the condition), subjects were asked to reevaluate the items. For the women who had to choose, would their choices (behavior) have any influence on these second ratings? The entries in Table III indicate that the answer to this question is definitely yes. When the items were rated the second time, the desirability of the

TABLE III
Changes in the desirability of consumer products as a consequence of subjects' choice of a product

Experimental conditions	RATINGS		Rating change
	Initial ratings	Second ratings[a]	
Choice			
chosen	6.19	6.45	+ .26
rejected	5.23	4.57	− .66
Gift	5.91	5.91	.00

After Brehm (1956).
[a] Values in this column are extrapolated from Brehm's data.

chosen items increased, whereas the desirability of the rejected items decreased. That is, somehow the women's differential behavior toward the chosen and rejected items caused them to change their estimates of those items' attractiveness, quality, and usefulness. It was clearly the act of choosing that produced these shifts, because Table III indicates that the other women who obtained something without choosing it (i.e., in the gift condition) did not change their estimates of its desirability. Here is pretty strong evidence that one's behavior toward an entity can influence one's affect and cognitions regarding that entity.

The act of choosing between attractive items is not the only sort of behavior that can influence cognition and affect. Cook, Pallak, Storms, and McCaul (1977) provide a more recent example wherein they first measured (on a 91-point scale) students' attitudes toward nuclear power plants and determined that their entire sample was more or less opposed to such installations. Next, the students were immediately asked to write an essay, either on the unfavorability (consistent essay) or the favorability (discrepant essay) of nuclear power plants. After the completion of the essays, their attitudes were measured again, and it was found that both versions of essay writing resulted in shifts in favorability ratings. Students who wrote a consistent essay shifted in a direction that indicated that now they were even more opposed to the matter (-1.54 units on the scale), whereas those who had written an essay discrepant with their original position showed a relatively large shift toward a more favorable reaction to the issue of nuclear power ($+12.38$). Again, as in the earlier Brehm study, behavior led to shifts in favorability. To put it another way, $B \rightarrow A + C$.

THE CONSISTENCY OF THE A AND C COMPONENTS AND BEHAVIOR

The next two chapters will examine in great detail the problem of predicting actual behavior from attitudes, but here it is worthwhile to mention that knowledge of the A and C components, and in particular their relationship to one another, takes us some distance toward understanding ATTITUDE–BEHAVIOR CONSISTENCY or inconsistency. In the preceding sections it was noted that there is a certain amount of consistency between the components themselves (e.g., $A \rightarrow C$, $C \rightarrow A$), but that, although strong, these relationships are hardly perfect. This finding means that humans have some capacity or tolerance for inconsistency among attitudinal elements. For instance, a person might think dogs are wonderful companions because of the security and comfort they afford, but, because of an irritating allergy, that same person might not want a dog for a pet. For some time researchers have been finding at least suggestive evidence about the role of such A–C consistency in the determination of attitude–behavior connections.

Norman (1975), for one, hypothesized that a person's affect regarding an attitudinal object would predict her or his behavior, *if* that affect was consistent with the individual's cognitive component relative to the object. Similarly, cognition would predict behavior if it was consistent with the affective component. Where there was inconsistency between these components, behavior would be less predictable.

To test this idea, Norman (1975) took separate affective and cognitive measures of students' attitudes toward volunteering to be a subject in a psychological research project. The affective measure showed the degree of favorability of such an activity; the cognitive index related the activity to the person's goals. To establish A → C consistency, the students were first rank-ordered for their affect for volunteering. That is, the person with the highest or most positive affect was ranked first, the individual with the lowest affect was ranked last, and the remaining students were located in the list according to their respective levels of affect. Next, these same persons were rank-ordered for the positiveness of their cognitions about volunteering, and the two rank orders were compared. A person occupying pretty much the same slot in the two orders was considered to be consistent; a person occupying different slots in the two orderings was considered to be inconsistent.

It was a simple matter to see which kind of student, consistent or inconsistent in terms of affect and cognition, would actually volunteer to be a subject. In general, those people whose affective and cognitive reports were consistent were the most likely to behave in a way that conformed to those components. For these consistent types, the correlation (r) between, for example, affective scores and actual behavior ranged from .47 to .62 over several independent studies, whereas the affective scores of inconsistent people were far less predictive of behavior, resulting in correlation coefficients that ranged from −.28 to .24.

Even so, Norman (1975) failed to find compelling evidence that *cognitions* predicted behavior in high-consistency subjects. And mixed, but suggestive, results have come in from other researchers. Fazio and Zanna (1978) were interested in whether subjects' prior experience (high or low) with an activity would predict their volunteering for further participation. They also measured affect–cognition consistency toward that activity, but they found that such consistency was predictive only for people with low prior experience. Finally, Chaiken and Baldwin (1981) found somewhat stronger evidence for the consistency position, in that subjects high in affect–cognition consistency where the environment was concerned were less susceptible to manipulated influences on self-perceptions about the environment than were low-consistency subjects.

In sum, if findings on the influence of level of consistency of affect and cognition are sometimes mixed, they are interesting enough to warrant further consideration and research.

The Construct Validity of the Tripartite (A-B-C) Model

Most of the studies just reviewed looked at the pairwise correspondence of components, but none was designed to investigate the CONSTRUCT VALIDITY of the complete A-B-C (tripartite) model. That is, are all three really real? Do we actually need three components when maybe two, or even one, might be at the base of what we take to be attitudes? What sort of experimentation or testing could be used to pin down answers to these questions? How could we find out if the constructs called A, B, and C are valid as independent entities? The first step is to break down the notion of construct validity into *its* components: CONVERGENT VALIDITY and DISCRIMINANT VALIDITY. These two kinds of validity will be discussed in turn.

CONVERGENT VALIDITY

Convergent validity is found when two methods of assessing the same component produce comparable results (Campbell and Fiske, 1959). This idea is simple, but powerful. It says that if two things are really different, one ought to be able to measure that difference in a number of ways. That is, the results of various kinds of measurements should converge on, or point to, a conclusion that the two things in question are not the same. Let us take an obvious example to illustrate this proposition. Imagine for the moment some elephants and mice. Are these two kinds of creatures really different? Using a convergent validity approach, we can find out. First we will require a variety of measures that can be applied to both sorts of beast: perhaps height, weight, food consumption, distance traveled daily, fetal gestation period, longevity, and others. It can be seen that these measures rate very different things. What is obvious, of course, is that all the measures just listed would reveal huge differences between elephants and mice. In other words, the various kinds of information at our disposal will point to—converge on—the same conclusion: namely, that elephants and mice are *not* the same thing.

If each of the A-B-Cs of attitudes could be measured by properties like height and weight, establishing their convergent validities would be a relatively easy task. But these particular measures are not feasible, because the concepts (constructs) in question are not physical but rather psychological in nature. In assessing the convergent validity of the components, a different approach will have to be taken, such as that adopted by Ostrom (1969) and Kothandapani (1971). These two studies are fairly similar and have earned about the same critical appraisals (cf. Bagozzi, 1978; Breckler, 1984), so I will concentrate on Kothandapani's.

Kothandapani (1971) used what is known as a MULTITRAIT–MULTIMETHOD MATRIX. A multitrait–multimethod approach in this context is fairly straightforward. First, the multitrait part can be understood by substituting the term *component* for the term *trait*. In a sense, the A-B-Cs are "traits" of attitudes. Second, the multimethod part has already been discussed in terms of convergent measures, as in the animal example. The multimethod aspect simply calls for the measurement of, say, the A component in more than one way. By extension, the B and C components would also be measured in a number of different ways.

The topic that Kothandapani used as a vehicle for his research were attitudes of women living in low-income housing toward birth control. He sought to measure the components of these attitudes with several different kinds of scales, such as those described in the previous chapter. Kothandapani developed a Thurstone (equal-appearing interval) scale, a Likert (summated ratings) scale, a Guttman-like (scalogram analysis) scale, and a self-report scale, all tailored to the A component. Next, he constructed these four kinds of scales for the B and for the C components, building 12 scales in all.

Having built the scales (methods) for these components (traits), Kothandapani could then set up the matrix. Such a matrix is seen in Table IV, which represents a part of his Table III in the original publication of 1971. Attention here will be limited to a comparison of the Thurstone scales with the Likert scales, since this simplifies things and does not distort any conclusions. The logic and power of the matrix is as follows. As a test for convergent validity, when the three components of attitude (A-B-C) are measured by different methods (here, Thurstone scale and Likert scale), a component should correlate higher with *itself* when measured by two scales than with another component when measured by the respective scales.

TABLE IV
A multitrait–multimethod matrix of correlation coefficients (r) that indicates the
convergent validity of the A-B-C components of attitudes

Likert scales	CORRELATION WITH THURSTONE SCALES		
	Affect (A)	Behavior (B)	Cognition (C)
Affect (A)	.58	.05	.34
Behavior (B)	.03	.49	.08
Cognition (C)	.20	.22	.50

After Kothandapani, 1971.
Note. Underlined coefficients in the table represent the critical comparison in that
particular row. In order to satisfy the criterion for convergent validity, the underlined
value should be the highest in that row; all the cases in this table do satisfy this criterion.
In other words, the components (A, B, and C) correlated more highly with themselves
than with other components over different methods of measurement.

To obtain information necessary to arrive at the correlational
analysis just outlined, Kothandapani measured women's feelings (A
component), intentions (B component), and beliefs (C component)
regarding contraceptives; he used the scales he had devised. The
intercorrelations of these measures for two of the scales are the
entries in Table IV. It can be seen in the table that the Likert A
scale correlated highly with the Thurstone A scale, but much less so
with the Thurstone B and C scales. Similarly, the Likert B scale
correlated strongly with the Thurstone B scale but not at all with the
other two kinds of Thurstone scales, A and C. Finally, the same sort
of scale-to-scale relationship is seen between the Likert and Thurstone C scales, but there is a lesser relation between the Likert C
and the Thurstone A and B scales. In sum, a component correlated
higher with itself when measured by two different scales than it did
with another component when measured by respective scales.

So, it appears that the A, B, and C components of attitudes could
be viable entities in light of the method of study employed by
Kothandapani (1971). His method of convergent validity looked at
each of the components from a different perspective or view (scale
type) but saw much the same picture from these various vantage
points. The three critical comparisons along the diagonal of Table IV
support the idea that A and B and C are different components. That
is, they correlate more highly with themselves than with any other
component over different methods of measurement. In fact, when
considering all four of the scales used by Kothandapani, it turns out

that there are a total of 18 such critical comparisons available (see his Table III), and *all* 18 are large enough to lend support to the separate validity of the A-B-C components of attitudes.

Discriminant Validity

We have just seen that convergent validity involves an examination of the *same* concept from different perspectives. On the other hand, there is an approach called DISCRIMINANT VALIDITY that has to do with the degree to which a concept *differs* from other concepts. A method for establishing discriminant validity is a statistical technique known as factor analysis, and a look at aspects of factor analysis is potentially useful for conceptualizing the tripartite (A-B-C) model.

One such test is called covariance structure analysis (Breckler, 1984). This form of analysis allows an estimation of relations among hypothetical, unobservable constructs called LATENT VARIABLES. In our parlance, three possible latent variables are the A-B-Cs in question. (These are unobservable constructs, because we never really expect to see them directly; they are psychological in nature.) However, there is another kind of variable in covariance structure analysis called MEASURED VARIABLES. These are observable and correspond to the types of scales we have been using throughout. The idea is that each latent variable is associated with (represented by) one or more measured variables (Breckler, 1984).

Figure 2 presents a diagram that shows a three-part structure in the terms of covariance structure analysis. By convention, latent variables are displayed within circles and measured variables within boxes. Our three latent variables are thus seen within circles in Figure 2, and nine measured variables (X_1 through X_9) are indicated in boxes. Notice in the example in Figure 2 that measured variables X_1 through X_3 are clustered near the latent variable of affect, X_4 through X_6 are associated with behavior, and X_7 through X_9 are clustered near cognition. In fact, specific measured variables are connected by arrows to particular latent variables. The arrows indicate that particular measured variables are associated (correlated) with a certain latent variable and not with the others.

We can compare the hypothetical tripartite (three-factor) model of attitudes represented in Figure 2 with a hypothetical one-factor model represented in Figure 3. There, all the measured variables are correlated with a single latent variable called "attitude." This one-factor model represents both a theoretically (conceptual) and statistically (empirical) competing model. The beauty of all of this is that, assuming there are usable data collected in a proper way, we can

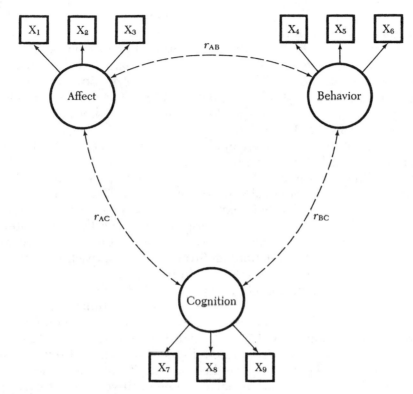

FIGURE 2
STRUCTURAL REPRESENTATION OF A TRIPARTITE MODEL of an attitude. Solid arrows indicate factor loadings and dashed arrows indicate interfactor correlations. (After Breckler, 1984.)

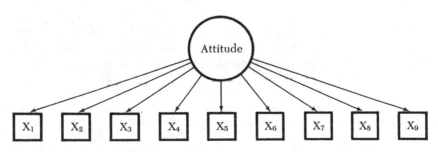

FIGURE 3
STRUCTURAL REPRESENTATION OF A ONE-FACTOR MODEL of an attitude. (After Breckler, 1984.)

enter those data into an appropriate computer program and the statistical output will tell us, explicitly, which model (one- or three-factor) best "fits" the data (Breckler, 1984). For our purposes it is enough to understand that there is a single statistical value called the "normed fit index" that expresses which of the two competing theoretical models best relates to data patterns. The normed fit index can range from 0 to 1, and the closer it is to 1, the better the fit (or the more plausible the model).

That is, if the three-factor model in Figure 2 meets the criterion of a fit of .90 or better, it can be said that various measured variables are "loading" on three different latent variables, thus, the A-B-C model would gain empirical support. Still, one other feature seen in Figure 2 must be clarified. Note the dashed lines between those variables. These represent correlations (r) between the three latent variables themselves. Common sense suggests that if these intercomponent (interfactor) correlations all turned out to approach 1.00, then, in effect, the three-factor model would be equivalent to a one-factor model, and the proposition of independent A-B-C factors would lose support. Do these correlations mean a necessary stumbling block to the A-B-C model? After all, almost everything we have seen heretofore in this chapter argued that the A-B-C components were consistent (correlated) with one another. Is the A-B-C model doomed to rejection because of this expected consistency? Not at all. The intercomponent correlations are expected to be positive, but not perfect. Thus, we look for two things from an actual factor analysis of appropriate data: (1) a *high* normed fit index and (2) *moderate* correlations between the factors.

The research. A stringent factor-analytic study contrasting a three-factor model with a one-factor model of attitudes was carried out by Breckler (1984). But before his findings were put into a computer, Breckler made sure things went right in the lab, where the data were to be collected. For the purpose of this account, he insisted on three conditions that in his view were essential to test the tripartite model's validity:

1. A variety of measures should be used, both verbal and nonverbal, because reliance on verbal reports alone (as in earlier studies) might inflate the interfactor correlations.
2. Dependent measures of affect, behavior, and cognition must be *responses* to an attitudinal object. That is, because the A-B-Cs can be considered to be alternative response categories, reliance on a cognitive representation of the object could again result in an overestimation of the interfactor correlations. To

guard against this false estimate, it is necessary that the object be *in* the situation so that it can be responded to.

3. Each A-B-C component should be tapped by multiple, different measures, because no single measure can be expected to capture the complete nature of what we have called a latent variable. Further, any given measure will necessarily produce some measurement error, and the multiple different measures will tend to cancel out each other's errors.

Breckler satisfied all of his own criteria, including the one that the attitudinal object be in the physical presence of a subject so that "responses" were literally elicited. In order to promote strong or clear responding, a live snake was used for the attitudinal object for all subjects. Breckler also saw to it that each of the components was measured in several different ways. In all, he used nine measures, three each for the three components. Breckler (1984) can be consulted for the details of these measures, but here it is sufficient to note that they consisted of (among others) conventional measures such as rating scales (for affect), reports of comfortable distances with respect to the object (for behavior), and semantic differentials (for cognition). We will label these nine measures simply affective measures 1, 2, and 3; behavioral measures 1, 2, and 3; and cognitive measures 1, 2, and 3.

The results. When Breckler entered the data he obtained from these procedures into the computer for analysis, he found strong evidence for the tripartite model of attitudes. The measured variables all correlated highly on their respective factors, as seen in Table V (A). (Note that these associations, called loadings, can range from 0 to 1.) In terms of the normed fit index, that overall value was reported as .92, which exceeds the .90 criterion level established earlier. In short, there was a good fit: the measured variables did load on three *different* latent variables. Further, Table V (B) indicates that the interfactor correlations were moderate, as expected. These moderate correlations, along with the high normed fit index (.92) support a tripartite model of attitudes. In contrast, a weaker normed fit index of .74 for a one-factor model led Breckler to reject it.

How are we to best understand Breckler's results? It should be pointed out that it was not for nothing that Breckler picked a snake for the attitudinal object in his study. He expected that most people would have had little direct experience with snakes, and thus affect, behavior, and cognition would be potentially alternative response categories toward such an object. Even so, the moderate interfactor correlations suggested some consistency across these components.

TABLE V
Factor loading values and interfactor correlations supporting a tripartite model
of attitudes

A. *Factor loading values*

Comparison	Estimate
Affect	
Measure 1	.92
Measure 2	.47
Measure 3	.54
Behavior	
Measure 1	.77
Measure 2	.63
Measure 3	.85
Cognition	
Measure 1	.64
Measure 2	.95
Measure 3	.59

B. *Interfactor correlations*

Comparison	Estimate
Affect/behavior	.50
Affect/cognition	.38
Behavior/cognition	.70

After Breckler (1984).

On the other hand, the high individual factor loadings seen in Table
V and the high normed fit index of .92 mean that we can consider
the latent variables of affect, behavior, and cognition to be separate
components. I take this to imply not that *all* attitudes conform to the
tripartite model but that a three-component scheme seems to be a
useful way to conceptualize many attitudes.

   In this context it will be useful to note that Bagozzi and Burnkrant
(1979) are identified as proponents of a two-component model of
attitudes: affect and cognition. Using state-of-the-art statistical procedures, they have found support for their position to the extent
that, in the sense developed above, a two-factor solution "fits" attitudinal data better than does a one-factor solution (see Bagozzi and

Burnkrant, 1985). Now, as I understand it, support for a two-component model does not necessarily rule out the possibility that there could also be support for a three-component model, or vice versa. What is perhaps most significant here is that both the two-component model of Bagozzi and Burnkrant (1985) and the three-component model of Breckler seem to be alternative ways to conceptualize "attitudes" (as defined in those respective studies) relative to a one-component model. Multicomponent models are apparently here to stay, even if a one-component model should be shown to apply to certain attitudinal domains (see, for example, Fishbein and Ajzen, 1974).

Persuasion and the A-B-C Components of Attitudes

The rather wide variety of research just reviewed indicates that it is useful to conceive of attitudes in terms of their separate components. Indeed, attention to these distinctions may well have practical implications. There are a great many people in this world trying to get us to form or change our attitudes, especially in connection with their clients' products or programs. We sometimes look with disdain upon commercial advertising and other PERSUASIVE COMMUNICATIONS that represent vested interests. But some propaganda amounts to education and is for our own good. Apparently, it is necessary to continuously inform the American public that it should not smoke or drink to excess, that it should drive safely, prevent forest fires, indulge in safe sex, vote at election time, and continue taking prescribed drugs for hypertension. All this persuasion requires a continuing investment of time, money, and energy; perhaps it could be done more effectively. One can speculate that such messages might have more impact if they impinged on all the components of attitudes simultaneously rather than being aimed at just one or another of the components.

One familiar source of persuasive communications are special interest groups. The recent flap in the summer of 1988 over the film *The Last Temptation of Christ* provides such an example (see Figure 4). Fundamentalist Christians and the Roman Catholic Church denounced the film as morally objectionable, and, from all appearances, seemed to want to convince everyone to shun it (Ansen, Murr, and Reese, 1988; "'Temptation' Tempest," 1988). The basis of the arguments against the film seemed to be one-dimensional and largely emotional, as evidenced in the picket signs in Figure 4. The statement of one detractor that the picture was the product of "Jewish

FIGURE 4
DEMONSTRATORS IN HOLLYWOOD protesting the film *The Last Temptation of Christ* in 1988.

cultural scum in Los Angeles" ("Movie Madness," 1988) may represent a "cognition," but it certainly is emotional in tone, too. That is, these messages seem to center on the "A" component of our attitudes toward the film. One wonders if the protesters and critics might have been more influential in blocking the picture if they had made a more rounded attack on our attitudes.

This wave of protest against *Temptation* was reminiscent of a similar but more conceptually balanced outcry of a few years ago over two other films that centered on the life of Christ. At the time, Rajecki (1982) reported on a real-life, three-pronged A-B-C message as seen in a television program titled "Those Sacrilegious Movies." This show had been prepared by an organization termed the Interfaith Committee against Blasphemy, and a letter from the head of the Committee (W. S. McBirnie, personal communication) estimated that it had been aired on U.S. and Canadian television some 644 times in the early 1980s. The point of the program was to urge the viewer to boycott two commercial films, *The Passover Plot* and *Many Faces of Jesus*. As an indication of the nature of the films, media reaction to the two movies is provided in Figure 5, a collage that was prepared by the Committee.

The Committee objected to the films because of their alleged blasphemous content. The program was staged as a panel show and in the main revealed the views of three discussants: Dr. McBirnie, a Baptist minister; Fr. Manning, a Catholic priest; and Mr. Howe, a layperson. The particular arguments against the films offered by each man are interesting, but even more so are the perspectives each adopted. That is, what was absorbing was the tone or theme that each represented.

An informal content analysis of the statements of the three discussants is presented in Table VI. The entries in the table were excerpted from recordings of the television program. These panel members were strongly individualistic, and the differences in their styles are evident in the table. Fr. Manning appeared to be the most emotional of the three and seemed to be the most personally upset

FIGURE 5
MEDIA TREATMENT in the early 1980s of two controversial films about the life of Christ.

TABLE VI
Informal content analysis of the affective, behavioral, and cognitive components of
the Interfaith Committee against Blasphemy panel discussion

Panelist and component	Sample statements
Fr. Manning: Affect	Now, if Jesus is not God, we're left completely hopeless, and I find that the idealism, and the reality of hope and life that can be moved in, are lost. If everybody says, oh well, Jesus was just kind of a pretend: a fake, we're going to believe that, and we're not going to have the power of his life and his love living in our hearts right now able to transform everything that we can do. It touches the heart of our whole existence. We can start to mobilize as Christians who have committed themselves to Jesus Christ and say I believe in him; I'm willing to be counted. I'm willing to stand up and say: Yes! I believe in him, and I don't want anybody running him down by saying that he's not God, that he's not the center of my life, that he's not the power of God eternal, . . . and showing us the real meaning of life.
Mr. Howe: Behavior	I'm not one to fight nudity or profanity to that degree like I feel about somebody mocking God . . . I think that's pulling the ground roots out from everybody, and I think we should smack them right back up side the head. I can't even believe that people out there will even let this kind of thing come down. I hope this is not the first time they've become aware of it, and I hope they're already fighting it, because it's a mess. . . . It's coming to the screens, and I think the best thing we can do is break the producer by not seeing his films, and discourage those kind of films.

(continued)

by the issue before the Committee. Mr. Howe was also evidently motivated, but in addition he was clearly a rugged individual and a man of action. Dr. McBirnie was the calmest of the three and was analytical and scholarly in demeanor.

Whether this discussion was spontaneous or scripted, it was highly engaging and effective. Part of its success, I think, is that the material included arguments concerning affect (from Fr. Manning), behavior (from Mr. Howe), and cognitions (from Dr. McBirnie). All the components of the viewer's attitude toward the films were assailed. Viewers not only got the point that the films were factually

TABLE VI (*continued*)

Panelist and component	Sample statements
	We, as a people, now have got to do something about it. Now, I've heard from everybody here (but) I'd really like to hear how we get out there and stop these dudes from making these kinds of movies, and how we stop them from going to the pictures. . . . I mean, it's going to decay the whole world. I mean, we're sitting here intellectualizing, but, boy, it's got to *stop now!*
Dr. McBirnie: Cognition	I wrote (my book: *The Search for the Twelve Apostles*) to find out by research, and took 32 trips to the Middle East and to Rome with the cooperation of the archeological authorities in all those countries to make one point; and that is, what became of the 12 apostles after the Biblical record was over? . . .
	I included (in my book) an extra five chapters, including a very carefully researched biography of St. Paul. I know where he was born; I went there. I know where he died; I've been there. I know what he did in various years. I know what his style is in the original Greek. I can tell you this: He wrote the books that bear his name.
	Having done the original work on the actual location of both the place of his death and his burial, I know what there is known. This is the total that is known among scholars about the tomb of Jesus. . . . This (film) is based purely on thin air. It has no basis in scholarship

wrong (cognition), but also were given reason to feel anxious and concerned about them (affect) and were further given guidelines for means of dealing with the problem (behavior). Of course, without a systematic program of evaluation, one cannot draw sound conclusions concerning the effectiveness of such a global assault on an attitude. However, the Committee argued that the program was working. "Our TV special has already forced a change in the advertising of 'The Passover Plot' and most people have been staying away from it because we have made it a public issue" (W. S. McBirnie, personal communication).

The Structure of Attitudes: I. Consistency with One Another

The panel discussants described in the previous section were consistent with one another in their attempts to persuade the viewer, and we have already reviewed a good deal of laboratory work that indicates consistency of attitudinal components *within* individual attitudes. Interest in consistency has also extended to the idea of consistency *between* attitudes. Indeed, social psychologists have long held that consistency is the rule in our social thinking; several volumes have been devoted exclusively to that topic (e.g., Abelson et al., 1968; Feldman, 1966; Zanna, Higgins, and Herman, 1982). Over the years a number of models or theories of such consistency have been developed; and it is useful to at least sketch these classics to increase our understanding of the nature of attitudes. In the section to follow, we will consider Heider's balance theory, Osgood's congruity theory, and Festinger's dissonance theory.

HEIDER'S BALANCE THEORY

Imagine that you are a member of a group of three people. You like the other two individuals and they, in turn, each think highly of you. However, in this example, it happens that the other two people cannot stand each other. How does this situation strike you? If you have ever found yourself in a real group similar to this hypothetical one, you probably recall how awkward the situation felt. According to Heider's (1958) terminology, the strain would arise because the attitudes within the group were in a state of IMBALANCE and there would be psychological pressure to restore BALANCE. There are several things that could be done to reduce the strain or awkwardness in the situation. To resolve the problem, you could get the two antagonists to change their attitudes and begin to like each other. Then everyone would be friendly and the group would be in harmony. Alternatively, you yourself might develop a dislike for one of the others, who would reciprocate and begin to dislike you. This shift would remove the condition of imbalance because you and your remaining friend would now have a common enemy or antagonist. Hence, either form of resolution would remove the imbalance or inconsistency in the situation.

This principle of balance and imbalance can be applied to any mental representation of a three-part social relationship. Consider another example: if you were attracted to someone because of their physical appearance but could not tolerate her or his political views, a state of imbalance would occur and you would desire to somehow modify the situation. There are a great many ways to resolve this inconsistency. However, the three most straightforward choices are to (1) decide that the political view was not really intolerable, (2) induce the person to change their political views, or (3) decide that the person was not so attractive after all.

Heider (1958) used the symbols P, X, and O to illustrate these kinds of relationships. P is the perceiver, O is some other person, and X can be a third person or some attribute of O. Figure 6 presents balanced and imbalanced states involving P, O, and X. The plus and minus signs in the figure indicate a sentiment or an attribute. For example, P + O would indicate that P likes O, whereas P − O would mean that P dislikes O. Similarly, O + X might mean that O owns X or says X or endorses X; O − X would indicate that O rejects X or criticizes X. In examining each three-part scheme in Figure 6, one can get an intuitive feeling for why it would be balanced or not. However, a general rule for determining which state (balanced or imbalanced) a triad represents is to multiply all the signs in a triad.

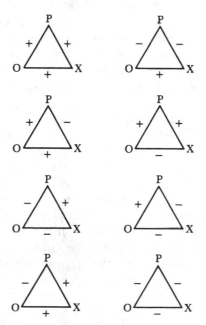

FIGURE 6
BALANCED AND IMBALANCED STATES or structures according to Heider's (1958) theory. Methods for determining whether a structure is balanced or imbalanced are discussed in the text.

In algebra, a plus times a plus yields a product that is plus; a minus times a minus yields a plus; and a plus times a minus equals a minus value. If the product of a triad's three signs is plus, that triad is balanced; if the product is minus, the triad is imbalanced. One can use this rule to discover the balanced and imbalanced triads in Figure 6 and can then match the rule-specified states against one's intuitive judgments.

Heider's model is a consistency model because it predicts the resolution of inconsistency. If a structure is imbalanced, there will be psychological pressure to modify some feature of the relationships. If a structure is already balanced, it will tend to remain in balance.

OSGOOD'S CONGRUITY MODEL

This model (Osgood and Tannenbaum, 1955) has to do with a more limited aspect of our social awareness, but one that is important nevertheless. It focuses on the manner in which we integrate communications concerning other persons (or any object or issue). Such messages could result in a condition of INCONGRUITY. For example, suppose that someone you disliked intensely (i.e., you would rate that person as a −3 on a scale from −3 to +3) says something good about another person for whom you have a high regard (rated at +2 on the scale.) This would be an incongruent and puzzling situation. You might well wonder why someone you dislike so much would go to the trouble of being nice to your favorite. Are they friends? Are they in cahoots?

Osgood's CONGRUITY model predicts that this state of affairs would cause you to change your attitude toward *both* people, the source and the object of the communication. Osgood and Tannenbaum (1955) offer a mathematical formula to calculate these changes, but for our purposes it is sufficient to say that your resulting attitudes will be a compromise between the initial polarities of your attitudes toward the two people before you heard the communication. A basic dictum of the model is that when a disliked person endorses a liked other, the resultant attitude will be the same toward both. By reason of association with each other, the person you liked previously will lose some of your esteem, but the person you initially disliked intensely will improve somewhat in your estimation. In terms of the current example, the model predicts that the final attitude toward both persons would be −1. (Details on the mathematics of the Osgood model are available from the original source, and a clear exposition can also be found in Kiesler, Collins, and Miller (1969).)

FESTINGER'S DISSONANCE THEORY

Festinger (1957) proposed a general theory of attitudinal consistency and argued that it was possible for a person to experience COGNITIVE DISSONANCE. Here, the meaning of the word *cognitive* is similar to its definition earlier in this chapter, but Festinger's use of the term is somewhat broader in that cognitive dissonance could also involve affective reactions.

According to the theory, cognitions are in a state of consonance when they follow from each other. For example, if I am aware that I am employed as a professor and judge that my work as a professor is interesting and the pay is good, it makes sense to go on being a professor. On the other hand, cognitions are in a state of dissonance when one does not follow from the other. To modify the preceding example, if I think my professorial duties are uninteresting and the pay is bad, does it make sense to continue in the field? The heart of Festinger's theory is that when cognitive dissonance occurs, that state makes one uncomfortable and there is a motivation to reduce the discomfort by *making* the cognitions more consonant. In the situation where the work was uninteresting and the pay low, just what psychological adjustments could be made to reduce the dissonance? Perhaps the work could be seen as interesting after all, and the pay not bad for this kind of job.

The idea of cognitive dissonance can be widely applied to many circumstances and to many attitudinal relationships. Of the consistency theories reviewed here, dissonance theory has received by far the most attention. Whereas most of the consistency theories get at least fairly high marks from critics (e.g., Kiesler et al., 1969), dissonance theory has attracted both dedicated adherents and insistent detractors. Because it can be viewed as one of the major theoretical developments in social psychology, Festinger's formulation is given detailed treatment in a subsequent chapter.

The Structure of Attitudes: II. Higher Order Organization

The consistency theories inform us that an attitude does not exist in a vacuum and that certain attitudes can have implications for other attitudes. However, it is possible, conceptually at least, to go far beyond the relatively simple dynamics captured by these particular consistency theories. To use an analogy, one can imagine an attitude as a planet in a system of other planets. Given the laws of physics, lesser or greater changes in one planet will have more or less serious consequences for the remaining bodies, depending where they are. Within the analogy, changes in a given attitude may have various implications for the other attitudes in that attitudinal system. But the laws of physics do not necessarily apply to psychological phenomena, so the usefulness of the planetary analogy has limits.

Fortunately, Bem (1970) has sketched a workable alternative idea of the higher order organization of attitudes in terms of what he called the vertical structure, the horizontal structure, and the centrality of beliefs. Because beliefs (cognitions) are certainly germane to the analyses presented elsewhere in this chapter, it seems reasonable to extend Bem's general scheme beyond beliefs to attitudes in the present meaning. Bem's analysis of belief structures rests on the use of syllogisms, but because attitudes are made up of more than beliefs, the syllogism approach will not be attempted here. Still, we are indebted to Bem for the basic conception. (For further work on consistency over beliefs, see Henninger and Wyer (1976); O'Malley and Thistlewaite (1980); Wyer (1974).)

Vertical Structure, Horizontal Structure, and Centrality

In discussing structure and centrality, let us begin with an attitudinal example close to everyday experience. Most of us have pretty strong convictions about the existence or nonexistence of what the Western world conceives of as God or a Supreme Being. It is not farfetched to state that a given person—say, someone who believes in God—has an attitude toward God. That person may love God; this emotional state reflects an affective component. That person may also feel that God is powerful, beneficent, and can work miracles; these ideas represent a cognitive component. Finally, that person may intend to act in certain ways out of the so-called fear of God (disinclination to give offense to God or to incur God's wrath), an intention that reflects a behavioral component.

Having established that our hypothetical person has a positive attitude toward God, it would not be surprising to discover that the person holds a related set of attitudes, as illustrated in the example in Figure 7. Many people who believe in God are also active in one or another kind of organized religion or faith. These believers presumably have a positive attitude toward their own organization and its dogma as the earthly manifestation of God's will or teaching. Finally, because most religions preach and practice some form of brotherly love (i.e., we are all God's children and we should help

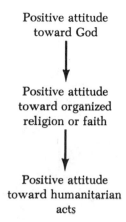

FIGURE 7
VERTICAL STRUCTURE culminating in a positive attitude toward humanitarian acts.

one another), it again would not be startling to find that our fictional person also has a positive attitude toward the policy or at least the notion of humanitarian acts, such as caring for the needy and comforting the sick.

Therefore, this final attitude toward humanitarian acts in this particular chain is based on a VERTICAL STRUCTURE. It is a higher order attitude because it is predicated or built upon *other* attitudes. (If it seems confusing that the higher order "humanitarian acts" are at the bottom of the figure, simply invert the page.) Bem (1970) might say that this was an elaborated or differentiated attitude, in the same sense that he speaks of an elaborated or differentiated belief.

An interesting characteristic of higher order attitudes is their apparent vulnerability. Consider our imaginary person's attitude toward humanitarian acts. That attitude is based on a prior attitude toward religion or faith, which in turn is based on a still prior attitude toward God. Should either of these prior attitudes undergo change, for whatever reason, it seems that the tertiary humanitarian attitude would invariably follow suit. But it turns out to be the case that a dramatic shift in one's attitude toward God or religion need *not* effect a marked change in one's humanitarian attitude, if that same attitude is anchored to other vertical structures of attitudes (see Figure 8).

The same higher order, tertiary attitude in this constellation is hooked to more than one elaborated series of prior attitudes. Here

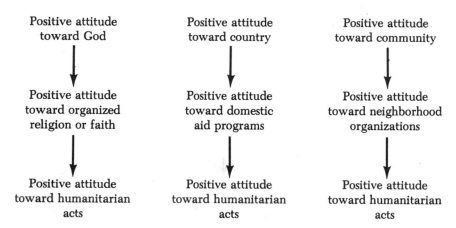

FIGURE 8
HORIZONTAL STRUCTURE culminating in a positive attitude toward humanitarian acts.

we can speak of the HORIZONTAL STRUCTURE underlying the higher order opinion concerning humanitarianism. In short, in this example the inclination toward humanitarianism is broadly based. Under these circumstances, should a person's attitude toward God completely reverse, it is still possible and even likely that the tertiary attitude would be maintained as usual by the horizontal structure (i.e., the remaining attitudes toward one's country or community). Therefore, changes in a given attitude can have more or less serious implications for other attitudes, depending on their location in vertical and horizontal structures.

Finally, a word on another structural characteristic is in order. Certain attitudes must, by some standard, be more important than others. The notion of CENTRALITY implies that there are some attitudes that are *central* to our basic concerns. Consider some attitudes about things that are right here, right now. By this stage the reader must have some attitude about this book, but that attitude can hardly be said to be central to the reader's concerns. If the reader is a student, he or she can drop the course and sell the book; if an instructor, he or she can adopt some other text or recommend this text to his or her colleagues. If one's attitude toward the book changed one way or another, probably few other attitudes would be affected. On the other hand, one's attitude toward God is probably much more central to basic concerns, and it is not uncommon to find a person's entire life organized around such an important attitudinal object (witness the conversion of Saul to St. Paul).

Further, let the reader consider his or her attitudes toward himself or herself. Doubtless, attitudes toward the self are central, for much of what we do or do not do is based on our judgments of our own capacities and strengths, limitations and weaknesses. If an attitude as central as those toward oneself underwent a drastic alteration, no doubt one's viewpoint on many other things would be changed as well. Since this consideration is so fascinating, an entire chapter has been devoted to it later in the book.

Higher Order Organization: A Domino Effect

To take an experimental perspective, one could generate a hypothesis that higher order attitudes would change as a result of a DOMINO EFFECT. When dominoes are stood on end a short distance apart in a column, knocking over the first (or last) domino guarantees that all the dominoes will fall over, in order. Therefore, if we could experimentally topple some prior attitude in the laboratory, we should see higher order or terminal attitudes topple accordingly. Indeed, evidence for such a domino-like effect comes from a study by Hendrick and Seyfried (1974). These writers were not speaking about domino effects as they have been identified here, nor were they explicit about higher order effects or structure. Nevertheless, these researchers have provided us with very useful data in this domain.

Hendrick and Seyfried's (1974) actual concern was whether procedures used to change attitudes in the laboratory really did change something or whether subjects only went along with a persuasive communication (for example) simply to please the experimenter. The basic strategy of their research was, first, to try to persuade some subjects to change their minds on an issue and, next, to see whether this new opinion influenced subsequent responses. It is these subsequent responses that are most interesting to us, because they were, in effect, reflections of higher order attitudes. To be more specific, Hendrick and Seyfried wanted to find out which type of person would ultimately be attractive to the subject. It is well known that, everything else being equal, people are highly attracted to others who share their own attitudes and opinions (Berscheid, 1985; Byrne, 1971). *This*, then, is the higher order attitude to which I have been alluding. If one's attraction to some stranger is based on a match between attitudes, then this very liking (which itself is attitudinal) is a higher order effect based on prior attitudes, because the terminal attitude is predicated on the prior attitudes. Hence, Hendrick and Seyfried's setup provides an ingenious and convenient (for us) test of the domino hypothesis. If their persuasive communication really changed a subject's prior attitude, would there then be related patterns of attraction later on?

The research. All college student subjects in that study were pretested in their regular classes for their attitudes toward the issue of students voting in local elections. Responses to the issue could range from 5 (con) to 25 (pro); most students were in favor of the idea as reflected in an overall sample mean of approximately 21. Pairs of students were then selected on the criterion that their individual scores matched closely. On a random basis, one member of each matched pair was assigned to an experimental group, and the other was assigned to a control condition.

The procedural difference between the two conditions was that there was an attempt at persuading the experimental subjects to change their minds about the issue of student voters. Individuals in the experimental group were called into the laboratory shortly after they had reported their original attitudes. Each was asked to read a three-page essay, ostensibly written by a student in an English class, that was strongly in opposition to students voting in local elections. Thus, this essay was a persuasive communication, and such communications often lead to attitude change. When a student had finished reading the essay, his or her *own* attitude toward the voting issue was assessed once again. To use the terms of Hendrick and Seyfried, the two indexes of attitude—before and after the persuasive communication—were called the pretest and posttest measures. There was quite a change in the students' attitudes as a consequence of reading the persuasive communication, as we shall see in a moment. The people in the control group also had their attitudes measured twice—pretest and posttest—but with no persuasive communication in between. Not surprisingly, the attitudes of the controls did not change from pretest to posttest.

Next, a critical step in the experiment occurred. Each subject once again returned to the laboratory after the posttest and was asked to examine certain attitudinal ratings on the issue of student voting that presumably reflected the attitudes of some other persons, two strangers. For a subject in the experimental condition, the attitude of one of the strangers was identical to that subject's pretest attitude, whereas the attitude of the other stranger was identical to her or his posttest attitude. The point of having the subject examine these purported attitudinal ratings was to see which stranger would be judged (on scales ranging from 2 to 14) as most similar and attractive to the subject. Recall that past research has shown that similarity of attitudes promotes attraction; thus, the subject's ratings of the similarity and attractiveness of the two strangers with different attitudes provides a check on whether the subject's own attitudes *really* changed as a result of reading the persuasive communication. Would a subject be most attracted to a person who held his or her pretest attitude on the issue or to one who held his or her posttest attitude on the issue? To use the terminology employed earlier, in viewing the subject's reaction to the strangers as an attitude, would this higher order attitude be influenced by changes in a prior attitude? As a guard against the possibility of simple chance shifts or preferences, each matched control subject was also presented with the purported attitudes of two strangers: one that was similar to a control subject's pretest attitude and one that was dissimilar to that attitude.

The results. Effects of these procedures and tests are presented in Table VII. The first row in the table indicates the attitudes and the amount of attitude change of the subjects in the experimental (persuaded) treatment and the control treatment. Because they were

TABLE VII
Average higher order similarity and attraction attitude scores as related to prior attitudes

| | GROUPS | | | |
| | Experimental (persuaded) | | Control (not persuaded) | |
Measure	Pretest	Posttest	Pretest	Posttest
Prior attitude:[a] voting issue	21.2	16.3	21.1	21.1
	Prestest stranger	Posttest stranger	Pretest stranger	Posttest stranger
Higher-order attitude:[b] similarity	8.3	12.1	11.7	8.0
attraction	9.3	11.3	11.6	8.9

After Hendrick and Seyfried, (1974).
[a] Scores could range from 5 (con) to 25 (pro).
[b] Scores could range from 2 (low) to 14 (high).

intentionally paired on the basis of matching pretest scores, the pretest means across the two groups turn out to be very close. However, the effect of the persuasive communication can be clearly seen in the posttest mean of the experimental group, which gives evidence of a shift away from those persons' original attitude in the direction of the position advocated in the essay.

It remains to be seen whether this shift in prior attitude would result in what we have been calling a higher order attitude. That is, would the attitude change of the experimental subjects lead to a related pattern of preference for strangers with similar versus dissimilar attitudes? The answer to this question is definitely yes. To begin with, as shown in Table VII, control subjects saw themselves as more similar to and more attracted to alleged strangers who had attitudes that were like those subjects' pretest (and by extension, posttest) attitudes. On the contrary, the experimental subjects judged themselves to be more similar to and were more attracted to alleged strangers that had attitudes that were like these latter subjects' posttest attitudes. In other words, the shift in attitudes for the experimental subjects did have a domino effect on their subsequent or higher order attitudes. A change in a presumably important attitude seems to have led to the outcome that related or terminal attitudes came into line.

In short, data like that reported by Hendrick and Seyfried (1974) support the long-standing idea of cognitive consistency in the area of our social mentality. These particular results tell us that such consistency can go beyond the bounds of adjustments within a given attitude. Processes of change and stabilization, termed a domino effect, occur across much wider attitude domains. Ralph Waldo Emerson's saying about consistency being the hobgoblin of little minds notwithstanding, it appears that most of our attitudes sort themselves out to reach some optimal state of harmony.

A Summing Up

In this chapter we have encountered an introduction to the components and structure of attitudes. It has proved useful to conceptualize attitudes in this fashion, for we now can better appreciate their complexity. However, while complex, attitudes are also "elegant" to an extent. By that I mean that attitudes seem to work in a limited, knowable number of ways. There apparently is consistency both within and between attitudes. Perhaps future research will discover anarchy and chaos in the workings of attitudes. But I doubt it. Short of pathological states, attitudes seem to "make sense." This brings us to the matters to be taken up in the next unit. Given the possibilities for defining and describing attitudes just discussed, what is the point? That is, does the study of attitudes tell us anything more than what attitudes are?

Part of the impetus for the study of attitudes lies in the assumption that attitudes predict future behavior or allow us to understand behavior that has already occurred. In the following two chapters we take up the important issue of attitude–behavior consistency.

THE RELATION OF ATTITUDE TO BEHAVIOR

There is a time-honored assumption among scientists and laypeople alike that knowledge of a person's attitudes permits a fuller understanding of his or her behavior. That is, the presence of a given attitude is thought to allow for the prediction of some future behavior or the interpretation of some past behavior. It is not surprising, then, to discover that a considerable amount of research and theorizing has been devoted to the issue of attitude–behavior consistency. Indeed, interest in this matter has become so broad as to require more than one textbook chapter for adequate coverage; thus, both Chapters 3 and 4 are devoted to this issue.

Chapter 3 traces certain historical developments in the field. Earlier in this century, attitude–behavior consistency was simply taken for granted, and there were some encouraging findings in this area. But by the late 1960s, there was more than a hint of gloom in the air concerning just how well behavior could be understood or predicted given information about attitudes. Again and again, researchers seemed unable to find strong connections between attitudinal and behavioral measures. However, the subsequent decade witnessed improvements and advances in attitude theory and methodology, with the result that there is renewed optimism regarding the attitude–behavior link. What Chapter 3 proposes is that attitudes and behavior *can* be seen to be related, provided one measures each of them properly.

In turn, Chapter 4 takes up recent approaches to the attitude–behavior issue. Here the general movement is toward the identification of variables that moderate consistency or inconsistency between attitudes and behavior. A number of important moderating factors have been identified, including situational influences, personality types, and experiential differences.

CHAPTER THREE

ATTITUDE–BEHAVIOR CONSISTENCIES

This chapter contains an exposition of basic issues related to attitude–behavior consistency and inconsistency. The organization of the material follows a beginning–middle–end theme. In the beginning (before midcentury), social psychologists were inclined to be enthusiastic about the potential of attitudes to allow the prediction or understanding of behavior. Such optimism is documented below in several quotes from writers of the time. Indeed, in certain areas of attitude–behavior research—such as opinions of candidates and voting—this early promise has been fulfilled. However, by the late 1960s (the middle of the story), evidence had accumulated that attitudes and behavior were often *in*consistent. These findings provoked something of a crisis in the field, and the status of "attitudes" as a useful concept was called into question by some. As a reaction to these theoretical concerns of the Sixties, recent work on attitude–behavior consistency has produced what appears to be a happy ending. By now, we better understand when and why attitudes and behavior are related, or not. Several recent advances in theory and method are discussed in the third section of this chapter.

A Beginning: A Success Story

When the phrase "attitude–behavior consistency" is used, there is the sense that attitudes predispose behavior. What does it mean to say that attitudes predispose overt behavior? Most social psychologists seem to view this as a question of the relation between what people say (their verbal responses to some person, object, issue, or event) and what they actually do (their nonverbal reactions to the entity in question). From a very simplified view of motivation, I assume that if a person says she likes yogurt (attitude), given the opportunity, she will eat yogurt (behavior). This sort of thinking appeared in early theoretical writings.

Some Quotes from Early Theoretical Writings

Recall from the first chapter Allport's time-honored 1935 definition of an attitude as

a mental or neural state of readiness, organized through experience, exerting a directive or dynamic influence upon the individual's response to all objects and situations with which it is related.

The part about "exerting a directive or dynamic influence upon the individual's response" is an expression of the idea that attitudes predispose behavior. Other writers sounded similar chords about the presumed connection between attitudes and behavior. For instance, Bogardus (1925) began his seminal article with the following declaration:

Social distance [as an attitude] refers to the degrees and grades of understanding and feeling that persons experience regarding each other. It explains the nature of a great deal of their *interaction*. It charts the character of social *relations* [emphasis added].

Similarly, Doob (1947) contended in his five-part definition that an attitude is:

1. An implicit response, which is
2. both (a) anticipatory and (b) mediating in reference to patterns of overt responses,
3. evoked (a) by a variety of stimulus patterns (b) as a result of previous learning or gradients of generalization and discrimination,
4. itself a cue and drive-producing, and
5. considered socially significant in the individual's society.

Thus, for Doob, the role of attitudes in behavior is stated explicitly in point 2 and is strongly implied in points 4 and 5.

Hence, for these theorists, knowledge of someone's attitudes might be useful in either predicting social behavior before it occurred or interpreting such behavior after it happened. If one searches for the basis of the assumption about an attitude–behavior link, one need not go much beyond common sense or everyday experience. Dollard's comment (1948) is particularly pertinent to the importance of *consistency* between words (attitudes) and acts in normal social life:

It [consistency] enables men to participate in organized social life with good confidence that others will do what they say they will do, will be where they say they will be. Valid prediction of behavior is not a mere luxury of morality, but a vital social necessity. Every man is under compulsion to keep his promises, and make his acts correspond with his verbal expressions. He constantly watches others to see that they do likewise.

ATTITUDES AND VOTING BEHAVIOR

This theoretical investment in the idea of attitude–behavior connections has paid large dividends in at least one important sector of our democratic social lives: POLITICAL VOTING. Influential reviews indicate that attitudes toward candidates—as measured by polls, surveys, or questionnaires—are highly predictive of voting behavior as reported by respondents (see Ajzen and Fishbein, 1977). Schuman and Johnson (1976), in their critique entitled "Attitudes and Behavior," went so far as to devote an entire section to the predictability of voting behavior from attitudinal measures and assigned it a glowing subheading—*A Nearly Ideal Model: The Act of Voting.*

As an example of such research, Fishbein and Coombs (1974) reported a study that focused on the 1964 presidential contest between Lyndon Johnson and Barry Goldwater. Respondents (Group 1 in the report) were interviewed shortly before and shortly after the actual election date. Prior to the election, voters' affect toward the candidates (called "A_o" by Fishbein and Coombs) was measured by the method of the semantic differential, thusly:

Candidate A
Good__:__:__:__:__:__:__:Bad

Several sets of bipolar endpoints were used, including wise–foolish, harmful–beneficial, clean–dirty, and sick–healthy.

Further, cognitions about the candidates were measured by having respondents evaluate each of several issues (called "a_i" in the original report), such as

Medicare
Good__:__:__:__:__:__:__:Bad

and beliefs about the candidates (called "B_i" in the article):

Candidate A is in favor of Medicare
Probable__:__:__:__:__:__:__:Improbable

A composite cognition for a candidate was arrived at by summing over a number of $B_i \times a_i$ products. Finally, voting intention was obtained by having respondents mark the following scale.

I will vote for Candidate A
Probable__:__:__:__:__:__:__:Improbable

After the election, the respondents' voting behavior was ascertained, and correlation coefficients were calculated to express the relationship between prior measures—affect, cognitions, and intentions toward the respective candidates—and voting patterns. Those correlations are presented in Table I. It is clear that for both candidates all the prior attitudinal and intentional measures were highly and positively related to the behavior of voting. In short, there is a great deal of attitude–behavior consistency seen in Table I.

Other researchers have enjoyed similar successes in predicting voting behavior from prior attitudinal measures (cf. Kelly and Mirer, 1974; Jaccard, Knox, and Brinberg, 1979). Indeed, one of the major success stories in the attitude measurement business is based on a long string of correct predictions of election outcomes from survey results. The Gallup Organization (and its forebears) have carried out polls prior to all presidential and congressional national elections since 1936. By 1985 there had been 25 such elections ("Gallup Poll Accuracy Record," 1985), and the Gallup Poll was right on every one, as indicated in Table II. Over the years, the average deviation of final Gallup surveys from election results was 2.1 percentage points. And it happens that the Gallup people are getting better at predicting election outcomes. The average deviation in the 1936–1950 era was 3.6 points; from 1952 to 1970, the mean error dropped to 1.7 points; and from 1972 to 1984, the deviation was an average of only 1.2 points. In this domain, it seems, attitude–behavior consistency can be taken for granted.

A Middle: Confusion—Some Notable Failures

Let us set aside voting for a moment and reflect a bit more deeply on the attitude–behavior issue. Is it not the case that written or

TABLE I
Correlation coefficients indicating strong, positive relationships between prior attitudinal measures and actual voting behavior in the 1964 Presidential election

	ACTUAL VOTE	
Prior measure	Goldwater	Johnson
Voting intention	.89	.79
Affect (A_o)	.70	.51
Cognition ($B_i \times a_i$)	.73	.72

After Fishbein and Coombs (1974).

TABLE II
Gallup Poll accuracy record in national elections from 1936 to 1984

Year	Gallup Final Survey		Election Results		Deviation
1984	59.0%	Reagan	59.2%	Reagan	−0.2
1982	55.0	Democratic	56.1	Democratic	−1.1
1980	47.0	Reagan	50.8	Reagan	−3.8
1978	55.0	Democratic	54.6	Democratic	+0.4
1976	48.0	Carter	50.0	Carter	−2.0
1974	60.0	Democratic	58.9	Democratic	+1.1
1972	62.0	Nixon	61.8	Nixon	+0.2
1970	53.0	Democratic	54.3	Democratic	−1.3
1968	43.0	Nixon	43.5	Nixon	−0.5
1966	52.5	Democratic	51.9	Democratic	+0.6
1964	64.0	Johnson	61.3	Johnson	+2.7
1962	55.5	Democratic	52.7	Democratic	+2.8
1960	51.0	Kennedy	50.1	Kennedy	+0.9
1958	57.0	Democratic	56.5	Democratic	+0.5
1956	59.5	Eisenhower	57.8	Eisenhower	+1.7
1954	51.5	Democratic	52.7	Democratic	−1.2
1952	51.0	Eisenhower	55.4	Eisenhower	−4.4
1950	51.0	Democratic	50.3	Democratic	+0.7
1948	44.5	Truman	49.9	Truman	−5.4
1946	58.0	Republican	54.3	Republican	+3.7
1944	51.5	Roosevelt	53.3	Roosevelt	−1.8
1942	52.0	Democratic	48.0	Democratic	+4.0
1940	52.0	Roosevelt	55.0	Roosevelt	−3.0
1938	54.0	Democratic	50.8	Democratic	+3.2
1936	55.7	Roosevelt	62.5	Roosevelt	−6.8

After *The Gallup Report*, #241, October, 1985.

spoken (or felt) attitudes toward an object are *not* precisely in the same class of things as behavior or action directed toward that thing? To take a trivial example, do you, the reader, have an attitude toward pizza (or chocolate cake, or ice cream)? Do you like pizza (or the other stuff)? Let us assume that the answer is "yes." Fine. Now, let us see how well this attitude predicts your behavior. Did you eat pizza at your previous meal? Are you eating pizza right now? Did you truly plan to have pizza for your next meal (before I brought the matter up)? If the answer to any of these last three questions is "no," how come your positive attitude toward pizza is such a poor predictor of your behavior toward pizza? Where is *your* attitude–behavior consistency?

There are lots of reasons for not eating pizza, no doubt, but the example does establish the possibility that even the most valid and reliable measures of attitudes just might not provide one with a basis for predicting an individual's behavior. In fact, just as there have been a number of proponents of the attitude–behavior consistency idea, there also have been opponents. As Wicker (1969) reminds us, the issue of ATTITUDE–BEHAVIOR DISCREPANCY surfaced almost as soon as the formal study of attitudes got under way. The firing of the first salvo is generally credited to LaPiere (1934):

> The questionnaire is cheap, easy, and mechanical. The study of human behavior is time consuming, intellectually fatiguing, and depends for its success upon the ability of the investigator. The former method gives quantitative results, the latter mainly qualitative. Quantitative measurements are quantitatively accurate; qualitative evaluations are always subject to the errors of human judgment. Yet it would seem far more worthwhile to make a shrewd guess regarding that which is essential than to accurately measure that which is to prove irrelevant.

Another early critic was Corey (1937):

> It is difficult to devise techniques whereby certain types of overt behavior can be rather objectively estimated for the purpose of comparison with verbal opinions. Such studies, despite their difficulty, would seem to be very much worthwhile. It is conceivable that our attitude testing program has gone too far in the wrong direction. The available scales and techniques are almost too neat. The ease with which so-called attitudinal studies can be conducted is attractive, but the implications are equivocal.

So many similar assaults on the consistency notion have been made through the years that they now represent a history-of-science vein in their own right. As Liska (1975) noted:

> While social scientists point to the central role of attitude in explaining behavior, they have been exceedingly slow to study this phenomenon systematically and have frequently assumed a consistent relationship between attitude and behavior. Yet, a discrepancy between attitude and behavior has been consistently "rediscovered" with each new generation of social scientists, and this generation is no exception.

What is it that gets rediscovered so often and that so concerned LaPiere and Corey as long ago as the 1930s? It is simply that measured attitudes often fail to predict or are inconsistent with relevant behavior. In a landmark review in 1969, Wicker pointed to over 30 separate attitude studies that found either weak evidence linking attitudes and behavior, or no evidence at all. A sampler of the studies in Wicker's review reveal these weaknesses under a wide variety of conditions that involve different subject populations, contexts, and issues (see Table III).

Some of the researches reviewed by Wicker will be discussed in detail below, but space limitations do not permit the inclusion of all of them. However, it may be helpful to know the stringent criteria Wicker applied in selecting studies to review:

(a) the unit of observation must be the individual rather than a group, (b) at least one attitudinal measure and one overt behavioral measure toward the same object must be obtained for each subject, (c) the attitude and the behavior must be measured on separate occasions, and (d) the overt behavioral response must not be merely the subject's retrospective verbal report of his own behavior (Wicker, 1969).

For instance, Wicker recounts that Bernberg (1952) found no relationship between employees' attitudes toward an aircraft company on the one hand and the work absences of those employees on the other. Having looked at a large number of such studies that fit his criteria, Wicker concluded that the strength of association (correlation) between measures of attitudes and behavior was rarely over

TABLE III
Sampler of studies on attitude–behavior inconsistencies

Source[a]	Subjects	Attitude measure	Behavioral inconsistency
Bernberg (1952)	plant employees	one's job	job absences
Bray (1950)	white college students	blacks, Jews	conforming to blacks' or Jews' judgments
Carr and Roberts (1965)	black college students	civil rights activities	participation in civil rights activities
Cattell, Heist, Heist, and Stewart (1950)	male college students	leisure activities	daily log of time or money spent
Corey (1937)	college students	cheating	cheating on self-graded exam
Dean (1958)	industrial employees	local labor union	attendance at local labor union meetings
Linn (1965)	white college students	blacks	willingness to have a photo taken with a black
Vroom (1964)	employees	one's job	job performance
Weitz and Nuckols (1953)	insurance agents	one's job	job resignations

[a] Full references to these entries can be found in Wicker (1969).

.30, and often close to zero. (For additional writers of this era who voiced strong concerns over the attitude–behavior discrepancy issue, see Festinger (1964), Deutscher (1966), and Abelson (1972).)

How bad can things get in the area of attitude–behavior consistency (or discrepancy)? To illustrate in some detail certain specific discrepancies between attitudes and behavior that are on record, we can turn to several interesting lines of research that are highly relevant to important social problems: racial discrimination in public facilities, the issue of law and order, and race relations.

RACIAL DISCRIMINATION IN PUBLIC FACILITIES

One of the first bits of evidence concerning a lack of connection between attitudes and behavior came from the work of LaPiere (1934), which began with an assessment of people's behavior toward an attitudinal object. The people (subjects) in question were staff members of various hotels, auto camps, tourist homes, restaurants, and cafes across the United States. The attitudinal object was a married couple, a young Chinese student and his wife. At the time, American sentiment toward the Chinese in general was not especially favorable, so LaPiere wanted to see how proprietors would react to the couple's requests for service or accommodations. On cross-country journeys, LaPiere and the couple stopped at 251 different establishments and were refused service on only one occasion. In other words, they were served in 99.6% of the cases. Indeed, La-Piere's impression was that they were "treated with what I judged to be more than ordinary consideration in more than 72 of them."

When the journey was finished, LaPiere undertook a measure of attitudes toward the Chinese. He sent a questionnaire to each place that had served them, asking, "Will you accept members of the Chinese race as guests at your establishment?" Replies were received from the staffs of 128 places, 92% of which said "No," with almost all of the remainder being uncertain. Clearly, the behavior of the proprietors toward the Chinese couple was different from their attitude toward the Chinese race.

This kind of attitude–behavior discrepancy has been observed in more recent times. Kutner, Wilkins, and Yarrow (1952) used the LaPiere procedure in a somewhat modified form. In the later research, a party of two white women arrived at a restaurant, were seated, and were subsequently joined by a third woman, a black. (Note that this study took place before federal civil rights laws had been enacted.) In 11 of 11 cases the party of three was served without incident. Following this, a letter was sent to each establishment requesting reservations for a mixed party of blacks and whites. The researchers then waited for over 2 weeks for answers to their letters, but no replies were received; yet none of their letters were returned as undelivered. When the researchers finally telephoned the 11 places, they were told on eight occasions that no letter had been received! Further, the staffs of most of the eating places were reluctant to discuss the matter of reservations for blacks. Transcripts of some of these telephone conversations are revealing concerning the attitudes of the staff.

RESTAURANT A: Didn't get any letter. We don't take large parties. We've got dancing after 6 P.M. (They actually don't.) Are you colored? (Yes.) I like everyone. My kitchen staff are colored and they are wonderful people. But we have a certain clientele here . . . This place is my bread and butter. Try in T_____ (next town).
RESTAURANT B: I didn't get your letter. We can't have you. It's against the law.
RESTAURANT E: I didn't get any letter. We don't take reservations. We take care of our regulars. A few Negroes come in just to eat. We *would* mind you coming.
RESTAURANT F: Yes I got your letter. I refuse to discuss it on the phone. What is the purpose of your party? What school did you attend? Why are you never home when I call? How many Negroes are in the party? (5 out of 10.) That's a large percentage, isn't it? (Insisted he call us, instead of vice versa.) (Adapted from Kutner et al., 1952).

Again, behavior and attitudes, as represented by actual service versus willingness to grant reservations, are not clearly linked here.

Even so, critics (e.g., Dillehay, 1973) have pointed out that the LaPiere paradigm may be inappropriate as a test of the attitude–behavior connection. If one assumes that the connectedness—correlational, or cause and effect relationship—is *in* the individual (or not), then the individual should be the level of analysis (see Davidson and Morrison, 1983, on this point). In LaPiere's study, he certainly could have identified who did the *behaving*; a log of clerks or waitresses could have been kept. But no one is sure who provided the *attitudinal* information, which was obtained via the returned questionnaires. In LaPiere's defense, Schuman and Johnson (1976) have pointed out that, criticisms aside, it was

not naive in 1934 to expect *some* consistency between the treatment of a Chinese couple in hotels and restaurants and the separate replies by owners of such establishments to a questionnaire about their acceptance of Chinese in general.

Mindful of the strengths and weaknesses of the LaPiere paradigm, we turn to another type of studies of the attitude–behavior link.

LAW AND ORDER

During the latter part of the 1960s, Americans were concerned about civil disorder and an alarming crime rate. One of the reactions of our political leadership was to get tough on offenders. A number of politicians advanced a policy of "law and order." We did have laws at the time, of course, but segments of the population (such as Vietnam-era draft resisters) were acting in defiance of the law out of moral outrage or a sense of alienation and were engaged in one or another form of civil disobedience or outright crime. The theme of law and order meant that those laws were going to be enforced, regardless of their popularity and regardless of whether the lawbreaking citizen was alienated from our society. To take the example of evasion of the military draft, the law-and-order view was that draft dodgers had no right to break the law and avoid induction just because they felt that the current law was immoral.

Naturally, the law-and-order issue surfaced in the 1968 American presidential election, and it was discussed to some degree by the three leading candidates: Hubert H. Humphrey, Richard M. Nixon, and George C. Wallace. Of the three, the most conservative candidate, Wallace, was the strongest advocate of the law-and-order position (Wrightsman, 1969). But were supporters of Wallace any more law-abiding than supporters of the other candidates? An opportunity to satisfy this curiosity occurred near the time of the national election. In a county in Tennessee, a local tax had been levied on automobiles. Residents had to each purchase a $15 "metro sticker" and affix it to their cars by November 2 of that year or be subject to a $50 fine. For various reasons, the new tax was very unpopular, and it had been criticized in the local press.

As the deadline for buying and attaching the sticker approached, would Wallace supporters be any more likely to abide by this law than would supporters of Humphrey or Nixon? To answer this question, Wrightsman (1969) and his assistants searched parking lots for cars that bore bumper stickers advocating the election of one or another of the presidential candidates. (The reader may have noted that putting a political bumper sticker on your car is a behavior, not a verbal attitude. However, once in place, the sticker amounts to a *statement*. So for now I will consider the presence of a political bumper sticker itself as an attitudinal index, and the act of *leaving it on* a behavior.) When an auto with a political bumper sticker was located, it was a simple matter to see whether it also bore a local tax sticker; the researchers then tabulated the proportion of each candidate's supporters who had failed to affix the tax sticker. When the findings were in, the results were telling. It turned out that the Wallace supporters were not more law-abiding than were advocates of Humphrey and Nixon. In fact, they were less law-abiding. The proportion of drivers that had failed to affix the tax sticker are shown in Table IV in terms of rates for Humphrey, Nixon, and Wallace supporters; it can be seen that the Wallace supporters showed the highest rate of noncompliance with the local tax law. Although Wallace himself advocated law and order, his supporters, in their own behavior, seemed to subscribe to it to a lesser degree than did the supporters of the other candidates. This result is further evidence for the existence of attitude–behavior inconsistency.

RACE RELATIONS IN THE LABORATORY

The aforementioned works of LaPiere, Kutner et al., and Wrightsman all took place in field settings, and that characteristic may have somehow contributed to attitude–behavior inconsistency. What about attitude–behavior consistencies in another type of setting, such as a laboratory? Would researchers find the consistency they seek in more controlled circumstances? Perhaps not.

In a classic paper, DeFleur and Westie (1958) reported a study involving white university students. As part of a sociology class, the students were asked to fill out a large questionnaire, within which were embedded several items that measured prejudice against blacks. The authors labeled their instrument the "Summated Differences Scale," based on the fact that scale items elicited responses from subjects to white or black figures in matched circumstances. For instance, at some point in the voluminous survey, the respondent encountered the following item:

I believe I would be willing to have a *Negro Doctor* have his hair cut at the same barber shop where I have mine cut.

The subject had an opportunity to indicate an attitude on a five-point scale that ranged from "strongly agree" to "strongly disagree." Some large number of extraneous items later, the respondent would encounter a related item to which to respond:

TABLE IV
Proportion of supporters of various political candidates who failed to comply with a local tax law

Supporter	Proportion (%) noncompliance
Humphrey	13.48
Nixon	13.49
Wallace	25.21

After Wrightsman (1969).

I believe I would be willing to have a *White Doctor* have his hair cut at the same barber shop where I have mine cut.

Sixteen such general items were involved, and a respondent's score was the summated numerical differences between responses to whites and blacks of similar occupation or status.

Next, DeFleur and Westie identified the 23 most prejudiced subjects (top quartile) and the 23 least prejudiced subjects (bottom quartile) from their total sample. Recall from Chapter 1 that selection of extreme groups is a technique that is supposed to help ensure that those individuals clearly have one or another attitude. Then, under an appropriate cover story, these people were given a chance to behave with regard to blacks. Subjects were asked whether they would be willing to pose for pictures with a black of the opposite sex. The precise behavior in question was whether a subject would sign certain "releases" for the use of the photos. The nature and level of each release is shown below. All began with the phrase: "I will allow this photograph to be . . ."

1. used in laboratory experiments where it will be seen only by professional sociologists.
2. published in a technical journal read only by professional sociologists.
3. shown to a few dozen University students in a laboratory situation.
4. shown to hundreds of University students as a teaching aid in Sociology classes.
5. published in the *Student Newspaper* as part of a publicity report on this research.
6. published in my home town newspaper as part of a publicity report on this research.
7. used in a nation-wide publicity campaign *advocating racial integration.*

Each of these levels also had a blank for a signature, and, obviously, each successive level demanded more of the respondent in terms of how much potential public exposure was involved.

The issue now is the nature of the relationship between attitudes as measured on the Summated Differences Scale and behavior as measured by signatures on releases. We already know that half the subjects were either prejudiced or unprejudiced. The authors further divided these people into those who signed a level of release below the experimental group ($N = 46$) average, or above that group average. A signed release below the average was taken to indicate low racial tolerance; a signed release above the average was understood as high racial tolerance. As always, the question is whether the two measures—attitude and behavior—matched.

Alas, the answer was "no." Even with the extreme groups involved, the match was far from perfect. Table V reveals some degree of consistency, but not enough to satisfy DeFleur and Westie, or later scholars. It was thought that too many cases fell in the wrong cells. Five of the prejudiced people, despite their "prejudice," nevertheless signed releases above the mean, and nine of the unprejudiced respondents signed levels below the mean. These "discrepant" cases amounted to 30% of the experimental sample, and such a sizable bloc "is too large a proportion to attribute to measurement errors" (DeFleur and Westie, 1958).

In sum, the sampler of studies seen earlier in Table III, plus the specific examples concerning racial discrimination in public places, the issue of law and order, and race relations all point to a serious problem with the idea that attitudes and behavior are necessarily consistent. On the basis of this sort of evidence, Wicker sternly concluded in his review that there was "little evidence to support the postulated existence of stable, underlying attitudes within the individual which influence both his verbal expressions and his actions" (Wicker, 1969). If Wicker is correct, then the tremendous emphasis on the study of attitudes in the social sciences may turn out to be nothing more than a gigantic scientific flop!

An End: Three Contemporary Perspectives

In 1935 Gordon Allport was hardly at a loss for words in extolling the virtues of the concept of "attitudes" in the social sciences. Recall from Chapter 1 that, for him, the concept of attitude was

elastic enough to apply either to the dispositions of single, isolated individuals or to broad patterns of culture. Psychologists and sociologists therefore find in it a meeting point for discussion and research. This useful, one might almost

TABLE V
Relationship between whites' racial attitude as measured by the Summated Differences Scale, and level of signed agreement to be photographed with a black person

Behavior (level of agreement)	ATTITUDE CATEGORY	
	Prejudiced	Unprejudiced
Below average	18	9[a]
Above average	5[a]	14

After Defleur and Westie (1958).
[a] Cases falling into these cells indicate attitude–behavior inconsistency.

say peaceful, concept has been so widely adopted that it has virtually established itself as the keystone in the edifice of American social psychology (Allport, 1935).

However, we have seen that by the late 1960s something seemed to have gone terribly wrong, and the concept of attitude was anything but peaceful. Had we witnessed the decline and fall of the attitudinal empire? The answer to this particular question is a resounding *no!* Ironically, perhaps, highly critical articles such as Wicker's proved to be a boon to students of attitudes, for these attacks forced them to pay particular attention to the issue of attitude–behavior consistency. The position of the critics turned out to be more of a challenge than an indictment.

Many writers took up the issue of the link between attitudes and behavior, and since the early 1970s the literature has proliferated. This surge was due to the undeterred enthusiasm on the part of many for the concept of social-psychological attitudes. Some of the response was positively buoyant; in 1974 Herbert C. Kelman published an article with the upbeat title of: "Attitudes Are Alive and Well and Gainfully Employed in the Sphere of Action." In that paper Kelman maintained that

in the years since publication of Allport's [1935] paper, attitudes have, if anything, become even more central in social psychology, largely because they have come to serve as *the* dependent variable par excellence for the major categories of social-psychological research: the sample survey, the questionnaire study, and the laboratory experiment (Kelman, 1974).

Current research and theorizing on the attitude–behavior issue is proceeding on several fronts. For our purposes, these advances will be organized into three basic perspectives:

1. Perspective of single-act criteria.
2. Perspective of multiple-act criteria.
3. Perspective of correspondence.

These three perspectives all focus on a central issue: What are the conditions under which attitudes and behavior *are* related? In other words, just *when* do attitudes predict behavior? There is a useful truism in scientific psychology that one gets answers only to the questions one asks. This limitation certainly applies to the issue of attitude–behavior discrepancies. Can one say with confidence that attitudes do *not* predict behavior? Which attitudes? Which behavior? Consider the methods of studying attitudes that were discussed in Chapter 1. All these techniques were developed by people in need of workable procedures; none of these methods is God-given or infallible. Perhaps the problem lies not within the conceptual link between attitudes and behavior but in the way we measure attitudes and the way we measure behavior (Ajzen and Fishbein, 1977).

For Ajzen (1982), the attitude–behavior consistency problem boils down to just what kind of behavior one wants to predict. He distinguished between SINGLE ACTIONS on the one hand and GLOBAL BEHAVIORAL TENDENCIES on the other. If the aim is to predict single actions, then attitudinal items tailored to *that* action are called for. We can call these BEHAVIORAL INTENTIONS. This sort of item would tap the individual's "evaluative predisposition to perform or not perform that particular behavior under consideration" (Ajzen, 1982). Contrarily, if the aim is to predict global behavioral tendencies, then the appropriate questions to be asked would involve GLOBAL MEASURES of attitudes. Further, it is meaningful and useful to ask about the semantic relationship between a written question about an individual's attitude and the procedural definition by which we record that individual's behavior. This topic is taken up later under the heading of "correspondence." Finally, after these perspectives have been discussed, we will apply the insights they yield to the earlier successes and failures to find attitude–behavior consistency.

PERSPECTIVE OF SINGLE-ACT CRITERIA

Imagine you are about to sit down to play a parlor game with another person. The game is an engaging one because your aim is to maximize your winnings. Of course, your opponent also wishes to maximize her or his outcome from the game. You and your opponent will make a sequence of simultaneous "moves." On any given move (or trial), you can engage in one of two contrasting tactics: the choices are to (a) cooperate or (b) compete. Not surprisingly, your opponent enjoys these options, too. It is the pattern of choices on each move that determines who gets what payoff. If you both cooperate on a trial, you both get the same, relatively modest payoff. But—and here is where it gets interesting—if on some trial your opponent chooses to *cooperate* while you choose simultaneously to *compete*, you receive a large payoff and your opponent receives a penalty! (Beware. The reverse applies as well. If you cooperate while your opponent competes, you lose some and he or she wins big.) Finally, if you both compete on a trial, you are both penalized a moderate amount.

This sort of game goes by various names, including "Prisoner's Dilemma." The point of bringing it up here is to focus on the attitude–behavior issue. Defining the behavior involved (call it *b*) is easy because it is so specific. In this case, b is taken to be a cooperative response on a given trial, or perhaps the proportion of cooperative responses over a series of trials. Now, what sort of attitudinal measure will best predict the b? In their research on this topic, Ajzen and Fishbein (1970) rhetorically suggested that a traditional approach would be to measure a player's attitude toward the other player (call the attitude A_o). Like many of the early researchers, one could use semantic differentials with endpoints such as wise–foolish, harmful–beneficial, good–bad, clean–dirty, and sick–healthy. "After all," the traditionally-oriented researcher might say, "if I am playing a game in which I can compete or cooperate, my attitude toward my opponent will determine my behavior." To use the symbols, b will be predicted by A_o, or

$$b \sim A_o$$

Well, maybe. Let us consider these elements in a bit more detail. Ajzen (1982) suggested earlier that the prediction of a specific act is done best by assessing an evaluative predisposition to perform that particular behavior. In our case the behavior *is* specific (b is a cooperative choice), but the semantic differential scales under consideration (A_o) seem diffuse and global. In any event, they apply to the opponent. Alternatively, Ajzen and Fishbein (1970) proposed a different prior self-report measure to predict b, and they called it BI, which stands for behavioral intentions regarding the behavior in question. BI was assessed by asking, "What are your intentions for this game?" with the subject then indicating the proportion of her or his responses that would be cooperative. Ajzen and Fishbein obtained such reports in the context of having subjects play two different versions of the Prisoner's Dilemma game, called Game 1 and Game 2. In short, they tested the hypothesis that behavior (b) would be predicted by behavioral intentions (BI).

Now the stage is set for a competition between formulations or theories. Where will consistency between attitudes and behavior occur? Will it be seen in the case of $b \sim A_o$, or in the case of $b \sim$ BI? The answer is found in Table VI. First of all, the $b \sim A_o$ entries are flops so far as attitude–behavior consistency goes. Prior knowledge of a player's attitude toward her or his *opponent* was quite weakly correlated with actual cooperative responses while playing the game with the opponent. These particular correlation coefficients (.26 and .09) are of an order that caused all the lamentations about attitudes and behaviors in the late 1960s. On the contrary, coefficients in the range of .80 to .90 are respectable in the social sciences. Thus,

.TABLE VI
Correlations between various prior attitudinal measures (BI and A_0) and subsequent behavior (b) by subjects in Prisoner's Dilemma games

Attitude–behavior comparisons[a]	PRISONER'S DILEMMA GAME	
	Game 1	Game 2
A_0 with b	.26	.09
BI with b	.85	.84

After Ajzen and Fishbein (1970).
[a] See the text for definitions of the terms in this column.

when BI was taken into account, very strong attitude–behavior links were in evidence. In other words, subjects who reported an intention to cooperate did cooperate; those who did not intend to cooperate did not.

Of course, this is precisely what Ajzen (1982) was talking about. If an investigator is interested in predicting (or understanding) single actions, then the individual's evaluative predisposition to perform or not perform that particular behavior is the thing to measure. Apparently, knowledge of behavioral intentions (BI) affords a great deal of predictability where a specific behavior (b) is concerned.

The measure of intentions for the purpose of predicting certain acts has been used successfully in areas of research such as occupational orientations, family planning, consumer behavior, and voting (see Ajzen and Fishbein, 1980). One detailed example of such practical application will suffice here. Manstead, Proffitt, and Smart (1983) wanted to find out whether women's prenatal *intentions* to breast-feed predicted their postnatal breast-feeding behavior. Also at issue was the predictability of more general *attitudes* toward the practice. During their pregnancies, hundreds of mothers-to-be filled out questionnaires that inquired about their intentions and their attitudes. The instrument that measured intentions was straightforward: it was a bipolar scale anchored at one end with the statement "I shall definitely breast-feed my baby" and at the other with the statement "I shall definitely bottle-feed my baby." As for attitudes, a number of scales were used, including one that read, "Using a feeding method [breast-feeding] that establishes a close bond between me and my baby is . . . 'very important to me,' or 'very unimportant to me.'" Having taken prior measures of these kinds, the researchers investigated the actual breast-feeding behavior of the mothers after delivery. As it turned out, the attitude instrument predicted behavior fairly well; the correlation between the measure and the behavior was .67. Further, the intention measure was that much more predictive, with an intention–behavior correlation of .82.

In sum, to predict any single behavior, we should directly measure the person's attitude or intentions toward *that* behavior. But is this altogether good news, or even progress? As Ajzen (1982) put it: "The objection has often been raised that this conclusion puts severe limitations on the utility of the attitude concept. If, for every behavior, we have to assess a different attitude, we appear to have gained very little."

Not to worry, because by now we have established certain important and useful propositions: attitudes toward behaviors do predict single acts; global measures of attitudes do not predict single acts (see Table V). However, even though global measures of attitudes might not predict single acts, those same global measures might serve very well to predict a more general index of behavior. It is to this possibility that we now turn in the following section on multiple-act measures.

PERSPECTIVE OF MULTIPLE-ACT CRITERIA

The use of the term *global measure* usually implies some non-specific, overall evaluation of an attitudinal object. Semantic differentials are one way to obtain this kind of estimation of a person's attitude. For instance, what do you think about the book you are looking at right now? Is it GOOD or BAD? HARMFUL or BENEFICIAL? HEALTHY or SICK? Note the contrast here with the single-act approach. Complete knowledge of whether you think this object is GOOD or BAD provides no information about any specific act you might engage in regarding the book. Assume for the moment that you think that the book is very GOOD. What can we expect you to *do* about it?

Well, you might do a lot of *different* things: At the end of the course, you might keep it rather than reselling it as you plan to do with your other texts. You might recommend it (or parts of it) to a friend or family member. You might look in the library for other titles by the same author. You might make favorable remarks about the text at the time of course evaluations. And what about some other person in the class who also thinks the book is very GOOD? He or she might go so far as to write to the author, or decide to major in the field. On the other hand, if someone felt the book was very BAD, that someone might disparage, discard, deface, or even destroy it! In short, even though global measures of attitudes fail to inform us about any single act, they should be associated with some general (broad) index of behavior. The best way to approximate that general index is with multiple-act measures.

Two studies very clearly found attitude–behavior consistencies at the level of global attitudinal measures and multiple-act behavioral measures. The first, by Fishbein and Ajzen (1974), was conducted in a laboratory, and the second, by Weigel and Newman (1976), was carried out in a field setting.

Fishbein and Ajzen (1974) were interested in the relationship between undergraduate students' global attitudes toward religion and the extent to which those students engaged in a number of religion-oriented behaviors. To begin with, the researchers made up a list of 100 items that represented behaviors connected with matters of religion. The list included entries such as "pray before and after meals," "take a religion course for credit," and "donate money to a religious institution," among 97 others. It was the subjects' task to check off on the list the behaviors that they had performed; hence this was a retrospective, self-report behavioral measure. Next, five global attitude scales concerning religion were administered to the same subjects. The first was a so-called Guilford self-rating scale that had the students indicate their attitude toward being religious by checking an 11-point dimension that ran from "extremely favorable" to "extremely unfavorable." Following the Guilford instrument, semantic differentials about religion were used. The final three scales were characterized as a Likert scale, a Guttman format, and a Thurstone scale (see Chapter 1).

Having measured behavior and attitudes in this extensive way, Fishbein and Ajzen (1974) could now determine what behaviors were connected with what attitudes. They used two procedures. First, they calculated the sum of all behavioral items checked off by a subject and compared that total value with the same subject's scores from each of the five attitude scales. This was termed the multiple-act criterion. The behavioral and attitudinal scores for all subjects in the study were entered into correlational analyses, one analysis for each scale type. High, positive correlations from these analyses would mean that global religious attitudes did predict a multiple-act measure of behavior. Reference to Table VII shows that this indeed was the result. Over the scale types, the correlations ranged from .61 to .71, all of which are impressive.

Second, Fishbein and Ajzen looked at the relationship between their global attitudinal measures (from the scales) and single acts

TABLE VII
Correlations of religious attitudes as measured by various global scales with behavior in terms of single-act and multiple-act criteria

Scale type	Single-act[a] criterion	Multiple-act[b] criterion
Self-report (Guilford)	.14	.64
Semantic differential	.15	.71
Guttman	.12	.61
Likert	.14	.68
Thurstone	.13	.63

After Fishbein and Ajzen (1974).
[a] Average correlation with 100 separate behaviors.
[b] Correlation with the sum over 100 behaviors.

(from the list). To do this they computed correlations between each of the scale scores and *each* of the 100 separate behavioral items. Each correlation value was termed a single-act criterion. (But this approach means that whereas there are only 5 coefficients in the "multiple-act criterion" column in Table VII, there would be all of 500 coefficients in the "single-act criterion" column. To avoid this clutter, Fishbein and Ajzen (1974) averaged the 100 coefficients associated with each scale and presented these averages.) The average single-act criterion correlations in Table VII range from .12 to .15, none of which is impressive.

Therefore, the Fishbein–Ajzen data lend credence to the propositions being established here: global measures of attitudes do a poor job of predicting single-act behavior but do a good job of predicting multiple-act behavior.

Impressive as these results are, Weigel and Newman (1976) had some reservations about the Fishbein–Ajzen procedures. They point out that self-reports of behavior were used and that these reports might be unreliable. Moreover, paper-and-pencil measures of both behavior and attitudes were obtained in a single session, so the subjects may have inferred what their attitudes were, based on what they reported about their behavior. Whatever the seriousness of these concerns, Weigel and Newman (1976) were motivated to work around them by conducting a field study on global attitude and multiple-act connections.

At the beginning of their field study, residents in a New England town were approached and asked to answer a 16-item questionnaire on environmental and pollution issues. Their responses were a measure of their global attitudes toward those issues. Many weeks later, and over a period of several subsequent months, the respondents were given a number of opportunities to *behave* with regard to the environment and to pollution. The way the researchers structured these opportunities to behave is quite interesting, and represents an appealing feature of their project, so I present their procedures in some detail.

The first opportunity to behave came when the residents were again approached (by a person different from the survey researcher) and were asked to sign petitions regarding environmental matters. Actually, there were four parts to this particular opportunity to behave: three types of petition—(a) offshore oil, (b) nuclear power, (c) auto exhausts—and (d) an opportunity for the resident to circulate more of the petitions. Since a resident could agree to do any or all (or none) of these things, it was possible to assign her or him a score of $+1$ (did it) or $+0$ (did not do it) on each, for a possible range of scores of 0 to 4 on this behavioral measure.

The second opportunity to behave occurred when residents were asked (by a new person) if they would (a) participate in a local litter cleanup, and whether they would (b) recruit a friend for the cleanup. So, on the litter pickup measure, scores could range from 0 to 2.

Finally, for a third behavioral opportunity, yet another person approached each resident and promoted a recycling program that would go on for 8 weeks. A resident could deposit recyclable material on each of 8 designated days. If material was forthcoming in a given week, the resident was assigned a score of $+1$ for that week, thus, total scores over the 8-week period could range from 0 to 8 for residents.

Having collected respondents' global attitudes toward the environment and pollution and having given these respondents ample opportunities to behave in connection with those matters, Weigel and Newman (1976) were in a position to analyze their data in about the same way as did Fishbein and Ajzen (1974). That is, they correlated respondents' global attitude scores with both multiple-act measures, summing over such measures, and single-act measures from the separate behaviors. (In this 1976 study, an intermediate level called categories of behavior was also identified.) All of this is summarized in Table VIII, and the findings there are much in line with the earlier report of Fishbein and Ajzen. When respondents' global attitudes were compared with the total behavior index (far right in the table) a strong correlation emerged (.62). Then as one

TABLE VIII
Correlations between global attitudes and single- and multiple-act behavioral measures

Single behaviors	r	Categories of behavior	r	General index	r
Offshore oil	.41				
Nuclear power	.36				
Auto exhaust	.39	Petitioning behavior scale (0–4)	.50		
Circulate petitions	.27				
Individual participation	.34	Litter pick-up scale (0–2)	.36	Comprehensive behavioral index (0–14)	.62
Recruit friend	.22				
Week 1	.34				
2	.57				
3	.34				
4	.33	Recylcing behavior scale (0–8)	.39		
5	.12				
6	.20				
7	.20				
8	.34				
Average r	.32		.42		.62

After Weigel and Newman (1976).

proceeds to the left in Table VIII, there is a regular diminution in the strength of the attitude–behavior relationship. The average correlation for the relatively small behavioral categories and global attitudes is .42; and for single behaviors and global attitudes, the average correlation is a weak .32.

Once again, the proposition is supported: global attitudes do not predict single acts particularly well, but global attitudes do predict some general (broad) index of behavior. Where global attitudes are concerned, multiple-act measures of behavior are called for.

The study by Weigel and Newman (1976) is particularly compelling because of its field setting and its thorough and clever methodology. However, recall that Weigel and Newman had some reservations about the prior Fishbein–Ajzen project. In turn, one is free to ponder parts of the Weigel–Newman paper. I have no strong reservations, but I am curious about one thing: How did they *know* to pick the particular single behaviors seen in the first column in Table

VIII? Now, we all realize that the study worked out fine, but how did they *know* that those behaviors would turn out to be so suitable? These researchers may have been prescient, or they may have been merely lucky; it doesn't matter which because nothing succeeds like success. But other researchers (or readers) may not yet be sure how to choose attitude objects and behaviors to compare in the attitude–behavior consistency business. The following section on CORRESPON-DENCE will address these considerations.

PERSPECTIVE OF CORRESPONDENCE

Another way to approach the problem of the apparent discrepancy between attitudes and behavior is to inquire as to just what it is that is discrepant. To illustrate this perspective, let us engage in a short exercise. Imagine that we are on a research team that wishes to determine what people will *do* as a consequence of their attitudes about nuclear power. We can and will ask respondents some questions about the desirability and feasibility of nuclear plants, but our basic concern is with the validity of those questions in terms of their ability—via the answers they elicit—to predict behavior. What kind of behavior should be linked to attitudes about nuclear energy? The reader ought to pause for a moment and consider making recommendations to our research team about behavior relevant to nuclear-related attitudes. However, as the senior member of this team, *I* will take the initiative and insist that the behavior we will examine is as follows: Do people with pro or con attitudes toward "nukes" eat their pizza with or without mushrooms? (Get it? "Nukes" and "mushroom" clouds.) That is, I judge that the validity of our attitude measures about nuclear power will rest on whether they predict pizza-eating behavior.

Ridiculous? Perhaps. Still, this exercise illustrates an important point. Insofar as I may be an "expert" in the area of attitudinal research, is there any merit in my judgment regarding what attitude should go with what behavior? Doubtless, in this case the reader will be inclined to mistrust my silly-sounding proposal concerning this particular behavioral measure. But the broader question becomes the extent to which we should trust *any* specification of the behavior that should or should not follow from a given attitude. As Ajzen and Fishbein (1977) put it,

it can be seen that a given behavior is assumed to be consistent or inconsistent with a person's attitude on the basis of largely intuitive considerations. In the absence of an explicit and unambiguous definition of attitude–behavior consistency, therefore, many tests of the attitude–behavior relation reduce to little more than tests of the investigator's intuition. From a theoretical point of view, such tests of the relation between arbitrarily selected measures of attitude or behavior are of rather limited value.

Because there is no obvious theoretical link between attitudes toward nuclear power and a taste for mushrooms, we are in a position to reject my proposal that pizza-eating could be an appropriate behavioral reflection of such attitudes. But what of the reader's recommendations? Did you propose that attitudes toward nuclear energy would be related to the way a person would vote in the next national election? Would it be the case that this sort of attitude predicts who will write letters to the editor? Would it be the case that an attitudinal measure could tell us which citizens might take part in protest demonstrations at nuclear plant sites? On the face of it, voting, writing letters, and demonstrating all appear to have some plausibility as behavioral measures that could reflect a person's attitude concerning nuclear power. Yet, each of these recommendations suffers from the same flaw that marred my suggestion regarding dietary preferences. Until we find rules for specifying which behavior should follow from which attitude, the choice of these measures will have to rely on somebody's intuition (see also Salancik, 1982, on this point). Happily, Ajzen and Fishbein (1977) have shown us a way out of this cul-de-sac by providing us with working guidelines for defining attitude–behavior correspondence.

Target, action, time, and context: Entities of attitudes and behavior. Ajzen and Fishbein's analysis begins with a conceptualization of the nature of attitudes and behavior. These authors define four "entities" that make up an attitude or a behavior. To begin with, an attitude at least implicitly involves a TARGET (the attitudinal object) and an ACTION (what one would like to do with the object), both of which exist in TIME (some temporal reference) and in a CONTEXT (some situational reference). By extension, any given behavior comprises the same four entities, because every act involves a target and an action and occurs in time and in a context. All of these entities are important in determining attitude–behavior consistency, but for the sake of clarity these theorists concentrated on the target and action entities.

Given the delineation of these entities, the Ajzen–Fishbein rule for defining attitude–behavior consistency was relatively simple and straightforward: "The central thesis . . . is that the strength of an attitude–behavior relationship depends in large part on the degree of correspondence between attitudinal and behavioral entities." For these authors, the term *correspondence* meant the degree of similarity between, on the one hand, the target entity of an attitude and the target entity of a behavior and, on the other, the action entity of an attitude and the action entity of a behavior. In the simplest case, if the target and action entities are identical across attitudinal and behavioral measures, then attitudes will indeed predict behavior. However, if either or both the entities of attitude and behavior are dissimilar, then one can expect little or no attitude–behavior consistency. To put this formulation in schematic form, consider the entries in Table IX. Three levels of correspondence are illustrated, which for our purposes can be labeled high, low, and none. The greatest amount of attitude–behavior consistency would be expected in the high-correspondence circumstance, whereas less consistency would be expected in the low-correspondence circumstance. Finally, there would be no reason to expect any consistency whatever (except for chance factors) in a situation where there was no correspondence.

How well does this correspondence formulation account for attitude–behavior consistency findings? In their impressive review, Ajzen and Fishbein (1977) analyzed 109 investigations within which a total of 142 attitude–behavior relations were reported (articles sometimes contain reports of more than one experiment). Numerical counts of these reports were displayed in a 3×3 (nine-cell) matrix. The horizontal axis of the matrix specified the degree of the attitude–behavior relation. Such relationships were classified as (1) statistically not significant (i.e., for our purposes, $r = 0$); (2) low, if their corre-

TABLE IX
Schematic illustrations of levels of correspondence between attitudinal and behavioral entities

Level of correspondence	Attitudinal entities	Behavioral entitites
High:	Target = A Action = X	Target = A Action = X
Low:[a]	Target = A Action = X	Target = A Action = Y
None:	Target = A Action = X	Target = B Action = Y

[a] Theoretically, low correspondence would also result if the action entities were identical, but the target entities differed.

lation (r) was less than .40 or there were inconsistent correlations across different measures or studies in a report; or (3) high, if their correlation was .40 or more. The vertical axis in the matrix was the level of correspondence between attitude and behavior entities in the studies, as judged by Ajzen and Fishbein. That matrix (their Table 1) is shown in Table X. Indeed, in the studies that were reviewed, there was a very strong relationship between the level of correspondence found in a report and the degree to which that report found an attitude–behavior relation. This analysis provides good evidence for the correspondence proposition.

Specificity: Application of the correspondence criterion. To reiterate, the basic Ajzen–Fishbein (1977) thesis is that the degree of attitude–behavior consistency would be related to the degree of correspondence between entities. A corollary is that one form of correspondence is the range of specificity or generality of the entities in the model. Evidence exists that degree of SPECIFICITY is related to the matter of attitude–behavior consistency under consideration. Two studies have demonstrated this point, and because they are fairly similar they will be treated here as companion pieces.

In the first, Weigel, Vernon, and Tognacci (1974) obtained people's reactions to certain things related to the environment. Subjects responded using four different scales, with each scale representing a different level of specificity regarding the target entity in question. The target was the Sierra Club, a national organization that focuses on environmental concerns. The four scales tapped respondents' reactions to (1) the importance of a pure environment, (2) pollution,

TABLE X
Pattern of attitude–behavior consistency reports by level of correspondence

	ATTITUDE–BEHAVIOR CONSISTENCY		
Correspondence level	Not significant	Low or inconsistent[a]	High[b]
Low	26	1	0
Partial	20	47	4
High	0	9	35

After Ajzen and Fishbein (1977).
[a] Low or inconsistent relations were defined as r less than .40 or were from reports of inconsistent correlations across measures or studies.
[b] High consistent relations were defined as r equal to or greater than .40.

(3) conservation, and (4) their attitude toward the Sierra Club itself. Five months after they had completed the scales, respondents were contacted by a representative of the Sierra Club and asked to do something (write a letter to the editor, join and pay dues) to support that organization. People's responses to the solicitation could vary, and a person was assigned a behavioral score of 0 if he or she refused further contact with the club, or a score of 1 to 3, depending on her or his willingness to help. When all this information was collected, it was empirically determined which of the four scales best predicted behavior that would benefit the Sierra Club. In a moment, we will examine the correlation between attitudes, as measured by the four scales, and behavior with reference to the club.

A similar study obtained information on consumer preferences for low-pollutant (lead-free) gasoline. Researchers recorded which motorists purchased regular gasoline and which purchased lead-free fuel (Heberlein and Black, 1976). The data was recorded in 1973, when the purchase of lead-free gas was voluntary—and costly as well, because regular gas was cheaper. As in the Weigel et al. (1974) project, Heberlein and Black employed four kinds of scales, and these varied in their specificity concerning the purchase of low-pollutant fuel. The various scales comprised questions about (1) environmentalism, (2) pollution, (3) the benefits of using lead-free gas, and (4) the respondent's own personal norms about using lead-free gas. Heberlein and Black then computed correlation coefficients between the driver's responses to the various scales and whether they actually went to the trouble to purchase lead-free fuel.

In both studies, there was virtually no relationship between the most general of the attitude scales and behavior with reference to the particular entities in question. People's attitudes toward a pure environment or environmentalism in general predicted neither how they would react to a plea to assist the Sierra Club (.06) nor whether they would purchase lead-free gasoline (.14; see Table XI).

For the remaining scales, however, the picture is different. As the scales are seen to be progressively more specific regarding a given entity, subjects' attitudes were more and more predictive of their behavior. To take an extreme example in Table XI, the correlation coefficient of .68 reported by Weigel et al. (1974) means that if a subject expressed a positive attitude toward the Sierra Club as a specific issue, it was very likely that subject would act in a way to assist the Club 5 months later. Similarly, Heberlein and Black (1976) found that the best predictors of people's purchases of lead-free gasoline were the attitudinal scales that tapped feelings about the

TABLE XI
Correlation coefficients between responses to attitude scales of varying specificity and behavior toward the Sierra Club and lead-free gasoline

Research report	Target of action entity	Scale type — attitude toward:	Correlation coefficient
Weigel et al., 1974	Sierra Club	1. pure environment	.06
		2. pollution	.32
		3. conservation	.24
		4. Sierra Club	.68
Heberlein and Black, 1976	Lead-free gasoline purchases	1. environmentalism	.14
		2. pollution	.26
		3. benefits of lead-free gasoline	.45
		4. personal norm to use lead-free gasoline	.54

After Weigel et al. (1974); Heberlein and Black (1976).

benefits of this specific practice or specific personal convictions regarding the use of such fuel.

In short, here is evidence that the specificity of an attitudinal measure, in terms of the notion of target and action entities, determines its predictive power where the entities of behavior are concerned. This idea is akin to the proposition that single-act behavior is best predicted by attitudes toward the act. Also bracketed is the proposition that global attitudes are predictive of a general index of behavior. Thus, the concept of correspondence is an important addition to our perspectives on the attitude–behavior consistency issue because it provides a way of understanding why those particular propositions seem to hold so well.

Earlier Successes and Failures Revisited

The preceding three perspectives provide considerable insight into the issue of attitude–behavior consistency *and* inconsistency. Let us briefly review some of the successes and failures already encountered in this domain, as informed by that insight. Why is voting as a behavior so often consistent with people's prior political attitudes? It seems plausible to say that, for example, Fishbein and Coombs (1974) assumed that voting is a single-act behavior (i.e., *b*). The best way to predict a single act is with an attitudinal measure about that act (i.e., BI). And certainly the Fishbein–Coombs study obtained a measure of BI, as indicated in Table I. Further, the reason that affect (A_o) and cognitions $(B_i \times a_i)$ are also related to voting in Table I is that the A-B-C components of attitude are expected to be connected (see Chapter 2). Certainly, by the time a person has decided to vote (or not) for a given candidate, that person must have gone a long way in sorting out affect and cognition to be consistent with that BI.

As for one of the purported failures to find consistency, DeFleur and Westie (1958) seem to have made the mistake of trying to predict single-act behavior (signing of photo releases) with a global measure of attitudes (Summated Differences Scale). We can speculate that had they used a multiple-act (general index) measure of behavior, the degree of attitude–behavior consistency in their work could have been more satisfactory.

Finally, what about the internally discrepant findings of LaPiere (1934) and Wrightsman (1969)? Here, it seems, the issue of correspondence comes in. It might be very helpful to represent the research of LaPiere (on ethnic bias) and Wrightsman (on law and order) in terms of the schemata used above in Table IX. When we have done so, it will become clearer why those researchers discovered attitude–behavior *inconsistency* rather than *consistency*. Table XII provides an outline of LaPiere's study, and reference to it provides a strong clue as to why the inconsistency may have occurred. There appears to be very little correspondence between the attitudinal target entity (the Chinese as a race "on paper") and the behavioral target entity (an actual Oriental couple), and just as little correspondence between the attitudinal action entity (grant a reservation) and the behavioral action entity (wait on people standing in the estab-

TABLE XII
Research of LaPiere and Wrightsman organized by the Ajzen–Fishbein correspondence criteria

Research report	Attitudinal entities	Behavioral entities
LaPiere (1934)		
Target	= Members of Chinese race	= Oriental man and woman
Action	= Accept as guests in future	= Serve present customers
Wrightsman (1969)		
Target	= Presidential candidate	= Local tax legislation
Action	= Apply inexpensive sticker	= Purchase unpopular sticker

lishment). Therefore, it is quite possible that the inconsistencies in LaPiere's results were due to the procedures he used and not to the social psychology of his subjects.

Much the same appraisal fits the 1969 Wrightsman project. Wrightsman, it will be recalled, checked automobiles for the presence of both a presidential campaign sticker (as an index of attitude) and a local road-tax sticker (as an index of behavior) and reached the conclusion that supporters of an enthusiastic law-and-order candidate were less law-abiding than were supporters of some other candidates. However, an inspection of Table XII suggests a different conclusion. It can be seen that neither the target nor the action entities match up very well across what can be considered to be the attitudinal and behavioral measures. Again, the results of this particular study may be due to the lack of correspondence between *measures*, apart from anyone's sentiments or responses concerning law and order on the local or national scenes.

Summary and Conclusion

The study of attitudes held great promise for students of social psychology early in this century. Doubtless, many of them lived long enough to hear the midcentury disappointment that was voiced concerning certain attitude–behavior inconsistencies or discrepancies. However, by the end of the century, the prospect of gainfully understanding social behavior via the study of attitudes has brightened. While it will always be healthy to keep the failures to find attitude–behavior consistencies in mind, the perspectives of single-act criteria, multiple-act criteria, and correspondence should serve researchers and theorists well in the attitude–behavior domain.

CHAPTER FOUR

NEW DIRECTIONS IN ATTITUDE–BEHAVIOR RESEARCH

In the previous chapter we saw one form of progress in the under-standing of attitude–behavior consistency. That progress was orga-nized around a beginning–middle–end theme and had to do mainly with methodological considerations. There have been advances on other fronts as well. This chapter focuses not so much on method-ology per se as on "variables" that *moderate* the attitude–behavior consistency relationship. It turns out that there are quite a few factors in our world that have an influence on when attitudes and behavior will match (or not). The organization of this chapter will be in the form of a general survey of the literature.

This chapter is divided into five sections. The first section takes up the issue of how attitudes might guide behavior. A major concept here has to do with the accessibility in memory of an attitude. The rule is that the more accessible the attitude, the more likely it is to control behavior. The next two sections introduce factors that influ-ence such accessibility: (1) direct experience with an attitudinal object and (2) one's own personality as it influences what is monitored in social situations. A fourth section takes up a different perspective: in some cases our social behavior is *not* under the influence of our attitudes; rather, it plays out "mindlessly," or according to social conventions (scripts). Finally, the chapter closes with an explora-tory recommendation of a special model for the study of attitude–behavior relations: food preferences, and, in particular, food rejec-tion. For now we turn to the first issue of how attitudes might guide behavior.

Accessibility and Attitude–Behavior Consistency

If there is real progress in theory and research in the social sciences, then one assumes that it can be marked or categorized in any of several ways. For instance, in a number of chapters in this book—such as the previous one—a beginning–middle–end theme is utilized to show certain steps in a given progression of ideas and findings. With specific reference to progress on the attitude–behavior consistency issue, Zanna and Fazio (1982) utilized a theme of another sort: the is–when–how generations, or eras, of progress. For them, the "*Is*" generation in the sequence occurs when someone asks, "*Is* there a relationship between X and Y?" That is, "*Is* there an effect or a phenomenon?" This question can be pinpointed in the "middle" section of Chapter 3, a time in social science history when critics were really not sure that attitudes and behavior were necessarily consistent.

The next generation is labeled "*When.*" If X and Y really are related—and should someone take the trouble to seek out that relationship—someone else will eventually pin down when (and to what extent) X is related to Y. Of course, we have a better idea of the "*When*" of attitude–behavior consistency by now. A large section of Chapter 3 showed us that attitudes and behavior can be related when you measure them properly. When the "*Is*" and "*When*" are established, the issue of "*How*" arises.

STUDIES ON THE "HOW" ISSUE

One approach to the "how" issue focuses on the ACCESSIBILITY in memory of an object–evaluation link. That is, attitudes can influence behavior only to the extent that they are likely to be retrieved from memory in the face of an opportunity to somehow deal with the attitudinal object. I take high accessibility to mean that the attitude is easy to locate in memory (as are my feelings about my current neighborhood) or that the attitude could automatically occur to the individual without effortful searching (as mine do when I hear a neighbor's loud dogs engage in their pointless barking). Indeed, accessibility as a concept is at the core of what is turning out to be a major development in the attitude–behavior domain. Let us look at an interesting study of real-life issues that got a handle on accessibility.

Attitude accessibility, perceptions, and behavior. As was noted in Chapter 1, voting behavior is quite predictable from attitudinal measures. Fazio and Williams (1986) hoped to find out something about the accessibility concept by studying attitudes, perceptions, and voting behavior in the 1984 presidential election. Reagan and Bush were the Republican candidates, and Mondale and Ferraro were the Democratic contenders. The respondents in the study were voting-age residents of the Bloomington, Indiana area. They were recruited through ads, in libraries, or in shopping malls.

In the initial phase of the research in June and July of 1984, two items (among others) were played to each respondent from a cassette tape recorder: "A good president for the next 4 years would be Ronald Reagan," and "A good president for the next 4 years would be Walter Mondale." Although the wording of these items seems a bit awkward, it was used for a reason. One clever part of this study in real-life settings is that Fazio and Williams were actually equipped with some sophisticated portable laboratory equipment with which respondents' attitudes were measured. In order to respond to an item, the respondent pushed one of five buttons on a panel. These were marked "strongly agree," "agree," "don't care," "disagree," and "strongly disagree." Of course, when a particular button was pushed in response, one bit of information critical to the study was automatically recorded. This was the attitudinal position (extremity) of the response that could range from "strongly agree" to "strongly disagree" with the statements about the candidates' merits.

However, of special importance was a second piece of information that was produced by a respondent's push of a button. That information was the LATENCY (delay interval) between the very last sounds in the two played items (the "gan" and the "dale" on the tapes) and the instant a button was pushed. Precise latencies were calculated and recorded by a microcomputer. The logic behind this procedure is that if one has an accessible attitude about a candidate, then one will need very little time to decide which button to push. On the other hand, if one is unclear on a candidate's merits, time will be used up in internal deliberations about the individual and the choice of a button will be delayed. Therefore, short latencies were taken to indicate accessible attitudes, and long latencies were judged to reflect less accessible attitudes.

The remaining phase of the study had to do with the important questions of how the two measures obtained in midsummer related to (1) the respondents' reactions to certain events later in the campaign and (2) how they voted in the election. Let us take up the campaign first. A debate between the presidential candidates took place on October 7, and a debate between the vice-presidential hopefuls occurred on October 11. Shortly after these television events, Fazio and Williams mailed questionnaires to the respondents who participated in the summer phase. Questions about particular debates were worded in the following format: "Reagan was much more impressive," "Reagan was slightly more impressive," "The two candidates performed equally well," "Mondale was slightly more impressive," "Mondale was much more impressive." As for voting behavior, beginning the day after the election the investigators attempted to telephone the summer participants to ascertain whether and how they actually voted.

The stage is now set for a look at the relationships between attitude extremity, attitude accessibility (latency), respondents' campaign perceptions, and respondents' voting behavior. However, first I want to clarify some points. Some of the summer respondents did not watch the debates, and some did not vote. Although Fazio and Williams (1986) were careful to distinguish the data from those who did and those who did not, for the sake of brevity I will present patterns of results only from actual watchers and voters. This selection does not affect conclusions in the least. Further, some of the correlation coefficients in the original tables are negative, but only by virtue of how responses were mechanically tabulated. For the sake of clarity, I will present the absolute values of the original coefficients. Again, interpretation is unaffected.

Were summertime attitudes ("strongly agree" to "strongly disagree" about Reagan and Mondale) predictive of respondents' later perceptions and behavior? The answer is clearly yes. Table I shows

TABLE I
Correlations between attitudes and campaign perceptions and between attitudes and voting behavior

Measure	Attitude toward Reagan	Attitude toward Mondale
Perceptions		
Presidential debate	.474	.436
Vice-presidential debate	.538	.358
Both debates	.566	.486
Voting	.782	.632

After Fazio and Williams (1986).
Note. A substantial, positive correlation indicates that respondents' initial attitudes are similar to their later perceptions and voting behavior patterns. All the coefficients in this table meet these criteria.

that attitudes toward Reagan in the summer were positively related
to perceptions of how the Republicans fared in the debates and to
how people actually voted in the election in November. The same
general pattern of correlations is also in evidence for people's attitudes and later reactions to Mondale and the Democrats, although
those relationships are a little weaker.

The finding that attitudes predicted perceptions and voting behavior is good news, but it is not big news because this was the
expected outcome. A more exciting question in this context has to
do with attitude *accessibility* and later attitude–perception and attitude–behavior relations. To determine how accessibility might have
had an impact, Fazio and Williams (1986) first identified Reagan and
Mondale supporters based on the attitudinal (agree–disagree) measure. Then, on the basis of the summertime latency-of-response
index, they divided each set of supporters into two subgroups: low
access (LA—*above* the median of response latency) and high access
(HA—*below* the median of response latency). (Recall that the longer
it takes to get the button pressed, the less accessible an attitude is.)

Is it possible that differences in response latency in June and July
could be related to differences in attitude–perception consistency
patterns in October and in attitude–behavior (voting) consistency
patterns in November? Amazingly, the answer to these questions is
also yes. Table II indicates that people in the HA groups showed
more consistency between their attitudes (button choice) and their
behavior (voting) than did people in the LA groups. For instance,
concerning Reagan supporters, those in the HA condition showed
more attitude–behavior (attitude–voting) consistency ($r = .891$) than
did those in the LA condition ($r = .663$). In sum, the idea that
accessibility of attitudes may be one important feature in "*How*"
attitudes guide behavior gains support from this field study in Indiana.

However, one point that cannot be addressed by the Fazio–
Williams field approach is how certain respondents' attitudes got to
be more or less accessible. We can now examine some laboratory
studies that provide the beginnings of an answer to that kind of
question.

Consolidation and attitude retrieval. A series of experiments by
Fazio, Chen, McDonel, and Sherman (1982) offer some clues on the
issue of the determinants of accessibility. They conducted four studies, but we will take up only their Experiments 2 and 4. In the first
of these, the researchers gave subjects either direct or indirect ex-

TABLE II
Correlations between attitudes and campaign perceptions and between attitudes and voting behavior within low-accessibility (LA) and high-accessibility (HA) groups

Measure	Attitude toward Reagan		Attitude toward Mondale	
	LA	HA	LA	HA
Perceptions				
Presidential debate	.394	.529	.437	.438
Vice-presidential debate	.410	.679	.312	.403
Both debates	.404	.738	.381	.587
Voting	.663	.891	.563	.658

After Fazio and Williams (1986).
Note. A substantial, positive correlation indicates that respondents' initial attitudes are similar to their later perceptions and voting behavior patterns. In general, the larger coefficients for the HA subjects indicate that they showed higher attitude–perception and attitude–behavior consistency.

perience with a set of five different types of visual puzzles. (As I will discuss in more depth in a later section, direct experience is expected to result in a higher level of attitude–behavior consistency.) Both groups of subjects saw a videotape in which the five puzzles were described and solved. The direct-experience group was given copies of the puzzles and was invited to try to come up with its own solutions as the tape progressed. The indirect-experience group was not given these materials and was instructed to simply watch the tape.

Eventually, all subjects would be asked to participate in a response-latency task similar to the one used in the field by Fazio and Williams (1986) The lab test will be described later. However, for half of each of the above groups, a second—and for us, critical—experimental variable was introduced. These two subgroups, one each from the direct- and indirect-experience groups, were given a chance to consolidate their attitudes prior to the latency task. CON-SOLIDATION is a term borrowed from learning theorists. In operational terms it means that a subject is given an opportunity to rehearse or otherwise contemplate an association that has just been formed so that it is entered into long-term memory. In the sense that the subjects in the Fazio et al. study had just learned their attitudes about the puzzles, these consolidation subgroups were allowed to rehearse them. Following the video tape, they were asked to express (rehearse) their judgments on a scale that ran from "boring" to "interesting"; only then were they allowed to go on to the latency task. In contrast, subjects in the no-consolidation subgroups went directly to the latency task at the end of the videotape. Therefore, the design of the experiment was a 2 × 2 factorial: two levels of experience (direct and indirect) crossed with two levels of consolidation (some and none).

The response-latency measure I have been mentioning was the dependent variable in the study. The subject's task was to push one of two buttons on each of ten trials. One button was labeled YES and the other NO. On a given trial, a picture of one of the five puzzles was projected on a screen, accompanied by an evaluative adjective (perhaps, "stupid" or "cute"). The subject had to make up her or his mind whether she or he agreed with this particular evaluation by pressing the appropriate button. Each of the puzzle pictures was presented twice, once with a positive adjective and once with a negative one.

The results of all this were quite revealing and are shown in Figure 1. The two experimental variables had independent and strong effects. It is clear in Figure 1 that the opportunity for consolidation helped subjects make up their minds faster regarding their agreement with the evaluative adjectives attached to the puzzles in the latency task. The same sort of facilitation was seen for the provision of direct experience; the subjects that had actually tried the puzzles also made up their minds more quickly.

What does all this mean? Well, it means that consolidation, or direct experience, or both in combination, did facilitate retrieval of attitudes from memory, and presumably a retrieved attitude is in a position to guide behavior. Unfortunately, the latency task did not measure any behavior with respect to the puzzles.

Consolidation and attitude–behavior consistency. In their Experiment 4, Fazio et al. tried to see whether some of these factors really would have an impact on attitude–behavior consistency. Subjects in this experiment were all given indirect experience (videotape only) with the five different puzzle types from the prior research. For half of them—the single-evaluation group—there was but one opportunity to evaluate the puzzles on the interesting–boring scale described above. For the other half—the repeated-evaluation group—there

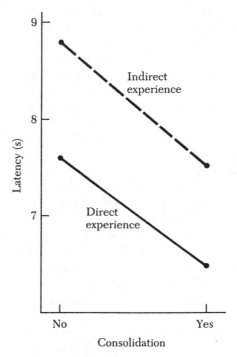

FIGURE 1
ATTITITUDE ACCESSIBILITY MEASURED BY LATENCY OF RESPONSE
as a consequence of direct or indirect experience and an opportunity for consolidation (rehearsal) of the attitude. (After Fazio et al., 1982.)

were three chances to fill out an evaluation. The rationale for these
multiple judgments was that the data had to go quickly to various
(fictitious) members of the research team and the experimenter had
found that it was easiest to have the subject duplicate responses on
three different versions of the same form.

Following the single or repeated evaluations of the puzzles, every
subject was given several copies of each of the five puzzle types, and
a 15-minute "free play" period ensued in which the subject could
work on any of the puzzles he or she cared to. The main dependent
measure was the correlation between prior interest scores and the
proportion of available problems from each type that were attempted
in the play situation. Here, it was found that attitudes were consistent
with behavior as mediated by the consolidation opportunity. For
subjects in the single-evaluation condition (low consolidation), the
average correlation coefficient between interest (attitude) and type

picked to play with (behavior) was only .22. Contrarily, for subjects in the repeated-evaluation condition (high consolidation), the correlation between attitude and behavior was a more substantial .47. In other words, something like variations in opportunities to rehearse one's attitudes seemed to have influenced how much those attitudes guided behavior.

A three-part conclusion can be drawn from the preceding Fazio et al. research:

1. Direct experience increased the accessibility of attitudes.
2. Consolidation increased the accessibility of attitudes.
3. Consolidation increased the strength of the attitude–behavior relationship.

Maybe we can take a shortcut through this three-part tangle. How about this?

Accessibility of attitudes is related to the attitude–behavior relationship.

Experiential Factors

DIRECT VERSUS INDIRECT EXPERIENCE

I noted earlier that people have attitudes for a variety of reasons and that these attitudes are formed or molded by a variety of circumstances. According to Fazio and Zanna (1981), the fact that various attitudes stem from different sources or experiences may have important implications for the attitude–behavior consistency issue. A dimension of special interest to them has to do with whether a person holds a particular attitude toward a particular object because of DIRECT or INDIRECT EXPERIENCE with that object. These writers employ a simple example to illustrate this possibility. In effect, they ask us to envision two children who have equivalent attitudes toward a certain toy. Perhaps they both rate that toy as 6 on a 7-point, 1 to 7 bad–good scale.

It is possible that the first child's attitude is a result of direct play with the toy. Conversely, the second child may have the same attitude as a result of seeing the toy advertised on television. Thus, even if these two attitudes were equally favorable in terms of self-reports, they do *differ* in their relation to past experience or behavior with the object. It was the thesis of Fazio and Zanna (1981) that the two attitudes would be differentially useful in the prediction of future behavior involving the toy. In short, their prediction was that attitude–behavior consistency would be greater in the context of a behavior-to-attitude-to-behavior sequence (first child) than in a simpler attitude-to-behavior sequence (second child).

In their review of the literature on this idea, Fazio and Zanna pointed to a number of studies that support their view. For example, a study by Fazio and Zanna (1978) obtained three separate bits of information from students enrolled in an upper-level psychology course: (1) each student's attitude about participating in the near future as a subject in psychology experiments, (2) their actual amount of past experience or participation as a subject in such psychological research, and (3) each student's willingness to sign up to be part of a subject pool for experimentation. This class of students was then divided up into three groups—high, moderate, or low—in terms of how much actual experience they had had. Next, attitude–behavior consistency within these three groups was expressed by correlation coefficients that indicated the relationship between attitude toward participating in the future and whether the person had volunteered for the pool.

In line with the hypothesis, an effect for the amount of past experience was found. Students who had minimal direct past experience as subjects showed, as a group, *no* attitude–behavior consistency, as indicated by an r of $-.03$ between current attitude and volunteering. On the contrary, students with a high amount of such direct experience showed substantially more attitude–behavior consistency, as reflected by an r of .42 between attitude and behavior. Finally, the group that had an intermediate amount of direct past experience showed an intermediate amount of consistency ($r = .36$).

Mediating influences of direct experience. Why should direct experience with an attitudinal object or issue produce more attitude–behavior consistency than indirect experience does? Fazio and Zanna (1981) explored this question in considerable detail in their chapter, but here a summary of their deliberations will serve:

1. Direct experience may simply make more information about the object available to the individual and hence may result in a more accurate or stable attitude.

2. Direct experience may cause the person to focus on his or her very behavior during that experience, and thus this behavior itself may become an element on which to base an attitude (e.g., "Did I act as if I liked it or disliked it?").

3. Direct experience of a voluntary sort may involve repetition or rehearsal

and may lead to an attitude that is more easily or accurately retrieved from memory.

LEVEL OF INFORMATION

As just noted, the amount of direct experience a person had with an attitudinal object could determine the amount of information he or she possessed about that object. Presumably, the more information one has about something at some $Time_1$, the less impactive on one's attitude will be new information received prior to some $Time_2$. Hence, people with higher levels of information or experience about an attitudinal object at $Time_1$ (attitude measure) will show more consistency with some second sort of measure at $Time_2$ (behavior measure). Two studies by Davidson, Yantis, Norwood, and Montano (1985) bear out such reasoning. Because the populations and the issues in the two studies are very different, I will sketch both to show the generality of the effect.

A voting study. In the first (their Study 2), introductory psychology students were surveyed regarding two initiatives in an upcoming local election. The issues were whether the city should (a) lift a ban on homosexual cohabitation by amending its open housing ordinances and (b) establish a fixed-fee dog and cat spay/neuter clinic. These two measures were selected because of their diversity in importance, emotional impact, and media coverage.

Eight days prior to the actual election, Davidson et al. obtained measures of attitudes and of levels of information from their respondents. From the sample of undergraduates, registered voters were asked how they intended to vote on the two issues, pro or con. Those who were not registered or who indicated no intention to vote were asked to answer "as if" they were going to vote. This pro or con sentiment constituted the attitudinal measure. Further, the students were asked to indicate how informed they were about each issue on a scale that ranged from 1 (completely uninformed) to 4 (extremely well informed).

Then, a day after the election, students were asked how they had actually voted (if they had voted) or how they would have voted (if they had not voted). As expected, there was attitude–behavior consistency for some but not all respondents, so it is possible to examine the relationship between level of information and the consistency/ inconsistency distinction. That relationship is shown in Table III,

TABLE III
Information levels for attitude–behavior consistent and inconsistent subjects on two local election initiatives

Subjects	Consistent	Inconsistent
Homosexual discrimination initiative		
Voters	3.00	2.40
Nonvoters	2.59	2.32
Spay–neuter clinic initiative		
Voters	2.38	1.77
Nonvoters	2.11	1.76

After Davidson et al. (1985).
Note. Ratings were made on a 4-point scale; 1 indicates low levels and 4 indicates high levels of information.

where the patterns for voters and nonvoters are presented separately. For both issues and for both voters and nonvoters, the relation of level of information to attitude–behavior consistency or inconsistency is clear. In all cases, consistent respondents reported themselves as having more information about the two initiatives prior to the election. Thus, in this study Davidson et al. (1985) found support for the role of information in the attitude–behavior consistency phenomenon in the area of voting.

A vaccination study. In a second study (the Davidson et al. Study 3), U.S. veterans (average age = 63.5 years) who were identified by the Veterans Administration as at risk from flu were the respondents. These male and female patients had been contacted by the VA with the recommendation that they obtain a flu shot at a local VA medical facility. Davidson et al. also contacted the veterans prior to the flu season and asked them for three bits of information: (1) an attitudinal measure of whether they intended to obtain a flu shot during the year, (2) how well informed they were about the flu shot on a scale that ran from 1 (completely uninformed) to 7 (completely informed), and (3) a prior-experience index of whether they had ever had a flu shot in the past.

When the flu season had passed, Davidson et al. determined—on the basis of self-reports and VA records—just who actually had obtained a flu shot. Given that the researchers had already recorded attitudinal, informational, and experiential measures from the respondents, it was possible to see how these premeasures were related to that behavior. These relationships are shown in Table IV. There, both level of information and experience were positively related to attitude–behavior consistency in the area of vaccinations, an outcome that fits nicely with the Zanna–Fazio (1982) position.

DIRECT EVIDENCE OF THE MEDIATION OF DIRECT EXPERIENCE

A visual analogy. It was stated above that, presumably, the more information—obtained through direct experience—one has at some $Time_1$, the less impactive on one's attitude will be new information received prior to some $Time_2$, and that it is on this basis that prior information mediates the attitude–behavior consistency relationship. Let me try to show my understanding of this proposition with the visual analogy seen in Figure 2. In Case I, the high $Time_1$ level of $Information_X$ overwhelms the impact of the vector of New $information_Y$ and deflects it. $Attitude_X$ prevails at $Time_2$ and elicits $Behavior_X$. On the other hand, in Case II, low $Time_1$ level of $Information_X$ produces a weak vector over time, and the impact of the vector of New $information_Y$ is sufficient to change the recipient's position to $Attitude_Y$. Thus, from the perspective of the researcher (who usually measures only $Attitude_X$ and $Behavior_X$), in Case I attitude–behavior consistency is observed, whereas in Case II inconsistency occurs. (Remember, this is strictly a visual *analogy*.)

As suggested, the Davidson et al. (1985) studies that were just reviewed support the notion found in the analogy, but they do not test it directly. To do so, a different and more elaborate research design would be required. Happily, such a design was undertaken by Wood (1982). She did not do the usual kind of testing of $Attitude_X$ and $Behavior_X$; instead, she did a thorough job of examining factors that mediate *attitude–attitude* consistency in the face of new infor-

TABLE IV
Information and experience levels for attitude–behavior consistent and inconsistent subjects regarding flu shots

Measure	Consistent	Inconsistent
Information[a]	5.25	4.49
Experience[b]	0.76	0.51

After Davidson et al. (1985).
[a] Ratings were made on a 7-point scale ranging from 1 (completely uninformed) to 7 (completely informed).
[b] Scores ranged from 0 (no prior flu shot) to 1 (prior flu shot).

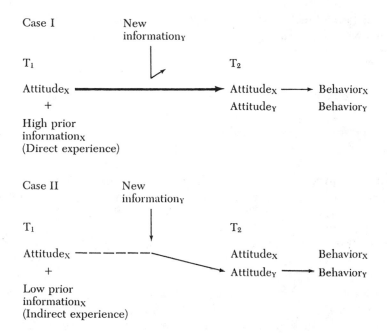

FIGURE 2
VISUAL ANALOG of the relationship of high or low prior information (and direct or indirect experience) on attitude–behavior consistency or inconsistency.

mation. Reference to Figure 2 suggests that this is an important first step in the evaluation of the analogy. Attitude–attitude consistency would seem to be a prerequisite for attitude–behavior consistency.

Measuring instruments for Time$_1$. Wood's (1982) research is useful and important. It is also rich and complicated, so we will examine it carefully and at length. The heart of the study was her measure of psychology students' attitudes toward the preservation of the environment. She called this measure "Opinions." It amounted to a 15-point scale anchored by the endpoints of "very favorable" and "very unfavorable." This instrument was applied in an initial session during which the student provided answers to five other questions, as listed and annotated here:

1. "Self-perception of previous reactions." Respondents indicated frequency of prior thoughts about, actions regarding, and positive and negative reactions to the environment.
2. "Self-perception of knowledge." The students indicated how well-in-

formed they thought they were and how frequently in the past they had sought or encountered information on the environment.

3. "Self-perception of involvement." Respondents indicated how important preservation was to them and how involved they were in the topic.

4. "Belief retrieval." Respondents were asked to list the characteristics and facts they believed to be true about the issue of the preservation of the environment. They could list from 0 to 6 beliefs.

5. "Behavior retrieval." Respondents were asked to list specific instances of times when they had engaged in actions related to preservation. They could list from 0 to 6 behaviors.

Results from Time$_1$. Before we go on to a consideration of attitude–attitude consistency in the face of new information, let us look at Wood's (1982) results from this preliminary session, for they certainly have a bearing on the broader direct-experience/information domain. Wood seems to have been principally interested in her "belief retrieval" and "behavior retrieval" measures, because she organized most of the rest of her findings around these factors. As a first step, subjects were divided into two groups on the basis of each kind of retrieval. That is, the median number of beliefs offered by the respondents was 3.70, so those that had written down more than the median were assigned to a "many beliefs" group, and those that had submitted fewer than the median were assigned to a contrasting "few beliefs" group. Similarly, all the subjects were reconsidered with respect to the median of 2.73 on the behavior question and were correspondingly assigned to "many" and "few" groups. (Please note that Wood found a weak correlation ($r = .30$) between the belief and behavior measures, so she always analyzed them separately in their relation to other variables.)

Wood initially determined that the number of behaviors retrieved from memory was clearly related to most of her other measures. Table V (Wood's Table 1) shows that those subjects who reported many behaviors also reported more thoughts, actions, feelings, knowledge, and involvement. All of the comparisons of the individual values in the left column in Table V with those in the right are statistically significant. Here, then, is a rich harvest of information for workers in the direct-experience area. The amount of direct experience is clearly related to other important factors.

The new information. Having obtained all this preliminary information, Wood introduced new information to the respondents 1 or 2 weeks later. Under a harmless deception, each respondent was given the impression that he or she was reading a transcript of an

TABLE V

Average reported thoughts, actions, feelings, knowledge, and involvement as related to level of behavioral retrieval

	BEHAVIORS RETRIEVED FROM MEMORY[a]	
Measure	Few	Many
Frequency of previous thought	10.16	11.93
Frequency of previous action	7.69	9.88
Frequency of previous feelings	10.46	12.04
Degree of knowledge	8.25	10.11
Extent of involvement	9.58	11.43

After Wood (1982).
Note. Scores in the table are average ratings on 15-point scales. Higher values indicate more frequent thoughts, actions, and feelings, and more knowledge and involvement.
[a] These were recollections of specific instances of behavior related to preservation. Over subjects the range of recollected instances was 0 to 6, with a median split of 2.73 into "few" and "many" subgroups.

interview. The person allegedly interviewed was one Jim H., a graduate student in biology who was interested in the issue of the preservation of the environment. Therefore, he was established as expert and as a credible communicator. Actually, Wood's aim was to hit the respondents with a powerful persuasive communication, and all the characteristics of the message were tailored to this end. Jim established that "he was not very strongly in favor of current efforts to preserve the environment" and went on to make the following negative points:

(a) preservation has a negative impact on the economy, (b) the energy problem justifies lowering environmental standards to allow the burning of coal, (c) preserved land is needed for housing and farming, and (d) preservation is unnecessary because it is possible to reclaim polluted areas (Wood, 1982).

You could say that Jim was no bleeding heart where the environment was concerned.

Behavior, belief, and attitude–attitude consistency. When the respondents finished reading the transcript of the interview, Wood remeasured their attitudes toward the preservation of the environment. Once again they responded to the "Opinion" item seen earlier. Because the communication was so strongly negative, one could expect overall negative shifts in attitudes toward the environment; and this occurred. However, a much more interesting question is whether attitude shifts were related to specific variables such as behavior retrieval and belief retrieval. Wood (1982) made these comparisons in her Table 2, and they are presented here in Table VI. The numbers in Table VI represent Time$_2$ shifts in attitudes; the bigger the number, the more the attitude change. It can be seen in Table VI that not all subgroups shifted equally. According to Wood,

analyses of these data indicated that as predicted, subjects who listed many behaviors changed their opinions less in response to the persuasive message than those who listed few behaviors . . . Those who listed a large number of beliefs changed their opinions less than those who listed few beliefs (Wood, 1982).

SUMMARY

Certain experiential differences are thus seen to be mediators of attitude–behavior relationships. And we see that the more social psychologists learn about people's characteristics or histories, the clearer becomes the solution to what was deemed a disturbing puzzle only a few decades ago. Attitudes and behavior can be meaningfully linked, and one is able to find that link if one knows where to look.

Individual Differences

I will continue to pursue this general approach by turning to some studies on the way certain individual differences (personality characteristics) can have an effect on the attitude–behavior relationship.

SELF-MONITORING

Self-monitoring defined. Obviously, two factors that have the potential to influence a person's behavior are (a) internal dispositions

TABLE VI
Average opinion change scores as a function of belief and behavior retrieval

Beliefs retrieved from memory	BEHAVIORS RETRIEVED FROM MEMORY	
	Few	Many
Few	5.68	3.92
Many	4.33	3.26

After Wood (1982).
Note. Higher numbers indicate greater opinion change after having read the persuasive communication.

such as attitudes and (b) the particular situation one happens to be in. In social psychology's recent past something of a heated debate has occurred regarding the relative strengths of these influences (see Epstein, 1979). However, by now it is becoming clearer that the issue goes beyond a matter of simply pitting the situation against the disposition to determine which is the more potent influence on behavior. Current thinking is that individuals *differ* in the extent to which either the situation or their dispositions guide their behavior. This personality factor has been termed *self-monitoring,* and people are said to be relatively HIGH SELF-MONITORS or LOW SELF-MONITORS (Snyder and Monson, 1975).

Because it is easy to become semantically confused about the technical meaning of low, as compared with high, self-monitoring, care must be exercised to keep things straight. Before I define the dimension, I will explain how people are sorted into the two categories. As in most tests of personality type, scales are used to obtain respondents' self-reports. On the basis of patterns of their responses, people are assigned to one or another category. Here are a few of the scale items that would be endorsed (agreed to) by a *low* self-monitor:

- "I can only argue for ideas that I already believe."
- "I rarely need the advice of my friends to choose movies, books, or music."
- "I have trouble changing my behavior to suit different people and different situations."
- "My behavior is usually an expression of my true inner feelings, attitudes, and beliefs."

On the other hand, here are a handful of items that would be endorsed by a *high* self-monitoring individual:

- "When I am uncertain how to act in a social situation, I look to the behavior of others for cues."
- "In different situations with different people I often act like very different persons."
- "I am not always the person I appear to be."
- "I laugh more when I watch a comedy with others than when alone" (Snyder and Monson, 1975; Snyder and Tanke, 1976).

Now for the definitions. According to Snyder and Monson (1975),

[low] self-monitoring individuals have less concern for the appropriateness of their social behavior and attend less to situational cues as guides to their social behavior. Their behavioral choices in social situations seem to be guided from

within by dispositions and other personal characteristics rather than by situational and interpersonal specifications of social appropriateness. As a consequence, these individuals ought to be relatively consistent across situations.

At the other end of the dimension of self-monitoring, we find a very different individual:

[High] self-monitoring individuals, out of concern for the situational and interpersonal appropriateness of their social behavior, are particularly sensitive to the expression and self-presentation of others in social situations and use these cues as guidelines for managing their own social behavior. As a result, these persons should show considerable situation-to-situation discriminativeness or variability in their behavior (Snyder and Monson, 1975).

The key to avoiding confusion between these two personality types is to realize (and memorize) *what* is being monitored. High self-monitors watch *themselves* and adjust their behavior to fit better with particular situations, whatever a given situation happens to be like. For them, it is a matter of saying "when in Rome, do as the Romans do." Their concerns regarding situation-specific cues to behavior override the guiding force of their dispositions, traits, or attitudes, and they operate on a situation-by-situation basis. On the contrary, low self-monitors are not concerned about watching themselves to see how well they fit in. They seem to be saying, "let your conscience be your guide." These individuals continue to behave in line with their attitudes or dispositions, and they do so over (across) situations.

Self monitoring and behavior–attitude consistency. It did not take long for researchers to see the relevance of the self-monitoring formulation to the issue of attitude–behavior consistency. If low self-monitors were true to their dispositions, then one would expect to see more attitude–behavior consistency on their part, compared with that of high self-monitors. An early effort to evaluate this possibility was carried out by Snyder and Tanke (1976). The subjects in that study were university students, and the attitudinal issue was how much control students should have over courses. The bipolar scale used to measure this attitude ranged from NO CONTROL to COMPLETE CONTROL, and responses were correspondingly scored from 60 to 0. The researchers had baseline (control) data that indicated that most students wanted some control over courses; thus, in that population a low average score around 21.50 would be expected.

Note, however, that Snyder and Tanke did not begin their study by applying the attitude scale and then checking for consistent behavior. Although the issue here is attitude–behavior consistency, where the attitude is thought to precede the behavior, they provided an interesting twist on this by checking for behavior–attitude consistency. People sometimes bring their attitudes in line with their behavior, as we will see in a later chapter. The experimenters first induced their subjects to behave in a way that was counter to their assumed attitudes about student control. That is, subjects were made to write "counterattitudinal" essays stating that students should indeed have *less* control over such matters, and then their attitudes toward student control were assessed.

The subtle part here is how the subjects were induced to do this. The main experimental conditions were perceived "no choice" and "choice" about writing the essay. In the no-choice condition the instructions to the subject gave the impression that the writing of a counterattitudinal essay was a mandatory part of the task, no buts about it. In contrast, in the choice condition the instructions gave a different impression. There the subject would read a statement to the effect that

we are asking students to write essays about how much control students have over courses. You have a choice whether to argue for more control, or less control. However, because most students choose to argue for more control, we are really short on essays arguing for less control. Since we need about an equal number of each type of essay, we were hoping you would write one about why there should be less student control over courses. Remember, the choice is up to you.

Under these circumstances, most subjects will write an essay arguing for less student control (Snyder and Tanke, 1976).

Only after the subjects had completed their essays did Snyder and Tanke apply the attitude scale. How would the presumably counterattitudinal behavior influence attitude ratings under the choice and no-choice conditions? The first prediction was that there would be higher scale scores—indicating an attitude of *less* desire for student control—in the choice condition than in the no-choice condition. The reasoning behind this is that if I am *forced* to write an essay that contradicts my positive attitude toward student control, then I have no reason to examine or adjust my attitude because I have justification for saying what I did: I am forced to. On the other hand, If I am under the impression that I voluntarily *chose* to write an essay that contradicts my original positive attitude, then maybe I do not feel so strongly positive after all. This prediction will be checked in a moment.

At the heart of the topic of this section is the question, How would self-monitoring interact with the experimental manipulations of no choice and choice? Recall that high self-monitors seem to adjust their behavior to a situation without too much regard for their dispositions or attitudes, whereas low self-monitors act according to their feelings about things. Because low self-monitoring individuals are more likely to adjust their behavior to their attitudes, the intriguing possibility is that they might also be more likely to adjust their attitudes to their behavior. Within the no-choice and choice conditions of the Snyder-Tanke study, the subjects were trichotomized into high, moderate, and low self-monitors on the basis of a previous test; their postbehavior attitude scores are shown in Figure 3. Two striking and interesting findings are illustrated in Figure 3. First,

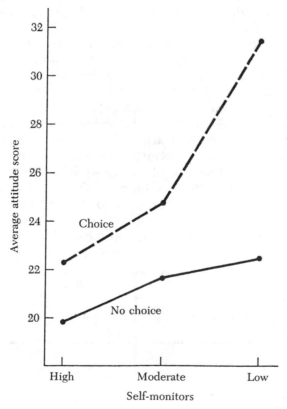

FIGURE 3
BEHAVIOR–ATTITUDE CONSISTENCY as related to level of self-monitoring (personality) and choice condition following a counterattitudinal essay. (After Snyder and Tanke, 1976.)

the prediction about the impact of choice on attitude adjustment was borne out. Students who "voluntarily" argued for less student control over courses had less positive attitudes (higher scores) toward control than students who were ordered to make such arguments. Second, the strongest relation between counterattitudinal behavior and presumed attitude shift occurred for low self-monitoring people in the choice condition. In other words, these low self-monitors showed the clearest consistency in the behavior–attitude link, which is in line with the general self-monitoring formulation.

Self-monitoring and attitude–behavior consistency. Having established the personality dimension of self-monitoring as a mediator of behavior–attitude consistency, let us turn to the possibility of its mediation of attitude–behavior connections in the real-life domain of religion-oriented behavior. Zanna, Olson, and Fazio (1980) made a dual prediction that attitude–behavior consistency would be higher among low self-monitors than among high self-monitors *and* that consistency would be higher in those individuals whose past behaviors relevant to religion had been relatively invariant, that is, in individuals with low rather than high behavioral variability.

The basic experimental design that follows from this theorizing is a 2 × 2 scheme (Figure 4). Having formulated the hypothesis, the researchers then obtained appropriate measures of subjects' (1) level of self-monitoring, (2) degree of variability of religion-oriented behavior in the past, (3) attitudes toward religion, and (4) reports of religion-oriented behavior subsequent to the attitude measure and other measures. The main dependent variable here is the correlation (r) between religious attitude and post-attitude-measure religious

	Self-monitoring	
Variability in past behavior	**Low**	**High**
Low	Prayed: $r = .52$ Used drugs: $r = -.59$	Prayed: $r = .34$ Used drugs: $r = -.21$
High	Prayed: $r = .38$ Used drugs: $r = -.06$	Prayed: $r = .29$ Used drugs: $r = .18$

FIGURE 4
ATTITUDE–BEHAVIOR CONSISTENCY as related to variability in past behavior and level of self-monitoring. (After Zanna et al., 1980.)

behavior. For example, praying was viewed as consistent with pro-religious attitudes and might be positively correlated with such attitudes. Contrarily, drug use (abuse) was generally viewed as inconsistent with traditional religious attitudes and might be negatively correlated with such attitudes. Of interest, of course, are the dual effects on these correlations of variability of past behavior and especially—for this section—of level of self-monitoring.

The correlations of interest can be seen in Figure 4. As was hypothesized, the greatest attitude–behavior consistency (i.e., the set of largest correlation coefficients) is seen in the upper left cell representing people low on both past variability of religious behavior and self-monitoring. In other words, attitudes were most predictive of behavior for subjects whose variability and self-monitoring scores placed them in this particular cell. Therefore, the Zanna–Olson–Fazio dual hypothesis gained support, and we have more evidence that individual differences can mediate attitude–behavior consistency.

AVAILABILITY, RELEVANCE, AND ATTITUDE–BEHAVIOR CONSISTENCY

So far, we have seen that the personality dimension of self-monitoring mediates attitude–behavior relationships (see also Snyder and Swann, 1976), but no one has said that low self-monitors will always show consistency or that high self-monitors will always show inconsistency. This section will close with a treatment of the increasing sophistication with which researchers have studied individual differences in this area. The single such advance to be considered here involves the issues of the AVAILABILITY and RELEVANCE of attitudes as guides to behavior. (For another, related approach, see Ajzen, Timko, and White, 1982.)

Before an attitude can guide one's behavior, one has to be aware of it. That is, the attitude has to be *available*. However, even if an attitude were available, it might have little impact on behavior if it is not *relevant*. For a given situation or circumstance, other factors —such as peer pressure, norms, or sheer physical conditions—might control the behavior, and thus a person would ignore or override her or his attitude. However, if the attitude were relevant—if its application made sense—that would be a sufficient condition for also making it available, and it would then have the potential to influence behavior (Snyder and Kendzierski, 1982).

A convincing demonstration of the importance of these concepts was provided by Snyder and Kendzierski (1982) in the context of research on the self-monitoring phenomenon in attitude–behavior patterns. The attitude in question was a subject's reaction to affirmative action. In a pretest a subject was asked whether he or she felt favorable or unfavorable about items of this sort: "Women and minorities should be given preference in hiring over others when choosing between two applicants who are equally qualified for the same position."

Two weeks after this initial assessment, the subject returned to participate as the juror (in a one-person jury) in a mock trial. The trial was presented in booklet form and had to do with an affirmative action lawsuit concerning a Ms. Harrison versus the University of Maine. A Mr. Sullivan and she had applied for the same assistant professor job in biology, but Ms. Harrison had been rejected and so was suing the school for discrimination. The subject/juror was told to carefully study both sides of the case, to weigh the evidence, and to arrive at a verdict. These mock trials took place under three experimental conditions that Snyder and Kendzierski called the basic situation, the attitude-available situation, and the attitude-relevant situation. (A given subject took part in only one of the situations.)

The basic situation. The basic situation has just been described. The juror's task was established as a problem-solving matter. He or she was to concentrate on the facts, and no reference to his or her attitude was ever made.

The attitude-available situation. Here, before any exposure to the court case, the subject was given three minutes to reflect on his or her personal attitude toward affirmative action. A list of questions was presented right in the booklet, such as: "Is it important to you that everyone is given equal opportunity in obtaining employment?" Participants were confronted with about a half-dozen similar prompts. Thus, a person's attitude was evoked prior to the deliberation of the case.

The attitude-relevant situation. This situation was created after the presentation of evidence but before the verdict was called for. The juror found in the booklet a "judge's charge to the jury." It pointed out that the verdict in this particular case had implications for others of a similar nature, was setting legal precedents, and might have an impact on the affirmative action program itself. Hence the subject/juror's attitudes were assumed to be relevant in this case, because the verdict could result in consequences that would be consistent with his or her attitudinal orientation. (Recall that the theory has it that if an attitude is relevant, it is assumed that it will become available.)

Results. Following the mock trials with these conditions or situations, subjects were asked to reach a verdict that had several components. They could find for Ms. Harrison (or not), award her damages (or not), declare that she was competent (or not), declare that they personally would have hired her (or not), among other things. These various components were combined in a single behavioral (or behavioroid, if you will) index, and that index was compared in a correlational analysis with the initial measure of attitude toward affirmative action that had been obtained a fortnight earlier. Correlations between attitudinal and behavioral measures in the three situations are shown in Table VII. Of course, because Snyder and Kendzierski were interested in the influence of individual differences, the correlations are further subdivided on the basis of the high and low self-monitors in those conditions.

The resultant pattern is very interesting, indeed. It shows that under the basic situation, *neither* the high nor the low self-monitors showed very much attitude–behavior consistency. This is the predicted result, because in this situation attitudes presumably were not available to people with either personality type. Next, in the column for the attitude-available situation, we find the traditional difference between the two kinds of self-monitors. The low self-monitors showed substantial attitude–behavior consistency, whereas the high self-monitors did not. Finally, entries under the attitude-relevant situation heading are equally interesting because *both* personality types showed strong attitude–behavior consistency. Apparently,

TABLE VII
Correlation coefficients showing the degree of attitude–behavior consistency for low and high self-monitors under various conditions of attitude salience

| Self-monitoring level | SITUATION | | |
	Basic	Attitude-available	Attitude-relevant
Low	.18*	.47**	.45**
High	−.17*	.18*	.60**

After Snyder and Kendzierski (1982).
* Minimal correspondence; ** substantial correspondence.

when attitudes are relevant to the situation as created by Snyder and Kendzierski (1982), high self-monitors will use them to guide their behavior. Table VII, then, shows how the interplay of situational characteristics and this type of individual difference (personality) can produce patterns of attitude–behavior consistency—or inconsistency.

SELF-MONITORING: CURRENT STATUS

In due time, the concept of self-monitoring as a personality variable came under moderately heavy fire. Criticisms were of two kinds, empirical and theoretical. The empirical form of attack was that subjects who measured low in self-monitoring did not always show that much more consistency between their attitudes and their behavior than high self-monitors did (e.g., Zuckerman and Reis, 1978). The theoretical form of attack was that the scale itself was flawed and did not measure a single "person variable." Rather, a technique known as factor analysis showed that the scale tapped more than one dimension (e.g., Briggs and Cheek, 1986).

Even so, Snyder and Gangestad (1986) were able to provide an energetic and thorough response to such criticisms. I do not want to leave the impression that the debate on these matters is over, but for the time being there is no need to hurriedly abandon the concept and measurement of self-monitoring and how it is related to other social phenomena. After presenting a long list of studies that found an association between people's self-monitoring scores and some facet of cognitive, behavioral, or interpersonal responding, Snyder and Gangestad (1986) simply observed that "in a phrase, the measure empirically *works*."

Indeed, recent studies employing self-monitoring measures have produced clear and interesting results in areas connected with the attitude–behavior consistency issue. For instance, self-monitoring and attitude accessibility are related. We know from earlier sections of this chapter that accessible attitudes can be elicited with shorter latencies and are predictive of behavior (see Tables I and II and related discussion). It turns out that low self-monitors can express their attitudes (involving hundreds of attitudinal objects) faster than high self-monitors can (Kardes, Sanbonmatsu, Voss, and Fazio, 1986).

And there continue to be discoveries that self-monitoring is connected with our behavior in important ways. A recent example is that level of self-monitoring in college students is associated with reported sexual behavior in the past and with anticipated sexual activity in the future (Snyder, Simpson, and Gangestad, 1986). For both men and women, high self-monitors indicated a larger number of "different partners in the last year" and higher estimates of "different partners foreseen in the next 5 years" (see Table VIII). One interpretation of this pattern is that low self-monitors prefer sex with persons that are psychologically close to them, hence would experience sexual contact mostly in the contexts of commitments or relationships. High self-monitors, on the other hand, do not limit their sexual contact with psychologically close others, hence would more likely engage in the activity with casual partners. In any event, level of self-monitoring as a moderator of the attitude–behavior relationship still seems like a worthy candidate for study.

SUMMARY

So far, all of my efforts have been devoted to finding a connectedness between attitudes and behavior. Concepts like "availability," "relevance," and "accessibility" have been developed to allow us to better understand when and how attitudes and behavior will be consistent. No doubt, more research and new concepts along these lines will be forthcoming, and this is all to the good because such progress justifies the investment social science has made in the study of attitudes and public opinion. Table IX provides a sampler of some other lines of research on mediating factors in attitude–behavior patterns; for a fairly recent annotated bibliography, see Canary and Seibold (1984).

Scripts and Mindlessness

To fully understand the relationships between mediating factors and attitude–behavior patterns, we must also examine factors that have

TABLE VIII
Sexual behavior patterns of high and low self-monitors

Behavior	SELF-MONITORING LEVEL			
	High		Low	
	Male	Female	Male	Female
Number of different partners in the last year	2.30	1.67	1.55	1.17
Number of different partners foreseen in the next 5 years	7.02	3.74	4.30	2.21

After Snyder et al. (1986).

TABLE IX
Sampler of variables studied in related lines of research on attitude–behavior consistency

Variable(s)	Author(s)
Social pressure	Andrews and Kandel (1979)
Self-awareness	Beaman, Klentz, Diener, and Svanum (1979)
Belief relevance and personal experience	Borgida and Campbell (1982)
Objective self-awareness	Carver (1975); Diener and Wallbom (1976)
Self-focused attention	Gibbons (1978)
Centrality, extremity, and intensity	Petersen and Dutton (1975)
Deindividuation	Prentice-Dunn and Rogers (1980)
Self-focused attention	Pryor, Gibbons, Wicklund, Fazio, and Hood (1977)
Certainty, direct experience, stability, and vested interest	Raden (1985)
Certainty	Sample and Warland (1973)
Temporal instability	Schwartz (1978)
Vested interest	Sivacek and Crano (1982)
Salient guides to action	Snyder and Swann (1976)

the potential to disrupt or bypass attitude–behavior connections. Two of these factors are known as scripts and mindlessness.

SCRIPTS

What governs our social behavior as it actually unfolds? Surely, some of what we do is based on intense concentration and analysis, but, apparently, some of what we do is fairly automatic. According to Abelson (1981, 1982), many of our social interactions are based on social-psychological "scripts." These are not exactly the scripts we encounter when we read a play; still, there is some similarity. A SCRIPT is an organized set of assumptions or expectations about a sequence of events. These events are usually a series of actions by particular individuals in a particular mundane setting. Scripts dictate our behavior in places such as restaurants, laundromats, and super-markets, and on occasions such as weddings and dinner parties. If you enter a supermarket as a shopper, you will act out the shopper script; if you enter as a bag boy, you will act out the bag-boy script.

To "behave a script" (Abelson's phrase), one must have a stable cognitive representation of the specific script, and conditions must exist to evoke it. Equally important is the *commitment* of the actor to the script. That is, starting a script implies that one will finish the script. One does not usually leave the chair until the dentist is finished, nor does one readily walk out of a friend's house in the middle of a sit-down dinner. However, commitment to a particular script is contingent on what has been termed an ACTION RULE. "An action rule consists of a set of criteria which if affirmed will lead the person to enter the script, but if negated will lead the person not to enter the script" (Abelson, 1982).

As an example, consider the script of a hotel manager. A potential guest presents herself or himself and asks for accommodations. Before the manager behaves according to his room-renting script, the action rule is checked. This rule has two parts: whether (a) a room is available and (b) the potential guest appears able to pay. If the answer on both counts is positive, the manager is well practiced at saying yes and carrying out the steps of registration; if either count is negative, the manager has no difficulty in offering a polite refusal.

Now, these script-based behavior patterns do not immediately strike one as exciting matters for study, until one realizes that without them our daily lives would be chaotic. But if scripted behavior is useful in everyday life, it can raise havoc in the domain of attitude–behavior consistency research. Let us take a familiar report of attitude–behavior *in*consistency and use a script analysis to clarify it.

Recall the classic findings of LaPiere (1934). This was the case where he and a Chinese couple toured the country and received accommodations at almost every placed they stopped. When LaPiere later wrote to those establishments about the possibility of reservations for Orientals, he received almost universal refusal. How would scripts lead us to an understanding of this inconsistency?

We have already seen that the action rule for hotel managers (and headwaiters) centers on available space and on the ability of the client to pay. If these counts check positively, it is very likely that the proprietor will carry out the script. Further, "liking" a guest is not a good action rule for a commercial establishment, thus attitude is not relevant in the commitment decision about engaging in welcoming behavior. In Abelson's (1981) words:

Even if a negative attitude exists toward a particular rare minority, this attitude (with some exceptions) is not practiced as a reason for nonaction. Emergent doubts have little chance of deflecting scripted behavior when standard action criteria are satisfied.

Therefore, script behavior overrode the prejudice of the hotel managers in the situation involving direct confrontation (by following the action rule) but not in the situation of the indirect confrontation (mail inquiry).

Abelson (1982) provides another example where an appeal to scripts makes sense of an otherwise confusing situation. Consider a script for going to a major department store to shop for clothing. In this kind of script the action rule usually has to do with the characteristics of the clothing to be examined, and this rule does not say anything about the snubbing of certain sales personnel.

Thus attitudes toward types of clothes should correlate well with the behavior of buying those clothes, whereas attitudes toward categories of sales persons need not correlate at all with the behavior of buying from those sales persons. This point seems obvious enough, but the finding some years back that the racial integration of the sales force at Macy's department store . . . had no effect on the purchasing behavior of prejudiced buyers occasioned a great deal of surprise at the time (Abelson, 1982).

Therefore, scripts can confuse the unwary investigator. If a racially prejudiced customer buys clothes from a minority clerk on the basis of a clothes-buying script, it does *not* mean that the racial attitude and the behavior toward the minority individual are inconsistent. It simply means that in this particular case the attitude and the behavior are irrelevant.

Mindlessness

For Abelson (1981, 1982), scripts involve cognitions and action rules. On the other hand, for Langer (Langer, Blank, and Chanowitz, 1978; Langer, Chanowitz, and Blank, 1985), scripts imply MIND-LESSNESS. That is, social behavior is accomplished much of the time without the need for thoughtfulness, or the need to pay attention to the substantive details of information in the environment. Mindlessness arises in familiar situations:

Through repeated exposure to a situation and its variations, the individual learns to ignore and remain ignorant of the peculiar semantics of the situation. Rather, one pays attention to the scripted cue points that invite participation by the individual in regular ways (Langer et al., 1978).

Consider a commonplace event. You have just arrived at a copy machine and are about to deposit a coin to begin your copying. Someone approaches you and asks to use the machine first. What do you do in response? Well, according to Langer et al. (1978), it depends on how the request is phrased and, in turn, what script you are using for that situation. Let us assume that your script for responding to requests for small favors looks something like this:

Favor X + Reason Y = Comply

On the face of it, this looks like a fairly thoughtful script. But is it? If you are using the script mindlessly, *any* Reason Y will fill the bill to compute the equation.

Langer et al. (1978) tested this mindlessness proposition by using what can be called the copy-machine paradigm. In a field experiment, unsuspecting subjects were interrupted just as they were about to deposit a coin in a copier. An experimenter approached them and asked to use the machine first. That request was made in one of three ways:

1. Request only. "Excuse me, I have 5 pages. May I use the Xerox machine?"
2. "Placebic" information. "Excuse me, I have 5 pages. May I use the Xerox machine, because I have to make copies?"
3. Real information. "Excuse me, I have 5 pages. May I use the Xerox machine, because I'm in a rush?"

On the basis of logic, requests 1 and 2 are equivalent, because they do not differ in the amount of actual information presented to the subject. However, in terms of the script presented earlier, requests 2 and 3 are equivalent because they both provide *some* Reason Y for mindless compliance. Indeed, when Langer et al. (1978) calculated the proportion of subjects who complied with each of the three types of requests, requests 2 and 3 were equivalent, and far more effective than request 1. The proportions of subjects who yielded the copy machine in response to requests 1, 2, and 3 were 60%, 93%, and 94%, respectively.

The potential for mindlessness to confuse conclusions about attitude–behavior relations should be clear. If a researcher measured subjects as high or low on altruism (as an attitude) and then recorded their behavior when approached for a favor at a copy machine, their responses would depend in an important way on how the request was made. If a mindless script was engaged by the request, there would be no reason to expect any connection between the altruistic attitude and the compliant behavior.

It is now known that not *all* is lost to mindlessness. Langer and Piper (1987) found that mindlessness could be reduced when requests were made in ways that allowed creative possibilities, as opposed to ways that evoked conventional responses. Further, Kitayama and Burnstein (1988) found that subjects could recall details of simple requests at levels higher than expected from generic knowledge, a finding showing that they were paying attention to some extent. Even so, both papers reported considerable evidence *for* mindlessness, under the right circumstances.

In sum, scripts and mindlessness have the potential to obscure attitude–behavior relationships. Future research and theorizing in the area should take these possible influences into account and guard against them. On the other hand, I have a sense that in a certain area there is an extremely strong link between attitude and behavior. What is this area, and what are the data upon which it is based? These are questions to be asked of a historian (or textbook writer). I am happy to be such a historian, but occasionally there is the temptation to be an oracle. Therefore, in this final section I offer some exploratory ideas about food preferences and food aversions as a model for attitude–behavior consistency considerations.

Food Preferences: A New Model of Attitude–Behavior Consistency

I propose that the "when" and especially the "how" of attitude–behavior consistency be given further study. What would be the best circumstance under which to carry out that study? It certainly would be nice to discover an area of human psychology where attitude–behavior consistency was almost *guaranteed*. Then the connection could be closely scrutinized. Alas, given all the powerful factors that mediate or obscure such connections, could there ever be guaranteed consistency? I think so. Consider the following observation:

Americans eat oysters but not snails. The French eat snails but not locusts. The Zulus eat locust but not fish. The Jews eat fish but not pork. The Hindus eat pork but not beef. The Russians eat beef but not snakes. The Chinese eat snakes but not people. The Jale of New Guinea find people delicious (Robertson, 1977).

No one would dispute the fact that people in different cultures eat different types of foodstuffs and that it would be a fairly straightforward matter to get data to match preferences (attitudes) with eating (behavior). Just ask yourself the following questions: "How many times have I had locusts for supper this year?" or "How many times have I had snake for breakfast this month?" Huge cultural differences in what constitutes acceptable food are further illustrated in Figure 5. Those things in the tree and in the bowl on the left side of the figure are mopane worms, the four-inch-long larva of the emperor moth. The South African woman seen there is picking a nice batch of these worms for human consumption. She might prepare them for eating in a number of ways: frying, drying, or stewing. Some people even eat them raw. The man in the right panel of Figure 5 is enjoying his worms stewed, in, as it says on the can's label, a "medium chilli tomato sauce." Apparently, this insect's popularity is on the rise as a fast food among urbanites in South Africa (Brandon and Bannister,

FIGURE 5
HARVESTING AND EATING MOPANE WORMS in South Africa. (From Brandon and Bannister, 1987.)

1987). How would you like *your* worms prepared? How many worms do you want on your plate?

FOOD REJECTION AS AN ATTITUDE

This, then, may be our access to *guaranteed* attitude–behavior connections. Pronounced and easily detectable attitude–behavior links doubtless can be found in the area of FOOD PREFERENCES and, especially, FOOD AVERSIONS or FOOD REJECTIONS. Of course, anthropologists have long been concerned with the understanding of cultural variations in dietary habits (see, for example, Harris, 1985). Recently, however, more and more attention has been paid to the psychology of likes and dislikes for food and other things that might be ingested (see Rozin and Fallon, 1987).

The growing literature on food preferences has links to mainstream attitudinal work based both on intuitive reasons and on theoretical grounds. Rozin and Fallon (1981) provided a taxonomy of potential foodstuffs in American culture that is based on primary reasons for acceptance or rejection. Three main elements make up the acceptance/rejection dimension: (1) a "sensory–affective" factor having to do with taste (flavor) and distaste, (2) an "anticipated consequences" factor having to do with beneficial and dangerous characteristics, and (3) an "ideational" factor based on the appropriateness or inappropriateness of certain substances. Their first factor, the "sensory–affective" factor, has affinities to the affective component A in the A-B-Cs of attitudes, and their second and third elements, "anticipated consequences" and "ideational [factors]," are surely linked to the cognitive C component (see Chapter 2). Although the B (behavioral) component is not explicitly identifiable in the Rozin–Fallon taxonomy, it is people's very behavior that the scheme is meant to explain. Hence, for Rozin and Fallon (1981), an attitude–behavior consistency (our terms) would simply be assumed.

DISGUST AS AN ATTITUDE TOWARD (CERTAIN) FOODS

In addition to distaste (e.g., spoiled milk, rotten meat), danger (e.g., suspected carcinogens, cholesterol), and sheer inappropriateness (e.g., sand, wood) as bases for rejection of potential or established foods, Rozin and Fallon (1987) highlight a little-studied reaction: DISGUST. Disgust is an interesting attitudinal response because it clearly involves affect and cognition. Indeed, Rozin and Fallon offer it as a "model for cognitive–affective linkages." This is so because disgust is a type of rejection that is spurred by ideational (appropriate versus inappropriate) factors. Further, disgusting items have offensive properties, and there is a presumption (i.e., an idea not necessarily based on experience) that the item would taste bad. Hence, disgust also involves the sensory–affective factor. Think back on the mopane worm snacks in Figure 5. Are big worms *appropriate* finger food in your culture? On a good–bad scale, what would be your estimate of how they would *taste* (or feel) in your mouth?

DISGUST, CONTAMINATION, AND BEHAVIOR

Disgusting substances have a strong potential to contaminate otherwise acceptable foods. This CONTAMINATION comes about by actual physical contact (e.g., a human hair in a bowl of soup) or by association (e.g., a bowl of soup stirred with a sterile flyswatter). But how do people behave with respect to disgusting or contaminated things? Surprisingly, there are very few articles that report behavior; almost all rely on ratings of some sort. However, there is an anecdote related by Rozin and Fallon (1987) wherein nurses in a certain children's hospital were at fault for drinking glasses of juice meant for the children. This problem was eliminated by serving the juice in new, clean urine-collection bottles. The nurses stopped drinking the juice. This is attitude–behavior *consistency!*

In a more systematic approach, Rozin, Fallon, and Augustoni-Ziskind (1985) offered children the opportunity to actually *sip* some fruit juice or *take a bite* of a cookie. Note that these are measures of *behavior*. The catch was that on certain occasions the juice was either contaminated by the experimenter's dirty (used) comb or by a dead grasshopper; and the cookie was contaminated by "grasshopper powder" (a mixture of sugar, flour, and food coloring). Figure 6 shows the percentage of children in three age groups that were willing to

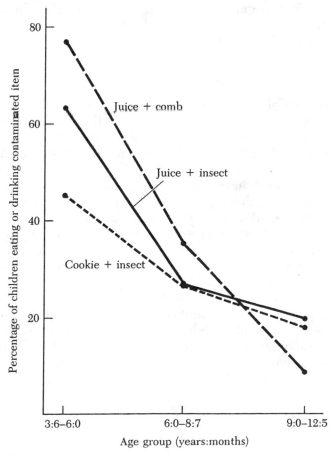

FIGURE 6
BEHAVIORAL AVERSION TO CONTAMINATED FOODS as a function of age group. (After Rozin et al., 1985.)

sip or bite the items after contamination. In terms of their behavior, the youngest children were the least bothered (disgusted) by the contaminating events, and the oldest children the most so. The children's behavior in these circumstances probably reflected their own attitudes about what is ingestible and what is not. Refusal to ingest contaminated items took place despite urging by the experimenter to sip or bite the material, and even though the experimenter acted as an exemplar by ingesting the contaminated food herself.

In sum, there is every reason to expect that in older children and adults, at least, strong attitude–behavior links would be very likely in the domain of food aversions. If social scientists can better understand why affect, cognition, and behavior are so tightly linked here, perhaps they can then apply this understanding to other domains in which such links are not so tight.

A General Summing Up

This chapter offered a view of five selected aspects of the attitude–behavior consistency issue. These were (1) the role of accessibility, (2) the impact of some experiential differences (history), (3) the mediation by individual differences (personality), (4) the confounding or confusing influences of scripts and mindlessness, and (5) a model for a reliable attitude–behavior relationship: food preferences and aversions. Progress on these particular fronts, as well as advances in methodological matters as reviewed in the previous chapter, have served to demystify the concerns about attitude–behavior inconsistencies that emerged in the late 1960s. This is not to say that we should be content to rest on our laurels in this domain. I hope there will be continued investment in the study of the attitude–behavior consistency issue. However, as I look ahead to the tremendous amount of attitude research and theory that makes up the rest of this book, I have a sense of confidence that it is probably worthwhile for me to write about it, and for you the reader to read about it. Attitudes can predict behavior, and they often do.

BEGINNING–MIDDLE–END: ADVANCES IN ATTITUDE THEORY AND RESEARCH

There is excitement in learning about the latest, state-of-the-art methods and findings of a social science. However, it is also illuminating to discover what steps and progressions were necessary to reach current levels of expertise. One can think of these scientific histories as stories, each having a beginning, a middle, and an end. The beginning of a story in scientific psychology is some point in time when an interesting or important phenomenon has first been identified and given an interpretation. The middle of the tale occurs when the original observation or interpretation is challenged by new information or by alternative explanations. Finally, an end is identifiable when there is a resolution of the conflict of information or theory and the original idea is refined, modified, or rejected.

Three such stories are offered in this third unit. The first, in Chapter 5, has to do with attitudinal effects of mere repeated exposure. Next, Chapter 6 discusses group influences and the polarization of attitudes. Finally, Chapter 7 deals with social cognition, cognitive dissonance, and attitude change.

CHAPTER FIVE

ATTITUDINAL EFFECTS OF MERE
REPEATED EXPOSURE

Several things will be accomplished in this chapter. First, we will trace the early history of a phenomenon known as the "mere exposure effect." Simplified, the basic proposition underlying the effect is "the more you see it, the more you like it." Developments in this domain from the late 1960s to the late 1970s are interesting and informative. Not only will we learn a great deal about the attitudinal consequences of familiarity, we will also encounter a beginning–middle–end theme. The literature that will be reviewed constitutes a brief but informative history-of-science progression.

Following this historical treatment, some practical applications of mere exposure theory and research will be discussed in the areas of interpersonal attraction, politics, and food preferences.

Finally, current advances in the study of attitudinal effects of mere repeated exposure on theoretical and empirical levels will be presented, and a new beginning–middle–end theme will be identified. The chapter will finish with an up-to-the-minute (and concise) review of 134 published articles on research on mere exposure effects.

A Beginning: Original Propositions and Findings

Most theories of attitude formation and change assume that an individual's psychological reaction to an object or event is caused, at least in part, by the information conveyed by that object or event. Indeed, we have seen in Chapter 2 that cognitions about the functions or consequences of attitudinal objects are important components of attitudes. It seems to follow from this assumption that if some stimulus object had no discernable function or consequences, then one would hardly be expected to have any measurable attitude toward that stimulus. However, there is one important theory that argues for the possibility that people *will* form an attitude toward such an unlikely target and that under some very simple circumstances such attitudes can be expected to be relatively positive. This theoretical position was proposed in an impressive monograph by Zajonc (1968) in which he stated this hypothesis: *The repeated mere exposure of a stimulus is a sufficient condition to enhance an observer's attitude toward that stimulus.*

Two of the words in this hypothesis ("repeated" and "mere") are especially important. First, in contrast to the old saying that familiarity breeds contempt, we find the assertion that the repetition of a stimulus leads to an improvement in one's reaction to it. Second, the conditions surrounding this repeated exposure need not have any special properties. That is, exposure has merely to occur and need not be accompanied by or followed with something pleasant or rewarding in the environment (i.e., there need be no consequences). Exposure itself is enough to modify the observer's attitude about the exposed thing. Hence, this idea became known as the MERE EXPOSURE HYPOTHESIS. Upon consideration, this form of exposure is by no means rare in real life, for many commercial advertisements seem designed to simply increase our *awareness* of the names or appearance of certain products or brands.

Of course, Zajonc had a theory for why there should be a relationship between frequency of repeated exposure or familiarity and attitude, but before this explanation could be taken seriously it was important to demonstrate that exposure and liking were actually positively related, that is, that more exposures led to more favorable attitudes. Zajonc offered evidence for his contention from two sources: correlational studies and laboratory experiments. We will also consider data from a third source from about the same period —field experiments.

CORRELATIONAL STUDIES

Correlational evidence in Zajonc's 1968 monograph was based on the fact that in everyday life people naturally encounter some things more often than others. For example, in reading and writing, people encounter certain letters of the alphabet (e.g., E, R, or T) much more frequently than other letters (e.g., Q, V, or X), and in a similar fashion whole words appear with differing regularity. The reader could demonstrate these differences in frequency of exposure for herself or himself by making a count of all the separate words in this book. Once information about frequency of exposure exists, one could perform a test of the mere exposure hypothesis based on the following logic. If we favor familiar things over those that are less familiar, then words that appear more frequently than others should be liked more by readers of this book. To empirically test this hypothesis, a researcher could select words from this text that were relatively high, medium, and low in frequency of appearance and then ask subjects to tell the experimenter, by ratings of the stimulus words on semantic differential scales (e.g., good–bad) how much they like each word, or how good or pleasant each word is. If subjects liked the higher frequency words more than they liked the lower frequency words, Zajonc's hypothesis would be supported.

To answer this correlational question, it will not be necessary for anyone to actually count the words in this book, for we can estimate their frequency of appearance or occurrence from earlier counts of words in print (e.g., Thorndike and Lorge, 1944). Zajonc picked relatively high-, medium-, and low-frequency words from such a word count and asked people to indicate their reaction to them on bipolar adjective scales, where larger scale values indicated more positive attitudes toward the words. The results of this procedure are shown in Table I, where it can be seen that respondents' attitudes or evaluations were clearly and positively related to the frequency of appearance of the word stimuli. Over many sets of words, such as the names of flowers, trees, vegetables, cities, and countries, the correlation coefficient (r) between frequency of appearance and subjects' evaluations reached or exceeded .80, which indicates a very strong relationship.

The reason that this word-count approach is *correlational* is that, although it indicates that the factors of frequency of appearance in print and liking for certain words are clearly related, there is no easy way to tell which caused which. That is, does the high rate of appearance of certain words cause liking for them, or vice versa? It seems reasonable to speculate that writers in general may have been more avid to discuss corn rather than parsnips, simply because of the preferred taste of corn. Further, correlations can be spurious or false in that two factors (say, A and B) can be independent but still highly correlated because of some factor C. Consider your own age and the number of nuclear weapons in the world. The older you became (factor A), the more weapons there were in existence (factor

TABLE I
Average ratings for fruit and vegetable names and estimates of their frequency
of appearance in print

Fruit name	Frequency of appearance	Rating[a]	Vegetable name	Frequency of appearance	Rating[a]
Apple	220	5.13	Corn	227	4.17
Cherry	167	5.00	Potato	384	4.13
Strawberry	121	4.83	Lettuce	142	4.00
Pear	62	4.38	Carrot	96	3.57
Grapefruit	33	4.00	Radish	43	3.13
Cantaloupe	2	3.75	Asparagus	5	2.33
Avocado	16	2.71	Cauliflower	27	1.96
Pomegranate	8	2.63	Broccoli	18	1.96
Gooseberry	5	2.63	Leek	3	1.96
Mango	2	2.38	Parsnip	8	1.92

After Zajonc (1968).
[a]Responses were obtained using a 7-point scale; larger values indicate more positive
attitudes tward the words.

B), a relationship that represents a very strong positive correlation.
But you did not influence the stockpiling of the weapons and neither
did they cause you to mature. Rather, the passage of time (factor C)
can account for the parallels in these two unrelated trends.

LABORATORY EXPERIMENT DATA

The mere exposure hypothesis posits that exposure causes liking.
This idea was "supported" by the correlational evidence, but that
data could not speak to cause-and-effect relationships. To more
clearly specify the causal direction of the effect, Zajonc (1968) turned
to laboratory experimental research. The procedure he used was
simple but compelling. In the laboratory he showed people certain
stimulus configurations more often than others. The preliminary information given to the subjects was skimpy. Where appropriate, the
people in the study were simply told that the research involved
"pronouncing foreign words" (when the stimuli were nonsense words)
or "visual memory" (when the stimuli were pictorial).

During the exposure period when particular stimuli (on slides,
usually) were briefly shown 1, 2, 5, 10, or 25 times, nothing was said
or done to any subject, thus this method approximated a condition

of mere exposure. Following the exposure session, the subjects were asked to evaluate the various stimuli on bipolar attitude scales. For example, in an experiment where nonsense words were used as stimuli (e.g., NANSOMA, AFWORBU, CIVADRA, IKTITAF, LO-KANTA, among others), the subjects were told that they had been shown Turkish adjectives and were asked to rate each on a good–bad scale to indicate whether they felt that an adjective meant something good or bad. In another study that employed photographs of men's faces as stimuli, respondents were instructed to rate how much they might like the man in each photograph (Zajonc, 1968).

Several other important features of this research deserve mention. First, the stimulus material to be exposed was chosen because it was judged to be both novel and neutral to the undergraduate population from which subjects were drawn. Therefore, attitudinal reactions to the materials could be attributed to the frequency at which it was exposed in the laboratory and not necessarily to the inherent properties of such stimuli. Second, as an additional precaution against the possibility that some types of material might just be inherently more attractive than others (say, NANSOMA compared with IKTI-TAF) slides were rotated from one frequency category to another across different subjects. For example, if for Subject 1 Slide A_1 was shown at high frequency (e.g., 25 times) and Slide A_2 was shown at low frequency (e.g., 1 time), then Subject 2 was scheduled to see Slide A_2 more frequently than A_1. If there were three slides, then three subjects were required to completely shuffle the assignments, and so on, depending on how many slides were involved. In practice this method is called the PARTIAL COUNTERBALANCING of slides to frequency categories.

Finally, and what is more important, in the laboratory the subject had no control over which stimuli were seen more or less frequently. That is, a subject could not choose to see a preferred object over one that was not preferred simply because it was the experimenter who determined the frequency of exposure of all the stimuli. This factor is the critical advantage that experimental studies enjoy over those that are correlational. In the lab, cause and effect can be determined.

These rather stringent experimental procedures seemed to have considerable success in demonstrating that frequency of exposure indeed causes an enhancement of the observer's attitude, just as the hypothesis suggested (Zajonc, 1968). The composite results of several independent laboratory experiments are displayed in Figure 1, where there is a plot of subjects' attitudinal (affective) reactions to several

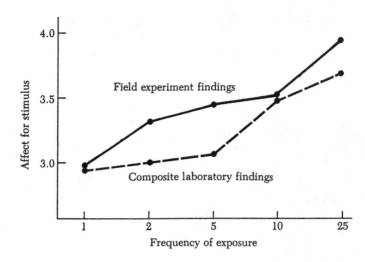

FIGURE 1
REPEATED MERE EXPOSURE EFFECTS on attitudinal ratings from laboratory and field studies. (After Zajonc and Rajecki, 1969.)

types of stimuli such as nonsense words, Chinese-like characters (letters), and photographs of men's faces taken from a university yearbook. These laboratory data show that the repeated exposure of at least certain kinds of visual material seemed to enhance observers' positive affective reactions to the stimuli seen most frequently (cf. Stang, 1974b). Such exposure effects have also been obtained for musical selections (Heingartner and Hall, 1974).

FIELD EXPERIMENT DATA

Similar findings were demonstrated outside the laboratory in a number of field experiments (Crandall, 1972; Rajecki and Wolfson, 1973; Zajonc and Rajecki, 1969). For example, campus newspapers at Michigan State University (in East Lansing) and the University of Michigan (in Ann Arbor) were employed to expose readers to 7-letter, 3-syllable nonsense words of the sort that had previously been used in the laboratory research. Over a one-month period, certain nonsense words were plainly printed 1, 2, 5, 10, or 25 times in the newspapers (see Figure 2 for a sample exposure). The employment of two papers allowed the partial counterbalancing of stimuli in frequency categories; words printed frequently in East Lansing were printed infrequently in Ann Arbor, and vice versa for the other words. After the exposure period, hundreds of respondents were

FIGURE 2
MERE EXPOSURE OF A NONSENSE WORD in a campus newspaper in the
Zajonc–Rajecki field experiment on the mere exposure hypothesis.

asked to rate the words on affective scales in questionnaires circulated
in classrooms on the respective campuses and by mail. As in the
laboratory studies, the results were clear. There was a positive relationship between frequency of exposure of the nonsense words*
and the affective ratings each received (Figure 1).

*The reader may have noticed a certain similarity between one class of stimuli
used in this phase of mere exposure research, and the last name of the author of
this book (e.g., NANSOMA, IKTITAF, CIVADRA, LOKANTA, RAJECKI). Well,
some respondents in the Zajonc–Rajecki (1969) field study did, because his name
and address were printed on the questionnaires used to obtain affective ratings.
These respondents drew little good–bad scales near his name and rated it in the
manner employed for the other nonsense words. The truth to tell, my name received
the worst ratings of all, which was taken as further support for the mere exposure
hypothesis since we assumed the name was unfamiliar to the respondents. What
some of us will go through for the sake of science (or Zajonc)!

THEORY

To account for the finding that the repeated mere exposure of a stimulus led to more positive evaluations of that stimulus, Zajonc and his colleagues proposed that the effect was attributable to a reduction in RESPONSE COMPETITION. That is, whereas the experimental stimuli were relatively novel and neutral to begin with, nothing is entirely new to adults. By the time we reach college, any given thing has the capacity to remind us of something else. When a subject first saw one of the somewhat complicated experimental stimuli, such as NANSOMA in Figure 2, it is conceivable that a number of responses could be evoked: NAN (a woman's name?), SO (so?), or MA (mom?). However, because the stimulus was seen but briefly (exposure duration was only a couple of seconds in the laboratory) and its literal meaning was intentionally made ambiguous, no particular response would be prepotent over others. Assuming that we want to give a single appropriate response to every stimulus we encounter, we could say that these multiple potential responses are in a state of competition. Further, this state of response competition would be relatively uncomfortable, not unlike the feeling one has when some fact is on "the tip of the tongue," while it remains oddly inaccessible to consciousness. Recall the feeling you had when you wanted to introduce two acquaintances to each other, but could not think of the name of one of the individuals.

The reason mere exposure leads to increased liking, according to this theory, is that multiple exposures provide an opportunity to reduce the response competition that is elicited by an ambiguous stimulus. As a thing is encountered more and more often, it is more and more likely that some single response will become associated or attached to that stimulus. When a person finally settles on a single response to one of the experimental stimuli (e.g., "Oh, yes, NANSOMA reminds me of the 'soma' in Huxley's novel, *Brave New World.*"), the conscious or subconscious annoyance with the word abates. When the subject is subsequently asked to evaluate a repeatedly exposed stimulus on a bipolar adjective scale, it is "liked" or viewed as more "pleasant" than some other related configuration that has been encountered less often and for which response competition is relatively high.

Support for the idea that a reduction in response competition caused the attitudinal effects of mere exposure came from a number of sources. Harrison (1968) operationally defined response competition as the amount of time (latency) it took a subject to generate a free association to the Chinese character (letter) stimuli. The logic is that if response competition for a particular stimulus is high, it should take a person longer to react (e.g., "That reminds me, I guess, of, uh, a tree.") to that object than to another object for which response competition has been reduced (e.g., "Horse!"). After showing the Chinese letters to subjects 1, 2, 5, 10, or 25 times, Harrison asked them to respond to a subsequent display of each stimulus by saying the first word that occurred to them. Support for the response competition notion was found in that response latency was negatively related to exposure frequency.

Similarly, Matlin (1970, 1971) produced evidence for this formulation by attempting to actively *manipulate* response competition. In one condition she required that subjects pronounce some of the nonsense word stimuli in a consistent fashion by having them emphasize the same syllable over and over again on repeated trials (i.e., *NANSOMA*, *NANSOMA*, and *NANSOMA*). It was expected that in this condition response competition would be reduced. On the other hand, in a second condition the subjects had to emphasize different syllables over trials (i.e., *IKTITAF*, *IKTITAF*, and *IKTITAF*); here response competition would be maximized. Matlin found that affective ratings were higher for words in the consistent condition than they were for words in the inconsistent condition; this finding provided support for the theory.

A Middle: Competing Hypotheses and Alternative Explanations

The mere exposure effect and the response-competition analysis were not received with universal enthusiasm among social psychologists. Critics were quick to come forward with a number of alternative explanations, any one of which, if correct, would undermine the theoretical importance of the exposure effect as a phenomenon worthy of study. For convenience we will consider these critiques under two categories: (1) exposure effects as an artifact of the experimental situation and (2) exposure effects as just another manifestation of simple learning.

Mere Exposure as an Artifact

This criticism is especially problematic to anyone disposed to take the exposure effect seriously, for it raises the issue of whether mere exposure has a real influence on the observer's attitude at all. This position holds that although subjects, by their ratings, indicate responses that *seem* to reflect the formation or change of attitude as a consequence of exposure, in reality their attitudes have been unaffected, and the resulting scale marks are a consequence of some other influence called the demand characteristics of the experimental setting. DEMAND CHARACTERISTICS include any feature of a research setting or procedure that might indicate to the subject how he or she "should" act in the situation. In particular, demand characteristics refer to those features of a study that might give a subject ideas about what phenomenon the experimenter is investigating and what outcome or result the experimenter hopes to record (Orne, 1962). Because of a desire to be a good subject, a person in a study may then act or react to give the investigator this presumed outcome, regardless of the person's true attitude (in this context). In sum, the results of experimentation with humans may not be valid if the methods and procedures dictate the responses to be made rather than objectively assessing spontaneous responses.

It is not hard to see how this criticism could be applied to the early exposure studies. As noted, the procedures in those studies were quite straightforward. Subjects were shown discriminable stimuli at various frequencies and were summarily requested to evaluate them. Subjects possibly inferred that because the experimenter had gone to the trouble of showing different stimuli different numbers of times, perhaps the psychologist wanted them rated differently. As Suedfeld, Epstein, Buchanan, and Landon (1971) suggested, if a subject is asked to judge how "good" (on a good–bad scale) the experimental stimuli are, that person may assume a mental set or disposition to assign more extreme ratings to the material he or she has the most information about, namely, the high-frequency stimuli. Indeed, when Suedfeld et al. (1971) asked subjects to rate how "bad" (on a bad–good scale) the stimuli were, they observed an inverted-U-shaped result as a consequence of 1 to 25 exposures of Chinese characters (see Figure 3). That is, when the subjects rated words in the framework of their "badness," high frequency of exposure did not lead to enhanced attitudes toward the stimuli. The pattern of ratings from the "bad"-set condition in Figure 3 thus lends some support to the Suedfeld et al. proposition that more extreme ratings are assigned to high-frequency stimuli, depending simply on what dimension the rater has in mind.

Further support for the notion that exposure effects are artifacts of demand characteristics comes from research by Stang (1974a). In one type of study Stang (1974a, Experiments 1 and 2) asked subjects to *imagine* that they were in a study and were being exposed to

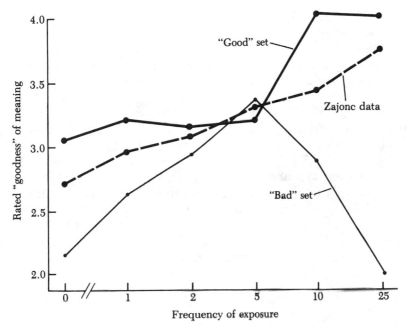

FIGURE 3
EXPOSURE EFFECTS as a consequence of rating the "badness" versus the "goodness" of the experimental stimuli. The zero-frequency point refers to ratings of stimuli not shown during the exposure session. (After Suedfeld et al., 1971.)

nonsense words 0, 1, 2, 5, 10, or 25 times and then to *imagine* how they would react to these stimuli on affective scales. When these imaginary ratings were actually expressed and analyzed, it was found that this procedure produced a clear "frequency" effect and one that was statistically indistinguishable from earlier laboratory findings. In a second type of study Stang (1974a, Experiments 3 and 4) actually showed subjects standard kinds of stimuli at differing frequencies and then obtained their affective ratings of the material. This procedure, of course, represents a typical mere exposure study. However, in addition to the usual ratings, Stang also asked the people to guess what the purpose of the experiment was and provided them with responses from which to choose, including (a) "the words seen most will be the most pleasant," (b) "the words seen most will be the least pleasant," (c) "the words seen an intermediate number of times will be the most pleasant," and three other, less relevant options. Not surprisingly, Stang obtained a positive exposure effect, but what is noteworthy in this context is that the effect was strongest for subjects who picked option (a). That is, subjects who seemed to have "guessed" the exposure hypothesis showed the best exposure effect, an outcome seemingly in line with the criticism that exposure effects are caused by the demand characteristics of such research.

MERE EXPOSURE EFFECTS AS LEARNING

For Zajonc and other social psychologists, the literature dealing with effects of mere exposure appeared to be a unique way to conceive of one mode of the formation and change of attitudes. Certain critics, however, doubted that this approach offered anything really new and sought to account for the so-called mere exposure effect by appealing to more traditionally accepted psychological mechanisms. A paper that was most explicit in this regard was published in 1971 by Burgess and Sales, who put forward the position that the positive relationship between familiarity and affect was the result of classical conditioning.

Context and associations. Burgess and Sales reasoned that for many subjects the typical laboratory setting provided a "highly positive context" in which to conduct mere exposure research and that each exposure of an experimental stimulus (a nonsense word, a Chinese-like letter, or whatever) constituted a learning trial in which an association could form between the general context around the subject and the particular stimulus seen by the subject. Because that context was assumed to be positive, the more often a stimulus was encountered in such a setting, the more positive would be a subject's reaction to it, via an association formed by classical conditioning. Hence, frequently exposed experimental stimuli are later assigned higher affective ratings than less familiar objects because the eventually familiar stimulus "increasingly assumes the affect which is aroused by the context" (Burgess and Sales, 1971).

Burgess and Sales produced some data that seemed to support their contention. In their Study 1, they exposed subjects to different nonsense words at various rates and indeed obtained the usual positive exposure effect. But in addition to these standard results, they also asked subjects to indicate their reaction to the experiment in general, and respondents were then divided into two groups: those who felt relatively positive versus those who felt relatively negative about the whole experimental context. The splitting point was the median of the entire sample of responses to the context question. From this procedure it was found that a very clear frequency of exposure effect emerged for the "positive" group, whereas virtually no such effect emerged for the "negative" group, a result that Burgess and Sales took as support for their learning hypothesis.

A second study (Burgess and Sales, 1971, Study 2) provided further confirmation for this position. In that study nonsense words were paired with meaningful words and were exposed to subjects at different frequencies. The nature of the meaningful words is important here, because they were selected on the basis of previous research that indicated that certain of them would evoke strong positive affective reactions, whereas others would evoke strong negative affective reactions. In addition, words that would elicit either moderately positive reactions or moderately negative reactions were also used in this study. Thus, four different groups of subjects were put through the typical exposure procedure and were shown certain nonsense words at various frequencies, except that in this study the nonsense stimuli they saw were associated (paired) with the real words that were highly positive, moderately positive, moderately negative, or highly negative. The results of this method seemed to be in agreement with the Burgess–Sales analysis. The two groups of subjects provided with positive meaningful word associates showed a positive frequency effect. That is, the more often a nonsense word was seen, the better it was subsequently rated, with a stronger positive effect for the stimuli paired with the highly positive meaningful words. Similarly, the two groups of subjects provided with negative meaningful word associates showed a negative frequency effect. In this case, the more often a nonsense word was seen, the less it was liked, with the stronger negative effect for the stimuli paired with the highly negative meaningful words. These effects are illustrated in Figure 4.

Social status symbols. The work of a second set of authors, Perlman and Oskamp (1971), can be included in this section on learning. Although these latter writers were more enthusiastic than Burgess and Sales regarding the special or unique influence of mere exposure as apart from conditioning per se, Perlman and Oskamp nevertheless argued that the *content* of the information in the exposed stimulus might have an important bearing on an individual's reaction to that stimulus configuration. The Perlman–Oskamp position stemmed, in part, from a concern that media exposure of minority persons in low-status (negative content) roles such as maid, janitor, or porter might lower rather than raise the viewer's attitude toward members of that minority. To test this idea, they prepared photographs of men of

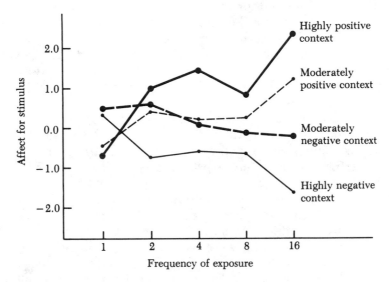

FIGURE 4
ATTITUDINAL RATINGS OF STIMULI as a consequence of being associated
with positive or negative words. (After Burgess and Sales, 1971.)

various races in clothing that was meant to convey the impression of
different statuses (or roles). For example, a given man (model) was
photographed either in (1) prison garb, (2) street clothes, or (3)
clerical or medical dress—to convey low, moderate, or high social
status, respectively. When subjects were repeatedly exposed to these
types of stimuli, the results were similar to those of the Burgess and
Sales Study 2. As seen in Figure 5, the most positive frequency of
exposure effect on affective reactions occurred for the high-status
stimuli, the low-status stimuli produced the lowest ratings, and the
intermediate-status pictures produced an effect that was roughly
intermediate to the two extreme conditions.

In sum, the ideas and data presented by Burgess and Sales and
by Perlman and Oskamp can be viewed as inimical to the position
of Zajonc and other proponents of the attitudinal effects of mere
repeated exposure. If Burgess and Sales are correct, the so-called
exposure effect is simply one more manifestation of the consequences
of classical conditioning. If exposure and conditioning are synony-
mous, the rule of scientific parsimony would instruct us to discard
the redundant or less elegant concept, which in this instance would
be the exposure hypothesis. Moreover, if Perlman and Oskamp are

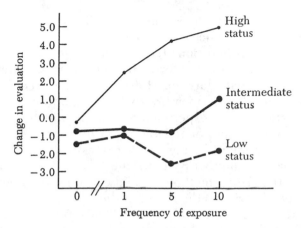

FIGURE 5
ATTITUDINAL RATINGS OF STIMULI as a consequence of being associated with high, intermediate, or low social status symbols. The zero-frequency point refers to ratings of stimuli not shown during the exposure session. (After Perlman and Oskamp, 1971.)

correct, then the "mere" part of the mere exposure hypothesis loses ground. Because it seems inconceivable that in the real world a stimulus or event could occur independently of some context or content, it remains to be seen what sort of influence "mere" exposure could have, if any at all.

An End: Resolution of Issues and Current Standing of Ideas

We seem to be in an impossible situation regarding the alleged effects of repeated mere exposure on attitudes and the possible mechanisms underlying these effects. However, even though the situation seems impossible, it is certainly not an uncommon one in scientific psychology or in any other science. In fact, the controversy that has just been aired can be viewed as a healthy condition insofar as the advancement of knowledge is concerned. Things are heating up: people are disagreeing, the issues are out in the open, critical thought is being devoted to them, and new information is being produced. With luck, the process by which this heat is generated will also give off some light.

THE ARTIFACT EXPLANATION RECONSIDERED

It should be clear from a reading of earlier sections of this chapter that both types of criticism, artifact and learning, attacked the mere exposure idea on methodological grounds. This is an entirely proper way to proceed in a science like social psychology, for psychologists find answers only to questions they ask and even the forms of the answers are dictated by the way the questions are framed. For example, we saw that Harrison (1968) was interested in response competition, but what he measured with his stopwatch was latency of free association to the experimental stimuli, which critics may or may not accept as a valid or reliable index of response competition. (A better measure might be the *number* of associations generated in response to each stimulus.) By the same token, it is warranted that we scrutinize the critics' methods of study also, for the power of their criticisms relies heavily on the merits of their own empirical analyses.

Moreland and Zajonc (1976) raised this point in considering Stang's (1974a) claim that the apparent "attitudinal" effects of mere exposure were caused by an artifact or the demand characteristics of the research setting. Recall that Stang used a procedure whereby new subjects were given information about the experiences of previous subjects, a method that has been termed an INTERPERSONAL REPLICATION by Bem (1967). In his first two experiments Stang gave subjects *only* the information that they would be seeing (or that they were to imagine they would see) different stimuli at different frequencies, and then he immediately asked them to provide affective judgments of those stimuli. In a subsequent study Stang actually *showed* people standard experimental stimuli at various frequencies and obtained their affective reactions to these stimuli; then he asked these subjects to "guess" the experimenter's hypothesis by choosing among hypotheses provided in a questionnaire.

In considering these details, Moreland and Zajonc (1976) were quick to note that although Stang's procedures produced results that seemed to support the demand characteristic interpretation, these very procedures *did not match* the procedures in a typical exposure experiment! Insofar as there was a discrepancy between Stang's method and the others, the results from Stang's approach might well be irrelevant to a critical analysis of earlier findings. As a matter of fact, the differences between Stang's methods and the typical exposure study are many and striking. In the first place, Stang (1974a, Experiments 1 and 2) told subjects to imagine seeing things at different rates and actually told them those frequencies would be 0, 1, 2, 5, 10, and 25 exposures. On the contrary, subjects in the real exposure research were not given this information and may have been only minimally aware of the differences in frequencies of exposure. Second, Stang's subjects had only the information on frequency to deal with, whereas actual subjects had every aspect of the experiment to sort out for themselves, including any perceived characteristics such as quality, duration, or pattern of exposures. Finally, with respect to guessing the experimenter's hypothesis, the real subjects were more or less on their own and were *not* provided with a written catalogue of ready hypotheses from which to choose, whereas Stang's subjects did have a catalogue of options (Stang, 1974a, Experiments 3 and 4).

To try to resolve these discrepancies, one of the counter-approaches taken by Moreland and Zajonc was to use the interpersonal replication method employed by Stang (1974a) but to structure their replication in a fashion that was truer to the experiences of the prior subjects in the actual exposure researches. Within the more elaborate of these Moreland–Zajonc interpersonal replications (unpublished, but described in Moreland and Zajonc, 1976), subjects were asked at various points to make an open-ended judgment: "At this point, do you have any ideas at all about what the experimenter is trying to prove in this experiment? (That is, what is the imaginary experimenter trying to prove in the imaginary experiment?)" This query was made after four stages in the imaginary experiment, as follows.

The first stage of the Moreland–Zajonc interpersonal replication was a description of the typical experience of a student who is a voluntary subject in a psychological study at a university. The subject was asked to imagine being called on the phone, agreeing to participate, showing up at the research site, entering the experimental room, and being briefed about the procedure. At the end of this stage (and also at the end of the subsequent three stages), the replication subject was asked to guess the experimenter's intent, as outlined in the query in the preceding paragraph.

For the second stage, Moreland and Zajonc asked the subjects to imagine their first reaction to the beginning of the exposure sequence when it becomes apparent that the experimental stimuli are, in this case, the Chinese-like characters or letters. However, the third stage is most important for our purposes, for in it the subject was asked to imagine a lot of things that might go on in a person's mind during a typical laboratory exposure sequence. That is, it was suggested that the subjects might imagine that the following things about the stimuli are noticed:

1. Some of the slides seem more pleasant to you than do others.
2. There are some differences in the quality of the slide material.

3. There are some indications of sequences or patterns in the slide presentations.

4. Each of the slides seems to be on the screen for about the same amount of time.

5. Some of the slides seem to be shown more often than others.

6. The length of time between the presentation of one slide and the next seems to be constant.

7. There seems to be a definite limit on the number of slides you are seeing.

8. There are some differences in the size of the drawings on the various slides.

9. Some of the drawings seem to remind you of other things you have seen before.

10. There are some differences in the complexity of the drawings on the slides you are shown.

Finally, in stage four of the Moreland–Zajonc replication the subjects were told that the experimenter would ask for affective ratings of the experimental stimuli and were shown scales typically used for this purpose, including those labeled PLEASANT–UN-PLEASANT, GOOD–BAD, and LIKE–DISLIKE. This description was followed, like every other stage, with the query about the experimenter's purpose.

The differences between the Stang interpersonal replication procedure and the Moreland–Zajonc interpersonal replication procedure should be clear. Whereas Stang provided subjects with only a minimal (if critical) amount of information in one lump, Moreland and Zajonc provided the same information, along with a great deal of other information subjects would routinely pick up in a real experiment. Further, they gave this information to subjects in a piecemeal fashion, which would also typify how things went in an actual laboratory sequence. Given that the Moreland–Zajonc subjects were provided with much to think about, as are actual subjects, it remains to be seen how many of them (on their own, as it were) came up with the mere exposure hypothesis as an answer to the question dealing with what the experimenter was trying to prove.

The subjects' replies to the queries at the end of the four stages were assigned by judges to one of ten predetermined categories, as shown in Table II. The most interesting category is number 6, "repeated exposure increases positivity of affective ratings," which is a paraphrasing of the exposure hypothesis. Out of the 40 undergraduate women who served as subjects in this study, *none* guessed this hypothesis after the first stage of the Moreland–Zajonc interpersonal replication, *none* guessed it after the second stage, *none* guessed it after the third stage, and only *one* subject came up with this hypoth-

TABLE II
Subjects' guesses about the experimenter's hypothesis in the Moreland–Zajonc interpersonal replication

Hypotheses	STAGE OF REPLICATION			
	I. Experimental setting	II. Stimulus characteristics	III. Frequency of exposure	IV. Affect ratings
1. Reactions or feelings toward the stimuli	7.5	5.0	25.0	32.5
2. Associations or meanings of the stimuli	7.5	2.5	10.0	7.5
3. Memory recognition or recall	30.0	35.0	7.5	0.0
4. Reactions to the experimental setting	7.5	5.0	2.5	5.0
5. Perceptual processes	7.5	2.5	7.5	10.0
6. Repeated exposure increases positivity of affective ratings	0.0	0.0	0.0	2.5
7. Repeated exposure increases negativity of affective ratings	0.0	0.0	0.0	2.5
8. Frequency of exposure is related to affective ratings	0.0	0.0	0.0	5.0
9. Miscellaneous responses	7.5	5.0	27.5	25.0
10. No hypothesis given	35.0	52.5	42.5	20.0

Unpublished table, courtesy of R. L. Moreland.
Note. Values are the percentages of the subjects guessing a particular hypothesis at various stages in the procedure. The numbers in the columns need not equal 100 because the subjects were free to guess more than one hypothesis. $N = 40$.

esis after the fourth stage, as indicated in Table II. Of course, subjects did have some ideas about what was going on, but even after the fourth stage, when they had the most information, fully 45% of the sample either gave no hypothesis or gave one that could only be coded in a miscellaneous category. Clearly, when the interpersonal replication technique conformed to the steps of a standard exposure study, it was not so clear to the subjects what the experimenter was after. This study seems to indicate that only a tiny minority of subjects might guess the exposure hypothesis as a result of the actual demand characteristics of exposure-research settings. And even if all the people who did guess or figure out the mere exposure hypothesis were willing to simply comply with the researcher's desired outcome, the fact that they are but a small subset of the sample of subjects tested makes it unlikely that they alone could produce the fairly strong effects seen in many reports on the attitudinal effects of exposure.

This reconsideration of Stang's (1974a) demand characteristic analysis reveals that it is based on two critical assumptions: (1) that subjects become aware that *different* stimuli are exposed at *different* frequencies and that this awareness forms the basis for their differential affective ratings, and (2) the decision rule that subjects operate on is that "more is better" or that the high-frequency-of-appearance items should be assigned the higher affective ratings. To the contrary, there is evidence against each of these assumptions. First, all the exposure studies we have seen so far have employed procedures whereby the subject sees different stimuli at different frequencies of exposure, say 1, 2, 5, 10, or 25 times. This method is termed a WITHIN-SUBJECTS EXPERIMENTAL DESIGN, because the entire experimental manipulation (variations in the amount of exposure) takes place "within" a given subject. Obviously, Stang's (1974a) criticism is based on an analysis of the possible artifactual consequences of this "within" form of experimental design. However, further research undermined this position.

Moreland and Zajonc (1976) reported an experiment in which the frequency of exposure was varied, not on a subject-by-subject basis, but on a group-by-group basis. When the different experimental treatments are applied to subjects in various categories or groups (and not all individual subjects), the method is referred to as a BETWEEN-SUBJECTS EXPERIMENTAL DESIGN. In their study, any given subject saw a number of stimuli, each of which was shown an *equal* number of times. However, across several experimental treatments, subjects in different groups saw those stimuli either 3, 9, or 27 times. And when subjects' reactions to the exposed stimuli were measured, affect was positively related to frequency of exposure, even in this case where a particular subject did not see different slides at different frequencies. Therefore, it seems that Stang's (1974a) analysis is inapplicable to the procedure of Moreland and Zajonc (1976), and the exposure effect they obtained remains unexplained by Stang. One possible accounting for their results might be that it was caused by a reduction of response competition elicited by the stimuli.

Regarding the second assumption inherent in Stang's (1974a) analysis, is it really the case that a person would operate on the assumption that things seen at higher frequencies of exposure should be better? This proposition was examined in a study by Gerard, Green, Hoyt, and Conolley (1973), who wondered whether stimuli that were positive (highly likable), neutral, or negative (highly unlikable) would influence subjects' estimates of how often they had been seen. That is, would subjects think, all else being equal, that a positive or highly likable stimulus had been seen more often than a negative or highly unlikable one? For an evaluation of this notion, Gerard et al. (1973) obtained slides of men's faces from a yearbook and had these stimuli rated for both likability and memorability. The researchers then used sets of slides that could be remembered with equal ease but that fell into positive, neutral, or negative categories. Undergraduate women were shown these stimuli at a frequency of 11 exposures of each picture. In short, the stimuli were seen an equal number of times.

To test the idea that the affective category of a slide would influence a person's judgment of its frequency of appearance, Gerard et al. (1973) asked their subjects to estimate how often they had seen the positive, neutral, and negative stimuli. Based on an assumption that people naturally associate better things with higher frequencies of appearance (Stang's assumption), one would predict that subjects in the study by Gerard et al. would underestimate their exposure to negative stimuli, be more or less accurate about neutral stimuli, and overestimate their exposure to positive stimuli. That is, according to the assumption, exposure estimates should be a linear function of the affective category of the stimuli. To the contrary, these subjects underestimated the prior amount of exposure to neutral stimuli and overestimated their amount of exposure to both negative and positive stimuli. Thus, the obtained effect was not linear but curvilinear in a U-shape. On the basis of this finding, we must question the conclusion that people automatically or always assume better judgments should always go with higher frequencies of exposure.

Summarizing the artifact interpretation. This reconsideration of the artifact, or demand characteristic, analysis of the exposure effect has revealed, as Moreland and Zajonc (1976) put it, that "the role of demand characteristics in mere exposure research has been misunderstood in several ways." Although one has to recognize that there *are* demand characteristics in any research setting, the attitudinal effects of mere exposure cannot be attributed to such effects alone. We have seen that in interpersonal replications that approximate the methods used in typical exposure studies, subjects are not very good at guessing the experimenter's hypothesis on their own. Further, repeated exposure effects occur even when subjects do not know that frequency of exposure is being manipulated, such as in the study that employed a between-subjects design. Finally, whatever subjects assume, guess, or figure out about the relationship between exposure and evaluation, their logic or psycho-logic does not invariably dictate that frequency and affective ratings are positively linked. In sum, whereas attention to artifacts, demand characteristics, and other flaws of the experimental method should be and are a continuing concern of researchers on attitudes, an analysis based exclusively on these factors does not give a satisfactory accounting of all the attitudinal effects of mere exposure.

THE LEARNING EXPLANATION RECONSIDERED

Let us now reconsider the relationship between mere exposure (and its possible influence on response competition) and learning as concepts that may be useful in explaining attitude formation and change. It seems quite clear, as noted earlier, that Burgess and Sales (1971) wished to supplant the idea of the effects of repeated mere exposure with a more traditional interpretation based on the principles of learning theory. However, it is not the case that the reverse intention was held by the advocates of the mere exposure position. That is, although they were doubtless aware that learning was implicated in the area of attitudes in important ways (for example, see Staats and Staats, 1958), Zajonc, Harrison, Matlin, and others unquestionably conveyed in their writings the impression that they were advancing a new way to think about attitudes that could not be found in other approaches. But this cannot be interpreted to mean that proponents of the mere exposure hypothesis wished to do away with other theories or explanations. Still, the challenges presented by Burgess and Sales and by Perlman and Oskamp prompted a closer examination of the relationship between the methods of mere exposure research and the procedures required to study learning.

Tacitly admitting that the principles found in the literature on mere exposure told one virtually nothing about the important phenomenon of learning, Zajonc and his colleagues rhetorically inquired about how much knowledge of learning procedures informed one about the possibility of mere exposure effects on attitudes. Very little was the answer, according to Saegert, Swap, and Zajonc (1973). Saegert et al. (1973) reflected on the studies of Burgess and Sales (1971) and concluded, on logical grounds, that the experiments reported in the Burgess–Sales paper might be of little value in evaluating the propositions attending the exposure hypothesis. In the first place, Saegert et al. (1973) judged that the results of the first study by Burgess and Sales were too ambiguous to support even the Burgess and Sales conclusion that it was liking for the experimental setting that caused subjects to learn to like, via classical conditioning, the high-frequency-of-exposure stimuli. That is, because subjects' affective ratings of both the repeatedly exposed stimuli and the experimental setting in general were obtained after the exposure session,

it was not clear from their data whether the subjects' elation over taking part in a psychological experiment enhanced the attractiveness of the stimuli, or whether finding themselves liking the stimuli more at the end of the session than at the beginning, the subjects viewed their participation in retrospect to have been rather pleasant (Saegert et al., 1973).

With respect to the second study in Burgess and Sales (1971) in which nonsense and meaningful stimuli were repeatedly paired (see Figure 4), Saegert et al. concluded that this method was well known to produce the learning of attitudes by association (as noted, Staats and Staats, 1958), but that it certainly did not represent an approximation of *mere* exposure; therefore the findings could not directly contradict the mere exposure hypothesis.

Mere exposure and context. Even so, it was the case that context, content, or other information could have an influence on the outcome of exposure to stimuli, as seen in the results of Perlman and Oskamp (1971). However, if learning effects and mere exposure effects were independent, or at least separable influences on attitudes, it should be possible to demonstrate their separate effects where both are operating in the same situation. In particular, it might be possible to demonstrate that mere exposure (via reduction in response competition, perhaps) might result in an enhancement of affect for stimuli despite the context in which the stimuli are encountered.

As a step in this direction, Saegert et al. (1973) studied the formation of interpersonal attraction under *pleasant* and *unpleasant* conditions by making it appear that they were researching taste responses to flavored liquids. A subject was taken to a cubicle where she was shown (1) a large bottle containing the liquid to be judged, (2) rating scales for the judgments, and (3) paraphernalia for handling the solution. Several such cubicles housed different kinds of liquids. The flavors of the liquids to be tasted were the basis for making the situation pleasant or unpleasant for the subjects in those respective conditions. For subjects in the pleasant treatment, the solutions in the bottles were flavors of a commercial soft drink; for those in the unpleasant condition the solutions were weak concentrations of vinegar, quinine, and citric acid. Further, because the equipment in each cubicle was unwieldy, it was explained to the subject that she would have to move to various other cubicles to complete her judgments of all the solutions under study. This design provided a mechanism for manipulating frequency of exposure to other people, because as the subject moved from cubicle to cubicle she encountered other subjects who were also moving about to complete their ostensible taste tests. Following a precise schedule, the experimenters made sure that a given subject ran into particular others a fixed number of times, a protocol that resulted in 1, 2, 5, or 10 exposures to four different fellow-subjects.

Shortly after the subjects were exposed to one another under either pleasant or unpleasant taste conditions, all subjects from a given test group were brought to a large room and, as part of a "general information" questionnaire, were asked to rate one another for favorability. The result for the pleasant condition (wherein the subjects gave the flavors an average rating of 3.54 on a 7-point scale) was that the favorability of the other people was a positive function of the number of times those people were encountered during the exposure session. More interesting, in the case of the unpleasant condition (where the flavors were given an average rating of 1.62), it was also found that favorability of other people was a *positive* function of the number of times those people were encountered. Thus, this study demonstrated that a positive exposure effect is possible even if the context in which the exposure occurs is negative. This result supports the idea that the effects of mere exposure and learning may be distinct, because the two theories would have made presumably opposite predictions for the outcome of the Saegert et al. (1973) procedure.

Mere exposure and negatively valued stimuli. Although suggestive, the Saegert et al. results do not yet provide a direct assessment of either response competition reduction (which, according to the original authors, underlies the mere exposure effect) or the influence of the value of the stimulus (positive or negative) on liking after repeated exposure. Could it be that even a negatively valued stimulus or object would become more attractive after such exposure? Learning theory is obliged to predict that repeated exposure to negative stimuli would increase our dislike for them through an association process; this prediction will be discussed in a subsequent section. But there is nothing in the mere exposure hypothesis that makes originally negative stimuli an exception to the rule that exposure enhances liking. A resolution of the apparent problem of negative stimuli and the mere exposure effect was put forth by Zajonc, Markus, and Wilson (1974).

Zajonc et al. (1974) began their analysis by pointing out two important consequences of repeated mere exposure: the SLOPE and the INTERCEPT of the attitudinal effect. That is, if one examines a typical mere exposure finding, such as that depicted in Figure 1, one sees that the functions are tilted, because stimuli that were more frequently shown received higher affective ratings. In statistical terminology, the tilt is termed the slope and is related to values on the horizontal axis. The other feature is the intercept of the function, which is simply the point on the vertical axis where the slope of the effect begins. For positive effects, the intercept would be the affective rating assigned to the least preferred stimulus, which in this case would be the low-frequency stimulus (Figure 1).

Having focused on these two important properties of mere exposure effects, Zajonc et al. (1974) inquired about the factors that would influence slope and intercept. They reasoned that slope could be influenced either by the formation of associations, as proposed by the learning theorists, or by a reduction in response competition. The point of intercept, on the other hand, was probably a result of the stimulus value of the material that was exposed. To illustrate how stimulus value might influence intercept, imagine that subjects are shown a photo of a stranger and are asked to rate how good, or handsome, or honest, or likable that stranger is. Given that this photo is of a stranger, the frequency of exposure to that person, prior to the rating trial, would be zero (0). However, if some subjects were told that the person in the picture was a prominent scientist such as a chemist, a biologist, or an archeologist, doubtless that subset of subjects would report a more favorable impression than some other subjects who were told that the stranger was a known criminal such as a kidnapper, a murderer, or an arsonist. These first impressions (ratings) of an infrequently exposed person can be viewed as the intercept of some exposure function; certainly the positive person would receive better ratings than the negative person. Thus, the intercept for a collection of positive stimuli would be higher than the intercept of a collection of negative stimuli.

The preceding paragraph says that, once established, the value of a stimulus would influence the intercept of an exposure function. The interesting issue becomes one of what would happen to the ratings of such a photograph after some repeated exposures. If on every subsequent exposure we reminded the respective subjects that the person was either a criminal or a scientist, then from the perspective of learning theory we would expect the positive photo (scientist) to become more and more favorable as a consequence of a stronger and stronger association between the face and the occupation and the negative photograph (criminal) to become less and less favorable for the same reason. But it has already been pointed out that procedures designed to show "learning" may have little bearing on the idea of mere exposure. Therefore, it would be interesting to see how exposure would influence ratings of positive and negative stimuli that are *merely* exposed, with no additional references during the exposure to the characteristics that contributed to their original categorization or value. Following such *mere* exposure, would originally negative stimuli become more negative or more positive? If the reduction of response competition as a consequence of repeated exposure influenced reactions to negative stimuli as well as positive stimuli, then ratings or the originally negative stimuli need not become more negative, and a positive slope over frequency of exposure might even result.

These propositions were tested by Zajonc et al. (1974, Experiment 2), who arranged conditions to match those suggested. The stimuli to be exposed were slides of the faces of Oriental men, taken from the book *Who's Who in China, 1936.* Half the undergraduate subjects to see these slides were told that the men were criminals and the remaining half were told that they were scholars and scientists, a protocol that established the initial negative and positive values of the stimuli. Both sets of subjects saw the very same slides. After receiving the bogus information about the men's "occupations," subjects saw either various criminals or various scientists 0, 1, 2, 5, 10, or 25 times. To get an idea how reduction in response competition might enter into liking for the men's faces, the subjects in the negative and positive conditions were further broken down into subsamples termed "consistent" or "inconsistent."

Consistency refers to a second type of stimulus that was presented along with each slide. These additional stimuli were auditory and consisted of a tape-recorded set of letters of the alphabet. In the consistent condition the same letter was voiced every time a man's face appeared on the viewing screen during the exposure series, whereas in the inconsistent condition a different letter was voiced each time a face appeared. The notion was that subjects might have an easier time attaching a specific response to a visual stimulus associated with a single letter, compared with subjects who were trying to attach a response to a stimulus associated with many letters. Thus, on the basis of a response competition analysis, we might expect to see more positive ratings of the high-frequency stimuli in the consistent–positive than in the inconsistent–positive condition (scientist), but it remains an open question how all of this might influence ratings in the negative (criminal) conditions.

Answers to all these speculations were provided by subjects' affective ratings of the slides following the exposure session. The people in the study were asked to rate how good, handsome, honest, and likable each of the men was. The results of those judgments are seen in composite form in Figure 6 In the first place, it is clear that stimulus values influenced intercept, with the two subsets of subjects that viewed "scientists" showing higher overall ratings than subjects that viewed "criminals." Second, subjects in the consistent–positive

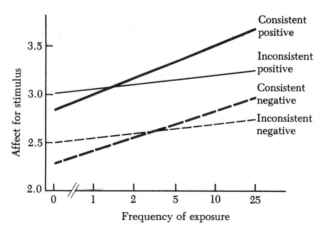

FIGURE 6
SLOPE AND INTERCEPT of attitudinal ratings as a consequence of positive or negative stimulus properties and mere exposure effects. The zero-frequency point refers to ratings of stimuli not shown during the exposure session. (After Zajonc et al., 1974.)

condition evidenced a steeper slope of affective ratings over frequency of exposure than did the raters in the inconsistent–positive
condition, a finding that is in line with the idea that a consistently
presented letter would facilitate reduction in response competition
and thereby enhance affective ratings. Finally, and what is most
interesting for our present purpose, the two slopes in the negative
conditions are nicely parallel to the slopes in the positive conditions.
This outcome means that although the intercepts of the negative
conditions were lower than those in the positive conditions, both
repeated exposure and response competition factors had about the
same influence on reactions to the negative stimuli as they did on
reactions to the positive stimuli. It is worth noting that a similar set
of findings was found by an independent set of researchers (Hamm,
Baum, and Nikels, 1975), thus confirming the result. Here is good
evidence that the repeated exposure of even negatively valued stimuli can, in the absence of reminders or associations to those qualities
that made them negative, enhance observers' attitudes toward those
stimuli.

SUMMARY

The mere exposure effect and the mere exposure hypothesis seem
to have survived in good order the first shock of criticisms and
alternative explanations* in the 1970s. One can now find statements
that in 1968 Zajonc created "a classic monograph" (Colman, Best,
and Austen, 1986). As we will see in a later section of this chapter,
the early exposure investigations of the 1960s and 1970s stimulated
another beginning–middle–end cycle that has extended into the late
1980s. But before we take up the rather technical details of this new
cycle, it will be worthwhile to take a different, nonlaboratory slant
on the attitudinal effects of exposure. For a bit, attention will be
devoted to the real world.

Real-World Exposure Effects

At least three interesting real-world exposure effects have been
published and will be touched on here. The first has to do with

---

*Please note that the artifact and learning interpretations of the exposure–
attitude data are not *theories* of exposure effects. As labeled in the text, they are
alternative explanations. One exposure theory that we have encountered thus far
had to do with response competition, and others we will encounter are the Birnbaum–Mellers model and the Moreland–Zajonc model (see Figure 7). By now there
are yet other theories for such effects, but these are beyond the scope of the current
treatment. Readers interested in theory should consult Bornstein (1989), Harrison
(1977), and Sawyer (1981).

people's preferences for faces, the second concerns exposure effects in politics, and the third touches on the phenomenon of food neophobia.

PREFERENCES FOR FACES

Although few people may realize the fact, each of us has two faces, and these may not be equally attractive to everyone. Let the reader consider her or his own two faces. The first of your faces is the one seen by the people around you. When some associate looks into your face, his or her right eye looks into your left eye and his or her left eye looks into your right eye. For convenience, we will call this your "true" image. However, when you look into your own face, as when seeing your reflection in a mirror, your right eye looks into your right eye and your left eye looks into your left eye; you see your "mirror" image. A quick inspection of your own face will reveal that its features are not perfectly symmetrical around your nose, so you and your friends are accustomed to seeing two different versions of you! Because people rarely look into mirrors together, it would follow that your associates would be more familiar with your true image, whereas you would be more familiar with your mirror image.

Could it be that something as simple as the distinction between the mirror image and the true image of a face could influence preferences for those images? The mere exposure notion would predict that we would have a preference for the familiar version, depending on whose face it was. Mita, Dermer, and Knight (1977) tested this idea with photographs of subjects' frontal faces. The researchers prepared two prints of the photos, a true print and a mirror print, which can be easily obtained by turning over the negative of the true print. Subjects and their friends or lovers indicated which photograph (mirror or true) he or she liked better. The results of these tests showed that there were clear preferences. Friends and lovers had a higher likelihood of choosing the true image of the subject, whereas the subjects showed an opposite tendency to pick their own mirror image!

EXPOSURE EFFECTS AND POLITICS

Next, what about mere exposure effects and politics? As Grush, McKeough, and Ahlering (1978) point out, American candidates for political office advertise their campaigns, which is a kind of exposure. They do so in order to obtain votes, which is a form of evaluation on the part of the voters (observers). However, Grush et al. note that only certain campaigns would qualify for mere exposure analysis.

Basically, there should be several candidates for an office, just as there are typically several stimuli exposed in the laboratory. Moreover, these candidates should all be relatively unknown at first, just as generally novel and neutral stimuli have been employed in past attitudinal research. Finally, a test of the mere exposure hypothesis is possible if different candidates spend different amounts of money on their campaigns, which presumably would result in differential exposure rates.

Not all political campaigns meet these requirements, so not all are suitable as tests. For example, the national election of an American president usually involves only two serious candidates, both of whom are quite well known before the final campaign begins. On the other hand, Grush et al. (1978) argue that many congressional primaries do meet the test conditions, and these writers concentrated on an analysis of such primaries in 1972. Some of the 1972 congressional primaries fit the description of experimental research, so Grush et al. classified these as belonging to a test category, with "test" implying that they could be used to test the exposure hypothesis. Other categories of primaries were uncovered that might also be useful in evaluating the effects of exposure, even though they did not satisfy the requirements of the experimental studies. One of these was termed the incumbency category, in which one of the candidates was the current holder of the sought-after office; another type was called the notoriety category, because one of the candidates had previously held some high political office or for other reasons was visible on the political scene. Obviously, the exposure theory would predict that incumbent or notorious candidates would have an advantage over other candidates, based on their relatively greater familiarity.

The results of a large sample of primaries were in line with the exposure hypothesis. In the test category (those primaries that met the requirements of mere exposure research), 29 of 51 contests were won by the leading spenders, which is a highly unlikely chance outcome given the large number of candidates that ran in those races. Equally striking, 38 of the 42 incumbency-category primaries were won by the incumbent, and 22 of the 26 primaries in the notorious category were carried by the notorious candidate (Grush et al., 1978). (For related work on candidate name exposure and voting, see Schaffner, Wandersman, and Stang, 1981.)

FOOD NEOPHOBIA AND EXPOSURE

FOOD NEOPHOBIA is a term that connotes a dislike of or a reluctance to ingest an unfamiliar food (cf. Crandall, 1985; Pliner, 1982).

At some point in our lives almost all foods are new to us. But by the time we grow older, we each prefer certain things to eat. How is it that people in different regions of the country, or in other countries, have different food preferences? One train of thought is that people who grow up in a certain region are exposed to the type of food available to that region and, literally, acquire a taste for it (Rozin and Schiller, 1980). In a lab study, Pliner (1982) tested this idea by having undergraduate men taste unfamiliar (and unpopular) tropical fruit juices either 0, 5, 10, or 20 times. As a result, ratings showed an exposure effect because the more frequently a juice was tasted, the more it was liked. Thus, unfamiliar juices were given low ratings and repeated exposure reduced this dislike.

Beyond the laboratory, Crandall (1985) provided an interesting test of the exposure hypothesis in connection with unfamiliar food. The site of her field study was a seasonally operated fish cannery in Alaska, and her unsuspecting subjects were over 200 people who worked there one season. This was a live-in situation; the cannery was a self-contained installation that provided work, food, recreation, and housing for its employees. Doughnuts are not part of the regional cuisine where Crandall did the study, so she used that pastry as a novel food. The unfamiliar doughnuts (prepared from a mix) were simply set out on display during the several coffee breaks (local term: "mug-ups") in a given day, and the dependent measure was the number of doughnuts that were consumed over the 1-month period of study. When Crandall made the doughnut counts, the results were fairly clear: an increased rate of consumption corresponded to the number of trials subjects had with the food. Food neophobia had given way to the exposure effect.

It is worth further mention that parents of young children can take heart from the effects of exposure on food neophobia. Even 2-year-olds show increased preferences for formerly novel food based on repeated tastings (Birch and Marlin, 1982). And cat owners can be similarly optimistic, because the effect also obtains when cats are repeatedly exposed to the odors of a new food (Bradshaw, 1986).

SUMMARY

The several studies just reviewed found what appear to be exposure effects in the domains of familiar faces, political campaigning, and food preferences. It is a matter of speculation whether these particular effects are caused by a reduction in response competition or some other factor attending the process of familiarization. Nevertheless, familiarity breeds something and that something is not always contempt.

Epilogue: Another Cycle

If it can be said that everything encountered so far in this chapter constitutes a kind of "beginning" in our scheme, it might be possible to identify another cycle of a "middle" and an "end." Once the exposure phenomenon was firmly established by the late 1970s, researchers began inquiring ever more closely into the reasons why such attitudinal effects should occur and into the mechanisms on which they are based. Disagreement occurred in short order.

COMPETING MODELS

One set of proponents had it that the real cause of attitudinal effects of repeated mere exposure is a single mediator, SUBJECTIVE RECOGNITION. That is, a person's impression that the object or stimulus is familiar produces expressions of liking and, of course, expressions of familiarity (Birnbaum and Mellers, 1979a,b). The Birnbaum–Mellers model is shown in the left panel of Figure 7. On the contrary, other theorists argued that two factors account for expressions of liking and familiarity; these are, respectively, subjective recognition and SUBJECTIVE AFFECT (Moreland and Zajonc, 1977, 1979; also see Zajonc, 1980, 1984). The Moreland–Zajonc model is seen in the right panel of Figure 7. There, the recognition factor produces familiarity,

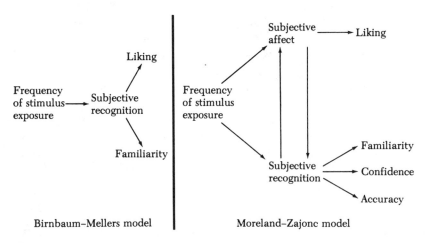

Birnbaum–Mellers model   Moreland–Zajonc model

FIGURE 7
COMPETING THEORIES (models) as explanations for the attitudinal effects of repeated mere exposure. (After Birnbaum and Mellers, 1979a,b; Moreland and Zajonc, 1977, 1979.)

accuracy, and confidence in frequency estimates. Liking, on the other hand, is mediated by subjective affect. Although subjective affect and subjective recognition can simultaneously occur and be mutually influential (Figure 7), the important difference in the two models is that liking in the Moreland–Zajonc formulation does not necessarily depend on recognition. It may sound paradoxical, but their model says that objectively (de facto) familiar things will be preferred over those that are objectively novel, even if the observer could not correctly identify the old or the new stimulus.

Thus, we quickly arrive at a new kind of "middle" in this domain. At the time, each camp claimed empirical support for its own model based on complicated reanalyses of existing data. Then new kinds of data started to come in, and the weight of evidence began to tilt more and more in the favor of one of the sets of proponents.

MASKED AND SUBLIMINAL EXPOSURE RESEARCH

Auditory exposures. One of the first studies in the new era was that of Wilson (1979) who wanted to expose subjects to certain stimuli *without* their awareness. To accomplish this feat, Wilson (1979, Experiment 2) used a stereo headphone to present a voice reading a literary passage to the subject's right ear. The subject's task was to listen to the passage and repeat the words aloud. At the same time, the subject was further required to check off mistakes in an error-filled written copy of the passage. This was a very difficult set of tasks that required intense concentration on the voice in the recording. So much attention was required that Wilson was confident that the subject would not be aware that there was a different auditory stimulus being presented to the unattended channel, the other ear.

Once the subject was engaged in monitoring the voice, Wilson presented 6 of a total of 12 discriminable tone patterns to the person's unattended ear. These tones were unannounced; subjects had been given no inkling that tones would be part of the experience, yet these constituted the experimental stimuli. Following the MASKED PRESENTATION of the tones, the subjects were told that they had actually been exposed to such stimuli. The subject's next duty was to listen to all twelve tones (unmasked) and to indicate which tones seemed old (heard previously) or new (not heard previously).

If subjects could correctly recognize the six familiar stimuli, then all of these deserved the label "old." But if subjects really could not recognize the objectively familiar stimuli, then they were relying on guesswork to assign tones to categories. Pure guesswork would result, in the long run, in declaring three of the familiar tones "old" and three "new." And it was this chance pattern that appeared. Subjects correctly labeled an average of only 3.17 of the really familiar tones as "old," an outcome that indicates they probably could not really recognize them and had guessed.

Would true familiarity have any effects under these conditions? Wilson found that indeed it did. When he obtained subjects' attitudinal ratings of the tones, it was revealed that the objectively familiar stimuli received better ratings than did the objectively novel items. This response occurred even when the subject's impression was that the familiar pattern was "new" and that the unfamiliar pattern was "old" (see Table III). Therefore, objective familiarity, and *not* subjective recognition, seems to have produced increased liking, a finding that is inconsistent with the Birnbaum–Mellers position but is compatible with the Moreland–Zajonc formulation (see Figure 7).

Visual exposures. Following Wilson's (1979) lead, a number of investigators have systematically exposed various visual stimuli to people *without* the subjects' awareness of such exposure. By using a special timing machine, visual stimulation can be presented subliminally. That is, the subject really is shown something like a geometric figure but does not know he saw it, nor can he recognize it when asked to pick it from a pair of such stimuli: the one he just saw and one he was not shown. The likelihood that a subject can or cannot report having seen a short visual presentation depends on several factors such as room illumination and the contrast of the stimulus with its background. Acknowledging these considerations, a SUBLIMINAL EXPOSURE standard we will adopt is 4 milliseconds (1 millisecond is one thousandth of a second).

At 4 milliseconds of exposure, subjects cannot be expected to

TABLE III
Average attitudinal ratings as a consequence of objective (de facto) familiarity (old–new) and subjective familiarity ("old–new") of auditory stimuli

| | SUBJECTIVE FAMILIARITY | |
Objective familiarity	"Old"	"New"
Old	3.61	3.87
New	3.08	3.06

After Wilson (1979).
Note. Responses on the attitude scale could range from 0 to 6, with larger numbers reflecting better or more favorable attitudes.

reliably identify truly familiar (old) stimuli from novel (new) ones, even when the exposure is repeated a number of times. But subjects *do* have a preference for the stimuli they encounter subliminally. When subjects are asked to express a preference between old and new stimuli, they reliably prefer the ones they have seen before! Again, this outcome supports the Moreland–Zajonc model in Figure 7; a stimulus elicits affect even if recognition is not involved. In fact, by now this subliminal effect has become fairly commonplace. It has emerged in three independent laboratories, based on the use of three slightly different methodologies (cf. Bornstein, Leone, and Galley, 1987; Kunst-Wilson and Zajonc, 1980; Seamon, Brody, and Kauff, 1983). Of course, the only problem with the subliminal paradigm is that critics are beginning to wonder what all of this has to do with exposure effects in real life. Just a few paragraphs ago we were eating increasingly familiar doughnuts in Alaska, and now we are looking at 4-millisecond presentations of abstract figures in a lab. How much do these experiences have in common?

Quite a bit, it turns out. I will demonstrate this with a brief look at Experiment 3 from the Bornstein et al. (1987) paper. In that study a real subject was asked to discuss some poems with two other young men, who happened to be experimental confederates (employees). The confederate subjects (call them A and B) were instructed by Bornstein to disagree about the poems, so the subject was in a position to favor one or the other person. Now, the heart of the study is what happened to the real subject just prior to meeting the confederates for the discussion. He (all were male) was given a cover story about being shown some material relevant to the poems to be discussed. Actually, the subject was given five 4-millisecond exposures to a picture of one or the other confederate.

The hypothesis was that if five 4-millisecond exposures were enough to influence a positive affective response to a given confederate, then in the subsequent discussion the subject might show more agreement with that particular confederate than with the one not exposed. Interestingly, that is the way things worked out. Table IV shows the number of subjects agreeing with either Confederate A or Confederate B, in terms of which one had been seen subliminally. This response is certainly a powerful behavioral effect. Even if we wish to see such a finding replicated for conservatism's sake, for the moment it certainly provides support for the Moreland–Zajonc model. In a sense, then, this state of affairs could be said to represent an "end" to this particular scientific progression regarding subjective affect versus subjective recognition.

TABLE IV
Number of subjects agreeing with Confederate A or B in the poem task as
related to prior subliminal exposure to pictures of those individuals

Prior subliminal exposure	Subjects agreeing with Confederate A	Subjects agreeing with Confederate B
Confederate A[a]	15	6
Confederate B[b]	7	13

After Bornstein et al. (1987).
[a] $n = 21$.   [b] $n = 20$.

A Major Review

The closing of this particular chapter has been made easier for
me by virtue of the recent appearance of a major technical review of
the exposure literature from 1968 to 1987. Bornstein (1989) conducted a meta-analysis of 134 published articles that reported a total
of 208 independent studies or experiments. He included in his review
studies that (1) were conducted on human subjects, (2) employed
unreinforced exposure to visual or auditory stimuli (i.e., mere exposure), and (3) involved some dependent measure of affect following
stimulus exposures.

Of interest in the review are the effects of certain variables or
procedures, such as the number of exposures involved, the duration
of exposure, the age of subjects, and others. On the basis of a
thorough and detailed analysis, Bornstein (1989) reached the following selected conclusions:

1. When *all* 208 studies were taken into account, there was definitely good
evidence in support of the mere exposure hypothesis.
2. The number of exposures in a study had a definite influence. The strongest effects occurred when the number of presentations was from 1 to 9, intermediate exposure effects obtained when presentations ranged from 10 to 99,
and the weakest effects occurred when there were 100 or more presentations.
3. Exposure effects occurred when heterogeneous (random) sequences of
stimuli were used and did not occur when homogeneous (massed, or blocked)
presentations were employed.
4. The duration of exposures in a study had a definite influence. The
strongest effects occurred when exposure duration was less than 1 second, lesser
effects obtained with 1- to 5-second exposures, and even weaker (and somewhat
irregular) effects occurred at longer exposure durations.
5. The age of the subject matters: exposure effects are very likely when
adults are tested and unlikely when children are involved.

The benefits from a review such as that of Bornstein are twofold. First, we gain confidence that the concept of mere exposure in the area of attitude formation and change merits further consideration. Second, past, present, and future theories in the domain can be evaluated against such a broad empirical base.

A Summing Up

Two decades ago the publication of Zajonc's 1968 monograph on the mere exposure hypothesis started us on a trip down a very interesting scientific path. We have gained two kinds of benefits from this journey. First, it seems reasonable to state that mere exposure effects *do* occur. They can be detected in the laboratory and appear to be important in sectors of everyday life. We now understand more about our attitudes than before the concept was introduced. Second, the controversies that have attended the development of theories explaining the effects of mere exposure have inspired critics and proponents alike to higher levels of methodological sophistication. Happily, these scientific conflicts have provided us not only with heat but with light as well.

CHAPTER SIX

GROUP DISCUSSION AND THE POLARIZATION OF ATTITUDES

One active area of research regarding social influences on attitudes concerns the impact of group discussion on individual sentiments. We often engage in exchanges of ideas on current topics and sometimes even go so far as to seek information from our associates to clarify vague or troubling matters. Of course, discussion of any attitudinal object or domain is a fit subject for study, but a certain dimension has come under a veritable microscope of investigation. This domain has to do with an individual's preferred method of solving everyday problems. Most problems or dilemmas we face can be characterized as having several solutions, the outcomes of which are more or less desirable and more or less chancy. In other words, the *riskiness* of our solutions to problems can be defined by the consequences of differing courses of action. A risky preference or attitude is revealed by a choice of a resolution that would lead to an attractive but unlikely outcome. A cautious preference or attitude is revealed by a choice of resolution that would lead to a more likely but less attractive outcome. The question is, How might social or group pressure influence an individual's preference for such risks?

The plan for this chapter is to review both historical trends in the literature on riskiness and contemporary advances in theory and research that were the result of the groundwork laid by the early risk researchers. Risk preference may seem like a narrow dimension on which to base a chapter, but as we will see, the vigorous research of one era led to unexpected, large-scale advances in a subsequent one. This review will take us through a beginning–middle–end progression on what has been termed the "risky shift" and then will focus on recent developments in the broader domain of the polarizing effects of group discussion.

A Beginning: Original Propositions and Findings

Expressing one's attitude toward risk as an individual is one thing; expressing that attitude as a member of a group (or having discussed it in a group) is often quite another. There are several reasons why a private reaction might change when expressed in a group situation. One possible reason for this difference is that individual risk attitudes may shift toward the mathematical average of all group members. That is, because there is a tendency toward conformity in groups, members with extremely cautious or risky stands on an issue may feel group pressure to adopt a more moderate position. An alternative possibility is that the groups' final consensus could be more cautious than the mathematical average of all the original attitudes. This could happen because a risky stand may make one appear foolish to others, so individuals in groups may be expected to adopt safer views than those they held originally to help preserve their image of competency. A third possible outcome is that individuals in a group may show shifts toward more risky policies, because groups are empowered to do things not open to individuals. Of these three alternatives, Wallach, Kogan, and Bem (1962) felt that the last eventuality was the least likely—but that was before they did their research.

To assess these possibilities, let us imagine that we first measure people's individual attitudes toward their own inclination to recommend risky or cautious solutions to problems. Then we will get them together in a group to discuss the merits of those recommendations. Further, we will insist that ultimate recommendations be the product of a group consensus. ("Consensus" in this chapter implies unanimity.) Next, we will measure the individuals' attitudes once more, either while they are still in the group or some time thereafter.

Shifts to Caution or Risk?

Wallach et al. decided to study the possibility of group influence on individuals' attitudes and, in particular, to examine this influence on individuals' preference for risky or cautious solutions to certain problems. As suggested, interest in the riskiness of group decisions is certainly warranted because as a society we trust many of our most difficult and ominous decisions to groups. We look daily to committees, commissions, and panels for guidance; one need only think of certain decision-making groups in the Federal Government, such as the military Joint Chiefs of Staff or the Supreme Court, to appreciate the magnitude of these decisions.

Wallach's team started on a more modest level; before taking on the captains of industry and government, they looked at group influence on risk-taking by average citizens. This level of study is also important because we routinely look to panels of our peers for decisions, most notably in the form of trial juries. The researchers based their study on an unpublished master's thesis written by J. A. F. Stoner in 1961. Stoner had studied the riskiness of graduate students of industrial management in and out of groups and, to the surprise of many, found that people in groups showed a shift to recommending solutions more risky than their original individual recommendations. To put it another way, Stoner detected a "RISKY SHIFT." Because this result was unexpected, Wallach decided to follow it up, but not by using specialized management trainees. The management trainees may have acted the way they did because it was expected of them given their training. The question was whether the shift to risk would be the outcome in groups composed of other sorts of people. The type of person Wallach et al. studied was the college student.

The choice dilemma questionnaire. A situation like the one described at the opening of this section was set up. Students' tendencies toward caution and risk in decision-making were first assessed; then they were assembled in small groups with instructions to discuss the problems and to reach a group consensus on each decision. Finally, the groups were disbanded, and each individual's attitudes were measured again. Other people served as controls and merely indicated their attitudes at two points in time in the absence of any group discussion. The possibility of shifts in the retest scores is the matter of interest here.

The actual method of measuring attitudes toward risk is central to the interests of this book; in this particular case the choice of method made by Wallach et al. proved to be momentous for later research and theory in the area. Therefore, we will examine it in some detail. Essentially, the instrument was a scaling device that the authors called an "opinion questionnaire" but that has subsequently come to be named the CHOICE DILEMMA QUESTIONNAIRE (CDQ). In using the CDQ, the respondent might be asked to think that he or she was in a position to give advice to someone else who was facing a problem or a dilemma. The twelve items in the original questionnaire are listed here (Wallach et al., 1962):

1. An electrical engineer may stick with his present job at a modest but adequate salary, or may take a new job offering considerably more money but no long-term security.

2. A man with a severe heart ailment must seriously curtail his customary way of life if he does not undergo a delicate medical operation which might cure him completely or might prove fatal.

3. A man of moderate means may invest some money he recently inherited in secure "blue chip" low return securities or in more risky securities that offer the possibility of large gains.

4. A captain of a college football team, in the final seconds of a game with the college's traditional rival, may choose a play that is almost certain to produce a tie score, or a more risky play that would lead to sure victory if successful, sure defeat if not.

5. The president of an American corporation which is about to expand may build a new plant in the United States where returns on investments would be moderate, or may decide to build in a foreign country with an unstable political history where, however, returns on the investment would be very high.

6. A college senior planning graduate work in chemistry may enter University X where, because of rigorous standards, only a fraction of the graduate students receive the PhD, or may enter University Y which has a poorer reputation but where almost every graduate student receives the PhD.

7. A low ranked participant in a national chess tournament, playing an early match with the top-favored man, has the choice of attempting or not trying a deceptive but risky maneuver which might lead to quick victory if successful or almost certain defeat if it fails.

8. A college senior with considerable musical talent must choose between the secure course of going on to medical school and becoming a physician, or the risky course of embarking on the career of a concert pianist.

9. An American prisoner-of-war in World War II must choose between possible escape with the risk of execution if caught, or remaining in camp where privations are severe.

10. A successful businessman with strong feelings of civic responsibility must decide whether or not to run for Congress on the ticket of a minority party whose campaign funds are limited.

11. A research physicist, just beginning a 5-year appointment at a university, may spend the time working on a series of short-term problems which he would be sure to solve but which would be of lesser importance, or on a very important but very difficult problem with the risk of nothing to show for his 5 years of effort.

12. An engaged couple must decide, in the face of recent arguments suggesting some sharp differences of opinion, whether or not to get married. Discussions with a marriage counselor indicate that a happy marriage, while possible, would not be assured.

It should be noted that in responding to an item the subject is asked to consider the risky option and to make a judgment as to what probability or odds for success would be required before she or he would recommend that risky option. For example, in terms of item 4, how much of a sure thing would the risky winning play have to be to cause the football captain to give up the virtual guarantee of a safe tie? The probabilities available to the subject were 1, 3, 5, 7, 9, and 10 chances of success in 10 for the risky option. A choice of 10 would mean that it would have to be a completely sure thing, and a choice of 9 in 10 would mean that the risky option would have to be almost a sure thing before it could be recommended. These choices of 10 in 10 and of 9 in 10 would mean that the subject was being quite cautious and willing to take little risk. On the other hand, a choice of 1 in 10 would mean that the risky option was so attractive that it was worth going for in the face of almost certain failure, a very risky course of action. If a person became more inclined to be risky after a group discussion of the item, he would pick lower odds, so Wallach et al. expressed shifts *to* risk as minus values (i.e., a shift from 9 in 10 to 7 in 10 would be expressed as −2) and shifts *away* from risk as plus values (i.e., a shift from 5 in 10 to 7 in 10 would be expressed as +2).

The result: the risky shift. The basic results of the study are shown separately for men and women in Table I. These results, like the CDQ itself, deserve close scrutiny. Recall that a minus score means that a shift toward risk (lower acceptable odds) has occurred. Indeed, there was a shift to risk on the vast majority of the items for both men and women. In adding up all the plus and minus entries in Table I, the grand net amount of change is −18.6. The grand net amount of change for the control subjects who did not undergo discussion was −0.7, which is almost no change. Therefore, something that went on in the groups is accountable for the shift to risk seen in the experimental subjects. Further, follow-up tests from 2 to 6 weeks later showed that the new postdiscussion riskiness was stable. That is, subjects did not go back to their original positions even after a lapse of an extensive period of time.

However, it may be noteworthy that two of the items in the CDQ (numbers 5 and 12) did not show a shift to risk in either men or women. Tuck this fact away in your memory for now; later in the chapter we will discover the hidden significance of these seemingly trivial departures from the general pattern of the shift to risk.

SETTING THE STAGE FOR COMPETING HYPOTHESES

The Wallach et al. (1962) study became something of a prototype for a wave of similar research that followed. Fads in research are not uncommon, but the research on the risky shift blossomed in an

TABLE I

The shift to riskier choices on the choice dilemma questionnaire (CDQ) following group discussion

Item number	SUBJECTS	
	Male	Female
1	−1.0	−0.9
2	−0.6	−0.7
3	−1.1	−0.6
4	−1.7	−1.4
5	+0.1	+0.6
6	−1.1	−0.8
7	−1.8	−1.7
8	−1.1	−1.2
9	−1.1	−0.5
10	−0.3	−0.7
11	−0.8	−0.9
12	+0.1	+0.7

After Wallach et al. (1962).
Note. A minus (−) entry indicates an average shift in preference toward a riskier solution to that particular dilemma; a plus (+) entry indicates an average shift toward a more conservative (less risky) solution.

extraordinary way because researchers were attracted to the effect for a variety of reasons. In the first place, the phenomenon itself was and is important. As noted, there are groups making momentous decisions everywhere, and if these decision-makers invariably become more risky as a consequence of working in groups, perhaps some alternative forum for rendering judgments should be sought. Second, the early results were strong and above all counterintuitive. Nobody expected to find a risky shift, but, from Stoner on, such shifts kept appearing. Third, the risky shift seemed to be a general, basic phenomenon, not restricted to men, women, or management trainees. Finally, some researchers may have been attracted to the topic for practical reasons. The instrument (CDQ) was well established, the general paradigm was straightforward, and the research instruments were cheap: paper and pencils. Given the simple requirements to research the risky shift, anyone who had access to adult subjects could run a study to test a favorite hypothesis about the basis for the shift to risk.

A *Middle: Competing Hypotheses and Alternative Explanations*

Ten years after the first shift had been measured, Cartwright (1971) was in a position to say that "rarely in the history of social psychology has a single study stimulated as much research as the master's thesis by Stoner . . . which reported the discovery of 'the risky shift'." There are therefore many avenues for tracing the rise and fall of various competing hypotheses for, and alternative explanations of, the shift to risk in this voluminous literature. Indeed, one could write several variations on the beginning–middle–end theme of this particular story, but here we are restricted to a single one of these strains. Of central interest are the evaluations of four different but plausible competing hypotheses (after Clark, 1971). These alternative accounts can be labeled the leadership hypothesis, the familiarity hypothesis, the diffusion-of-responsibility hypothesis, and the risk-as-value hypothesis. The method to proceed through these various hypotheses will be to define or describe a particular mechanism that might produce a shift to risk and then find a study or two that provides a reasonable test of that proposition.

Ordinarily we would seek more than one or two studies to evaluate an hypothesis, but here one or a few more will be sufficient when it is understood that more such evidence is available but is largely redundant. This approach represents a working compromise between breadth of coverage of various hypotheses on the one hand and depth of attention to any given hypothesis on the other. Because so many hypotheses are being tested, it may be useful to keep a scorecard of whether the data cited support a particular position. If a hypothesis gains support, then we can credit it with a plus (+) and consider it further. But if the results fail to support that notion, then we have to fault it with a minus (−) and go on to seek a more supportable interpretation.

THE LEADERSHIP HYPOTHESIS

The LEADERSHIP HYPOTHESIS for the risky shift goes something like this. There are probably individual differences in the proneness to risk-taking in the population, with some people being generally more risky than others. There are probably other traits that go along with a person's level of riskiness and one of these might be certain qualities of leadership. After all, leaders are known to strike out in new directions and foster innovative solutions to problems, which might be a reflection of their greater riskiness. When we assemble people in groups, such as in the risky-shift paradigm, we are bound to get some high-risk subjects and some low-risk subjects. When the group discussion of the CDQ items begins, the naturally more risky leaders come to the fore and their arguments for more risky recommendations have weight over those of the more cautious members by virtue of their leadership skills or tactics. Thus, we generally see shifts to risk rather than to caution because leaders (who are more risky anyway) tend to get their way. (Interestingly, it was originally suggested by Wallach et al. (1962) that conservative people might be more likely to be leaders, but that was back in the days when shifts to caution were expected.)

Testing the leadership hypothesis. In testing the leadership hypothesis, Vidmar (1970) used a logic that was impeccable. He pointed out that in order to have leaders, there must also be followers; if there is no one to follow, who is there to lead? To put it another way, before leadership can be effective in producing the typical shift to risk, the group composition must be heterogeneous on this dimension rather than homogeneous or there will be no one to follow anyone else's lead. If the members are heterogeneous with respect to their riskiness, the more cautious persons can be induced to the more extreme position of the risk-prone leaders, and a general shift to risk would be measurable. But even in heterogeneous groups the most risky members will not shift, for if the shift is a result of the influence of leadership, who is there to lead the leaders? Two specific predictions can be derived from this consideration:

1. Groups whose members are initially similar will *not* show the shift to risk.
2. The riskiest member of any sort of group will *not* show a shift to risk.

To test these subhypotheses, Vidmar (1970) used the standard individual/group discussion/individual CDQ procedure. However, before any discussions took place, he took care to create special groups. First, he measured initial individual riskiness with 10 of the 12 original CDQ items. (He omitted completely the two pesky items, numbers 5 and 12, that were likely to elicit cautious shifts. As promised, we will return to this point later on.) An individual's score on the first test could range from 10 to 100 (odds per item × 10 items). Based on their scores, Vidmar selected groups of five high risk-takers (H) with initial preferences ranging from 22 to 48 (mean = 40.3; standard deviation = 7.3), groups of five medium risk-takers (M) with a range of initial scores of 49 to 60 (mean = 55.3; standard deviation

= 3.5), and groups of five low risk-takers (L) whose scores ranged from 61 to 97 (mean = 69.4; standard deviation = 7.4). Additionally, he composed mixed groups (Mx) of risky or cautious people whose first scores ranged from 22 through 97 (mean = 54.6; standard deviation = 13.5). Inspection of these groups' standard deviations (i.e., average deviations from the mean) shows that the scores of the members of the H, M, and L groups were much more clustered around their respective means than were the scores of the members of the Mx groups, which were more heterogeneous than the others.

Vidmar let these groups discuss the items and retested individual risk preferences a second time. Therefore, in terms of shifts to risk, Vidmar's first subhypothesis can be expressed thusly:

$$Mx > H \simeq M \simeq L = 0$$

That is, the heterogeneous groups (Mx) should show a shift, but there should be no shifts in the homogeneous groups (H, M, L) where discussion-induced changes should be near zero (0).

Next, Vidmar's second subhypothesis concerning who should shift within a group can be operationalized as follows. Within any given group of five, the members (S_k) can be rank-ordered in terms of their original risk choices. We can assign the riskiest member to the first rank (S_1), the second riskiest member to the second rank (S_2), and so on to the most cautious member (S_5). We can express Vidmar's second subhypothesis thusly:

$$S_5 > S_4 > S_3 > S_2 > S_1 = 0$$

That is, the originally more cautious members (S_5, S_4, S_3, S_2) should show the most shifting to risk in that order, but S_1, who is the riskiest, should show no shift, for he or she is already the risk leader and there is no one for him or her to follow.

Support for the leadership hypothesis? Having expressed Vidmar's subhypotheses symbolically, it is a simple matter to consult his results to see whether they offer support for these ideas. He calculated risky shifts by comparing initial preferences to those seen after group discussion; these were converted to minus values to be comparable to the patterns seen in Table I. Vidmar's (1970) findings across groups are shown in Table II (upper panel) as the average total shift over the ten CDQ items. Based on a formal statistical analysis, the outcome in the top part of Table II can be expressed in this way:

$$Mx > H \simeq M \simeq L \neq 0$$

TABLE II
Shifts to risk after group discussions between and within groups

Category	Shift[a]
Between groups[b]	
High risk groups (H)	−7.73
Medium risk groups (M)	−6.12
Low risk groups (L)	−10.17
Mixed risk groups (Mx)	−14.15
Subjects within groups[c]	
S_1 (most risky)	−3.57
S_2	−3.83
S_3	−8.06
S_4	−10.61
S_5 (most cautious)	−11.92

After Vidmar (1970).
[a] The minus (−) entry indicates an average shift in preference toward a riskier solution.
[b] Groupings were based on initial risk preferences of members.
[c] Rankings were based on initial risk preferences of members.

Therefore, although there was more shifting in the heterogeneous (Mx) groups, there was nevertheless real shifting in the other kinds of groups as well. Accordingly, Vidmar's first subhypothesis receives only partial support at best (i.e., Mx > H, M, L), and the part that does not receive support (i.e., H ≃ M ≃ L ≠ 0) may be the most damaging.

The second subhypothesis can be evaluated by examining the amounts of risky shifting by the various individuals within groups, which are also shown in Table II (lower panel). These results can be expressed as follows:

$$S_5 > S_4 > S_3 > S_2 > S_1 \neq 0$$

Again, these results lend partial support to the prediction (i.e., $S_5 > S_4 > S_3 > S_2 > S_1$), but not the entire prediction (i.e., $S_1 \neq 0$). In other words, the riskiest individuals in these groups also shifted, even though they were the presumed leaders, with no one to lead them on to greater riskiness.

A minus (−) for the leadership hypothesis. The predictions from the leadership hypothesis received partial support, but only for certain outcomes that might be better accounted for by other hypotheses. The more critical predictions, that groups having homogeneous initial risk preferences would not shift and that the riskiest members of any group would not shift, were flatly unsupported, because significant shifts occurred in both cases (see also Hoyt and Stoner, 1968, for such shifts in homogeneous groups). In the absence of strong support to the contrary, it appears that the leadership hypothesis as stated is untenable; we will give it a mark of (−) and discard it.

THE FAMILIARITY HYPOTHESIS

Basically, the FAMILIARITY HYPOTHESIS says that the group discussion is actually irrelevant to the risky-shift effect, in the sense that such shifts might be produced by means other than group discussion. In essence, shifts could occur any time subjects become more familiar with the problems at hand. That is, most people are not accustomed to dealing with problems such as those offered in the CDQ, and when they first confront these decisions they are inclined to be hesitant and cautious. If subjects are then permitted to talk over the issues, by the time they are finished discussing the items with their peers they have gained more experience in these matters and subsequently proceed to decisions that are made more briskly and that are more risky. However, any source of familiarity, whether it comes from a group discussion or something else, should produce shifts to risk. Whereas an inexperienced college student might hesitate regarding the football item (number 4) in the CDQ, a seasoned football player might not pause for an instant in going for a win over a tie.

Therefore, according to the familiarity hypothesis, if we make the subject more familiar with the problem, we should see a shift in her or his riskiness. One activity that increases familiarity is rehearsal or practice, but it remains to be seen whether familiarity produced in this fashion produces the typical shift to risk.

Testing the familiarity hypothesis. The work of Teger, Pruitt, St. Jean, and Haaland (1970) offers an abundant testing of the familiarity hypothesis as established here. Their article reports the results of five separate experiments. Generally, the studies had quite a bit in common, and for our purposes we can lump them together. In each, the subjects first gave their reactions to some of the shiftier CDQ items (numbers 1, 6, and 7) and were then asked to rehearse solutions to these by writing down anything they thought might be used for or against a given decision or to merely think about these things for a few moments. Their CDQ reactions were then measured again.

Support for the familiarity hypothesis? Perhaps the simplest way to convey the results of the Teger et al. 1970) studies is to quote their article's abstract verbatim:

A total of 226 subjects at three universities participated in five separate studies which measured the effect on individual risk taking of increased familiarity with the problem situation. The results of all five studies failed to replicate the finding that individuals will take increased risk after they are given an opportunity to become more familiar with the problem. These failures to replicate cast doubt on the hypothesis that the increase in risk after a group discussion is due to increased familiarity with the problems rather than to the effect of group interaction.

A minus (−) for the familiarity hypothesis. Things do not look promising for the familiarity hypothesis. Although some studies (e.g., Bateson, 1966) have provided support for the relationship of familiarity to risky shifting, many more have not or have produced contradictory evidence (e.g., Bem, Wallach, and Kogan, 1965). As Teger et al. (1970) put it, "although a familiarization procedure has, in some instances, produced an increase in risk, it appears that the effect is too inconsistent to be acceptable as the basis for the risky shift." In other words, for a phenomenon as ubiquitous as the shift to risk, we need an explanation much more robust than the familiarity hypothesis has proved to be. In the absence of strong support to the contrary, it appears that the familiarity hypothesis as stated is untenable, and we will give it a mark of (−) and discard it.

THE DIFFUSION-OF-RESPONSIBILITY HYPOTHESIS

It may be the case that the shifts to riskier decisions after group discussion are due to a diffusion of responsibility in a group, hence the DIFFUSION-OF-RESPONSIBILITY HYPOTHESIS. As in the metaphor where concentrated gases become more diffuse in larger spaces, an individual's personal liability for a decision may become less concentrated in herself if she can spread it out or share it with other group members. Potential failures based on risky recommendations may be easier to bear when others are implicated in the decision process. If a person is thus made less responsible, he or she may be inclined to be more risky in actions. According to Pruitt and Teger (1969), their review of the writing on diffusion of responsibility seemed to indicate that diffusion would "take place only when group members feel affection toward one another in addition to seeing each other implicated in the final decision." But note there is no mention in the preceding quote that discussion of the decision items themselves is necessary, only that "group members feel affection toward one another" and that they must see "each other implicated in the final decision."

Testing the diffusion-of-responsibility hypothesis. Pruitt and Teger (1969) endeavored to test this proposition using a measure that differed somewhat from the standard CDQ items but was fundamentally related to those items. Gambling on a roulette wheel or betting at a race track is like choosing CDQ options. In the questionnaire, there are more or less attractive forced choices, but the more attractive picks always have a higher potential for loss. The same thing can be said of betting on a long-shot number or horse. When long shots win, they pay off handsomely. But because long shots rarely win, they seldom pay off, so again the more attractive picks represent more potential for loss.

Pruitt and Teger used a betting situation to see whether choices in that context were susceptible to the shift to risk. Undergraduate female subjects were assessed for their initial bet preferences in a laboratory situation. They were given $2.00 to bet with (and to keep) and were told that wins would be added to this amount and losses deducted. Subjects next had an opportunity to bet on roulette numbers that had the following probabilities of winning: 1 out of 3, 1 out of 6, or 1 out of 10. Having indicated the amounts of their $2.00 stake that they wished to bet on these options, some subjects were collected into groups and were asked to reach a consensus about the size of bet to be made at each odds level; they were told that this consensus would be binding on their personal wagers. Additionally, there was the typical control group in which preferences were reassessed without intervening discussion.

The results of the Pruitt–Teger procedure produced the usual pattern. In the first place, for the no-discussion controls there were no meaningful shifts to risk and, if anything, small shifts toward caution. On the other hand, for the discussion condition, there was the traditional risky shift. The upper panel of Table III presents the pre- and postdiscussion bet sizes in dollar amounts for the options of various odds. There was a net shift toward risk at each odds level, and an overall increase of $.07 per bet after group discussion. This outcome means that the women were willing to risk $.07 more per bet than they were before the discussion.

TABLE III
Shifts to risk in the dollar amount bet as a consequence of actual group discussion of the choice options or conditions of diffusion of responsibility surrounding betting

Measure	ODDS OPTIONS		
	1/3	1/6	1/10
Actual group discussion			
Initial risk measure (A)	.64	.48	.45
Second risk measure (B)	.69	.56	.54
Shift to risk (B − A)	+ .05	+ .08	+ .09
Average shift		+ .07	
Diffusion of responsibility			
Initial risk measure (A)	.64	.52	.44
Second risk measure (B)	.57	.52	.42
Shift to risk (B − A)	− .07	.00	− .02
Average shift		− .03	

After Pruitt and Teger (1969).
Note. Entries are dollar amounts; a plus (+) shift is a shift to risk.

Support for the diffusion-of-responsibility hypothesis? By establishing that their type of betting measure was sensitive to the risky shift, Pruitt and Teger (1969) were in a position to evaluate the diffusion-of-responsibility hypothesis. They did so by replicating the experiment outlined above, but with some important modifications. The new experiment had the following crucial steps:

1. Initial bet preferences were established in private, as before.
2. The subjects were brought together in groups and were asked to discuss something, but *not* their betting preferences. This step was taken so that some sort of actual discussion would lead to a sense of group cohesion and affection, which is one of the prerequisites for diffusion of responsibility as noted in the definition.
3. After these irrelevant (to betting) discussions, private bet preferences were again assessed, but this time the individual subject was informed that her own bet preference would be averaged with those of all the other women who had been in the discussion group and that this averaged amount would determine everyone's wins and losses. Clearly, this allowed each of them to see one another implicated in the final decision, which is the second required factor to elicit diffusion of responsibility.

The only thing left to do is to see whether a risky shift occurred under these conditions of affection and implication in the final decision; the results are given in the lower panel of Table III. For better or worse, no risky shift is evident in the diffusion-of-responsibility experiment. If anything, subjects became more cautious under this experimental manipulation.

A minus (−) for the diffusion-of-responsibility hypothesis. Like other hypotheses before it, the diffusion-of-responsibility hypothesis does not seem to have fared particularly well under the rigorous conditions of the laboratory. The instruction that the women would all have a hand in the final decision in Pruitt and Teger's (1969) second study certainly set the stage for sharing (diffusing) responsibility for riskiness among the group members. In addition, the group discussion of nonbetting matters produced social ties among members in the second study that were just as strong as those in the first as revealed by independent cohesiveness ratings. Still, there was no evidence of the shift-to-risk phenomenon in the absence of a group discussion of the betting items. Without this discussion feature, diffusion of responsibility alone did not produce the usual risk effect. In the absence of strong support to the contrary, it appears that the diffusion-of-responsibility hypothesis is untenable; we will give it a mark of (−) and discard it.

THE RISK-AS-VALUE HYPOTHESIS

It seems that in our society there is something of an attraction to risk-taking. The adventure story is popular among young and old, people pay good money to go to circuses and fairs to see daredevil acts, and explorers such as astronauts are highly admired. Therefore, having a reputation for being at least moderately risky is desirable, and few of us would welcome the label of being timid. The RISK-AS-VALUE HYPOTHESIS is based on the assumption that there is a premium on boldness and that each of us wants to appear to be properly bold. According to this hypothesis, when a risky-shift study is undertaken, people pick initial risk preferences in terms of what they *think* the norm is. However, when the group discussion begins, some of the individuals discover that they are more or less timid in comparison with others. Fearing for their reputations, they engage in impression management by adjusting their own expressed riskiness upward to match the societal standard—hence, the shift to risk after group discussion of CDQ-like problems.

Testing the risk-as-value hypothesis. One certainly could test this hypothesis by using CDQ items, and we will see such a test shortly. However, because it is known that betting patterns may be sensitive to influences that produce shifts to risk on the questionnaire, it is not unreasonable to turn to another betting study as a test of the risk-as-value hypothesis. McCauley, Stitt, Woods, and Lipton (1973) studied betting in a real-life situation, a race track. They assessed shifts in risk preferences by recruiting as subjects male bettors who had just finished making a $2.00 bet on the next race. The only stipulation was that the bettor had to reveal the horse on which he had just bet for the forthcoming race and had to come to a unanimous decision with two other bettors regarding a horse in that race on which they would all place their gratis $2.00 bets. In other words, subjects entered into a group discussion of what risk to take on their next bet (i.e., the odds on the horse they all agreed upon) after they had expressed their initial personal preference for risk (i.e., the odds on the horse they had bet on privately). A control group of bettors were simply given a free $2.00 ticket to bet without any group discussion. It was then a simple matter to calculate the difference between the riskiness of the pre- and postdiscussion bets to determine whether there was a shift to risk.

Support for the risk-as-value hypothesis? The results of the McCauley et al. field experiment are shown in Table IV in terms of the frequency of risky, zero, or cautious shifts relative to the original bets. Most bettors in the individual control condition did not shift at all, and of those that did, very few shifted in the risky direction. On the contrary, most groups did show a shift and a vast majority of these shifts were in the cautious direction. Hence, if the risk-as-value sentiment permeates other areas of our culture, it does not appear to have reached as far as the race track, where caution is the apparent product of group discussion.

But from the beginning we have had an inkling that people are

TABLE IV
Incidence of individual and group shifts in risk at a racetrack

Condition	TYPE OF SHIFT		
	Cautious	Zero	Risky
Individual[a]	6	13	3
Group[b]	16	1	5

After McCauley et al. (1973).
[a] $n = 22$.   [b] $n = 22$.

not always more risky after group discussion and here one could make reference to items 5 and 12 in the CDQ. The discrepancy between these items and the others was not taken seriously at first, and as we have seen some researchers simply stopped using them in their attempts to study "risk." However, the distinction between the two kinds of items on the CDQ—those that yield a shift to risk and those that do not—has persisted and can be easily demonstrated. As part of a course on attitudes and public opinion at the University of Wisconsin at Madison, this author had students respond in private to items 1, 4, and 12 from the CDQ using the standard 1-in-10 to 10-in-10 recommended odds measure. The students then talked about the problems there in the classroom; and, when the discussion was finished, rated the items again. In several such exercises the results were always the same. Items 1 and 4 (known risky items) showed risky shifts from $-.7$ to -1.5; item 12 (known cautious item) showed consistent cautious shifts that ranged from $+.5$ to $+.8$. Therefore, one still has to account for the finding that people reliably show shifts to caution in some circumstances, no matter how often they show risky shifts in other places.

A *minus* $(-)$ *for the risk-as-value hypothesis.* The risk-as-value hypothesis does not seem to be a very good general explanation for shifts in attitudes after group discussions. If risk-as-value produces the risky shift, then an explanation of caution-as-value is also needed to account for cautious shifts. In fact, years of research with the CDQ has revealed that item 2 is neutral and generally does not provoke shifting at all (Vinokur and Burnstein, 1978). To account for this, we might posit a neither-risk-nor-caution-as-value hypothesis. Unfortunately, this sort of tacking on of explanations could go on forever and becomes tautological. Better that we drop the risk-as-value hypothesis and seek some other. Therefore, in the absence of strong support to the contrary, it appears that the risk-as-value hypothesis as stated is untenable, and we will give it a mark of $(-)$ and discard it.

An End: Resolution of Issues and Current Standing of Ideas

We seem to be in the awkward position of having tested ourselves out of hypotheses. It may be the case that had some other writer compiled this review, one or another of the hypotheses might be treated more kindly. (Readers interested in alternative accounts of this part of the history of social science are referred to Lamm and Myers (1978) and to Miller (1978).) Still, negative reviews of this literature are more the rule than the exception. My evaluation is consistent with that of Cartwright (1973):

As time went by . . . it gradually became clear that the cumulative impact of these findings was quite different from what had been expected by those who produced them. Instead of provoking an explanation of why "groups are riskier than individuals," they in fact cast serious doubt on the validity of the proposition itself.

The problem, as Cartwright (1973) saw it, was a matter of labeling. Once the phenomenon was tagged the "risky shift" or the "shift to risk," researchers and theorists seemed to have assumed that *risk* was what they were studying and were not inclined to question the connotation of that term. "The term, risky shift, placed the phenomenon in the domain of risk-taking rather than other possible ones, such as group problem solving, group decision making, social influence, or attitude change" (Cartwright, 1973)—hence, the flurry of hypotheses that directly implicated risk instead of some other dimension or process. How different would this literature look if it had been christened with some other name?

As the enterprise of finding the source of the so-called risky shift became more and more questionable, it became apparent that the whole problem would have to be thought through again. A hint of some basic flaws in the original explanations came when researchers began to take a closer look at the CDQ itself (cf. Teger and Pruitt, 1967; Myers and Arenson, 1972). It has long been known that the 12 items of the CDQ varied as to the amount of shifting each yielded, but what was further revealed was that the amount of shifting on various items was consistently associated with *initial* preferences for riskiness on that item. That is, the direction and amount of shifting was correlated with the items' initial risk means. This pattern is shown in Figure 1, which is adopted from Myers and Arenson (1972).

Figure 1 indicates the important fact that the amount of shifting results from something about the items themselves. This observation cuts across all four competing hypotheses considered previously. If the items themselves generate differences in shifting one way or the other, what matter the leadership, familiarity, diffusion, or value hypotheses? I venture to say that if the relationship of initial riskiness on an item to shifts in riskiness had been more widely known early on, many of the foregoing hypotheses would not have received consideration and other lines of research and theory would have emerged instead. As a matter of fact, as the several risky-shift propositions began to run into dead ends, a new paradigm surfaced that elegantly accounted for the risky shift itself, and for a whole lot more. This new paradigm was the group polarization phenomenon.

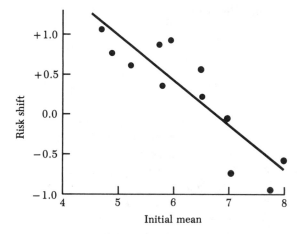

FIGURE 1
SCATTER PLOT showing the correlation between initial risk ratings and degree of risky shift per CDQ item following group discussion. The vertical axis indicates shifts toward risk (plus values in this figure) or toward caution (minus values in this figure). The scatter plot shows that initially risky items were associated with shifts toward risk, and that initially cautious items were associated with shifts toward caution. (After Myers and Arenson, 1972.)

POLARIZING EFFECTS OF DISCUSSION IN GROUPS

Considering the relationship between original risk choices and subsequent shifting seen in Figure 1, one might express the pattern thusly. If people in a group are already inclined toward a course of action (or hold a certain attitude), group discussion will serve to make them even more extreme on that dimension. If they are originally risky, they will become even more risky. If originally cautious, the change will be to even greater caution. That is what the picture in Figure 1 shows. But before we further consider a theory for *why* shifts in different directions occur, it will be quite useful to look at some of the empirical work of Myers and his colleagues on this topic.

Myers and Lamm (1975, 1976; and see also Moscovici and Zavalloni, 1969) have described a phenomenon termed the GROUP POLARIZATION EFFECT. Basically, this phenomenon is thought to emerge under the following circumstances. Individuals' attitudes on any dimension predict the direction toward which they will shift as a consequence of group discussion. Measure people's attitudes toward anything—political parties, race relations, environmental concerns (or risky decisions, for that matter)—and then assemble them in a group to discuss the issue. If it is the case that the initial attitudes of most people in the group are on one or the other side of the neutral point of the scale employed, then group discussion will polarize their attitude toward the end to which they were originally disposed. Figure 2 illustrates this proposition, using a semantic differential scale for racial feelings. It suggests that people originally on the positive side will become even more positive, whereas people on the negative side will become even more negative. Myers and Lamm next discussed data that supported the prediction of polarization.

Polarization of racial attitudes. Myers and Bishop (1970) tested the proposition by first measuring high school students' racial attitudes. They used an instrument called the Multifactor Racial Attitude Inventory for measuring white attitudes toward black people. An item in this scale and the method of scoring are provided in the following example. "Some people recently have been saying that 'white racism' is basically responsible for conditions in which Negroes live in American cities. Others disagree. How do you feel?" To answer the query, the respondents used a scale that ranged from +9 (white racism is responsible), through 0, to −9 (white racism is not responsible). Here, the lower the score, the more prejudiced the subject.

After students' initial attitudes toward the minority had been measured, they were assembled into two groups, one having an

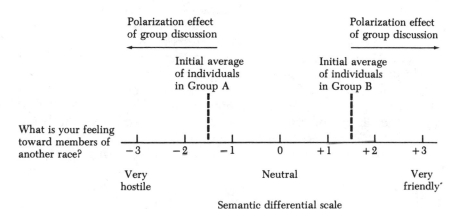

FIGURE 2
GROUP POLARIZATION process in homogenous groups depicted in schematic form.

average of individuals' scores that was above the neutral point of zero (i.e., 2.94) and the other having an average of individuals' scores that was below the neutral point of zero (i.e., −1.70). Each item on the racial attitude inventory was then discussed for 2 minutes and the group tried to reach a consensus during that time. Following the discussion, each subject again filled out an individual inventory so that the pre- and postdiscussion scores could be compared. As might be expected, there were also prejudiced and unprejudiced control individuals who did not discuss the scale items but who responded to the scale at two points in time.

The results of the Myers–Bishop procedure were clear. Controls who were originally unprejudiced showed a change of −.32 toward more prejudice, whereas controls who were originally prejudiced showed a change of +.16 toward less prejudice. These small shifts can be written off as a "regression to the mean," but in any event they do not represent polarization, because they are shifts toward the neutral point. However, group discussion did produce rather large shifts in attitudes and resulted in polarization as predicted. The unprejudiced students shifted from 2.94 to 3.41 (+.47), and the prejudiced students shifted from −1.70 to −3.01 (−1.31), shifts that are both *away* from the neutral point. In short, the predictions illustrated in Figure 2 were borne out. Group discussion did lead to further polarization of preexisting attitudes in the groups.

Polarization of jury decisions. Recall that the explanation of the polarization effect is meant to apply to almost any attitudinal dimension. The decision of a jury is attitudinal in nature, being based at least on affective and cognitive factors, and just possibly open to the influence of group discussion because jurors must reach a unanimous decision. Myers and Kaplan (1976) arranged a clever test of this possibility. Groups of people (mock juries) read court records that implied that some defendants were probably not guilty whereas others were probably guilty. The individual mock jurors were asked to give their initial private impressions of the defendants' guilt based on a scale that ranged from 0 (innocent) to 20 (guilty). They were also asked to assign punishment to each defendant that ranged from 1 (minimum) to 7 (maximum). The jurors were then assembled into groups (juries) to discuss to consensus the innocence or guilt of some of the defendants; other defendants' cases were not discussed and served as controls.

The logic is that because a given defendant was made to *appear* either innocent or guilty by experimental manipulation, most jurors would have similar attitudes toward particular parties prior to the group discussions. The average initial impressions of the guilt and innocence of the respective parties is shown in Figure 3. And Figure 3 shows that assigned punishment varied according to a defendant's presumed guilt. However, group discussion had its expected polarizing impact. For the low-guilt cases, estimates of guilt and assignment of punishment decreased on the final ratings, whereas for the high-guilt cases, the opposite pattern was seen. For the cases that were not discussed, no such shifts were seen.

The risky shift as polarization. The stage is now set for what is perhaps the proper interpretation of the so-called risky shift after group discussion. We have seen that certain items on the CDQ reliably elicit *initially* risky or cautious reactions or recommendations, and these respective items also produce the largest shifts to risk or caution (see Figure 1). Let us take a look at the dilemma of the football captain facing a tie (item 4) and the couple facing a shaky

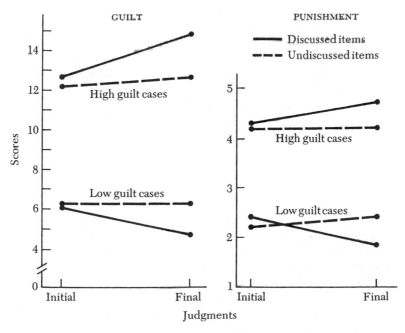

FIGURE 3
DISCUSSION-BASED POLARIZATION of guilt and punishment scores assigned to presumably innocent or guilty defendants. The fact that the solid-line dots are farther apart after discussion (final) than before (initial) indicates the polarization effect. Such shifting did not occur on items that were not discussed. (After Myers and Kaplan, 1976.)

marriage (item 12) as risky and cautious items, respectively. Most people reading the football item privately react in a risky fashion. After all, there is the glory of the win set against the ignominy of the tie. On the other hand, most people reading the marriage item privately react in a cautious manner. It is all well and good to be married, but the emotional and financial cost of a failed marriage can be overwhelming. Next, when we assemble these people into groups for the sake of discussion, most people bring their private risky attitudes toward item 4 and their own cautious attitudes toward item 12 along with them. In other words, given the general tendencies in the population, we are bound to form groups with an initial mean attitude that is below the neutral or midpoint of the odds scale (1 in 10 to 10 in 10) for number 4, and, similarly, we will end up with groups with an initial mean attitude above the scale midpoint for item 12.

From here on the analysis is simple. The group polarization formulation says that any time there is a discussion among individuals whose attitudes are already polarized in the same direction, those attitudes will polarize even further. Thus, because most people are already feeling risky about item 4, they end up shifting in a risky direction. By the same token, because most people are already feeling cautious about item 12, the postdiscussion shift is in the cautious direction. Therefore, as suggested, in using the polarization explanation we can account for the group risky shift without necessary reference to any of the four hypotheses reviewed in the section on alternative explanations. The factor of "riskiness" is just one more attitude dimension sensitive to the polarization effect.

POLARIZATION OR DEPOLARIZATION? ACCOUNTING FOR SUCH EFFECTS

Vinokur and Burnstein (1978), following the lead of Myers and Lamm (1976), point out that there are two basic ways to account for the polarization effect, NORMATIVE INFLUENCE and INFORMATIONAL INFLUENCE. In some circumstances, predictions from theories of normative influence are the same as predictions from theories of informational influence, but in other circumstances predictions from these positions are contradictory. Let us first examine definitions and elaborations of these forms of influence, then see when and where they make the same, or differing, predictions.

Normative influence. This position is based on the assumption that there is a certain amount of ambiguity as to the "proper" attitude to hold on a particular issue. People then use one another's attitudes as social comparisons with which to gauge the appropriateness of their own attitudes. The notion of risk-as-value mentioned earlier is a narrow variant of the many kinds of social comparisons there are. In further assuming that relatively extreme values may generally be more desirable than others, normative influences would cause moderates to shift toward the endpoint of the dimension, whatever that dimension happened to be.

Informational influence. This position states that an attitude can be thought of as being made up of a limited pool of arguments (i.e., the cognitive component). These arguments may vary across people in terms of their availability (whether they come to mind) and their persuasiveness. To illustrate the influence of such information, Vinokur and Burnstein (1978) ask us to imagine that there are two alternatives to an issue, say J or K, and that there are a total of six possible arguments in favor of J (a, b, c, d, e, and f) and a total of three possible arguments favoring K (l, m, and n). If we form a group of three individuals and let them discuss the issues for which J and K are potential alternatives, there may be shifts toward J *or* K, depending on the number and pattern of arguments brought forth by the discussants. If all three of the people thought of exactly the same arguments, their prior attitudes would have been identical and there is no basis for change as a result of discussion. If, however, arguments a, b, and m were contributed by one member; c, d, and m by a second member; and e, f, and m by a third, there would be a marked group shift to J (and no shift to K) even though their original attitudes were quantitatively similar, each having two new arguments that were pro-J. After the discussion, all the members would have six pro-J arguments at their disposal. On the other hand, polarization to K would occur if one discussant contributed a, b, and l; the second a, b, and m; and the third a, b, and n. Here, each brought up the same two pro-J arguments and a different pro-K argument. Of course, the amount of shift to K in the latter case would be less than the amount of shift to J in the former, as fewer arguments are involved.

Applicability of normative and informational influences. If the group that is to discuss an issue is relatively homogeneous with respect to its individuals' prediscussion attitudes, then either the normative-influence or the informational-influence formulations make the prediction of polarization of those attitudes. First, the very similarity of the individuals would define them as a group whose members could use one another as standards for comparison and matching (normative influence). Second, given the possibility that each member may hold the same *number* but not the same *kind* of arguments, there is the possibility that group discussion will add to the argument collection of all the members (informational influence). Thus, where there is relative homogeneity, both positions predict polarization.

On the other hand, if the group is relatively heterogeneous regarding its individuals' prediscussion attitudes, then the normative and informational formulations make very different predictions. When there are two clear subgroups in opposition to each other on an issue (one pro-J and one pro-K, for example), normative-influence theory predicts that each subgroup would reject its rival as a proper basis for social comparison and matching and would look increasingly to their own kind for standards to match. In heterogeneous groups, normative influences would again lead to polarization—in this case, bidirectional polarization. The pro-J people would shift toward J and the pro-K people would shift toward K.

But note, this is where the predictions of the two formulations diverge, because informational-influence theory would predict that the heterogeneity of subgroups would lead to massive DEPOLARIZATION between these elements. Here, depolarization means a reduction in the attitudinal "gap" between subgroups involved in a heterogeneous group discussion. This happens because, in terms of the pro-J and pro-K examples, most of the pro-J group are already familiar with most of the pro-J arguments (a, b, c, d, e, and f), so they will not polarize extensively when these arguments are raised. Similarly, most of the pro-K arguments (l, m, and n) will be familiar to the pro-K group, so airing them will not polarize the pro-Ks too much. But at the same time, arguments a, b, c, d, e, and f may be brand-new to the pro-K element, and, by the same reasoning, l, m, and n may be novel to the pro-J faction. According to this perspective, the polarization of both subgroups based on ingroup information will (everything else equal) be more than countered by depolarization based on information available from the outgroup. Therefore, the distinctions between the dynamics of homogeneous and heterogeneous discussion groups highlight the need to take these factors into consideration when analyzing attitude change after discussion.

Testing for polarization and depolarization. Vinokur and Burnstein (1978) correctly asserted that virtually all the previous research demonstrating attitude polarization effects had relied on homogeneous groups (e.g., Myers and Bishop, 1970). This situation prompted Vinokur and Burnstein to study polarization and depolarization in heterogeneous groups. In their Experiment 1 they identified subgroups by measuring initial preferences for risk with traditional CDQ-type items. They used several such items, but for simplicity of exposition we will limit our attention to two representative issues: a "risky" item (their item A) and a "cautious" item (their item E). Subjects' initial cautious or risky reactions were assessed privately and then discussion groups were formed on the basis of these private reactions. In the group discussing the risky item, half the members of the group had had an initial risky reaction, whereas the remainder of the group had been relatively cautious. In the group discussing the cautious item, there were again some risky and some cautious people assigned to the group. The original differences between these respective cautious and risky subgroups were substantial. There was an average gap between their initial private risk preferences of about 5.5 units on the 1-in-10 to 10-in-10 odds scale. The groups then discussed each item until each group reached a unanimous decision regarding their recommendations on the CDQ problems, and later each person was asked for a final private reaction.

Again, the question was whether the results would show polarization or depolarization of attitudes in such heterogeneous groups. The answer was that on the surface *both* effects seem to have occurred. Polarization was in evidence because there was an overall (whole group) shift in the direction known to be standard for an item; that is, there was a risky shift for a risky item and a cautious shift for a cautious item. Depolarization was also in evidence in that the prediscussion gap in attitude between the risky and cautious subgroups was reduced (narrowed) as a result of the discussion. Table V presents these patterns. Overall, there was a net polarization on both the risky item (−1.21) and the cautious item (+0.99). In other words, postdiscussion choices on the risky issue were for odds lower than those chosen initially; the corresponding choices on the cautious issue were for odds higher than those chosen originally. At the same time there was an impressive amount of depolarization between the initially divergent subgroups. The gap between the risky and cautious people on the risky item was reduced by 3.09 units, and on the cautious item this reduction was 3.37 units. The attitudes of the two subgroups were far more similar after group discussion than before.

How could there be both polarization *and* depolarization in the same groups of subjects? The solution to this apparent paradox lies

TABLE V
Effects of polarization and depolarization of attitudes following discussions by heterogeneous groups.

Item type	WHOLE GROUP POLARIZATION			SUBGROUP DEPOLARIZATION		
	Before[a]	After[a]	Shift[b]	Before[a]	After[a]	Gap[c]
Risky	4.71	3.50	−1.21	5.09	2.00	−3.09
Cautious	6.22	7.21	+0.99	5.96	2.59	−3.37

After Vinokur and Burnstein (1978).
Note. Polarization refers to shifts on an item by the discussion group considered as a whole; depolarization refers to changes in the distance (gap) of the distinct subgroups from one another on the attitudinal measure.
[a] Values are average scores indicating preference for risk or caution on the 1 in 10, to 10 in 10 scale.
[b] A negative value indicates a shift to risk on an item; a positive value indicates a shift to caution.
[c] A negative value indicates a narrowing of the gap between the subgroups as a consequence of discussion. For example, on the risky item the initial gap was 5.09 units, whereas after the discussion this gap had been reduced to 2.00 units.

TABLE VI
Effects of discussions by heterogeneous groups by item type and subgroup type.

Item type	RISKY SUBGROUPS			CAUTIOUS SUBGROUPS		
	Before[a]	After[a]	Shift[b]	Before[a]	After[a]	Shift[b]
Risky	2.16	2.50	+0.33	7.26	4.50	−2.76
Cautious	3.25	5.91	+2.66	9.21	8.50	−0.70

After Vinokur and Burnstein (1978).
[a] Values are average scores indicating preference for risk or caution on the 1 in 10, to 10 in 10 scale.
[b] A negative value indicates a shift to risk; a positive value indicates a shift to caution.

in the fact that Table V masks some very important differences between the risky and cautious subgroups. These critical differences are made more clear in Table VI. There was indeed a marked risky shift, but it was on the part of the cautious subgroups (−2.76) and not on the part of the risky subgroup (+0.33). Conversely, the cautious shifting that occurred is attributable to the risky subgroup (+2.66) and not to the cautious faction (−0.70).

In terms of the competing hypotheses for possible shifts in heterogeneous groups, apparently under the conditions of the study the normative influence could not hold out over the informational influence. The risky subgroups seem to have been greatly influenced by the arguments for caution presumably advanced by the cautious subgroups. The original risky people evidenced a huge shift to caution on the cautious item and even some shift to caution on the risky item. The corresponding pattern held true for the initially cautious subgroups. They showed a large risky shift on the risky item and even a small shift to risk on the cautious item. Therefore, although *overall* tallies of change for items indicated that attitudes in the group as a whole were becoming more polarized, the subgroups were actually moving closer together and were shifting by different degrees on different items. The risky subgroups were becoming far more cautious on the cautious item than were the cautious subgroups becoming risky on this item. Similarly, the cautious subgroups were becoming far more risky on the risky item than were the risky subgroups becoming cautious on this item.

Depolarization and familiarity. The idea of Vinokur and Burnstein (1978) that depolarization is due to the receipt of new information was tested in their Experiment 2. They reasoned that the more familiar a person was with an issue, the less likely that person would be to show an attitude shift—either polarization or depolarization—toward that issue. Vinokur and Burnstein asked certain undergraduate respondents to consider three kinds of attitudinal items: (1) *factual* (having to do with geography, population statistics, and energy requirements); (2) *personal taste* (having to do with preferred sports and colors); and (3) *values* (having to do with civil rights and capital punishment). The undergraduates indicated how many ideas they had about these three kinds of issues, how often they thought about or discussed them, and how interesting each was. This index of "familiarity" showed that the respondents had the most commerce with values, a moderate amount concerning taste, and the least amount regarding the facts.

When they did their main Experiment 2, Vinokur and Burnstein followed the procedure of their Experiment 1. For each of the three types of attitudinal items, they identified and formed groups of subjects who had divergent and relatively extreme reactions. In other words, the researchers constructed discussion groups in which there were large initial gaps between subgroups. Based on the results of Experiment 1, it was expected that a great deal of depolarization would occur between previously extreme subgroups as a result of discussion, and so it did. However, what was of interest here was to find the relationship between the amount of depolarization (expressed as the proportion of the reduction of the initial gap) and the subjects' presumed familiarity with the three item types. Recall that the order of familiarity of the independent sample of respondents was, from most to least, value, taste, and fact. As it happened, that was also the rank order of the magnitude of depolarization over the item types. Proportional gap reduction was .18, .35, and .81 for the value, taste, and fact items, respectively. In sum, subjects showed the most depolarization on items they were presumably least familiar with, and the least amount of depolarization on the items they were most familiar with. This pattern nicely fits the Vinokur–Burnstein formulation on the influence of information.

Summary on polarization and depolarization. Vinokur and Burnstein (1978) were right to point out the distinction between the dynamics of attitude shifts in groups with homogeneous or heterogeneous memberships. So far as we know, the discussion of members holding homogeneous attitudes produces polarization toward the extreme already favored by the group. This polarization can be caused by either, or both, normative influences or informational influences in homogeneous groups.

However, the analysis is vastly different in groups where members hold heterogeneous initial attitudes on the issue to be discussed. That is, where there are ingroups and outgroups within the discussion group as a whole, the normative and informational influences would oppose one another. The normative influence, usually seen as an effect of the ingroup on itself, would lead to bidirectional polarization between the two subgroups. On the contrary, informational influence would cause depolarization, because the arguments provided to each other by the outgroups might contain more new information than the contrary arguments that the ingroups provide for themselves. The question of which effect would obtain, polarization or depolarization, is largely an empirical one that depends on the circumstances. In the situation employed by Vinokur and Burnstein (1978), the informational influence appeared to far outweigh the normative influence, and massive depolarization was seen in that study.

INFORMATIONAL VERSUS NORMATIVE INFLUENCES:
ISSUE TYPE AND DECISION RULE

In the last line of the preceding paragraph, I intentionally used the clause "the informational influence appeared to far outweigh the normative influence." This statement implies a theoretical confrontation concerning the predominance of one over the other type of influences, which is reflective in a way of the literature in the area. Generally, informational influence has produced more frequent and stronger discussion-based shifts than has the normative sort (see Kaplan and Miller, 1987). However, as Kaplan and Miller (1987) point out, this may be a misleading distinction. For these writers, it is a matter not of which influence category is "stronger," but of which type of influences is attempted by discussants in which kind of situation. By and large, the Kaplan–Miller definitions of normative and informational influence are consistent with those offered above, as follows:

Normative influence . . . is based on the desire to conform to the expectations of others. Judgment shifts are assumed to result from exposure to others' choice preferences and from subsequent conformity to the norms that are implicit or explicit in these preferences.

And,

informational influence . . . is based on the acceptance of information from others as evidence about reality. Shifts are attributed to the sharing of relevant arguments and factual information about the judged issue.

Now, it would depend on the *type* of issues as to which kind of arguments (influence) would be forthcoming and presumably influential. Continuing with definitions, Kaplan and Miller (1987) outline one dimension along which issues might fall: intellective compared with judgmental matters.

At one end of the continuum are *intellective* issues, for which there are, or are considered to be, demonstrably correct answers. At the other end of the continuum are *judgmental* issues, which involve behavioral, ethical, or esthetic judgments for which there are no demonstrably correct answers. For intellective issues, the group's task is to discover the "true" or "correct" answer, whereas for judgmental issues, the group's task is to decide the "moral," "valued," "proper," or "preferred" position.

It would seem that intellective issues would call forth informational statements and that judgmental issues would stimulate normative arguments.

Finally, a second situational feature that requires attention is the decision *rule* under which a group happens to be operating. That is, it might make a big difference whether the group must come to a majority decision or to a unanimous decision. Kaplan and Miller (1987) point out that past research has shown that reaching a unanimous decision is more difficult than reaching one that is based on a majority. In keeping with their distinction between intellective and judgmental issues, they expected that under conditions of unanimous decision-making there would be a high likelihood that certain influences would be brought to bear on certain issues. That is, for intellective issues there would be more informational than normative pressure under the demand of unanimity, whereas for judgmental issues the opposite would occur and more normative than informational arguments would be made.

The research. To test these ideas, Kaplan and Miller set up a jury-like situation for small groups of undergraduate female subjects. These student–jurors were asked to award damages in a civil suit. The plaintiff had been injured by a faulty furnace, and the manufacturer was clearly negligent. Half the subjects were charged with awarding "compensatory" damages. This type of damages decision was thought to represent an intellective issue, because a kind of arithmetic can be applied to monetary amounts such as the plaintiff's medical expenses and loss of past and future earnings. The other half of the subjects were asked to award "exemplary" damages. These damages are punitive in nature and are determined by how much the defendant deviated from social norms and values regarding public welfare and justice. Here, a judgmental issue confronted the jurors, because matters of what is "moral" and "proper" were at hand. In addition to issue type, a second experimental variable was the decision rule imposed on the juries. Half were required to reach a majority decision, and half were required to reach unanimity. Thus, the basic design was a 2 × 2 factorial that crossed issue types with decision rules.

The results. The juries' deliberations were recorded and later coded for the kinds of statements—informational or normative—that the jurors had made. Remember, the prediction was that on an intellective issue (the compensatory damages condition) more informational than normative statements would be in evidence, whereas for the judgmental issue (the exemplary damages condition) more normative than informational statements would occur. Furthermore, if unanimity rather than a majority decision was required of subjects, these contrasting patterns would be even more extreme. And the results of the study, as shown in Figure 4, bear out these predictions. Under the compensatory condition, there were more informational statements offered compared with normative ones under the majority rule, and even more so for the unanimous condition. A similar pattern occurred in the exemplary situation, where more normative than

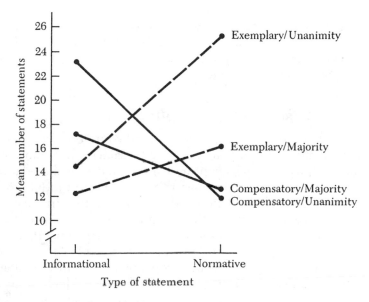

FIGURE 4
NORMATIVE AND INFORMATIONAL INFLUENCE STATEMENTS as related to type of issue and decision rule. (After Kaplan and Miller, 1987.)

informational statements were forthcoming, and again more so under the demand for unanimity.

OPINION CHANGE IN THE REAL WORLD ON REAL ISSUES

Setting aside the contrast between informational and normative influences, let us return for a moment to the study by Vinokur and Burnstein (1978). That research has been characterized thusly:

The one experimental study [Experiment 2] in the group polarization literature that focused on members' familiarity with the issues found that the largest shift in opinion occurred on issues with which the members had little familiarity, and the smallest shifts, on issues with which they were very familiar (Vinokur, Burnstein, Sechrest, and Wortman, 1985).

Following this lead, Vinokur et al. (1985) measured the amount of change of opinion and behavior (practice) of medical experts who participated in high-level National Institutes of Health panels on various topics such as cervical cancer screening, coronary surgery, Reye's syndrome, and others. Of interest here, as in the case of the Vinokur–Burnstein Experiment 2 (above), was the relationship between the novelty of the information the experts received and the amount of change in their opinions and practices. Based on self-reports, novelty of information was positively related to change in attitude ($r = .73$) and practice ($r = .63$). Thus, in this real-world setting involving presumably intellective issues, informational influence was very much in evidence.

Group Polarization: Current Standings

When I look around me, I see people endlessly engaged in discussion. Some of this amounts mostly to palaver, but some of it is serious and intense. In this chapter, I have tried to make you aware of the fact that such discussion has the potential to produce polarization or depolarization of attitudes, depending on the circumstances. What is the current standing of theory in this area? In a recent meta-analysis of the polarization literature, Isenberg (1986) points out that in 1971 there were as many as 11 overlapping explanatory accounts for choice shifts, a subset of which you saw earlier in this chapter. By now this list has been reduced to two, both of which, according to Isenberg's (1986) meta-analysis, enjoy considerable empirical support. One of these is termed PERSUASIVE ARGUMENTS THEORY (PAT), and I have traced some of its developments in the preceding pages. According to Isenberg (1986),

PAT holds that an individual's choice or position on an issue is a function of the number and persuasiveness of pro and con arguments that that person recalls from memory when formulating his or her own position . . . Group discussion will cause an individual to shift in a given direction to the extent that the discussion exposes that individual to persuasive arguments favoring that direction.

The second current model for polarization effects is called SOCIAL COMPARISON THEORY (SCT). In Isenberg's (1986) words,

According to this perspective, people are constantly motivated both to perceive and present themselves in a socially desirable light. In order to do this, an individual must be continually processing information about how other people present themselves, and adjusting his or her own self-presentation accordingly . . . Once we determine how most other people present themselves, we present ourselves in a somewhat more favorable light. When all members of an interacting group engage in the same comparing process, the result is an average shift in a direction of greater perceived social value.

Note that in the SCT position, discussion and arguments are not strictly necessary to produce choice shifts—any of several sources of information could produce an effect. However, both the PAT and SCT formulations are applicable where discussion is a feature of the social situation. Taken together they go a long way in allowing us to understand the polarizing influence of group discussion.

CHAPTER SEVEN

COGNITIVE DISSONANCE VERSUS
SELF-PERCEPTION AND ATTRIBUTION:
A COMPETITION BETWEEN THEORIES

In this chapter I will trace theoretical developments connected with a phenomenon called cognitive dissonance. Cognitive dissonance research is deep in the mainstream of contemporary social psychology. The journey will follow a beginning–middle–end path that will cover theoretical and empirical contributions of historical and recent vintage.

A Beginning: Original Propositions and Findings

In 1956 a book entitled *When Prophecy Fails* was published. Authored by a team of social psychologists, Leon Festinger, Henry W. Riecken, and Stanley Schacter, it told the story of an actual group of people who had become convinced that one of their members was receiving messages directly from God. The central theme of the messages was ominous. Within the year a substantial part of the world was to be destroyed by an enormous flood. The good news was that the members were also told that they were "chosen ones" who would be rescued from the flood by flying saucers and transported to a safe place. The flood would occur, they were told, on December 21 of the year in question.

The leaders of the group initially tried to proselytize by various means; late in the summer they sent out 50 copies of a press release that was entitled "An Open Letter to American Editors and Publishers." Unfortunately for their purpose, there was no reaction to the release except for a derogatory treatment by a local newspaper. Eventually, however, the group's claim was met with something other than simple skepticism. One of the most prominent members, a Dr. Armstrong, was fired from his post at a nearby university as a direct consequence of his unorthodox convictions.

Reactions to these more or less serious rebuffs were understandable, if unpleasant. If the group did not quite go underground, its members certainly became very circumspect about advertising their ideas. For example, after several such reversals, Dr. Armstrong became quite hesitant about recruiting. In answer to a student's question about the problem of proselytizing, he replied with phrases like "you can't explain the prophecy or the coming catastrophe to anyone who isn't ready" and "it will be up to them, individually, to decide what to do." But when it was made known that Armstrong had been fired for his beliefs, *he* became news and whether or not he wanted to talk with reporters on the issue, they certainly wanted to talk with him. In the face of this opportunity to disseminate the group's convictions, the doctor was very reluctant to open up to the media. He told reporters "he was not a street-corner evangelist; he was not interested in saving the world; and he didn't want to persuade anybody to join anything . . . "

Although the group members were now reserved about the publication of their beliefs regarding the December flood, those beliefs remained unshaken. Indeed, as the fateful day approached, everything they did pointed to their deepening convictions. If the world as we know it was about to end, they reasoned, why continue to bother with earthly concerns? Following this line of thought, the people in the group abandoned their worldly burdens and treasures by quitting their jobs or their studies and by giving away their possessions. Although these examples are impressive, last-minute preparations were even more so. On the eve of the predicted rescue, someone got the idea that people could not wear any metal in a flying saucer (their means of rescue from the flood), so they divested themselves of coins, keys, jewelry, and belts. This also meant that eyelets had to be removed from shoes, tinfoil had to be unwrapped from sticks of gum, and zippers had to be ripped from trousers!

As the reader can guess, not a single flying saucer appeared to pick up the chosen ones before the date of the predicted flood, and, to make matters worse, there was no flood. By the morning of December 21, it was painfully clear to the group that the prophecy had failed to come true. Despite a tremendous investment and commitment to the prophecy, the members were stuck with the reality that nothing had happened. What could they do in such a bind? For several hours the membership sat around brooding. Then the unexpected occurred. According to Dr. Armstrong, an extraordinary set of messages sent from God arrived at about 5:00 that morning, indicating that the world had been spared the catastrophe because of the group and that this information should be *immediately released to the press!*

Now put yourself in Dr. Armstrong's place. As one of the leaders of the group, he had already been publicly humiliated and persecuted for his belief, so he and the others had withdrawn to the privacy and mutual support afforded by one another's company. In spite of this retreat and entrenchment, however, that belief was in danger of being shattered in light of the strong evidence that the prophecy had failed. Yet, this man and the others were currently being asked to return to the spotlight of publicity with another improbable story. Would they do it or had they had enough?

The stalwarts of the group responded without hesitation. Within 2 hours of the receipt of the most recent messages, group members had phoned not only the local newspapers, but the Associated Press and United Press International as well. Indeed, this apparent desire for publicity continued unabated for several days. Press releases concerning the prophecy and related matters were sent out regularly, taped interviews with reporters were granted, callers were treated to lengthy discussions, and every sort of crank and practical joker was admitted to the group's quarters and welcomed warmly, all in an effort to spread the word. How can social psychology account for this immediate and complete reversal of policy regarding proselytizing, publicity, and recruiting? We saw that before the failure of the prophecy the group was very tight-lipped about the whole affair, but following the failure there seemed to be no limit on their efforts at broadcasting the news.* A plausible solution to this puzzle comes from the theory of COGNITIVE DISSONANCE.

THEORY AND RESEARCH ON COGNITIVE DISSONANCE

Not long after the appearance of *When Prophecy Fails*, Festinger published another book called *A Theory of Cognitive Dissonance* (1957). In it he argued that an important part of our psychology of attitudes had to do with our cognitions concerning reality. Festinger's

---

*But for a case in which a failed doomsday prophecy did not lead to proselytizing, see Hardyck and Braden (1962).

definition is close to that of a cognitive element in an attitude (see Chapter 2). Festinger went on to argue that there were certain relationships between cognitions. Basically, the relationships were irrelevance, consonance, and dissonance. To take simple cases, two or more cognitions are in a state of (1) IRRELEVANCE when they have virtually nothing to do with one another (e.g., Donald Duck's girlfriend is named Daisy and the price of family homes keeps increasing), (2) CONSONANCE if one follows from the other (e.g., the temperature this morning was −20 degrees Fahrenheit and my car would not start), and (3) DISSONANCE if one does not follow from the other (e.g., I am in favor of saving energy and I drive a gas-guzzling car). Generally, consonance can be viewed as consistency and dissonance as inconsistency.*

Festinger's main point is that we usually strive for consistency or consonance between our cognitions. He went so far as to declare that "the existence of dissonance, being psychologically uncomfortable, will motivate the person to try to reduce dissonance and achieve consonance." In principle, a person can reduce dissonance simply by ordering or adjusting her or his cognitions so that one does follow from the other. In the dissonance example above, it would only be necessary to get rid of the car. Unfortunately, in practice (real life) the changing of cognitions is not always an easy task or a simple process. The problem is that some cognitions are more or less bound up with reality, and in many instances reality is very resistant to change (without changing other cognitions that protect our psyches). However, because the definition of cognitions also encompasses categories of information termed beliefs (insofar as we view our beliefs to be "correct"), this theory has a tremendous potential for increasing our understanding of the dynamics of attitude change.

*When Festinger's writing is discussed, there has been a general tendency to treat the term "cognition" rather loosely. For instance, consider this recent passage from Quattrone (1985): "According to the theory of cognitive dissonance (Festinger, 1957), an individual who holds two or more cognitions (i.e., *beliefs* or *evaluations* [emphasis added]) . . . " In this, I think Quattrone adequately conveys Festinger's original intent. But if I am to be true to the tripartite model I advocated in Chapter 2, equating "beliefs" and "evaluations" seems to violate the distinction between "cognition" and "affect." In other words, I feel that what Festinger really developed, technically speaking, was a theory of cognitive/affective dissonance. However, because I do not think the world is ready to accept my meddling with the name of a classic theory, I hope to finesse this semantic bind by declaring the following ground rules. On the one hand, if I say something like "I *like* to eat zucchini," this is a statement concerning affect. On the other hand, if I say something such as, "Eating zucchini *causes* me to have a feeling of liking for zucchini," this is a statement concerning cognition. Therefore, in this chapter I will concentrate on *cognitive* dissonance without reference to the potentially confusing element of "evaluation."

SOME TRADITIONAL DISSONANCE PARADIGMS

In a few pages I will take up a formal representation of cognitive dissonance theory and its implications for changes in attitudes. This formal model will then be applied to the phenomenon that was seen earlier in the *Prophecy* book. However, before I do this, I want to present some early laboratory studies that were designed to test and elaborate the theory. Knowledge of the procedures and results of selected studies will help make the theory's elements clearer. These studies each represent a particular dissonance "paradigm." That is, cognitive dissonance could presumably be produced by any number of real-life circumstances, and the paradigms represent laboratory analogs of those situations.

The Festinger–Carlsmith counterattitudinal behavior study. What if someone had an attitude toward something but then acted in a way that was contrary to that attitude? He or she would then be faced with the cognitions concerning the original attitude and the contrary behavior. Would cognitive dissonance result from this COUNTERATTITUDINAL BEHAVIOR, and if so, what would happen to the cognitions involved? Festinger and Carlsmith (1959) conducted an experiment to answer these questions. In general, they structured the situation so that they could be fairly sure that subjects would have a *negative* attitude toward certain events in the laboratory and then induced (tricked) those subjects into praising those same events. The experimenters managed this induction in a way that made it appear to at least certain subjects that they had pretty much volunteered to praise the disliked thing. Following this manipulation, subjects' attitudes toward this attitudinal entity were assessed.

Individual subjects (male college students) were told that the experiment had to do with "measures of performance." Actually, the task would bore anyone to tears. Twelve spools had to be repeatedly placed on a tray, dumped out, and so on, for a full half-hour. This boring activity was followed by a second tedious half-hour-long task involving turning pegs in a pegboard. When the tasks were completed, each subject was further told that the purpose of the experiment was to compare the behavioral effects of a preexperimental introduction or briefing about the tasks with the effect of no introduction to the tasks. A subject was reminded that he had been in the condition where no introduction had been provided (all subjects were told this). At this point, a subject in the control condition—no counterattitudinal behavior—was ostensibly dismissed from the

study and was sent to an office that housed a departmental representative who wanted to get his reaction to whatever experiment he had
just been in. The representative was made to appear to be independent of the "measures-of-performance" experiment, so that subjects
would be honest in their evaluation of their experiences.

Subjects in the remaining two conditions also showed up at the
representative's office eventually, but they had an intervening experience along the way. A person in one of these conditions was told
that the next subject was scheduled to be briefed but that the assistant that was regularly responsible for this activity was not currently
available. The experimenter then asked the subject if he would stick
around and brief the next person. The subject would be required to
tell the next person that *his own* reaction to the experiment was
along these lines: "It was enjoyable, I had a lot of fun, I enjoyed
myself, it was very interesting, it was intriguing, [and] it was exciting." Surely, it is plausible that these statements (behavior) went
against the subjects' true attitudes toward the miserable tasks. In a
sense, these subjects were asked to tell a lie about the experiment.
However, what distinguished the two experimental conditions in the
study was that some of the subjects were told that they would receive
only $1.00 in payment for dissembling; the others were told that
they would receive $20.00 for their equivalent services. Having
learned of their duties and payoffs, each subject was given an apparent choice in the matter and was asked, "Do you think you could do
that for us?"

Most subjects agreed and actually briefed the next subject (a
confederate of the experimenter), then reported to the departmental
representative who asked them to give their evaluation of their experimental participation (the presumably boring tasks). Two items in
the departmental questionnaire are of interest here.

1. Were the tasks interesting and enjoyable?
2. Would you have any desire to participate in another similar experiment?

Subjects answered these questions by using bipolar scales that ranged
from −5 (no) to +5 (yes), as had the control subjects. So, which sort
of subject had the best or most positive attitude toward the spool
and peg tasks by the time they responded to the representative's
questionnaire? Was it the subjects in the control group who had not
engaged in counterattitudinal behavior or the subjects that did so
and received either $1.00 or $20.00 for their efforts? The answer to
this question can be found in Table I, where reactions of the control

TABLE I

Subjects' evaluation of their research participation as a function of experimental condition

Questionnaire item	Control group	COUNTERATTITUDINAL GROUPS	
		$20.00	$1.00
Tasks enjoyable?	−0.45	−0.05	+1.35
Participate again?	−0.62	−0.25	+1.20

After Festinger and Carlsmith (1959).

Note. Values are from scales that ranged from −5 (no) to +5 (yes).

group represent our best estimate of persons' reactions to the boring tasks, everything else equal.

Indeed, the negative numbers in the control group column indicate that these subjects did not find the tasks particularly enjoyable, nor were they especially inclined to participate again. A similar pattern is in evidence for the $20.00 group, and a statistical analysis showed that this group and the control group did not reliably differ. Conversely, subjects in the $1.00 condition showed a very different pattern and actually indicated a positive attitude toward the tasks. Shortly, we will see how dissonance theory accounts for this outcome.

The Aronson–Mills severity-of-initiation study. Many organizations treat new members to a rather rude welcome. Traditionally, induction into the military or into societies such as college fraternities involves a good deal of harassment or hazing of the inductee. What might be the consequences of a severe initiation? How would a person react to such rough treatment? Would he or she feel resentment toward the group or would that person's attitude be otherwise?

Aronson and Mills (1959) examined the consequences of SEVERITY OF INITIATION on women's evaluations of a group they had recently joined. The subjects were to participate in alleged group discussions on the psychology of sex. As a basis for varying the severity of initiation into the group, the experimenter told the subject that potential participants had to be screened. That is, the subject was told by the male experimenter that she would be required to pass an "embarrassment" test. For women in the control condition, simply agreeing to take such a test was sufficient, but more was required in two kinds of initiation conditions. In a mild condition, women had to read aloud from a list of words that were related to sex, yet were not obscene (e.g., *prostitute, virgin, petting*). In a severe condition, subjects had to say obscene words (e.g., *fuck, cock, screw*). Presumably, saying vulgar words in the presence of a male experimenter would be stressful to typical undergraduate women.

Following the variations in initiation, the women were introduced to their group and were given an opportunity to evaluate that group. They were told that they would neither participate directly during their first exposure nor would they actually see the group members. Rather, they would listen to the group's discussion on that day via earphones. This procedure was carried out so that the researchers could be sure that women in all three conditions heard exactly the same discussion, which, as a matter of fact, was a tape recording.

The taped discussion of sex was purposely scripted to be banal and boring. It was filled with contradictions and non sequiturs and the quality of the speaking was poor. When the discussion was over, the subjects were asked to rate both the group and its discussion. Several scales were used and subjects' evaluations were expressed as the sum of their ratings, where larger values represent more positive attitudes. When the data were analyzed, it was clear that attitudes were related to the kind of initiation a woman received. The average scores were 166.7, 171.1, and 195.3 for the control, mild, and severe conditions, respectively. That is, the more difficult the initiation into the group, the more likely the women were to have a positive attitude toward the group.

A FORMAL REPRESENTATION OF COGNITIVE DISSONANCE THEORY

We have seen some seemingly odd outcomes in the foregoing examples. In the *Prophecy* book the apparent smashing of a belief led to renewed efforts to gain converts to that belief; in the Festinger–Carlsmith study subjects who were paid the least to lie had the greatest change in sentiment, and in the Aronson–Mills research the subjects who had the toughest time getting into the group liked the group best. Does any of this make sense? According to Festinger's cognitive dissonance theory, it does.

All of the behavioral phenomena discussed thus far in this chapter can be visualized in a model or flowchart that terminates in some form of cognitive adjustment or attitude change (see Figure 1). The first element in the model is represented by the dissonance paradigms, or whatever circumstances are sufficient for evoking dissonance between cognitions. The second element is a quasi-mathematical expression that allows us to specify the presence or absence of dissonance and to some extent the intensity of the dissonance.

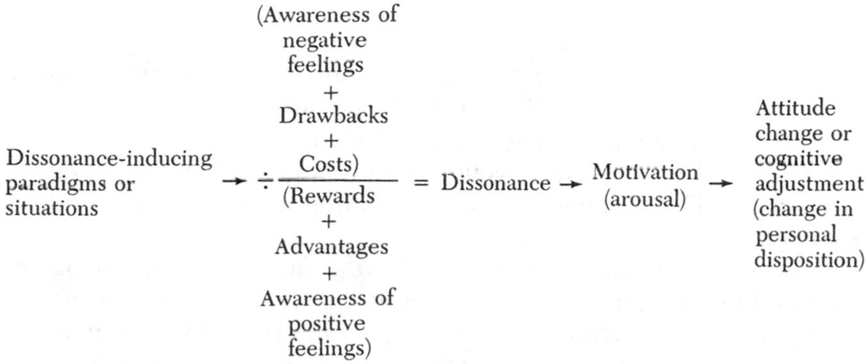

Dissonance-inducing paradigms or situations → ÷ $\dfrac{\text{(Awareness of negative feelings + Drawbacks + Costs)}}{\text{(Rewards + Advantages + Awareness of positive feelings)}}$ = Dissonance → Motivation (arousal) → Attitude change or cognitive adjustment (change in personal disposition)

FIGURE 1
MODEL FOR ATTITUDE CHANGE or adjustment (or change in personal disposition) as a function of cognitive dissonance. (After Festinger, 1959.)

This second element (or fraction, or ratio) requires elaboration, which will be presented shortly. Next, as the model indicates, should dissonance exist, it will lead to a condition of motivation—Festinger's point on the "psychologically uncomfortable" state—which in turn will lead to some form of attitude or cognitive change that will serve to reduce the dissonance.

The computation of dissonance. One way to symbolize the mechanics of cognitive dissonance is to represent a person's thinking about an attitudinal object as a metaphorical fraction. By convention, we assign all the bad or undesirable things about the object to the numerator and all the good or desirable things about the object to the denominator. Basically, the formula for the computation of dissonance is BAD/GOOD = DISSONANCE (or BAD divided by GOOD = DISSONANCE). Now, by assigning numerical values to these good and bad entries, it is a simple matter to calculate the theoretical amount of dissonance our hypothetical person will experience at any given moment.

To take an example, suppose you had an attitude toward "X," and whereas there were 10 good characteristics that were associated with "X," there were 0 (zero) bad things connected with "X." The computation would be 0/10, which is equal to 0. In this circumstance there would be no dissonance and no pressure for attitude or cognitive change. On the other hand, if for some other entity "Y" there were three bad features and only one good feature, the computation would be 3/1, which would indicate 3 units of dissonance and presumably considerable pressure for cognitive or attitude change. Could one ever find oneself in a situation where the computation could approach something like the 3/1 value? Unfortunately, one is often likely to find oneself in such straits. Imagine you took a job because you liked the money (1 good thing), but then discovered that you disliked the hours, your duties, and your fellow workers (3 bad things). This is a commonplace situation, and dissonance would occur.

How could one reduce dissonance in this job example? Obviously, the numbers chosen for the preceding examples are somewhat arbitrary, and the statement concerning "units" of dissonance is more of a convenience than a meaningful estimate. Still, it can be seen that the ideal state is where dissonance is equal to 0. Theoretically, this is so because of Festinger's (1957) argument that dissonance is psychologically uncomfortable. To borrow a phrase from algebra, the individual would want to "set his dissonance to zero" (or as close to 0 as possible) to rid himself of the psychological discomfort. There are two ways to modify a mathematical fraction to get it to approach the value of 0 or at least to reduce its magnitude. One can either increase the value of the denominator or decrease the value of the numerator (or both). Psychologically speaking, these are also two ways to reduce dissonance. One can either increase the good things associated with an object (entries in the denominator) or decrease the bad things associated with an object (entries in the numerator).

The failure of prophecy and dissonance theory. To apply the above formulation, consider the thoughts of Dr. Armstrong about the prophecy at the moment he became convinced that there would be neither flying saucers nor flooding on that December morning. In terms of the numerator of the hypothetical dissonance fraction in Figure 1, he certainly would be aware that the failure had caused him negative feelings, there would be drawbacks aplenty in terms of the social pressure *against* his belief that stemmed from his critics, and his belief had already cost him his job. On the other hand, in terms of the denominator of the scheme, an advantage was the social pressure (support) for his belief that came from his fellow-believers, there were potential rewards (rescue and salvation), and there was also his awareness that his belief had caused positive feelings stemming from involvement in a monumental enterprise.

We can only speculate that, given the gloom that attended the disconfirmation, it seems reasonable that Dr. Armstrong and the other members of his circle were in a state of cognitive dissonance. That is, the bad things associated with the belief (the numerator) outweighed the good things (denominator), at least for the moment. What could someone in their position do? Let us consider tinkering with the metaphorical fraction in Dr. Armstrong's mind to reduce the fraction's (ratio's) magnitude and rid him of some or all dissonance. First, he could not ignore the absence of the flood, because it was painfully obvious that it had failed to materialize. Second, he could not dismiss or diminish the impact of his critics, for their criticisms were not under his control. Third, he could not ignore the costs involved, because he was still out of a job.

Well, if the entries in the metaphorical numerator are impervious to change, then let us see whether we can meddle with the denominator. It probably was not feasible for him to exaggerate his awareness or expectations about positive feelings about the enterprise as a whole, because it was by no means clear whether they were still in business. Similarly, he could not point to the prospect of rescue and salvation, because their most recent hope of deliverance had proved empty. Finally, there remained the possibility of enlarging the circle of fellow-believers. This would increase the amount of social support available to the veteran members of the group and would offset the disappointment, embarrassment, and hardships that went along with holding the belief. This was the road taken by Dr. Armstrong and the others in an attempt to reduce their cognitive dissonance. The burst of proselytizing was an effort to gain converts to compensate for all the new problems associated with the disconfirmation.

Counterattitudinal behavior, severity of initiation, and dissonance. The same kind of analysis can be applied to the subjects' reactions to the $1.00 and $20.00 manipulations in the Festinger–Carlsmith study. Which of the subjects in those conditions would have experienced the most dissonance? Probably all those people had a negative reaction to the boring tasks, yet they found themselves praising the merits of those activities. We can assign more or less arbitrary values to the metaphorical fraction (Figure 1) to allow us to estimate the extent of dissonance. First, in the numerator we can assign an equal amount of awareness of the originally negative feelings to both groups, say 10 units worth. Second, we can imagine that there were few or no drawbacks or costs for engaging in the counterattitudinal behavior, so each group will receive 0 for those entries.

In the denominator, it might be reasonable to guess that neither group originally held many positive feelings toward the task, so those entries will also be 0.

To this point the two groups are equivalent. However, when we consider the amount of reward each group got for engaging in the counterattitudinal behavior, the picture changes. If we enter a value of a reward of 1 for the $1.00 group and a value of 20 for the $20.00 group and then compute the value of the fractions, we see that the estimation of dissonance (in this exercise) for the $1.00 group will be 10.00, whereas for the $20.00 group it will be 0.50. Because the $20.00 group presumably experienced relatively little dissonance (= 0.50) as a consequence of their behavior, there was little need for them to adjust their attitudes or cognitions about the tasks. On the contrary, the $1.00 subjects probably experienced considerable dissonance. But what cognitions could they modify to rid themselves of this annoying condition? The one thing they could not possibly change was the value of their $1.00 payment. Rather, they seemed to have either reduced their awareness of their negative feelings or increased—fabricated—their awareness of positive feelings (or both), a process that would result in a net change in attitude toward the tasks as seen in Table I.

The same form of analysis can be applied to the reactions of the women in the Aronson–Mills initiation study. In particular, the women in the severe condition had paid a relatively high price to join the group, so there doubtless was a large value in the cost entry of the metaphorical fraction that represented their thinking. A way to reduce the resulting dissonance would be to offset that cost by increasing one's valuation of the group, which presumably accounts for the finding that the women in the severe-initiation condition had the most positive attitudes, eventually. In this case, as in the case of the size of reward for the $1.00 subjects in the Festinger–Carlsmith study, it was probably best to change the attitude by manipulating some of the cost or reward cognitions in the metaphorical fraction.

REFINEMENTS IN DISSONANCE THEORY

The basic dissonance theory has undergone some refinements since 1957. By and large these changes amount to additions to the original scheme depicted in my fashion in Figure 1. The first such revision was the claim that COMMITMENT, choice, or volition were essential to the generation of dissonance. That is, dissonance would be produced only if a person felt responsible for her or his behavior or felt bound by certain cognitions (Brehm and Cohen, 1962). A second revision was an argument that, in the case of counterattitudinal or insincere behavior, the presence or absence of CONSEQUENCES of that behavior determined whether dissonance would be produced. That is, dissonance would not occur unless there were serious implications stemming from the behavior (Cooper and Worchel, 1970).

Bad/good × *commitment* × *consequences.* Further, Calder, Ross, and Insko (1973) went on to speculate that the variables of commitment and consequences were each insufficient to produce dissonance in isolation from each other. In other words, these two variables would "interact." This revised formulation begins with the familiar metaphorical fraction and is completed by the commitment and consequences factors:

$$\text{bad/good} \times \text{commitment} \times \text{consequences} = \text{dissonance}$$

In this form, dissonance theory becomes a MULTIPLICATIVE MODEL, and the amount of intensity of cognitive dissonance is seen as the product of the three terms in the model. Thus, if any of the individual terms is equal to 0, then the product (dissonance) is also zero. It follows that in the absence of either commitment or consequences there is no dissonance.

Calder et al. (1973) tested this multiplicative model in an experiment. They manipulated subjects' cognitions by using the procedure of the familiar Festinger and Carlsmith (1959) study wherein subjects engaged in a boring task and then, during briefing, told other people that the task was actually interesting. The researchers varied commitment by telling some of the subjects that the briefing of (lying to) the next subject was a standard part of the experimental routine and that they were obliged to do it. Other subjects were permitted to choose to do the briefing. Finally, consequences were varied by having the next subject (a confederate) either decline to participate in the study (no consequence) or seem to be persuaded to participate instead of using the time to prepare for an exam (consequence).

The results of this study were represented as changes in attitude toward the task and were in line with the predictions of the multiplicative model. According to Calder et al. (1973), the results indicated that for dissonance to occur, a chosen, insincere behavior (telling a waiting subject that a dull task was interesting) must have aversive consequences, such as the loss of study time. Given aversive consequences, a cognitive dissonance effect occurred only in the case where the subject had a choice whether to perform the insincere behavior.

Internal states and behavior. For Festinger and other theorists, dissonance can lead to an internal state of attitude change, and, as we know from Chapters 3 and 4, attitudes can lead to behavior. In theory, then, it ought to be possible to detect both behavioral (external) and attitudinal (internal) consequences of dissonance, and these should pretty much match. However, in practice this has not always been the case.

As it happens, there are a number of studies in which this internal–external match was not found. To take one instance, Weick and Penner (1969) extended the literature on the severity of initiation into a group. As a first step, subjects were placed in a *competitive* situation with two confederates; the stooges ganged up on the individual subject and caused him to lose on all trials in this phase. Next, dissonance was induced in half the subjects by giving them a choice whether to continue with the two stooges on a *cooperative* task. Dissonance theory would predict higher liking for the group by those in the choice condition than by the control subjects who were forced to continue on the cooperative task. Indeed, the cooperative-task performance of the choice subjects seemed to follow from this prediction: they worked faster and were more accurate than were the no-choice subjects. However, when attitudes toward the respective groups were measured after this second task, there were no differences in liking across the choice and no-choice conditions! Behavioral (external) and attitudinal (internal) measures did not match.

Results such as these caused perplexity for some reviewers (e.g., Nisbett and Wilson, 1977), but a solution to the apparent mismatch across internal and external standards was offered by Quattrone (1985). He pointed out that the opportunity to behave *after* a dissonance manipulation but *before* a measurement of attitude could have consequences for that attitude. The phrase he used was "internal states erased by behavior." An experiment by Mansson (1969) serves to illustrate Quattrone's point. Two groups of dissonance (low-justification) subjects were placed in high and low conditions by their commitment to abstain from drinking water for either 24 or 4 hours. Those in the 24-hour group should have experienced the most dissonance, and Mansson found that they did. Following the dissonance manipulation, three measures were taken in quick succession: (1) a measure of thirst (internal) immediately after the subjects' commitment, (2) an opportunity for an actual drink of water (external), and (3) another measure of thirst (internal) after the drink of water. The results of the first two of Mansson's (1969) measures supported dissonance theory. Subjects in the 24-hour group reported themselves less thirsty and actually drank less water than those in the 4-hour group. Presumably, they made themselves feel less thirsty as a way to reduce the dissonance from having agreed to go without water for so long, and their actual consumption was mediated by this impression of thirst. However, at step 3, the second thirst measure, there was *no* difference between the two groups on reported thirst. And when you think about it, why should there be any difference on this second thirst measure? If I do not think I am very thirsty (for whatever reason), why should I drink very much water? I will drink only as much water as is necessary to slake my thirst. And when I am finished drinking, I will no longer experience any thirst.

All of this sounds very straightforward, of course, but it illustrates Quattrone's (1985) position in a convincing way. Notice, he points out, that if we considered only measures 1 and 2 in Mansson's research we would come away convinced that dissonance produces matching internal and external dependent variables. However, if we considered only measures 2 and 3, we would reach the very different conclusion that external and internal measures mismatch. But the troublesome mismatch is perfectly understandable in light of the idea that "internal state effects [can be] erased by behavior." The reason that Mansson's internal measures 1 and 3 are not the same is that measure 3 was mediated by measure 2, the external measure. Subjects in the low (4-hour) or high (24-hour) dissonance conditions had different subjective thresholds for the satisfaction of their respective thirst levels, and by drinking more or less water they reached those thresholds. In other words, the very behavior involved in measure 2 made it impossible that there would be group differences on measure 3. Why would anybody be thirsty anymore?

By extension, this type of analysis can also be applied to the study by Weick and Penner (1969) cited earlier. I speculate that subjects who chose to continue to work with the nasty confederates probably experienced dissonance over their choice. But because they had a chance to behave right away, they worked hard and accurately to gain the advantages and rewards (see Figure 1) associated with success. If advantages and rewards balanced out their negative cognitions about the confederates, there was no need to change their minds about how nasty those people were. If there had *not* been an opportunity to behave in this manner, then attitude change toward the confederates might well have occurred.

The message here for dissonance theorists and researchers is this: by all accounts dissonance, attitude, and behavior are bound up in a kind of dynamic package. If some *measurement* procedure (such as step 2 in the Mansson study) can have an impact on that package, we would do well to understand this implication and treat measurement with care in the future.

A Middle: Competing Hypotheses and Alternative Explanations

Over the years dissonance theory and research attracted many adherents because it seemed to apply to a wide variety of situations involving attitudes and it made predictions that were unavailable from other theories. This popularity notwithstanding, in 1967 Daryl Bem, a psychologist, launched an impressive attack on dissonance theory as a useful conceptual tool. Bem's attack was based on another important development in social psychology that occurred at about the same time. A number of theorists and researchers were tackling the problem of how people come to draw inferences from the behavior of other persons. This line of work came to be known as ATTRIBUTION THEORY. Bem argued that something like attribution theory could (and should) completely supplant dissonance theory.

THEORY OF ATTRIBUTION

The things people do and say are important in our everyday lives. However, sometimes it is not the behavior itself that really matters but the motivation that prompted the act. For example, suppose you learn that Mr. X shot Mr. Y. On the basis of this act, try to estimate Mr. X's feelings about Mr. Y. It would be very helpful, of course, to know the circumstances surrounding the shooting. If the event occurred in a wilderness area during a hunting season, you might not impute malice to Mr. X. On the other hand, if the event occurred in a friendly neighborhood tavern, then it is fairly certain that Mr. X intended to do Mr. Y some harm. But how, in general, do we reach such inferences from behavior? What rules do we use?

From another perspective, when we turn on a television set, it is common to encounter celebrities, such as star athletes, who are trying to sell us all manner of things. The celebrity usually endorses or praises the product or otherwise indicates that he or she favors its use. Are we therefore expected to believe that this person really prefers a particular brand of chewing gum, automobile, beer, or breakfast cereal? By what logical or psychological steps do people come to a decision about the motivation underlying an act such as an endorsement, or any other claim about opinions or attitudes?

Conceptually, there are two sets of pressures that account for why anybody does anything. Behavior is governed by either internal or external factors. The internal factors could be feelings, desires, dispositions, or any type of attitudes, whereas the external factors could be environmental demands, laws, societal norms or expectations, or any type of coercions. In our social lives it is often very important to determine whether a particular act is under the control of internal or external factors. Several theoretical models have been developed to suggest how we arrive at these determinations. Here we will take up one of these, a theory put forth by Kelly G. Shaver.

Shaver's three-stage model. When we see someone behave in a certain manner, we ask questions at particular stages in a particular sequence until we can, or cannot, arrive at an attribution to a personal disposition to commit the act (Shaver, 1975). By using the example of a celebrity who has endorsed a product, we can see how Shaver's model of this process works (see Figure 2).

Stage 1 asks whether the behavior was observed. This stage may seem trivial, but if we have not observed (or learned of) the act, then we have nothing to analyze. In this example the answer to the Stage 1 question is yes, because we heard the celebrity make the endorsement. Note that in the flowchart in Figure 2, a "yes" answer at Stage 1 allows us to proceed to Stage 2, which asks whether the act was intended. Did the celebrity appear to know what is going

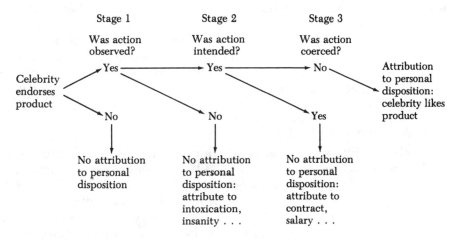

FIGURE 2
THREE-STAGE ATTRIBUTION MODEL of imputing an act to a personal disposition. (After Shaver, 1975.)

on? Did he look lucid and in control of himself, or did he seem drugged, intoxicated, or deranged? Because our imaginary celebrity seemed to be in good shape, the answer to the Stage 2 question is yes, the act appeared to be intended.

Stage 3 asks, Was the act coerced? There did not appear to be a gun pointed at the celebrity's head, but physical threat is not the only form of coercion. Clearly, the need for a paycheck can get us to do all sorts of undesirable things that we might not do voluntarily. We know that celebrities command huge salaries for their endorsements, and because we are watching a commercial advertisement, it seems likely that payment is involved. Because the answer to the Stage 3 question is yes, that coercion in the form of salary is probably involved, we have gone as far as we can in the model; in this case we cannot attribute the celebrity's acts exclusively to his personal dispositions. He may really like the product or he may not. Because coercion (money) is a likely external cause of his behavior, we cannot make a confident estimate of his own internal feelings.

Let us consider a related example to see when the model would permit the attribution of an act to a disposition. Suppose that you are sitting on a bus and overhear a conversation between two people sitting in front of you. They are obviously friends and they are discussing home appliances. One person remarks that Brand-X is the best personal computer she has ever encountered. What could you infer about her feelings toward the Brand-X machine? Shaver's model would predict that you would judge that she really admires the Brand-X computer because her act of endorsement was observed, intended, and not obviously coerced by rewards or threats of punishments. In other words, our tendency to attribute acts to dispositions depends on the *circumstances* in which the acts occur. In order to make an attribution to a disposition in an actor, the observer has to be able to rule out external or situational forces on the behavior.

RESEARCH ON ATTRIBUTION

In this middle section on competing hypotheses and alternative explanations the aim is, as it is in similar sections elsewhere in the book, to trace history-of-science developments. There is something to be gained from studying controversies in the context of the era in which they occurred. As noted, it was in 1967 that Bem proposed an alternative explanation for some of the so-called dissonance phenomena. Bem could only argue from what was known or thought about attributions by then, and his supporters or critics could do no better. Therefore, in reviewing selected research on attribution I will limit consideration to material and ideas of that era. Since then, of course, a great deal of research and theoretical work on attribution and social cognition has been done, and the interested reader is referred to the texts, collections, or reviews of Fiske and Taylor (1984); Harvey, Ickes, and Kidd (1976–1981); Harvey and Weary (1981); and Ross and Fletcher (1985).

EARLY RESEARCH ON ATTRIBUTION

Attributions and role demands. One of the things that has a tremendous potential for exerting external demands on your behavior is the job you hold. For example, if you heard the nation's vice president praise the policies of the chief executive, you could not tell how he (or she) actually felt about those policies, because it is part of that job to promote and support the actions of the administration. On the contrary, if the vice president publicly condemned the president's actions, you could be very sure of his feelings toward his superior's policies, because he had said critical things despite the pressure of the job to act in some other fashion.

Are attributions to dispositions influenced when an actor conforms to job or role demands or when an actor violates those demands? Jones, Davis, and Gergen (1961) conducted an experiment in which the dispositions in question were how the actor felt about being around people in general. Two tape recordings were prepared in which the actor was allegedly replying to an interviewer's queries. On one tape, the actor's replies made it appear that he was a very outgoing, socially oriented person. This behavior was labeled "other-directed," and examples of these responses follow.

- "I always like to support the majority."
- "I would like to be a door-to-door salesman."
- "I like to know how other people think I should behave."
- "I like to settle the arguments and the disputes of others."

For the second tape, the same actor was made to appear to be quite a loner, and he said "inner-directed" things.

- "I like to feel free to do what I want to do."
- "I would like to be a forest ranger."
- "I avoid situations where I am expected to behave in a conventional way."
- "I like to attack points of view that are contrary to my own."

The question posed by Jones et al. (1961) was whether subjects would believe the claims made on the two tapes concerning the actor's real degree of sociability. That is, would observers attribute the acts (replies) they heard to the actor's personal dispositions or to something else, such as role or job demands placed on the actor? The subjects were told that the actor was being interviewed because he had applied for special training as either a submariner or an astronaut. The reader will recognize that the rigorous demands of either job would probably call for candidates with very different personalities or dispositions. In a submarine, many people are in close confinement for long periods of time. Contrarily, in 1961 astronauts were being orbited in one-man spacecraft that put them literally out of touch with humanity. It would be reasonable to assume that the candidate would also be aware that certain jobs would demand certain dispositions or personalities and these are the role demands in the situation.

To see how the implicit job requirements might influence people's attributions, different subjects were assigned to one of four experimental groupings: astro-other, astro-inner, sub-other, and sub-inner. In the first condition subjects heard the other-directed replies given by a candidate for astronaut training, whereas in the second condition they heard inner-directed replies given by an astronaut candidate. The remaining two conditions were similar, except that subjects thought they were listening to the replies of an applicant to submarine school. After they heard the tape, the subjects were asked to rate the actor on the dimensions of affiliation and conformity, where higher scale values represented estimates of greater sociability.

The results of the procedure are shown in Table II. Crucial comparisons are between the astro-other and sub-other groups and between the astro-inner and sub-inner conditions. Subjects rated the other-directed person differently, depending on whether they thought he was applying for an astronaut or a submariner position. The same holds for the inner-directed person. The most extreme sociability ratings were given to interviewees that acted in a fashion that was inconsistent with or violated the role demands of the job.

In terms of Shaver's model, we can see why the sub-other tape did not get higher sociability rating and why the astro-inner tape did not get lower ratings. Presumably, when people reached Stage 3 in the attribution process for these particular tapes they were inclined to think that the interviewee's replies (actions) were coerced by the demands of the situation. A "yes" answer to the Stage 3 question

TABLE II
Subjects' ratings of the sociability of job applicants as a function of the applicants'
statements and the nature of the job

Sociability dimension	EXPERIMENTAL CONDITION			
	Astro-other	Sub-other	Astro-inner	Sub-inner
Affiliation	15.27	12.00	11.12	8.64
Conformity	15.91	12.58	13.09	9.41

After Jones et al. (1961).
Note. Impressions of affiliation and conformity were obtained using two different 10-point scales for each dimension. Apparently, the values are the summed averages from the two respective scales.

(see Figure 2) means that the observers could not confidently attribute the actor's actions to his personal dispositions and hence the moderate rating for these conditions where the behavior conformed to role demands.

Attributions and choice. In the example of the celebrity endorsement, mention was made of holding a gun at someone's head to induce that person to do something. In that case coercion would be obvious, and the model predicts that no attribution to personal disposition would be made. On the other hand, if it were clear that the actor chose his or her actions, internal attributions would be possible. To demonstrate these effects, Jones and Harris (1967) had subjects read essays that were either pro-(Fidel) Castro or anti-Castro in tone. Some of the subjects were told that the writer (purported to be a student) had been *instructed* to write a pro or con paper; other subjects were given the information that the writer had the *option* to do either a pro or con essay.

Having read one of the essays, the subjects were asked to estimate the writer's true feelings about Castro. The findings were clear. Subjects gave the most extreme ratings of true feelings to essay writers who had a choice and much less extreme ratings to writers who had none. Like the subjects in the Jones et al. job-requirement study, the observers in this experiment apparently could not be confident about the sentiments of an actor where coercion—here in the form of an instruction to write a particular kind of essay—could account for the behavior. (For an interesting study on attributions about the *self*, see Storms and Nisbett, 1970.)

An Attack on Dissonance Theory: Dissonance or Self-Perception?

It seems to be established that we use rules to decide whether to attribute some other person's behavior to external causes or to internal dispositions. But what about our awareness of our own dispositions? For Bem (1967), the process by which we infer the dispositions of others and the process by which we are aware of our own dispositions are similar processes. That is, the steps through which an observer can arrive at the attitudes of an actor are functionally equivalent to the steps a person would use in evaluating her or his own attitudes. This is true because (in Bem's view) the self is just a special case where the observer and actor reside in the same skin. For example, I (the writer) could observe my own behavior in the same way that you (the reader) could observe my behavior. Then we both could use something like Shaver's three-stage attribution model to decide what my true attitude or disposition was, or whether to attribute my act to external forces. In Bem's words,

the present analysis of dissonance phenomena, then, will rest upon the single empirical generalization that an individual's belief and attitude statements and the beliefs and attitudes that an outside observer would attribute to him are often functionally similar in that both sets of statements are partial "inferences" from the same evidence: the public behaviors and accompanying cues.

(It should be pointed out that the terminology employed in Bem's (1967) paper was not derived strictly from attribution theory but rather was associated with the radical behaviorism of Skinner (1957). Nevertheless, the two terminologies are compatible on these issues.)

Interpersonal replications. If someone inquired whether or not you like brown bread, your answer might be, "I guess so, I eat it all the time." Then if someone asked your housemate whether you like brown bread, she (or he) might respond, "I guess so, he (or she) eats it all the time." In both cases an inference about your feelings about brown bread could be drawn from your overt behavior (Bem, 1967). Now let us extend this kind of attributional analysis to a representative dissonance experiment, such as the counterattitudinal study by Festinger and Carlsmith (1959). If, after he has briefed the next subject, we ask someone in the $20.00 condition whether he really enjoyed the task, he might reflect thusly: "I did say I liked the task, but I may have been coerced by the large reward for making the statement, so I am not confident that the statement reflects my true feelings about the task." On the other hand, if we ask the same question of someone in the $1.00 group, he might reply: "I did say I like the task, and there was not much coercion to do so, so I guess I really do like the task." Thus, in both hypothetical cases the subjects have drawn inferences about their own dispositions in the same way an observer would infer their dispositions.

But the question remains whether observers can conclude that someone who received $1.00 for endorsing the Festinger–Carlsmith task really did like the task, so Bem conducted an interpersonal replication of that 1959 study using fresh subjects. In other words, the new subjects did not directly experience the conditions of the research but only heard descriptions of the procedures via tape recordings. The boring task was described and two different groups of subjects heard an enactment of a "briefing" either under the $1.00 condition or under the $20.00 condition. A third group of replication subjects heard a description of the control procedure. After listening to the tapes, the new subjects were asked to estimate how the actor on the tape actually felt about the task. In a sense, they were requested to make an attribution of the act of praising the task to a personal disposition (attitude) or to some external factor (money).

The interpersonal replication subjects' estimates are shown in Table III, where we can find the answer to the question of whether the tasks were enjoyable. The original data from the Festinger–Carlsmith study are also presented in Table III for comparison. It can be seen in the table that although the original results were not precisely duplicated, the same general relationships between conditions did emerge in Bem's replication study. Replication subjects gave estimates of the most positive attitudes for actors in the $1.00 condition and estimates of negative attitudes for the $20.00 and control groups.

TABLE III
Results of the original Festinger–Carlsmith (1959) study and Bem's (1967) interpersonal replication of subjects' evaluation of research participation

Item: tasks enjoyable?	Control group	COUNTERATTITUDINAL GROUPS	
		$20.00	$1.00
Original study	−0.45	−0.05	+1.35
Interpersonal replication	−1.56	−1.96	+0.52

After Festinger and Carlsmith (1959); Bem (1967).

Dissonance and motivation? This success, and others, at interpersonal replications of so-called dissonance phenomena put Bem in
a position to make very telling arguments against a central tenet of
dissonance theory. Recall that Festinger's theory holds that dissonance produces an unpleasant motivational state and that a person
changes her or his cognitions in order to reduce dissonance and thus
alleviate the concomitant distress. Bem wondered, rhetorically, why
it was necessary to posit this motivational state at all. If observers
could reasonably estimate an actor's dispositions without themselves
experiencing anything like dissonance and motivation, why is it that
actors experience dissonance while estimating their own attitudes?
To put it another way, if I use an attribution process to figure out
your personal dispositions, there is no reason for me to agonize
during the process. By the same token, if I use the same mechanism
to figure out my personal dispositions, why should there be any need
for me to agonize during that particular attribution process?

Bem's point can be illustrated schematically. A casual inspection
of the dissonance model (Figure 1) and the attribution model (Figure
2) may suggest that they are very different. However, when the two
formulations are juxtaposed as they are in Figure 3, important com-
monalities emerge. These common features are identified in boxes
containing certain model components. The elements common to both
formulations are connected by broken lines.

Obviously, both models lead to an estimation of a personal disposition, so they have that feature in common. Further, the first two
stages of the current attribution model concerning the observation
and intent of an act seem to be represented in the paradigms section
of the dissonance model, in which an actor observes himself acting
and intending to act. Finally, the third stage of the attribution model
seems to find its counterpart in the quasi-mathematical fraction in
the dissonance formulation. In a real sense the question of coercion
is represented in the fraction in terms of advantages and rewards for
an act or a cognition. For example, if someone stuck a gun in your
ribs and told you that you had better say that you like brown bread,
it would be of great advantage to you to make that statement, whatever your true feelings.

Most of the features of dissonance theory are represented in one
way or another in the attribution scheme, and vice versa (and for
another treatment of parallels between the two models, see Nisbett
and Wilson, 1977). But there are two critical elements in the dissonance picture that are missing from the attribution outline: dissonance and motivation. This observation brings us directly to the heart

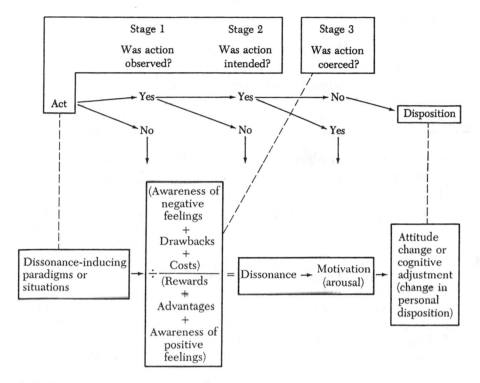

FIGURE 3
COMMON ELEMENTS BETWEEN DISSONANCE AND ATTRIBUTION
THEORIES.

of Bem's argument. Scientists strive for parsimony in their theories. Simple and elegant explanations are favored over those that are complicated and cumbersome. If attribution theory, through the self-perception analysis, can make all the predictions of dissonance theory with fewer working parts (so to speak), then dissonance theory should be discarded. On this issue Bem was not inclined to mince words:

It remains our conviction that the appeal to hypothetical internal states of the organism for causal explanations of behavior is often heuristically undesirable. Such diversion appears only to retard and deflect the thrust of the analysis that is required (Bem, 1967).

An End: Resolution of Issues and Current Standing of Ideas

This bold attack caught dissonance theorists somewhat off balance, for on one point it seemed to be correct. The motivational state that was supposed to accompany dissonance could well be viewed as "hypothetical," simply because there was little direct evidence that such a state really existed. Similarly, there was very little, if any, direct measurement of cognitive dissonance itself, because most researchers had employed some sort of attitudinal measure to indirectly reflect the dissonant state. Because the measurement of attitudes could be used to support either dissonance or attribution theory, new information was needed to distinguish between the two theories.

AROUSAL PROPERTIES OF DISSONANCE MANIPULATIONS

This heading is borrowed from the title of a scholarly review by Kiesler and Pallak (1976). Because their focus was on the issue raised by Bem, these authors used the terms "arousal" and "motivation" interchangeably. They sought information on the relationship between dissonance manipulations and physiological or psychological measures of arousal (i.e., motivation). Kiesler and Pallak identified a number of lines of evidence concerning the relationship of dissonance to motivation, two of which will be reviewed here: (1) response competition and verbal performance in task situations, and (2) physiological correlates. Almost all the material reviewed by Kiesler and Pallak relied on indirect evidence or inference. We will end this section with recent, direct evidence concerning dissonance and arousal.

Dominant and subordinate responses, arousal, and dissonance. It is a widely established fact that levels of general motivation or arousal can have an impact on patterns of verbal responses, even when the responses themselves have nothing to do with the source of the arousal (Kiesler and Pallak, 1976). To put it generally, DOMINANT RESPONSES—those with a relatively high probability of emission—become more frequent under higher levels of arousal; whereas SUBORDINATE RESPONSES—those with a relatively low probability of emission—become less frequent under higher levels of arousal (Cottrell, 1972). On the basis of this knowledge, Cottrell, Rajecki, and Smith (1974) employed a procedure that was sensitive to changes in verbal behavior attributable to changes in arousal level. This procedure, known as a PSEUDO-RECOGNITION TASK, allows for an estimate of subjects' level of motivation without their awareness.

Another advantage of the pseudo-recognition task is that a subject's dominant and subordinate responses can be developed right in the laboratory. To do this, naive subjects are given an opportunity to pronounce nonsense words, such as AFWORBU or IKTITAF, at different rates during a training session. A certain subject might be asked to pronounce IKTITAF some 25 times and AFWORBU 10 times or less. By definition, IKTITAF would be the dominant response and AFWORBU the subordinate, if only by virtue of likelihood of retrieval from memory. (But do not confuse this procedure with the mere exposure research discussed in Chapter 5.) Later, under test conditions of baseline-level arousal, the subject would be expected to voluntarily say IKTITAF a certain number of times and AFWORBU fewer times. However, under conditions of heightened arousal (motivation), the rate of emission of IKTITAF would go up and that of AFWORBU would go down.

Why would a subject bother to say these silly-sounding words at all? That is where the pseudo-recognition task comes in. The experimenter shows the subject an unintelligible blur on a screen, insists that he has displayed one of the training words, and further insists that the subject report the word, even if he or she has to guess at it. In this situation subjects are more likely to guess a dominant (high training frequency) nonsense word than some other. As suggested, an exaggerated rate of such dominant responses emerges under conditions known to produce arousal, such as incentive instructions (Zajonc and Nieuwenhuyse, 1964) and the presence of an audience (Cottrell, Wack, Sekerak, and Rittle, 1968).

Cottrell et al. (1974) used a pseudo-recognition measure to see whether cognitive dissonance would produce anything like an arousal effect. Female subjects were first run through a forced-choice dissonance paradigm and were given the choice between two desirable objects *immediately* preceding the arousal measure. Because of the choice, these subjects should have experienced dissonance, and if motivation or arousal is associated with dissonance, then the task performance should have been affected. As a control, other subjects were given a gift prior to the task; these subjects did not choose or act on their own volition and therefore should not have experienced dissonance.

Did dissonance occur, and did it produce arousal or motivation? The answer to the first part of this question is yes. When the subjects reevaluated the items later, only those who had been forced to choose showed an increase in liking for the chosen item and a decrease in liking for the rejected item, the classic dissonance effect. The answer to the second part of the question is shown in Figure 4, and that answer is also yes. The emission of dominant responses was higher in the dissonance group than in the control group. Because this finding is akin to earlier results where known sources of arousal were

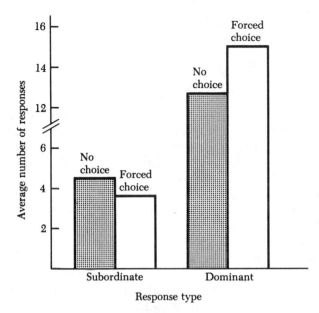

FIGURE 4
PSEUDO-RECOGNITION TASK RESPONSES indicating the arousal properties of a forced-choice dissonance manipulation. (After Cottrell et al., 1974.)

studied, we can conclude that Figure 4 presents evidence for the motivational properties or consequences of cognitive dissonance.

Physiological correlates of dissonance. Can the reduction of cognitive dissonance reduce stress as well? Because stress is a well-known influence on verbal behavior and because stress is detectable by physiological measurement—such as GALVANIC SKIN RESPONSE (GSR)—this question can be explored. Zimbardo, Cohen, Weisenberg, Dworkin, and Firestone (1969) utilized this information in a study where subjects experienced stress and were also induced to have cognitive dissonance about that stress. The source of stress was electrical shock. To assess the impact of stress per se, Zimbardo et al. tested some subjects in dissonance-free control conditions.

Subjects were required to learn lists of words by the serial anticipation method, which is roughly the way one might memorize a poem. After they had worked on a practice list in relative comfort, some subjects worked on a second list while receiving high-intensity (45-volt) shocks, and then worked on a third list while continuing to receive this high level of pain. These people were labeled the high-to-high shock subjects. We can expect noxious stimulation to interfere with verbal learning, and this is exactly what occurred. As seen in the left panel in Figure 5, under shock they needed more trials to master the material, compared with their success on the practice list. Another group of control subjects also received the 45-volt shocks on the second list, which substantially interfered with their learning (see Figure 5). However, when this second group went on to the third list, the experimenters reduced the intensity of the shock to 22 volts. This group, labeled the high-to-moderate shock subjects, showed a marked improvement in their learning when the discomfort was reduced, which would have been predicted.

Subjects in two dissonance groups also went through these steps, and it is very important to note that when shock was applied to these people it was *always* at the 45-volt level. For these latter two groups, cognitive dissonance was manipulated between the second and third lists. When they mastered the second list (see Figure 5), subjects in both dissonance conditions were informed that the experiment was over, but they were asked whether they were willing to stay and work on another list. People in the low-dissonance condition were given a great deal of justification for staying: they were told that the additional information that would be gained by this extra work was of personal importance to the experimenter, of theoretical importance

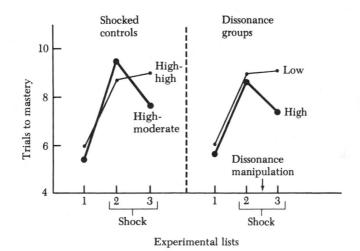

FIGURE 5
LEARNING RATE as a function of experimental conditions. (After Zimbardo et al., 1969.)

to science, of practical importance to the government's space program, and of general value to the subject. In contrast, subjects in the high-dissonance condition were told that the experimenter was merely trying out some procedures that in fact might not add very much to what had already been found. The reader will recognize the conceptual resemblance of these manipulations to the $20.00 and $1.00 conditions in the classic Festinger–Carlsmith study.

The impact of the dissonance manipulations is shown in the right panel of Figure 5. As was the case with the control subjects, the application of painful shock during the work on the second list interfered with the learning of that material. This interference carried over to the third list for the subjects in the low-dissonance group, whose general pattern of scores matched those of the high-to-high shocked controls. However, the picture is quite different for the high-dissonance condition. After dissonance was induced, the learning of these people *improved*, even though they continued to receive the 45-volt shock! The pattern of learning scores for the high-dissonance group closely resembles that of the high-to-moderate shocked controls. Like that particular group of controls, the high-dissonance subjects were able to work on the third list as if they were more comfortable than the low-dissonance group or the high-to-high shocked controls.

These data indicate that subjects who presumably experienced dissonance about their research participation also suffered less discomfort from the physical properties of that situation. Consider what might have gone on in the minds of the subjects in the high-dissonance condition: "I am in an unpleasant situation and I have little justification for being here. Perhaps the situation is not so unpleasant after all." This sounds, of course, like a rationalization, but we would call it an attempt to reduce cognitive dissonance. Still, were the high-dissonance subjects really less uncomfortable as a consequence of their cognitive adjustments?

An answer to this question is available in the physiological data from the GSR measure of Zimbardo et al. Figure 6 shows changes in GSR level from the second list to the third. Positive changes indicate increases in stress, and negative changes mean a decrease in stress. For the control groups, it is clear that the subjects in the high-to-moderate condition were more relaxed during the third list than were their high-to-high shocked counterparts. After all, the former control subjects were experiencing considerably less pain by the third list. Subjects in the high-dissonance condition, unlike the people in the low-dissonance group, also showed this pattern of

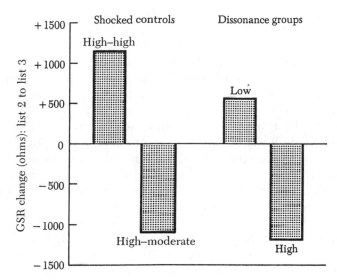

FIGURE 6
CHANGE IN GALVANIC SKIN RESPONSE (GSR) of subjects learning word lists under shock stress. (After Zimbardo et al., 1969.)

reduced stress. Therefore, Zimbardo et al. (1969) have provided both behavioral and physiological evidence that the manipulation of cognitive dissonance produces concomitant effects on motivational or arousal states. These dissonance-induced states have the capacity to materially influence related motivational systems, such as those involved in the perception and tolerance of noxious stimulation.

Manipulated arousal and the mislabeling of arousal states. It follows from Festinger's original formulation that if arousal from cognitive dissonance is motivating, then people adjust their cognitions or attitudes to reduce that specific arousal. This consideration raises two interesting and important points. First, is arousal necessary for attitude change following one or another experience within the dissonance paradigms? Second, if arousal did actually stem from certain dissonant cognitions, but was *misattributed* (labeled as stemming from some other source), would attitude change still occur? We will examine these two issues in turn.

Concerning the first issue, Cooper, Zanna, and Taves (1978) wondered whether arousal is a necessary condition for attitude change following induced compliance. The first thing to consider is the means by which these researchers *directly* manipulated their subjects' actual physiological arousal. Subjects were told that they were part of an experiment having to do with the influence of certain drugs on memory processes. The three types of drugs under study were described as being a stimulant (amphetamine), a tranquilizer (phenobarbital), and an inert placebo (milk powder). Each subject was informed that he or she was to be given the placebo, but in fact only some subjects were given the placebo; others actually received the stimulant or the tranquilizer. In sum, administration of one or another specific drug was the means by which each individual subject's arousal was manipulated, even though the subjects expected no change in arousal.

Next, dissonance was induced in the subjects. Here we will limit our attention to those persons who engaged in counterattitudinal behavior under the impression that they themselves had chosen to do so (the high-choice group in Cooper et al., 1978). While the subjects waited for the next step in the ostensible memory experiment, they were asked rather casually whether they would be willing to participate in an attitude study on a political issue. At about the time of the study, former President Nixon had received a pardon from President Ford for alleged wrongdoing in the Watergate scandal. The Nixon pardon was unpopular in many circles, as revealed by a check on the researchers' campus: an independent sample of dormitory students indicated a low average rating of the pardon at 7.9 on a 31-point scale. Assuming that their subjects also looked with disfavor on the Nixon pardon, the experimenters asked them whether they would be willing to write an essay favoring the pardon, which would amount to counterattitudinal behavior that should have led to dissonance.

Following the writing of the counterattitudinal essays, all of the experimental subjects rated the Nixon pardon on the 31-point scale, and the average ratings (along with those of the dormitory control sample) are shown in Table IV. The control group mean was 7.9; if we take that value as the population baseline against which to assess the impact of the experimental treatments, we find a noticeable effect of arousal on attitude change. The average rating of the Nixon pardon by subjects who received a tranquilizer was 8.6. Thus, tranquilized subjects whose arousal was reduced by chemical means showed virtually no attitude change when compared with baseline subjects. Conversely, the mean post-essay score of 14.7 for people in the real placebo group whose arousal had not been manipulated (limited) indicates a shift in attitude. Even more striking, for subjects in the stimulant treatment group whose arousal had been artificially in-

TABLE IV
Subjects' average ratings of the so-called Nixon pardon (from Cooper et al., 1978) and a ban on campus speakers (from Zanna and Cooper, 1974) after writing counterattitudinal essays under actual or ostensible (see text) drug conditions

Control sample	DRUG CONDITION[a]		
	Tranquilizer	Placebo	Stimulant
Cooper et al., 1978			
7.9	8.6	14.7	20.2
Zanna and Cooper, 1974			
2.3	13.4	9.1	3.4

Note. All ratings were made on a 31-point scale; the larger the entry, the more favorable the attitude.
[a]Entries are from the high-choice condition in the Cooper et al. (1978) study and from the high-decision-freedom condition in the Zanna and Cooper (1974) research.

creased, there was the highest positive attitude (mean = 20.2) compared with the other groups.

In short, the Cooper et al. (1978) results indicate that arousal *is* a necessary condition for attitude change following induced compliance, because drug-produced increases resulted in the most attitude change, and drug-induced decreases were related to the least change. This conclusion regarding the role of arousal in dissonance-related shifts in attitudes leads directly to the second question, namely, whether arousal misattributed to sources other than dissonant cognitions would lead to attitude change involving those cognitions. In other words, if one experienced cognitive dissonance and its presumed attendant arousal but mistakenly thought that the arousal stemmed from some other agent or cause, would the cognitive dissonance lead to attitude change or not?

Zanna and Cooper (1974) attempted to answer this question and used a general procedure very much like that of the Cooper et al. (1978) study. Basically, Zanna and Cooper told subjects that the true focus of their study was the effect of drugs on memory tasks. In this research, all subjects were actually given a placebo (milk powder), but were informed that the drug they had taken would have certain "side effects." Some of the subjects were led to believe that they would feel aroused, others were led to expect that they would feel relaxed, and still others were given to think that they would experience no side effects as a result of their drug. Of course, these expectations are the equivalent of the real effects of the drugs in the Cooper et al. research, but remember that the subjects in the Zanna–Cooper study did not have their levels of arousal chemically manipulated. They were only *told* such effects would occur.

For the dissonance manipulation, subjects were asked whether they would mind participating in an attitude study while they waited for the next step in the memory experiment. Here the issue was a proposed ban on inflammatory speakers on campus, a ban that was unpopular with most students as revealed by the low average rating of 2.3 (on a 31-point scale) from a nonexperimental control sample. Again, the experimental subjects were asked whether they would write a counterattitudinal essay on the issue of the ban. We will examine the attitudes of those subjects who had a choice whether to do so (the high-decision-freedom condition in Zanna and Cooper, 1974).

Following the writing of the pro-ban essays, subjects in the three bogus drug groups—alleged tranquilizer, placebo, or stimulant—provided their opinion of the ban; these means (along with that of the control group who wrote no essay) are presented in the lower panel of Table IV. Now, although the drug condition headings apply to both the upper and lower panels in Table IV, the numbers in the experimental cells hardly match in pattern. In the Zanna–Cooper study, subjects who thought they would be feeling relaxed (tranquilized) by their drug showed the most positive attitude toward the ban, whereas people who thought they would feel aroused (stimulated) gave the lowest rating. In a sense, this result is the opposite of that seen in the Cooper et al. data in the upper panel. How could the Zanna–Cooper study, so similar to that of Cooper et al., produce findings that are apparently so dissimilar?

The answer to this puzzle lies in an analysis of the subjects' experiences in the two studies. In the Cooper et al. project, people probably did or did not feel real arousal, because those states had been directly manipulated by chemical means. In the Zanna–Cooper research, on the other hand, people only expected to feel one way or another. Presumably, all did feel aroused to some extent as a result of experiencing cognitive dissonance. The issue is, to what did the various subjects attribute their sensations?

In the case of a Zanna–Cooper subject who expected no side effect (placebo condition) there was nothing to which the arousal could be attributed other than the dissonant cognitions. Accordingly, these subjects seemed to have changed their cognitions (attitudes) in order to reduce this arousal. The subjects in the Zanna–Cooper stimulant group had an opportunity to attribute their dissonance-induced arousal to their drug's alleged side effect and apparently did so. This attribution of arousal to the drug is inferred from the fact that they evidenced little attitude change. Apparently, they felt little need to change their attitudes because they did not have to view their dissonant cognitions as the source of their tension. Finally, having accounted for these attitudinal effects, we still have to interpret the high degree of attitude change on the part of the group that expected to be relaxed or tranquilized. Because they expected to feel relaxed, yet probably did feel the arousal that is said to accompany dissonance, people in this group must have felt an urgent need to reduce arousal, since it seemed that their dissonant cognitions had produced such great tension that they could overpower a tranquilizing drug. Therefore, these particular people seem to have made a great effort to reduce their arousal by engaging in a great deal of cognitive or attitude change.

Direct measurement of dissonance-based arousal. The results of all the studies seen so far in this section—Zimbardo et al., Cooper et al., and Zanna and Cooper—support the idea that dissonance is associated with increases in arousal or motivation. Unfortunately, another thing they have in common is that they only allow us to *infer* that motivation was involved. None offers a direct measurement of physiological activity at the moment of dissonance induction. Happily, such direct measurements are now available. In a recent study, Elkin and Leippe (1986) used galvanic skin response (GSR) as the index of arousal and the counterattitudinal paradigm to induce dissonance.

Elkin and Leippe took special pains to ensure that their subjects would not misattribute their dissonance-based arousal to the fact that they were wearing electrodes for the GSR measure. In their Experiment 1 many filler tasks were completed ahead of the dissonance manipulation, and stable GSR baselines were established. To produce dissonance, half the subjects were induced to write a counterattitudinal essay (about parking fees) under a high-choice condition, while the other half of the participants wrote the same sort of essay under a low-choice condition. By now the reader should be able to predict that there would be more dissonance and attitude change expected in the former subjects than in the latter subjects.

And that was precisely the outcome. Figure 7 shows the amount of attitude shift from a premeasure to a postessay measure for subjects

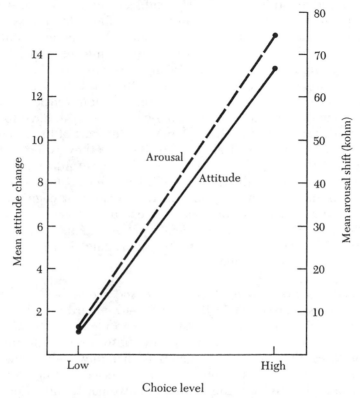

FIGURE 7
ATTITUDE CHANGE AND AROUSAL SHIFT as a consequence of cognitive
dissonance. (After Elkin and Leippe, 1986.)

in the low-choice and high-choice conditions, based on a 31-point
scale. That is, having written essays that favored increased parking
fees, subjects in the high-choice condition rated the proposition more
favorably than did the subjects in the low-choice group. Moreover,
average arousal shifts conformed to the same pattern. Figure 7 also
shows that there were substantial shifts in the high-choice group and
virtually none in the low-choice group. In fact, the overall correlation
(*r*) between attitude change and arousal shift was a strong +.73. A
second experiment by Elkin and Leippe (1986) confirmed these findings; thus there seems to be good evidence for arousal consequences
of dissonance as revealed by direct measurement.

Closing Thoughts on Dissonance and Self-Perception Theory

By way of summary of past work and a look to the future of the concept of cognitive dissonance, one would do well to reiterate the basic issues, as set down by Zanna and Cooper (1976).

Dissonance theory sees man as aroused by inconsistencies among his cognitions. As in classical arousal theories of experimental psychology . . . , man is motivated to rid himself of the drive-like, uncomfortable tension that accompanies perceived inconsistency. Attribution models, on the other hand, see man in a constant process of making sense out of his environment. In such models, man is viewed as a scientist, using attributional rules to infer causality in an otherwise chaotic world of social stimuli.

If a key issue in the contention between dissonance and attribution theorists is the matter of the motivational state produced by dissonance, then this issue can be closed for now. The review by Kiesler and Pallak (1976) indicates that respectable evidence for such a state has been accumulating from a time well before the appearance of Bem's 1967 article (e.g., Brehm and Cohen, 1962), and we have seen here that researchers continue to provide such documentation (e.g., Elkin and Leippe, 1986).

On a more conciliatory note, there are reasons to believe that both dissonance theory and attribution theory are useful in furthering our understanding of aspects of social cognition. Each has its special characteristics and each captures a different phenomenon. Fazio, Zanna, and Cooper (1977) argue that, far from being in competition, attributional and dissonance processes are complementary in providing a way to understand the influence of behavior on attitudes. In their view, dissonance theory is most appropriately applied when behavior is discrepant with a previous attitude, which of course is its traditional application. Dissonance would engender cognitive change to reduce the discrepancy in *direction* between attitude and behavior. As for attribution theory, Fazio et al. urge that it be applied to cases where the behavior in question is consistent with, but more extreme than, a previous attitude. Here, attributional processes would engender changes in self-perception that would reconcile differences in *degree* of attitude and behavior, when attitude and behavior are otherwise compatible (and see also Bem, 1972).

Even so, if dissonance theory did weather the attack from the self-perception position, that does not mean it will be forever immune to charges from other quarters. There is a controversy developing over whether dissonance is the sole or major basis for attitude change in certain of the traditional paradigms. A current conceptual contestant for such effects is "impression management." For example, in the classic Festinger–Carlsmith method involving boring tasks, a subject might feel that he looked foolish in the eyes of *others* for endorsing the inane activity. In order to maintain a credible image in the eyes of the researchers, that subject might feign a positive attitude toward the tasks. The difference here is that while dissonance involves personal (intrapsychic) variables, impression management involves public (interpsychic) factors. So far the returns are mixed as to which explanatory device is to be preferred, but at the rate research is appearing we may have an answer before long (cf. Malkis, Kalle, and Tedeschi, 1982; Paulhus, 1982; Rosenfeld, Giacalone, and Tedeschi, 1983, 1984; Stults, Messe, and Kerr, 1984; and Tetlock and Manstead, 1985).

Postscript: The End of the World (Again)

Recall that in the Festinger et al. book, *When Prophecy Fails*, a certain Dr. Armstrong and his fellow believers predicted that the world would end as the result of a flood on December 21 of a particular year, and that this conviction earned them a dose of cognitive dissonance. "Armstrong" was a pseudonym used by the authors of *Prophecy* to protect the identity of a real person, who I now have reason to believe was actually Dr. Charles Laughead, a lecturer at a college in Michigan. According to a 1983 report by an eminent British astronomer, Patrick Moore, Laughead was converted by a mystic, predicted December 21 as the date of floods and UFO visitations, and was fired from his job. The year was 1954.

Some 30 years later we might be facing the same sort of problem confronted by Armstrong (Laughead) and his group! In 1986, Richard W. Noone published a 358-page book titled *5/5/2000 Ice: The Ultimate Disaster*. The "5/5/2000" in the title refers to the fifth of May in the year 2000, and "ice" refers to his prediction that on that date certain planets (Jupiter, Mars, Mercury, Saturn, and Venus) will be "aligned" with our planet for the first time in many thousands of years. The result of this alignment, in conjunction with a buildup of ice at the South Pole, will (according to Mr. Noone) send many tons of water and ice surging across the face of our planet. Noone's sources are the Bible, Freemasonry, Nostradamus, Egyptology, the Shroud of Turin, and Albert Einstein, among others.

What to do? Well, *some* people are prepared. The book in question tells us that residents in two American communities (A_____,

Texas and S_____, Illinois) have organized themselves in order to obtain technology sufficient to orbit 250,000 people some 74,000 feet above the Earth's surface during the flooding. When the destruction is over, they intend to return. (If the reader is interested, there are photographs of the people in S_____, Illinois on pages viii and 271 of Noone's volume.)

Now, Patrick Moore's (1983) book recounts as many as 17 end-of-the-world scares from A.D. 1000 to 1982, so it is just possible that the predicted cataclysm will fail to occur on May 5, 2000. Will the residents of A_____, Texas and S_____, Illinois experience cognitive dissonance on that spring day? We certainly hope so.

UNIT 4

MAINSTREAM THEMES

Some topics in the domain of attitude research wax and wane in popularity, or at least in the number of journal pages that are devoted to them. On the other hand, there are certain subjects that always seem to generate interest, possibly because they are so central to our daily social lives. I have chosen the label "mainstream themes" to mark these areas. Several such relevant matters are taken up here. Chapter 8 treats the bases for intergroup bias and the dynamics of social stereotypes. Next, the effects of persuasive communications on attitudes are discussed; Chapter 9 deals with the conceptually distinct issues of the source of a persuasive communication, the content of the message, and the intended audience. Finally, Chapter 10 covers perspectives on attitudes toward the self, coping, and survival.

CHAPTER EIGHT

INTERGROUP BIAS AND
SOCIAL STEREOTYPES

In commenting on the "hot, bloody little wars that have plagued the world in the last few decades," an anonymous editorial writer for *The New Yorker* magazine made the following observation:

The most enduring cause of the organized violence we call war is not ideology or greed or politics but the potent mixture of fear and allegiance which breeds intense tribal rivalries . . . Rivalries of this kind have a life of their own, independent of the particular issues that may bring them to the surface at a given moment ("Notes and Comment," 1976).

Warring peoples are not the only groups that display INTERGROUP BIAS. It is a fair working hypothesis to say that any time two groups are aware of each other's existence there is a potential for some type of bias and the possibility for discriminatory behavior ranging anywhere from mild disdain to open warfare.

However, the scope of this chapter, while broad, is finite. The reader should be aware of what types of coverage are *not* attempted here so that he or she will not be disappointed in the end. I will not give a broad survey of thought on real-world group relations; for that type of treatment, see, for example, *Theories of Intergroup Relations* by Taylor and Moghaddam (1987). Neither will I dwell on real groups in contact; for that purpose, consult, for example, *Contact and Conflict in Intergroup Encounters* by Hewstone and Brown (1986) or *Groups in Contact: The Psychology of Desegregation* by Miller and Brewer (1984). Finally, I cannot dwell on real-world racial attitudes; to that end, see, for example, *Prejudice, Discrimination, and Racism* by Dovidio and Gaertner (1986b) or *Racial Attitudes in America* by Schuman, Steeh, and Bobo (1985).

What is left? Plenty. This chapter will be occupied with the explication of processes that presumably underlie most of the material listed in the preceding paragraph. I will focus on some basic and universal aspects of intergroup relations and attitudes. The next section will present the phenomenon known as ingroup/outgroup bias as based on the concepts of shared fate and sheer social categorization. Following this, the topic of social stereotypes will be introduced, and a classic theory of stereotypes will be explained and evaluated. There will then be a treatment of how stereotypes can and do influence behavior. Finally, several contemporary theories of intergroup bias and stereotypes will be taken up and assessed.

Sources of Intergroup Bias

Because there is a high potential for intergroup bias and because such bias can lead to social ills, finding the causes for these phenomena becomes an urgent practical matter as well as one of considerable theoretical interest. Many contributing sources of bias are intertwined in everyday life, so for the purpose of clarity it will be useful to distinguish among them. Recognized factors are competition, mutual frustration, and shared fate.

COMPETITION

Competition occurs any time two parties, whether individuals or groups, are pursuing the same goal. To put it another way, COMPETITION is a zero-sum game, where the gain to one party (+) represents a loss to the other (−), the sum of the outcomes being zero. It is not difficult to see how competition can engender hard feelings between the competing parties. Normally, two suitors cannot both win the hand of the lone local beauty nor can two applicants usually win the same job position, so someone is bound to be disappointed. Angry brawls are quite common in highly competitive sports like professional ice hockey, and in some countries literally thousands of spectators riot over unpopular judges' decisions at soccer matches.

MUTUAL FRUSTRATION

There is potential for MUTUAL FRUSTRATION when two parties have different goals but each may cause the loss of the other's goal. An example of mutual frustration is close at hand. Students want good grades from a course to put on their transcripts and professors want good student evaluations from a course to add to their vitae. Grades are useless to a professor's career aims and student evaluations have no place on a student's transcript. But professors are in a position to give low grades, and students are in a position to give poor evaluations. It does not take much reflection to sense the potential for ill feelings based on mutual frustration between students and their professors.

SHARED FATE

As if the effects of competition and mutual frustration were not bad enough, research has uncovered yet another source of bias between groups. This third source was sought by Rabbie and Horwitz (1969) after they discovered that the first two causes were insufficient to account for all the bias that they could observe. In particular, they report pilot studies in which competition and mutual frustration were *eliminated* in their laboratory setup. Nevertheless, even under these benign circumstances, the offer of help by one group to another was viewed by the latter as condescension, and when one group offered a suggestion, it was viewed as an ultimatum. Because competition and mutual frustration had been ruled out experimentally, something else must have promoted the bias reflected in the unfriendly reactions to help and suggestions.

Testing for shared fate. Rabbie and Horwitz (1969) offered the notion of SHARED FATE as a basis for intergroup bias; through an ingenious experiment they provided empirical support for their hypothesis. A discussion of the meaning of shared fate will be more fruitful if we first take a look at their research. Basically, these researchers wanted to assess the consequences of group membership per se. That is, they wanted to assemble people into more or less arbitrary groups that had no history or common ends and to determine what factors might promote bias between such simple social units. To do this they enlisted as their subjects high-school students from widely scattered locations in a large European city. When eight such students arrived at the lab, they were randomly divided into two groups of four strangers and were seated around two tables that were separated by a large screen. The experimenter, standing at the head of the screen, could see and address both groups, one of which he called the "blues" and the other the "greens." The point of all this was to see what further conditions might make people in this austere circumstance favor their own "group" over the other, which is the typical intergroup bias effect or phenomenon. In all, groups were observed under four experimental conditions termed control, group "vote," experimenter, and chance.

For the control condition, the screen between the two groups was removed at some point and all the subjects were asked to evaluate their own group (i.e., the people seated around their own table) and the other group (i.e., those seated at the other table). They were asked to indicate whether each group was, for example, friendly, hostile, productive, or cohesive, or whether each had other desirable or undesirable characteristics. The higher the overall rating, the more favorable the impression of one or the other group.

For the remaining three experimental treatments, something much more dramatic happened prior to the subjects' ratings of one anothers' groups. In these treatments the experimenter announced that because he was so grateful for the students' participation, he had a bonus to offer and was going to give away some miniature transistor radios. (Subsequent measures revealed that these radios were enormously attractive to the students.) The experimenter had to admit, however, that whereas there were eight students present at the session, he had only four radios to give away. What to do in this dilemma? The experimenter's various "solutions" to this problem of distributing the radios constituted the remaining conditions in the research design.

The group "vote" condition. For some groups of blues and greens, the experimenter stated that the fairest and most democratic thing to do was to have a vote to determine which group of four would get the radios and he brusquely asked which group would care to do the voting. Before anyone could so much as move, the experimenter acted as if one of the groups had volunteered, let us say the blues in this case. The blues voted, but their ballots were covertly discarded and replaced by others prepared by the researchers. And, sure enough, the experimenter announced that the blues had voted for themselves! In other instances (other fresh sets of eight subjects), when the greens were given the voting duties, the rigged balloting made it appear that the greens had voted for themselves. When the "voting" and distribution of the radios were completed, the screen was removed and group evaluations were obtained as in the control condition.

The experimenter condition. For other groups of blues and greens, the experimenter stated that because he was in charge it was up to him to make the hard decisions, so he promptly awarded the radios to either the blue group or the green group based on his inclination at the moment. Over successive groupings of eight new subjects, the blues got the radios at some times and the greens got them at others. As usual, following this manipulation, the screen was removed and ratings were taken.

The chance condition. In a final experimental treatment the experimenter stated that the only really fair way to decide who would get the radios was to let chance decide. Because most people are familiar with coin flipping as a basis for making chance decisions, the experimenter produced a coin, assigned "heads" to one group and "tails" to the other, and flipped the coin. The radios went to one or the other group on the basis of whether the coin came up heads or tails, the screen was removed, and evaluations commenced.

The grounds for bias. Let us consider the possibilities for intergroup bias in the four Rabbie–Horwitz treatments. In terms of the control condition, there should be little bias because no radios were involved and therefore there was no competition, no mutual frustration, or anything else to spark ill-feelings. However, bias certainly is possible in the group "vote" condition, because that manipulation made it look like one of the groups (the voters) entered into competition for the prizes and used their advantage to ensure the prizes for themselves. At this point in the consideration, the experimenter and the chance treatments become especially interesting. Here, there was no competition (and certainly no mutual frustration) because the distribution of the prizes was not at the discretion of anybody in either group. Rather, the agent of distribution was either the experimenter or chance. Would intergroup bias emerge under these latter two conditions, and if so, why? Following the distribution of the radios, subjects were asked to evaluate their own and the other group; these evaluations are shown in Table I. Recall that the larger the entry, the more favorable the evaluation.

It can be seen in Table I that people in the control group did not favor their own group over the other, as indicated by a nearly equal amount of favorability assigned to each. On the other hand, bias was reflected in the ratings of the group "vote" subjects in a way that favored their own group over the other, as expected on the basis of the apparent competition there. Indeed, intergroup bias was also made manifest by the experimenter and chance subjects, even though in these latter two cases the group members themselves were not responsible for the distribution of the radios.

TABLE I
Subjects' ratings of their own group and some other group as a function of experimental treatments

	GROUP	
Treatment	Own	Other
Control	4.28	4.41
Group "vote"	4.54	4.10
Experimenter	4.56	4.24
Chance	4.85	4.26

After Rabbie and Horwitz (1969).
Note. Responses were obtained using a 7-point scale; the higher the value, the more favorable the evaluation.

How can one account for the bias that emerged under the experimenter and chance conditions? This is where the notion of shared fate comes into play. By the time the radios had been given out, the gatherings of blues and greens in the experimenter and chance conditions were no longer such arbitrary collections of strangers. Now, whether they had received radios or not, all the blues had something *in common*, as did all the greens. Within each group of four they were either "haves" or "have nots," and in a real sense they had, for better or worse, shared a fate. There now was a basis for belongingness. The respective groups of blues and greens were thus "all in the same boat," a phrase implying that people in the same boat should look out for one another's welfare, perhaps even at the expense of people in some other boat. A feeling of "being in the same boat" may simply be another way of expressing the idea of intergroup bias.

INGROUP/OUTGROUP CATEGORIZATION

The conditions in the Rabbie–Horwitz study were quite austere, but although those groups hardly approximated the richness and complexity of actual social life, there was apparently a basis for bias. This finding brings us to a consideration of the very minimal conditions under which intergroup bias might emerge. Tajfel, Billig, Bundy, and Flament (1971) were also interested in exploring the minimums of bias-producing situations. If the Rabbie–Horwitz approach was austere, that of Tajfel et al. (1971) was absolutely stark.

They attempted to study intergroup bias under the following restrictions:

1. There should be no face-to-face interaction between persons within groups or between persons in different groups.
2. Complete anonymity of membership was to be preserved. Subjects were to be told only that they were categorized in a group with some others, but that is all they were to be told.
3. There should be no logical link between the basis for being in the group and the means for the expression of bias while in that group.
4. Responses that potentially reveal bias should have no direct utility for the individual subject making those responses. That is, if bias was expressed, it should not be self-serving.

Could bias emerge even under such circumstances? To find out, Tajfel et al. (1971) assembled a large number of subjects in a room and had them look at slide presentations of more or less dense patterns of dots. The subjects' ostensible task was to estimate how many dots were shown in a given slide. After several slides had been shown, the subjects' dot estimates were collected and covertly discarded. Then, on a completely random basis, subjects were given bogus feedback about their ability to judge numbers of dots. Some were told that they were better than average, and some were told that they were worse than average. This manipulation represented an INGROUP/OUTGROUP CATEGORIZATION. INGROUP refers to members of one's own social unit, and OUTGROUP refers to persons excluded from that social category. For every ingroup there is an outgroup. To put it another way, one person's ingroup is another person's outgroup. Whatever the subjects' bogus feedback, they were told that somewhere there were others like them (better than average on dots) in their group and that there were others unlike them (worse than average on dots) in another group, or vice versa.

This method of categorization satisfied the first two of the listed stringent standards. People had been given the information that groups existed and that they were in one or the other, but they had been given no idea of who else was actually involved. The next step was to assess these subjects' intergroup bias, if any. Each subject was informed that he could reward either his own group (ingroup) or the other group (outgroup), but that the awards he assigned to either group would not accrue to him personally. The reward system had nothing to do with the reason for being in a particular group (counting dots), so the third and fourth criteria had been met. Subjects distributed awards through the use of a set of matrixes, such as the one shown in Figure 1. Basically, in using this particular matrix,

Most equitable choice

Choice number	1	2	3	4	5	6	7	8	9	10	11	12	13	14
Ingroup reward	1	2	3	4	5	6	7	8	9	10	11	12	13	14
Outgroup reward	14	13	12	11	10	9	8	7	6	5	4	3	2	1

Reward matrix

FIGURE 1
REWARD MATRIX used in laboratory studies of ingroup and outgroup bias based on social categorization. (After Tajfel et al., 1971.)

the subject had 15 units of award to distribute on each of several trials; he could give some of these units to members of the ingroup or to members of the outgroup, according to his wish. If the subject consistently picked choice 14 (see Figure 1), he would be extremely generous to the ingroup, giving awards to that ingroup at a ratio of 14 to 1 over that given to the outgroup. A consistent choice of number 1, on the contrary, would be extremely generous to the outgroup. As can be seen in Figure 1, an average pick of 7.5 (choice 7 on one trial and 8 on the next, over successive trials) would be the fairest of all.

But would subjects *be* fair in the face of an opportunity to be biased in favor of an almost arbitrary ingroup over an equally arbitrary outgroup? It turns out that they were hardly fair at all. Overall, approximately 82% of the subjects gave more units of award to the anonymous ingroup. This discriminatory tendency is also evident in their average matrix choice number of 9.2, which clearly indicates bias in favor of the ingroup. Hence, even under the stringent conditions prescribed by Tajfel et al. (1971), intergroup bias emerged.

SUMMARY

People in groups seem ready to show their intergroup bias at the drop of a hat, so to speak. When we consider that the conditions of shared fate and group categorization are often accompanied by either competition or mutual frustration, it becomes less than surprising to find so much social conflict between groups. Of course, the studies just reviewed speak only to the identification of certain minimal or basic conditions for the formation of bias (for a review of other such studies, see Brewer, 1979; and for an extension of categorization theory, see Turner, Hogg, Oakes, Reicher, and Wetherell, 1987). In the real world many complicated factors are involved in intergroup relationships (see Taylor and Moghaddam, 1987). However, because elemental features such as categorization and shared fate are conceivably involved in any and all group conflict, continued study of these concepts is required.

Social Stereotypes

The great thing about ethnic and national characteristics is that people in various cultures *are* different from one another to some extent, and any society that successfully assimilates such diversity benefits from a kind of hybrid vigor. Unfortunately, these real differences are also at the base of much bias and prejudice between groups. Some of the most widespread expressions of such bias are SOCIAL STEREOTYPES. By thumbnail definition, stereotypes are overgeneralized attitudes based on too little experience or knowledge about individuals. One creates or engages in a stereotype when one is willing to ascribe a feature that may exist for a subset of some group to *any* member of that group. To put it another way, when we stereotype an unfamiliar (or even hypothetical) individual, we first assign that person to a category and then react to the category rather than to the individual. Therefore, even with no accurate information about a particular outgroup person, one may be willing to assume a variety of things about that person on the basis of his or her group membership.

Whether the word "stereotype" is used as a noun or a verb, most social stereotypes of outgroups have a pejorative quality about them. That is, the mental picture one group has of another usually demeans or disparages the outgroup. For example, it has been said that professors are absentminded, students are lazy, and athletes are stupid. One may or may not agree with these miniature portraits, depending on one's role as a professor, a student, or an athlete, but one gets the flavor. The disparagement of the outgroup becomes a far more serious matter in the areas of racial and ethnic conflict. The tendency to paint a negative picture of those in a rival group can go so far as to define the enemy as something less than human. According to Eibl-Eibesfeldt's (1977) analysis of intergroup aggression and warfare in man,

in a process of self-indoctrination, each group speaks of itself as "the real men . . . " Others are not considered to count as full members of mankind, or even as human beings; men then act accordingly. By cultural definition, intraspecific aggression [man–man] gets shifted to the level of interspecific aggression [man–animal] . . . Facilitated by communication barriers and by armament which kills quickly and often at a distance, man shuts himself off against all appeals normally releasing the fighting inhibitions which are subjectively experienced as pity.

KERNEL OF TRUTH AND RECIPROCAL DESCRIPTIONS

In other words, if my stereotype of the enemy is that he is no more than an animal, why should I have any qualms about his slaughter? This tendency to disparage the outgroup to the point of dehumanization seems to receive its most intense expression in wartime propaganda (Keen, 1986; Rhodes, 1983), as suggested in Figure 2. Even so, much more mundane stereotypes also involve negative evaluations of persons in outgroups. How do these everyday patterns come about? One plausible answer has to do with a theory about "kernels of truth" and "reciprocal descriptions" as put forth by Donald Campbell.

The perception of group differences. Campbell's (1967) analysis of intergroup stereotypes rests on the fact that groups are different

FIGURE 2
PROPAGANDA POSTERS depicting the enemy as subhuman. The panel on the left from the U.S.S.R. shows the United States as a spider creeping over Spain; the panel on the right from Southeast Asia shows Richard Nixon as a vulture descending on Vietnam. (From Keen, 1986.)

from each other on a number of dimensions. If they were not, there would be only one group, not two. Consider a hypothetical Martian space traveler who stops off in England for a while and then visits the United States. This perceptive being might well report that the English are relatively formal, reserved in public, and generally respectful of the privacy of others. Americans, in turn, might be described as friendly, outgoing, and openhearted. Assuming that our space visitor has been completely objective and accurate at arriving at these profiles or descriptions of the two peoples, what implications are there for intergroup attitudes in the face of such real group differences? The English are perfectly capable of viewing both our behavior and their own, and we Americans can observe their demeanor as well as our own. All of us thus have a sense of the "reserved Englishman" and the "outgoing American." These facts provide us with a KERNEL OF TRUTH about each group that will lead to the formation of *mutually pejorative* social stereotypes in the two sets of nationals. Why?

The next step in Campbell's (1967) analysis tells us that these kernels of truth undergo a process he terms RECIPROCAL DESCRIPTIONS. The general workings of reciprocal descriptions are shown in Table II. Group A is described *by* members of Group A as desirable and good. Similarly, Group B is viewed as admirable *by* members of Group B. On the contrary, Group A is seen as being bad from the standpoint of members of Group B, and Group B is disparaged by members of Group A. Campbell fleshes out his scheme with the example of Americans and Englishmen. Whereas the English take pride in themselves for being reserved and having respect for the privacy of others (good), Americans might well take the view that the English are cold, snobbish, and unfriendly (bad). Reciprocally, whereas Americans pride themselves on their friendly, outgoing, and

TABLE II
An illustration of Campbell's formulation on the reciprocal descriptions of the kernel of truth in social stereotypes

Descriptions by	DESCRIPTIONS OF[a]	
	Group A	Group B
Group A	Good	Bad
Group B	Bad	Good

After Campbell (1967).
[a]Note that this heading could also read "Descriptions given to."

openhearted style (good), the English might conclude that we are intrusive, forward, and pushy (bad). Of course, elements of reciprocal descriptions based on a kernel of truth can be found in real life. For example, in a study of stereotypes in the 1970s, both white and black respondents characterized lower-class blacks as being "rebellious." However, further probing revealed that while white respondents felt that this trait was unattractive, blacks thought it attractive (Smedley and Bayton, 1978).

The potential for enmity based on reciprocal descriptions has even made its way into children's literature. A recent (1984) Dr. Seuss book, *The Butter Battle Book*, is a cautionary tale about the dangers of an arms race between superpowers. Two peoples, the Yooks and the Zooks, have armed themselves to the point of mutual annihilation. It all started with what would appear to be a fairly harmless kernel of truth, as told by a Yook grandparent to a Yook child:

> "It's high time that you knew
> of the terribly horrible thing that Zooks do.
> In every Zook house and in every Zook town
> *every Zook eats his bread*
> *with the butter side down*!
> But we Yooks, as you know,
> when we breakfast or sup,
> spread our bread," Grandpa said,
> "with the butter side *up*.
> That's the right, honest way!"
> Grandpa gritted his teeth.
> "So you can't trust a Zook who spreads bread underneath!
> Every Zook must be watched! He has kinks in his soul . . . !"

It all ends with a Yook and a Zook confronting each other with their respective versions of a doomsday machine, the "Big-Boy Boomeroo."

In short, social stereotypes can be based at least in part on real group characteristics (kernels of truth) that are subject to distortion, or open to interpretation and disparagement (reciprocal descriptions). Group features, then, are important not for what they *denote* but for what they *connote* about those groups. The ingroup is praised; the outgroup is insulted (Campbell, 1967). This analysis is especially useful, because it instructs us that, although stereotypes may be distortions of reality, they are by no means delusions or complete fabrications. Because they seem to be based on some kernel of truth, any remedy for intergroup bias will have to take this consideration into account. Not the least important is that Campbell's position gives us a way of understanding how stereotypes might change over time. One need only imagine that as the kernel of truth behind any stereotype changed or was modified (for whatever reason), the stereotype itself could change accordingly.

The kernel of truth and dynamics of stereotypes over time. There have been enormous changes in the ethnic makeup of America in this century; because of the World Wars and the expansion of higher education and the mass media, we know more and more about one another as groups. If the kernel-of-truth idea has merit and if such kernels can be modified by domestic and international developments, then we might be able to trace meaningful and interpretable changes in stereotypes over time. An opportunity to do this has been afforded by the work of Katz and Braly (1933), Gilbert (1951), and Karlins, Coffman, and Walters (1969).*

All these researchers went to Princeton University in search of the ethnic and national stereotypes held by male students there. At each assessment over the various decades, the students were provided with a catalog of 84 traits (such as *industrious, superstitious, sly, intelligent,* and *methodical*) and a booklet containing blank pages labeled with the names of national or ethnic groups (such as Armenians, Italians, and Negroes). The respondents' basic task was to write down under each label the five most characteristic traits in the catalog that applied to all Germans, for example, or to all Chinese, or to whatever group. The researchers then simply calculated what proportion (percentage) of their respondents selected a given trait for a given group. The more often a certain trait was chosen by the Princeton students, the more importantly that trait figured into the stereotype of that particular national or ethnic group.

The pattern of respondents' selections of those traits over 30-odd years can be seen in Table III. For instance, in 1932, 48% of the students who were surveyed thought Americans were industrious. By 1967, though, only 23% of the respondents listed this trait, so its place in the stereotype had diminished. On the other hand, whereas 33% of the 1932 sample thought that Americans were materialistic, by 1967 that proportion had doubled to 67%. These changes may well constitute evidence that the kernel of truth for the stereotype of "Americans" was undergoing real change. Loss of productivity in this era *is* known to have been part of the U.S. economic problem

*The years just listed are the publication dates of the respective articles. Inspection of the reports reveals that Karlins et al. obtained their data in 1967, Gilbert's work was done in 1950, and Katz and Braly had completed their measures sometime prior to mid-1932. For the sake of historical accuracy, the dates of data collection will be used in the text.

TABLE III
Changes in American college students' stereotypes of various ethnic and national groups from 1932 to 1967

Trait	PERCENTAGE OF SUBJECTS SELECTING TRAIT		
	1932	1950	1967
Americans			
Industrious	48	30	23
Intelligent	47	32	20
Materialistic	33	37	67
Ambitious	33	21	42
Progressive	27	5	17
Pleasure-loving	26	27	28
Alert	23	7	7
Efficient	21	9	15
Germans			
Science-minded	78	62	47
Industrious	44	10	9
Stolid	44	10	9
Intelligent	32	32	19
Methodical	31	20	21
Nationalistic	24	50	43
Progressive	16	3	13
Efficient	16	—	46
Chinese			
Superstitious	34	18	8
Sly	29	4	6
Conservative	29	14	15
Tradition loving	26	26	32
Loyal to family ties	22	35	50
Industrious	18	18	23
Meditative	19	—	21
Reserved	17	18	15
"Negroes"			
Superstitious	84	41	13
Lazy	75	31	26
Happy-go-lucky	38	17	27
Ignorant	38	24	11
Musical	26	33	47
Ostentatious	26	11	25
Very religious	24	17	8
Stupid	22	10	4

After Karlins et al. (1969).
Note. The dates over the columns are the years in which the data were collected, not the years in which they were subsequently published (see the text). Entries are the percentages of respondents who indicated that a particular trait was characteristic of that group. Blanks (—) indicate that data were not reported in the 1951 study, *not* that the percentage is zero.

of inflation, and American materialism in the 1950s and beyond has long been a target of critics and observers of our society (e.g., Hine, 1986). The shift in "alertness" (Table III) from 1932 to 1950 is also instructive. Perhaps the success of the Japanese surprise attack on Pearl Harbor in 1941 no longer permits us to see Americans as alert.

There are interesting changes in other panels in Table III. Whereas the successive generations of students saw the Chinese as less sly, a growing number of these respondents believed that Chinese were loyal to family ties, while the Germans were becoming more nationalistic and more efficient in their eyes. No less interesting are changes in patterns of stereotypes of black people ("Negroes" in the table, as in the originals). There were marked declines in the listings of unflattering traits such as "superstitious," "lazy," and "ignorant." Indeed, in 1967 the only trait for blacks in Table III that showed an increase above its 1932 level was "musical."

I am inclined to take the kernel-of-truth idea seriously and to attribute this increase in "musical" up to 1967 to blacks' disproportionate success as performing artists and famous entertainers during that period. That is, a case could be made that, at the time, blacks were statistically overrepresented in popular music. The 1970 U.S. census estimated that blacks made up about 11% of the American population at that time (see Table IV in Chapter 1). However, even casual reference to archives of popular music of that era supports the idea of black overrepresentation. For example, the dust jacket photo of Henry Pleasants's (1974) book, *The Great American Popular Singers* (see Figure 3), shows 11 superstars of the genre, 4 of which are black. Four of 11 is over 36%, which makes the point about overrepresentation relative to the 11% estimate for the population. An examination of the table of contents of Pleasants's (1974) book further supports this view. Of his 22 substantive chapters—each devoted to a single artist—fully 10 are devoted to black stars, which is an even stronger 45%. For another source, the Smithsonian Institution of Washington, D.C. recently offered a "historical album" from about the period under consideration. The cartoon (by Al Hirschfeld) on the cover of the album showed 8 performers, 3 of which are black (38%). If these estimates are approximately correct, students' stereotypes of blacks as "musical" could have come from their awareness of the success of blacks as popular musicians. No doubt, the ascendance in the 1950s and 1960s of predominantly black rhythm and blues, soul music (Guralnick, 1986), and the Motown sound (Waller, 1985) added to this impression.

FIGURE 3
BOOK COVER indicating a statistical overrepresentation of blacks in popular music in the 1950s and 1960s (see text).

Kernel of truth—an update. So far as I know, no research beyond 1967 has been carried out on the topic of Princeton students' stereotypes. However, comparable data were collected at Colgate University in 1982 (Dovidio and Gaertner, 1986a). Parts of these more current stereotypes—along with earlier data for comparison—are shown in Table IV. As continuations of earlier trends, Americans were seen as even less intelligent in the early 1980s, but just as materialistic. Further, an interesting development in the profile of stereotypes of blacks was the continuing downward trend in respondents' listings of unflattering traits. This response is consistent with positive shifts in other white attitudes toward blacks that have been reported elsewhere (Schuman et al., 1985). But in connection with the case made earlier, there was a drop in the listing of "musical" for blacks. Again, I feel this may well reflect a change in the kernel of truth based on blacks' representation in popular music. One's impressions are that from the mid-1960s to well into the 1970s rock music largely supplanted earlier forms and that rock was a predominantly white genre

TABLE IV
Changes in racial stereotypes over time

| Trait | PERCENTAGE OF SUBJECTS SELECTING TRAIT | | | |
	1932	1950	1967	1982
Attributed to "Negroes" (1933, 1951, 1969) or black Americans (1982)				
Superstitious	84	41	13	6
Lazy	75	31	26	13
Happy-go-lucky	38	17	27	15
Ignorant	38	24	11	10
Musical	26	33	47	29
Attributed to white Americans				
Industrious	48	30	23	21
Intelligent	47	32	20	10
Materialistic	33	37	67	65
Ambitious	33	21	42	35
Progressive	27	5	17	9

After Dovidio and Gaertner (1986a); Karlins et al. (1969).

(cf. McDonough, 1985; Stallings, 1984; *The Superstars of Rock*, 1984), Further, during this phase of pop music development, the so-called rock and roll movies mainly involved white performers (Burt, 1986). Therefore, given the infusion of white acts, the proportion of black performers in the business was probably less than it had been in previous years. Perhaps this was the basis of the 1982 impression of blacks as less "musical" than in 1967.

In sum, all of us pick up kernels of truth about the various outgroups in our lives. We get these bits and pieces through personal experience, interpersonal communication, and exposure to the media. The working hypothesis was that as our knowledge of reality changes, so do our stereotypes. A case was developed that the actual proportion of minority performers in popular entertainment could serve as a kernel of truth upon which to base part of a stereotype of that group. "Athletic" was *not* one of the 84 traits made available to Princeton students in the 1932 Katz–Braly study, so subsequent researchers did not include it. That is too bad, because given the tremendous television coverage of sports events these days, and the current statistical overrepresentation of minority-group athletes in many professional sports, I would not be surprised to learn that "athletic" was part of outgroup stereotypes of certain U.S. minorities today.

Reciprocal descriptions—An East African survey. Although the comparisons in Tables III and IV are quite valuable and instructive with regard to the dynamics of stereotypes and the kernel-of-truth notion, they tell us nothing about the role of reciprocal descriptions. Happily, Campbell and a colleague (Brewer and Campbell, 1976) provide us with some excellent information on the existence of reciprocal descriptions between real groups. These field workers sought such stereotyping among members of various tribes in the East African countries of Uganda, Kenya, and Tanzania. Within Tanzania there were 10 such tribes; because the findings from the peoples in Uganda and Kenya were virtually identical with those from Tanzania, elaborate discussion of the Uganda and Kenya data is unnecessary.

In Tanzania, a quota sample of respondents was asked to assign traits to their own tribe or to some other tribe, wherever the trait applied most appropriately. Such traits included terms like *dirty, clean, strong, weak, handsome, ugly, friendly, cruel, hardworking, lazy, peaceful, quarrelsome,* and many more. Obviously, some of these traits are desirable or good and could be signified by a plus (+) mark. But some of the traits are undesirable or bad and could be signified by a minus (−) mark. Basically what Brewer and Campbell did with their data was to tally how many plus and minus traits tribe members assigned to their own tribe and to the other tribes in the region. The actual formula they used for this tally was rather complicated, but it need not detain us here. It is sufficient to say that if reciprocal descriptions occurred across these tribes, we would find people assigning many plus traits and few minus traits to their own group (tribe) while at the same time assigning more minus traits and fewer plus traits to the outgroups. Even more interesting, a tribe might assign itself a large number of plus traits even when it was held in very low esteem by all the other tribes. This possibility follows from Campbell's (1967) idea that, whereas others may view our group's characteristics as bad, we see the selfsame characteristics as good.

The outcome of the survey in Tanzania is shown in Table V. It should be noted that none of the tribes are named in this particular table, because Brewer and Campbell refused to identify them by name in the original report. The reader will soon see the reason for the authors' discretion and reticence. The horizontal axis in Table V indicates ratings given *to* the 10 tribes, here assigned the nominal labels of A through J. The vertical axis indicates ratings given *by* the various tribes, again labeled A through J. (Note that this orientation of *by* and *to* matches that in the earlier Table II used in the expli-

TABLE V
Intergroup evaluative ratings given by ten tribes

Tribe giving ratings	RATING GIVEN TO TRIBE									
	A	B	C	D	E	F	G	H	I	J
A	+72	+62	+39	+4	−5	+16	+3	−12	−122	−5
B	+11	+110	+22	0	−4	+72	+22	−33	−195	−33
C	−4	+26	+203	+4	+2	+16	+3	−24	−43	−12
D	−16	+29	+8	+73	−50	+42	+40	−37	+4	−12
E	+2	+31	+11	+18	+5	+43	+67	−33	−80	−15
F	−14	+3	+20	−9	0	+159	+87	−45	−95	−16
G	−8	+13	+23	−2	0	+47	+182	−33	−112	−40
H	+48	−5	−5	−14	−7	−2	−5	+87	−46	−8
I	+16	0	−4	−33	+40	−34	−21	−1	+143	−26
J	+12	+16	+6	+2	0	+14	+52	−13	−152	+111

After Brewer and Campbell (1976).
Note. Plus entries (+) indicate favorable evaluations; negative entries (−) indicate unfavorable evaluations. Underlined entries are tribe members' evaluations of their own tribe.

cation of reciprocal descriptions.) It can be seen, for example, that tribe A assigned itself +72 net units of favorable marks, gave tribe B +62, tribe C +39, and so on. Apparently, members of tribe A did not much like the people of tribe I, to whom they assigned an insulting score of −122 marks.

Tribe B was even more generous to itself (+110) and even more disparaging to tribe I (−195). Further, a quick scan of the entire table reveals that in virtually all of the cases, the highest marks assigned by a tribe were to itself, the ingroup. The only exception to this observation is tribe E, whose members do not seem to have cared one way or the other. However, out of the 30 or so tribes studied in the entire survey (in Tanzania, Uganda, and Kenya), tribe E in Tanzania was one of only three that failed to favor themselves!

Another interesting feature in Table V are entries associated with tribe I. It seems that the other tribes living in Tanzania thought rather poorly of tribe I. Even the indifferent tribe E managed to muster enough malice to assign it a score of −80 (and see the remainder of the column for tribe I). A glance at the feelings of the members of I toward the other peoples (row) shows that there was little love lost between them. But tribe I thought itself just fine, assigning itself a respectable score of +143. Witness the power of reciprocal descriptions in intergroup bias! We can see why Brewer and Campbell (1976) refused to explicitly identify the tribes arrayed in Table V; if they had, they might have started tribal warfare.

OTHER MEASURES, OTHER STEREOTYPES

Bogus pipeline approach. Is the problem of racial or ethnic stereotypes really so serious in the United States and other industrial societies? In this day and age of integration, extensive higher education, and pervasive mass media, can we still harbor distorted images or perceptions of the groups in our society? Sigall and Page (1971) attempted to answer this question by using a bogus pipeline technique like the one described in Chapter 1. As a reminder, a bogus pipeline method is one through which the respondent or subject is convinced that it is futile to lie or withhold true feelings. This technique is markedly different from the traditional method in attitudinal research whereby the respondent is merely asked for his opinion or reaction and that answer is taken at face value.

The main interest of Sigall and Page (1971) was the possibility that the two kinds of measurement techniques might yield contrasting findings where stereotypes were concerned. At the time of their study, it was probably unflattering to be seen as a bigot on many college campuses; if asked about their racial prejudices, white students might cover them up and provide answers that were designed to make them appear publicly tolerant. At the same time (the Vietnam War era) it was fashionable among many groups to be critical of American foreign and domestic policies (see Chapter 12). It is fair to say that the media kept the war protesters and civil-rights advocates in plain view. A student, asked for his reactions to "Americans," might have been likely to give a negative-sounding evaluation just to be in vogue. In both the cases of civil rights and the antiwar movement, the respondent's true attitudes would be masked, so Sigall and Page measured such attitudes using a bogus pipeline method as well as the traditional rating method.

White male college students were given a list of traits such as those seen in Table VI and were asked to consider "Americans" or "Negroes" and the extent to which a trait applied to these people. Responses could range from −3 to +3. A −3 response meant that the trait was uncharacteristic of people in that group, whereas a +3 reaction meant that it was characteristic. Some subjects were given a traditional rating scale method to express their attitudes, whereas others were queried via a bogus pipeline procedure that also recorded responses in the range from −3 to + 3.

The results showed that there was a marked difference in whites' attitudes toward both Americans in general and blacks across the two measurement methods (Table VI). Although these students were somewhat more favorable toward Americans in general than toward blacks when assessed by the traditional paper-and-pencil method, these contrasts became much more sharp when the truth-inducing bogus pipeline technique was used. On every trait listed in Table VI, the bogus pipeline measure indicated that Americans in general were actually viewed more positively than revealed by the traditional method and that the contrary was true for reactions to black Americans. In the latter case the traditional method produced an apparently contrived positive picture of whites' feelings toward blacks, compared with the bogus pipeline as the more accurate or reliable of the two measures.

In sum, racial stereotypes on the part of whites about blacks were there and became evident when one used an appropriate or sensitive measure. I wager the same thing can be said of blacks' attitudes toward whites, Chicanos' views of Anglos, French-speaking Canadians' feelings toward English-speaking Canadians, or whatever com-

TABLE VI
Stereotypes by white male college students of "Americans" and "Negroes" as
revealed by rating-scale and bogus-pipeline measures

Trait	"AMERICANS"			"NEGROES"		
	Rating Scale	Bogus pipeline	Net differential	Rating scale	Bogus pipeline	Net differential
Honest	−0.27	0.60	+0.87	0.67	−0.33	−1.00
Ignorant	−0.07	−0.53	+0.46	0.20	0.60	−0.40
Intelligent	1.00	1.73	+0.73	0.47	0.00	−0.47
Lazy	−0.40	−0.80	+0.40	−0.73	0.60	−1.33
Physically dirty	−1.53	−1.67	+0.14	−1.33	0.20	−1.53
Sensitive	0.07	1.47	+1.40	1.60	0.87	−0.73
Stupid	−0.20	−1.07	+0.87	−1.00	0.13	−1.13
Unreliable	−0.40	−0.73	+0.33	−0.67	0.27	−0.94

After Sigall and Page (1971).
Note. Responses for the rating scale and the bogus pipeline procedure ranged from −3 (trait is uncharacteristic of group) to +3 (trait is characteristic of group). A net differential of a plus (+) indicates a more favorable attitude as revealed by the bogus pipeline when compared with the traditional rating method. A net differential of a minus (−) indicates a less favorable attitude.

bination of groups is considered. The fact that such stereotypes can be undercover, so to speak, only means that they are that much more difficult to deal with.

Conditional-probability approach. There are methods beyond that of the bogus pipeline for determining the extent and content of stereotypes, and these methods reveal interesting aspects of this attitudinal phenomenon. One such method is based on the idea of CONDITIONAL PROBABILITY. Without looking out of the window, what is the probability (p) that it will rain (R) today? The range of answers to this question is from .00 (will definitely not rain) to 1.00 (will definitely rain), and any given estimate can be expressed as $p(R)$. However, to make such a prediction more accurate, it would be quite useful to know whether there were some clouds (C) in the sky. If we assume that there are some clouds in the sky, what then is the probability of rainfall? This new estimate could be expressed as $p(R/C)$, that is, the probability of rain given some cloud cover.

Let us apply this concept of conditional probability to the content of a particular stereotype. For example, are German people seen as any more or less efficient than the rest of the world's population? To answer this question, McCauley and Stitt (1978) asked American college-age women to give their estimates of the *percentage* of Germans that they judged to be efficient. This version of a conditional probability estimate is like asking for the probability of a given German person being efficient, yet in this percentage form it is probably easier to understand and answer. In either case, the answer could be expressed p(efficient/German)—the percentage of people who are judged to be efficient by virtue of the fact that they are German.

The women in the study gave their estimates of the conditional probability (by percentage) that people would be efficient if German, but, as McCauley and Stitt point out, this is still insufficient evidence to determine whether judges saw the quality of being efficient as pertaining to Germans in particular as part of the nationality's stereotype. What is required is another bit of information, namely, the base rate of efficient people in the total human population. Therefore, the researchers also asked their respondents the percentage of all the world's people who are efficient; this estimate can be stated as p(efficient). From this point on, it is relatively straightforward to determine whether Germans were estimated or judged to be any more or less efficient than everyone else. We simply need to compute a "diagnostic ratio" by dividing p(efficient/German) by p(efficient).

The DIAGNOSTIC RATIO (the term used by McCauley and Stitt, 1978) indicates whether Germans were seen as being more or less efficient than other peoples. Note that if the ratio were equal to 1, "efficient" would not be seen as particularly characteristic of German people one way or the other, for the percentage estimate for this group would be equal to the worldwide percentage. On the other hand, if the ratio were reliably greater than 1, that trait would be judged more likely in Germans than in the rest of the population. Finally, if the diagnostic ratio were substantially less than 1, that trait would be viewed as uncharacteristic of Germans because the rate in other people would exceed that of the group in question.

The results of the McCauley–Stitt procedure are shown in Table VII. According to the results, the women in the study had a stereotype of Germans as characteristically efficient, extremely nationalistic, industrious, and scientifically minded. In addition, Germans were seen as being anything but ignorant, impulsive, pleasure-loving, or superstitious, at least when compared with the rest of us. In sum, the conditional-probability approach, along with the bogus pipeline technique and others, also reveals that many people do maintain

TABLE VII
An American stereotype of Germans as revealed by the conditional probability method

Trait	p(trait/German)	p(trait)	Diagnostic ratio[a]
	Characteristic traits		
Efficient	63.4	49.8	1.27
Extremely nationalistic	56.3	35.4	1.59
Industrious	68.2	59.8	1.14
Scientifically minded	43.1	32.6	1.32
	Uncharacteristic traits		
Ignorant	29.2	34.0	0.86
Impulsive	41.1	51.7	0.79
Pleasure-loving	72.8	82.2	0.89
Superstitious	30.4	42.1	0.72

After McCauley and Stitt (1978).
[a]Diagnostic ratio = p(trait/German) ÷ p(trait).

measurable stereotypes of certain ethnic, racial, and national groups, in this case Americans' stereotype of Germans. It would therefore not come as much of a surprise to discover that Germans have a stereotype of Americans.

There seems little doubt that racial, ethnic, gender, and other kinds of stereotypes exist and can be measured. It was said earlier that stereotypes were one manifestation of intergroup biases. What of manifestations of stereotypes themselves? One possible way in which they are made manifest is through behavior, and it is to this possibility that we now look.

The Self-Fulfillment of Social Stereotypes

To this point we have seen that the perception of group differences indeed leads to biases and stereotyping. In this section we will examine some *implications* of these widespread phenomena. Chapters 3 and 4 on attitude–behavior consistency showed that given certain circumstances attitudes indeed predict behavior. Thus, the very pervasiveness of social stereotypes as attitudes suggests a great potential for behavioral influence. Here we will take up investigations on several different kinds of stereotypes, all having in common the potential that such attitudes can and do have an impact on behavior of both the holder (perceiver) and the target of the stereotype.

Several approaches to the study of stereotype-based behavior will be taken up. The first mechanism involved in such attitude–behavior consistency has been termed the behavioral confirmation of social stereotypes, and the case in question has to do with men's biases toward women's appearance. The second approach is here termed the behavioral mediation of stereotype-based behavior, and in the current instance has to do with racial prejudice. Finally, a third approach to the phenomenon of consistency examines stereotypes as normative expectations for behavior; this approach focuses on traditional and untraditional women's self-concepts. In all of these the emphasis is on how the existence of a stereotype in the perception of a holder actually leads to behavior by its target that is in line with that stereotype, regardless of whether the behavior is flattering to the targeted individual.

The Behavioral Confirmation of Social Stereotypes

What is beautiful is good. The foregoing phrase is the title of a research paper in which Dion, Berscheid, and Walster (1972) reported that when given only photographs as the basis for their judgments, respondents rated physically attractive people as having nicer personality traits (e.g., being genuine, sensitive, sincere, warm, kind, poised) than unattractive persons. Subjects also estimated that attractive people have higher occupational status and more marital competence, all on the basis of their photographs alone. This positive bias toward attractive people—or negative bias toward unattractive people—also applies to adults' impressions of children. Student teachers made estimates of the likelihood that a child accused of a certain transgression would err in the future. The most lenient estimates were given to attractive children, especially when the child was accused of a severe past transgression (Dion, 1972). By now, whole books have been written about the role of personal appearance in social life (cf. Hatfield and Sprecher, 1986; Herman, Zanna, and Higgins, 1986).

This generally held attitude that attractive people are somehow better than their less attractive counterparts certainly can be classified as a stereotype. Even if we do not know the person, assignment to the "attractive" category opens the way to a reaction to the category rather than to the individual. Such reactions can influence the behavior of the perceiver, and, in turn, the behavior of the target.

Consider the physical dimension of height. A popular song, "Short

People" by Randy Newman (copyright 1977, Hightree Music, BMI), openly derided diminutive individuals, indicating that they had "grubby little fingers and dirty little minds" and a desire to "get you every time," among other unfortunate features. This characterization is all very amusing to taller types, but what about the influence of this kind of bias on actual behavior directed at short people? It turns out that there are important differential reactions toward tall and short individuals. Taller men, for example, tend to land better jobs, to make more money within given jobs, and to win more votes in elections (Keyes, 1980). In some societies, such as the Mehinaku tribe in tropical Brazil, relative shortness is a clear barrier to full participation in social life. The prevailing attitude in that society is that a man's shortness is a highly undesirable trait and that such shortness results not from some genetic legacy but from an inability to curb one's sexual activities during adolescent initiation phases. Thus, not only are small men short, they are immoral as well. Of course, this attitude has an impact on the behavior of the taller men in the group toward those that are shorter. Short men are continually derided behind their backs, are almost openly cuckolded if married, and seldom get to be chief (Gregor, 1979).

On further reflection, how might this unfair treatment influence a Mehinaku man's *self*-perception or *self*-esteem? One such short individual in this tribe seems to have come to agree with the others' impression of him.

Itsa, one of the shortest men in the village, has apparently accepted the villagers' disrespect and made himself a kind of village fool and jester. When he wrestles, the men shout mock advice at him from the bench in front of the mens' house, and he exaggerates the style of the more successful wrestlers to earn their laughter (Gregor, 1979).

What is beautiful is good is confirmed. In the description of Itsa, the short Mehinaku man, the tribe's stereotype concerning the demerits of small stature seems to have come true in that he himself behaved in a foolish and self-demeaning manner. In other words, that stereotype seems to have been a prophecy that fulfilled itself. Stereotypes can indeed be self-fulfilling prophecies through a process of behavioral confirmation. BEHAVIORAL CONFIRMATION occurs when a holder of a stereotype behaves consistently with that attitude and elicits the expected behavior from the target, whether or not the target really has a personal disposition to act in that fashion. For example, if person A has a stereotype of person B that maintains that B is unfriendly, A might act rudely toward B, thus eliciting real unfriendly behavior from B and confirming the stereotype in the process. An experiment based on this analysis was undertaken by Snyder, Tanke, and Berscheid (1977) in an attempt to document the behavioral confirmation, or the self-fulfilling nature, of the social stereotype that what is beautiful is good.

To validate the behavioral confirmation concept, two people— strangers to each other—were asked to interact socially in the form of a telephone conversation. These two subjects, a man and a woman in different rooms, had been told that the experimenter was studying the acquaintance process; therefore, before the phone conversation started, he asked them to write down some general background information on a form. These forms were to be exchanged as an aid to getting acquainted. When the man received the woman's form, he found a photograph attached to it, ostensibly that of his conversation partner. However, this was *not* a photo of his actual partner; rather, it was a picture of a paid model and it established the experimental manipulation in the study. There were two such photos used in the research. Some male subjects received a picture of a model that had been previously given an average rating of 8.10 on a scale from 1 to 10 (where 1 was unattractive and 10 was attractive). Other male subjects received a photo that had been given a prior average rating of 2.56 on the same scale. Therefore, about half the male subjects were given the impression that their interactant was very attractive, whereas the rest thought she was quite unattractive. It is important to note that the woman's own appearance was completely unrelated to the type of picture her male partner was given. (There was no picture on the form given to the woman.)

Two interesting questions emerge at this point. First, would the males' impressions evoke the typical stereotypes linked with beauty and would they behave accordingly? Second, would the males' impressions influence their partners' behavior and the impression that the *women* gave in the actual conversation? In other words, would the holder's or perceiver's (man's) behavior influence the target's (woman's) behavior in a way that would confirm the stereotype associated with her purported attractiveness?

To see whether one or the other of the two types of pictures actually evoked the traditional stereotype in the man, immediately upon receiving a picture he was given an impression-formation questionnaire that included 27 traits (e.g., friendliness, enthusiasm, worthiness, social adeptness) that are usually differentially ascribed to attractive and not so attractive persons.

The result was that men faced with the prospect of talking to an attractive woman prejudged her to be a sociable, poised, humorous, and socially adept person, while the men expecting to talk to an unattractive woman quickly formed images of an unsociable, awkward, serious, and socially inept partner. In all, there were a total of 21 personality traits on which there was a large initial difference between the ratings of the men in the attractive versus unattractive conditions.

Finally, after all this preparation, the two people did engage in a free-form (unstructured) 10-minute conversation on the phone. The experimental setup was such that this conversation could be recorded on a two-channel stereo recording device. The man's part of the exchange was recorded on channel 1 and that of the woman on channel 2. This distinction is important, because it means that Snyder et al. (1977) could now play back the woman's part of the conversation to naive (new) judges, in order to obtain the impression of these judges as to just how socially poised, humorous, and otherwise socially adept the woman on the tape seemed to be. These new judgments could be made in the absence of knowledge of what the man said, and, of course, without any knowledge of the woman's true or purported appearance. That is, given that the original male perceivers were inclined to expect (or not expect) their interlocutor to be sensitive, intelligent, or friendly, would naive judges "hear" different degrees of these qualities in the women's tapes?

They certainly did! Recall that there were 21 traits that distinguished the mental picture of the male perceivers in the attractive condition from that of the male perceivers in the unattractive treatment. Well, almost the same picture emerged in the minds of the new judges. A woman who had talked with a male perceiver who thought she was attractive came across as relatively sociable, poised, and adept. As for the other condition, a woman who had talked to a male perceiver who thought she was unattractive came across as relatively unsociable, awkward, and inept. In all, 17 of the 21 traits that had distinguished the original perceivers' stereotypes also distinguished the impressions of the subsequent judges who scored the tapes. In sum, if a woman had conversed with a man who thought she was attractive, she gave the impression that she *was* attractive. The opposite held true for women whose partners thought they were unattractive.

What mediated the women's behavior so that they gave these very different impressions? Apparently, it was the men's behavior, based on what type of person they thought they were conversing with. Other judges listened to the male parts of the taped communications and sensed a difference there, too. The men themselves in the attractive condition were judged to be more sociable, sexually warm, interesting, bold, and socially adept than men in the unattractive condition. And the women subjects were certainly sensitive to these differences. When asked, women in the attractive condition rated their perceivers' image of them as more accurate than did women in the unattractive condition. Moreover, women in the unattractive condition felt that the treatment they received from their perceivers was not typical of the way men generally treated them. (Note again that a woman's actual appearance was totally unrelated to her assigned experimental condition.) As Snyder et al. (1977) put it, "these latter individuals, perhaps, rejected their partners' treatment of them as unrepresentative and defensively adopted more cool and aloof postures to cope with their situations"—hence, behavioral confirmation.

BEHAVIORAL MEDIATION OF STEREOTYPIC BEHAVIOR

The Snyder et al. work indicates that stereotypes might be self-fulfilling even when the stereotyped person is not necessarily flattered by the biased picture. It was noted that most stereotypes present a pejorative picture of the target, and it seems reasonable that people would actually avoid enacting such unfavorable portraits. Even so, through BEHAVIORAL MEDIATION a person may be induced to act in accordance with someone else's prejudice. Recall the evidence in Table VI that "Negroes," compared with "Americans," were stereotyped by white subjects as less honest, less intelligent, less reliable, and generally less attractive as revealed by the bogus pipeline method. A person holding such a prejudice might therefore expect blacks to fare less well in, say, job interviews. Could this set of expectations on the part of whites influence their own behavior (posture, eye contact, seating distance) vis-à-vis blacks to make the behavior of blacks objectively appear less successful than that of whites in this context?

To test this idea, Word, Zanna, and Cooper (1974) set up a laboratory situation that resembled a typical job interview. The essence of the research was an attempt to (1) document differences in behavior on the part of white interviewers toward black versus white candidates and (2) determine whether such discriminatory behavior could have a measurable influence on the success of any given candidate. In order to carry out highly controlled tests of these possibilities, the researchers conducted a series of two experiments. The first study (Study 1) was meant to address point 1 in the above proposition. Here, *naive* white interviewers interviewed *trained* black and white candidates. The second study (Study 2), addressing point 2, used *trained* white interviewers who interviewed *naive* white candidates. The rationale for these combinations will be appreciated once the two studies are explained.

As for Study 1, a good, trained interviewer would probably guard against her or his own prejudices, so instead Word et al. employed *naive* white male college students (subjects) to interview black and white male high-school students (candidates) for a certain job. We can assume that the white subjects were motivated to give a good account of themselves as interviewers because they were made to understand that there would be a prize for the best performance. However, given that they were inexperienced interviewers, it is possible that their prejudices toward blacks and whites in general might be reflected in different behaviors toward black and white candidates. The experimenters were able to constrain or equalize the verbal behavior of these interviewers by requiring that they all ask the same list of 15 questions of each and every candidate. Thus, if prejudice existed, it would have to be revealed in other mediating behavior, if at all.

Of course, the researchers wanted to hold the influence of particular black and white candidates constant. That is, they did not want the behavior of any candidate to uniquely influence the behavior of an interviewer. Therefore, all candidates (blacks and whites) had been carefully pretrained to act in a standardized way. They had been coached to respond to the interview questions with a predetermined set of replies, to sit with a certain posture, and to maintain a specific amount of eye contact with the interviewer. Thus, if the subject/interviewer acted in a certain way toward a black or white candidate, it could be attributed to the interviewer's inclinations rather than to the behavior of a particular candidate. For purposes of comparison, each white interviewer in Study 1 was confronted on separate occasions with one black and one white candidate.

Several nonverbal and related behaviors were employed as measures of prejudice in Study 1; of these, we will consider those that showed the clearest differences between the interviewers' handling of black and white candidates. There are three distinctions of main interest: the distance an interviewer placed his chair from a particular kind of candidate, the length of the interview in minutes, and speech error rate (e.g., repetitions, stutters, incoherent sounds). These records were made without the awareness of the subjects and revealed strong racial differences (see Table VIII). Clearly, white interviewers

TABLE VIII
Average behavior of white interviewers as related to the race of job candidates

Behavior	RACE OF CANDIDATE	
	Black	White
Seating distance (in inches)	62.29	58.43
Interview length (in minutes)	9.42	12.77
Speech error rate (per minute)	3.54	2.37

After Word et al. (1974).

sat closer to white candidates than to those who were black, and they spoke longer and more correctly to whites than to blacks. All in all, this pattern indicates a degree of prejudice against blacks.

Would such differences in nonverbal and related behavior have an influence on the behavior of the two types of candidates and lead them to self-fulfill the stereotype or bias in question? Because the candidates in Study 1 were confederates trained to respond in certain ways, one cannot look to their behavior to answer this question, so Word et al. conducted the second study in the series. In Study 2, white confederates were trained as interviewers. They were rehearsed to act in a manner that closely corresponded to the various patterns of behavior seen in the naive interviewers in Study 1 regarding seating distance, interview length, and speech errors. These trained, white interviewers then interviewed naive white candidates. In this second study, it is these naive candidates (college students) who were the subjects, because the main interest is in whether whites' interviewing style can influence a candidate's success.

Half the new white candidates were involved in interviews that mimicked the experiences of black candidates in Study 1. Their white interviewers' seating distance, interview length, and speech clarity matched the values seen in the "Black" column of Table VIII. The rest of the new white candidates encountered white interviewers whose behavior matched the values seen in the table's "White" column. The advantage of the use of white persons as both interviewers and candidates in Study 2 should be clear. Here, race itself is irrelevant. Rather, what is at issue is how new white candidates will respond to the distinctive treatments afforded black and white candidates in Study 1. In particular, in considering the "success" of the new candidates *as* candidates, which interviewer style might produce the better-looking candidate?

A number of measures were taken to evaluate these possibilities. The interview was allowed to proceed for 5 minutes to establish the tone or style of the two types of interviewer manipulations. Then there was an apparently accidental interruption of the interview. Actually, the interruption occurred by design and set the stage for a second starting point. Now the subject/candidate's seating distance from the interviewer and own speech error rate were covertly recorded on videotape. Further, subsequent to the interview the subjects reported their mood and feelings of friendliness toward the interviewer on paper-and-pencil scales. Finally, independent judges scored the videotapes for the quality of the subject/candidates' performance and composure.

All of these measures revealed differences that favored candidates who had received white candidate–style interviews over candidates who had received white interviewers' black candidate–style interviews, as shown in Table IX. In other words, white candidates who were treated as the whites in Study 1 had been treated were more successful than those who were treated as the blacks in Study 1 had been treated. Apparently, the new candidates detected and reciprocated the differential styles of their interviewers to the relative detriment of those in the latter condition.

TABLE IX
White job candidates' behavior as a consequence of being exposed to interview styles elicited by previous black or white candidates

	PREVIOUS INTERVIEW STYLE	
Behavior	Black	White
Subjects' responses		
Seating distance (in inches)	72.73	56.93
Speech error rate (per minute)	5.01	3.33
Self-ratings[a]		
Mood	3.77	5.97
Interviewer friendliness	4.33	6.60
Judges' responses		
Ratings of candidate[b]		
Performance	1.44	2.22
Demeanor	1.62	3.02

After Word et al. (1974).
Note. On all rating scales employed, the bigger the number, the better the rating.
[a]Self-ratings were based on 7-point scales.
[b]Judges' ratings of candidates were based on 4-point scales.

In conclusion, the Word et al. (1974) study provides an apt demonstration of the self-fulfilling nature of social stereotypes or prejudice. Of course, this assertion is based on the assumption that the white interviewers in their Study 1 were more prejudiced against blacks than against whites, and there is evidence in Table VIII that this was so. Perhaps these initial interviewers behaved in the fashion they did because they *expected* that the black candidates would be relatively more unsuccessful than the white candidates. In any event, the treatment that was afforded blacks, when applied to whites in Study 2, seems destined to elicit behavior that fulfills a particular stereotype.

STEREOTYPES AS NORMATIVE EXPECTATIONS FOR BEHAVIOR

When one first encounters a stranger of a given gender, NORMATIVE EXPECTATIONS come to mind about how that person is likely to act. These expectations fit the thumbnail definition of a stereotype: overgeneralized attitudes based on too little knowledge or experience with that individual. There is considerable evidence that in general women are *thought* to be more conforming and less intelligent than men. However, there is also evidence that these presumed sex differences may not be based strictly on biology but may be specific to certain situations. This latter possibility is raised by additional findings that women are indeed more conforming than men on *male*-related issues but that men are more conforming than women on *female*-related issues (Sistrunk and McDavid, 1971). Thus, if women do conform more than men, this behavior may be caused by situational rather than biological factors.

This pattern of findings led Zanna and Pack (1975) to hypothesize that sex-role stereotypes may provide powerful normative expectations about the way the stereotyped person should behave, given the situation. One circumstance that would promote the enactment of the stereotype on the part of the stereotyped person would be the case where an attractive other person was known to hold the stereotype or expectation. The stereotyped person (target) would then be motivated to act out the stereotype in order to reap the social rewards that often accompany appropriate, normative, or expected behavior. In short, this behavior would represent an interpersonal self-fulfillment of a stereotypic prophecy, wherein the stereotyped person would be aware of the holder's (perceiver's) stereotype and would act accordingly to gain social reinforcement.

To test this idea, Zanna and Pack first employed a questionnaire whereby university women's self-concepts were measured. These self-concepts were organized around certain dimensions commonly included in the traditional sex-role stereotype for females. Each was asked to indicate the extent to which she agreed with the following set of statements: I am the kind of person who is . . .

- very interested in her own appearance.
- very career oriented.
- not at all aggressive.
- not at all dependent on other people.
- very sentimental.
- very objective.
- a very strong believer in women's liberation.
- very tender.

A subject's responses to these items were scored on a scale in which higher numbers indicated her agreement with a traditional female stereotype (i.e., interested in own appearance, not career-oriented, not aggressive, dependent on other people, sentimental, not objective, not believing in women's liberation, and tender).

About 3 weeks after this pretest, individual subjects returned to the laboratory to be in a study purported to deal with person perception and impression formation. A woman was told that she soon would be introduced to a young man (a fictitious person, actually) who was a university student. Before the introduction, however, the woman was given a description of the man, allegedly to facilitate their meeting. In truth, the nature of the description allowed the researchers to test hypotheses regarding the impact of two variables: (1) the attractiveness of the young man (attractive or unattractive), who would turn out to be the holder of a stereotype of women, and (2) the kind of stereotype (traditional or untraditional) that he held. This resulted in a 2 × 2 experimental design as illustrated in Table X.

In the description of the attractive man, he was said to be a 6-foot-1-inch-tall senior who liked sports, owned a car, and was looking for a girlfriend. The description of the unattractive man included the information that he was a 5-foot-5-inch-tall freshman who did not like sports, did not own a car, and already had a girlfriend. Presumably, the women would find the first individual more attractive or desirable than the second and would be more likely to seek social reinforcement from that kind of person.

Concerning the nature of the young man's stereotype of women,

TABLE X
Average change from women's self-conceptualization to their self-presentation
as a function of their male partner's stereotype view and his desirability

Partner's desirability	PARTNER'S STEREOTYPE	
	Traditional	Untraditional
Low	−0.60	−0.60
High	2.35	−5.05

After Zanna and Pack (1975).
Note. Positive entries represent shifts toward a traditional stereotype of women; negative entries represent shifts toward an untraditional stereotype.

a woman was given a copy of a questionnaire that this fictive person had presumably filled out. In the conditions where the man was to hold a traditional stereotype, the phony questionnaire indicated agreement with the following statements: The ideal woman would . . .

- be very soft.
- be concerned with how she looks.
- be very passive.
- be very emotional.
- not be independent.
- not be competitive.
- not be ambitious.
- not be dominant.

On the contrary, in the conditions where the stereotype was to be untraditional, the fictitious man was made to appear to have checked off reactions that were the opposite of the traditional pattern (e.g., "The ideal woman would not be soft, not concerned with how she looks, not passive").

Having been armed with this information about a man they were about to meet (attractive or unattractive; harboring a traditional or untraditional stereotype about women), the women were tested to see whether their behavior would conform to the man's alleged normative expectations, as related to the level of his attractiveness or desirability. At this point a subject filled out a questionnaire about her own attitudes toward the "ideal woman." Zanna and Pack (1975) considered these questionnaire responses to be behavioral or self-presentational, because the women in the study had been given the impression that their questionnaire would be passed on to their male counterpart (the young man) prior to contact. The key items in this questionnaire were duplications of the items the women had answered in the pretest three weeks earlier. The question was, Would their current self-presentation differ from their initial self-conceptualization as a consequence of the various manipulations?

The answer to this question can be seen in Table X. The entries in the table are average *change* scores from the pretest self-conceptualization responses to the experimental self-presentational responses. Negative scores represent shifts away from a traditional stereotype; positive scores indicated changes toward the traditional view. Two interesting patterns are seen in the table. First, when the fictional male was described as undesirable, the women's self-presentation did not strongly shift to conform to his expectations, the difference in the influence of the two stereotypes for this kind of person being nil ($-.60$ versus $-.60$). Contrarily, when the other person's desirability was high, his own particular stereotype had a marked effect on subjects' self-presentation. The attractive man with traditional views elicited presentations that were much more traditional than would have been expected on the basis of the earlier self-conceptualization reports, whereas the attractive man with untraditional views provoked the opposite trend.

Therefore, there is support from the Zanna–Pack (1975) study for the hypothesis that social stereotypes may operate in part as normative expectations to which we conform in order to gain social reinforcement. The women in the experiment tailored their behavior (self-presentation) to be in line with the stereotype of an individual that was presented as attractive and hence in a position to dispense social rewards. On the other hand, when the individual was depicted as unattractive, his stereotype had little influence on the women's self-presentations. In sum, perceivers' stereotypes of traditional or untraditional women can be self-fulfilling when the stereotyped person *wants* to fulfill them.

Old Biases and New Theories

Most of the work covered to this point on ingroup–outgroup bias and social stereotypes was predicated on the assumption that there is a pervasive tendency among humans to simply favor the ingroup over the outgroup. For example, Campbell's (1967) kernel-of-truth and reciprocal-description analysis is based on this premise. While this assumption has stood the test of time and research, there is no reason to exclude the possibility that other mechanisms or processes also underlie intergroup attitudinal relations. Recently, Jussim, Coleman, and Lerch (1987) provided a review and empirical assessment of three contemporary theories of stereotypes and bias. Their review is both clear and comprehensive, so I will follow its outline here. The three positions to be outlined are termed (1) complexity–extremity theory, (2) assumed-characteristics theory, and (3) expectancy-violation theory. There is no claim that these theories are mutually exclusive, but the reader will see that each brings a special perspective to the area.

COMPLEXITY–EXTREMITY THEORY

It is generally the case that people have more contacts and interactions with ingroup members than with outgroup members. As a consequence, a person has more information about the ingroup than about the outgroup as a whole. When making judgments about individuals in these respective groups, more dimensions are available upon which to evaluate an ingroup member. Given this complexity of ingroup information, judgments of ingroup individuals tend to be less than extreme. Knowledge about bad features on some dimensions is balanced or canceled by knowledge about good features on other dimensions. On the other hand, fewer dimensions or smaller amounts of information are available upon which to make judgments of an outgroup person. More extreme evaluations of an outgroup member are thus more likely, because conclusions drawn from a few dimensions could result in a perception of all bad, or all good (see Linville, 1982; Linville and Jones, 1980).

One hypothesis that follows from this theory is that the *range* of evaluations of outgroup members would be wider than the range of evaluations of ingroup members. Since Jussim et al. worked in the domain of whites' stereotypes of whites and blacks, let us follow their lead. Consider this possibility. White subjects encounter and evaluate upper-class white targets and lower-class white targets. These white subjects also encounter upper-class black targets and lower-class black targets. Whatever the main effect of race of target, the theory predicts that whites would assign a wider range of evaluative scores across the two classes of black targets (outgroup) and a narrower range of scores across the two classes of white targets (ingroup).

ASSUMED-CHARACTERISTICS THEORY

According to this theory, a consequence of a stereotype is that it provides the holder with assumed characteristics about a given target. That is, if one is merely provided with a group, ethnic, or gender label, such as "student," "professor," "black," "white," "man," or "woman," there is a widely documented tendency to assume that certain traits are more or less likely to be possessed by the labeled individual. For people in general, there is an assumption that there are more desirable traits within the ingroup than within the outgroup, hence bias arises.

However, the theory states that if further direct and relevant information about the labeled individual is provided, these "background characteristics" should override the attitudinal reaction to sheer group membership or label. (Added information of this type has also been termed DIAGNOSTIC, or INDIVIDUATING INFORMATION.) This idea is known as the ELIMINATION-OF-BIAS HYPOTHESIS. Concerning whites' ratings of blacks and whites, whatever the main effect for reactions to race per se, there should be an even stronger effect for the provision of individuating or diagnostic background characteristics (see, for example, Locksley, Borgida, Brekke, and Hepburn, 1980; Deaux and Lewis, 1984).

EXPECTANCY-VIOLATION THEORY

This position is akin to the assumed-characteristics theory, but it makes somewhat different predictions. The analysis begins with the recognition that group labels do lead to assumptions about traits possessed by the labeled individual. But when it is learned by the perceiver that the individual's actual characteristics *violate* the expectancy derived from the stereotype, evaluations should become more extreme in the direction of the violation. That is, individuals who are found to possess more desirable traits than expected will be evaluated more positively than comparable individuals who were expected to be evaluated positively all along. Further, individuals who are found to possess more undesirable characteristics than expected will be evaluated more negatively than comparable individuals who were expected to be evaluated negatively.

Regarding the stereotypes held by whites about blacks (outgroup) and whites (ingroup), Jussim et al. (1987) state that

expectancy-violation theory predicts that whites will evaluate blacks more favorably than similar whites if either (or both) of two conditions are true: (a) blacks have an unexpected positive characteristic or (b) whites have an unexpected negative characteristic.

This is an interesting prediction, because other theories of stereotypes would lead one to believe that the ingroup would invariably be favored over the outgroup. Here, "group-ness" is not so much the determinant of evaluative reactions as is the *fit* between expectations and information. This situation leads to what from other perspectives would be a paradox: depending on circumstances, members of the outgroup could receive more favorable evaluations than members of the ingroup (see, for example, Smedley and Bayton, 1978).

AN EMPIRICAL ASSESSMENT

Jussim et al. carried out an experiment to test all three propositions just noted. The subjects were white undergraduate students at a large midwestern university who were asked to make judgments about white and black job applicants. The supposed applicants were black or white male confederates who had been photographed at various points in a staged interview. The subjects saw slides of the interviews and heard tapes of the applicants' verbal responses to questions (also contrived). The appearance of the job applicants in the slides and the style in which they responded represented the independent variables in the study.

As noted, some of the applicants were black, and some were white. This setup in effect provided ethnic or racial labels for the subjects; presumably, stereotypes would be evoked in a subject given the knowledge that a black person or a white person was applying for a job (as in an earlier section of this chapter). Beyond race, certain visual information was conveyed by the slides. Some of the applicants were presented as having "upper-class" socioeconomic status: they were conservatively and tastefully dressed. Other applicants were shown as "lower-class" individuals: their dress was out of fashion and shabby. As for the taped verbal responses, some of the job applicants were presented as speaking Standard English, and some were heard using Nonstandard English. For example, in response to the interviewer's question "Why do you want the job?" the two kinds of speech came out thusly:

STANDARD ENGLISH: This is the kind of job I have been trained to do. At my old job I wasn't able to use all of my skills. This job would allow me to use more of my skills, while learning some new ones at the same time.
NONSTANDARD ENGLISH: Dis is da kinda job I been trainin ta do. At ma ole job I wasn able to use all a ma skills. Dis job'd llow me ta use maw of ma skills while learnin some new ones at da same time (Jussim et al., 1987).

In all, the experiment was a 2 × 2 × 2 design, which yields eight conditions. That is, there were two levels of race, crossed with two levels of social class, and further crossed with two levels of English dialect. Various subjects were exposed to parts of the design. All subjects completed ratings of the candidates they happened to see.

These dependent variables were estimates of an applicant's intelligence, job suitability, interpersonal warmth, and likability, among others. By my reckoning, total scores could range from 11 to 105, with higher values representing more favorable evaluations.

The results of these manipulations are shown in Figures 4 and 5; we will use them to assess the three theories reviewed by Jussim et al. (Technically, findings of this type should be displayed in a table or in a bar graph, but for ease of exposition line graphs have been employed here.)

Complexity–extremity theory. This theory would predict that for these subjects (whites) the range of reactions to the ingroup (white targets) would be narrower than that for the outgroup (black targets). Such a difference in range can be seen in Figure 4. The most favorable average rating of upper-class, Standard English–speaking, white targets was 72.45, and the least favorable rating of lower-class, Nonstandard English–speaking whites was 42.64, which is a range of

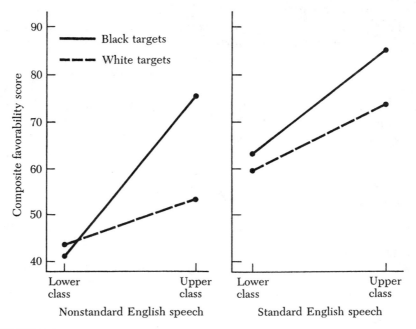

FIGURE 4
AVERAGE COMPOSITE FAVORABILITY SCORES assigned by white subjects to black or white targets as a function of targets' social class and dialect. (After Jussim et al., 1987.)

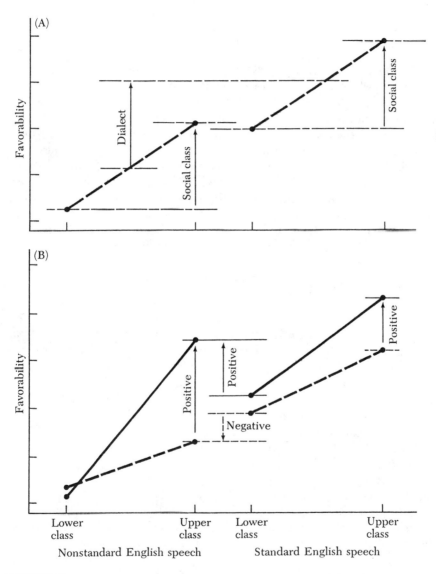

FIGURE 5
SIMPLIFIED VERSIONS OF FIGURE 4 showing (A) the effects of "background information" and (B) "expectancy violations" on whites' average ratings of black or white targets.

29.81. In comparison, the most favorable rating of black targets was 84.02, and the least favorable was 41.68, which is a range of 42.34. As predicted, the range for the ingroup was found to be narrower than that for the outgroup, thus the complexity–extremity theory receives support.

Assumed-characteristics theory. Recall that this theory states that a group label prompts the perceiver to assume certain characteristics about the labeled individual, but that background, diagnostic, or individuating information should override these assumptions. In the Jussim et al. research, race was such a label, to which the background information of socioeconomic class and dialect was experimentally added. Figure 5A is a simplified version of Figure 4, with ratings collapsed (averaged) over black and white targets. It is clear in Figure 5A that background information had its expected impact. Within dialect conditions there was a clear effect for social class, and across dialect conditions there was also a strong effect. These differences are indicated by the vertical arrows between ratings assigned to the various targets as a consequence of the independent variables and are all in the predicted direction. Therefore, the assumed-characteristics theory gains support.

Expectancy-violation theory. Figure 5B shows how the data bear on this theory. The finding that upper-class black targets were more favorably rated than their white counterparts supports the theory. Apparently, when white subjects encountered black applicants with upper-class characteristics, this discovery positively violated their expectations of blacks, and ratings were polarized as a result. This trend is indicated by the upward-pointing arrows in Figure 5B. It is as if the white subjects expected blacks to be somehow handicapped or disadvantaged in the interview situation, but the appearance of such prosperous dress suggested exceptional individuals who had overcome such obstacles (after Kelley, 1971). Similarly, upper-class black targets who spoke Nonstandard English were rated higher than lower-class black targets who spoke Standard English. Apparently, the dress of the former positively violated expectations based on dialect, and ratings polarized upward as a result. On the other hand, the Nonstandard English dialect of upper-class white targets seems to have negatively violated expectations, with the result that those targets were rated *lower* than lower-class, Standard English–speaking white targets (downward-pointing arrow). In any event, these are the interpretations placed on the data by Jussim et al. (1987), and the patterns lend support to the expectancy-violation theory.

Critique. The only part of the Jussim et al. (1987) results that is not informative is the absence of differences in ratings of lower-class black and white targets. Perhaps the only thing that can be said is that expectancies for blacks, or whites, or both were not violated by this manipulation. Alas, it must be lamented that Jussim et al. did not obtain a measure of subjects' attitudes toward race labels *before* the background information about class and dialect was administered, so we cannot be sure that class had no differential effect. Still, the rest of their data are quite useful and do show support (at least in part) for the three contemporary theories in question.

Closing Comments

Several lines of theory and research on social stereotypes and group bias have been developed. The traditional view is that somehow the ingroup is automatically favored over the outgroup, whereas more recent perspectives tell us that reactions to outgroup members can be more complex, depending on what information is available to a perceiver. To my way of thinking, these different-sounding positions are not incompatible. In the first place, the more traditional analysis (say, Campbell's) admits of the influence of information as represented by the concept of the kernel of truth, and an argument was presented here that as the kernel changes, so does the stereotype. Second, background, individuating, or diagnostic information about a particular target may change one's opinion about *that* target but not necessarily about the *group* from which the target is drawn. We have all heard the bigot say: "Hell, some of my best friends are _____." Therefore, there is probably room for many kinds of theories about stereotypes and bias, for there surely is enough bias to develop theories about.

CHAPTER NINE

PERSUASIVE COMMUNICATION AND ATTITUDES

The study of the impact of persuasive communication on attitudes and behavior has a long tradition in social psychology, and current times are no exception. Recently, a number of books have appeared that bear out this contention: *Attitudes and Persuasion: Classic and Contemporary Approaches* (Petty and Cacioppo, 1981); *Communication and Persuasion* (Petty and Cacioppo, 1986); *Influence* (Cialdini, 1984); *Persuasion* (Simons, 1984); and *Propaganda and Persuasion* (Jowett and O'Donnell, 1986). Obviously, I cannot pretend that a single chapter in a general text on attitudes will encompass all of this new literature, much less that of the past. However, the aim is to give a respectful nod to both traditional and modern contributions to the domain. Tradition will be served by the use of long-standing formulations or models of the persuasion process and by the citation of certain classic findings. Modernity will be recognized in the form of up-to-date findings. In this way, a balanced presentation of contributions to the field will be achieved.

The structure of the chapter will follow a long-standing outline of the persuasion process. Conceptually, the comprehensive study of persuasive communication requires attention to three elements: (1) the communicator or source, (2) the audience or recipient, and (3) the communication or message. In any real-life persuasion attempt, these three elements are simultaneously and interactively involved. In short, it matters a great deal who says what to whom. The persuasion process cannot be said to exist if one of the elements is missing. Nevertheless, the process is rarely studied as a whole, and

300

elements are often researched in a certain amount of isolation from one another.

The reason for this reductionism is easy to understand. First, an experiment that incorporates a large number of source, audience, and message variables in a single grand design would of necessity be complicated and expensive, and not all researchers are in a position to afford such luxury. Second, at times a researcher is interested in testing only a specific question with respect to one of the elements. Involving all of the elements in every single study may not be in her or his best interest. Lastly, reductionism and fractionalization seem endemic to social psychology, and maybe for good reason. If, ultimately, we need a *grand* theory of persuasive communication, in the meantime we probably also need *mini*-theories concerning sources, audiences, and messages. The plan for this chapter is to take up the elements of source, audience, and message in turn.

The Persuasive Source

CREDIBILITY

One of the factors that is known to affect the persuasive influence of a source is "credibility." It should not surprise the reader to discover that the more credible the source, the more persuasive the communication. CREDIBILITY can be discussed in terms of perceived competence, status, expertise, intelligence, sheer moral standing, or other such dimensions. We find that audiences are more persuaded by a respected medical authority than by a quack, and that they are more influenced by the claims of scientists than those of crackpots. There are many studies that show this sort of relationship of credibility to persuasion, and excellent reviews are available (McGuire, 1969; Eagly and Himmelfarb, 1978).

Along these lines, certain events in mainstream U.S. culture in recent years have accentuated the importance of the role of credibility in persuasion and leadership. Just prior to and during the presidential campaign of 1988, the concept of the "character issue" emerged. Political fortunes were lost on the basis of this issue, as indicated in Table I. Joe Biden, Douglas Ginsburg, and Gary Hart — who at some point were all impressive aspirants to their respective governmental posts—had their aspirations dashed by losses of credibility due to revelations about allegedly questionable behavior. Even some of the final major players in that campaign were menaced by the "character issue." The Democratic presidential candidate Michael

TABLE I
Consequences for national figures resulting from an erosion of their credibility due to certain problems with images

Figure	Role or occupation	Year	Problem	Consequence
Bakker, Jim	Televangelist	1987	Sexual indiscretion	Ministry lost
Biden, Joe	Presidential candidate	1987	Plagiarism	Candidacy withdrawn
Ginsburg, Douglas H.	Supreme Court nominee	1987	Restricted-substance use	Nomination withdrawn
Hart, Gary	Presidential candidate	1987	Sexual indiscretion	Candidacy withdrawn
Swaggart, Jimmy	Televangelist	1988	Sexual indiscretion	Ministry suspended
Tower, John	Cabinet candidate	1989	Drinking, womanizing	Candidacy defeated
Wright, Jim	Speaker of the House	1989	Finances	Resignation

Note. References to the entries are Bakker: Watson, Smith, and Wright (1987); Biden: Alter and Fineman (1987); Ginsburg: Press, McDaniel, DeFrank, Clift, McKillop, and Hutchinson (1987); Hart: Morganthau, Warner, Fineman, and Calonius (1987); Swaggart: Rosellini (1988); Tower: Martz, Clift, and Fineman (1989); Wright: Drew (1989).

Dukakis was obliged to defend his mental health (Range, Goode, Borger, Baer, and Walsh, 1988), and the Republican vice-presidential hopeful, Dan Quayle, was made to squirm regarding his choice of safe military service during the war in Vietnam (Alter, Padgett, King, and Noah, 1988). Of course, ethical issues ruined two highly visible politicians in 1989: John Tower, a candidate for Secretary of Defense, on the basis of alleged womanizing and drinking; and Jim Wright, the Speaker of the House, for questionable financial dealings.

In the related arena of religious leadership and popularity, famous televangelists Jim Bakker and Jimmy Swaggart lost to some degree their lofty positions and popularity in their respective ministries, again for what can be called the "character issue." Clearly, "credibility" is not merely some trivial explanatory concept dreamed up by social scientists to account for some inconsequential laboratory findings. In real life, credibility matters!

Discounting Cues and Disassociation

As noted, audiences are generally more persuaded by credible than by implausible sources. Those audiences nevertheless learn or retain about the *same* amount of the content of the persuasive message from either (McGuire, 1969)! For example, if two audiences heard the same speech about the effectiveness of pesticides in controlling insects, those people who thought they were listening to a Nobel Prize–winning chemist would be more persuaded than those who were under the impression that they were listening to a high-school chemistry student. But if pressed, both audiences could reveal about the same amount of *information* about pesticides and their alleged effectiveness. Therefore, the simple availability of information is not what necessarily determines the effectiveness of a persuasive communication. The actual cause of the attitudinal differences appear to be DISCOUNTING CUES, which are any characteristics or features of the source that undermine its persuasiveness. Discounting cues lead to the process of DISCOUNTING, which is the suppression of whatever initial attitude change accrued from the persuasive communication. This discounting occurs when the theme of the message is paired with other information (the discounting cues) "that causes subjects not to accept the message conclusion to the extent that they would if they had received the message alone" (Gruder, Cook, Hennigan, Flay, Alessis, and Halamaj, 1978). Apparently the absence of credibility is one discounting cue that leads to the suppression of attitude change that would otherwise stem from the persuasive communication.

On the other hand, DISASSOCIATION refers to a process whereby there is a breakdown of the pairing of the message theme and the discounting cues. This breakdown is thought to be spontaneous and could be traced to one of the normal bases for forgetting such as disuse, decay, retrieval difficulties, or interference. Should disassociation occur and should the audience retain the message content, one's attitude after disassociation would depend on how much residual influence the message conclusion carried at the time of disassociation.

THE SLEEPER EFFECT

The important implication of the process of disassociation is that a person may retain the information contained in a persuasive communication, but that over time the source of that information might be forgotten or misidentified. If a person's attitude is assessed immediately after the communication and again after disassociation has had an opportunity to occur, two very different attitudinal pictures might emerge. Any such improvement in an attitude over time is known as a SLEEPER EFFECT, which is a process whereby a persuasive message may have a greater delayed impact than the initial effect on subjects' attitudes. (A "sleeper" by definition is something unpromising or unnoticed that suddenly attains prominence or value, as, for example, a race horse that suddenly wins after a history of poor performance.)

A classic study. One of the earliest studies on source credibility and the sleeper effect was conducted in a regular history course at Yale University (Hovland and Weiss, 1951). The researcher was presented as a guest lecturer; the rationale to the students for conducting research in this setting was that it would provide information that would be useful to a class discussion later. In its essential aspects, the experimental design involved two types of communicators: those with high credibility and those with low credibility. For example, in a communication on the feasibility of U.S. atomic submarines, the high-credibility source was said to be Robert J. Oppenheimer, a noted American authority on nuclear matters. His opposite, the low-credibility source concerning information about the U.S. Navy, was said to be *Pravda*, the official Soviet communist newspaper.

The basic plan was to measure the students' opinions on the submarine issue (along with several other issues) at three critical points: (1) before a persuasive communication by a high- or low-credibility communicator, (2) immediately after such communications, and (3) 4 weeks after the communications. This timetable would enable Hovland and Weiss to ascertain shifts in attitudes as a function of persuasive communication and the passage of time. The critical credibility manipulation turned out to be successful in that fully 90% of the subjects in the high-credibility condition rated that source as trustworthy, whereas a scant 11% of the subjects in the low-credibility condition thought that source was trustworthy.

The central findings from these procedures are shown in Figure 1, in terms of net change in attitude from before the communication to immediately after, and again a month later. The high-credibility subjects showed an immediate shift of 23 percentage points toward the position advocated by the source, whereas the low-credibility condition evidenced a change of merely 7 percentage points at this time. Parenthetically, it is interesting to note that there was no difference across these groups in the amount of information learned at the point of the immediate postcommunication measure, so it was not how *much* the students knew that influenced their attitudes. Rather, the difference in attitude at the first opinion measure must have been caused by something like discounting cues (in the low-credibility condition) discussed earlier. Even so, when the students'

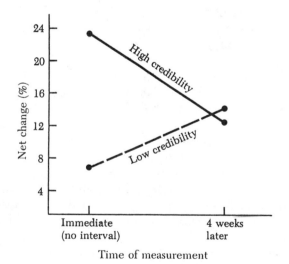

FIGURE 1
SLEEPER EFFECT in persuasive communication. The values on the vertical axis represent the amount of change in attitude from before to some time after a communication, as a function of the credibility of the communicator. (After Hovland and Weiss, 1951.)

attitudes were again measured 4 weeks later, the difference in attitude shift had disappeared, presumably as a result of disassociation.

A modern study. A comprehensive and compelling laboratory
study of the sleeper effect is available from Gruder et al. (1978).
These researchers noted certain failures to find the effect in the past,
so they set out the following conditions that need to be met for any
study of sleeper-like attitudinal phenomena:

1. The persuasive communication that is employed must be strong enough
to have a significant initial impact on attitudes.
2. There must be a discounting cue powerful enough to inhibit significantly
the amount of change in attitude that would otherwise be caused by the message.
3. The discounting cue and the message conclusion must have time to
become disassociated before the subsequent (second) attitudinal measure is
taken.
4. The level of attitude in a message-only (no discounting cue) control group
must be higher at the time of the subsequent (second) measure than is the level
of the discounting cue group immediately after exposure to the message. In
other words, the cue and the message have to be disassociated quickly enough
so that the message still has some impact when disassociation occurs.

To meet the first of these four requirements, laboratory subjects
(college students) were exposed to a pretested communication known
to be effective in changing attitudes. The written message argued
against a recent revision in traffic laws that permitted a right turn on
a red signal. For the second requirement, some subjects found that
the message was followed by a "Note to the Reader," which restated
the message conclusion but labeled it as being false and further
refuted the message by saying it was inaccurate. That is, these particular subjects were exposed to discounting cues regarding the message (as if it had come from a noncredible source). To meet the third
condition, the experimenters measured the attitude of the subjects
toward the traffic light message immediately after they read the
message and again 5 weeks later, an interval that provided an opportunity for the disassociation of the message from the discounting
cues. The scaling device used by the researchers ranged from -60
(least favorable to the message) to $+60$ (most favorable to the message). Concerning the fourth requirement, in addition to the discounting-cue group, two control groups were tested. One control
group read no message at all (no-message controls); the other group
read the message in the absence of discounting cues (message-only
controls). The favorableness of these subjects toward the traffic light

message was also measured, and these data provide an opportunity to check for a sleeper effect.

We can look for that effect in Figure 2, where it can be clearly seen that at the time of the immediate postmessage measurement, the message-only controls were much more favorable toward the message than were the discounting-cue subjects. These subjects were no more favorable to the message than were the no-message controls. This initial, large difference between the two message groups can be traced to acceptability (discounting cues). However, after 5 weeks, the picture had changed. The attitude of the no-message controls remained fairly stable, for there was no reason that it should change. On the contrary, there was a strong positive shift in the attitude of the discounting-cue group, which represents the classic sleeper effect. This positive shift was presumably caused by the disassociation of the discounting cues from the message content (and a subsequent experiment by Gruder et al., 1978, showed that something like disassociation does take place). Finally, there was the expected dissipation or decay of the message for the message-only controls after some time had passed. It is sufficient to say, however, that the data from these controls satisfies the fourth requirement in the list by Gruder et al. of conditions for the proper study of sleeper effect phenomena.

In summary, the presence of discounting cues, which reduced

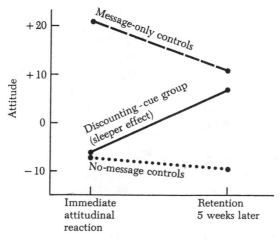

FIGURE 2
SLEEPER EFFECT in persuasive communication. (After Gruder et al., 1978.)

the message's acceptability, seems to have inhibited attitude change that the message would otherwise have produced (witness the message-only control attitude). Still, 5 weeks later something like disassociation of the cues from the message seems to have taken place, with the result that by the time of the second measurement the attitude of the discounting-cue group had markedly improved— hence, the sleeper effect.

A current study. Yet another set of authors has echoed the difficulty of demonstrating a sleeper effect. In a review of dozens of fairly recent publications, Pratkanis, Greenwald, Leippe, and Baumgardner (1988) credit only Gruder et al. (1978) with having done so. However, for Pratkanis et al. (1988), the difficulties stem from the way the topic has been studied rather than with the importance or viability of the phenomenon. In what must be one of the most definitive lines of research in social psychology, Pratkanis and his coworkers carried out a series of 16 separate experiments involving 478 subjects in an attempt to isolate variables (e.g., timing of the identification of the source before or after the message; length of measurement delay) that would produce a sleeper effect. Although it is impossible to review such a large body of work in this single chapter, it is very useful to present the conclusion that the researchers reached:

A sleeper effect can be obtained reliably when subjects (a) note the important arguments in a message, (b) receive a discounting cue *after* the message, and (c) rate the trustworthiness of the message communicator immediately *after* receiving the discounting cue (Pratkanis et al., 1988; emphasis added).

Apparently, other combinations or levels of these variables may have effects, but they do not generate what is taken to be the classic sleeper effect. It is particularly important to note the influence of the *timing* of the discounting cue. In their 16 studies Pratkanis et al. (1988) never found a sleeper effect if the cue was presented *before* the persuasive communication. The import of this finding will be discussed after we review their last experiment.

Having reached the multipart conclusion cited above, Pratkanis et al. showed faith in their own propositions by conducting a seventeenth study as a test. The persuasive communication they used was a 1,000-word message on the drawbacks of a 4-day work week. It cited problems with such schedules, including employee dissatisfaction. Subjects' agreement with the communication was measured twice: immediately following their reading of an article that contained the message, and again 6 weeks later. Scores could range from −60 (strong disagreement) to +60 (strong agreement).

A discounting cue was given to subjects in two of the four conditions that will be covered here, as follows:

Since this article went to press, new research evidence on this topic has been released. In our next issue we will report the findings of a comprehensive study that demonstrates the conclusion of this article is false, and, in fact, the opposite is true—namely that the 4-day work week does not produce major problems and increases employee satisfaction.

Having established the message and the cue (to be used where appropriate), I will now outline the four conditions in Experiment 17: (1) message-only controls, (2) no-message controls, (3) cue-after-message experimentals, and (4) cue-before-message experimentals. As it happens, conditions 1, 2, and 3 are similar enough to the Gruder et al. (1978) research that we can review the data in Figure 2 to see what to expect from Pratkanis et al. The message-only controls (1) should show relatively high agreement immediately following the communication and some decay of this agreement by the 6-week measure. For their part, the no-message controls (2) should show relatively low agreement on the immediate measure and not much change 6 weeks later. Next, if all goes well for the sleeper effect, the cue-after experimentals (3) should show low agreement upon immediate measurement and a sharp increase in agreement 6 weeks later. The only effect that cannot be predicted from the Gruder et al. data in Figure 2 is the effect for the cue-before subjects (4), because that treatment was not included in the earlier study.

By and large, these predictions are borne out in the results shown in Figure 3. Further, there is an interesting difference between the pattern for the cue-after and the cue-before treatments. Pratkanis et al. thought that there would be a sleeper effect only for the cue-after condition, and they were correct. It is on this difference between cue-before and cue-after effects that those authors arrived at a revised theory of sleeper effects in persuasive communication. Their model was based not on the concept of disassociation but on the concept of decay.

DISCOUNTING CUES AND DECAY

The observation that a cue-before manipulation does *not* lead to a sleeper effect (see Figure 3) presents difficulties for an interpretation that says that sleeper effects happen because the message and the source become disassociated over time. In the first place, presenting the cue before the message does not even produce very low

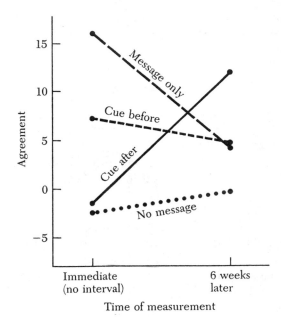

FIGURE 3
SLEEPER EFFECT in persuasive communication showing effects of cue-before and cue-after procedures. (After Pratkanis et al., 1988.)

agreement with that message at the immediate measurement. Then, the passage of time does not make for enhanced agreement. Thus, the cue-before effect looks more than anything else like a weakened message-only effect. But before we grapple further with the results of this particular condition, let us see how Pratkanis et al. (1988) account for sleeper effects that *do* occur.

The differential-decay explanation. According to this model, a sleeper effect occurs when subjects (a) note the important information and points in a communication and (b) receive a discounting cue *after* the communication. It is assumed—and supported by results just discussed— that the communication and the discounting cue have opposite and almost equal impacts. The message and the cue are said to be "not well-integrated in memory" (Pratkanis et al., 1988). I take this to mean that because of the order of presentation, the communication and the subsequent cue have an independent and perhaps successive influence on agreement or attitude. To put it another way, there would be two "memories" about the issue: the memory of the original communication and the memory of the discounting cue. These opposing forces and their net, resultant impact are presented in theoretical form in Figure 4.

As time passes, both the message effect (memory) and the cue effect (memory) begin to decay, where "decay" implies some form of forgetting or loss of retention. According to the theory, there is a slower rate of decay for the first element in the sequence (the communication) than for the second (the discounting cue). These differential rates are seen in the respective slopes beyond the point of the discounting cue presentation in Figure 4. If an attitudinal measure were taken some time well past the discounting cue presentation, positive shifts in net agreement would be detected—hence, the resultant sleeper effect.

But what about the absence of a sleeper effect for the cue-before procedure? Pratkanis et al. (1988) understand that result thusly:

According to the differential decay interpretation, a sleeper effect is not likely to occur when discounting information precedes the message. In such cases

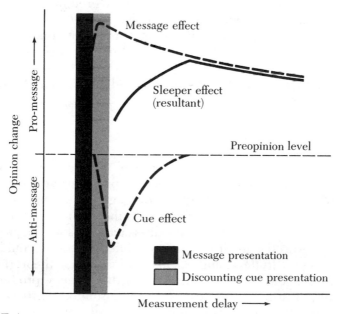

FIGURE 4
DIFFERENTIAL DECAY INTERPRETATION of the sleeper effect. The discounting cue has immediate counterpersuasive impact, but this negative effect decays more rapidly than does the positive effect of the message. (After Greenwald et al., 1986.)

subjects may be more disposed to counterargue with the message as they read. Thus, the persuasive impact of the message is attenuated, and the message and source [cue] are more likely to form a unit in memory.

In other words, the relatively low agreement of the cue-before subjects at the immediate measure (about +6 or +7 scale units in Figure 3) was due to the fact that the discounting cue and the communication became well integrated as the communication was received. Rather than independent influences on agreement or attitude, the message and the cue became part of a single influence. Because there would be only one memory concerning the issue, it is not possible to speak of differential rates of decay, and neither could there be any kind of "resultant" shift over time—hence, no sleeper effect.

SUMMARY

Source characteristics, such as credibility, certainly have to be taken into account in assessing the impact of persuasive communications. In some arenas, such as politics at the national level, credibility may be everything. But on all levels, credibility comes into play sooner or later. The research on sleeper effects indicates that credibility has its strongest influence sooner rather than later. This outcome is due to some feature of the psychology of the recipient of a message.

Let us now consider the role of the audience as an active factor in the persuasion process.

The Persuaded (or Not) Audience

Implied in any discussion of "persuasion" is the goal of establishing in a person an attitude where one did not previously exist, or, more commonly, the goal of changing, modifying, or shifting an attitude that already exists. A further implication is that the attitude advocated by some communication has to be discrepant to some degree from the existing attitude, for if it were not different there would be no possibility for attitude change. This notion raises theoretical and empirical questions as to just how much discrepancy produces the most change. But even if we can determine some objective distance between two attitudinal expressions, there remains the problem of subjective estimates of that distance. Humans are anything but infallible judges, and it is known that judgmental processes, including judgments of attitudes, have built-in errors or natural distortions about them. In this section I will take up the topics of (1) assimilation and contrast, (2) latitudes of acceptance and rejection of messages, and (3) an area of theory known as the elaboration likelihood model. All of these address the role of the audience in persuasive communications.

ASSIMILATION AND CONTRAST

Using a very simple psychophysical task, Sherif, Taub, and Hovland (1958) demonstrated assimilation and contrast in such judgments. Subjects were given a set of several weights that ranged up to 141 grams and were asked to sort these weights into six different slots or categories. When *no* reference, or anchor point, was provided (i.e., no explicit standard to establish the meaning of "heavy"), the subjects did a fairly good job of spreading the various weights evenly over the range of available categories, as indicated in the top part of Figure 5. However, when anchors were provided, the picture of the distribution of the very same weights changed! For instance, on one trial the subjects were provided with an anchor of 141 grams. That is, they were told that 141 grams represents "heavy." In this instance many more weights in the set were judged to be "heavy" than before, as seen in the middle illustration in Figure 5. At other times, when

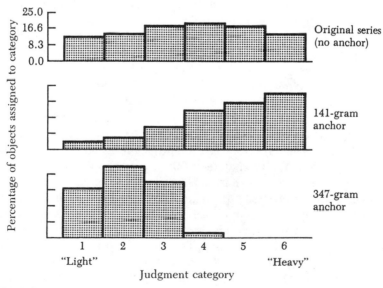

FIGURE 5
ASSIMILATION AND CONTRAST EFFECTS related to anchor weights. (After Sherif et al., 1958.)

a weight as heavy as 347 grams was used as the anchor for "heavy," many of the original set of weights were judged to be "light" (Figure 5, bottom).

When judging the heaviness of any object, it matters very much what sort of standard or anchor stimulus is being considered. Apparently, when the anchor is at or near the high end of the series or assortment in question, weights in the series are actually perceived as being more similar to the anchor than is really the case. That is, we make a perceptual error and *assimilate* nearby weights into or toward the category marked by the anchor; this process is termed ASSIMILATION. On the other hand, when the anchor is a considerable distance from the series, most of the weights are perceived as being even more different from the anchor than is really the case. Here we make another kind of perceptual or judgmental error and tend to perceive a greater *contrast* between these weights and weights in the category marked by the anchor; this process is termed CONTRAST. In other words, stimuli at some close distance to an anchor are seen as more similar to that anchor than they really are (assimilation), whereas stimuli at some distance from an anchor are seen as more dissimilar to that anchor than they really are (contrast).

What does all this have to do with persuasive communication and attitudes? A great deal if we consider one's own attitudinal position as an anchor against which is judged the attitudinal position found in any given message. A familiar example, along with an illustration, will help clarify this possibility. Imagine a person (who will be our subject) at a university social gathering. Conversation in the group has centered on one of the school's more visible teams, say, the women's volleyball team, which is scheduled to play 10 tough varsity games in the forthcoming year. Our subject happens to feel that the team will neither win every competition (100% wins) nor lose every competition (0% wins). In fact, the subject feels that the team probably will win 5 of its 10 matches (50%). Thus, our subject's current attitudinal anchor in this matter is 50%.

Further imagine that one or another person at the party voices his or her strong conviction concerning the team's chances for future success and that this expression can be viewed as a persuasive communication as much as any other. This outside opinion (to our subject) could range anywhere from 0% to 100%, but for the moment say it is 50%. Upon hearing this 50% communication, should our subject's attitude change? No, because we have already accepted the assumption that audience–message discrepancy is a prerequisite for change. But what about cases where the message may have advocated 0 to

40% wins, or 60 to 100% wins? Reference to Figure 6 provides a look at some possibilities. According to a principle that can be drawn from known assimilation effects, attitudinal positions that are close to the subject's anchor will be judged as *nearer* to his or her own attitude than they really are. That is, assimilation will reduce (psychologically) the discrepancy between 40% and the anchor, and 60% and the anchor. Recall again that if there is no or very little audience–message discrepancy involved, one cannot expect much attitude change.

Next, at the most extreme distances from the subject's 50% anchor—the 0–10% and 90–100% ranges—one would expect a similar outcome (no attitude change), but one based on a principle derived from known contrast effects. Assuming these distances to be far enough, our subject would contrast (exaggerate) the difference between his own attitude and that of the extreme communication and would see those attitudinal positions as further from his own than they are in reality. (One can imagine the subject coming away from such a gathering and reporting to an acquaintance, "You know,

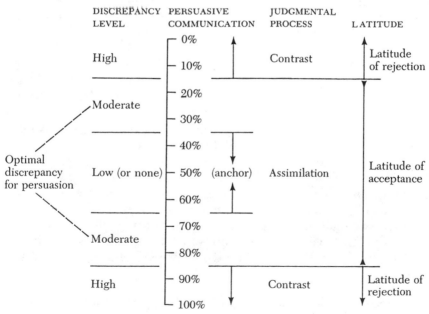

FIGURE 6
LATITUDES OF ACCEPTANCE AND REJECTION as they relate to the concepts of assimilation and contrast.

there was some fool at the party who really believes the volleyball team is going to win every game this season. He must be crazy!" There is a strong sense of exaggeration or contrast here.) Therefore, attitude change under circumstances of extreme messages is unlikely because there is not only the true mathematical distance between our subject's anchor and the message content, but also the added psychological distance due to contrast effects. When discrepancy is *too* high, attitude change will not be forthcoming, because extremely discrepant positions will strike the subject as completely implausible or unfeasible.

That leaves a consideration of the impact of messages that are moderately discrepant from the subject's initial anchor. Although it is strictly an empirical question in real life, in the example, messages that call for 20–30% wins, or 70–80% wins are probably neither close enough to the anchor to become involved in assimilation nor far enough from the anchor to engender contrast. It is toward these ranges that the attitude about the team's chances might well shift, all else being equal. Thus, an attitude change theory that is based on assimilation and contrast effects would predict most attitude change in the presence of moderate audience–message discrepancies. (Of course, the current analysis is indebted to the seminal work on social judgment theory by Sherif and Hovland, 1961.)

LATITUDES OF ACCEPTANCE AND REJECTION

Let us look further at research on the question of audience–message discrepancies and use the notions of assimilation and contrast to understand data already presented. Before we do so, however, it will be useful to explore the impact of persuasive communications on attitudes from a slightly different orientation. We still expect little attitude change toward the extreme positions in Figure 6, so we can call the area occupied by these extremes the LATITUDE(S) OF REJECTION. Contrarily, although aware that the remaining positions are not equally persuasive as messages for change, we can call the area occupied by these intermediate positions the LATITUDE OF ACCEPTANCE. Given this new map, so to speak, it is possible to write a short, two-part summary of all that has been said so far on latitude effects.

1. Persuasive communications that fall within a person's latitude of rejection on an issue will usually not change her or his attitude.
2. Persuasive communications that fall within a person's latitude of acceptance may change her or his attitude, generally as a positive function of audience–message discrepancy (cf. Hovland and Pritzker, 1957; Sherif and Hovland, 1961; Sherif, Sherif, and Nebergall, 1965).

Latitude width and assimilation and contrast. A classic study on latitude and assimilation–contrast effects was carried out by Hovland, Harvey, and Sherif (1957). The real-world controversy studied by Hovland et al. was the prohibition of the sale of alcoholic beverages in one state in the United States that was "dry" at the time. That is, the sale of such beverages in that state was illegal. To ensure a wide range of attitudes on the topic for their study, real-world groups of "drys" (pro-prohibition people) were assembled from members of the Women's Christian Temperance Union and the Salvation Army (long-standing opponents of alcohol consumption), whereas groups of "wets" (anti-prohibition people) were gathered from "cases personally known to the [experimenters] or their assistants." Finally, a group of people of no known persuasion were included in order to represent more moderate stands on the issue.

The latitudes of acceptance and rejection of the subjects were estimated by using the scale shown in Figure 7. Respondents were asked to indicate (1) which items came closest to their own view, (2) which items were at least acceptable to them, and (3) which items

---

A. Since alcohol is the curse of mankind, the sale and use of alcohol, including light beer, should be completely abolished.

B. Since alcohol is the main cause of corruption in public life, lawlessness, and immoral acts, its sale should be prohibited.

C. Since it is hard to stop at a reasonable moderation point in the use of alcohol, it is safer to discourage its use.

D. Alcohol should not be sold or used except as a remedy for snake bites, cramps, colds, fainting, and other aches and pains.

E. The arguments in favor of and against the sale and use of alcohol are nearly equal.

F. The sale of alcohol should be regulated so that it is available in limited quantities for special occasions.

G. The sale and use of alcohol should be permitted with proper state controls, so that the revenue from taxation may be used for the betterment of schools, highways, and other state institutions.

H. Since prohibition is a major cause of corruption in public life, lawlessness, immoral acts, and juvenile delinquency, the sale and use of alcohol should be legalized.

I. It has become evident that man cannot get along without alcohol; therefore, there should be no restriction whatsoever on its sale and use.

FIGURE 7

REPRESENTATIVE CONTEMPORARY STATEMENTS ON PROHIBITION. These statements range from strong advocacy of prohibition (Statement A) to strong advocacy of repeal of prohibition (Statement I). (After Hovland et al., 1957.)

were definitely objectionable. It was found that differences in latitude width were related to the extremity of the respondent's own stand. Table II indicates that people holding extreme stands (wet or dry) accepted fewer items and actively rejected more items than did people holding more moderate views.

Further, as a measure of assimilation and contrast processes, each respondent was asked to concentrate on statement F in Figure 7 and to place it, according to her or his own reaction, on a graphic scale that ranged from extremely dry to extremely wet positions. Given that the researchers already knew the individual respondent's own preferred item on the scale, they were in a position to see whether the respondent might be inclined to place statement F closer to (assimilation) or further away from (contrast) his or her own preference than would be warranted by the objective qualities of statement F. If all the respondents placed statement F where it belonged on an objective basis, all the data points would lie along the horizontal broken line seen in Figure 8. However, if contrast and assimilation occurred, the pattern of data points should roughly conform to the wavelike solid line running across the figure.

In scanning from left to right across Figure 8, it can be seen that people who personally preferred statements A or B tended to see statement F as fitting in near the G and H portion of the scale. That is, these extreme "drys" gave evidence of a contrast effect and displaced the moderately wet F-statement *away* from their own stands. Nearer the middle range of the abscissa, something of an assimilation effect occurred, with a partial displacement of the item toward the

TABLE II
Average number of statements that were judged acceptable (latitude of acceptance) or objectionable (latitude of rejection) to respondents as a function of the extremity of their own stand on the issue

	MEAN NUMBER OF STATEMENTS	
Respondent's own most acceptable statement	Actively accepted	Actively rejected
Extreme wet or dry (A, B, G, H, I)	2.81	4.71
Moderate (C, D, E, F)	3.05	3.70

After Hovland et al. (1957).
Note. The statements used in this study are listed in Figure 7.

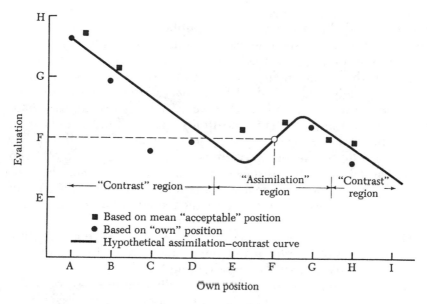

FIGURE 8
AVERAGE EVALUATION OF THE MODERATELY WET COMMUNICA-
TION (Statement F in Figure 7) by respondents holding various personal positions on the issues (A through I in Figure 7) plotted against a theoretical
assimilation–contrast curve (wavelike line). If all the respondents had placed
Statement F where it belonged on an objective basis, all data points would lie
along the horizontal broken line in the figure. However, contrast and assimilation occurred, as revealed by the pattern of data points that roughly conform
to the wavelike solid line running across the figure. This assimilation–contrast
effect is generally seen for the respondents' own preferred position (circles) and
for positions that respondents found acceptable (squares). (After Hovland et al.,
1957.)

individual's own stand. Finally, as the respondents' own stands in
Figure 8 became more extremely wet, there is the beginning of a
tendency to again displace the position of statement F away from
one's own position, which is another contrast effect.

Hovland et al. (1957) thus provided an early demonstration of
assimilation and contrast effects as related to latitudes of acceptance
and rejection. More recent investigators have also documented the
phenomena. Eagly and Telaak (1972) measured subjects' latitude of
acceptance on an issue related to sexual behavior. These researchers
assembled a scale of items that represented a wide range of reactions
to the policy and practice of birth control. For example, a highly

favorable item read: "Birth control devices should be available to everyone, and the government and public welfare agencies should encourage the use of such devices." From the opposite perspective, a highly unfavorable item read: "All birth control devices should be illegal and the government should prevent them from being manufactured" (Eagly and Telaak, 1972). In addition to these extreme statements, there were others that were more or less intermediate, making up a scale that had nine items spaced about evenly in an order from "for" to "against." A subject was asked to indicate how many items he or she agreed with; thus, width of latitude of acceptance was taken as the distance in scale units between the most opposing and the most affirmative statement agreeable to the subject. Additionally, the subject indicated which single item was most preferred.

On the basis of this information, the subjects were divided into three categories of latitude of acceptance: narrow, medium, and wide. These groups were identified by dividing the distribution of widths for the entire sample into thirds (i.e, the distribution was trichotomized). Next all subjects read a number of persuasive messages about birth control and again picked a most preferred item from the 9-point scale previously described. Attitude change on the issue was the shift in scale value between the most preferred item on the pretest and the most preferred item on the posttest. These attitude change scores are presented in Table III, where positive values represent shifts toward the message content and negative scores are changes in the opposite direction. It can be seen that there were clear differences in the amount of attitude change across levels of attitude width, as predicted by the theory. Subjects with a relatively

TABLE III
Average attitude change in response to a persuasive communication as related to subjects' width of latitude of acceptance on the issue of birth control

Latitude width	Attitude change[a]
Wide	+.80
Medium	+.09
Narrow	−.11

After Eagly and Telaak (1972).
[a]Responses were obtained using an 11-point scale. Positive numbers indicate an attitudinal shift toward the message content; negative numbers indicate a shift away from message content.

wide latitude of acceptance showed the most shifting toward the message, while subjects with a relatively narrow latitude showed shifting away from the message.

Current research examples. The concepts of assimilation and contrast are in active use in guiding and interpreting research on aspects of attitudes (e.g., polarization of judgments: Romer, 1983; formation of stereotypes: Manis, Paskewitz, and Cotler, 1986). Here, I will concentrate on an interesting application of the concepts of latitudes of acceptance and rejection for an analysis of changes in self-esteem. A person can certainly be said to have attitudes about herself or himself, and the whole of Chapter 10 will be devoted to this topic. For now, we will examine the work of Rhodewalt and Agustsdottir (1986) on the effects of self-presentation (behavior) on self-esteem (attitude).

Self-esteem can be defined as a person's self-conceptualization along an evaluative dimension. Our concepts about ourselves stem from many sources, including how other people feel about us and how we judge our own behavior. It is thought that self-esteem is fairly constant over the long run. However, because there is a huge amount of information we use as a basis for our respective self-concepts, it is impossible to hold it all in awareness at any given moment. Thus, momentary, short-term changes are conceivable and can stem from inputs such as persuasive communications, the topic of this chapter. Consider these possibilities. If you were to praise yourself to some other person, would your glowing self-presentation enhance your own self-esteem? On the other side, if you were to criticize yourself in the presence of a listener, would your gloomy self-presentation diminish your own self-esteem?

For Rhodewalt and Agustsdottir, the answers depend on several factors, including the widths of the latitudes of one's acceptance and rejection for communications or information regarding the self. As Rhodewalt and Agustsdottir see it, the phenomenal self (level of self-esteem) of a nondepressed individual can be located somewhere on a dimension ranging from unfavorable to favorable, as seen in Figure 9A. For a certain person—say, someone who is not particularly depressed as a rule—both extremely unfavorable *and* favorable messages would be dismissed as falling into latitudes of rejection. But for this sort of person, who is not chronically critical of himself, it is theorized that the latitude of acceptance would extend further toward the favorable pole of the dimension rather than toward the unfavorable pole, as illustrated in Figure 9A. As a consequence, for a non-

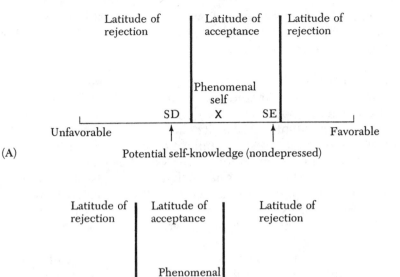

(A)

(B)

FIGURE 9
LATITUDES OF ACCEPTANCE AND REJECTION for self-knowledge for (A) nondepressed individuals and (B) depressed individuals. SD = self-deprecating message; SE = self-enhancing message. (After Rhodewalt and Agustsdottir, 1986.)

depressed person, a moderate self-enhancing message (SE in the figure) would be likely to fall into the latitude of acceptance, and a moderate self-deprecating message (SD) would be likely to fall into a latitude of rejection.

For some other individual—say, someone who does experience mild chronic depression—extreme messages would also be dismissed. But for this type of person, who is chronically critical of himself, it is theorized that the latitude of acceptance would be shifted toward the unfavorable pole, as illustrated in Figure 9B. As a consequence, for a depressed person, the self-deprecating message would be accepted and the self-enhancing message would be rejected.

Rhodewalt and Agustsdottir (1986) began an operationalization of these concepts by using established scales to pretest college students for their levels of self-esteem and levels of mild chronic depression.

Selected subsets of these students were invited to participate as subjects in an experiment, and nondepressed versus depressed was one of the main experimental variables. The subjects were given an opportunity to make a presentation about themselves to an interviewer. Half the subjects were instructed to make a positive, self-enhancing presentation ("Think of yourself on a day when you are really up, when you are in a good mood, you feel really good about yourself"). The other half were instructed to make a negative, self-deprecating presentation ("Think of yourself on a day when you are really down, when you are in a bad mood, you really feel inadequate, unloved, incompetent"). Type of presentation was thus a second important variable in the study. Finally, a third variable was whether a subject was given the impression that he or she had a choice in the matter of making a presentation, or that he or she had no choice but to make the presentation under the dictates of the experimentation. (This last manipulation sounds suspiciously like a dissonance research ploy, which is exactly what it was, as we shall see.) Once a presentation was made, each subject's self-esteem was again measured and the scores were used to calculate pre- to postexperimental shifts.

Having set things up in this fashion, what did Rhodewalt and Agustsdottir expect to find? The full design of the part of their study that we are examining is shown in Table IV. (Readers of the original article will note that I am ignoring the control subjects there, but that does not change anything about the current exposition.) Based

TABLE IV
Self-esteem change scores from pre- to postexperimental measures as a function of level of depression, self-enhancing and self-deprecating presentation, and choice

Presentation	Choice	No choice
Nondepressed subjects		
Self-enhancing	19.0	19.6
Self-deprecating	−8.0	8.7
Depressed subjects		
Self-enhancing	23.8	1.5
Self-deprecating	−13.3	−14.1

After Rhodewalt and Agustsdottir (1986).
Note. Positive entries represent shifts toward higher self-esteem; negative entries indicate shifts toward lower self-esteem.

on the hypothesized differences in latitudes of acceptance across nondepressed and depressed subjects depicted in Figure 9, the authors expected to see positive shifts after the self-enhancement presentations for nondepressives and negative shifts in self-esteem after self-deprecating presentations for the depressives. Because the SE and SD messages were expected to fall into the respective latitudes of acceptance, there was no expectation that level of choice would come into play, and reference to Table IV shows that this was the case. There were average positive shifts in self-esteem under self-enhancement for both the choice (+19.0) and the no-choice (+19.6) nondepressives and negative shifts in self-esteem for both the choice (−13.3) and the no-choice (−14.1) depressives under self-deprecation.

But what about a nondepressed person who makes a self-deprecating presentation or a depressed person who makes a self-enhancing one? These are interesting cases, because the "messages" (behavior) should fall outside the respective latitudes of acceptance for these people (see Figure 9). Nevertheless, a person making such a conflicting presentation is confronted with the cognition that he or she indeed behaved in a certain way. As noted, this sounds like a dissonance-inducing situation, and that is why the researchers included the choice/no-choice manipulation in their design. Dissonance theory would predict that for nondepressives, having *no* choice in the matter of making a deprecating self-presentation would relieve that person of any psychological responsibility for that action, and self-esteem would not be markedly influenced. This analysis would also apply to the depressives who had no choice but to make a self-enhancing presentation. In these two cases there would be no dissonance, and hence no psychological pressure to align self-esteem with the behavior in question. On the other hand, for subjects that were given the impression that they had chosen to behave one way or another, there would be pressure to align their cognitions. This prediction is also borne out in Table IV. The nondepressed subjects who made self-deprecating presentations showed much more negative shifting in self-esteem under the choice condition (−8.0) than they did under the no-choice condition (+8.7). Similarly, the depressives who made self-enhancing presentations under the choice condition showed more positive shifting (+23.8) than those in the no-choice group did (+1.5).

In sum, the pattern of scores in Table IV would be hard to understand if we could not turn to concepts like the latitudes of acceptance and rejection (and the now-familiar notion of cognitive dissonance). People are not passive recipients of just any bits of information concerning attitudinal objects; they will accept some and reject others. The active role a person can play regarding the impact of persuasive messages is even more clearly brought to light in the next section on an elaboration likelihood model of persuasion effects.

THE ELABORATION LIKELIHOOD MODEL (ELM) OF PERSUASION

The recipient of a persuasive communication can deal with the information in several ways. These reactions include rejection or counterargumentation. Indeed, people can be prepared to deflect the impact of messages by the provision of prior information. For example, there is a line of research on ATTITUDE INOCULATION. In the sense that we can be immunized against a severe disease by a mild dose of that same disease, an attitude or belief can be safe-guarded against massive persuasion attempts if the recipient is first given a mild challenge to the attitude. The weak challenge stimulates the person to defend the attitude, and he or she is thus prepared to fend off a later, stronger attack (McGuire, 1964). This process seems similar to *forewarning*, where prior information that persuasion is forthcoming permits the recipient some rehearsal of the rejection of the source or the message (McGuire, 1985).

Perhaps the most elegant analysis of recipient features can be found in a number of recent publications by Richard E. Petty and John T. Cacioppo. They put forward a theory they call the ELABO-RATION LIKELIHOOD MODEL (ELM) of persuasion (e.g., Cacioppo and Petty, 1987; Petty and Cacioppo, 1981, 1986). The term "elab-oration" in the title refers to the extent to which a recipient of a persuasive message studies, analyzes, and evaluates issue-relevant information in the communication, as related to information already available in memory. In some cases this kind of elaboration is high: the recipient engages in a great deal of scrutiny of the central issues and tends to ignore what the authors term "peripheral matters" such as source credibility. In other cases this kind of elaboration is low: the recipient does not or cannot engage in processing the message per se and may rely on peripheral factors to form or change her or his attitude. Hence, persuasion can have its influence through one of two metaphorical channels: the CENTRAL ROUTE, or the PERIPH-ERAL ROUTE. In our terms, these routes represent audience variables in the persuasion process. In the words of Cacioppo and Petty (1987),

in some persuasion situations, the likelihood of message elaboration and issue-relevant thinking is high. In these situations people are (a) highly *motivated* to devote the cognitive work necessary to evaluate the message, perhaps because the message has direct personal relevance, personal responsibility is high, or they are the kinds of people who typically enjoy thinking, . . . and (b) highly *able* to evaluate the message, perhaps because the message is repeated several times, distractions are few, or they have considerable issue-relevant knowledge . . . In other situations, however, motivation and/or ability to process issue-relevant information is quite low. In these situations simple cues may induce agreement without argument scrutiny.

A flow chart illustrating the ELM is presented in Figure 10. In general, the central route is laid out on the left side of Figure 10, and the peripheral route is seen on the right. The interconnections between the two routes are also indicated. This theory makes some interesting and useful predictions where agreement with a persuasive communication might be the result of either central or peripheral processing, or a combination of the two. Consider the following possible combinations of factors: (a) persuasive communications can contain strong or weak arguments, (b) these messages can be associated with positive or negative cues such as source credibility, and (c) different recipients might engage in low, medium, or high levels of elaboration, as represented by respective levels of motivation and ability. What would the ELM predict in this complicated and potentially confusing mix of variables?

Hypothetical data sets have been used to construct Figure 11, which shows that the theory would make quite straightforward predictions. If elaboration were low, the peripheral route would be utilized to appraise the messages, and cue effects would override the unscrutinized argument factors (Figure 11A). Next, if elaboration were moderate, the argument factors would come into play and diminish the impact of the peripheral cues, as seen in Figure 11B. Finally, if elaboration were high, the power of the arguments would determine the amount of agreement with the messages and would override the impact of the peripheral cues altogether (Figure 11C). Thus, although there seemed to be considerable potential for finding "inconsistent" and "confusing" effects for message type and cue, the hypothetical findings in Figure 11 suggest that such findings would be quite consistent and not at all confusing when level of elaboration is taken into account.

A research example. The findings of a number of experiments have supported predictions from the ELM. Consider the recent study by Wu and Shaffer (1987). They based their research on earlier findings that direct versus indirect experience with an object produces variations in attitudes toward that object (as noted in Chapter

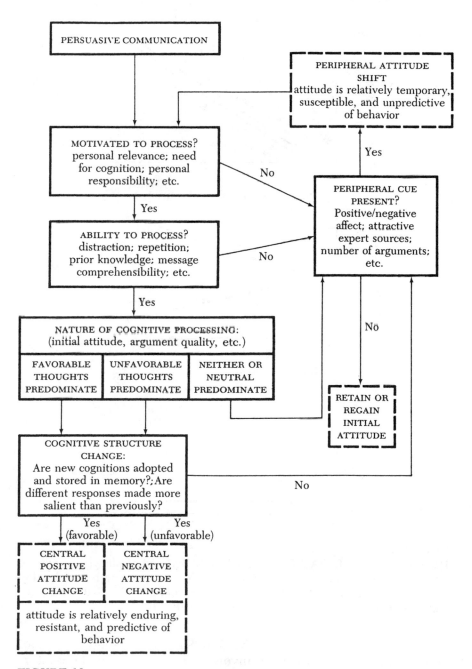

FIGURE 10
ELABORATION LIKELIHOOD MODEL (ELM) in schematic form. The six boxes on the left represent the central route to persuasion, and the three boxes on the right represent the peripheral route to persuasion. (After Petty and Cacioppo, 1986.)

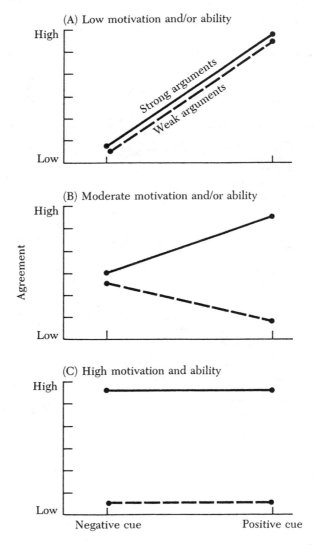

FIGURE 11
HYPOTHETICAL DATA SETS BASED ON THE ELM showing predicted
interactions between source credibility (cue), argument strength, and level of
elaboration. (A) Low level of elaboration, (B) moderate level of elaboration, (C)
high level of elaboration. (After Cacioppo and Petty, 1987.)

4). The attitudinal object in the Wu–Shaffer project was peanut
butter. There were two types involved: Product X and Product Y.
Some subjects were given an opportunity to form an attitude toward

the products by actually tasting them. Thus, these people were in a direct-experience condition, and whichever jar they preferred was called Product X. Other subjects had an opportunity to form an attitude about Product X by reading about its superiority over Product Y; they were in an indirect-experience condition.

Wu and Shaffer (1987) reasoned that people who had direct experience with the product would be more likely to follow the central route in the persuasion process, because their attitudes would have "evolved from a thoughtful elaboration of self-generated information that is likely to be clear, involving, and accessible." On the other hand, for people with attitudes based on indirect experience, such sentiments would be "less likely to have been extensively elaborated and, thus, are less clear, involving, or accessible." Hence these latter people would be more likely to follow the peripheral route in the process.

Once attitudes had been formed by direct or indirect experiences, subjects were confronted with a persuasive communication that argued that Product Y was actually the better type. Half the subjects in each attitude-formation condition received this message from a highly credible source: a trained tester who had repeatedly tasted the two products. The other half got the message from a less credible source: a tester who had not tasted the two peanut butters. The question was, Which subjects would show agreement with the persuasive communication about Product Y? The prediction was that people in the indirect-experience condition would be the most influenced in general. Further, these indirect-experience subjects would be more likely to be influenced by peripheral route features such as source credibility.

The results were very much in line with these predictions. Table V shows that there was more agreement with the persuasive communication about Product Y in the indirect-experience group and an especially high level of agreement in those particular subjects who had heard from a highly credible source. In sum, a formulation like the ELM permits us to understand the differential impact of a persuasive communication in terms of audience variables.

SUMMARY

Obviously, the audience plays an active role in the domain of persuasive communications. Whether we conceptualize this role in terms of assimilation and contrast, latitudes of acceptance and rejection, or elaboration processes, the workings of the recipient must be taken into account in theory and practice. We often view commu-

TABLE V
Average agreement with a persuasive communication as a function of method
of attitude formation and of communicator credibility

	COMMUNICATOR CREDIBILITY	
Method of attitude formation	Low	High
Direct experience	2.71	2.34
Indirect experience	3.71	5.00

After Wu and Shaffer (1987).
Note. Agreement could range from 1 (completely disagree) to 9 (completely agree).

nications as a way to manipulate or exploit an audience, thus audience
variables can be considered a kind of "defense" against such assaults.
But in some cases benevolent communications are meant to educate
or counsel. Even so, the proclivities of the audience do not go away
simply because of the good intentions of the communicator. This
point is illustrated in the next section, having to do with the nature
of certain persuasive messages.

The Persuasive Message

FEAR APPEALS

From the foregoing pages, one gets the impression that a persuasive communicator should not go "too far" with the content of a
given message lest the information end up in the audience's latitude
of rejection or be otherwise discounted. This is generally not a serious
problem, because it is relatively easy to be restrained while com-
posing messages designed to get people to buy a certain brand of
soap or enlist in a certain branch of the armed forces. However, the
exercise of such restraint appears to be much more difficult in areas
where the communicator is (perhaps rightly) desperate to persuade
the audience. Cases that easily come to mind are in the domains of
health and safety practices. Unfortunately, in the next few years
millions of people will suffer agony because of accidents, cancer,
venereal disease, heart problems, and drug abuse, among other
potentially avoidable problems. What could be more humane than
to try to persuade some of these potential victims, before it is too
late, that they should drive more slowly, smoke or drink less, and
guard against infection? Perhaps people could be *scared* into compliance? How best to frighten them for our ends?

Such practices are in active use, and in certain cases they have been used by communicators that are driven by moral concerns. One of the most salient issues in the United States in the latter part of the 1980s was the antiabortion movement (McLoughlin, 1988). Perhaps fear or other strong emotional reactions could be produced in pregnant women to cause them to forgo an abortion? Apparently, this was a tactic adopted by certain antiabortion agencies. In a report on women in three different American cities, it was noted that when a prospective abortion client entered what she assumed was a bona fide clinic it turned out that the aim of the staff was actually to try to dissuade her from having an abortion. In St. Louis a woman was shown a slide of a bloody fetus in a bucket; in Atlanta a woman was shown a video of babies with "their insides hanging out"; and in Houston a woman got a slide show of human body parts in a pail. These scare tactics were apparently intentional and were aimed at changing women's minds about having an abortion (Uehling, Underwood, King, and Burgower, 1986).

Other current users of fear appeals are fueled by ideological motivations. Perhaps the most visible of these is the National Rifle Association (NRA). Beginning in September of 1987, the NRA began to run a special series of six ads concerning citizens' rights to protect themselves—that is, the right to own guns. The ads in question were frankly self-admitted FEAR APPEALS. In discussing the ads, the NRA was explicit in pointing to a focus on the "actual emotional and physical anguish of crime victims," in a "frightened [and] angered America" ("NRA's Violent Crime Ads," 1988; and see also "Go Ahead, Make Our Day," 1988). One of the ads is pictured in Figure 12.

Evaluating fear appeals in the laboratory. I. Smoking. Do appeals (communications) such as these work? Do they have their intended effect? As things stand, there is a great mix of findings on the efficacy of fear appeals. This controversial literature will be reviewed in a later section on field studies, where much of the work was carried out. For now, though, consider one of the first laboratory studies on fear appeals, and one with a most interesting result.

Will a strong fear appeal be any more effective than a weaker one in changing people's attitudes toward smoking? A laboratory study by Janis and Terwilliger (1962) attempted to answer this question. As a measure of initial attitude toward smoking, a subject (in one of two conditions) was asked to imagine himself smoking a cigarette and to freely verbalize his thoughts and feelings while doing so. These verbalizations were later coded as being for or against smoking. A

FIGURE 12
FEAR APPEAL in an advertisement by the National Rifle Association.

fear appeal message followed this initial assessment. There were two types of appeals, one weak and one strong. The weak fear appeal was characterized as merely calling attention to the fact, in highly objective and abstract terms, that one of the consequences of smoking was the danger of contracting cancer. The strong fear appeal included all of the information on cancer and smoking that was contained in the weaker one but went on to elaborate on painful symptoms, body damage, and high rates of death associated with the disease. Following a brief rest at the end of the communication, the subject provided a second expression of his attitude toward smoking, using the role-playing technique. Assessing change in attitude from before to after the communication is, of course, at the heart of this study.

Beyond that, the researchers also wanted to determine people's psychological reaction to the fear appeals themselves at the moment they encountered the messages. To accomplish this end, the subject was given the respective message in bits of one paragraph at a time. Upon finishing a paragraph, the person was asked to make free associations to it. The associations were recorded and later coded (analyzed) as to any emotional disturbance they revealed and also as to the frequency of evaluative statements therein. Janis and Terwilliger scored the subject's comments as being unfavorable (category of "major criticism"), or favorable (categories of "minor favorable comments," or "paraphrasing") toward the communication.

Several data of interest from these procedures are found in Table VI. In the first place, fear in the stronger appeal had an interpretable effect, because more subjects in that condition revealed emotional upset than did the weak fear appeal group. However, the strong fear manipulation was *less* effective than the weak one in inducing anti-smoking sentiment. The reason for the inferior attitudinal effect for the strong fear treatment might be found in the data presented in the bottom panel of Table VI, which reveals that the strong appeal evoked more criticism and less favorable commentary than did the appeal that was less frightening. In short, the strong fear appeal in this study was the less effective of the two where attitude change is concerned.

Evaluating fear appeals in the laboratory. II. Driving. Consider the following abstract from an article in the journal called *Accident Analysis and Prevention:*

[Psychological tests] were administered to 58 college students before and after viewing a 5-minute film segment, portraying graphic documentary scenes of automobile accident victims, and part of a pathologist's autopsy of a road victim.

Presentation of this high-threat stimulus induced an intense elevation in several emotional and motivational states. Most changes implied a generalised psychological disorientation and concomitant diminution in motor skills. In accord with previous evidence, the present findings suggested that fear appeals are probably ineffective in augmenting safer driving behaviors (Boyle, 1984).

So much for spatter-film education.

Evaluating fear appeals in the field. I. Hygiene. In the preceding laboratory studies it was found that a strong fear appeal seemed to be less successful than a weaker one. It happens that this is generally the result of the first field study on the topic, as reported by Janis and Feshbach in 1953. Their study was conducted in a Connecticut high school and employed the freshman class as subjects.

The experimental design involved a before-and-after measure of attitudes toward dental health practices. Between the two attitudinal measures, either some sort of fear appeal (minimal, moderate, or strong) was communicated to the students, or no message at all was given to a control group. Each of the appeals was based on a lecture about the unfavorable and dire consequences of improper dental hygiene. Difficulties such as cancer, paralysis, infection, cavities, loss of teeth, painful dental work, and ugly teeth were mentioned. Some idea of the strength of these fear appeals comes from a tabulation of the number of unfavorable consequences mentioned at each level. The minimal fear appeal mentioned 18 of the awful outcomes, the

TABLE VI
Emotional, attitudinal, and critical reactions to strong and weak fear appeals

	FEAR APPEAL	
Measure	Strong	Weak
Percentage of subjects		
Display of emotional upset	79	12
Attitudinal shifting to		
antismoking position	36	69
Frequency of evaluative comments[a]		
Major criticisms	3.86	2.24
Minor favorable comments	0.93	1.83
Paraphrasing	0.29	1.30

After Janis and Terwilliger (1962).
[a]Values are the average number of various comments in reaction to a standardized set of 15 paragraphs on the unfavorable consequences of smoking.

moderate appeal stated a total of 49, and the strong appeal contained 71 such problems. Moreover, in the minimal appeal only abstract representations of dental problems (x-rays, diagrams) accompanied the text, whereas the moderate appeal was accompanied by pictures of mild oral pathology, and the strong appeal was illustrated by vivid pictures of cavities and infections.

In addition to the fear-inducing material in the various conditions, each type of message advocated a common recommendation (across all levels) to brush one's teeth in a certain fashion: up and down gently for at least 3 minutes daily and after meals rather than before. Having heard one of the higher levels of fear appeal, would the students necessarily be more likely to endorse this method of hygiene than before? The answer is no. Figure 13 indicates that the net change in conformity to the recommendation from a week before the communication to a week after the communication was higher in the minimal and moderate groups than it was either in the no-message control condition or in the strong fear appeal group. Could it be that the highest fear appeal simply did not "take" the way it was supposed to? The answer to this question is also no, for a manipulation check revealed that freshmen in the high fear appeal condition had been the *most* disturbed by what they had heard or seen in the illustrated lecture on dental care (Janis and Feschbach, 1953). Like the outcome of the 1962 laboratory study by Janis and Terwilliger (see Table VI),

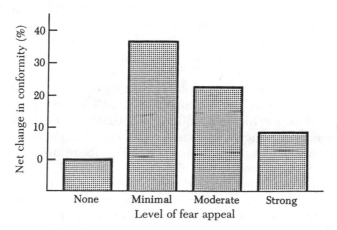

FIGURE 13
FEAR APPEALS AND CONFORMITY TO THE MESSAGE. (After Janis and Feshbach, 1953.)

the most fearful subjects in this fear appeal study in the field did not show the most attitude change (see Figure 13).

Evaluating fear appeals in the field. II. Delinquency. The periodical titled the *World Press Review* reprints foreign news articles for U.S. readers. Two items from Russia appeared in the November 1987 issue. One of these ("Teen-age Attitudes," 1987) reported that 17-year-olds in Moscow felt that the shady professions of black marketeer and profiteer were the most lucrative (compared with auto mechanic or restaurant worker). In counterpoint, within the same issue ("In the Labor Camps," 1987) a repentant, 17-year-old convicted burglar wrote that "Soviet schools should show films of labor camps to students to deter them from straying into crime." It seems that the young inmate was advocating what we would call a fear appeal. Exposure to the awfulness of prison life would convince others to forgo illegal activity. Or would it? A field experiment of sorts in the United States was addressed to this question.

The year 1979 witnessed what surely must be the most massive fear appeal project in history. The audience for this huge effort was potentially all (or almost all) of the teenagers in the United States! It was not aimed at getting people to brush their teeth properly; rather it insisted that one should not lead a life of crime, especially if one were a teenager. Now, if you think this project's audience and message were unusual, the source involved was certainly no less so, for the communicators were convicted murderers and armed robbers who were currently serving life sentences for their crimes in Rahway, a New Jersey prison. Of course, not every teenager in the United States was expected to get to New Jersey to hear the appeal in question, so a professional film of the source's message was prepared and aired nationwide on commercial television.

Appropriately enough, the film's title was "Scared Straight," and it amounted to a blatant fear appeal. The title referred to a rehabilitation program for juvenile delinquents that was predicated on the assumption that the fear of the consequences of a criminal conviction and incarceration would influence delinquents to abandon a life of crime. The film showed a small group of tough East Coast delinquents that were to be "scared" into "going straight." By extension of this assumption, any delinquent, or potentially delinquent, viewers in the national audience would also be "scared straight."

The "scare" part was accomplished by having a small group of self-admitted juvenile criminals visit the real prison and encounter real prisoners. The prisoners themselves had concocted a program of "lectures" on the evils of prison life. However, these lectures were unlike anything one would ever hear in a classroom or in a psychological study. First, the youths were actually locked in the prison with the inmates, who were free to rove about in a room and mingle with the juvenile offenders. Soon these hardened convicts began to portray the day-to-day horrors of prison life. Whereas prison tales about frequent extortion, homosexual rape or subjugation, beatings, and killings were upsetting enough, the style of the delivery of this information was stunning and truly frightening. Short of direct physical assault, the prisoners acted in the most abusive, aggressive, and brutal fashion imaginable. The vocabulary used was undistilled street language, with none of the impurities removed. As seen in the nationally televised film, the hapless teens were savagely cursed, insulted, taunted, and vilified by a succession of highly vicious speakers. All in all, it *was* impressive.

What was the outcome of this sort of heavy-handed fear appeal? At first, the film's backers and promoters were optimistic and claimed that from 80 to 90% of the youths that actually endured the prisoners' lectures indeed went straight. However, as social scientists were able to make more systematic estimates of the program's success (or nonsuccess), the picture became much more gloomy. The investigations of Finckenauer (1982) tell a story that has begun to be familiar to us in this section on fear appeals.

Finckenauer, a professor in the School of Criminal Justice at Rutgers, used court records to follow up the behavior of delinquents who had taken part in the Scared Straight program. He was further able to identify delinquents who had not been exposed to the prisoners and also a sets of nondelinquents who had or had not been scared. (Finckenauer estimates that 14,000 teenagers were sent to Rahway for a scaring. Some of these came not from the ranks of juvenile delinquents but from church and other youth groups.) Each of these teens was coded as a "success" or a "failure." Failure in this context meant that a youth had a further recorded offense in a 6-month follow-up period.

The sample sizes and patterns of successes and failures for the four groups of subjects are shown in Table VII. Several things in the table are striking. Nondelinquents who were not scared mostly stayed straight; this looks like a fairly reasonable baseline against which to gauge the impact of the project. Unhappily, nondelinquents who were scared did not fare so well. Of those, 32% got in trouble with the law. As for the delinquents who were not scared, success was fairly high at 79%. Most unhappily, of the delinquents who visited Rahway, almost half quickly got into trouble again.

These data do not speak well for the Scared Straight program. If

TABLE VII
Rates of success and failure (trouble with the law) for nondelinquents and
delinquents who were or were not "scared straight"

Condition	Success (%)	Failure (%)	n
Nondelinquents			
Not scared	95	5	21
Scared straight	68	32	19
Delinquents			
Not scared	79	21	14
Scared straight	52	48	27

After Finckenauer (1982).

anything, Finckenauer's (1982) evaluation suggests that this form of
rehabilitation only made things worse. Like some other studies we
have seen, a strong fear message in Rahway prison may not have had
its intended effect on some members of the audience. Indeed, it may
have been the case that the prisoners served as role models for
delinquents and nondelinquents alike.

   Review of fear appeal research. Do fear appeals ever work? If
not, why is it that they fail? To answer these questions we will look
at a brief review of the literature and then examine some theories of
fear appeals.
   Fear appeals have been employed in the contexts of smoking,
dental hygiene, tetanus shots, safe driving, fallout shelters, population growth, mental health, cancer, roundworms, school grades, tu-
berculosis, staring at the sun, army life, donating blood, and others.
Some reviewers of this flurry of activity were optimistic about the
efficacy of fear messages, as seen in Higbee's (1969) conclusion that
"most relevant research has indicated that high threat is superior to
low threat in persuasion." Other scholars have been a bit more
cautious. Even if there are studies that do claim a positive effect for
higher levels of fear appeals (e.g., Chu, 1966; Dabbs and Leventhal,
1966; Insko, Arkoff, and Insko, 1965), there are, in addition to the
four that were reviewed in detail above, several that have failed to
show a positive effect (e.g., Leventhal and Niles, 1964; Leventhal
and Watts, 1966) or have shown an effect on verbal or written attitudes but no effect on behavior (e.g., Leventhal, Jones, and Trembly,
1966; Leventhal, Singer, and Jones, 1965; Leventhal, Watts, and
Pagano, 1967). Finally, there are studies that show that fear appeals

are beneficial to some personality types or individuals (e.g., "copers," people who habitually try to cope with their problems) but probably harmful to others (e.g., "avoiders," people who habitually try to avoid their problems) (Goldstein, 1959).

Perhaps it was this mixed bag of results that led certain reviewers to be cautious or conservative about the overall fear appeal picture, as seen in the following example:

> While fear arousing communications often lead to reductions in smoking, subjects exposed to both high and low fear messages reduce their smoking more than do control subjects . . . [but] there are relatively fewer studies that show high fear messages leading to more smoking reduction than do low fear messages (Leventhal, 1970).

What this passage suggests is that *some* message is perhaps better than *no* message in certain cases, a statement that in itself is hardly a stirring recommendation for a strong fear appeal approach. In fact, one writer went so far as to characterize much of the fear appeal literature as an "intractable pattern of conflicting results" (Rogers, 1975).

CURRENT THEORIES OF FEAR APPEALS

But maybe we have started off on the wrong foot. Rather than simply inquiring *whether* fear appeals work, it might be far more productive to inquire *why* such communications might influence our attitudes and behavior, and *when*. That is, we could well use a theory about the potential impact of fear appeals. Happily, several such theories are now available, and they will be taken up in turn.

The three-legged model. One of the reasons Finckenauer (1982) undertook his evaluation of the Scared Straight program was that he was testing what he called a THREE-LEGGED MODEL OF DETERRENCE. Imagine a three-legged stool. If one or more legs were missing, the stool could not fulfill its function; it would merely fall over. This is the kind of analogy that Finckenauer brought to the deterrence of juvenile crime. If a program of persuasion was to be successful in deterring criminal behavior, it had to stand on three legs regarding what it said about the consequences of crime: namely, punishment. For Finckenauer, these legs were

1. The swiftness of consequences.
2. The certainty of consequences.
3. The severity of consequences.

As was the case with the stool, if any of these legs was missing, the persuasive program would not fulfill its function either. And that is how Finckenauer (1982) understood the apparent failure of the prisoners' program at Rahway. He pointed out that in their harangues the inmates concentrated almost exclusively on the severity of the consequences. While they might have done a very good job on that leg, the other two were virtually ignored—and hence the failure to rehabilitate.

The protection-motivation theory. Rogers (1975) offers a similar but more general theory of critical features of fear appeals. According to Rogers, the three most crucial variables in a fear message amount to three *different* kinds of information that are conveyed:

1. Information about the magnitude of the noxiousness of the problem to be avoided, such as the discomfort associated with cancer, injury, or imprisonment.
2. Information about the conditional probability or likelihood that the event will occur (e.g., disease) given that no corrective activity is performed or the appeal is ignored.
3. Information about the relative effectiveness of a coping response that might avert or minimize the problem.

In Rogers's model, this kind of information enters into a cognitive mediating process that results in the generation of some greater or lesser amount of PROTECTION MOTIVATION, the name he gives to his theory. On the basis of the degree of protection motivation that is generated, a more or less strong *intent* to adopt the recommended action (i.e., attitude change) occurs. Rogers's scheme is depicted in Figure 14. If a fear appeal contains enough information about the magnitude of noxiousness, probability of occurrence, and efficacy or recommended response, then protection motivation is likely to result, and intent (attitude change) will be in evidence. However, if one or another type of information is omitted, or stated to be low or near zero, then protection motivation will not result.

To test this protection-motivation theory, Rogers and Mewborn (1976) systematically manipulated the components of fear appeals listed in the left-most column of Figure 14 by using a 2 × 2 × 2 experimental design. In the study, some smokers were given information about the highly noxious outcomes of smoking, whereas others were told about less noxious outcomes; some subjects were informed that the probability of the outcomes was rather high, and other subjects were informed that this probability was rather low;

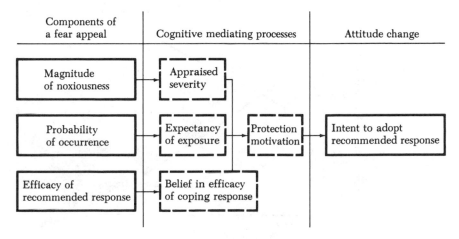

Components of a fear appeal	Cognitive mediating processes	Attitude change

FIGURE 14
PROTECTION MOTIVATION MODEL. (After Rogers, 1975.)

and finally, some people were told that the recommended corrective behavior was highly effective, but other people were told it was not.

When Rogers and Mewborn asked subjects to rate, on a 10-point scale, their intent to adopt the recommended response, there generally was a slightly higher intent under the more noxious condition. What is more interesting is an interaction that emerged between probability of occurrence of outcome and relative efficacy of the recommended response, as shown in Figure 15. Under conditions of low probability, there was an intermediate level of intent to adopt the recommended response, which was unaffected by level of efficacy. On the other hand, under the dual conditions of high probability and high efficacy, there was an especially *high* level of intent; whereas under the dual conditions of high probability and low efficacy, there was an especially *low* level of intent. (This latter finding reminds me of the negative effects sometimes seen following strong fear appeals. When you scare someone but do not give them a way to fix the problem, the message is apparently rejected.) Thus, Rogers's theory gains support.

Recent research has provided further support for the protection motivation theory and has led to certain revisions. For instance, in a study by Maddux and Rogers (1983) the researchers manipulated (1) levels of the probability of occurrence of a noxious outcome related to smoking, (2) levels of the efficacy of a response (quitting smoking) to avoid that outcome, and (3) a new variable—levels of self-efficacy:

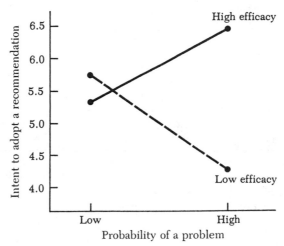

FIGURE 15
ATTITUDE CHANGE (intent to adopt a recommendation) as related to probability of a problem and the efficacy of solutions to that problem. (After Rogers
and Mewborn, 1976.)

some smokers were told that quitting would be easy for them,
whereas others were told it would be hard. What these investigators
found was that if any two of the above independent variables were
high, then adding information about the third variable did not further
influence smokers' intentions to try to stop smoking. In other words,
if a certain *threshold* of information was reached, then additional
input did not have a further effect. This recognition that fear appeals
(and other persuasive messages) can be broken down into essential
or critical elements is an important contribution of Rogers and his
colleagues.

The subjective expected utility (SEU) theory. It happens that
developments in the literature on fear appeals may be bypassing fear
to a large extent. That is, modern thinking in the area recognizes
that people have to be made aware of the seriousness of certain
health and safety precautions, so certain undesirable outcomes (disease, injury) will have to be included in educational material. But
the "fear" this information might arouse may be incidental to the
objective the communicator wishes to reach. Indeed, fear of an
unavoidable outcome could well block intentions to do anything
about the situation. Instead, current recommendations are that we
should concentrate not only on scaring the audience but also on

giving the audience a sense that something can be done to manage the problem (which is essentially the Maddux–Rogers position). As one set of reviewers put it,

two fundamental beliefs are seen as comprising perceived threat control: *response efficacy*, which is the perceived ability of the recommended coping action(s) to reduce or control the threat; and *personal efficacy*, which is the person's expectation of being able to perform the recommended threat-coping action(s) successfully . . . Empirical support . . . indicates that . . . personal efficacy is a more important determinant of protective health behavior than response efficacy (Beck and Frankel, 1981).

This idea is compatible with a formulation known as SUBJECTIVE EXPECTED UTILITY (SEU) theory as outlined by Sutton and Eiser (1984). For Sutton and Eiser, the fact that a fear appeal might cause fear is largely immaterial; fear might have an influence, or it might not. What is important is whether the message (such as an anti-smoking film) influences at least intentions to modify one's behavior for health's sake. In the Sutton–Eiser framework, the information in the message could have impact on two kinds of cognitions that should mediate intentions: (1) the utility of avoiding disease or harm and (2) the subjective probability of successful coping. They called this second factor "confidence."

To test the SEU theory, the researchers showed British smokers an antismoking film called "Dying for a Fag." Following the film, self-reports were taken on the utility of avoiding lung cancer, confidence in one's ability to stop smoking, and intention to stop smoking. Approximately 3 months later, subjects were contacted and were asked whether they had stopped smoking or had tried to cut down. According to a regression analysis, confidence mediated (predicted) intention, and intention in turn mediated (predicted) actual behavior. Thus, the idea that Beck and Frankel earlier called "personal efficacy" gained encouraging support.

However, it should be pointed out that Sutton and Eiser (1984) also measured "fear" in their subjects ("When you were watching the film did you feel frightened? tense? sick?") and that level of fear also mediated intentions independently of confidence.

OVERVIEW AND SUMMARY ON FEAR APPEALS

In their review, Beck and Frankel (1981) provide a concise history of trends in fear appeal theorizing. The earliest theory was known as the "drive model," and it was attributed to Hovland, Janis, and Kelley (1953). For this model, it was assumed that the contents of a fear appeal created emotional tension in the subject and that the subject rehearsed or adopted the message's recommendation in order to reduce that tension. This early model has not gained much support.

Later, Leventhal (1970) offered what was called the "parallel response model." According to this formulation, a fear message certainly has the potential to make a person react emotionally (one response category), but that same message would elicit a cognitive appraisal of the danger involved (the parallel response category). These reactions occur simultaneously, not in a sequence. To quote Beck and Frankel, "from this perspective, health threat messages may make people fearful, but protective actions result from a desire to control the danger, not to reduce fear." Even though it was seen as an advance over the drive model, the parallel response model was evaluated by Beck and Frankel as untestable, because it did not specify the stimulus conditions that were necessary to produce the separate emotion or danger elements.

Of course, this leads us to the era of the 1980s, where we have found Finckenauer's three-legged model, Rogers's protection motivation theory, and Sutton and Eiser's SEU model. In all three of these modern treatments the impacts of affect (emotions) and cognitions are recognized, and in one way or another behavior is taken into account. Now this somehow reminds me of the panel discussion described in Chapter 2 having to do with the portrayal of Christ in lewd films. Do you recall that *that* persuasive communication included all of the A-B-C components? I speculated in those pages that a communication containing information on all three of the components—rather than some subset—would be the most powerful or effective. This speculation seems to have been borne out to a certain extent in the recent literature on fear appeals. Is it so unfair to say that the fear appeal researchers have merely rediscovered the A-B-Cs of attitudes? I think it is to their credit.

Postscript: Some Perils of Persuasion

Early in this chapter it was shown that the credibility of a source is a key factor in his or her persuasiveness. As the reader will recall, Table I presented a list of people who fell from real or potential power and leadership because of a loss of credibility. Other prominent names could be added to that list, such as that of Pete Rose, the ex-manager of the Cincinnati Reds who was banned from baseball for gambling, and that of Marion Barry, the discredited mayor of Washington, D.C. who was allegedly involved in illegal drug use. It is sad to see people topple in this fashion, for each could have been a force for the good, and perhaps we should not excessively exploit their loss and distress. However, since there is so much trivial persuasive communication in the air at all times, one can engage in the enjoyable (and harmless) game of watching certain people or organizations discredit *themselves*. I am thinking in particular of advertising campaigns that fail, either because the ads themselves contain some "blooper" that undermines their intended message or because a celebrity who has made an endorsement commits some faux pas. Let us look at some examples.

I recently received a direct-mail catalog, the March, 1990 *Book-of-the-Month Club News*. An announcement on the cover touted a bonus 1990 road atlas. Since I meant to do some traveling, I turned to the page that described the book, the *Rand McNally Road Atlas 1990*. Part of the written persuasive communication about the book said in bold print that there had been "19,536 changes since the 1989 edition," and to the left of this headline was a sample map. However, it was very difficult at first to ascertain what territory the map depicted; it was oddly strange and familiar at the same time. Suddenly, the nature of the map became clear: it was a map of the continental United States *printed backwards!* The east and west coasts had been reversed in the image so that the Florida peninsula was pointing down toward my left hand as I held the page. That is certainly one impressive change from the 1989 edition, but I was not sure I cared to learn about the other 19,535 revisions in the 1990 edition.

Persuasive communications have also been used recently in attempts to modify people's food preferences or attitudes. There have been several national publicity campaigns about meat of late. The message is, You are supposed to *eat* it, not avoid it! Both the National Pork Producers Council and the Beef Industry Council have recently sunk millions of dollars into such promotions (Miller, 1987). For example, over the slogan, "Beef. Real Food For Real People," the red-meat marketers had certain celebrities make endorsements. Cybil Shepard said, "I know some people who don't eat hamburgers. But I'm not sure I trust them." James Garner said, "I never liked the way the vegetables always fell off between the sirloin on my beef kabobs. But I fixed that. I don't put any vegetables on." Finally, a food wholesaler in Oklahoma City distributed a poster to supermarkets that was apparently designed to link patriotism and meat-eating. It showed a young blond cowboy, wearing a tie (a *tie?*), looking off to his left, with his left hand on his hip and his right hand holding the staff of an American flag. The text at the bottom of the poster read "America's Meat Roundup." One supposes that the promoters behind all these efforts were quite satisfied with their propaganda campaigns.

Alas, the meat campaign seems to have run aground. First, Cybil Shepard was later quoted as saying she "never ate the stuff" ("Red Meat and Red Faces," 1988). This is not perjury; she never claimed to eat the stuff in the ad, either. Next, spokesperson James Garner entered a hospital for heart surgery. Finally, some people noticed an odd similarity between the food wholesaler's poster and a certain *earlier* poster, a 1930s Nazi propaganda poster painted by Ludwig Hohlwein. This poster also depicts a young blond man, wearing a tie, looking off to his left, with his left hand on his hip. However, his right hand holds the staff of a Nazi flag, and the text reads, "The German student fights for the Führer and the people" (Rhodes, 1983). By all appearances, the 1980's artist had simply traced his modern cowboy picture from the Nazi version. (To compare the two images for yourself, see "Red Meat and Red Faces," 1988.)

The offending posters were quickly removed from supermarkets and the food wholesaler subsequently denied my request to reprint the cowboy poster here. Who could blame them? Maybe the 1980's artist was having a little joke on the hapless wholesaler client, but the affinities between the two posters are hardly conducive to persuasion at the meat counter. If the red-meat industry wants to use persuasive communications to change our attitudes about its product, it is going to have to attend to matters of credibility first. In any event, the reader is encouraged to do her or his own checking on the credibility of everyday persuasive communications. Good hunting, and have fun!

CHAPTER TEN

ATTITUDES TOWARD ONESELF

The great bulk of scientific work on attitudes has focused on the psychological relationship between an individual and another person, a concept, an object, or an event. Of course, a person's own characteristics, such as her or his pattern of past behavior, have entered into the analysis of attitudes, as seen in the work on cognitive dissonance and self-perception. However, even work in these areas mostly concentrates on an individual's feelings about something other than the self. But what about the possibility that an attitude toward *oneself* could influence one's behavior? Is this a legitimate use of the term "attitude"?

The answer to this question is definitely yes, as reference to the A-B-Cs of attitudes will show. In terms of the A, or affective component, there seems little doubt that most of us evaluate ourselves as worthwhile people. I can only speculate, but the reader probably thinks of herself or himself as a decent individual, a reasonable person, a good friend to have, and not unattractive at that. To paraphrase the commercial slogan, most of us feel that "it may be expensive, but I'm worth it." As for the C, or cognitive component, we are all aware of our individual strengths and skills. Just about everyone can do *something* most other people cannot do well at all, such as participation in athletics, creative work, entertaining in one's home, or public speaking. Finally, the behavioral, or B component, is represented in attitudes toward the self, as reflected in common reactions such as pride or guilt. Who among us has not experienced the thrill of victory or the agony of defeat? That is, we feel very differently about ourselves when our behavior is above or below some standard of excellence. The fact that you are reading these lines, perhaps as part of routine class assignment, means that as a tuition-paying student you are behaving appropriately, which is likely to engender feelings of self-satisfaction.

Indeed, several other writers voice this position. For instance, Greenwald and Pratkanis (1984) described what they termed the "affective aspects of self" (our A component), the "conative aspects of self—self as task orientation" (our B component), and the "cognitive aspects of self" (our C component). As they put it, "perhaps the most prominent feature of the self is the positive affect normally attached to one's own actions, attitudes, attributes, and memories. The self is thus the object of an *attitude*" (Greenwald and Pratkanis, 1984, emphasis in the original).

In a similar vein, Linville (1982) has inquired into the interrelatedness of cognition and affect within the self. She feels that processes by which we make judgments of ourselves have a fundamental similarity with processes by which we judge others. Basically, the complexity of one's representation of another or oneself determines the extremity or variability of one's reactions to new information about those targets. To take an example concerning the self, imagine one young woman who has a "simple" self-representation: she views herself as (1) a daughter and (2) a college student. Contrast this relatively simple self-portrait with another young woman who has a "complex" self-representation: she views herself as (1) a daughter, (2) a college student, (3) a community volunteer, (4) an amateur musician, and (5) an avid golfer. Suppose both women receive the information (cognition) that they have failed an important examination at school. Linville's (1982) theory has it that the first young lady will have a strong negative affective reaction to this outcome because much of her "self" (50%) will be engulfed by the failure. The second woman should experience less of an affective swing because a smaller part (20%) of her "self" is affected (see also Linville, 1985, 1987).

Thus, there seems to be theoretical justification for applying the notion "attitude" to personal reactions to ourselves. And, insofar as there is a causal link between attitudes and behavior, the study of self-directed attitudes would be essential in understanding behavior in general. Given that most of us take ourselves more or less seriously, egocentric attitudes can be expected to be quite powerful. The only issue that remains is to choose aspects of the self for study. Social-psychology texts offer a host of concepts prefixed with "self-," as in self-concept, self-schemata, self-esteem, self-efficacy, self-awareness, self-consciousness, self-perception, self-evaluation, self-assessment, self-enhancement, self-handicapping, self-consistency, self-presentation, (and as we have seen elsewhere) self-monitoring (e.g., Forsyth, 1987). No doubt, all of these topics are worthy of attention, but of necessity our attention will have to be somewhat limited. In the pages that follow I will focus closely on the concepts of "locus of control" and "perceived control." Laboratory and field studies have shown that these features of self-directed attitudes are powerful influences on an individual's behavior and well-being.

Locus of Control

I–E ORIENTATION

This chapter will concentrate mainly on the C (cognitive) component of self-directed attitudes. Cognitions, as defined earlier, have to do with the assumed instrumentality, consequences, or efficaciousness of the attitudinal object. When considering myself, it is possible to ask what accounts for the things that happen to me. That is, what controls the experiences, outcomes, or reinforcements in my life? There is a wide range of answers to this question. Some people, including both children and adults, feel that they themselves are in control of important events in their lives. On the contrary, other people have the impression that the things that happen to them are under the control of external agents or forces. In the literature this dimension has been treated as an individual difference, or in the domain of personality (Lefcourt, 1976; Phares, 1976). No doubt this is proper, but authorities have also labeled "the perception of control as an enduring attitude" (Lefcourt, 1982).

This attitude about who or what governs a person's own reinforcements has been termed the LOCUS-OF-CONTROL ORIENTATION. People who view themselves as clearly in control have traditionally been termed INTERNALS or as having an I orientation, whereas people at the other extreme have been identified as EXTERNALS or as having an E orientation. The paper-and-pencil tests that have been developed to measure this orientation are known as I–E SCALES.

The first I–E scale to be widely used was published by Rotter in 1966. Since that time a number of different scales have been developed; some are suitable for different age groups, others are tailored to demographic categories of the adult population. A sampler of questions from four such I–E scales is provided in Figure 1, along with the group of persons for which each test was designed. Typical scales offer the respondent a choice of options with which to complete a sentence stem. One of the options reflects an internal orientation,

Scales for children

Stanford Preschool I–E Scale (Mischel, Zeiss, and Zeiss, 1974).

Item: When your father reads a book to you, is that
      a. because you want to hear the story, or
(E)   b. because he likes to read?

Intellectual Achievement Responsibility Questionnaire (Crandall, Katkovsky, and Crandall, 1965).

Item: If a teacher passes you to the next grade, would it probably be
(E)   a. because she liked you, or
      b. because of the work you did?

Scales for adults

I–E Locus of Control Scale (Rotter, 1966)

Item: I more strongly believe that
      a. becoming a success is a matter of hard work, luck has little or nothing
         to do with it.
(E)   b. getting a good job depends mainly on being in the right place at the
         right time.

Extended I–E Scale (Gurin, Gurin, Lao, and Beattie, 1969).

Item: (pick one)
(E)   a. Many Negroes who don't do well in life do have good training but
         the opportunities just always go to whites.
      b. Negroes may not have the same opportunities as whites but many
         Negroes haven't prepared themselves enough to make use of the
         opportunities that come their way.

FIGURE 1
A SAMPLER OF ITEMS FROM VARIOUS I–E SCALES. Item choices marked with an (E) indicate an external orientation.

and the other option reveals an external orientation. By convention, if a respondent picks an external option on an item, a score of 1 is assigned to that item. An internal choice would be scored as 0. The scores for all the items are summed, and the total score reveals the subject's locus-of-control orientation. For example, the maximum externality on the Rotter (1966) I–E scale is 23, because the scale has 23 items.

A typical range of scores on Rotter's scale in a college sample was reported in a study by Gregory (1978). He had students from an introductory psychology class fill out the Rotter scale and found the

average score to be 10.03. For experimental purposes he then trichotomized the distribution of scores to arrive at internal, moderate,
and external subsamples. People with a total score of 0 to 8 were
labeled Internals; those with a score of 9, 10, and 11 were termed
moderates; and those with totals of 12 to 23 were declared Externals.
Using these cutoffs, he found that about a third of the entire sample
fell into each grouping.

   This example indicates that the average for the population as a
whole is somewhere near the midpoint of the scale (see also Phares,
1976). More important, Gregory's procedure illustrates the way researchers have usually classified respondents. Obviously, to be declared an Internal or an External means your answers must indicate
that you think either that your actions predominantly govern your
outcomes (as in the case of the Internals), or that other people, or
luck, or fate control your reinforcements (as in the case of the Externals). Such a scale requires but a few minutes to complete. Is it
possible that instruments as seemingly simple as these can really tell
us much about such a pervasive and profound element in our psychological makeup?

   Apparently, the answer to the this question is affirmative. There
have been many hundreds of research reports on the I–E dimension,
and their results have been generally consistent. In a typical study,
the experimenter obtains a subject's score on an I–E scale and then
observes the subject in a standardized test situation, the nature of
which depends on the hypothesis under evaluation. The list of such
articles is long, as noted, but we are fortunate to have available
excellent comprehensive reviews of the literature (Lefcourt, 1976,
1982; Phares, 1976), and some general conclusions can be gleaned
from these extensive works. Based on what has been reported, there
is agreement that Internals differ from Externals in at least the ways
shown in Figure 2. This is an impressive list of differences; and it
speaks to the sensitivity of the I–E scales and the importance of the
trait or attitude that they measure.

ORIGINAL RESEARCH ON THE I–E DIMENSION: SELECTED TOPICS

   Some sense of the power of the I–E attitude can be had from
Figure 2, but perhaps an even deeper appreciation comes from an
exposure to original research reports. In the sections that follow,
selected topics will be reviewed.

   Orientation, attribution of success and failure, and anxiety. The
entries in Figure 2 raise the possibility that there may be a relationship between externality and psychological maladjustment. If a per-

Internals are superior to Externals in their ability to cope with experimental tasks, a difference which seems to be mediated by Internals' greater cognitive skills.

Internals are better than Externals in acquiring information and retaining it, and are less content with the extent of information they have amassed at any given point.

Internals, compared with Externals, are superior in creating rules to process information and devote more attention to useful information available in the environment.

Internals have more self-discipline and self-control than do Externals.

Internals are more reliant on their own judgments, compared with Externals.

Internals are more accepting of communications when the information has merit, and are less likely to be swayed by the communicator's prestige.

In children, Internals generally do better in terms of grades than do Externals, and Internals appear to be better able to delay gratification.

Internals are less likely to violate social norms under pressure and are more likely to help others than are Externals.

FIGURE 2
A SAMPLER OF DIFFERENCES BETWEEN PEOPLE with internal or external locus-of-control orientations.

son senses chronically low personal control over events that are important to her or him, then life may seem to be much more threatening and stressful. Indeed, there are data that show that External college students suffer more anxiety than do their Internal counterparts, even under the relatively benign conditions of a laboratory experiment. Lefcourt, Hogg, Struthers, and Holmes (1975) measured the locus of control of undergraduates and then had them participate in an anagram test in which the subject's task was to identify words from jumbled letters, such as OPFRESSRO.

OPFRESSRO is relatively easy to identify as PROFESSOR, but what about a jumble like CTHUROLAY? In fact (so far as I can tell), this second anagram is insoluble because there is no English word made up of those letters. This is precisely the kind of difficulty faced by subjects in the Lefcourt et al. (1975) study. Early in the experimental session, the anagrams they worked on were fairly easy to solve. However, as the session progressed, the anagrams got harder, and in a final segment the students found puzzles that could not be solved. In other words, as the experiment progressed, all subjects met with early success, then began to fare less well, and finally ended up failing miserably. The question is, How would Internals and Externals react to these experiences? For our purposes two questions were asked in this situation: To what would Externals and Internals attribute their success and failure, and to what extent would Externals and Internals feel anxious as a consequence of their varied experiences?

To answer the first question, subjects were queried after initial successes, and after total failure. They were asked whether success on such tasks depended mainly on luck or mainly on ability, and they expressed their feelings on a scale that ranged from 10 (mainly luck) to 0 (mainly ability). On this measure the Externals and the Internals were quite different, as seen in the upper panel of Table I. Success or failure did not much change Internals' estimates of the cause. In contrast, Externals saw luck as more involved overall and, having failed, were even more likely to place responsibility for their outcomes on something other than their own capacities.

The second question in this study centered on anxiety. To put it simply, Did the Externals gain any relief from the discomfort or stress that accompanied failure or frustration by shifting the burden of responsibility from their own capacities to luck? One way to estimate such anxiety is to score the subject for "adaptors." It seems that people that are nervous or anxious behave in special ways. They engage in relatively high rates of hand-to-body movements such as grooming, rubbing, and sucking on the fingers, or they press the

TABLE I

Average outcome attribution score and adaptor rate under outcomes of success and failure for individuals with internal or external locus-of-control orientations

	OUTCOME	
I–E orientation	Success	Failure
Outcome attribution score[a]		
Internal	2.93	2.97
External	3.96	4.82
Adaptor rate[b]		
Internal	.112	.159
External	.180	.248

After Lefcourt et al. (1975).
Note. Entries are unweighted means collapsed over high- and low-confidence subjects in the original Lefcourt et al. Tables 1 and 2.
[a]Values could range from 0 (mainly ability) to 10 (mainly luck).
[b]Values are the proportion of test time in which the behavior was observed.

teeth against the lips or tap themselves with objects such as pencils. These acts are called ADAPTORS. Lefcourt et al. expressed adaptor rate as the proportion of time in tests during which such behaviors were observed, as shown in the lower panel of Table I.

It can be seen that for Internals the adaptor rate increased from success to failure, a result that in common-sense terms means they were more bothered by failure than by success. But what about the Externals? Recall that they fared just as well (or badly) as the Internals but that they had a stronger tendency to place responsibility for their outcomes on outside forces (luck). Did this sort of external attribution get them off the emotional hook? Apparently not, for even during success the adaptor rate for Externals exceeded that of the Internals. Further, when the Externals had failed—and were presumably blaming something other than themselves for their failure —they used adaptors at the highest rate of all (Table I). The fact that Externals were less willing than Internals to accept personal responsibility for their performance on the anagram test did not mean that they felt any less concerned for their failures. Therefore, we might extrapolate from this pattern and suggest that for Externals, their failures in this experiment may have been just one more bit of evidence that their outcomes were more or less beyond their control. However, this "knowledge" made the Externals less comfortable rather than more comfortable with their performance.

Orientation and reliance on experts. If Externals are less likely to attribute their outcomes to their ability, then it may follow that they would attach more importance than Internals to the judgment of experts for the solution of problems. It happens that there is considerable evidence for this trend. Let us see how certain researchers have arrived at this important result.

In the first study of a series, the problem-solving behavior of black boys (ages 10 and 11 years) in an inner-city school was examined (Baron and Ganz, 1972). The problem the boys had to solve was a modified version of the old carnival shell game. On a given trial the child was shown three boxes, similar to one another except that one was marked with a triangle, another with a square, and a third with a circle. Under one of these boxes was a hidden object, a checker. Each subject was given 30 different trials to figure out which box hid the checker. This goal was attainable, because for a given child the object was always under the same box, although the position of the boxes was changed from trial to trial. The heart of the experiment was the manner in which the child gained information about the location of the object. In the first of two experimental conditions, called the intrinsic reinforcement condition, the subject himself picked up the box he had chosen and discovered for himself whether he had made the correct choice. On the contrary, in the extrinsic reinforcement condition, a small screen was placed between the subject and the boxes following the subject's indication of a choice, and the *experimenter* lifted the box and *told* the boy whether that particular choice was correct. Half the subjects in each reinforcement condition had previously been assessed as Internals, and the other half were Externals; thus, the basic experiment was a 2 × 2 design yielding four values: Internals' performance under intrinsic or extrinsic conditions, and Externals' performance under those two treatments. It is worth noting that the Externals and Internals in this study did not differ on measured intelligence, so any difference in their performances can safely be attributed to their I–E orientation and the kind of reinforcement they received.

The results of the Baron–Ganz study are shown in Table II. The two largest numbers in the table indicate that the Internals did the best under the intrinsic reinforcement condition, and the Externals excelled under the extrinsic treatment. In a sense this means that the Internals trusted their own discovery of information more than the information that they received from the experimenter (or expert). That is, if an Internal was in the condition where he was *told* he was correct in making a choice (extrinsic reinforcement), he may or may not have made that same choice later. However, if some other Internal was in the condition where he could *see* that his choice was correct (intrinsic reinforcement), he was likely to make that same choice later. Conversely, the opposite pattern obtained for the Externals, who seemed to trust the experimenter's claims more than their own discoveries. Hence, the Internals seemed to rely on what they *knew* to be the correct choice, whereas Externals seemed to

TABLE II
Rate of correct choices as a function of reinforcement type and I–E orientation.

I–E Orientation	REINFORCEMENT	
	Extrinsic	Intrinsic
External	20.1	15.9
Internal	12.2	21.9

After Baron and Ganz (1972).
Note. Values are average number of correct choices out of a total of 30 trials.

place more weight on what they *were told* was correct, that is, on the "expert" judgment of the experimenter.

One important aspect of this finding is that under the appropriate information or reinforcement circumstances, Externals and Internals do about equally well and that under the inappropriate circumstances they do about equally poorly. This finding seems to correct the impression that may have been conveyed earlier that Externals are somehow inferior to Internals. It seems more reasonable to say that people in the two categories pay attention to different things. Indeed, these findings have been buttressed by an extension of this work that revealed that the interaction pattern seen in Table II holds for white boys—and for white college students as well (Baron, Cowan, Ganz, and McDonald, 1974). However, given that most Western cultures are meritocracies based on capitalism, it seems that there would be an inevitable bias to construct research problems in a certain way and to conclude that Internals "show higher levels of adaptive functioning" (Crandall and Crandall, 1983).

I–E Orientation and xenophobia: paper-and-pencil measures. XENOPHOBIA is an adverse reaction to strangers that can range from simple wariness or fear to overt aggression. Such reactions are well documented in a wide variety of species and also can be quite pronounced in human infants and adults (Rajecki, 1983, 1985). The relationship between xenophobia and locus-of-control orientation is potentially important. If the analysis already suggested is correct, then Externals may be even more concerned about strangers than are Internals. Because strangers are inherently unpredictable because of their unfamiliarity, a person who views himself or herself as low on personal control of a situation is likely to be more wary than someone who has a perception of high personal control.

One way to operationalize such a possibility is to measure the INTERPERSONAL DISTANCE, or PERSONAL SPACE, that various personality types find desirable. The idea of interpersonal distance, or personal space, is that each of us has an envelope of space around us that represents a psychological extension of our being. Under everyday circumstances, the penetration of this space by certain people is theoretically aversive or discomforting; in fact a great deal of evidence exists that this is the case (Hall, 1966; Rajecki, 1977; Sommer, 1969).

Duke and Nowicki (1972) used a paper-and-pencil test to estimate comfortable interpersonal distances. They asked subjects to pretend that they were standing in the middle of a room, with the floor represented by a sheet of paper. Eight 80-millimeter radii emanating from a central point were drawn on the sheet. The subject's task was to imagine standing on the central point, with various people, one at a time, approaching along the different radii. The subject indicated by pencil how close certain individuals could approach them, down to a distance that made them feel uncomfortable. The distance at which the subject asked a certain type of imaginary person to halt was the comfortable interpersonal distance for that class of individual.

The types of imaginary "intruders" that approached the subject are of interest. In one study the subject was asked to think that he or she was being approached by a parent, a friend, or a stranger; in a second study new subjects thought about parents, professors, and the United States president (who at that time was Richard Nixon). In both studies, the comfortable interpersonal distance between the subject and the intruder increased as the familiarity of the intruder decreased. However, what is especially interesting is that there was a differential reaction to strangers based on I–E orientation. There are several ways to express this finding, and Duke and Nowicki (1972) reported a correlational analysis. In the first experiment they found that the correlation (r) between externality and comfortable distance for parents was effectively zero, whereas I–E score and distance for strangers resulted in an r of .40, which is a reliable effect. This finding was replicated in the second experiment in which the I–E/distance correlation for parents was again near zero, but for professor and president the respective coefficients were .47 and .48, both of which are more extreme and highly significant. What these correlations tell us is that our I–E orientation does not influence our reactions to familiar people like our parents, but the more external a person is, the more he or she reacts to the presence of a stranger.

Another way to depict this difference between Externals and Internals on comfortable interpersonal distance between familiar and strange people is shown in Table III. The values in the table represent the *difference* between I and E individuals on the distance measure. The larger the number, the greater the distance desired by Externals compared with Internals. In the first experiment Externals and Internals responded similarly in their desire for distance between themselves and their parents, but as familiarity with the target person declined, the Externals' desire for greater distance increased. This pattern was duplicated in the second experiment. Thus, the preferences for additional space on the part of the Externals

TABLE III
Differences in comfortable interpersonal distance as a function of
I–E orientation and the identity of the oncoming person

Intruder	Extra distance (mm) desired by Externals
Experiment 1	
Parent	+0.97
Friend	+3.12
Stranger	+8.60
Experiment 2	
Parent	+0.97
Professor	+16.93
President	+27.81

After Duke and Nowicki (1972).
Note. Plus (+) values mean that Externals desired a greater interpersonal distance between themselves and approaching persons (intruders) of various types than did Internals.

indicates that one way to deal with such a threat is to avoid it as much as possible by installing a buffer between oneself and the stranger.

I–E Orientation and xenophobia: behavioral measures. Unfortunately, in some social situations it is impossible to move others or oneself around at will, yet even in these more fixed circumstances one might expect an I–E difference in reactions to strangers. To examine this possibility, Rajecki, Ickes, and Tanford (1981) adopted a procedure known as the UNSTRUCTURED DYADIC SITUATION. Developed by Ickes and Barnes (1977) to study the impact of personality on social behavior, the unstructured dyadic situation brings two unfamiliar people (hence, the dyad part) into a situation where there are no instructions or obvious guidelines for how to behave (hence, the unstructured part). Basically, two subjects are brought to a room, are told that the experiment will begin shortly, and are temporarily deserted by the experimenter. Any behavior that the subjects engage in is therefore based largely on their dispositions or expectations. During this brief period the subjects' spontaneous responses are covertly recorded on video tape for later analysis.

We used this technique to study I–E differences in reactions to strangers. Undergraduate men were screened for I–E orientation in their classrooms and were later invited to participate in an experiment. Pairs of people were scheduled to arrive at the laboratory at the same time. These pairs were of three types: two Internals (I+I dyad), an Internal and an External (I+E dyad), and two Externals (E+E dyad). The individuals, strangers to each other, were brought to the experimental room at the same time, were asked to sit on the same couch (actually, the only piece of furniture in the room), and were told that the experimenter had to leave for a bit in order to fetch some questionnaires. The experimenter then exited, leaving the two men to their own devices (or dispositions) for a 5-minute period. During this time their behavior and verbalizations were recorded on tape with a hidden camera. The experimenter returned, debriefed the subjects, and obtained their permission to use the tapes for data analysis (Rajecki et al., 1981).

On the basis of the Duke and Nowicki (1972) studies discussed earlier, we would expect that behavior across the dyad types would vary, but because this situation was very different from that used in the Duke–Nowicki studies, it was not immediately clear *how* they would be different. Accordingly, a number of behavior patterns were scored from the playbacks of the tapes. Several of these measures detected strong and significant differences between dyad types. Directed gazes (at each other), mutual gazes, and vocalizations by the E+E dyads exceeded those by the I+I dyads (see Table IV). In

TABLE IV
Responses of internally and externally oriented individuals in an unstructured dyadic situation.

Response type	Dyad type	Response rate[a]
Directed gaze	Internal–internal	5.32
	Internal–external	7.55
	External–external	11.23
Verbalization	Internal–internal	8.03
	Internal–external	10.67
	External–external	15.21
Mutual gaze	Internal–internal	3.25
	Internal–external	5.50
	External–external	7.79

After Rajecki et al. (1981).
[a]For directed gaze and verbalization responses, values are time samples of 2-second intervals in which the behavior was recorded; for mutual gaze responses, values are number of discrete events.

general, the I+E dyads were intermediate in their response rates for these particular measures.

The dyadic data in Table IV reveal that Externals initiated or maintained social interaction much more than their Internal counterparts. What is the meaning of these differences? From the perspectives we have encountered, there could be two important reasons for the differential behavior. First, we have seen in an earlier section that Externals tend to rely on others' opinions when things are somewhat ambiguous. The situation in which the Externals and Internals found themselves in the Rajecki et al. study certainly was ambiguous, so perhaps the Externals conversed in order to gain the views of their partner as to just what was going on. Second, and more germane to the topic of xenophobia, Externals may have talked and interacted more in order to gain information about their partner. It was noted that strangers are unfamiliar and hence unpredictable, and this unpredictability would be more discomforting to Externals than to Internals. One way to reduce the unpredictability of anyone is to ask them questions, and these questions can be about anything, really. As long as the answers are civil and intelligible, one can be confident that one is in the company of a normal person, as opposed to a monster or a dangerous idiot.

I–E ORIENTATION IN THE REAL WORLD

So far we have seen an impressive array of data that shows that I–E orientation makes a big difference in how people react under laboratory conditions. That is very interesting, but of equal interest is how this attitude dimension or personality factor might figure into reactions to the domains of real life. I have three topics in mind: (a) coping with natural disasters, (b) alcoholism, and (c) consequences of early socialization experiences.

I–E orientation and coping with natural disasters. On the eve of the writing of the first draft of this section, there was a violent thunderstorm in the midwestern community where I resided. The late afternoon sky was prematurely and ominously dark; wind and rain lashed the house; television programs were repeatedly interrupted by nervous-sounding local weatherpersons announcing a tornado warning; and between these live interruptions, written notices of the severe weather warning were superimposed on ongoing programs like mismatched English subtitles on a foreign film. Worst of all, the local siren system suddenly began to wail, meaning that someone in a nearby area had spotted a funnel cloud. All in all, I can testify that the experience was quite frightening.

I am telling this story to indicate to those readers who do not live in tornado-prone areas that the conditions surrounding the potential occurrence of most twisters are pretty obvious and would be hard to miss even if one were without electronic media or lived in an isolated locale. The foregoing weather disturbance quickly abated, and the storm passed our neighborhood without serious incident; in the adjacent area, the funnel cloud caused only minor injuries to five people. However, many tornado warnings are followed by much more severe results, and every year many Americans lose their lives in such storms. Most of the deaths occur around an imaginary line that stretches from Dallas, through Topeka, and ends in Detroit (Sims and Baumann, 1972). However, not everyone living in this zone is equally likely to die in a tornado. Sims and Baumann (1972) describe a differential regional risk thusly:

We begin with this fact: the number of tornado-caused deaths in the South is strikingly higher than it is in the remainder of the nation. This is best documented by Linehan [1957]: "Compared with all others, Region I [the South] is characterized in superlatives. In every tornado-death attribute selected, Region I outranks each of the other three, usually by a very wide margin . . . Region I has nearly 12 deaths per 1000 square miles, more than three times the comparable figure for the next ranking region; its 23 deaths per 100,000 inhabitants is over five times greater."

There might be many reasons why southerners are more jeopardized by tornadoes than are people who live elsewhere, and Sims and Baumann discuss some of the more plausible of these. It may be that (1) tornadoes in the South strike areas that are more densely populated than the afflicted areas of other regions, or (2) there may be more nocturnal tornadoes in the South, which would mean that residents of that region would be caught unaware more often, or (3) the lighter construction of southern buildings makes them less likely to withstand a storm's ravages and therefore less likely to protect inhabitants. The interested reader will discover that Sims and Baumann (1972) are able, by careful analysis of relevant data, to *dismiss* all of these as prime factors underlying the differential death rate. Rather, Sims and Baumann turn to a psychological interpretation of the phenomenon.

Figure 3 shows both sides of a wallet-sized card distributed by civil defense agencies. The information on the card is clear and doubtless would be of value in saving lives in tornadoes (and, presumably, in other less-than-natural disasters). But these instructions

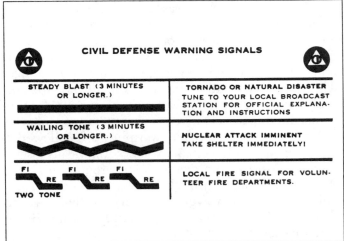

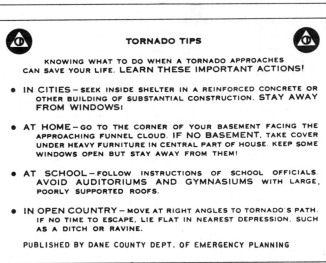

FIGURE 3
CIVIL DEFENSE WARNING SIGNALS and tips on surviving tornadoes. Tips
are printed on a wallet-sized card.

would have an effect only if followed. What sort of people would be
most likely to heed such advice? Sims and Baumann (1972) hypothesized that a distinction might lie along the Internal–External locus-
of-control orientation. We know from several reviews that internally

oriented persons are often better at solving laboratory problems, and it may be that Internals are also better at dealing with awesome problems such as coping with the threat of a tornado. If this is so, the North–South mortality difference could mean that more southerners than northerners are externally oriented.

To test this hypothesis, Sims and Baumann (1972) interviewed several hundred people in the United States. Of special interest are samples of respondents from Illinois and Alabama, who were selected from counties that had experienced about equal numbers of occurrences of tornadoes, potential casualties, and actual rates of tornado-caused deaths. Furthermore, all the respondents were white women between the ages of 31 and 60, matched on education and family income. These women were asked a number of questions, including some that resemble I–E scale items and some that sought their reactions to the threat of a tornado. The percentages of women in each state's sample that gave certain responses are listed in Table V. It can be seen in the table that Alabamans gave general replies indicating that there may be more externally oriented women residing in the South than in northern regions and that their respective reactions to potential tornadoes per se are more passive.

TABLE V

Percentage of women from a northern and a southern state giving certain responses to questions concerning I–E orientation and tornadoes

Response	STATE	
	Alabama	Illinois
As far as my life is concerned, God controls it.	59	36
I believe that luck is very important to me.	29	6
Getting ahead in the world results from God willing it.	46	9
During the time when a tornado watch is out, I watch the sky.	29	9
The best way of identifying tornado weather is listening to the radio.	4	42
The job done by the weather bureau in forecasting tornadoes is excellent.	13	46

After Sims and Baumann (1972).
Note. Since these are only selected responses, no two or more proportions in this table need sum to 100.

The data in Table V suggest that part of the differential rate of tornado-caused deaths between the South and other regions of the country may be the result of the fact that southerners are more fatalistic in their reaction to threatening weather. This fatalism presumably leads to a lower likelihood of precautionary steps toward self-protection. If future research shows this to be a reliable finding, then the job of educating the citizenry will become more complex but perhaps more effective. Finding ways to convince people that they *can* do more to help themselves must be one of the more challenging tasks confronting psychologists who study attitudes.

I–E orientation and alcoholism. Once armed with a concept like locus of control and a yardstick like an I–E scale, the temptation is to rush out and make tests of every human condition worth testing. If something like I–E orientation is involved in surviving disasters, it must surely have a role in coping with other calamities such as disease, divorce, defeat, and decrepitude. Maybe the key to understanding why some folks sail through life while others sink rests in simple measurement. Naturally enough, investigators have applied I–E scales to persons with chronic but presumably tractable problems, such as alcoholism. The logic seems straightforward enough: if alcoholics, compared with nonalcoholics, are markedly external in orientation, then therapeutic or prevention programs can be designed to take advantage of this information. Of course, we might find that alcoholics are highly internal in orientation, even if this might be illusory on their part. Still, the information would be useful in dealing with the problem.

However, while seeming to hold much promise, much of the first decade of such work produced disappointing results. According to a review by Donovan and O'Leary (1983), there is considerable evidence for each of the following three conclusions: (a) alcoholics are more external than nonalcoholics, (b) alcoholics are more internal than nonalcoholics, and (c) alcoholics and nonalcoholics do not differ as groups with regard to their locus-of-control orientation. The literature in general contains so many conflicting findings that Donovan and O'Leary were reduced to alluding to Keller's Law concerning trait research in alcoholism:

The investigation of any trait in alcoholics will show that they have either more or less of it.

One supposes that there could be a Keller's Second Law:

The broad enough investigation of any trait in alcoholics will show that they have both more and less of it.

According to an analysis by Donovan and O'Leary (1983), the trouble with the preceding literature is that many of the investigators employed measures of *generalized* expectancies of control, such as the original Rotter I–E scale. These reviewers point out that scores from such general instruments might well predict behavior in general. But as an individual gains experience with a specific activity—such as drinking—increased familiarity with the settings and motivations involved would make the measure of generalized locus of control a relatively ineffective predictor of alcohol-related behavior.

As an alternative approach, Donovan and O'Leary (1978, 1983) point to what is called the drink-related locus-of-control (DRIE) scale. This scale has items that deal more or less specifically with the antecedents and consequences of drinking for alcoholics. The scale's items seem to tap three separate dimensions in the psychology of alcoholism. Using the proper statistical techniques, Donovan and O'Leary found that three kinds of factors have a role in problem drinking: intrapersonal control, interpersonal control, and general control. These factors, and some scale items that represent each, are listed in Figure 4. It can be seen in the figure that the intrapersonal

---

Intrapersonal control

When I see a bottle, I cannot resist taking a drink.
I cannot feel good unless I am drinking.
Once I start to drink I can't stop.
Drinking is my favorite form of entertainment.

Interpersonal control

I feel so helpless in some situations that I need a drink.
Trouble at work or home drives me to drink.
I get so upset over small arguments that they cause me to drink.
I just cannot handle my problems unless I take a drink first.

General control

Without the right breaks one cannot stay sober.
Staying sober depends mainly on things going right for you.
Sometimes I cannot understand how people control their drinking.

FIGURE 4
EXTERNAL RESPONSE ALTERNATIVES for some of the DRIE scale items (see text) that represent intrapersonal control, interpersonal control, and general control. (After Donovan and O'Leary, 1983.)

control items reveal how much or how little control the individual has over her or his own psychology. Next, the interpersonal items generally show degree of control of the self in certain situations. Finally, the general control items reflect a more global perspective.

Donovan and O'Leary (1978) sought an empirical validation of the DRIE. In one study they compared the DRIE scores of alcoholics and nonalcoholics and found that the problem drinkers had significantly more external scores. In another project they compared alcoholics that had external DRIE scores with alcoholics that had internal DRIE scores. In the authors' words,

those with external DRIE scores tended to drink in a more sustained, obsessive fashion, had previously utilized more outside resources in an attempt to stop drinking, had experienced more physical and perceptual symptoms during withdrawal, and evidenced significantly greater physical, psychosocial, and psychological deterioration as a consequence of drinking (Donovan and O'Leary, 1983).

In sum, alcoholics *are* more external, at least as measured by the DRIE, which is what I suspected all along. This section has offered another good object lesson on an issue raised again and again in this book, namely, that psychologists only get answers to the questions they ask. We saw in Chapter 3 that general attitudes predict multiple-act criteria but that the prediction of a single act requires the measurement of attitude toward *that* act. Apparently, the same rule applies where locus of control and alcoholism (as a single act) are concerned.

I–E orientation and childhood socialization. How do people acquire their I–E orientation? In the second part of this chapter having to do with perceived control, it will be seen that certain traumatic events or major life changes give people the impression that they are more or less helpless in coping with life's demands. But I–E orientation seems more subtle and stable than a reaction to a certain event. Recall that this concept originated in the domain of personality theory. The impression is that I–E orientation is based somehow on the sum of past experience, and perhaps especially on early experience. This notion has led researchers to inquire about the impact of childhood socialization experiences on orientation.

In their review, Crandall and Crandall (1983) identify several types of research designs for such investigations, as presented in Table VI. One of these—which I have labeled Type I—provides for the *direct* observation or rating of actual parent–child interactions and also for a concurrent or subsequent I–E measure of the child as a child or adolescent. This design reveals the short-term influence

TABLE VI
Outlines of research designs employed in estimating the effects of parent–child
interactions on a child's childhood or adulthood I–E orientation

Research design	Parent–child interaction	Childhood I–E orientation	Adulthood I–E orientation	Number of reports
Type I	Observed	Observed	—	7
Type II	Recalled	—	Observed	9
Type III	Observed	—	Observed	1

Note. These outlines are based on the review of Crandall and Crandall (1983).

of parental treatment. Crandall and Crandall cite seven such studies.
A second design (Type II in the table) obtains a measure of a person's
I–E orientation as an adult and then estimates parental treatment
from the subject's *recall* of her or his parents' behavior. These retrospective studies provide an estimate of long-term influences of
early experiences, and the Crandall–Crandall review identifies nine
such investigations. Finally, there is a third type of study (Type III)
in which parental behavior is directly observed and then later related
to I–E orientation when measured in the child as an adult. This type
is rare, and we will turn to the single such project after a look at the
results from the 16 other studies.

The results of the first 16 studies identified by Crandall and
Crandall (1983) were consistent and clear. According to the reviewers,

in summary, with the exception of protectiveness, relatively consistent parental
antecedents have been found for I–E assessed in child, adolescent, and adult
samples. For all age levels, a cluster of behaviors reflecting parental warmth,
involvement, and supportiveness seems to function as a major determinant of
internal perceptions. Consistency of discipline and independence training also
appear to influence I–E development. For studies of children and adolescents,
data on parenting derived from verbal reports have been corroborated in observations of parents.

Thus, parental warmth and supportiveness are seen as positively
and, presumably, causally related to internal-control orientation, a
finding found consistently in studies of Types I and II. Similarly, in
a separate review on familial influences, Lefcourt (1982) concluded
that an "attentive, responsive, critical, and contingent milieu"
seemed to be the precursor of the emergence of an internal view.
But what about that lone Type III study in Table VI? Here, Crandall
and Crandall (1983) used their own data from a Fels Institute longi-

tudinal project. The households of 63 children were visited regularly from the birth of the child until it reached 10 years of age. After each home visit, observers rated aspects of the mother's behavior with standardized Fels Behavior Rating Scales and also filed a narrative report of mother–child interactions. Therefore, Crandall and Crandall were armed with a rich and detailed history of their subjects' socialization experiences. Then, when the children in question approached or reached adulthood (aged 18–26 years), they were invited to return to the institute for a battery of tests that included I–E scales.

The outcome of this study was that Crandall and Crandall (1983) found a strong *negative* relationship between internal locus of control and parental warmth. These most recent findings were in direct *contradiction* to the 16 investigations that preceded them. Nevertheless, the Crandall–Crandall data were very strong and clear. For internally oriented female subjects, the childhood measures clearly showed that the mothers had been lacking in affection and were somewhat rejecting and punitive. For males, the childhood indexes showed pretty much the same thing: mothers of internal young men were less affectionate and more rejecting than were the mothers of external young men.

How can one reconcile these conflicting results? Because the identification of the antecedent to I–E orientation is an important matter in personality and social psychology, I am not inclined to simply dismiss the Crandalls' study as a fluke, or to dismiss all the earlier projects as flukes, either. Instead, the total body of literature seems to suggest some interesting lines for future research, two of which I suggest here:

1. Antecedents of childhood and adolescent I–E orientation may not be the antecedents of adult orientation. The child's world and the adult's world are very different places. Parental treatments that give a child a sense of internal control (in Type I studies) may not have a parallel impact when that child faces the demands of an adult existence (in Type III studies). It is known that I–E orientation can change in the face of environmental pressures. Doherty and Baldwin (1985) found a clear shift to externality in women in a longitudinal study over the 1960s and 1970s, whereas men showed no such shift in this period. Presumably, the women reacted to the realization of external constraints on their ability to meet their goals in the work force, whereas men did not experience similar changes in perceptions.

2. However, adult internals in Type II studies *recall* more parental warmth than do externals. How could this be if their parents were

actually low on warmth? The answer is that it may be a *mis*perception on their part. Crandall and Crandall (1983) point out that internals consistently report themselves as being better adjusted and having more of a sense of well-being than do externals. They suggest that it may be that internals' perception of their own positive characteristics leads them to infer erroneous attributions of superior (warmer) childrearing practices on the part of their parents.

In any event, these possibilities are worth tracking down. Continuing research on the antecedents of I–E locus of control promises to provide us with interesting future findings.

SUMMARY

As noted, research and theory on internal or external locus-of-control orientations is a bridge between the areas of personality and the social psychology of attitudes. This bridge is a welcome one, for the study of these two domains have much in common (Ajzen, 1988). Knowledge of a person's control orientation as an attitude provides us with an improved ability to understand and predict behavior, which is a goal of modern scientific psychology.

Perceived Control

Another research bridge exists between the areas of social psychology and clinical psychology in the matter of PERCEIVED CONTROL. Advances in this domain have come from work in laboratory and field settings; we will begin with the former.

LEARNED HELPLESSNESS

"If at first you don't succeed, try, try again." This line may contain sound advice in the abstract, but it is an empirical question whether people actually behave this way in the laboratory or in the real world. One of the most common psychological ailments is depression. Sometimes we feel just bogged down and unable to go on, and in extreme cases this feeling can lead to suicide. When we see people down in the dumps because of the loss of a spouse, a lover, a pet, a job, or some important goal, it seems easy to offer uplifting advice. There are, after all, plenty of other people around to serve as spouses or lovers, all the dogs and cats anyone could want, other jobs for the taking, and many alternative goals to pursue. Still, we have seen that some people view outcomes to be more or less independent of their actions, and if this sort of out-of-control attitude is part of a clinical depression, then recovery from such a state may be neither automatic nor easy.

We will begin our survey in the laboratory. Because depression is a serious problem, it is important to develop many ways of studying the condition, including lab analogs. One of the most noteworthy laboratory paradigms for studying depression or depressive-like states is that of Seligman (1975) and his colleagues, who developed a way of inducing LEARNED HELPLESSNESS in the laboratory. The Seligman paradigm is relatively simple and involves two parts or stages. During the first part, which will be called the *training* stage, subjects are provided with information concerning the relationship between their responses and the effects of those responses in a certain situation. In the second part, or *test* stage, subjects are assessed for their ability to cope with a new situation.

An animal study. Some of the earliest and most influential studies on learned helplessness were conducted with animals. I will begin at the test stage (part two) of an experiment by Seligman and Maier (1967): the final task required of canine subjects was to jump across a low barrier from one compartment of a box to the other on signal, which was the dimming of the lights in the unit. The reason the dogs bothered to jump was that the light signal was followed 10 seconds later by a powerful electric shock delivered through the compartment's grid floor for a total of 50 seconds. If the dog failed to jump, it would experience almost a minute of extremely noxious stimulation per trial.

Most dogs new to the apparatus quickly learn to jump on signal and usually experience only a small amount of shock on the first few trials. However, some dogs in the Seligman–Maier study failed badly on this jumping test, depending on certain experiences during the prior training stage of the experiment. Of interest are two of these experiences, the escapable and the inescapable shock conditions. In the former condition, a dog was placed in a harness or sling so that its feet could not touch the floor. The animal's neck was placed in a stock like a pillory, and panels resembling oversized blinders were installed on either side of the animal's head. To make things worse, shock-generating electrodes were attached to one of the dog's legs, and a machine was programmed to deliver 64 painful shocks, of 30 seconds duration each.

The dogs in the escapable shock condition could turn off—or "escape"—the shock by nudging either of the head panels. A touch on a panel terminated the shock on that trial, and the subjects could reduce their discomfort by reacting quickly. If they reacted within 1 second on all 64 trials, a minimum of 64 seconds of shock was achievable. In fact, the dogs rapidly learned to turn off the shocks as they came on, and the animals in this condition received an average of only 226 seconds of shock out of a possible 1,920.

But there was a second set of dogs trained in the harness, and these were termed the inescapable shock group. These animals received almost the same training as the escapable group; they too received 226 seconds of stimulation over 64 trials. However, the experience of the inescapable animals was different from the others in one important respect: nothing they did had any influence on the shock they received. In other words, whereas the animals in the escapable shock condition learned that they could terminate aversive stimulation while in the harness, the dogs in the inescapable group learned that they could not turn off the shock.

The dogs were then removed from the harness, rested, and then tested in the barrier apparatus 24 hours later. Recall that, first, none of the dogs in the escapable or inescapable conditions had ever been in the test apparatus before, and, second, if a dog failed to jump on any test trial, it received a total of 50 seconds of painful stimulation on that trial. How did the dogs cope with the problem in the test unit? In fact, animals in the escapable (stage 1) condition did rather well. Their overall average latency to jumping the barrier after the light signal came on was 27 seconds, and they failed to escape on an average of only 2.63 trials out of 10. In sharp contrast, the mean latency for the animals in the inescapable condition was 48 seconds (which was almost the maximum possible latency), and they completely failed to jump on seven and more trials. Clearly, the animals in the inescapable training condition did not cope well with the subsequent test problem, compared with the escapable group, even though individuals in both groups had an equal opportunity to do so. It was as if training with inescapable shock had taught those animals that there was little they could do to relieve themselves of shock, anywhere—hence the term "learned helplessness."

A human study. Actually, knowledge of the Seligman–Maier procedure with dogs makes for an easy transition to an early study of learned helplessness in humans, because Hiroto (1974) used those same methods on introductory psychology students. For the training phase, Hiroto used a headset (earphones) in place of a body harness and substituted aversive noise for aversive shock. For the test stage, the humans did not have to jump over a barrier; rather, they had to turn a lever that resembled an automobile gearshift.

Beyond that, the student subjects faced a situation similar to the one confronting the dogs. Subjects were brought to the laboratory and were told that the study involved listening to a loud noise (a

110-decibel, 3,000-hertz tone) through a headset. This type of sound is unpleasant and above many persons' threshold for pain. The subjects first heard the following recorded message, which was their only clue as what to do in the situation:

Listen to these instructions carefully, I am not allowed to give you additional information other than what is given to you now. So please listen and do not ask me any questions. From time to time a loud noise will appear. When the tone comes on there is something you can do to stop it (Hiroto, 1974).

In front of the subject was a small panel containing a spring-loaded red button. Once the series of thirty 5-second tones began, the subjects commenced to push the button avidly. But as the reader may have guessed by now, pushing the button did not have the same effect or consequence for all subjects. For the people in an escapable condition, pushing the button immediately terminated the noise on that trial. These humans could do something to "escape" the aversive stimulation. Other subjects in an inescapable condition had to listen to a total of 150 seconds of scheduled noise because pushing their button accomplished nothing. Like the dogs in the inescapable condition, these particular subjects were confronted with the fact that their own behavior was ineffective in terminating their discomfort.

Following the training session, the subjects (with headsets in place) were taken to a different table in the laboratory where their coping was assessed in a test stage. There, they found the gearshift lever and a cue light, and like the dogs' problem, the light served as a warning for the onset of the aversive tone. Again, subjects were given minimal information concerning their options.

You will be given some trials in which a relatively loud tone will be presented to you at different intervals. Now here is the important part, and I want you to listen carefully. Whenever you hear the tone come on there is something you can do to stop it (Hiroto, 1974).

Thereafter followed 18 trials wherein the light preceded the tone by 5 seconds. Protection from the tone was possible if the person moved the lever from one side to the other on alternative trials. As was the case with the dogs, humans in the escapable and inescapable training conditions were now on an equal footing in this test stage, but they did not act that way. Subjects in the escapable condition completely avoided the aversive stimulus on 87% of the test trials, whereas individuals in the inescapable group protected themselves on only 50% of these trials. Latencies to responding during this series of 18 trials also revealed differences that showed that the escapable group was responding much faster. So, although we know that everyone had equal opportunities to cope with the demands of the test stage, there was something about the subjects who had gone through the inescapable training experience that prevented them from coping optimally. Hiroto therefore concluded that learned helplessness could be induced in human beings as well as in other animals.

Generalization of learned helplessness. However, these findings from the human research are open to a number of interpretations. Were the subjects in the inescapable condition really feeling somewhat helpless, or could it be that there were other factors influencing their behavior in the test situation? To mention just a few alternative accounts, maybe the training convinced those subjects that they were just bad on motor tasks, or that they were having a bad day, or even that the laboratory equipment was unreliable and out of order. That is, how comparable were their feelings on that occasion with the general impression of lethargy and reluctance associated with depressive states? To put it another way, did this method produce a *state* (temporary reaction to a particular circumstance) or a *trait* (persevering reaction to circumstances in general)? Hiroto attempted to answer this question in collaboration with Seligman.

Hiroto and Seligman (1975) tested subjects for the generalization of learned helplessness effects. If for the moment we consider the Seligman and Maier (1967) dog study and the Hiroto (1974) human experiment, it is clear that subjects had no opportunity to show the generalization of the effect. In both cases the training and test stages involved motor tasks. Therefore, Hiroto and Seligman (1975) first had to determine whether the helplessness phenomenon could occur for some task other than one demanding a motor response. Basically, they ran four experiments, as illustrated in Table VII. These experiments involved four different tasks for humans, the two motor tasks with which we are familiar and two cognitive tasks: a visual discrimination puzzle and an anagram (jumbled letters) task. In Table VII, experiment A was a replication of Hiroto's study and experiment B served to establish learned helplessness using cognitive tasks. Experiments C and D are the crucial ones, for they represented tests of the generalization of the effect. If subjects were made to succeed or fail on one kind of task, would that success or failure generalize to a very different task?

Without going into too much detail, the answer to the question is clearly yes, according to the conclusion of Hiroto and Seligman (1975).

Learned helplessness was found with all four experiments. Both insolubility and inescapability produced failure to escape and failure to solve anagrams. We suggest that inescapability and insolubility both engendered expectancies that

TABLE VII
Features of the four experiments in research on the generalization of the learned
helplessness effect

	STAGE	
Experiment	Training	Test
A	Motor (button pushing)	Motor (lever moving)
B	Cognitive (visual puzzle)	Cognitive (anagram test)
C	Motor (button pushing)	Cognitive (anagram test)
D	Cognitive (visual puzzle)	Motor (lever moving)

After Hiroto and Seligman (1975).

responding is independent of reinforcement. The generality of this process
suggests that learned helplessness may be an induced "trait."

It is also worth noting that the generalizability of such effects has
been replicated by Cohen, Rothbart, and Phillips (1976).

Epilogue. The studies just noted emerged in the context of inquiries into depression. By now, there has been considerable debate
as to the merit of the learned helplessness approach in understanding
depression per se. For instance, Depue and Monroe (1978) faulted
the theory for not taking into account the complexity and variety of
actual clinical depression. In reaction to such criticism, Seligman
(1978) argued that there is a subclass of experience-induced depression that cuts across mild and clinical divisions of the disorder. But
for the reader of this book, the issue does not begin or end with
concerns about a particular diagnostic category. Our concerns in this
chapter are with attitudes toward the self. Although we recognize
that the applicability of the notion of learned helplessness has its
limitations, the research that this concept has inspired definitely tells
us that something about one's perceived control in a given situation
can influence one's behavior. Taken far enough, a person's willingness
or ability to cope may be profoundly influenced by such perceptions.
This claim will be scrutinized in the following section on institutionalization.

CONTROL, WELL-BEING, AND SURVIVAL IN ELDERLY INDIVIDUALS

The methods used to induce human learned helplessness in the laboratory are relatively harmless, at least when compared with some of the more traumatic events of real life. We are susceptible to trauma at all points in the developmental span and become especially vulnerable in old age. Elderly persons sooner or later are faced with a number of major changes in their lives, some of which can be viewed as events having the potential to induce learned helplessness, depression, and even early death. Rowland (1977) reviewed the literature on the adverse effects of retirement, loss of a spouse, and institutionalization on the aged and found that the latter two events, at least, were definitely linked to premature death.

In this section we will concentrate on institutionalization. Relocation can be difficult for anyone, and being institutionalized must rank as one of the more trying kinds of change. When an elderly person is installed in a nursing home, vast disruptions in their lifestyle are imposed. Familiar faces are replaced by those of strangers, surroundings are new, and normal routines are replaced by regimens and schedules dictated by the staff. It is important to note that the negative effects of such moves are not necessarily attributable to a lessening in the physical quality of life; rather, *change* itself is related to mortality. Rowland (1977) found that change from one institution to another resulted in an increase in the death rate, even when the receiving unit had comparable or superior facilities.

It is quite plausible that the experience of institutionalization conveys to the individual that he or she is no longer completely in control of his or her outcomes or reinforcements. Coupled with the literal helplessness (infirmity) that often accompanies advanced age, the addition of psychological helplessness can be viewed as unnerving and as a contributing factor in morbidity and mortality. Still, there could be a brighter side to all of this. That is, if helplessness can be induced via learning or experience, then that trait might be modified by additional learning or other experiences. How would an institutionalized, elderly person react to a reinstatement of her or his control over outcomes or reinforcements? Would this shift in contingencies result in any change in well-being?

This was the essential question asked in a number of seminal field experiments conducted by Ellen Langer and Judith Rodin and by Richard Schulz. Their studies are interesting and noteworthy because of the manner in which they established elderly persons' control over important parts of the environment and because of the extensiveness of their longitudinal work.

Control, predictability, and well-being: short-term effects. The subjects in the Schulz (1976) study were of an advanced age (the average was 81.5 years) and were residents of a retirement home. Schulz assigned people in the home to four different treatment groups, groupings that determined how much "control" each resident had over some person on the research team. The people in the home were visited by one of Schulz's undergraduate research assistants. In one experimental group, termed the control-visitor condition, the resident was given the privilege of telephoning one of the assistants and having him or her visit as often as was wished and for as long as desired. Patients in this group could literally control the behavior of some other person. For a second group of subjects (residents), the rate and duration of visits was matched to those in the control-visitor condition. Therefore, if a certain resident in the control-visitor group had had three 15-minute visits in a given week, his or her counterpart in the second group also received three 15-minute visits in that week. However, although this second group of people did not have the power to arrange the visits, they were at least forewarned (by telephone) well in advance when a visit would take place. Accordingly, this second condition was termed the predict-visitor group, because the subjects could predict when an assistant would show up.

Schulz used these conditions to provide residents with control or predictability over some person. To assess the impact of this predictability and control, two more conditions were established: the random-visitor and the no-visitor treatments. In the random-visitor condition, a third subset of residents were matched to those of the control-visitor and predict-visitor groups (as in the example of three 15-minute visits per week), but they were given no advance warning about any of the visits and the assistants arrived on an apparently random basis. Finally, in the no-visitor group, there simply were no visits.

A large number of measures were obtained by Schulz (1976) to evaluate the possibility that giving elderly persons the ability to control or predict important events—such as visits—might influence their well-being. These measures were taken before and after the month-long (or so) field experiment during which the visiting took place for the appropriate groups. It was a straightforward matter to calculate changes in a person's status or outlook as a consequence of the various treatments. Certain of these changes in scores are presented in Table VIII, where positive values represent improvement and negative scores indicate the opposite. According to Schulz's statistical analysis, the major finding in Table VIII is that although the control-visitor and predict-visitor conditions did not differ from each other and produced roughly equivalent positive effects, these effects were superior to those that resulted from the random-visitor and no-visitor treatments (which also did not differ from each other). Therefore, establishing a resident's capacity to control or predict a visitor seems to have been crucial to any beneficial consequences that might accrue from such visits. Random visits, on the contrary, did not have much more of a positive influence on well-being than did no visits at all.

Responsibility and well-being: short-term effects. Turning to the Langer and Rodin (1976) study, the location of their research was a highly rated nursing home in Connecticut. The researchers' intent was to convey to some of the residents that they themselves had the right and the *responsibility* to be influential in their own lives. These people were informed in no uncertain terms that they could and should make decisions about the use of resources and about the nature of their day-to-day activities while in the institution. By contrast, another sample of the resident population was given equivalent information about the resources and activities available to them while in the home, but there was no suggestion that the use or enjoyment of these features was at the exclusive discretion of the individual resident. For this second group, it was implied instead that the staff

TABLE VIII

Change scores on various measures as a consequence of visitor treatments

	TREATMENT			
Measure	Control visitor	Predict visitor	Random visitor	No visitor
Health status	+6.90	+6.10	+4.70	+5.10
Level of hope	+.42	+.20	−.07	−.31
Activity index	+.50	+.27	.00	−.60

After Schulz (1976).
Note. The different measures (health status, level of hope, activity index) were made with different scales, so it is not appropriate to make comparisons across scales. The appropriate comparisons in the table are across treatments. Plus scores indicate improvement; negative scores indicate deterioration.

maintained jurisdiction in these matters. This differential information was given to residents of two different floors of the nursing home in the form of a briefing or a pep talk by the director. Because the difference in the two talks constituted the whole of the experimental manipulation in the study, their contents are reproduced verbatim

---

Talk for responsibility-induced group

I brought you together today to give you some information about Arden House. I was surprised to learn that many of you don't know about the things that are available to you and more important, that many of you don't realize the influence you have over your own lives here. Take a minute to think of the decisions you can and should be making. For example, you have the responsibility of caring for yourselves, of deciding whether or not you want to make this a home you can be proud of and happy in. You should be deciding how you want your rooms to be arranged—whether you want it to be as it is or whether you want the staff to help you rearrange the furniture. You should be deciding how you want to spend your time, for example, whether you want to be visiting your friends who live on this floor or on the other floors, whether you want to visit in your room or your friends' room, in the lounge, the dining room, etc., or whether you want to be watching television, listening to the radio, writing, reading, or planning social events. In other words, it's your life and you can make of it whatever you want.

This brings me to another point. If you are unsatisfied with anything here,

---

Talk for comparison group

I brought you together today to give you some information about the Arden House. I was surprised to learn that many of you don't know about the things that are available to you; that many of you don't realize all you're allowed to do here. Take a minute to think of all the options that we've provided for you in order for your life to be fuller and more interesting. For example, you're permitted to visit people on the other floors and to use the lounge on this floor for visiting as well as the dining room or your own rooms. We want your rooms to be as nice as they can be, and we've tried to make them that way for you. We want you to be happy here. We feel that it's our responsibility to make this a home you can be proud of and happy in, and we want to do all we can to help you.

FIGURE 5
THE DIFFERENT PEP TALKS heard by residents in the Langer–Rodin field experiment. (Quoted from Langer and Rodin, 1976.)

in Figure 5. The reader should carefully examine the contents of Figure 5 before proceeding further in the text.

On the basis of the two pep talks, the residents of the respective floors were termed the responsibility-induced group and the comparison group. In order to determine whether the induction of re-

---

you have the influence to change it. It's your responsibility to make your complaints known, to tell us what you would like to change, to tell us what you would like. These are just a few of the things you could and should be deciding and thinking about now and from time to time everyday. You made these decisions before you came here and you can and should be making them now.

We're thinking of instituting some way for airing complaints, suggestions, etc. Let [nurse's name] know if you think this is a good idea and how you think we should go about doing it. In any case let her know what your complaints or suggestions are.

Also, I wanted to take this opportunity to give you each a present from the Arden House. [A box of small plants was passed around, and patients were given two decisions to make: first, whether or not they wanted a plant at all, and second, to choose which one they wanted. All residents did select a plant.] The plants are yours to keep and take care of as you'd like.

One last thing, I wanted to tell you that we're showing a movie two nights next week, Thursday and Friday. You should decide which night you'd like to go, if you choose to see it at all.

This brings me to another point. If you have any complaints or suggestions about anything, let [nurse's name] know what they are. Let us know how we can best help you. You should feel that you have free access to anyone on the staff, and we will do the best we can to provide individualized attention and time for you.

Also, I wanted to take this opportunity to give you each a present from the Arden House. [The nurse walked around with a box of plants and each patient was handed one.] The plants are yours to keep. The nurses will water and care for them for you.

One last thing, I wanted to tell you that we're showing a movie next week on Thursday and Friday. We'll let you know later which day you're scheduled to see it.

sponsibility had any special influence on that group, information about both groups was obtained 1 week before and 3 weeks after the briefings. The sources of these dependent measures were varied and included residents' self-reports, the researchers' impression of each resident, and nurses' impressions of the residents. No matter what the source of the information, however, it was clear that by the end of the field experiment the people in the responsibility-induced group were better off than those in the comparison condition. This difference is reflected in changes in their well-being from before to after the experimental manipulation, as seen in Table IX. By all accounts, the residents in the responsibility-induced condition improved, presumably as a result of their rediscovered capacity to make decisions, whereas over the same period the well-being of the comparison group declined. All the differences between the two groups are statistically significant.

Long-term effects. If the short-term results of the Langer and Rodin (1976) field experiment were impressive, the results of their later follow-up (Rodin and Langer, 1977) were no less so. These researchers returned to the nursing home 18 months after the director had given his talks (see Figure 5) and were able to obtain addi-

TABLE IX
Change scores on various measures from before to after the experimental treatment (pep talk)

	TREATMENT	
Measure[a]	Responsibility-induced	Comparison
Self-report:		
happy	+0.28	−0.12
active	+0.20	−1.28
Interviewer rating:		
alert	+0.29	−0.37
Nurses' rating:		
general improvement	+3.97	−2.39
time visiting others	+2.14	−4.16

After Langer and Rodin (1976).
Note. A positive (+) change score indicates an improvement or an increase, whereas a negative (−) change score indicates a deterioration or a decrease.
[a]The different measures (self-report, interviewer and nurses' ratings) were made with different scales, so it is not appropriate to make comparisons across measures. The appropriate comparisons in this table are across treatments.

tional information about the well-being of the residents. One of the things they discovered about the surviving residents was that there continued to be a difference between the responsibility-induced group and the comparison group. Nurses provided new impressions that indicated that people in the responsibility group were happier, more actively interested in things, and more sociable, self-initiating, and vigorous than were individuals in the other group. Further, the medical records of the two groups showed that the responsibility-induced residents were healthier.

Finally, even the death rates of the two groups were affected by the difference in experimental manipulation. In the 18-month period before the beginning of the study, one-fourth of the entire population of the home had died. That is, the best estimate of the death rate in the home is that 25% of the residents would die in any given 18-month period. However, in the 18 months following the pep talks (Figure 5) the death rate of the comparison group was 30%, whereas the corresponding rate in the responsibility-induced group was only 15%. This difference in death rate adds a grim note of validity to the ratings reported earlier.

When Schulz completed a 3.5 year follow-up check on his elderly residents, he also encountered some grim long-term statistics. Recall that in his 1976 paper the control-visitor and predict-visitor subjects were in better shape than were the random-visitor and no-visitor controls (Table VIII). However, by 42 months after the experimenters (visitors) had departed, these previously superior residents had shown a precipitous decline in physical and psychological well-being, so much so that they were worse off than other residents (random- and no-visitor subjects), who showed much less steep declines over the same period (Schulz and Hanusa, 1978). Moreover, the death rate in the control-visitor and predict-visitor groups was higher ($n = 7$) than in the other two groups ($n = 0$). All of this shows a *reversal* of the short-term gains produced by the visitor manipulations and provides a picture in stark contrast with that of Rodin and Langer (1977).

Predicting long-term effects from theory. Given the correspondence in short-term effects for the respective Langer and Rodin (1976) and Schulz (1976) field-experimental manipulations, how could the long-term effects seen by Rodin and Langer (1977) and by Schulz and Hanusa (1978) be so diametrically opposed? One possible answer can be found in a theory of learned helplessness. Abramson, Seligman, and Teasdale (1978) set forth a theoretical position on learned helplessness that was based on an attributional analysis of reactions to uncontrollable events, or cases where a person discovers that outcomes are not contingent on her or his behavior. The Abramson et al. argument is that the degree of subjective helplessness is determined by attributions about the cause of the noncontingency. These attributions are made along three independent dimensions: internal/external, stable/unstable, and global/specific.

1. Internal/external. When one accounts for a noncontingency due to a personal characteristic, then the attribution will be to an internal factor; when some environmental feature is to blame, then the attribution will be to an external factor.

2. Stable/unstable. When that thing that accounts for the noncontingency is thought to be enduring, an attribution to a stable factor will occur; if the accountable thing is unenduring, an attribution to an unstable factor will take place.

3. Global/specific. When helplessness deficits can be expected to occur in a wide range of situations, then the individual will make an attribution to a global feature; if they are expected in a narrow range of situations, there will be an attribution to a specific feature.

To illustrate how this theory would predict behavior due to the discovery of a noncontingency between behavior and an outcome, let us take an example of a student confronted with a morning math test (this example is borrowed, with slight revision, from Abramson et al., 1978). Our student studied diligently for the test, was motivated to get a good grade, and worked quite hard on the test problems. However, when the exam was scored in that same class period, our hypothetical student learned to his disappointment that he had utterly *failed* the math test. Now, the question is, How will this student fare on a second test that day? How will his experience in math influence his behavior during an English examination that afternoon? The answer depends on the factors to which he attributed his earlier failure. Did he make internal versus external, stable versus unstable, or global versus specific attributions?

These possibilities are illustrated in Table X. In the example in the table we would not expect our student's unhappy morning experience to carry over to his efforts in the afternoon if he made external, specific, and unstable attributions. On the other hand, if his attributions about his morning's fate were internal, global, and stable, then we might well expect him to have cognitive or motivational deficits in English class. In general, the more internal, stable, and global the attributions concerning the failure were, the more we would expect carryover effects to the second test.

TABLE X
Attributional dimensions and examples from a hypothetical case of a student
who failed a math exam

I–E orientation	Global	Specific
Internal		
Stable	I have a low IQ.	I lack math ability.
Unstable	I have a cold.	I am tired of math problems.
External		
Stable	Profs are unfair.	Math profs are unfair.
Unstable	Today is Friday the 13th.	The math test was the wrong test.

After Abramson et al. (1978).

It seems reasonable to try to apply this sort of formulation to the circumstances experienced by certain subjects in the Schulz and Hanusa (1978) report. Recall that residents in the control-visitor and predict-visitor conditions had a good deal of predictability or control regarding visits for a time, but then the visiting volunteer(s) left, never to return. Abruptly, these residents were confronted with the information that they could no longer control or expect visits from, say, volunteer X. That is, however much they might want to try to arrange for a visit, it would not be forthcoming. Table XI shows some

TABLE XI
Application of attributional dimensions to the residents in the Schulz–Hanusa
follow-up who could no longer control or predict visits from volunteer X

I–E orientation	Global	Specific
Internal		
Stable	I am unimportant.	I am unimportant to volunteer X.
Unstable	I seem to be unimportant today.	I seem to be unimportant to volunteer X today.
External		
Stable	People are uncaring.	Volunteer X is uncaring.
Unstable	Volunteer X is uncaring.	Volunteer X is sometimes busy and uncaring.

After Schulz and Hanusa (1978).

possible reactions to this turn of events. Just as in the case of the student who failed a math test, residents' reactions would depend to an important degree on the attributions they made about their situation. If they made external, specific, and unstable attributions, then we would not expect their disappointment to carry over to other areas of their lives. Unfortunately, it must have eventually dawned on the subjects that the visitors were *not* coming back and that no one else was coming to take their place. Under these circumstances, it seems plausible that the residents made internal, stable, and global attributions about their inability to receive visitors. These inimical judgments may well have carried over to other areas of their existence, influencing their health, general morale, and longevity.

DEPENDENCY IN ELDERLY INDIVIDUALS

Of course, the application of theories of learned helplessness to the plight of institutionalized elderly people implies that there is an absence of contingency between residents' behavior and many of their important outcomes. However, this does not mean that all outcomes are completely independent of their behavior. Indeed, social scientists' reconstruction of the experience of institutionalization shows that certain outcomes and certain behavior are closely linked, but perhaps in a way that is inimical to the well-being of residents in the long run:

Upon entry, the individual, who rarely chooses to be there, gives up control over the most mundane daily activities, when to sleep, wake, visit, perform toileting activities, bathe, and shop. The patient is exposed to infantilization and numbing bureaucratic and health routines that are of obscure purpose due to the invariably poor communication and misinformation given to placate the patient . . . The staff may treat aggressiveness of the patient with drugs, punishment, or increased response time to the demands of the patient and the implied threat of not providing the best possible care. The patient sees his or her being on the best possible terms with the staff as imperative and as *demanding passive and dependent behavior* (White and Janson, 1986; emphasis added).

What this White–Janson passage implies is that while it is clear that an elderly resident of an institution loses control over many of the daily routines of the past, that resident certainly does not enter an environment that is devoid of contingencies between behavior and outcomes. It turns out that a great deal of controllable reinforcement is available to old people in nursing homes. Over the past decade Margaret M. Baltes and her colleagues have documented the nature of that reinforcement.

Baltes and Reisenzein (1986) provide a review of a number of studies on the "psychosocial control toward dependency" in long-term-care institutions. It is their thesis that older residents of such institutions are indeed reinforced for behaving in certain specific ways and that the mode of responding most often reinforced is that which fosters the dependency of the resident on the staff. The method often employed in this line of research is direct observation. For example, in a typical study Barton, Baltes, and Orzech (1980) placed observers in a ward of elderly nursing home residents during morning care hours (6:30 to 9:00 A.M.) when there were frequent interactions between staff and residents with regard to self-care. The observers carefully recorded what went on in the ward, including two categories of the behavior of the elderly residents.

Independent behavior refers to a resident's self- or other-initiated execution of bathing, dressing, eating, grooming, and toileting tasks or components thereof without assistance.

Dependent behavior refers to a resident's request for or acceptance of assistance in bathing, dressing, eating, grooming, or toileting.

Similarly, two kinds of staff behaviors were recorded.

Independence-supportive behavior refers to staff verbal encouragement of or praise for a resident's execution of personal maintenance tasks without help. It also refers to staff discouragement of or scolding for a resident's request for assistance or nonattempts of execution of self-maintenance tasks.

Dependence-supportive behavior refers to staff assistance in a resident's personal maintenance, praise for a resident's acceptance of assistance, or discouragement of a resident's attempts to execute personal maintenance tasks without help (Barton et al., 1980).

At the outset of such a study, the observers made note of the frequency of these four categories of behavior and compared those rates to the remaining activities of the residents and staff. In other words, baseline rates of all behaviors were empirically determined. However, of particular interest are the patterns or sequences of such response categories. If a resident engaged in an independent behavior, what would be the behavioral reaction of a staff member? What would happen if a resident engaged in dependent behavior? By extension, how would a resident react to a staff member's independence-supportive or dependence-supportive behavior?

In order to answer these questions, the researchers fed their raw data into appropriate computer programs. The computer output indicated the probability of a certain behavioral consequence of a particular behavioral antecedent. Reference to Table XII shows the result of one such analysis. When staff members engaged in inde-

TABLE XII
Probability of consequent resident self-care behavior following antecedent staff
behavior

	CONSEQUENT RESIDENT BEHAVIOR	
Antecedent staff behavior	Independent self-care	Dependent self-care
Independence-supportive	.48	.16
Dependence-supportive	.04	.65
(Base rate resident behavior)	(.16)	(.03)

After Baltes and Reisenzein (1986).

pendence-supportive behavior, residents were sensitive to this and reacted with independent self-care with a probability of .48. Similarly, when staff members engaged in dependence-supportive behavior, the residents reacted in kind with dependent self-care with a probability of .65. Resident behavior did not depart from baseline values (shown in parentheses) when a staff behavior was not germane.

One could point out that the .48 value seems to belie the notion that there is "psychosocial control toward dependency." But let the reader beware. What the .48 probability statement really means is that *if* a staff member behaved in an independence-supportive manner, then it was very likely that a *resident* would behave independently in turn. What that number does *not* tell us is how likely staff independence-supportive behavior was. To determine that rate, refer to Table XIII where it can be seen that it was very rare indeed. No matter how residents behaved, staff members were very unlikely to react with independence-supportive behavior. On the contrary, if a resident acted in a dependent self-care fashion, it was highly likely that a staff member would support that dependency. In effect, dependence was reinforced and independence was ignored (.48 in Table XIII).

Why would the pattern of staff behavior seen in Table XIII emerge? It might be that independent self-care on the part of residents would be ignored because it simply conformed to a societal norm or expectation, as argued by Baltes and Reisenzein (1986). On the other hand, fostering dependency might be a way to expedite the daily personal-care chores or routines in a home. To use another age group for insight, anyone in a hurry who has watched their toddler try to dress herself or their preschooler try to make his own sandwich knows the urge to foster dependency by taking over.

TABLE XIII
Probability of consequent staff supportive behavior following antecedent resident behavior

	CONSEQUENT STAFF BEHAVIOR	
Antecedent resident behavior	Independence-supportive	Dependence-supportive
Independent self-care	.00	.02
Dependent self-care	.05	.48
(Base rate staff behavior)	(.01)	(.03)

After Baltes and Reisenzein (1986).

But what is so bad about fostering dependency in the aged? According to a further, more detailed analysis by Baltes and Reisenzein (1986), most dependent behaviors were found to be compliant in nature: they were usually not refusals or requests; rather, they seemed to be passive reactions. Now, these passive reactions did gain the supportive behavior of the staff (as seen in Table XIII), and that *is* a kind of control over the social environment. But Baltes and Reisenzein are concerned that "dependent behaviors when experiencing contingencies should be considered as providing the experience of *passive* rather than *active* control." The problem here is that

passive control leads to a decay of productive action systems. Consequently, passive control through dependent behaviors implies that independent behaviors are less often used and practiced by the elderly than they could and should be. The fact that disuse induces decay is often cited in the aging literature in order to explain functional decline in the elderly . . . Consequently, even if dependent behaviors yield passive control . . . , in the long run they might have the same detrimental effects as no control at all, at least [where] performance deficits are concerned (Baltes and Reisenzein, 1986).

Summary. Whether an elderly person's attitude toward herself or himself is more influenced by a perceived loss of control or by training toward dependency is a moot point. Depending on the circumstances, one or the other process could have an adverse effect, and there seems to be nothing to prevent them from acting in concert. Institutionalization potentially holds many hazards for elderly residents' psychology and their attitudes toward themselves.

Conclusion

In this chapter we have examined attitudes toward the self from the perspectives of locus-of-control orientation as a personality factor and of perceived control as a consequence of contingencies between behavior and outcomes. These two approaches by no means exhaust the ways theorists and researchers have analyzed the issues. For other psychological perspectives on the matter of control in general, see the volume by Langer (1983), and for views on the matter of control and aging, see the volume edited by Baltes and Baltes (1986). However, regardless of the approach taken, attitudes toward the self concerning the concept of control will doubtless continue to be a focus of interest. I have a hunch that developments will bring something of a merger between personality theorists and social psychologists. Their joint products will further tell us about the role of attitudes toward the self.

UNIT 5

SOCIETAL ISSUES

For various reasons, it is interesting and useful to inquire into the attitudes of large aggregates of people or to look at the effects of vast cultural forces on attitude formation and change. Although many of our opinions are related to unique personal experiences in intimate groups, we are all also part of a larger group known as society. This society influences us, and each of us—to some degree—influences it.

There are many concerns about the impact of society on our daily lives. Not infrequently we hear questions like: "What effect does television have on my children?" or "How good a job is the government doing these days?" Issues such as these are taken up in this fifth unit. Chapter 11 takes a broad view of various media as both causes and effects of our attitudes. Then, Chapter 12 looks at national sentiments in terms of Americans' roller-coaster swings of opinion about their federal government and its personalities, policies, and actions. Topics of special interest are public sentiments about the Vietnam War, the "patriotic revival" of the 1980s, and attitudes toward the presidency.

CHAPTER ELEVEN

THE MEDIA: CAUSE AND EFFECT OF ATTITUDES

The estimates vary, but they are always astonishingly high. People's lives, in this culture at least, are saturated by the media. According to one estimate, by the time most American children finish high school they will have spent only 11,000 hours in the classroom and as much as 20,000 hours in front of a television set! How could a child manage to accumulate that much viewing time? Well, investigators estimate that the average American watches more than 3 hours of television per day and that in the average household the set is on over 6 hours per day (McGuire, 1986). Six hours times 365 is 2,190, so if a child started watching at age 6, he or she could conceivably accumulate 20,000 hours by age 16. Television notwithstanding, when all media are taken into account, it is estimated that over 20% of the waking time of the average American involves some kind of exposure. This is twice the amount of time we spend directly interacting with one another (McGuire, 1986).

The question arises, What are these media, what sorts of information or misinformation do they offer, and what is the impact of that information on our attitudes and social behavior? To answer the first part of the question, in my view there seem to be many influential media, and I am open to learning about them all. In the sections to follow we will make reference to movies and other popular entertainments, television programming and commercials, magazine and newspaper ads and stories, and children's books, and we will even consider what is shown on the front of a box of breakfast cereal.

As for the second part of the question, different media tell us different things, and the same media tell us different things at different times. For example, how could one answer the question, What is the impact of television? The answer would depend on what is shown and who is watching. For instance, in Table I we find that the content of prime-time television has varied wildly in the last 20 years. Many of the top ten shows in the 1964–65 period suggest that those viewers were seeking (or were being fed) escapist fantasy and lily-white, laundered sitcoms (situation comedies). All of that changed in the 1974–75 period, when the civil rights movement, social reformers, and the antiwar movement seem to have raised the viewers' (or the networks') social consciousness. Many of the 1974–75 offerings were based on ethnic, gender-related, or political themes. However, by 1984–85, all that changed again, and we seemed to be back to escapist fantasy and voyeurism, now deliciously tinged with sleaze, muck, sex, and violence. As to the impact of all of this on viewers, take a look at the top show in 1974–75. The central character of "All in the Family" was Archie Bunker, a confirmed bigot. As we shall see, the impact of this show depended very much on certain characteristics of the people who watched Bunker's racist antics.

Concerning the third part of the opening question, my inclination is to be liberal in seeking out the social effects of media. As it says in the ad in Figure 1, children believe what their parents tell them. It seems probable that at least some of the time adults as well as children believe what other people tell them, especially if they have no better information, or if they are inclined to believe the message anyway. But this book is about attitudes. How narrow should the selection of dependent measures be? Again, I am inclined to be liberal. I take part of my lead in this from an influential writer in the field of attitudes, William J. McGuire. In a recent article on media effects, McGuire made the following sweeping assertion: "Second only to providing entertainment, the major social function of the mass media is to influence the receiver's cognitions, attitudes, or behavior in some desired direction" (McGuire, 1986). This statement seems very much in line with the A-B-C analysis in Chapter 2 of this book, especially if one substitutes the word "affect" for "attitude" in McGuire's sentence. I think, therefore, that our dependent measures could include all of "social influence," where that term includes a potential or measured impact on affect, cognition, or behavior. In fact, in some instances behavior is the only measure available, as in the case of possible media influences on suicide rates. In such cases I will simply fall back on the assumption that attitudes mediated the behavior.

In more concrete terms, this chapter has three major sections.

TABLE I
Top ten prime-time television shows at three points in U.S. history

1964–65	1974–75	1984–85
1. "Bonanza" (NBC)	1. "All in the Family" (CBS)	1. "Dallas" (CBS)
2. "Bewitched" (ABC)	2. "Sanford and Son" (NBC)	2. "Dynasty" (ABC)
3. "Gomer Pyle, U.S.M.C." (CBS)	3. "Chico and the Man" (NBC)	3. "60 Minutes" (CBS)
4. "The Andy Griffith Show" (CBS)	4. "The Jeffersons" (CBS)	4. "Crazy Like a Fox" (CBS)
5. "The Fugitive" (ABC)	5. "M*A*S*H" (CBS)	5. "The Cosby Show" (NBC)
6. "The Red Skelton Hour" (CBS)	6. "Rhoda" (CBS)	6. "Simon & Simon" (CBS)
7. "The Dick Van Dyke Show" (CBS)	7. "The Waltons" (CBS)	7. "The A-Team" (NBC)
8. "The Lucy Show" (CBS)	8. "Good Times" (CBS)	8. "Falcon Crest" (CBS)
9. "Peyton Place" (II) (ABC)	9. "Maude" (CBS)	9. "Family Ties" (NBC)
10. "Combat" (ABC)	10. "Hawaii Five-O" (CBS)	10. "Hotel" (ABC)

After *Harper's Magazine* advertising brochure (n.d.).

FIGURE 1
PRINT MEDIA AD pointing out the impressionable nature of children.

The first two, Minority Portrayals in the Media, and Gender and Other Demographic Stereotypes in the Media, obviously have to do with what kinds of information the media are wittingly or unwittingly handing us now, or have handed us in the past. The third section, Attitudinal and Behavioral Effects of the Media, presents some attempts to gauge the quantitative impact of various media on the social world.

Minority Portrayals in the Media

Members of potentially oppressed groups—typically women, minorities, the politically disenfranchised—have good reason for concern about how they are portrayed in the media. In an earlier chapter it was argued that kernels of truth are at the heart of many powerful stereotypes and that exposure to media or education could provide the content of such kernels. If, by design or otherwise, the media convey an inaccurate or distorted image of the truth, then resultant attitudes would reflect that distortion. This proposition is very much in line with the theme of *Ethnic Notions,* a recent video documentary on traditional racial prejudice in America.

ETHNIC NOTIONS: BLACK PEOPLE IN WHITE MEDIA

Produced and directed by Marlon Riggs and narrated by Esther Rolle, *Ethnic Notions** (Riggs, 1987) provides a brilliant treatment of the painful history of whites' stereotypes of blacks, focusing on the period from just before the U.S. Civil War, to the postbellum Reconstruction and beyond. The documentary makes piercing points about the nature and *function* of caricatures of blacks in that politically turbulent time. Prior to the Civil War, the motivation of many whites was to justify the paradoxical institution of slavery in a free society, and the *media* of the time—songs, novels, stage entertainments, among others—were powerful tools used to achieve this justification. Before emancipation, four distinct stereotypes emerged that were suited to proslavery whites' aims in the prewar era. Two of the caricatures of male slaves were the "Sambo" and the "Uncle Tom." The Sambo was presented as a simple, carefree, pleasure-loving person, whose life was one of childlike contentment. The Uncle Tom, faithful and hard-working, illustrated the presumed paradise-like conditions on plantations where slaves were happy and masters were kind. Similarly, for female slaves, the "Mammy" stereotype came into being. The Mammy was the counterpart to the Uncle Tom; she was portrayed as being docile, happily obedient to her master and mistress, and protective of the white household. All in all, these first three stereotypes in the media of that time helped resolve what we might call the cognitive dissonance of allowing slavery in a democratic culture (and for another treatment of the Sambo phenomenon, see Boskin, 1986). Examples of images of the Mammy and Sambo caricatures are shown in Figure 2.

But, of course, the Sambo and the Uncle Tom images could not be made to fit black freedmen in the North. Their very existence and successes in white society must have constituted a threat to the premise that slavery was the only institution or social niche suitable for blacks. To counter this threat, a fourth antebellum stereotype emerged: "Zip Coon." White minstrels (in blackface) portrayed the Zip Coon as an ostentatious and pretentious dandy, who was also a

Ethnic Notions (1982) is also the title of a catalog of an exhibition of Afro-American stereotype and caricature objects and items from the collection of Janette Faulkner. The collection was shown at the Berkeley Art Center in 1982.

FIGURE 2
MAMMY, SAMBO, AND PICKANINNY CARICATURE ILLUSTRATIONS.
(From *Ethnic Notions*, 1982.)

perfect buffoon, completely incapable of imitating, for example, intelligent white speech. Hence, the Zip Coon had no chance of being
assimilated into white ways.

Taken together, these four antebellum stereotypes that were
available to whites provided a powerful base on which to build other
attitudes toward blacks. To quote the narrator of the video *Ethnic
Notions:* "Together Zip Coon and Sambo [and the others] provided
a double-edged defense of slavery: Zip Coon, proof of blacks' ludi-
crous failure to adapt to freedom; and Sambo, the fantasy of happy
darkies in their proper place."

However, after the Civil War and the emancipation of the slaves, these particular four stereotypes as a basis for white domination of blacks began have restricted usefulness. Surely, they could be (and were) applied to former slaves who were now faithful retainers, but generations of blacks came into being who had not "known the domesticating influence of slavery." Under these circumstances, two *new* black stereotypes emerged to justify presumed white ascendancy: the "Brute" and the "Pickaninny." Both of these were based on the premise that without the kindly and beneficent guidance of whites (read: slavery) blacks were reverting to savagery. The Brute, as suggested in the very term, constituted a "black menace." Portrayed as vicious, violent, and aggressive, the rebellious black male was an offense to civilization. Predictably, the black Brute was a peril to white virgins, even surfacing in D. W. Griffith's famous film *Birth of a Nation*, wherein a white girl commits suicide while being pursued by a black man.

As for the other postwar media caricature, a Pickaninny (black child) was cute in appearance, but the message that this stereotype conveyed was anything but. Pickaninnies were *always* in danger. Typically shown by a river, they were partially clad, dirty, and unkempt. Much worse, these babies were harassed and threatened by wild animals—usually alligators—hence the need for the river as a backdrop (see Figure 2). Otherwise, Pickaninnies led violent lives. *Ethnic Notions* (Riggs, 1987) recounts three stanzas from a period poem titled "Seven Little Niggers:"

> Seven little niggers playing with bricks,
> one was it most all de time,
> den dey was but six.
> Five little niggers playing dere was war . . .
> Boom went de cannon
> Den dey was four . . .
> One little nigger in the scorchin' sun,
> soon dey was the smell of smoke,
> and den dey was none.

One gets the idea. A Pickaninny living in constant association with dangerous animals and violence was dehumanized and seen as animal-like. If the Pickaninny was nothing more than a little beast, what need to extend to it (or its kin) the rights and considerations owed to decent human beings?

All in all, *Ethnic Notions* (Riggs, 1987) is an informative and moving documentary.* It is highly recommended.

*At this writing, video purchase and rental information about the film documentary *Ethnic Notions* (Riggs, 1987) is available from California Newsreel, 630 Natoma Street, San Francisco, CA 94103.

MINORITIES AND REACTIONS TO THE MEDIA

Amos 'n' Andy. As we have seen, the media can be used to create or reinforce images in a powerful way, and once an image is formed, its revision or eradication would be difficult. It is therefore no wonder that contemporary minority members and their leaders are so sensitive about ethnic and racial portrayals in the media and are willing to take steps when they judge these to be offensive or inaccurate. One modern example of minority pressure on a medium to curtail the broadcast of negative stereotypes is the famous case of the CBS television show "Amos 'n' Andy."

As described in a history written by Andrews and Juilliard (1986), "Amos 'n' Andy" was a popular television situation comedy in the early 1950s. At the time, its unique feature was that all the principal players were black. The central characters were Amos (played by Alvin Childress), Andy (played by Spencer Williams, Jr.), and King-fish (played by Tim Moore), as shown in Figure 3. These characters went through a series of misadventures on a weekly basis, acting out shows with titles such as "Andy Goes into Business," "Kingfish Buys a Chair," "The Broken Clock," "Getting Mama Married (Parts I and II)," and "Kingfish Sells a Lot" (Andrews and Juilliard, 1986). Perhaps a fair characterization from my own recall of many of these episodes is that Kingfish tried to take advantage of Andy, Andy let himself be duped, and Amos acted as a wise moderator to redress any wrongdoing.

Another salient feature of the program was the terrible butchering of the English language by some of the characters, accompanied by bombastic phrasing and dialect. To briefly illustrate this, what follows is an exchange from an earlier, radio version of the show upon which the television series was based. In this instance, Kingfish was played by Freeman Gosden, and his wife, Sapphire, was done by Ernestine Wade.

SAPPHIRE: George Stevens [the Kingfish], I done made up my mind that I'm gonna have a husband that dresses good, knows nice people, and is got a steady job.
KINGFISH: Sapphire, you mean to say that you is gonna leave me?
SAPPHIRE: George, I know why you're a no-good bum. It's on account of your association with Andy Brown. Why don't you try to meet a nicer class of men?
KINGFISH: Well, I ain't got da opportunity to meet em, they's all workin'.
SAPPHIRE: Well, that Andy Brown is the cause of it all. What has he ever accomplished?
KINGFISH: Well, yesterday, he had a run of thirteen balls in da side pocket without leanin' on da table.

FIGURE 3
CENTRAL CHARACTERS OF THE AMOS 'N' ANDY TELEVISION SHOW:
left, Spencer Williams, Jr. (Andy); center, Tim Moore (Kingfish); right, Alvin
Childress (Amos).

SAPPHIRE: Now, that's exactly what I mean: Andy hangin' around a pool table
all day. Why don't he go to a cultured place like a public library?
KINGFISH: They ain't got no pool table dere (Andrews and Juilliard, 1986).

Well, many people thought that this sort of thing was funny,
including blacks such as Flip Wilson and Redd Foxx. But many
people did not, including blacks such as Richard Pryor and Bill
Cosby. Assuredly the National Association for the Advancement of

Colored People (NAACP) was not amused and began protests within
a week of the first television episode of "Amos 'n' Andy." A formal
suit against CBS listed specific objections to the show's content:

- It tends to strengthen the conclusion among uninformed and prejudiced
  people that Negroes are inferior, lazy, dumb, and dishonest.
- Every character in this one and only show with an all-Negro cast is either
  a clown or a crook.
- Negro doctors are shown as quacks and thieves.
- Negro lawyers are shown as slippery cowards, ignorant of their profession,
  and without ethics.
- Negro women are shown as cackling, screaming shrews, in bigmouth
  closeups using street slang, just short of vulgarity.
- All Negroes are shown as dodging work of any kind.
- Millions of white Americans see this "Amos 'n' Andy" picture and think
  the entire race is the same (Andrews and Juilliard, 1986).

Maybe so. This list certainly is reminiscent of the "message" conveyed by the stereotyped figures revealed in the *Ethnic Notions*
video documentary. In any event, the NAACP got its way, eventually.
The "Amos 'n' Andy" television show ran on the national CBS network from Thursday, June 28, 1951, to Thursday, June 11, 1953. The
program was dropped by CBS for a number of reasons, including a
boycott of the sponsor's product and pressure on the Federal Communications Commission. However, a complete victory for the
NAACP in this matter was a long time in coming, because CBS
continued to produce episodes to be distributed for broadcast by
affiliates in the United States and by stations abroad. It was not until
1966 that the last of the "Amos 'n' Andy" shows were finally removed
from commercial television (Andrews and Juilliard, 1986).

As an epilogue of sorts, a San Diego lawyer named Michael Avery
produced a documentary history of the show titled *"Amos 'n' Andy":
Anatomy of a Controversy.** It is a balanced presentation and endeavors to show both sides of the controversy over the show. However, when it was aired in Los Angeles in 1984, it drew the following
attack from Willis Edwards, the president of the local NAACP chapter: "We are appalled at the apparent insensitivity of the television
station [KABC] to reopen old wounds inflicted years ago by a tele-

*A version of this documentary is (at this writing) available on video cassette
from Avery Home Video, copyright 1986.

vision series fraught with flagrant stereotypes and demeaning black characterizations" (Andrews and Juilliard, 1986).

He may have had a point.

MINORITIES IN OTHER MEDIA

Movies. Fans of old movies will recognize the stereotypes available in a series of popular films like the one touted by the poster shown in Figure 4. Several sorts of stereotypic information were depicted in the long string of so-called Chan films. First, the old-world Chinese character (Charlie Chan, played here by Sidney Toler) was portrayed as inscrutable, aloof, and unflappable. Second, younger, westernized Chinese characters (such as Number One Son or Number Two Son, played here by Benson Fong) were depicted as shallow, opportunistic, and bumbling. Finally, the black character (Birmingham, played by Mantan Moreland) was excitable, expressive, and quite easily frightened. Moreover, the status of these characters in civilized society was clearly conveyed. Charlie Chan was sometimes a minion of the law or an agent serving the interests of a white client. Birmingham was a servant, a chauffeur to the Chan family. According to an actor who appeared in a number of the films, "the Chan movies of the Forties and the Fifties were onscreen/

FIGURE 4
FILM POSTER portraying ethnic characters in a stereotyped fashion.

offscreen double-vision parables of racist order with whites on top, blacks on the bottom, and two kinds of Chinese in between" (Chin, 1973).

Television: the golden age of sitcoms. Recall from Table I that in the 1974–75 period many of the top-ranked television programs had to do with social issues such as race relations and antiwar sentiment. At about that time, Reid (1979) conducted an analysis of stereotypes or ROLE PORTRAYALS in programs with predominantly black, white, or racially mixed casts. The one category of program that allowed her to do this in 1977 (when she collected the data) was the situation comedy. For black shows, she chose "The Jeffersons," "Good Times," and "Sanford and Son." Mostly white casts were seen in "All in the Family," "Happy Days," and "One Day at a Time." Mixed-cast shows were represented by "Chico and the Man," "Fish," and "Welcome Back, Kotter." Using a standardized scoring method, black observers and white observers recorded the behavior of the programs' characters on the basis of a time sample. That is, 30-second segments of videotape were shown, and it was noted whether a character exhibited actions such as aggression, deference, dependence, or any of many other categories of response (Reid, 1979).

When the tallies were completed, the results of the study were revealing in terms of the stereotypes portrayed by both black and white characters. One of the clearer findings was that the depiction of black women was much different from that of white women, and in turn the depiction of women in general was very different from that of men in general. Table II presents some selected ratings of characters' self-esteem and dependence relations to others. Black women characters of that era were rated as lowest on succorance (need to be taken care of) and highest on nurturance (need to take care of). Further, they were seen as being more dominant than white women. On the contrary, white women characters were rated as highest on succorance and lowest on dominance. This pattern, according to Reid, seemed consistent with the stereotypic pictures of the dominant, independent, and supportive black woman and the submissive, dependent white woman. Men in these shows were seen as far more dominant and far less nurturant than women.

In addition, Reid (1979) presented data on the impressions of white characters' demeanor across sitcoms of one or another type of predominant racial casting, and these ratings are shown in Table III. Compared with their depiction on predominantly white and mixed shows, whites seen in predominantly black shows were more defer-

TABLE II
Some stereotypic behavior of black women and white women as revealed by analysis of television situation comedies

Rating category	RACE AND SEX		
	Black women	White women	Combined males
Succorance (need to be taken care of)	1.16	5.05	2.74
Self-recognition	.12	.58	.87
Dominance	6.84	4.36	10.60
Nurturance (need to take care of)	14.01	8.71	5.19

After Reid (1979).
Note. The absolute magnitudes of the values are almost arbitrary and depend on the scoring system used. Meaningful comparisons can be made within rows.

TABLE III
Depictions of white characters in television situation comedies having casts that are predominantly black, white, or mixed

Rating category	PREDOMINANT CASTING		
	Black	White	Mixed
Deference	9.06	4.25	1.56
Autonomy	0.00	4.11	0.96
Achievement	0.83	2.45	2.29
Aggression: males	17.40	9.76	7.65
Aggression: females	8.00	6.86	1.20

After Reid (1979).

ential, had less autonomy, exhibited lower levels of achievement, and expressed higher levels of aggressive behavior. This pattern suggests to me that the individuals representing the minority— whites in black shows, blacks in white shows—served as vehicles for the expression of racial tension. Such tension was part of the appeal of this genre. Consider for a moment the unveiled racial slurs of the American television character Archie Bunker (played by Carroll O'Connor in "All in the Family") when he spoke of "your Coloreds," or the bigoted black character George Jefferson (played by Sherman Hemsley in "The Jeffersons") when he referred to some nonblack as "honky," "whitey," or "zebra." "Zebra" was an epithet applied to children born of racially mixed marriages. What is the impact of presenting these models? Do people become more tolerant when they see such comic portrayals of intolerance? Perhaps not. Vidmar and Rokeach (1974) sampled the reactions of prejudiced and unprejudiced young people to the reactionary antics of Archie Bunker. Subjects already prejudiced against minorities tended to see Bunker's racial insults as justified and admired his derogatory statements.

A similar study on the role of subject variables in the impact of "All in the Family" was carried out by Surlin (1974). In this case Surlin assigned subjects to high, middle, and low dogmatic categories on the basis of how they had answered dogmatism scale items such as "There are two kinds of people in this world: those who are for truth and those who are against truth," and "Of all the different philosophies which exist in this world, there is probably only one that is correct." The basic hypothesis under test was that high dogmatic viewers would come to *like* characters with which they agreed and *dislike* characters with which they disagreed. No such effects were predicted for low dogmatic subjects. Since the Archie Bunker character was quite dogmatic and his son-in-law Mike was not, differential liking by high-dogmatic viewers for the two characters would support Surlin's (1974) position. The data in Table IV reveal support for that hypothesis. Further, Surlin found more agreement with Archie Bunker for those subjects comparatively low in education, low in income, and low in occupational status. Again, all of this bears

TABLE IV
Average agreement with and liking for the "All in the Family" characters Archie and Mike, related to subjects' level of dogmatism

Character and scale	DOGMATISM LEVEL		
	High	Middle	Low
Archie			
Agreement with	2.2	3.4	4.0
Liking for	1.8	2.2	2.1
Mike			
Agreement with	3.0	2.8	2.3
Liking for	2.7	2.4	2.2

After Surlin (1974).
Note. The agreement and liking scales ran from 1 (strongly agree/strongly like) to 5 (strongly disagree/strongly dislike); therefore, smaller numbers indicate more favorable reactions.

out the contention that it makes a difference *who* hears or sees what
in the media.

OTHER MINORITIES, OTHER SLURS

Black people are not the only minority persons to be maligned
in the media by characters such as Archie Bunker. I, for one, am
addicted to old-time cartoon shows such as the "Tom and Jerry
Show," "Bugs Bunny and Friends," and "Bugs Bunny and Pals." If
one watched these programs long enough, it would be possible to
catalog characters or depictions that slur blacks, Native Americans,
Hispanics, and Jews. Sometimes these caricatures are drawn out,
and at other times they are quick and transient. I am sure many
readers can remember cartoons where something (a large firecracker,
say) in a character's hand explodes and the character is briefly shown
in blackface and is made to look like a Pickaninny. Cartoon American
Indians seem invariably cast in clown roles, and some of the supporting "actors" in the "Speedy Gonzales" series are hardly role
models for Hispanics. As more and more older cartoons from the
Thirties and Forties surface on cable TV, I more frequently encounter
the following shtick, usually at the cartoon's finale: someone (or a
chorus) asks the central character a loaded question, and he replies
in a heavy "Yiddish" accent, "Mmmmmm, could be."

Of course, it is no news that Jews have been maligned in various
media for millennia, and that this treatment has prompted the formation of organizations such as the Anti-Defamation League of B'nai
B'rith (ADL). Apparently, there is a need for the sensitizing influence
of the ADL, for insensitivity to Jews crops up in the most unexpected
places. Consider the following quotes from the 1988 presidential
election campaign.

- "It was an obscene period in our nation's history." Dan Quayle, offering
  his view of the Holocaust in which millions of Jews were murdered by
  the Nazis in WWII.

- "I didn't live in this century." Dan Quayle explaining his gaffe on the
  Holocaust.*

- "I hope I stand for antibigotry, anti-Semitism, antiracism. This is what
  drives me." George Bush campaigning (see "Glitches, Gaffes, and Mud,"
  1989).

*Mr. Quayle has favored other ethnic groups with his brand of observation. In
an address to members of the United Negro College Fund he stated: "What a waste
it is to lose one's mind—or not to have a mind. How true that is" ("Overheard,"
1989). The correct saying is: "A mind is a terrible thing to waste." Further, the Vice
President described the people of American Samoa as "happy campers" (Rosellini,
1989).

All of this can seem to be amusing except, perhaps, if you feel a
need for the ADL. Other, potentially insidious slurs of Jews are
available for review. Consider the left panel of Figure 5. This is the
front of a box of General Mills' "Count Chocula" cereal found on
grocers' shelves in 1987 and 1988. What has this silliness got to do
with anti-Semitism? Well, look more closely at the computer enhanced picture from the old film about a vampire called Count
Dracula (played by Bela Lugosi). That character is wearing some kind
of medallion, and, surprise to behold, it appears to be the Star of
David. In short, the implication is that Count Dracula was a Jewish
vampire! Is this implication anti-Semitic, or is it merely stupid? In
some circles it was taken to be anti-Semitic, no doubt given the
history of "blood libels" that are part of historic stereotypes of Jews.
From the middle ages to early in this century, Jews were accused of
kidnapping and murdering Christian children for their blood (Ozick,
1988; Steiner, 1989; and see also the 1985 novel *Blood Libels* by
Clive Sinclair). The Star of David in connection with the ghoulish
Dracula evokes this stereotype, hence the strong complaints directed
at General Mills.

FIGURE 5
MEDIA DEPICTIONS taken by some observers to be tinged with anti-Semitic
content.

In defense of General Mills, a spokesperson said that "we are not anti-Semitic. Our intent was merely to use Dracula's likeness in a fresh and entertaining way" ("Quotes of the Week," 1987). But wittingly or not, such insensitivity has the potential to evoke or reinforce bias. Another possible example of an unwitting anti-Semitic slur is seen in the right panel of Figure 5. Apparently, enough readers took exception to this July 4, 1988 cover of *The New Republic* to prompt an editorial comment in the August 22, 1988 issue of that periodical. The editors disagreed with the complaints but did reprint the cover with their comments so that the reader could decide for herself or himself. I am afraid that for me, it is all too easy to hear the cigar-chomping figure say, "Mmmmm, could be."

The point here is not to single out General Mills or *The New Republic* for criticism. Rather, the point in displaying the pictures in Figure 5 is that it is fairly easy to find examples of images that some people would be inclined to see as tinged with anti-Semitism (or some other variety of racial or ethnic slurs). And, for me, this business about whether such colorations are witting or unwitting does not matter. It would be easy to convince me that a majority of the white minstrels in nineteenth- and early twentieth-century America thought nothing of their malicious treatment of blacks' images, but what a powerful influence they must have been on other whites' attitudes! As noted, children believe what you tell them, and often, so do adults.

CONCLUSION

I think one could demonstrate that minorities, including blacks, have received increasingly better treatment in the media over the last century. In my own mind I can see a trend in upward social mobility of certain black media characters beginning with Uncle Remus as a happy slave and Buckwheat (Billy Thomas) of the "Our Gang" series as a kind of Pickaninny, through Birmingham as a servant, George Jefferson as a businessman, Virgil Tibbs (Sidney Poitier) and Alex Foley (Eddie Murphy) as policemen, and ending with Cliff Huxtable (Bill Cosby) as an obstetrician. Such trends are also seen in more systematic analyses. According to the abstract of a paper by Humphrey and Schuman (1984) on the portrayal of blacks in magazine ads from 1950 to 1982,

the occupational level of blacks portrayed has risen considerably, and blacks are no longer presented as maids or servants. However, white authority figures are still frequently shown aiding poor blacks or supervising black children. Furthermore, ads show friendly and informal social relationships between individual whites much more frequently than they show such relationships between whites and blacks. Finally, in an extended analysis the frequency of black ads in 1980, 1981, and 1982 is examined for *Time, Newsweek*, and [*Ladies' Home Journal*]. Blacks are still somewhat underrepresented (Humphrey and Schuman, 1984).

Relatively low rates of depicted interactions between blacks and whites had also been reported for prime-time television (Weigel, Loomis, and Soja, 1980). However, by the late 1980s, blacks were seen in ads more frequently and in more authentic ways (Marby and Adams, 1989), and it has been suggested that TV's color line is disappearing (Sanoff and Thornton, 1987). But let us turn from minority and ethnic considerations for now and find out how certain media treat gender and other demographic categories.

Gender and Other Demographic Stereotypes in the Media

FUN WITH DICK AND JANE

For much of the time that I spent in elementary school, television as we know it today simply did not exist. The socializing media to which my childhood friends and I were exposed were radio programs, movies, and, principally, books. Apart from comic books, most of our reading material was encountered at school, and one set of readers that I recall quite vividly was the series that featured Dick and Jane (and Sally and Spot and others). I suppose my schoolmates and I should be grateful for the Dick-and-Jane-type primers, since everyone in my circle did learn how to read. But as things turned out, we may have learned much more than that. For example, look at Figure 6. If no one had ever suggested to us before that boys and girls are different (or are *supposed* to be different), we would surely have gotten that idea from this section. Of course, Figure 6 presents but two pages from a single reader. Other writers have made far more extensive analyses.

In 1972, and again in 1975, an organization called Women on Words & Images (WOWI) published a book called *Dick & Jane as Victims* that focused on SEX STEREOTYPING in children's readers. They did this because of the following concerns:

Some station is transmitting a clear message to our children about their place in life. They have been tuned in from birth to a frequency that directs everything they attempt, from skipping rope to getting a Ph.D. Something ensures that any deviation from the norm will be fraught with personal hazards and traumas. If Janey does become a doctor, she will feel guilty at not being a Mommy, or

Dick said, "Go, little pony.
Go fast! Go fast!
I want a fast ride.
I want a good ride.
A fast ride.
A good ride.
Go, little pony, go fast."

Away went Dick on the pony.
Away, away he went.

52

Dick said, "Come, Jane and Sally.
Get on the pony.
Jump on! Jump on!
It is fun to ride on the pony."

Jane said, "Oh, little pony.
Please do not go fast.
Sally and I do not want
to ride fast."

53

FIGURE 6
PAGES FROM A DICK AND JANE READER are taken by some observers
to indicate a sexist bias.

as good a Mommy as she "ought" to be. Johnny will not feel at all guilty about
being a doctor whether he is a Daddy or not. Dick will say girls are stupid, and
most girls will agree with him, except for Janey, who is thereby on the way to
becoming an "aggressive" woman. Dick himself will feel no guilt at his remark.
Sally, however, would feel very bad indeed if she called Dick stupid, for it
might wound his self-esteem, which, even at the age of nine, Sally knows is a
very serious thing. Johnny will spend much of his working and playing life with
boys, whom he expects will be much more fun than girls; his wife, locked into
domesticity, will be even less fun as a result of her confinement. Sally, being a
complete Mommy, will drive her children from one achievement to another,
imprison them in a spotless home, and project her own ambitions onto them
in a classic smotherlove pattern until they finally break for freedom. Then Sally
will find herself out of a job, frustrated, and "growing old," often before her
chronological time (*Dick & Jane as Victims*, 1975).

Is it possible that children get locked into such rigid sex roles by
what they encounter in elementary school readers? Just what is in
those readers, anyway? In order to answer the second question, the
WOWI group obtained 134 elementary school readers (by 14 differ-

ent publishers) that were in active use in New Jersey at the time. Based on a standardized coding scheme, the 2,760 stories the books contained were searched for a sexist bias. And it was there! In terms of frequency of offerings, some striking ratios were discovered:

Boy-centered stories to girl-centered stories	5:2
Adult male main characters to adult female main characters	3:1
Male biographies to female biographies	6:1
Male animal stories to female animal stories	2:1
Male folk or fantasy stories to female folk or fantasy stories	4:1

Other pronounced gender biases were also found. For example, women in the stories were depicted in only 26 different occupations, whereas men participated in fully 147 different jobs. This presentation clearly implies that the range of careers for women is much more limited than that for men. Of course, the authors were able to demonstrate many sexist trends in stories about children themselves, including differences in active mastery themes such as ingenuity and cleverness, strength and bravery, and adventuresomeness and imaginative play. This difference was also found for secondary sex themes such as passivity and pseudo-dependence, and rehearsal for domesticity. A summary of the WOWI 1975 findings is shown in Table V. The numbers are impressive, and so is the bias.

In answer to an earlier question, yes, it appears that children might get locked into rigid sex roles by exposure to the contents of elementary school readers, in combination with other socializing pressures. At least that is the thesis of Raphaela Best's book, *We've All Got Scars: What Boys and Girls Learn in Elementary School.* According to the book's back-cover blurb,

this book shows how little girls become second-class citizens—psychologically, socially, sexually—at the hands of a system run by caring adults. It shows how little boys become victims of a macho tradition and how both girls and boys are socialized by our society and our school system to become incomplete people (Best, 1989).

Never mind "Run Spot run." It ought to be "Run Dick run," and "Run Jane run." Run for cover from these influences. (For analyses of children's sex-role stereotyping on television, see Liebert and Sprafkin (1988); Sternglanz and Serbin (1974); Welch, Huston-Stein, Wright, and Plehal (1979); and for a general review of the development of sex-role stereotypes in children, see Weinraub and Brown (1983).)

TABLE V
Frequency of dominant themes found in child-centered stories in children's readers

Themes	Boys	Girls
Traits implying active mastery		
Ingenuity, cleverness	131	33
Industry, problem-solving ability	169	47
Strength, bravery, heroism	143	36
Routine helpfulness	53	68
Elective of creative helpfulness	54	19
Apprenticeship, acquisition of skills, coming of age	151	53
Earning, acquisition, unearned rewards	87	18
Adventure, exploration, imaginative play	216	68
Secondary traits		
Passivity and pseudodependence	19	119
Altruism	55	22
Goal constriction and rehearsal for domesticity	50	166
Incompetence, mishaps	51	60
Victimization and humiliation by the opposite sex	7	68

After *Dick & Jane as Victims* (1975).

EVEN MORE FUN WITH DICK AND JANE

If Dick and Jane were real, they would have grown up by now. At least this is the contention of writer and artist Marc Gregory Gallant, who published *More Fun with Dick and Jane* in 1986.

In Gallant's clever book, Dick and Jane are middle-class, middle-aged, and middle-of-the-road. They both have careers and children of their own. Beyond this, the 1980s version has distinct similarities to the primers of an earlier time. In the backs of the original series of readers were lists of new vocabulary words. The 1940 edition of *Fun with Dick and Jane* that I had access to listed, for example, "fast," "dog," "children," "under," "school," and others. Similarly, in the back of Gallant's book, there is a helpful vocabulary list of new words not seen in any of the earlier D&J readers: "pooper-scooper," "L. L. Bean," "awesome," "128K," "quiche," and others.

More to the point, as in the originals, Gallant (1986) gave Dick and Jane quite different personalities or roles to play. The mature Dick is described thusly:

Dick, now almost forty, is a systems engineer for a public utility. Married to Susan, a minor character from the original series, Dick is a quiet, well-meaning father of three boys—Brad, Rick and Adam. Dick works tirelessly, pays his bills promptly and has a fascination for gadgets; he is also an avid golfer with a secret ambition to get a hole in one.

As for his sister,

Jane is a thirty-eight-year-old divorcée. She lives with her two daughters Robin and Jessica, in an impeccably clean house in a suburb of Dayton, Ohio (about a half hour drive from her brother Dick). By day Jane works as a loan officer in a downtown bank; after hours she brings incredible zeal to her job as a direct distributor for Amway. Jane is focused, serious and very independent (Gallant, 1986).

Note the parallels with the originals. Dick is still a hands-on kind of guy; Jane is in a service role. Gadgets and golf matter for Dick; an impeccable household and cosmetics are salient for Jane. Jane is located geographically *in reference to* Dick (a half-hour drive away). Dick is married; Jane is divorced. (Not incidentally, Sally, the other sister is also unmarried, having been *twice* divorced. These women cannot even handle relationships!) Jane managed to make two girl babies (good); Dick managed to make *three* boy babies (better). Even the cover of *More Fun with Dick and Jane* reinforces the notion of different, rigid roles for the genders (see Figure 7). Clearly, Jane is still a second-class citizen. Of course, Mr. Gallant is making a parody of a series that is already self-parodying, so we cannot take his treatment as independent evidence for gender bias in the media. However, the very fact that all this is pretty funny illustrates how accustomed we have become to the idea that Dick and Jane are expected to do different things and behave in different ways. What is perhaps less amusing is that if the roles of Dick and Jane are clichés, then many of us are also acting out these clichés. Think about it.

In their 1975 book, *Dick & Jane as Victims*, the WOWI group lamented the fact that despite their earlier protestations in 1972, "a series of readers that is nonsexist has not yet been found." Should they have got their hands on *More Fun with Dick and Jane*, that conclusion would not change (see also Best, 1989). In the late 1960s, women looked to the Women's Liberation Movement for hope in their struggle for parity with men in our society. By now, it is clear they have not achieved that parity.

FIGURE 7
BOOK COVER of a contemporary parody of a Dick and Jane reader. (From Gallant, 1986.)

ADVERTISING, STEREOTYPES, AND THE WOMEN'S LIBERATION MOVEMENT

Let us now turn to other media for treatments of gender difference, with particular reference to the period of social reforms in the sixties. For better or worse, these days one notices a trend in titles of books about the feminist movement. For example, there are *The Failure of Feminism* (Davidson, 1988), *Why ERA Failed* (Berry, 1986), *Why We Lost the ERA* (Mansbridge, 1986), and perhaps others. Indeed, the Equal Rights Amendment was the first and only constitutional amendment submitted to the states by Congress that did not become ratified (Hoff-Wilson, 1986). A sense of disappointment in all of this is summed up on the inside dust flap of Sylvia Hewlett's (1986) book, *A Lesser Life:*

Hewlett, in provocative and unforgettable prose, describes the often harsh reality of contemporary women's lives. In doing so, she destroys some favorite myths. Did you know that the gap between male and female earnings is precisely the same as it was in 1939? Can you believe that 50 percent of fathers never see or support their children in the wake of divorce? Do you know that over half of all female executives remain childless while more than 90 percent of male executives combine their careers with children? Do you wonder why men can routinely expect to find fulfillment in love and work and women cannot?

Alas, women as a class may not have accomplished all they sought to gain during the social reform period of the late 1960s. Using that span of years as a focal point, let us begin an examination of the portrayal of women in various media. The point will be to determine whether the media reflect conditions that fit (or not) the rather gloomy tone of the blurb on Hewlett's book.

Magazine ads. One thing that the women's movement has failed to achieve is a complete reform of the way women are portrayed in magazine advertisements. During the mid-1960s, organizations such as NOW (National Organization for Women) staged protests against national magazines—*Ladies' Home Journal, Playboy, Newsweek, Time*—in response to the industry tendency to project a narrow portrait of women that did not reflect the reforms that were thought to be happening (Venkatesan and Losco, 1975).

As Betty Friedan (1963), a popular and influential feminist author observed at the time,

an American woman no longer has a private image to tell her who she is, or can be, or wants to be. The public image in the magazines and television commercials is designed to sell washing machines, cake mixes, deodorants, detergents, rejuvenating face creams, hair tints. But the power of that image, on which companies spend millions of dollars for television time and ad space comes from this: American women no longer know who they are . . . As the motivational researchers keep telling the advertisers, American women are so unsure of who they should be that they look to this glossy public image to decide every detail of their lives.

What was this image, and how was it influenced by the social rights movement?

In an attempt to answer these questions, Venkatesan and Losco (1975) analyzed 14,378 magazine ads over a period from 1959 to 1971. They chose this range of years to bracket the Women's Liberation Movement. For these authors, 1959 to 1963 constituted a pre-women's movement period; 1964 to 1968 was the active civil and equal rights period; and 1969 to 1971 represented what they called the "awareness" period. The results of the study were grouped by these units of time. Further, Venkatesan and Losco were careful to survey magazines from three different classifications. One class was labeled "general magazines" and included *Reader's Digest, Time, Saturday Review,* and *Life.* Another class was "women's magazines" and included *Harper's Bazaar, Cosmopolitan, Ladies' Home Journal,* and *Better Homes & Gardens.* A third class was "men's magazines"; it contained *Argosy, Esquire, Sports Illustrated,* and *Evergreen Review.*

For our purposes, the portrayals of women in the ads were coded as falling into one (or more) of four categories:

1. Woman as dependent on man:
   - in order to complete a task woman needs male instruction
   - woman needs male encouragement or reinforcement
   - woman requires male for affection, instruction, happiness, leisure

2. Woman as overachieving housewife
   - woman is obsessed with menial tasks
   - woman concerned with ultimate cleanliness
   - woman concerned with being a good housewife

3. Woman as physically beautiful
   - woman concerned with cosmetic products
   - woman concerned with extraneous accessories to enhance physical beauty
   - woman concerned with looking more youthful, slimmer, more appealing

4. Woman as sexual object
   - woman in ad has no relation to the product
   - woman presented in ad performs no function, except decorative

The results of this extensive analysis are shown in Table VI, which presents assignment scores in terms of percentages. In the first place, magazines in the three classes revealed very different portraits of women. As can be seen in the table, men's and general magazine ads were far more likely to show women as dependent on a man or as a sexual object than were women's magazine ads. On the other hand, it was women's magazine ads that most frequently depicted the woman as physically beautiful. It was also women's magazine ads that revealed the highest rate of showing women as the overachieving

TABLE VI
Percentage of ads in certain magazines depicting women in various categories in the period from 1959 to 1971

Categories: Woman as	MEN'S MAGAZINES			WOMEN'S MAGAZINES			GENERAL MAGAZINES		
	59–63	64–68	69–71	59–63	64–68	69–71	59–63	64–68	69–71
Dependent on man	43	42	55	16	16	16	26	28	30
Overachieving housewife	1	1	3	23	12	10	9	7	8
Physically beautiful	2	3	5	43	58	63	8	11	9
Sexual object	57	56	52	17	16	12	68	63	66

After Venkatesan and Losco (1975).
Note. The percentages in the columns need not sum to 100 because a given ad could be scored for more than one category.

housewife, no doubt due to the preponderance of household products touted in such periodicals.

Perhaps the Women's Liberation Movement had an impact; there were changes, to a certain extent. In all classes of magazines, there was at least a diminution in the portrayal of women as sexual objects, and an increase in presenting them as physically beautiful. (Given the importance of appearance in social life, I am inclined to see this sort of change as a plus.) Further, in women's magazines there was a sharp drop in entries of women as overachieving housewives. But enthusiasm over these modest reforms must be tempered by other trends and figures. While there was a decline in women as sexual objects in ads in men's and general magazines, the rates of such portrayals were still quite high at over 50% (see Table VI). Moreover, ads falling in the category of "woman as dependent on man" *increased* in all classes of magazines, especially those for men. It is just possible that this category of ad simply *replaced* other sorts that were curtailed. What this means is that even after the social rights movement a random selection of ads from men's and general magazines would still show the presumed sexist bias against women. Certainly, women received better treatment in ads in women's magazines over the period of study. However, in the other classes of magazines, women in ads were not necessarily liberated, but merely reallocated to other sexist categories. What they got was the shift.

Television commercials. Of course, during the sixties the feminists also took issue with trends in television advertising. Dominick and Rauch (1972) reviewed several such complaints. For instance:

Feminist Germaine Greer berated the media for concentrating on ads for "things to squirt on women to stop them from being so offensive." Marijean Suelzle pointed out that commercials "endlessly show women helpless before a pile of soiled laundry until the male voice of authority overrides hers to tell how brand X with its fast-acting enzymes will get her clothes cleaner than clean" . . . And writer Caroline Bird summed up the situation by saying "our main quarrel with television is that it does not provide human models for a bright 13-year-old girl who would like to be something more than an ecstatic floor waxer."

To document the possibility of sexist bias in television ads, Dominick and Rauch (1972) conducted an analysis of the contents of prime-time commercials. Their eventual samples were 381 commercials that featured women and 235 that featured men. Two of the Dominick–Rauch analyses are of particular interest to us: (1) the settings in which men versus women were depicted and (2) the use of women as sex objects (as discussed earlier in the Venkatesan–Losco material). Table VII shows a clear sexist bias in the presentation of the two genders. Women were shown inside the home far more often than were men and, contrarily, men were shown outdoors far more often than were women. Depictions of business settings also involved men more frequently than women. Clearly, a woman's place is in the home, at least according to these ads.

The use of women as sex objects was also revealed in the Dominick–Rauch analyses. The characters in ads were coded as to their role or occupation. For women:

The most frequent role recorded was that of sex object/decoration. Some 32% of the females were in this role. The wife/mother characterization was next in frequency with 20% of the females judged to be in this category. Predictably,

TABLE VII

Percentage of women and men in early 1970s television commercials depicted in various settings

Setting	Women	Men
Indoors (house)	38	14
Outdoors	19	44
Business	7	14

After Dominick and Rauch (1972).
Note. The percentages in the columns do not sum to 100 because there were other settings in the original article not included here.

the frequency with which women were portrayed as sex objects, or for decorative purposes varied according to what sex generally buys the advertised product. In ads for products usually bought by men, 54% of the females were in this role. In ads for products bought generally by females or bought equally by both sexes, 25% of the females were in this category.

These patterns seem very consistent with those seen in Table VI concerning the variance in the use of women as sex objects according to the assumed gender of the reader.

FACE-ISM IN PRINT MEDIA

By now there is a long and clear line of evidence that men and women are consistently portrayed in biased ways in the media. Consider the following highlights from a review by Archer et al. (1983):

- Courtney and Lockeretz (1971): In an analysis of 312 ads from eight general magazines, it was found that 45% of the men were depicted in paid-work roles, while only 9% of the women were portrayed in this way.

- Sexton and Haberman (1974): From a study of 1,827 magazine ads, it was found that only 16% showed women in nontraditional situations.

- Miller (1975): An analysis of 3,661 news photos in *The Washington Post* and *The Los Angeles Times* (from 1973 and 1974) showed that (1) over 80% were exclusively of men; (2) while 75% of the men were shown in sport, professional, or political roles, women generally appeared as socialites, celebrities, or wives of famous men; and (3) fully 25% of the women shown in *The Washington Post* were brides.

Although such patterns may have become all too familiar, these days there is something of a "new look" in gender bias in the media. Following the lead of Goffman (1976), Archer et al. (1983) undertook a special sort of analysis of the photographs of women and men in various periodicals. Now, these researchers were not particularly interested in the roles or categories in which the two genders were presented. Rather, they combed the publications to find pictures of men and women so that they could measure them for what they termed FACIAL PROMINENCE. Archer et al. had the impression that it was not only roles that distinguished pictures of men from pictures of women, but that there might also be differences in *how much* of a male or female person was depicted. Their hunch was that men would be presented with more facial prominence than would women.

Why, given the apparent media bias against women, or in favor of men, might men be shown with more facial prominence? According to the authors,

if media depictions of men and women differ in terms of facial prominence, these differences may (wittingly or not) communicate something important about the relative importance for each sex of mind and body. Because the face and head are centers of mental life—intellect, personality, and character—the relative prominence of this part of the anatomy may be symbolically consequential . . . [Further,] facial prominence may both reflect and contribute to thematic conceptions about the relative importance for women and men of hearts and minds (Archer et al., 1983).

Thus, the traditional gender bias might be seen in a new guise.

The research. In order to quantify facial prominence, Archer et al. developed what they called the FACE-ISM INDEX. The calculation of this index is fairly straightforward, and we will do a few here, using the pictures in Figure 8. (Obviously, these covers were chosen especially for this exercise.) The first measurement required is the distance in any picture from the top of the person's head (including hair, I guess) to the lowest part of the chin in, say, millimeters. For reference, call this first value the numerator. Next, measure the same person from the top of the head to the lowest visible part of the body (clothed and unclothed parts are equivalent). Call this

FIGURE 8
FACIAL PROMINENCE of men and women on magazine covers.

second value the denominator. Then the face-ism index for the picture in question is obtained by simply dividing the numerator by the denominator. Theoretically, this index could range from a low of 0.00 (the face is not shown at all) to a high of 1.00 (the picture shows only the face). If the face and some lower part of the body are shown, the index will fall somewhere between 0.00 and 1.00. Before reading any farther, calculate face-ism indexes for the three people in Figure 8.

My estimate of the face-ism index for Mr. Reagan in Figure 8 is .74, and that for Mr. Gorbachev is .80. The picture of Candice Bergen in the figure scores considerably lower on facial prominence. From me, she would receive a face-ism index of .38. If you and I are off by a few percentage points, not to worry. As long as there was reasonable agreement between us (a concept termed INTEROBSERVER RELIABILITY), readers and critics would trust us. Still, any disagreement between a reader and this writer (or a reader and a classmate) points up the fact that while measurement in social psychology often sounds simple, in practice it seldom is. (Where *is* the lowest part of Mr. Reagan's chin in Figure 8?)

The results. Again, the pictures in Figure 8 were chosen for the sake of our exercise, and in and of themselves cannot be taken as evidence for "face-ism." However, the Archer et al. (1983) study did not suffer from this limitation, because they obtained a huge sample of over 5,400 photos from a total of 18 periodicals in 12 nations or regions. For instance, the five periodicals they examined in the United States were *Time, Newsweek, Ms., The San Francisco Chronicle,* and *The Santa Cruz Sentinel.* A face-ism index was calculated for each of the pictures, and the average indexes for men and women in the respective societies are presented in Table VIII. The table shows enormous support for the idea that there is gender bias in the media. For *every* society there was greater facial prominence in media photos of men than in those of women. Moreover, data such as these for face-ism are all the more impressive, because they are very much in line with the direction of the gender bias seen in earlier analyses.

Even so, it should be noted that gender trends in facial prominence may well be linked to the role or context of the person in any given photograph. Recent studies have found that there was little difference in the face-ism indexes for the three principal male candidates in the 1984 presidential election—Bush, Mondale, and Reagan—and the single female candidate—Ferraro (Sparks and

TABLE VIII
Face-ism index scores for women and men in photographs from periodicals in 12 societies

Society[a]	Women	Men
Chile	.34	.52
England	.49	.55
France	.41	.57
Federal Republic of Germany	.49	.60
Hong Kong	.56	.67
India	.45	.64
Italy	.41	.55
Kenya	.47	.72
Mexico	.49	.60
Middle East	.55	.72
Spain	.39	.58
United States	.45	.65

After Archer et al. (1983).
Note. Face-ism index scores can range from 0 to 1.00 (see text).
[a]For every society (row) listed, the difference in face-ism indexes across men and women is statistically significant at the .05 level or beyond. The entries for France and Italy are unweighted averages of separate indexes presented in Table 2 of Archer et al. (1983).

Fehlner, 1986). Further, male face-ism was less pronounced in pictures in publications oriented toward women's issues (Zuckerman, 1986). In this light, future inquiries into the face-ism issue should take into account just who is in the picture and what is going on.

SEXISM IN THE MEDIA: AN UPDATE

As noted, the women's movement in the late 1960s focused attention on the depiction of gender differences in the various media, and a large number of studies appeared in the movement's wake. As the 1970s unfolded, many of these researches yielded discouraging news about hoped-for changes in the biased portrayals of women (cf. Beuf, 1974; McNeil, 1975; O'Donnell and O'Donnell, 1978). Currently, media portrayals are still a matter of interest and concern (cf. Berry, 1988; CBS/Broadcast Group, 1988; Greenberg, 1988). Perhaps the most notorious of recent sexist communications was a 1989 advertising booklet distributed by Miller beer for insertion in campus newspapers. That 16-page pamphlet, titled *Beachin' Times*, had as its theme "babes," how to "scam them," or how "you can turn spring break into your own personal trout farm" (whatever that phrase is supposed to mean). One particular recommendation was to "Offer to apply sunblock anywhere she'll let you." Another was to "Act romantic. Use simple lines like 'let's walk along the beach at sunset and suck down some Miller Genuine Drafts,' or 'wanna get naked?'" Unfortunately for Miller beer, the slick ad eventually raised a storm of protest. Miller stopped the distribution of the insert and issued an apology (Riordan, 1989; "The Sexism Watch," 1989).

SEX STEREOTYPES IN THE MEDIA: NO LAUGHING MATTER

Media depictions of gender differences can be given a somewhat light-handed treatment, as has been the case here. However, there is a darker side to all of this, two aspects of which will be touched on. First, if the media (and our parents and teachers and peers) insist that we each conform to some societal standard or profile regarding a sex role, some of us are going to have more or less difficulty fitting in. This pressure could lead in some cases to maladjustment or neurosis. Second, some of the messages in certain media can be menacing, especially in the area of aggressive pornography and the potential for violence toward women. Let us consider these matters briefly.

Sex stereotypes and neuroses. In a seminal book, Allport (1958) argued that victims of prejudice could react psychologically in one of two basic ways. To use his terms, a victim could proceed along an "extropunitive" route (take it out on the oppressor) or an "intropunitive" one (take it out on one's self). If for some reason the latter avenue was chosen, self-hate, clowning, withdrawal and passivity, or NEUROTICISM might be the result. These possibilities seem borne out in our time. In 1983, two clinical psychologists, Violet Franks and Esther D. Rothblum, published an edited book entitled *The Stereotyping of Women: Its Effects on Mental Health*. In their introduction they point out that, despite changes in society, women are overrepresented in certain clinical problem areas. Chapters by various contributors to the book cover depression, agoraphobia, sexual dysfunction, assertiveness, and weight and health. According to the editors, "the book focuses on the negative effects of sex-role stereotypes about women . . . We shall examine how the pressures to be 'normal' by conforming to sex-role stereotypes result in . . . clinical problems" (Rothblum and Franks, 1983). Alas, more fun with Dick and Jane.

Pornography and the potential for sexual aggression. Thinking in the area of effects of PORNOGRAPHY is nothing if not controversial (Eysenck, 1984). Interested readers are referred to *Pornography and Sexual Aggression* (edited by Malamuth and Donnerstein, 1984), and interested readers with stamina are referred to the *Attorney General's Commission on Pornography* (1986). In perusing such material, the impression one gets is that nonviolent, sexually explicit material does not necessarily lead to harmful effects (Donnerstein, 1984). However, what is much clearer is that violent pornography *does*. According to the Attorney General's 1986 report, exposure to violent, sexually explicit materials

(1) leads to greater acceptance of rape myths and violence against women; (2) [has] more pronounced effects when the victim is shown enjoying the use of force or violence; (3) is arousing for rapists and for some males in the general population; and (4) has resulted in sexual aggression against women in the laboratory (*Attorney General's Commission on Pornography*, 1986).

(For more information on the workings of the Commission, see Koop (1987), and for certain social psychologists' reactions to its recommendations see Linz, Donnerstein, and Penrod (1987). Further, for an interesting review of pornography and the law, see McConahay (1988).)

Still, pornography in various media is not the only matter of concern in the area of violence toward women. For example, Briere and Malamuth (1983) investigated—through subjects' self-reports— why males might engage in rape or in sexual force. These researchers evaluated the predictive power of *sexuality* variables (frustration or maladjustment) versus *attitude* variables (blaming the victim or viewing sexual violence as arousing for women). The result was that the attitude variables were far more predictive regarding the likelihood of violent sex. Based on these and other findings, Briere and Malamuth concluded that rape is part of an attitudinal continuum of "aggression toward women" rather than a separate phenomenon. Where would some men acquire such an attitude? Maybe at the local newsstand. An analysis of detective magazines showed that 76% of the covers depicted the domination of women and fully 38% portrayed women in bondage (Dietz, Harry, and Hazelwood, 1986).

SUMMARY

There is reason to be concerned about, or at least alert to, the depiction of gender differences in the media. Such models are with us from childhood on. The focus here was on the portrayal of girls and women, but male readers should also be sensitive to this issue.

In a preceding section, clinicians Rothblum and Franks (1983) pointed out that women were overrepresented in "passive" clinical problem areas. However, they also mentioned that men are overrepresented in "acting out" areas such as alcoholism, drug abuse, and certain personality disorders. Maybe it is not so easy (or comfortable) to fill the bill offered to males. In any event, since we read, watch, and listen to the media so much anyway, we might do well to do so in a more critical fashion. For now, let us see what certain media offer us in the way of images of another important segment of society: the elderly.

AGE-ISM: THE INVISIBILITY ISSUE

The media bias associated with females is seen in the way in which women are *actively* depicted. Our exposures to these offerings presumably form or confirm our attitudes about women. However, another way the media can influence our opinions about members of certain demographic groups is to simply *withhold* their image. This is the matter of UNDERREPRESENTATION and SOCIAL INVISIBILITY (McGuire, 1986).

One demographic group for which this type of bias has been confirmed is the elderly. From samples of United States television programming from 1969 through 1978, Gerbner, Gross, Signorielli, and Morgan (1980) identified 1,365 programs and 16,688 characters. Through systematic analyses, they were able to determine the ages of these characters, and the frequency distribution of character age is shown in Figure 9. Of interest is a comparison of this fictional population with the American population at the time. The frequency distribution of Americans' ages (according to Gerbner et al.) is also presented in Figure 9. It is immediately obvious that the elderly (and children and adolescents) are underrepresented in television programs. Gerbner et al. (1980) reported that, even though people over 65 constituted about 11% of the U.S. population, they made up only 2.3% of the fictional population. Similar patterns of the underrepresentation of the elderly in magazine advertisements has also been reported (Gantz, Gartenberg, and Rainbow, 1980).

What might be the effects of these differences in representation? Gerbner et al. (1980) presented some suggestive findings. In a survey conducted by Louis Harris and Associates in 1974, respondents were asked questions regarding the number, health, and longevity of older people. The way things were set up, a high score on these indexes would reflect a belief that the elderly represented a diminishing rather than a growing segment of U.S. society. Interestingly, for

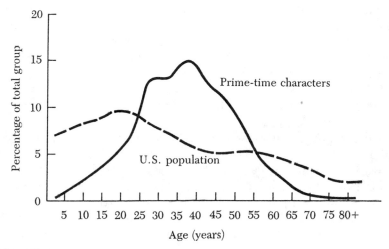

FIGURE 9
AGE DISTRIBUTIONS of television characters and of the U.S. population. (After Gerbner et al., 1980.)

viewers under 30, there was a positive and significant correlation (*r*) of .20 between level of TV viewing (light to heavy) and the impression that the aged were becoming a vanishing breed. In another study, school children were asked "at what age does a woman [man] become elderly or old?" Light TV viewers gave the age as about 57, whereas heavy viewers responded with the age of 51. The correlation between level of viewing and age estimates in this sample was −.21 (Gerbner et al., 1980). In sum, it seems that the relative invisibility of the elderly in the media might have influenced young persons' estimates of the number of the aged or the definition of aging.*

SUMMARY

From *Fun with Dick and Jane* in the 1940s to face-ism (and age-ism) in the 1980s, there seems to be no end to the expression of gender (and other demographic) biases in certain of the mass media, and all of this in the face of several recent cultural changes. The feminist movement was real and no doubt had a strong impact at some levels; witness the first female vice-presidential candidate in a national campaign (in what perhaps was an unwinnable election in 1984 for Walter

*Readers may be chafing at the report of correlations at the .20 level. Keep this thought until we encounter a section on "variance accounted for" a few pages from here.

Mondale and Geraldine Ferraro). And, despite my earlier mention
of recent books with pessimistic titles about reforms for women,
there are others that are more upbeat. For example, consider *The
Changing Lives of American Women* (McGlaughin et al., 1988), and
*The Sisterhood: The True Story of the Women Who Changed the
World* (Cohen, 1988). Even so, the Dick and Jane mentality has a
strong grip on our culture, and it would not surprise me to see media
gender messages continue.

Do these persistent biases mean that most of the public finds
media presentations of gender and other demographic stereotypes to
be at least tolerable? This raises the important issue of whether (1)
the media are the cause and our attitudes are the effect or (2) the
media are simply a reflection of widespread attitudes or cultural
values, or both. For the remainder of this chapter I will take up the
matter of measuring the attitudinal and behavioral impact of the
media.

Attitudinal and Behavioral Effects of the Media

There is no doubt that the media contain many messages that
have the potential to influence our attitudes and behavior. But just
what is the impact of such messages? Many special interest groups
would like us to believe that the impact is great. Concerning television, for instance, *friends* of the medium—the networks, advertisers, and advertising agencies—operate on the assumption that what
is aired has consequences, principally for our consumer behavior.
On the other side, *foes* of the medium—say, the National Coalition
on Television Violence—fear that certain program content can be
detrimental to individual viewers and to society as a whole. Certainly,
we *are* exposed to a great deal of televised material; the estimate
presented above was that children have spent as much as 20,000
hours in front of a television set by the time they finish high school.
As McGuire (1986) put it, "with all this watching, there must be
some effect." What is the evidence for these presumed effects?

According to McGuire (1986), the effects are weak. The first part
of the title of McGuire's paper reveals that position: "The Myth of
Massive Media Impact . . . " In his well-researched review, McGuire
took up six intended effects of the media:

- commercial advertising on purchasing
- political campaigning on voting
- public service announcements on personal or public betterment

- multimedia campaigns on change in life-style
- indoctrination effects on ideology
- mass media rituals in social control

He also covered six unintended effects:

- program violence and viewer aggression
- underrepresentation and social invisibility
- misrepresentation effects: stereotypes
- effects of erotica on sexual thoughts, feelings, behavior
- media affecting cognitive styles
- media affecting thought processes

Having evaluated the available data, McGuire reached the following conclusion:

We have reviewed and evaluated the evidence regarding the dozen types of media effects that have received the most mention and most study, six having to do with intended effects and six with unintended effects of the media. For each of the dozen areas of purported effects we concluded that the demonstrated impacts are surprisingly slight. Even in the areas with the most impressive results, including frequent statistically significant effects in methodologically adequate studies, the size of the impacts are so small as to raise questions about their practical significance and cost effectiveness (McGuire, 1986).

This conservative (and, perhaps to some, chilling) conclusion is based on an statistical approach termed "accounting for variance." Let us take some hypothetical examples of ACCOUNTING FOR VARIANCE to see how McGuire reached his conclusion. For example, the correlation coefficient (r) is a commonly reported statistic that expresses the strength of association between two variables. Recall that such coefficients can range in size from $+1.00$ to -1.00. Imagine that in a small sample of first-graders we find that the empirical correlation between their height and weight is $+1.00$. This relationship is very strong, because if we know which child is tallest, we also know that that child is the heaviest. Similarly, if we know which child is the shortest, we also know which child is the lightest, and so on for every point in between. That is, knowing about one variable (height) tells us everything we need to know about the other variable (weight). Statistically, this relatedness can be expressed by squaring the correlation coefficient. In this case, the square of 1.00 is 1, or 100%. In other words, in this example the variance of one variable "accounts for" all (100%) of the variance of the other variable.

Of course, it is rare to encounter correlation coefficients as large as +1.00 or −1.00, so usually the amount of variance accounted for is less than 100%, and Table IX shows the amount of variance accounted for by correlations of various sizes. (Note that there are appropriate techniques for expressing variance accounted for when other statistical tests are used.) Now, to return to the matter of McGuire's (1986) critique of the media-effect literature, let us take another hypothetical example. Suppose a researcher reported that in a large sample of people the correlation between (1) hours of television watched and (2) bottles of eyedrops purchased was .30. No doubt a correlation of .30 would be statistically significant, and a proper conclusion would be that there is a trend that heavy viewers purchase the most eyedrops. However, reference to Table IX indicates that a coefficient of .30 accounts for less than 10% of the variance. In other words, the strength of the association between the two variables is quite low. Knowing how many hours an individual watches television would be a *poor* predictor of how many bottles of eyedrops she or he would purchase. And this is McGuire's point: typical media effects are simply not strong, or, in his terms, "massive." Recall the correlations on the order of .20 reported by Gerbner et al. (1980) in a preceding section on age-ism. This type of finding is precisely what McGuire was talking about in his concern over the myth of massive media impact.

But to say that media effects are not strong or massive is not to

TABLE IX
Percentage of "variance accounted for" by correlation coefficients of various sizes

r	r^2	Variance accounted for (%)
1.00	1.00	100
.90	.81	81
.80	.64	64
.70	.49	49
.60	.36	36
.50	.25	25
.40	.16	16
.30	.09	9
.20	.04	4
.10	.01	1
.00	.00	0

Note. The same principle applies to negative correlations.

deny their potential importance. The impressiveness of a small correlation coefficient is often in the eye of the beholder. It certainly matters who is interpreting the statistic. Consider a view of media effects that is counter to McGuire's conservatism:

A persistent difference in the exposure to messages that cultivate perspectives [attitudes] need not result in a major shift in personal outlook and behavior to have profound consequences. A barely perceptible shift of a few degrees average temperature can lead to an ice age or make the desert bloom. A slight but pervasive tilt in the cultural climate can have major social and public policy implications. The closer a vote, a decision, a public policy issue, the smaller the shift needed for change, and the more rigid the forces of stability might be. This is one reason why we prefer to speak of the contribution of television to the cultivation of common perspectives rather than of its achieving any specific or preconceived goals, impacts, or effects (Gerbner, Gross, Jackson-Beeck, Jeffries-Fox, and Signorielli, 1978).

In fact, even McGuire (1986), after "savaging" (his word) the myth of massive media impact, offered as many as 33 methodological and theoretical points why such impacts might really be there, only to have been missed by the researches of the past. Our position here, then, will be a synthesis of those offered by McGuire on the one hand and by Gerbner et al. on the other. We will be cautious about the overinterpretation of weak or marginal media effects, while simultaneously appreciating their potential for influence due to the very scale of the industry. It is to a particular concern many people have about television that we now turn. Let us consider television violence and its impact on the viewer.

TELEVISION VIOLENCE

Television fare is nothing if not violent. No matter how they are expressed, the numbers are impressive. For instance, Gerbner et al. (1978) reported a survey of shows seen on prime-time and weekend daytime programming on the major networks from 1967 to 1977. Within that period, approximately 80% of the programs contained violence, and about 60% of the characters in the programs were involved in violence. Using U.S. census data, Gerbner et al. estimated that in the real world in that period there were 0.32 violent crimes per 100 persons, which means that any given person had a .003 chance of being involved in such violence. In contrast, television characters had a .30 (for supporting roles) to .64 (for central roles) chance of being involved in violence. Thus, violence was up to 213 times more likely on TV than in real life in that period! From another perspective, it has been estimated that by the time of high school graduation the average child will have witnessed 18,000 murders and any number of bombings and beatings (Hearold, 1986). The top panel of Table X provides a sampler of recent prime-time television offerings, as analyzed by the National Coalition on Television Violence (NCTV). Certain of the high-violence shows offer the viewer close to one violent act per minute ("Fall, 1988 Prime Time Network TV Monitoring," 1989). If all this media mayhem directed at adults is a bit much for the reader, perhaps we can turn to children's fare for relief. Also listed in Table X (lower panel) are some network cartoon shows. Alas, things are pretty rough here, too ("Wham! Pow! Bam!", 1988; for an estimate of the level of violence in comic books, see "Biff! Pow! Blowie!", 1989.)

TABLE X
Certain prime-time and cartoon shows seen in 1988, and the frequency of depictions of violent acts per hour

Show and network	Violent acts per hour
Prime-time shows	
"Miami Vice" (NBC)	54
"The Equalizer" (CBS)	51
"Crimes of the Century" (ABC)	50
"Paradise" (CBS)	46
"Something Is Out There" (NBC)	38
"Nightwatch" (ABC)	30
"Mission: Impossible" (ABC)	28
"Simon & Simon" (CBS)	26
"Sonny Spoon" (NBC)	23
"Midnight Caller" (NBC)	23
Cartoons	
"Mighty Mouse: The New Adventures" (CBS)	60
"Bugs Bunny and Tweety" (ABC)	49
"Gummi Bears" (NBC)	47
"Real Ghostbusters" (ABC)	37
"The Little Wizards" (ABC)	35
"Smurfs" (NBC)	29
"Hello Kitty's" (CBS)	26
"Dennis the Menace" (CBS)	25
"Teen Wolf" (CBS)	25
"My Pet Monster" (ABC)	24

After (for prime-time entries) "Fall, 1988 Prime Time Network TV Monitoring," 1989; (for cartoon entries) "Wham! Pow! Bam!", 1988.

A survey. Having established that there is indeed a lot of violence on the tube, Gerbner et al. (1978) set out to try to measure its impact. Reflecting on the fact that almost all U.S. households have television sets, these authors did not attempt to compare viewers' reactions with those of nonviewers. Rather, they divided viewers into three categories: light, medium, and heavy. Operationally, 2 hours or less viewing per day was considered light, 3 hours as medium, and 4 and more hours as heavy.

Respondents were reached by survey research teams from the National Opinion Research Center (NORC) of the University of Chicago and the Center for Political Studies of the Institute for Social Research at the University of Michigan. People were asked several questions regarding precautions they might have taken to protect themselves from the threat of violence. The rationale for the study was that if heavy viewers were exposed to more television violence than lesser viewers, they might have assumed that contemporary society *was* violent. If they did hold this assumption, perhaps they would take more precautions. Some of the questions that tapped the precautions issue were whether the respondent had bought a dog, installed new locks, or kept a gun. Further, since the prospect of violence often can produce a demoralized or fearful reaction, respondents were also checked for ANOMIE, a term denoting personal unrest or alienation. These questions had to do with the condition of the average man and whether it was fair to bring a child into this world under the circumstances.

The patterns of replies as related to level of television viewing are shown in Table XI. Anomie was generally the most prevalent among heavy viewers and the least prevalent among light viewers. For the three precautions listed there, a measurable relationship was also found. Of course, by some standards the differences in Table XI could be said to be unimpressive, which might be McGuire's (1986) evaluation. But when you add things up there were a *lot* more dogs, locks, and guns out there because of the heavy viewers, presumably as a consequence of their viewing habits.

Of course, one problem with the above interpretation is that it can easily be turned around. Rather than making the causal link that viewing produced precautions, one could conclude that people who were already concerned about social dangers would take precautions, one of which might be spending less time out on the street, especially at night. Hence, they would simply have more time to watch television at home. But, as in other areas of media effects, it does not seem to matter too much which came first, the precautions or the

TABLE XI
Percentage of respondents who took precautions to be safe from crime or who expressed anomie, by level of television viewing

	VIEWING LEVEL[a]		
Item	Light	Medium	Heavy
Precautions			
Bought a dog	10	12	16
Installed new locks	28	31	32
Kept a gun	19	21	29
Anomie			
Lot of average man getting worse	51	61	62
Unfair to bring child into world	34	41	46

After Gerbner et al. (1978).
[a]These levels were defined variously in the different surveys on which the table is based. For example, in the NORC 1977 General Social Survey, 2 hours or less was considered light, 3 hours medium, and 4 or more hours heavy.

viewing. If the heavy viewing caused the precautions, then we have a bona fide media effect. On the other hand, if the precautions caused the heavy viewing, this would serve to confirm the viewer's impression of the danger, and we would *still* have a bona fide media effect. And we would still have more dogs, locks, and guns.

A *meta-analysis.* Recently, Hearold (1986) carried out a meta-analysis of the effects of television on social behavior. Using a comprehensive search technique, she located a total of 230 empirical studies that reported 1,043 effects. Hearold's aim was to estimate the "effect sizes" in these studies. EFFECT SIZE is a statistical expression of the strength of the impact of an independent variable on a dependent variable. Let us create an imaginary media experiment and then see how Hearold would use our data.

For our hypothetical study, one group of subjects could be exposed to a 30-minute segment of "Miami Vice," "The Equalizer," or "Mighty Mouse" (see Table X). That would ensure that those subjects would see a lot of violence. Then, as a control, another group of subjects could be shown 30 minutes of some show that is very low on violence such as "Cheers" or "The Cosby Show" (for which the NCTV estimate is zero violent acts per hour). Following the exposures, we could measure everyone's attitude toward a controversial issue such as the right of citizens to possess guns. Imagine that the outcome of the study was that experimental subjects, who viewed violence, did endorse possession of arms more than the control subjects, who did not view violence. What we would have is the average attitude of the experimental subjects, which we will call M_1, and the average for the controls, which we will call M_2. Now the strength of the impact of the independent variable (program type) on the dependent variable (attitude) could be determined by subtracting M_2 from M_1: $(M_1 - M_2)$. Of course, the interpretation of a mean difference has to be tempered by the amount of error variance (overlap) in the two sets of data, so we will adjust the difference by dividing this difference by the average standard deviation of the two means. Thus, in practical terms, effect strength is calculated as follows:

$$ES = (M_1 - M_2)/s$$

Since effect strength (ES) is something of a statistical abstraction that rests on the parameters M_1, M_2, and s, it is not altogether easy to describe in everyday language. One way to get a handle on the concept is to talk about the ES of a known effect. We all know that as groups, men are taller than women. This is a very strong and reliable finding. According to Hearold (1986), the established ES of gender on height is 1.20. In any event, ES gave Hearold a way to standardize the results of many different kinds of studies having many different kinds of dependent measures. What we gain from this is the ability to directly compare various treatments in terms of their effects on behavior. That is, we can meaningfully ask the following sort of question: "What has more influence on subjects' antisocial behavior, watching the news or watching cartoons?"

Having assembled the 230 studies for meta-analysis, Hearold separated the independent variables used by the original researchers into antisocial treatments and prosocial treatments. The antisocial treatments included exposures to demonstrated behavior (such as in Albert Bandura's famous Bobo Doll aggression research with children), news, Westerns, sports, and cartoons. Prosocial treatments involved demonstrated behavior, public service ads, "Lassie," "Mr. Rogers' Neighborhood," and comedies. As for dependent variables, the subjects in the original studies were scored variously for antisocial behavior in terms of physical and verbal aggression, rule breaking, unlawful behavior, the perception of the world as violent, and other dimensions. Prosocial behavior was scored as altruism, cooperation, or affiliation, among other such categories.

It is reassuring that Hearold looked at both the brighter and the darker sides of media effects. So far we have been concerned only with the inimical effects of media, but there is no reason to think that because certain media effects might be viewed as bad, others could not be seen as good. In fact, her meta-analysis revealed both kinds of effects, as shown in Table XII. In terms of the concept of effect size, the strongest antisocial treatments were seen for demonstrated behavior and news shows. Cartoons have much less impact than does the news. Interestingly, even though they are meant to be comedies, shows like "Sanford and Son" and "All in the Family" do have the capacity to influence antisocial behavior. As for prosocial treatments, the strongest in this data set were for "Lassie" and demonstrated behavior. Also high in positive influence were public service ads and children's socialization shows such as "Mister Rogers'

TABLE XII
Average effect sizes for antisocial television material on subjects' antisocial behavior, and for prosocial television material on subjects' prosocial behavior

Treatment type	Average effect size
Antisocial	
Demonstrated behavior (made for research)	0.69
News	0.67
Commercials	0.46
Cartoons	0.41
Mixed movies	0.40
Westerns	0.35
Sports	0.27
Mixture of cartoons and comedy	0.26
Crime/detective	0.25
"All in the Family"/"Sanford and Son"	0.25
Prosocial	
"Lassie" (animal)	1.16
Demonstrated behavior (made for research)	1.02
Public service ads	0.79
Simulated programs (made for research)	0.79
"Mr. Rogers' Neighborhood"	0.68
"Sesame Street"/"Electric Company"	0.58
"Big Blue Marble"	0.57
Comedy	0.54
Mixed programs	0.18

After Hearold (1986).

Neighborhood" and "Sesame Street." Well, along with the bad news, we have some good news for a change.

In sum, Hearold (1986) has provided us with another demonstration of media effects, in this case the antisocial and prosocial influences of certain kinds of materials. To repeat the slogan, children and other people do believe what you tell them, at least some of the time. As consumers of the media or as parents of consumers of the media, it just might be a good idea to keep these data in mind when selecting viewing matter. While media effects may not be massive, they are definitely real and detectable.

However, any writer familiar with the literature on television and violence (or aggression, or crime) would be quick to point out that debate seems always to attend these issues. For a taste of current controversies, the interested reader is referred to Volume 8 of the *Applied Social Psychology Annual*, published in 1988. In Part III of that periodical—"Television Violence"—six noted researchers in the area present their views. Some think television and real-life violence or crime are causally connected, and some do not. But the point here is not merely to call for more research; doubtless that research is occurring in any event. Far more useful is the observation that readers sensitized to the possibility of adverse effects of television viewing can at least use discretion in choosing what is watched.

OTHER MEDIA IMPACTS: THE "WERTHER" EFFECT

The previous section on television violence opened with a discussion of made-for-TV mayhem. That is, dramatic and cartoon shows require writers, producers, directors, and actors (or artists), all working in concert to create images of violence for our entertainment, titillation, or mere distraction. However, there are other media sources that provide us with doses of violence, presumably for our *benefit*. Newscasters everywhere regularly serve up more or less detailed accounts of real-life violence directed at others (homicide) or directed at the self (suicide). One supposes that we need such information to monitor the condition of our society and the quality of life. But this sort of information is not always dispassionately received and objectively stored. Note in Table XII that Hearold (1986) found a strong effect size for the *news* on aggressive behavior. Such possibilities deserve further attention.

Indeed, the impact of the news has come under scrutiny, with chilling results. One salient line of research in this area has been carried out by David P. Phillips and his associates (Phillips, 1986a, 1986b). They documented what Phillips has called the WERTHER

EFFECT. Werther was a literary character (in a 1787 novel by Goethe) whose fictive suicide is thought to have led to imitative suicides by readers of the period. Astonishingly enough, some people today seem to be committing the same sort of imitative suicides! But they do not have to seek out Goethe's work; they can read about suicides in their local newspapers.

Here are the propositions that Phillips tests. Archival in nature, his research involves the identification of a publicized suicide. This task is done by a thorough recording of newspaper accounts. Then other public archives are used to follow rates of suicides before and after the specific report, and at comparable times in other years. It is hypothesized that the Werther effect will occur in a given period *after* a suicide's publicity, thus the other periods are used as "controls." Now, suicide can be accomplished in a number of ways, including the use of an automobile, so Phillips includes single-vehicle fatalities in the scope of the effect.

What is the evidence for the Werther effect where suicide is concerned? All this may sound pretty farfetched until one looks at the data. Here is a summary of some of Phillips's findings:

1. United States monthly suicides ([from the period] 1946–1968) increase significantly just after publicized suicide stories. This finding has been replicated with daily United States suicide data (1972–1976).
2. The greater the publicity devoted to the suicide story, the greater the rise in United States suicides thereafter.
3. The rise is greatest in those geographic areas where the suicide story is most heavily publicized.
4. California motor vehicle fatalities increase significantly just after a publicized suicide story.
5. Single-vehicle fatalities increase more than other types of fatality.
6. The driver in these single-vehicle crashes is unusually similar to the person described in the suicide story (but the passengers are not) (Phillips, 1986a).

There is even more such evidence—as in the finding that noncommercial air crashes increase after a publicized suicide—and it is all convincing. Further, Phillips (1986a) reports that prominent prizefights are shortly followed by an increase in homicides! Still, all is not gloom and doom; there is also the finding that following the publicizing of the execution or punishment of criminals there is a dip in homicides (Phillips, 1986a). Of course, few things about media influences remain noncontroversial for long, and by now there is a suggestion that the Werther suicide effect obtains only for celebrity deaths (Wasserman, 1984). Even so, the potential for such influence may be great, and investigations will surely continue.

Summary

Throughout this chapter we have seen considerable evidence that the media can be a force for evil, and some evidence that it can be a force for good. To the extent that we view them as evil, attitudes of racism, sexism, and what I have called age-ism can all be strengthened by biased representation in the media. Television violence is another concern, as are the supposed unintended consequences of news reports of suicide and murder, and other human violence. On the other hand, to the extent that we view them as good, prosocial sentiments about things like altruism and cooperation can also be influenced.

What do the media of the present and future hold for us? I personally do not expect any reduction of, for instance, the violence in films or on television, for I cannot identify much strong pressure against it. Certainly, the media will go on reporting murders and suicides. Worse, perhaps, we are witnessing the development of "trash TV," where sensationalism and violence seem to be the governing goals (Waters, McKillop, Powell, and Huck, 1988), as well as "crash TV," such as "Roller Games" (Waters, 1989).

However, the media can continue to be useful in promoting positive social ends. Leo (1989) suggests that social reforms can be achieved through the use of STIGMA (a mark of shame or discredit). His computer search of newspapers turned up hundreds of stigmas, some of the most successful of which are listed here:

- Antismoking campaigns. The antismoking forces have won in their efforts to devalue the burning and inhaling of dead plant matter.
- Antidrinking campaigns. Groups such as Mothers Against Drunk Driving have stigmatized drunkenness to the point that it is no longer seen as humorous or cute but connotes a loss of control and a pathetic, dangerous condition.
- Animal rights campaigns. Animal activists and protectionists have sensitized people to the wanton slaughter of animals for such luxuries as high-fashion furs and cosmetics testing.
- Antiabortion campaigns. According to Leo (1989), "the most dramatic stigma contest now being fought."

I am not saying where I stand on any of these issues. However, if you are an advocate, keep the faith. The effective use of stigmas in the media could get you somewhere.

CHAPTER TWELVE

PROTEST, PATRIOTISM, AND THE PRESIDENCY: MODERN TRENDS IN U.S. NATIONALIST SENTIMENTS

The period from the early 1960s to the present has been one of extensive and sometimes turbulent social activism in the United States. There have been a number of "movements," each deserving of capital letters: the Civil Rights Movement, the Antiwar Movement, the Environmental Movement, Women's Liberation, Gay Liberation, and even the Animal Rights Movement. The dynamics of attitudes and opinions underlying any of these would make for an interesting discussion, but for the present I will restrict my presentation to only a few aspects of nationalist sentiments.

Of course, any 3-decade segment of modern American history would produce volumes of information regarding attitude formation and change, so my attention will have to be selective. For this chapter, I have identified three topics that allow me to do a reasonable job of tracking Americans' attitudes about things American in the era in question. Although they are all interrelated, they can perhaps best be treated serially. The topics, and the order in which they will be taken up, are (1) the war in Vietnam, (2) the so-called Patriotic Revival, and (3) the American presidency.

The War in Vietnam

On the evening of October 7, 1986, Wyatt Andrews—a CBS Moscow correspondent—told viewers that the Soviet Union was experiencing its own "television war" in Afghanistan. Previously, the conflict had been officially ignored in the U.S.S.R., but a change in Soviet propaganda policy dictated that Soviet soldiers' sacrifices in that war should now be portrayed to the Russian people. Documentaries of the fighting, and news stories of the decoration of troops for heroism, began to be shown there for the first time. However, Andrews went on to point out that along with this rather tardy praise for the veterans, the Soviet press admitted indications of war-related problems at home. Draft evasion was mentioned, as was anger among Russian veterans who were confused by the apathetic society they had reentered. The segment closed with the statement: "This may be the Soviet Union's television war, but to Americans who remember Vietnam, it may seem like a rerun."

Indeed, that television news report was a reminder of major national events in the United States in the 1960s and 1970s. America's TELEVISION WAR in Vietnam had cost the country dearly, and not only in terms of bloodshed. As put by one set of observers: "This was the war that ruined one presidency and all but consumed another—a war that sapped the national will, subverted our trust in government and our sense of the rightness of the American cause" (Morganthau, Willenson, Walcott, Horrock, and Lubenow, 1985).

The war in Vietnam is often characterized as being "unpopular" among Americans. Just how unpopular was it? To begin to answer this question, and to provide some orientation, the briefest of sketches will be presented to outline some of the chronology of that conflict (after Karnow, 1983).

A BRIEF HISTORY

- 1961: Kennedy sends American equipment and advisers to South Vietnam.
- 1963: By the end of the year, there are 15,000 American advisers in Vietnam.
- 1964: Congress passes the Tonkin Gulf resolution; Johnson now has extraordinary power to act in the region.
- 1965: The first American combat troops arrive to defend Da Nang airfield.
- 1966: American troop strength reaches 400,000 by year-end.
- 1968: The communists launch the Tet offensive; American troop strength is 540,000, the highest in the entire history of the war.
- 1969: Massive antiwar demonstrations occur in the U.S.; the Mylai massacre is revealed; troop withdrawals begin.
- 1970: Nixon announces an incursion into Cambodia; large antiwar demonstrations spread in the U.S.; the Kent State killings occur.

- 1971: American troop strength is down to 140,000.

- 1972: Nixon bombs Hanoi; the Watergate break-in occurs.

- 1973: The last American troops leave Vietnam.

- 1975: Saigon is captured by communist forces.

Three kinds of evidence will be used to show the unpopularity of this string of events in Southeast Asia: (1) survey results regarding the loss of public support for the war, (2) an archival analysis of negative sentiments as expressed in antiwar demonstrations, and (3) survey results that indicate a general antigovernment sentiment in that period. These three sections will be followed by a more or less exploratory account of Americans' attitudes toward the veterans of the Vietnam War.

SURVEY RESULTS: ANTIWAR ATTITUDES

As the war gained momentum in the field and attention in the media, pollsters began to scrutinize the American people's support for U.S. involvement. Of relevance here are three sets or series of polls that are in quite good agreement about trends in war-related attitudes from the 1960s to the 1980s. The following paragraphs present descriptions of each and information about the nature of the questions that were asked of respondents. Differences in questions might account for certain slight differences in the results from the three projects. Because the questions differed in terms of grammar and syntax, for this exposition responses will be standardized in pro (pro-war) and con (anti-war) form.

The first report appeared in 1971 in the *American Political Science Review*. In it, Mueller (1971) utilized data from Gallup surveys carried out at the American Institute of Public Opinion. Surveys were carried out every year from 1965 to 1970. The actual question that produced the data was, "In view of the developments since we entered the fighting in Vietnam, do you think the U.S. made a mistake sending troops to fight in Vietnam?" Mueller's article reported both pro and con reactions.

The second report appeared in March 1985 in the *New York Times Magazine* and stated that 1,533 adults had been contacted in April of that year (Clymer, 1985). This report also included data from 1964, 1972, and 1983. The University of Michigan is credited with the first two of these prior studies, and a *New York Times*/CBS News Poll produced the third. The apparent question asked here was, "Did we do the right thing in getting into the fighting in Vietnam or should we have stayed out?" Clymer's article thus reports both pro and con reactions.

Finally, a third report appeared in April 1985 in *Newsweek* ("A *Newsweek* Poll," 1985). The Gallup organization is credited with carrying out a telephone survey during the previous month of a national sample of 1,021 adults. Data were also reported from 1965, 1966, 1967, 1968, 1969, 1970, 1971, and 1973. The question that was asked is not exactly clear. It was stated only that the results were "the trend percent saying 'Vietnam was a mistake.'" Here, only con responses were available.

The results of these three extensive reports have been plotted in a common graph (Figure 1). Because the raw data from the studies were not available, the plots in Figure 1 are only estimates. The figure was prepared from unweighted means from earlier tables and figures, so any errors or misrepresentations are not attributable to the original sources. Even so, a very consistent picture emerges in Figure 1. Early in the war there *was* public support for U.S. involvement. However, as involvement increased, public support decreased.

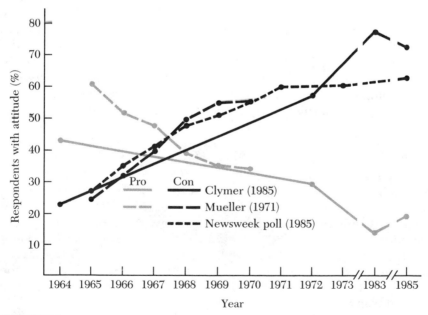

FIGURE 1
PERCENTAGE OF SUPPORT (PRO) AND OPPOSE (CON) ATTITUDES toward U.S. involvement in the Vietnam War. (From various sources; see text.)

The year 1968 witnessed the communists' Tet offensive, and 1969 produced the report of the massacre of civilians by American troops at Mylai. As the harsh realities and terrible human costs of the war became more apparent, fewer and fewer Americans were willing to express their support for it. It is also interesting to note that these trends persisted into the 1980s. There is no doubt that the war in Vietnam remains a bitter memory for many Americans, and we will take up these contemporary sentiments in a later section.

Did Walter Cronkite really lose the war? In the preceding section it was seen that Americans' support for the Vietnam War steadily declined almost from the outset of heavy troop involvement. What was the impetus for this massive attitude change? Some commentators argued that *television* lost the war: it was America's first television war; it was the first war that the country lost; therefore, television somehow caused America to lose that war. According to this theory, TV images of the fighting and broadcasters' handling of the material undermined the people's initial support for President Johnson's war policies and caused a national failure of will (Hallin, 1986). Two of America's military leaders of the period, Generals William C. Westmoreland and Maxwell D. Taylor, made this point explicitly in their respective memoirs (Lichty and Fouhy, 1987). Often cited in this connection is Walter Cronkite's CBS News coverage of the communists' Tet offensive in 1968, in which some 100 cities in South Vietnam were simultaneously attacked. The Vietcong were defeated, but Cronkite's assessment was that the war had become a "bloody stalemate" and perhaps it was time for America to get out (Hallin, 1986).

However, as analyzed by Lichty and Fouhy (1987), this theory appears to be untenable. These writers point to Gallup data that show that a sharp drop in public support began not in 1968 but much earlier in 1965 and 1966 (and see Figure 1). In fact, if anything, TV coverage was actually pro-war during the 1965–1967 period when positive attitudes were eroding and antiwar demonstrations were mounting (see below). For example, Hallin (1986) reported a count of statements presented on television from August 1965 to January 1968 that were favorable or unfavorable to various principals in the war (Table I). Clearly, this medium was pro-war then and was sending the Johnson administration's message in this era.

Even more to the point, Lichty and Fouhy (1987) reviewed an analysis that counted documentary or TV forum shows featuring "hawks" (proponents of the war) or "doves" (opponents of the war).

TABLE I
Numbers of statements presented on national television between August 1965 and January 1968 that were favorable or unfavorable to various principals in the war in Vietnam

Principal	NUMBER OF STATEMENTS ON FILM		NUMBER OF JOURNALISTS' COMMENTS	
	Favorable	Unfavorable	Favorable	Unfavorable
United States	65	31	11	3
South Vietnam	3	1	2	2
North Vietnam	2	8	0	20
U.S. domestic opposition	0	6	0	2

After Hallin (1986).

Before 1965, 90% of the guests on these programs were "hawks"; by 1968, there were an equal number of "hawks" and "doves"; and not until 1970 was there a majority of "doves." For these writers, then, the medium did not cause Americans' attitudes, it followed them.

ARCHIVAL RESULTS: ANTIWAR PROTESTS AND DEMONSTRATIONS

Why did pollsters start to measure Americans' attitudes toward the war in Vietnam in the early- to mid-1960s? They did so because it was becoming increasingly clear by then that not everybody was going to support the war. In fact, individuals and groups were going to actively oppose it. Different people did different things to express their opposition. A handful committed suicide in protest, sometimes through self-immolation by fire ("Scenes from a Nightmare," 1985). At home, certain citizens evaded the military draft by fleeing the country and other means. As evidence for this sort of resistance, on the day of his inauguration in 1977 President Carter pardoned as many as 10,000 Vietnam-era draft evaders (Karnow, 1983).

But the most popular form of expression was the PROTEST DEM-ONSTRATION. For those who remember the times, there seems to have been an endless number of mass meetings and marches, and people's participation was no doubt a reflection of their attitudes. As the war got longer, the demonstrations got bigger. For instance, Figure 2 gives an impression of the extent of a certain major demonstration. This particular 1967 protest was said to be the largest in U.S. history at the time (Dougan and Weiss, 1983), and the photo

FIGURE 2
ANTIWAR DEMONSTRATION in the streets of Manhattan on April 15, 1967.
(From Dougan and Weiss, 1983.)

shows that the participants represented a considerable mix of race,
gender, and age.

Taking part in a demonstration is arguably a meaningful indicator
of a person's feelings about something like the war in Vietnam.
Demonstrations then were dangerous to a degree. Arrests were commonplace, and physical clashes with authorities, like the one at the
1968 Democratic National Convention in Chicago, were not infre-
quent. In one case four demonstrators were killed (and others injured) by Ohio National Guard bullets at Kent State University in

May of 1970. Thus, tracing the number of demonstrations or the number of people attending demonstrations could serve as useful indicators of public sentiment over the years concerning the war and the government.

Alternatively, one way to quantify the emergence of political demonstrations is to inquire into media coverage of such events (following the precedent of Mueller, 1988). A survey of the *Readers' Guide to Periodical Literature* revealed that an increasing amount of page space was devoted to entries under the general heading of "Vietnamese war" in the early 1960s. In fact, by 1965 (in Volume 25) a special Vietnam War subheading had to be introduced to help organize a burgeoning set of a certain kind of article. That rubric was:

"Protests, demonstrations, etc, against"

Here, then, is a concise index of journalistic reaction to the demonstrations. If demonstrations were salient on the American scene, they would no doubt receive print coverage.

To compile such an index, one could simply count the number of articles in the *Readers' Guide* that were listed under the "Protests" rubric for every volume from 1965 (Volume 25) to 1974 (Volume 34). After 1974 the "Protests" heading was no longer used, presumably for lack of protests to write about. The pattern of protest articles per year in that era is plotted in Figure 3. Also plotted there are the numbers of U.S. troops in Vietnam over the same years, based on estimates from Karnow (1983). The fit between the two plots is fairly close. As troop involvement increased from 1965 to 1967, so did the amount of attention writers devoted to public protests of one sort or another. The dip in protest articles in 1968—an election year—may reflect the many campaign promises to end the war (Karnow, 1983), and protest pieces tailed off as troop involvement did.

In summary, the protest article index seen in Figure 3 represents good evidence for thinking that the war in Vietnam was unpopular. It was disliked so much that many people were willing to take to the streets to try to oppose it.

SURVEY RESULTS: ANTIGOVERNMENT SENTIMENTS

By the early 1970s a great many Americans were generally fed up with the way things were being run at the national level. The Vietnam conflict was being touted as America's "first military defeat" ("Vietnam in America," 1985). At home, the Watergate break-in was uncovered in 1972 and eventually led to Nixon's resignation from

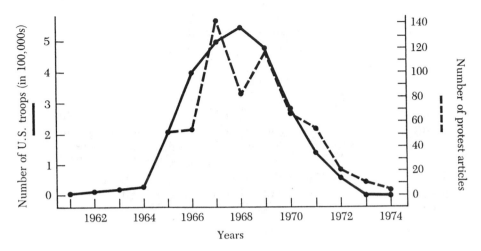

FIGURE 3
ARTICLES ON ANTIWAR PROTESTS listed in the *Readers' Guide* compared
with estimates of U.S. troop involvement in Vietnam.

the presidency in 1974. On top of all this, there was an energy crisis;
there were long lines at filling stations and inflation soared.

How deep was the discontent in the 1970s? One answer to this
question is revealed by changes in public support for military spending. By reviewing a number of national surveys over time, Kriesberg
and Klein (1980) showed that during America's involvement in Vietnam there was a sharp reversal of public opinion about military
spending. As seen in Figure 4, something about that conflict changed
people's minds dramatically, and it was not until 1977 and beyond
that sentiments returned to pre-Vietnam levels.

The war and the military were not the only sources of dissatisfaction on the American scene. Andrews and Withey (1976) reviewed a
great deal of survey data that was based on the question, "How do
you feel about the way our national government is doing [or oper-
ating]?" Respondents could pick one of seven response categories:
"delighted," "pleased," "mostly satisfied," "mixed," "mostly dissatis-
fied," "unhappy," and "terrible." Now, before we go on I want to
establish my view of this "scale" of responses. For coding purposes,
Andrews and Withey treated the "mixed" category as the midpoint
of their measure; they assigned it a score of 4 on a scale from 1 to 7.
I beg to disagree; my intuition tells me that the midpoint is somewhere between "mostly satisfied" and "mixed." This disagreement

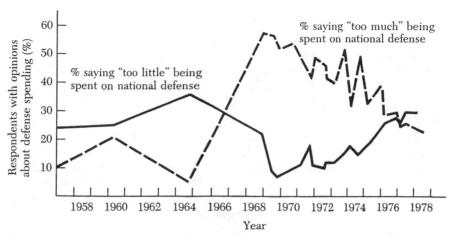

FIGURE 4
TRENDS IN OPINIONS ABOUT DEFENSE SPENDING from 1957 to 1978.
(After Kriesberg and Klein, 1980.)

revives the concerns about intuitive interval scales discussed in Chapter 1.

In any event, in 1972 the majority of respondents picked the gloomier categories to express their feelings about the nation. Fully 74% chose the slots between "mixed" and "terrible," and only the remaining 26% opted for "delighted," "pleased," or "mostly satisfied." By 1974 things were even worse: only 13% picked the three positive categories. By this time, 18% of the American population was "unhappy" about the nation, and 12% felt "terrible" about it. For a population as large as America's, 30% is a lot of upset people.

THE VIETNAM VETERAN AND PUBLIC OPINION: A RETROSPECTIVE ANALYSIS

Another aspect of public opinion about the war in Vietnam was the attention centered on the veterans of that war. For many Americans in the 1960s and 1970s, the image of the veteran took on the proportions of a myth, and an ugly one at that.

For example, many believe that the men who went to Vietnam represent a self-selected sample of misfits and dropouts who would never have fitted into society under any circumstances. Others hold that the experiences in Vietnam turned men into junkies or alienated them from the political mainstream . . . Perhaps the most popular and most damaging stereotype to emerge from the war—one that is perpetuated in movies, TV series, news bulletins, and newspapers—is that Vietnam Veterans are violent and lawless, that they are time bombs programmed to explode at the slightest provocation (Kadushin and Boulanger, 1986).

The point here is not to try to understand the Vietnam-era veterans' wartime experiences or postwar problems. Rather, the aim is to try to sketch changes in the public's opinion of the veteran. Based on the resources at hand, this may be an uneven and incomplete treatment, but there is a sense that some powerful indicators are there.

How would the public's opinion about the veterans form, and why would it change in a positive way? It is possible that the answers, as suggested in the above quote, come partly from what was available in the media. The first focus here will be on popular films of the 1970s and 1980s, a second focus will be on Vietnam documentaries available for home video in that period, and a final view will be of certain events in the nation's capital in the 1980s.

Vietnam vet as cinematic hero: a short filmography. Every film of this period cannot be mentioned, but some highlights are telling. A few of the early commercial films about returned veterans were indeed disturbing. One of these, released in 1972, was titled *Welcome Home, Soldier Boys.* Starring, among others, Joe Don Baker, it told the story of four vets (ex–Green Berets) traveling to the West Coast. They stop in a small town for gas and get into a ruckus with the owner of the station. He takes a shot at them. They take an arsenal of weapons from the trunk of the car and don their old uniforms, commit a gang rape, kill most of the town's inhabitants, and in turn are killed by the local National Guard (cf. Hyams, 1984; Maltin, 1986)! Somewhat more controlled but disturbing in other ways was *Taxi Driver*, released in 1976. Here, Robert De Niro played a lonely, crazed Vietnam vet who is depicted achieving catharsis through violence, or at least through the preparation of an assassination attempt (cf. Halliwell, 1987; Maltin, 1986).

These movies were followed by several other releases in the late 1970s that tried to deal more directly with combat in Vietnam. Kennedy (1987) includes among these *The Boys in Company C*, *The Deer Hunter*, *Coming Home*, and *Apocalypse Now*. However, for Kennedy (1987; and see also Christensen, 1987) a turning point in the genre came in 1982 with Sylvester Stallone's *First Blood*, in which a Vietnam vet fights back after being provoked by a local sheriff. In Kennedy's view, "John Rambo was one of the first cinematic Vietnam veterans who, when faced with adversity, did not become a wanton psychotic killer or a veteran vegetable. When *he* had flashbacks, he went out there and kicked some ass."

According to Kennedy (1987), there were two ramifications to such an approach. First, the film implied that if those guys—the vets—had been given a chance to win in Vietnam, they would have. Second, the Rambo phenomenon is a coupling of the censorious tone of the films of the 1970s with the action-oriented heroes of more recent films (e.g., Chuck Norris, Arnold Schwarzenegger). That is, "Hollywood became eager to tell the story of the *personal* side of the living room war combat." This theme was extended in the 1985 release of *Rambo: First Blood Part II*, in which the hero is sent back to Southeast Asia where he finds and rescues Americans still held prisoner, and was also seen in the 1983 film *Uncommon Valor* (Bayles, 1988). John Rambo's success in convincingly devastating the communists in *First Blood Part II* opens an interesting patriotic possibility: "Hollywood came up with a new twist—while America may have lost the war in Vietnam, it could win it on the movie screen" (Garland, 1987). Finally, for Kennedy, the culmination of the personalizing trend is seen in *Platoon*, released in 1987, which offers "war at its lowest common denominator, its most human." In sum, Americans were finally being shown Vietnam vets in human terms, with the result that they were made to look heroic. This dual theme—surrogate victory and the restoration of a heroic (human) image—has also been remarked on by Bayles (1988). (Of course, film exploitation of vets' wartime experiences could also produce some backlash. I recently saw a small car-window sign that said, "Vietnam was a war. Not a movie. Remember the vet.")

The television war redux: Vietnam videos and the vets. If the reader missed seeing America's television war the first time around, not to worry, because reruns are available. In an article in *Mother Jones*, Ehrenreich (1987) stated that she would be happy to answer foreigners' questions about America, except concerning "Vietnam, which is already available as a movie genre, [and] a videocassette industry." We have just seen what Ehrenreich meant about the movie genre, and she got the part about the videocassette industry correct, too. I have been able to purchase to date well over 40 different Vietnam War documentary videocassettes. These were all offered through magazine ads, direct mail catalogs, and television spots. Videos in this archive are listed in Table II. As it happens, dozens of additional cassettes have appeared since the table was constructed, and there does not seem to be any end of production in sight.

TABLE II
Sampler of Vietnam war documentaries available as home videos

Title	Copyright
Air War in Vietnam	1987 Command Vision Ltd.
Hearts and Minds	1975 Rainbow Pictures 1985 Embassy Home Entertainment
No Substitute for Victory	1987 United American Video
Prelude to Vietnam	1988 Films for the Humanities, Inc.
Television's Vietnam	1984, 1985 Accuracy in Media, Inc.
The Anderson Platoon	1966 Pierre Schoendorffer
The Vietnam War with Walter Cronkite	1985, 1986, 1987 CBS Inc.
Vietnam: A Television History[a]	1985, 1987 WGBH Educational Foundation
Vietnam: A Television History[b]	1985, 1987 WGBH Educational Foundation
Vietnam: Chronicle of a War	1981 CBS Inc. 1984 CBS/FOX Company
Vietnam Experience	1987 Green Mountain Post & Rag Baby Records 1987 MPI Home Video
Vietnam in the Year of the Pig	1968 Turin Film Corporation
Vietnam: Remember	1968 MPI Home Video
Vietnam: Time of the Locust	1986 MPI Home Video
Vietnam: The Secret Agent	1983, 1986 MPI Home Video
Vietnam: The Ten Thousand Day War	1980 TDW Copyright Holding Ltd. 1980 Embassy Home Entertainment
Vietnam: The War at Home	1986 MPI Home Video

[a]The original 13-part, 13-hour, award-winning series aired on PBS.
[b]A truncated, edited, repackaged 7-part, 7-hour version of the original PBS series (above) that was distributed by Time-Life Books.

Of course, it is possible to account for this deluge of commercially available Vietnam War footage in terms of the sheer video explosion of the 1980s, since that is when most of it was released or re-released (see Table II). Still, the marketing (and marketability) of Vietnam War subject matter may go beyond general trends in home entertainment. Watching a video of combat cannot influence anything about the Vietnam War, except the viewer's attitudes toward it or toward those who fought there. It may be that the videos—like feature films noted earlier—give the audience a chance to take the immediate perspective of the individuals involved in the fighting.

This again offers the possibility of "humanizing" the struggle: it may have been a bad war, but at least it was fought by (our) good people.

Such a possibility was suggested in a letter I received along with the first of the cassettes in *The Vietnam War with Walter Cronkite* series. That particular video is entitled "Courage Under Fire," and the letter opened thusly:

Dear Subscriber:

Courage!

That's the subject matter of the videocassette you're holding in your hands.

The courage to cut through a hail of fire in a Medivac chopper on a rescue mission.

The courage to court danger and risk death as a helicopter pilot in the Charley Horse platoon.

The courage to risk your life to save a wounded buddy.

In "Courage Under Fire," you'll see . . . hear . . . and *feel* [ellipses and emphasis in the original] the courage it took to fight in the Vietnam War through some of the most remarkable combat footage ever filmed.

There is no mention of "victory" or "defeat" in this CBS Video Library letter, because that is not the issue in this context. Legitimate documentaries—unlike movies—cannot create surrogate victories; at some level we are presumably past caring about whether the war was won or lost. What is being sold and bought here is not the success or failure of Americans in Vietnam, but their very *struggles*.

Vietnam vet as official hero: some monuments. Americans, in addition to being shown eventually in films and videos that the vets were heroes, were *told* that they were heroes. One of the first major national monuments to the Vietnam-era veterans was the erection and dedication in 1982 of the Vietnam Veterans Memorial (also known as "the Wall"), an imposing granite structure featuring the engraved names of just over 58,000 men and women killed while serving in the military in Vietnam. Set in Washington's Constitution Gardens in the shadow of the Lincoln Memorial, it is accompanied by a flagpole with an American flag, and an 8-foot statue of three infantrymen (Lopes, 1987). (Later it was proposed that a statue of a nurse—a woman—be added to the memorial (Leslie, 1988).) On the occasion of the dedication, President Reagan said that, "On behalf of the nation, let me again thank the Vietnam veterans from the bottom of my heart for their courageous service to America" (Erickson, 1985).

In another part of Washington, at Arlington National Cemetery, Mr. Reagan read on May 28, 1984 a graveside eulogy for the Unknown Soldier of the Vietnam conflict. According to Erickson (1985), early in the address Mr. Reagan said of the hero, "We may not know of this man's life, but we know of his character. We may not know his name, but we know his courage. He is the heart, the spirit, the soul of America." And later in the address Mr. Reagan concluded, "Thank you, dear son. May God cradle you in His loving arms." This is indeed fitting oratory for dead heroes.

Other perspectives on vets. There are other ways to get a sense of the status of the Vietnam vets as heroes in American public opinion today. For instance, it is estimated that between four and five million people visited the Wall in 1986 alone (Lopes, 1987). For another kind of number, you could read a recently published book, *The Navy Cross*, in which are printed the citations of the 483 men awarded that high honor in Vietnam between 1964 and 1973 (Stevens, 1987).

And there are still other indicators of the current popularity and standing of the vets. The *Catalogue of Official Coins and Medals* of the United States Mint (circa 1985 and 1986) offers on pages 6 and 7 a set of nine "Official Medals of the U.S. Mint." Some are more expensive than others, and one simply assumes that the Mint picked what it thought were marketable (popular or noteworthy) persons as subjects for the costly items. Those people and the respective top prices for the medals on which they appear are presented in Table III. It can be seen that the Vietnam vets are right up there with President Reagan, John Wayne, and James Baker (then Secretary of

TABLE III
Subjects and prices of certain medals offered by the United States Mint in 1985 and 1986

Medal subject[a]	Price ($)
Ronald Reagan	16.00
Vietnam Veterans	16.00
John Wayne	16.00
James Baker	16.00
Louis L'Amour	2.25
Joe Louis	2.25
Danny Thomas	2.25
Harry S. Truman	2.25
Roy Wilkins	2.25

[a]The order of the names presented here is the same as that presented in the mint's brochure (n.d.).

the Treasury). Finally, you can, if you want to, get at least one kind of Vietnam veteran credit card. This type of charge card is known as an "affinity" card, and they are available from a variety of sponsors (Bauer, 1987). An organization called Vietnam Veterans of America offers a Visa affinity card package through the Dollar Dry Dock Bank (see Figure 5). There is no annual fee, and the $20 annual membership supports vets with special medical or adjustment problems.

Cashing in on Vietnam (continued). These observations on the commercialization of aspects of the Vietnam experience have been nicely confirmed in a recent *Newsweek* article, "Cashing in on Vietnam" (Hammer, 1989). According to that report, sundry articles capitalizing on Vietnam tie-ins are available, including reproductions of M16 rifles, commemorative rings, cravats, T-shirts, ashtrays, customized medals, posters, bumper stickers, Frisbees, stationery, tote bags, a plastic model of the Memorial statue "Three Fighting Men," and even gravestones made from the same black granite used to build The Wall. The gravestones will go for $2,600 each (Hammer,

FIGURE 5
VIETNAM VET VISA CREDIT CARD held by a representative of the Vietnam Veterans of America.

1989). Further, a new magazine appeared in the spring of 1988: *Vietnam*. Its success is apparently phenomenal. As of the writing of Hammer's 1989 article, circulation had exploded to 250,000 in the first year of publication. Vietnam-era trading cards are also available ("Trade You," 1989).

"Miss Saigon": a musical about Vietnam. As if all of this manufacturing and publishing were not enough, a musical about the final days of the war had a smash opening in London in September 1989. Entitled "Miss Saigon," it tells a story along the lines of "Madame Butterfly" wherein a young Vietnamese girl and a U.S. marine fall in love. Apparently, this show is an instant classic (as the oxymoron goes). The musical drew nearly $8 million in advance sales alone. It is slated for a Broadway performance in 1990 (Kroll, 1989).

Vietnam and current politics. To close this section, it is worth mentioning that a special irony is currently developing with respect to the relationship of Vietnam-era activity on the part of young people then and the standing of those same maturing people in society today. During the 1988 presidential race, there was a terrific media flap over the military service of the Republican vice-presidential figure, Dan Quayle. Quayle's Indiana National Guard service in the late 1960s was tantamount to draft dodging to some journalists (Salholz, 1988). But Quayle was only one of many such baby-boom politicians who faced problems with their pasts, including avoiding the war and smoking marijuana (Kaus and Miller, 1988).

Indeed, it seemed that *whatever* one did during the war presented difficulties for aspiring young politicians. This was brought out nicely in a September 26, 1988 letter to the editor of *Newsweek*, written by one Alexander H. Carver.

For my generation, these are the options: (1) Served in Vietnam. Press response: murderer of innocent civilians. (2) Served in Vietnam but not in combat. Press response: coward for not murdering innocent civilians. (3) Served in the Reserves or the National Guard. Press response: cowardly privileged child who pulled strings to avoid Vietnam. (4) Did not serve in Vietnam, Reserves, or Guard. Press response: see category 3. (5) Fled to Canada, Sweden, etc. Press response: see category 2. Apparently, no member of the Vietnam generation can hope to qualify for public office.

Surely Mr. Carver exaggerates a bit, but his point is well taken that the place of the Vietnam veteran in contemporary politics, at least, is not altogether settled.

Summary. The point is not to overlook the fact that many Vietnam veterans had, and are having, terrible difficulties in dealing with postwar life. For example, of the 5,500 inmates in Michigan's Jackson prison in 1988, fully 1,200 served in Vietnam. This sort of statistic is taken as evidence that "an alarming number [of vets] have committed violent crimes" (Hackett and Zeman, 1988). Further, the reality of posttraumatic stress disorder seems beyond doubt (see Boulanger and Kadushin, 1986). However, despite these real problems, it is possible that the foregoing arguments about positive attitudinal shifts toward the men and women who took part in the Vietnam conflict are correct. The shifts occurred in part because of the factors that were mentioned, but there were other trends in this same period that could also have fostered the recognition of the vet's patriotic standing. A basic trend underway in America at that time was the so-called new patriotism, or patriotic revival, and it is just possible that the reputation of the vets was boosted by this groundswell.

The Patriotic Revival

By the summer of 1979, President Carter was moved to appear on national television to warn of a crisis of American strength, unity, confidence, and spirit. This talk became known as his "malaise speech," and Mr. Carter was on to something.

Americans did feel dispirited about their nation: cynical about its faded grandeur, alarmed by what felt like the beginnings of economic chaos and despairing of prospects of improvement. The notion of even a quiet national contentment and pride seemed quaint, implausible, slightly foolish (Andersen, Attinger, Blaylock, and Taylor, 1984).

But not for long. Figure 6 displays parts of ads by Chrysler Motors that appeared in *Newsweek* magazine on November 18, 1985 (left panel) and September 9, 1986 (right panel). They give an inkling that by the mid-1980s the pride *was* back. It seems that America might have experienced a PATRIOTIC REVIVAL. Other suggestions of this renewed national pride or patriotism come from certain familiar jingles from beer commercials of that period.

> Miller's made the American way,
> born and brewed in the U.S.A.,
> just as proud as the people who are drinking it today,
> Miller's made the American way.

And,

> You bring out the pride
> we all feel inside.
> It's more than just a job you do.
> You make America work and
> this Bud's for you.

FIGURE 6
ADS BY CHRYSLER MOTORS in 1985 and 1986, suggesting a patriotic revival.

Indeed, in certain articles in the print news media during the mid-1980s, the article titles themselves constitute a kind of index of such a patriotic revival. Consider this sampler:

- "America's Upbeat Mood" (*Time:* Andersen et al., 1984).
- "Jingo Bells" (*Rolling Stone:* Loder, 1985).
- "The New Nationalism" (*National Review:* McGlaughlin, 1984).
- "The New Patriotism" (*Harper's:* Lapham, 1984).
- "The New 'Patriotism'" (*World Press Review:* Simonov, 1985).
- "Patriotism is Back in Style" (*U.S. News & World Report:* Witkin, 1984).
- "A Rebirth of American Craftsmanship" (*Industry Week:* Pollock, 1984).
- "Showing the Flag. Rocky, Rambo and the Return of the American Hero" (*Newsweek* [cover blurb]: Goldman, McAlevey, Doherty, McCormick, and Maier, 1985).

The apparent revival of spirit remarked on here was, of course, related to characteristics and events of Ronald Reagan's first 6 years as U.S. president. The release of the American hostages from Iran on the very same day as Reagan's inauguration in 1981 was "the first patriotic lightning-bolt to strike the populace" (McGlaughlin, 1984). Improvements in the economy followed, as did Reagan's much-applauded (if relatively minor) military responses in Grenada and then Libya (Pfaff, 1986). Apparently, the "Vietnam syndrome"—the disinclination to employ military force in situations of foreign conflict—had gone into remission. Apparently, Mr. Reagan was justified when in 1984 the theme of his administration was "Morning in America" (see Drew, 1986; Schell, 1987), and the second-term slogan was "An American Renewal" (Shapiro, DeFrank, Clift, Thomas, and Greenberg, 1985). Indeed, in his farewell address to the nation on January 11, 1989, President Reagan made the point that one of the things he was proudest of in his 8 years in office was "the resurgence of national pride that I called the new patriotism."

But how to *quantify* this alleged patriotic revival? One could turn to certain survey data over this period. For instance, according to a Gallup poll, between 1983 and 1984 there was a sharp upward shift in people's satisfaction with the nation—from 24 to 50% ("Outlook Toward Nation," 1984). However, Rajecki, Halter, Everts, and Féghali (unpublished data) found that this positive change was highly correlated with an improvement in the national economy at the same time, so one cannot be sure whether "satisfaction with the nation" reflected a patriotic revival or an economic recovery. Instead, Rajecki et al. sought other kinds of data to test the idea that patriotism had blossomed during the early 1980s.

Rather than trusting retrospective surveys of people's attitudes, Rajecki et al.—writing in 1989—turned to archives as sources of information about such nationalistic sentiments in the recent and more distant past. They identified several archival bases, two of which will be reviewed here: (1) the covers of all the baseball World Series programs from 1903 to 1987, and (2) a count of the number of American-made "war movies" released annually from 1941 to 1986.

OVERVIEW

The rationale for the use of these archives was that if certain attitudinal developments in America were real, then these would sooner or later be reflected in the mass media, the marketplace, or otherwise in the popular culture. In a recent instance of such a reflection, Pope John Paul II visited the United States in September 1987, and several months earlier a host of papal paraphernalia and products was already on the market. According to one source, items with papal tie-ins were available in myriad forms, such as T-shirts, lawn sprinklers (called "Let Us Spray," and selling for $55.00), videos, comic books, rings, hats and masks, posters, pose-with-the-Pope pix, and Popesicles ("The Selling of the Pope," 1987). Even if one had never previously heard of Pope John Paul II, one could use this bonanza to correctly *infer* his enormous appeal and popularity. Similarly, trends in popular culture could reveal changes in nationalistic attitudes.

WORLD SERIES PROGRAM COVERS

The program covers for all the World Series were reprinted in the "Official 1986 World Series Program." Rajecki et al. obtained this program, and the subsequent one in 1987. The "patriotic content" of the covers was operationalized by the assignment of scores to certain national elements depicted there. For example, a score of 1 was assigned to the depiction of bunting, a score of 2 was assigned to a picture of the American flag, and a score of 3 was given for a picture of an American president. (The highest score of 3 for presidents was justified by Stimson's (1976) analysis that that office is symbolically linked with the very conception of American national government.) As an example, the 1986 program cover shown in Figure 7 displays a flag and some bunting. Next, the authors combined the years of the programs into decades and showed the average patriotic content by decade (Figure 8). The results were quite clear. The highest peak of such content was in the 1940s, the decade that witnessed America's involvement in World War II. This period was one of high patriotic feeling and popular support for the war (cf. Harris, Mitchell, and Schechter, 1984; Kennett, 1985; Meuller, 1973). Thus, Rajecki et al. made a claim for the validity of World Series program covers as a reflection of public opinion. Finally, there is another high peak in the 1980s, which they took to reflect the patriotic revival.

WAR MOVIES

A second archival source treated in the Rajecki et al. report was the film genre called "war movies." The special rationale here was that the public's tolerance (or enthusiasm) for war would be reflected in their willingness to pay to see war or military themes in popular entertainments such as movies. Or, to put it another way, the film industry, sensitive as always to cultural trends, would somehow sense consumers' feelings about military matters and invest in film production accordingly. This notion seems to hold for other industries: the automobile industry shifted to smaller models in the 1970s in response to consumers' concerns about fuel costs.

Rajecki et al. located two filmographies that were devoted entirely

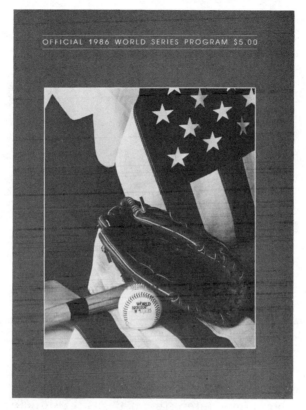

FIGURE 7
WORLD SERIES PROGRAM COVER displaying two types of patriotic content, a flag and bunting.

to war movies, both, coincidentally, having the title *War Movies*. One of these was by Hyams (1984) and the other by Garland (1987). Initially, the two were analyzed separately. Although they presumably covered the same material, these filmographers differed a bit in their tastes. Of the two, Hyams was more open to films made for television, while Garland was more tolerant in admitting service comedies and romances and futuristic treatments such as *Star Wars*. It was thought that a comparison of the two volumes might provide an interesting contrast. However, it turned out that the two collections were not that different after all. When Rajecki et al. counted all the American-made movies in each on an annual basis from 1940, it seems that both authors were sensitive to the same trends in production. The correlation (r), on a yearly basis, between the two

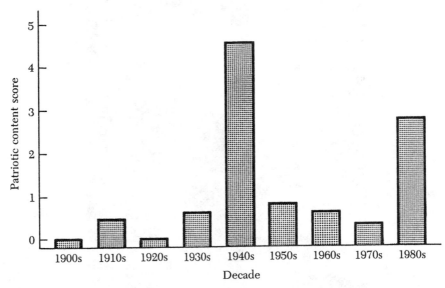

FIGURE 8
AVERAGE PATRIOTIC CONTENT SCORE from World Series program covers
over the decades.

counts was .79, so the annual entries of the two filmographies were
averaged, and those averages are presented in Figure 9.

Figure 9 shows some interesting patterns. First, note the peak of
production in 1943. If you had been a war movie buff in America in
1943, you would have had to go to the flicks at least once in about
every 12 days to take them all in! More to the point, this particular
high rate of production doubtless reflects the patriotic surge during
World War II that was alluded to earlier in the section on World
Series program covers. Hence, concerns about the validity of this
measure seem relieved. Subsequent to the Second World War, interest in war movies declined markedly until the onset, in 1950, of
the 2-year-long Korean War. The early 1950s also saw the development of the Cold War, which continued intermittently—as did the
production of war films—for decades. However, the war in Vietnam
did not seem to have the salutary effect on the production of war
movies seen during earlier conflicts. Instead, this war seems to have
effectively strangled the genre. According to one observer,

one of the first attempts by American film-makers to deal with the effects of
the Vietnam War on Americans, *Limbo* [1972] was ahead of its time. Its title is
an apt description of the place the Vietnam War occupied in the film industry

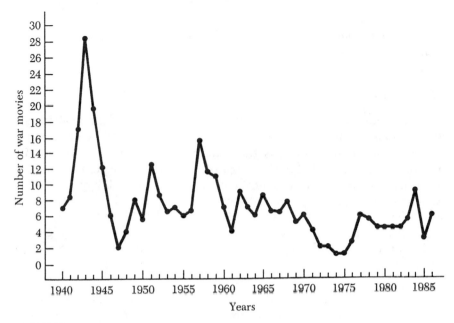

FIGURE 9
AVERAGE NUMBER OF WAR MOVIES released per year, as estimated by counting entries in Garland (1987) and Hyams (1984).

during the early years of the 1970s, for there were no major films about the Vietnam War until the last years of the decade. There were plenty of screenplays about Vietnam making the rounds of Hollywood studios, but no one dared touch the subject (Hyams, 1984).

Like the federal government, the film industry seems to have experienced its own "Vietnam syndrome."

In any event, the period past 1975 witnessed a renaissance in the genre. Figure 9 shows that by the mid-1980s war movie production had climbed back to pre–Vietnam War levels. Why? Well, apparently U.S. audiences by then had become more tolerant of war and military themes in their entertainments. (Rajecki et al. were able to show that the American revival of the war movie genre was not parallel to other trends in filmmaking in the United States or in foreign countries.) Of course, Rajecki et al. concluded that the film pattern, like the pattern for World Series program covers, was yet another manifestation of the patriotic revival.

Obviously, this so-called patriotic revival coincided with the presidency of Ronald Reagan, and he was not shy about taking credit for it, as seen in the above quote from his farewell address. Regardless of whether he really should take credit for the trend, we must acknowledge that the Office of the President *is* powerful, both materially and symbolically.

The Presidency

In previous sections we looked at various kinds of data on attitudes on a national scale, or at least on national issues. Another interesting aspect of national opinion is the public's relation to the president. As noted, one marker for the beginning of the patriotic revival was the release of the American hostages in Iran on the day of President Reagan's first inaugural, and thereafter he seemed to continue to symbolize and inspire the renewal in national pride. Obviously, the president is the country's central and influential figurehead, but it still matters greatly how he is viewed by the citizenry. As Stimson (1976) points out,

if the real power of the presidency is not directly proportional to the most recent Gallup popularity rating, it is not far from it. In an important sense, those who at a given moment "approve" of the president are his real constituency. And the size of that constituency plays a crucial role in the calculations of decision makers in the Washington community—not excluding Embassy Row. Congress, for example, is disposed to give a popular president—even of the opposition party—what he wants. The unpopular president may not even get hearings scheduled on important legislative proposals . . . Presidents of the past and present were vitally linked with children's earliest conceptions of government [and] it is not unreasonable to extrapolate a somewhat weaker symbolic linkage to adults . . . Thus to speak of presidential popularity or approval may well be, for many members of the mass public, to speak as well of the popularity or approval of American national government.

Thus, in this section we will take a look at aspects of the presidency from the perspective of attitudes and public opinion.

PRESIDENTIAL CANDIDATES: TO WHOM DO PERSONAL ATTRIBUTES MATTER?

In presidential politics, why do we, the electorate, vote for whom we vote for? One way to answer this question is to find out what the public focuses on during election-year campaigns. The point here is to discover not what is said by the candidates and their minions but what is on the minds of the voters. Let us pick an election year and find out. For example, in 1980 the Center for Political Studies of the University of Michigan conducted a survey as part of its National Election Study program. For our purposes, a respondent was asked several questions about each of the major candidates: "Is there anything in particular about Mr. Carter that might make you want to vote for him?" ("What is that?") And: "Is there anything in particular about Mr. Carter that might make you want to vote against him?" ("What is that?")

People's responses to such questions were used by Glass (1985) to test a hypothesis about the relationship between level of education and concern for candidates' personal qualities. In particular, are people with more education (college degree or higher) any more or less interested in a nominee's PERSONAL ATTRIBUTES than are those with relatively little education (eighth grade or less)? Actually, two predictions can be made. The first is that highly educated people would be *less* concerned about personal qualities—competence, character, personal attraction—because they would be more interested in issues and policies. On the contrary, it could also be predicted that highly educated people would be *more* concerned about personal attributes, because they are in a position to know that campaign rhetoric and promises fade quickly and it is the person of the president that must deal with the shocks and blows of the office.

Glass (1985) used the National Election Study data from 1980 and from several other election years to find out. Because respondents' answers to the questions detailed earlier were "open-ended," Glass first had to code or categorize them. He employed four categories; responses pertained to either (1) personal attributes, (2) policies, (3) group affiliations, or (4) party affiliations. Next, Glass recognized that level of education would probably be related to the sheer number of things a respondent said, so he adjusted for this possibility by using the proportion of personal attribute references—relative to those in all other categories— given by each person in a sample.

Those percentages are shown in Table IV, where two things are immediately clear. First, the more educated respondents were generally more likely to make reference to personal attributes than were the less educated, at least up to 1976. This outcome supports the latter prediction outlined above. Second, interest in personal attributes has declined since the 1950s. By the 1980s people at the extreme education levels did not differ in their level of expressed interest. It could be worthwhile to speculate why this decline occurred (Glass, alas, did not), but for now it is at least clear that highly educated respondents are not, and never were, any less interested than anyone else in the candidate's personal attributes.

AMERICAN PRESIDENTS: CYCLICAL PUBLIC SUPPORT

Personal attributes aside for the moment, what happens to a winning candidate's popularity after the election? Most of us probably assume that the public's support of American presidents is based

TABLE IV
Percentages of personal attribute references in presidential candidate evaluations, by level of education, from 1952 to 1984

Education level of respondents	YEAR									Row means
	1952	1956	1960	1964	1968	1972	1976	1980	1984	
College or more	68	71	73	55	55	39	60	43	28	55
Some college	61	68	64	46	52	33	57	39	27	50
High school	62	61	58	43	48	34	52	40	25	47
Eighth grade or less	57	49	58	34	40	32	46	41	25	42
Column means	61	60	61	44	48	35	54	41	26	

After Glass (1985).
Note. Values are taken directly from Glass's Table 1. The column and row means are apparently "weighted." That is, it seems likely that they were calculated from samples of different sizes. Therefore, respective means will approximate but will not necessarily equal "unweighted" means calculated directly from the values in a given column or row.

primarily on two factors: (a) political affiliation and (b) the particular achievements or failures experienced by a president. To some degree, these assumptions are warranted, but there are also strong trends in patterns of public support that may be more or less independent of these two particular features. A number of analysts have detected very reliable shifts in public support for presidents, and these swings require a theory that takes into account influences beyond party affiliation and an incumbent's record. There is *something* about the presidency itself that is associated with changes in public opinion. Our introduction to this topic will begin with the work of Stimson (1976), who described a CYCLICAL MODEL OF PUBLIC SUPPORT.

Stimson, who acknowledged the earlier work of Mueller (1973), pointed out that there was considerable regularity in the popularity of presidents over the course of their administrations. Generally, a president assumes the office with a great deal of public support but soon after begins to rapidly lose approval. This decline usually continues to the third or fourth year, when there is an upturn in approval.

Is this really a regular pattern? To demonstrate his impression, Stimson used data collected in Gallup polls. One question that the Gallup people routinely ask of respondents is, "Do you approve or disapprove of the way [the incumbent president] is handling his job as president?" From the raw data Stimson then constructed an index he called the RELATIVE APPROVAL RATING. This index was the percentage that approved as a proportion of those expressing an opinion, one way or the other. For example, if in a given survey 51% of the sample approved and 13% disapproved, the relative approval— 51/(51 + 13)—would be roughly 80%. (Most researchers in this subfield employ the relative approval index, so the reader will have to be careful when comparing their data with the original poll results.)

Using this procedure, Stimson amassed a large amount of information: he used Gallup poll relative approval ratings from Truman's first and second terms, Eisenhower's first and second terms, Kennedy's truncated term, Johnson's only full term, and Nixon's first term. These figures were fed into a computer and compared with a statistical standard for a parabolic function—that is, high initial popularity, followed by a decline, followed by a partial recovery. Figure 10 shows the result of this statistical processing. The dots are the individual relative approval ratings from the presidential data sets, and the curved line is the empirical parabolic curve for those values. It seems that Stimson's (1976) impression regarding cyclical patterns of support for presidents is pretty general after all. In fact, Stimson was moved to what some might see as an unsettling conclusion: "The extraordinary fit of parabolic curves to actual presidential approval leads to the suspicion that presidential approval may almost be wholly

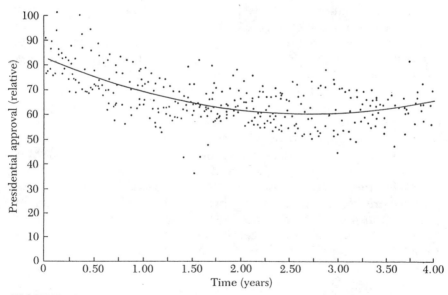

FIGURE 10
AGGREGATED PRESIDENTIAL RELATIVE APPROVAL fit to the parabolic statistical model. (After Stimson, 1976.)

independent of the president's behavior in office, a function largely of inevitable forces associated with time."

Beyond this, Stimson wondered whether factors other than sheer time might strongly enter into approval patterns. He identified three variables that might have some kind of an effect: (1) economic slumps, (2) rally points (as in "rally-'round-the-flag" events such as Nixon's 1972 trip to China), and (3) wars. The influence of these variables was assessed by means of the technique of multiple regression analysis. When approval was regressed on time, the correlation was .644, which is simply another way of expressing the empirical parabolic function seen in Figure 10. Then, in a second equation with rally points and time taken into account, the multiple correlation increased to only .662. Finally, with rally points, slumps and wars, and time all included, the final multiple correlation was .666. Thus, for Stimson, the answer to the question of whether anything other than time matters was, "nothing else matters *much*." (And for another downplay of the "rally-'round-the-flag" effect, see Brody and Shapiro, 1988.)

THE EXPECTATION/DISILLUSION THEORY

How are we to understand the relation between time and presidential approval ratings? According to Stimson, the story goes something like this. By the end of a successful presidential campaign, the winning candidate has promised us the world, and in a simplistic way. Since nothing succeeds like success, the newly elected person gains supporters even beyond his original core. Everyone has EX-PECTATIONS that the president can come through on his promises, so approval is generally high. However, it soon becomes more and more apparent that the expected achievements are not to be forthcoming, and as DISILLUSION increases, approval starts to slip. The decline continues until an "invariant 'bottoming out'" (Stimson's phrase) occurs, followed by a modest recovery as a first-term president actively manipulates opinions, or as the public loses some of its cynicism about a last-term president.

By far the most attention has been focused on the downward phase of presidential popularity. This is understandable, because this phase is the most dramatic and costly to an administration. To put things a bit more formally, Sigelman and Knight (1985) distilled (and I quote) four propositions from Stimson's arguments:

1. Over time, the decline in presidential popularity [approval] should be accompanied by an erosion in public expectations about what the president will achieve.

2. At any point in time, expectations and approval of the president should be closely interrelated.

3. Early in the president's term, the more educated (who are presumed to be more politically sophisticated) should have more realistic, and therefore lower, expectations than the less educated do.

4. As time passes, this gap should narrow considerably as the less educated become more disillusioned.

Points 1 and 2 seem to fall into one kind of package having to do with expectations, and points 3 and 4 seem to fall into a rather different package having to do with sophistication. Let us evaluate these two aspects, starting with points 3 and 4.

Sophistication and approval. Although several researchers have examined the propositions about sophistication (points 3 and 4), these have not received support (cf. Presser and Converse, 1977; Sigelman and Knight, 1983, 1985). Even so, a corollary to the sophistication notion might be that political affiliation could be related to changes in approval, and this notion does have some support. Members of the president's party might have more realistic expectations or ones that are different from members of some other party. This pattern was basically the finding of an analysis of Gallup poll data done by Presser and Converse (1977). They found that during the Johnson administration (a Democrat, 1965–1969) Republicans showed more of a decline in relative approval of the president than did Democrats, whereas in Nixon's first term (a Republican, 1969–1972) Democrats showed more of an approval decline than did Republicans. These relative (party) patterns are shown in Figure 11. These same relative patterns held during Nixon's second, truncated term (1973–1974) and Ford's (a Republican) years (1974–1976).

Expectations and approval. On the other hand, the relationship between expectations and approval (points 1 and 2) has been solidly established. Consider the study of Carter's term by Sigelman and Knight (1983). These researchers used CBS News/*New York Times* poll data. The advantage in using this source was that the CBS/*Times* pollsters not only asked respondents for their approval or disapproval of the president, but also asked (for instance), "Do you think Jimmy Carter will or will not be able to restore trust in the government?" (There were six additional questions concerning expectations about the success of Carter's actions, but these do not add or detract much from the analysis of the "trust in the government" measure, so I will concentrate on it.) The patterns of presidential popularity and ex-

Presidential approval by party identification

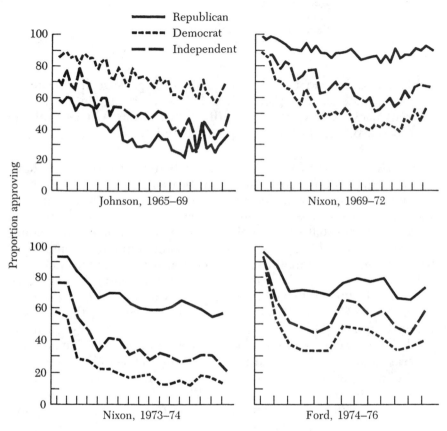

FIGURE 11
PRESIDENTIAL RELATIVE APPROVAL over four separate administrations, by party identification. (After Presser and Converse, 1977.)

pectations over time are shown in Table V, and it is clear that in the 2-year period they both declined steadily and in parallel. Also seen in Table V are the correlations—on a poll-by-poll basis—between approval and expectation. The correlations tell us that people who retained their expectations were the ones willing to express approval. However, while this relationship is strong and clear, keep in mind that it is correlational in nature, and thus cause and effect cannot be assumed. Sigelman and Knight (1983) suggested that the two— approval and expectation—might well be joint outcomes of people's

TABLE V
Presidential relative approval, expectations over time, and the correlation between the two measures

Measure	DATE OF SURVEY					
	4/77	7/77	10/77	1/78	1/79	6/79
Approval of Carter (%)	76.5	78.1	65.8	63.9	49.1	32.8
Expect Carter will restore trust (%)	76.9	69.5	56.8	58.1	38.0	28.9
Correlation coefficient (r)	.758	.788	.773	.625	.772	.809

After Sigelman and Knight (1983).

judgments of the *effectiveness* with which the president was carrying out his duties.

Summary. Broadly speaking, Stimson's findings have stood the test of time, at least for a decade. But what we have not yet seen is an attitudinal analysis of the Reagan presidency. By any standard Ronald Reagan was a very special president, one way or another. In the following section we will take a fairly detailed look at aspects of one of our most recent chief executives.

THE REAGAN PRESIDENCY

From the perspective of attitudes and public opinion, the Reagan presidency was interesting, and even paradoxical. No matter how one felt about Mr. Reagan, it was easy to find someone who would agree. As with most prominent political figures, there was a certain amount of polarization in various segments of society—Reagan was much less popular among women than among men—and reactions to him varied over time. We will begin this section with a look at some of the negative and positive impressions of the Reagan persona.

Negative images. On the negative side, journalists had a field day in bashing the president. Consider the following press selections from U.S. and other sources:

- The situation is worse now than usual. A lazy president [Reagan], out of his depth, is unable to reach accommodation with an unfriendly Congress or to rouse public opinion to his side (Hoggart, 1988).

- The panache of Reagan's style, the bravado of certain acts (Grenada, Libya) should not be allowed to disguise the reality that his "restoration" of American authority was illusory (Vanaik, 1987).

- Reagan was described variously by White House aides and others as "little more than a figurehead president," a "cue-card president," a "detached president" (Alter, 1987).

- [This] forms the basis for Reagan's spectacular "management style" (or "out-to-lunch") defense: he had nothing to do with making and executing policy on one of the central concerns of the administration ("The Smoking Gun Fallacy," 1987).

- A year ago, no longer the dodo of critical estimate, he had been recharacterized as a strong, sure, and popular leader, and the lush Fourth of July celebration at the Statue of Liberty was sort of a third inaugural. Now he has been re-dodoed (Greenfield, 1987).

- It seems that after eight years of Ronald Reagan, the country may have had enough vision for a while (Schneider, 1987).

Of course, one of the most persistent problems Reagan had with his image was his age. First elected at 70, he was the oldest U.S. president. Even during his campaign in 1980, the issue dogged him; he had to promise the electorate to undergo regular tests for senility in the event he was elected (Sheehy, 1987). While there never was anything reported in the press to indicate significant incapacity, Mr. Reagan's maturity did apparently betray him occasionally, at least by innuendo:

- Lieut. Col. Ollie North . . . was conducting his own one-man foreign policy in the White House basement while The Gipper dozed in the Ovaltine Office (Fotheringham, 1987).

- The press has pounced on Reagan's weak Venice performance, dismissing him as "stalled" or worse. The senility theme has made its third appearance, with Reagan's ability to complete his presidency again questioned (Freund, 1987).

The truth to tell, Mr. Reagan seems to have fallen asleep at several top-rank public appearances: once in a meeting with the Pope in 1982, once at a summit in Vienna in 1987, and twice at a summit in Moscow in 1988 (cf. Alter, 1987; Barnes, 1988; Chaze, Walsh, Chesnoff, Mullin, and Plattner, 1987).

The press was especially unforgiving of Reagan during the Iran-Contra affair, and magnified his foibles. Perhaps they could not resist when the president offered up targets such as his exchange with a woman reporter during a press conference.

Q: Mr. President, is it possible that two military officers who are trained to obey orders grabbed power, made major foreign policy moves, didn't tell you when you were briefed every day on intelligence? Or did they think they were doing your bidding?

A: Helen, I don't know. I only know that that's why I've said repeatedly that I want to find out. I want to get to the bottom of this and find out all that has happened and so far I've told all that I know. And you know the truth of the matter is, for quite some long time, all that you knew was what I'd told you.

According to Cockburn (1987), "this is fun to read, particularly if you rearrange it in blank verse, but it suggests a high score on the Alzheimer graph."

Mr. Cockburn may have had a point. By now, Mr. Reagan's speech patterns have come under even closer scrutiny. In 1980 Reagan and Carter engaged in a television debate, and in 1984 there were two separate television debates between Reagan and Mondale. Transcripts of these debates were obtained by Gottschalk, Uliana, and Gilbert (1988), a team of psychiatric and clinical researchers. Gottschalk et al. reasoned that debates were a good source for the study of the spontaneous mental performance of the politicians since there is only so much rehearsal of the debaters' give and take. These authors analyzed the speech patterns of the candidates and noncandidates involved in the debates using a diagnostic tool known as the Gottschalk–Gleser COGNITIVE IMPAIRMENT SCALE.

In using the Cognitive Impairment Scale, the utterances of a person are coded in terms of the nature and quality of her or his statements. By convention, positive scores are assigned to types of utterances known to be associated with problems such as aging, alcoholism, brain tumors, strokes, and body irradiation. For example, impairment would be in evidence if a person showed disorientation in interpersonal references or showed signs of disorganization such as incomplete sentences or repetition of ideas in sequence. On the other hand, negative scores are assigned to utterances that show good brain function, such as congenial and constructive thoughts.

In all three debates, Reagan's cognitive impairment scores were higher than those of his opponents and the noncandidates that were involved. Figure 12 shows the pattern in the first debate with Mondale in 1984. Gottschalk–Gleser scores greater than 2.15 are considered to be quite rare in normal populations (Gottschalk et al., 1988), and it is clear that Reagan exceeded that value on several occasions. Now, *I* am not prepared to argue that speech patterns, in and of themselves, are proof of "cognitive impairment"; I have given too many clumsy answers to questions in lecture to be willing to do that.

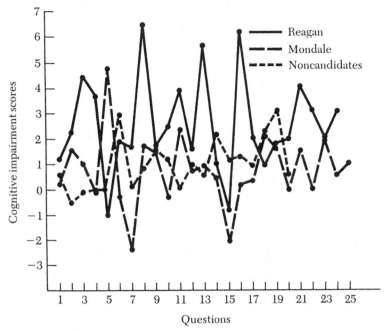

FIGURE 12

"COGNITIVE IMPAIRMENT" SCORES in response to questions in the first Reagan–Mondale debate in 1984. (After Gottschalk et al., 1988.)

However, the Gottschalk–Gleser method does seem to be an objective, reliable way to quantify verbal communication styles and skills. (In the May 1988 issue of *Harper's*, the editors named the Cognitive Impairment Scale "a presidential flubometer.") Even people without scientific training can hear these speech patterns, and such are the things, among others, from which a president's negative image comes.*

Positive images. On the contrary, there were people outside the administration who championed Mr. Reagan, at least occasionally. Consider this sampler of kudos:

*The close scrutiny of presidential candidates continues. A Boston College psychologist named Joe Tecce measured the blink rates of George Bush and Michael Dukakis during a televised debate in October, 1988. The normal rate of blinks per minute (BPM) is said to be 15, but the candidates must have been nervous because Bush was clocked on average at 67 and Dukakis at 75. BPM was related to specific issues. When asked about raising taxes Dukakis's rate jumped to 92, and when the topic was abortion Bush's BPM was 89 (Howard, 1988).

- After all the abuses and indignities he has suffered during the past two years, Ronald Reagan deserves a rousing cheer for his performance in Moscow (Gergen, 1988).

- When it counts—for instance, after the space shuttle disaster in January, 1986—Reagan rises to the occasion: "The future doesn't belong to the faint-hearted; it belongs to the brave." Coming from a victim of both cancer and a would-be assassin, this carries conviction ("Don't Write Him Off," 1987).

- It was clear that the picture of the Russian [Gorbachev] and the American [Reagan] sitting by the cold North Atlantic, contemplating massive cuts in nuclear stockpiles, sent a thrilling vision of a better world through the spirits of millions of human beings all over the globe (Wilkins, 1987).

Reagan and the expectation/disillusion model. In the face of these strong positive and negative personal attributes, is there any chance that Reagan's first term, at least, as president would be viewed by the public in accord with the expectation/disillusion theory we saw earlier? For the first term, the answer is clearly yes. Sigelman and Knight (1985) traced attitudes and expectations about Reagan's performance from January of 1981 to January of 1982, his first year in office. They employed data from CBS News/*New York Times* national telephone surveys. These surveys included the standard Approve question and other questions aimed at expectations. The results of the polls are shown in Table VI. The decline in popularity (relative approval) is pronounced, as is the lessening in certain expectations, and once again the expectation/disillusion theory is supported.

TABLE VI
Presidential relative approval and certain expectations over time (%)

Measure	DATE OF SURVEY				
	1/81	4/81	6/81	9/81	1/82
Approval of Reagan	80.0[a]	80.9	72.1	62.0	56.5
Expect Reagan will reduce unemployment	55.4	47.9	—	—	30.8
Expect Reagan will balance the budget	40.1	38.3	37.0	35.4	25.8

After Sigelman and Knight (1985).
[a]This value was not available in the original Sigelman and Knight (1985) report; it is an estimate from my own calculation of Reagan's relative approval based on Gallup data (see Figure 14).

There is also support for that theory from other polls during the initial Reagan administration. The Gallup Organization asked the Approve question of respondents in 79 separate surveys from January 1981 to December 1984 ("Reagan Popularity 1981–1984," 1984). There was at least one such poll per month during those 4 years. The relative approval rating (approval/ approval + disapproval) was calculated (by me) from each of the polls, and these calculations are presented in Figure 13. Clearly, there is solid support here for the expectation/disillusion theory of public opinion about the president as seen in the roughly U-shaped plot in Figure 13.

An afterthought on the expectation/disillusion theory. Regardless of what happened over the first administration, public opinion during the second Reagan administration does *not* seem to fit the Stimson (1976) statistical model. In the first 2 years of that term, the predicted rapid decline did not occur. The Gallup people conducted 23 surveys between January 1985 and October 1986 ("Reagan's Job Perfor-

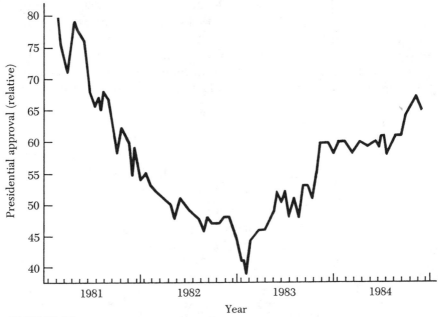

FIGURE 13
PRESIDENTIAL RELATIVE APPROVAL over the 4 years of Reagan's first term. (Adapted from "Reagan Popularity 1981–1984," 1984.)

mance," 1987). From these polls it was possible to calculate relative approval ratings, and their pattern was essentially flat over that period, with an unweighted average of a comfortable 68.4%. The relative approval rating in January 1985 was 68%, and in October 1986 it was 69%, with very little fluctuation in between. Of course, in December 1986 the president's Approval ratings diminished drastically, but the sharp drop in that month is attributable entirely to the revelation in November of the Iran-Contra scandal (see Chapter 2, Figure 1).

Why was there no decline in Reagan's relative approval in 1985 and 1986? Perhaps there are two answers. The first may be that the Stimson model is more applicable to first terms than to second terms of presidencies. The second possibility is that something about the "patriotic revival" in that era cushioned Mr. Reagan against the wear-and-tear of the early years of an administration. After all, Reagan became known as the "Teflon president" (Sheehy, 1987, "The First Four Years," 1985), in the sense that apparent blunders and miscalculations—such as the seemingly pointless loss of U.S. Marines killed in Lebanon in 1983 and the ill-advised visit to the Nazi cemetery in Bitburg, Germany in 1985—simply did not "stick" to him or tarnish his reputation. As noted earlier in this chapter, the Reagan presidency was interesting and paradoxical from the standpoint of attitudes and public opinion; perhaps future research will clarify the apparent contradictions.

Summing Up

We have seen some marked trends in national sentiments from the 1960s to the present. The study of these trends is always interesting (and sometimes entertaining), but continued attention to such fluctuations is also *important* for two reasons. First, in a democracy like the United States, public opinion is a powerful force at the national level. Presidents are made or broken as a result of the feelings of their constituencies, and the course of national actions— such as the involvement in the Vietnam War—can certainly be influenced. Further, people's attitudes about the nation and the national scene reveal a great deal about their subjective experiences. That is, how might the national posture or condition have an impact on a given person's personal satisfactions or frustrations? Thus, these areas are a fruitful meeting ground for the disciplines of social psychology, sociology, and political science.

Postscript

Having said all this about the power and importance of national sentiments in the United States, it perhaps should have come as no surprise in 1989 to see the mid-summer furor over the Supreme Court's ruling on the desecration of the American flag. In effect, the Justices' 5–4 vote indicated that the contemptuous act of burning the flag was protected under the Constitution's free-speech guarantee. Well, people were outraged. The Senate quickly voted 97 to 3 to condemn the ruling, and President George Bush called for a constitutional amendment that would prohibit the flag's physical desecration ("A Fiery Furor," 1989). Pro-flag critics of the court went so far as to publicly burn a judicial robe ("The High Court," 1989). Whatever the long-term consequences of these developments, they point up the fact that protests, patriotism, and political attitudes demand continued study.

Literature Cited

Abelson, R. P. (1972). Are attitudes necessary? In B. T. King & E. McGinnes (Eds.), *Attitudes, conflict, and social change* (pp. 19–32). New York: Academic Press.

Abelson, R. P. (1981). Psychological status of the script concept. *American Psychologist, 36,* 715–729.

Abelson, R. P. (1982). Three modes of attitude–behavior consistency. In M. P. Zanna, E. T. Higgins, & C. P. Herman (Eds.), *Consistency in social behavior* (pp. 131–145). Hillsdale, NJ: Lawrence Erlbaum Associates.

Abelson, R. P., Aronson, E., McGuire, W. J., Newcomb, T. M., Rosenberg, M. J., & Tannenbaum, P. H. (Eds.). (1968). *Theories of cognitive consistency: A sourcebook.* Chicago: Rand McNally.

Abramson, L. Y., Seligman, M. E. P., & Teasdale, J. D. (1978). Learned helplessness in humans: Critique and reformulation. *Journal of Abnormal Psychology, 87,* 49–74.

Ajzen, I. (1982). On behaving in accordance with one's attitudes. In M. P. Zanna, E. T. Higgins, & C. P. Herman (Eds.), *Consistency in social behavior* (pp. 3–15). Hillsdale, NJ: Lawrence Erlbaum Associates.

Ajzen, I. (1988). *Attitudes, personality, and behavior.* Chicago: Dorsey Press.

Ajzen, I., & Fishbein, M. (1970). The prediction of behavior from attitudinal and normative variables. *Journal of Experimental Social Psychology, 6,* 466–487.

Ajzen, I., & Fishbein, M. (1977). Attitude–behavior relations: A theoretical analysis and review of empirical research. *Psychological Bulletin, 84,* 888–918.

Ajzen, I., & Fishbein, M. (1980). *Understanding attitudes and predicting social behavior.* Englewood Cliffs, NJ: Prentice-Hall.

Ajzen, I., Timko, C., & White, J. B. (1982). Self-monitoring and the attitude–behavior relationship. *Journal of Personality and Social Psychology, 42,* 426–435.

Allport, G. W. (1935). Attitudes. In C. A. Murchison (Ed.), *A handbook of social psychology* (Vol. 2, pp. 798–844). Worcester, MA: Clark University Press.

Allport, G. W. (1958). *The nature of prejudice.* Garden City, NY: Doubleday.

Alter, J. (1987, November 23). Has Reagan changed? *Newsweek,* p. 20.

Alter, J., & Fineman, H. (1987, October 5). The fall of Joe Biden. *Newsweek,* p. 28.

Alter, J., Padgett, T., King, P., & Noah, T. (1988, August 29). Who is Dan Quayle? *Newsweek,* pp. 22–23, 25.

Andersen, K., Attinger, J., Blaylock, W., & Taylor, E. (1984, September 24). America's upbeat mood. *Time,* pp. 10–14, 16–17.

Andrews, B., & Juilliard, A. (1986). *Holy mackerel!* New York: E. P. Dutton.

Andrews, F. M., & Withey, S. B. (1976). *Social indicators of well-being.* New York: Plenum.

Andrews, K. H., & Kandel, D. B. (1979). Attitude and behavior: A specification of the contingent consistency hypothesis. *American Sociological Review, 44,* 298–310.

Ansen, D., Murr, A., & Reese, M. (1988, August 15). Wrestling with "Temptation." *Newsweek*, pp. 56–57.

Archer, D., Iritani, B., Kimes, D. D., & Barrios, M. (1983). Face-ism: Five studies of sex differences in facial prominence. *Journal of Personality and Social Psychology, 45,* 725–735.

Aronson, E., & Mills, J. (1959). The effect of severity of initiation on liking for a group. *Journal of Abnormal and Social Psychology, 59,* 177–181.

Asher, H. (1988). *Polling and the public.* Washington, DC: Congressional Quarterly Press.

Attorney General's Commission on Pornography: Final Report. (1986). Washington, D. C.: U.S. Government Printing Office.

Bagozzi, R. P. (1978). The construct validity of the affective, behavioral, and cognitive components of attitude by analysis of covariance structures. *Multivariate Behavioral Research, 13,* 9–13.

Bagozzi, R. P., & Burnkrant, R. E. (1979). Attitude organization and the attitude–behavior relationship. *Journal of Personality and Social Psychology, 37,* 913–929.

Bagozzi, R. P., & Burnkrant, R. E. (1985). Attitude organization and the attitude–behavior relation: A reply to Dillon and Kumar. *Journal of Personality and Social Psychology, 49,* 47–57.

Baltes, M. M., & Baltes, P. B. (Eds.). (1986). *The psychology of control and aging.* Hillsdale, NJ: Lawrence Erlbaum Associates.

Baltes, M. M., & Reisenzein, R. (1986). The social world in long-term care institutions: Psychosocial control toward dependency? In M. M. Baltes & P. B. Baltes (Eds.), *The psychology of control and aging* (pp. 315–343). Hillsdale, NJ: Lawrence Erlbaum Associates.

Barnes, F. (1988, June 20). In the evil empire. *The New Republic,* pp. 8–9.

Baron, R. M., Cowan, G., Ganz, R. L., & McDonald, M. (1974). Interaction of locus of control and type of performance feedback: Considerations of external validity. *Journal of Personality and Social Psychology, 30,* 285–292.

Baron, R. M., & Ganz, R. L. (1972). Effects of locus of control and type of feedback on task performance of lower class black children. *Journal of Personality and Social Psychology, 21,* 124–130.

Barton, E. M., Baltes, M. M., & Orzech, M. J. (1980). Etiology of dependence in older nursing home residents during morning care: The role of staff behavior. *Journal of Personality and Social Psychology, 38,* 423–431.

Bateson, N. (1966). Familiarization, group discussion, and risk-taking. *Journal of Experimental Social Psychology, 2,* 119–129.

Bauer, B. (1987, October 5). Comes the virtuous credit card. *U.S. News and World Report,* p. 82.

Bayles, M. (1988, July 18 & 25). The road to Rambo III. *The New Republic,* pp. 30–35.

Beaman, A. L., Klentz, B., Diener, E., & Svanum, S. (1979). Self-awareness and transgression in children: Two field studies. *Journal of Personality and Social Psychology, 37,* 1835–1846.

Beck, K. H., & Frankel, A. (1981). A conceptualization of threat communications and protective health behavior. *Social Psychology Quarterly, 44,* 204–217.

Bem, D. J. (1967). Self-perception: An alternative interpretation of cognitive dissonance phenomena. *Psychological Review, 74,* 183–200.

Bem, D. J. (1970). *Beliefs, attitudes, and human affairs.* Belmont, CA: Brooks/ Cole.

Bem, D. J. (1972). Self-perception theory. In L. Berkowitz (Ed.), *Advances in experimental social psychology* (Vol. 6, pp. 1–62). New York: Academic Press.

Bem, D. J., Wallach, M. A., & Kogan, N. (1965). Group decision making under risk of aversive consequences. *Journal of Personality and Social Psychology, 1,* 453–460.

Bernberg, R. E. (1952). Socio-psychological factors in industrial morale: I. The prediction of specific indicators. *Journal of Social Psychology, 36,* 73–82.

Berry, G. L. (1988). Multicultural role portrayals on television as a social psychological issue. *Applied Social Psychology Annual, 8,* 118–129.

Berry, M. F. (1986). *Why ERA failed.* Bloomington, IN: Indiana University Press.

Berscheid, E. (1985). Interpersonal attraction. In G. Lindzey & E. Aronson (Eds.), *Handbook of social psychology* (3rd ed., Vol. 2, pp. 413–484). New York: Random House.

Best, R. (1989). *We've all got scars: What boys and girls learn in elementary school.* Bloomington, IN: Indiana University Press.

Beuf, A. (1974). Doctor, lawyer, household drudge. *Journal of Communication, 25,* 142–145.

Biff! Pow! Blowie! (1989, July 24). *U.S. News and World Report,* p. 86.

Birch, L. L., & Marlin, D. W. (1982). I don't like it; I never tried it: Effects of exposure on two-year-old children's food preferences. *Appetite: Journal for Intake Research, 3,* 353–360.

Birnbaum, M. H., & Mellers, B. A. (1979a). One-mediator model of exposure effects is still viable. *Journal of Personality and Social Psychology, 37,* 1090–1096.

Birnbaum, M. H., & Mellers, B. A. (1979b). Stimulus recognition may mediate exposure effects. *Journal of Personality and Social Psychology, 37,* 391–394.

Blumenthal, M. D., Kahn, R. L., Andrews, F. M., & Head, K. (1972). *Justifying violence: Attitudes of American men.* Ann Arbor, MI: Institute for Social Research.

Bogardus, E. S. (1925). Measuring social distances. *Journal of Applied Sociology, 9,* 299–308.

Borgida, E., & Campbell, B. (1982). Belief relevance and attitude–behavior consistency: The moderating role of personal experience. *Journal of Personality and Social Psychology, 42,* 239–247.

Bornstein, R. F. (1989). Exposure and affect: Overview and meta-analysis of research, 1968–1987. *Psychological Bulletin, 106,* 265–289.

Bornstein, R. F., Leone, D. R., & Galley, D. J. (1987). The generalizability of subliminal mere exposure effects: Influence of stimuli perceived without awareness on social behavior. *Journal of Personality and Social Psychology, 53,* 1070–1079.

Boskin, J. (1986). *Sambo*. New York: Oxford University Press.

Boulanger, G., & Kadushin, C. (Eds.). *The Vietnam veteran redefined*. Hillsdale, NJ: Lawrence Erlbaum Associates.

Boyle, G. J. (1984). Effects of viewing a road trauma film on emotional and motivational factors. *Accident Analysis and Prevention, 16*, 383–386.

Bradshaw, J. W. S. (1986). Mere exposure reduces cats' neophobia to unfamiliar food. *Animal Behaviour, 34*, 613–614.

Brandon, H., & Bannister, A. (1987, March–April). The snack that crawls. *International Wildlife*, pp. 16–21.

Breckler, S. J. (1984). Empirical validation of affect, behavior, and cognition as distinct components of attitude. *Journal of Personality and Social Psychology, 47*, 1119–1205.

Brehm, J. (1956). Post-decision changes in the desirability of alternatives. *Journal of Abnormal and Social Psychology, 52*, 384–389.

Brehm, J. W., & Cohen, A. R. (1962). *Explorations in cognitive dissonance*. New York: John Wiley & Sons.

Brewer, M. B. (1979). In-group bias and the minimal intergroup situation: A cognitive–motivational analysis. *Psychological Bulletin, 86*, 307–324.

Brewer, M. B., & Campbell, D. T. (1976). *Ethnocentrism and intergroup attitudes*. Beverly Hills, CA: Sage.

Briere, J., & Malamuth, N. M. (1983). Self-reported likelihood of sexually aggressive behavior: Attitudinal versus sexual explanations. *Journal of Research in Personality, 17*, 315–323.

Briggs, S. R., & Cheek, J. M. (1986). The role of factor analysis in the development and evaluation of personality scales. *Journal of Personality, 54*, 106–148.

Brody, R. A., & Shapiro, C. R. (1988). A reconsideration of the rally phenomenon in public opinion. *Political Behavior Annual, 2*, 77–102.

Burgess, T. D. G., II, & Sales, S. M. (1971). Attitudinal effects of "mere exposure": A reevaluation. *Journal of Experimental Social Psychology, 7*, 461–472.

Burt, R. (1983). *Rock and roll: The movies*. Poole, Dorset: New Orchard Editions.

Byrne, D. (1971). *The attraction paradigm*. New York: Academic Press.

Cacioppo, J. T., & Petty, R. E. (1987). Stalking rudimentary processes of social influence: A psychophysiological approach. In M. P. Zanna, J. M. Olson, & C. P. Herman (Eds.), *Social influence* (pp. 41–74). Hillsdale, NJ: Lawrence Erlbaum Associates.

Calder, B. J., Ross, M., Insko, C. A. (1973). Attitude change and attitude attribution: Effects of incentive, choice, and consequences. *Journal of Personality and Social Psychology, 25*, 84–99.

Campbell, A., Converse, P. E., & Rodgers, W. L. (1976). *The quality of American life*. New York: Russell Sage Foundation.

Campbell, D. T. (1967). Stereotypes and the perception of group differences. *American Psychologist, 22*, 817–829.

Campbell, D. T., & Fiske, D. W. (1959). Convergent and discriminant validity by the multitrait–multimethod matrix. *Psychological Bulletin, 56*, 81–105.

Canary, D. J., & Seibold, D. R. (1984). *Attitudes and behavior*. New York: Praeger.

Cartwright, D. (1971). Risk taking by individuals and groups: An assessment of research employing choice dilemmas. *Journal of Personality and Social Psychology, 20,* 361–378.

Cartwright, D. (1973). Determinants of scientific progress: The case of research on the risky shift. *American Psychologist, 28,* 222–231.

Carver, C. S. (1975). Physical aggression as a function of objective self-awareness and attitudes toward punishment. *Journal of Experimental Social Psychology, 11,* 510–519.

CBS/Broadcast Group. (1988). Program standards for the CBS television network. *Applied Social Psychology Annual, 8,* 132–140.

Chaiken, S., & Baldwin, M. W. (1981). Affective–cognitive consistency and the effect of salient behavioral information on the self-perception of attitudes. *Journal of Personality and Social Psychology, 41,* 1–12.

Chaze, W. L., Walsh, K. T., Chesnoff, R. Z., Mullin, D., & Plattner, A. (1987, June 22). For Reagan, missed opportunities at a soufflé summit. *U.S. News and World Report,* pp. 20–21.

Chin, F. (1973, March). Confessions of a number one son. *Ramparts,* 41–48.

Christensen, T. (1987). *Reel politics.* New York: Basil Blackwell.

Chu, G. C. (1966). Fear arousal, efficacy, and imminency. *Journal of Personality and Social Psychology, 4,* 517–524.

Cialdini, R. B. (1984). *Influence.* New York: Quill.

Clark, R. D., III. (1971). Group-induced shift toward risk. *Psychological Bulletin, 76,* 251–270.

Clymer, A. (1985, March 31). What Americans think now. *New York Times Magazine,* p. 28.

Cockburn, A. (1987, April 4). Afterglow: All the president's men. *The Nation,* pp. 422–423.

Cohen, M. (1988). *The sisterhood: The true story of the women who changed the world.* New York: Simon & Schuster.

Cohen, S., Rothbart, M., & Phillips, S. (1976). Locus of control and the generality of learned helplessness in humans. *Journal of Personality and Social Psychology, 34,* 1049–1056.

Colman, A. M., Best, W. M., & Austen, A. J. (1986). Familiarity and liking: Direct tests of the preference-feedback hypothesis. *Psychological Reports, 58,* 931–938.

Converse, J. M., & Presser, S. (1986). *Survey questions: Handcrafting the standardized questionnaire.* Beverly Hills, CA: Sage.

Cook, D. A., Pallak, M. S., Storms, M. D., & McCaul, K. D. (1977). The effect of forced compliance on attitude change and behavior change. *Personality and Social Psychology Bulletin, 3,* 71–74.

Cooper, J., & Worchel, S. (1970). Role of undesired consequences in arousing cognitive dissonance. *Journal of Personality and Social Psychology, 16,* 199–206.

Cooper, J., Zanna, M. P., & Taves, P. A. (1978). Arousal as a necessary condition for attitude change following induced compliance. *Journal of Personality and Social Psychology, 36,* 1101–1106.

Corey, S. M. (1937). Professed attitudes and actual behavior. *Journal of Educational Psychology, 28,* 271–280.

Cottrell, N. B. (1972). Social facilitation. In C. G. McClintock (Ed.), *Experimental social psychology* (pp. 185–236). New York: Holt, Rinehart & Winston.

Cottrell, N. B., Rajecki, D. W., & Smith, D. U. (1974). The energizing effects of post-decision dissonance upon performance of an irrelevant task. *Journal of Social Psychology, 93,* 81–92.

Cottrell, N. B., Wack, D. L., Sekerak, G., & Rittle, R. H. (1968). Social facilitation of dominant and subordinate responses by the presence of an audience and the mere presence of others. *Journal of Personality and Social Psychology, 9,* 245–250.

Courtney, A. E., & Lockeretz, S. W. (1971). A woman's place: An analysis of the roles portrayed by women in magazine advertisements. *Journal of Marketing Research, 8,* 92–95.

Crandall, C. S. (1985). The liking of foods as a result of exposure: Eating doughnuts in Alaska. *Journal of Social Psychology, 125,* 187–194.

Crandall, R. (1972). Field extension of the frequency–affect findings. *Psychological Reports, 31,* 371–374.

Crandall, V. C., & Crandall, B. W. (1983). Maternal and childhood behaviors as antecedents of internal–external control perceptions in young adulthood. In H. M. Lefcourt (Ed.), *Research with the locus of control construct* (Vol. 2, pp. 53–103). New York: Academic Press.

Crandall, V. C., Katkovsky, W., & Crandall, V. J. (1965). Children's belief in their control of reinforcements in intellectual academic achievement behaviors. *Child Development, 36,* 91–109.

Dabbs, J. M., & Leventhal, H. (1966). Effects of varying the recommendations in a fear-arousing communication. *Journal of Personality and Social Psychology, 4,* 525–531.

Davidson, A. R., & Morrison, D. M. (1983). Predicting contraceptive behavior from attitudes: A comparison of within- versus across-subjects procedures. *Journal of Personality and Social Psychology, 45,* 997–1009.

Davidson, A. R., Yantis, S., Norwood, M., & Montano, D. E. (1985). Amount of information about the attitude object and attitude–behavior consistency. *Journal of Personality and Social Psychology, 49,* 1184–1198.

Davidson, N. (1988). *The failure of feminism.* Buffalo, NY: Prometheus Books.

Dawes, R. M. (1972). *Fundamentals of attitude measurement.* New York: John Wiley & Sons.

Dawes, R. M. (1977). Suppose we measured height with rating scales instead of rulers. *Applied Psychological Measurement, 1,* 267–273.

Dawes, R. M., & Smith, T. L. (1985). Attitude and opinion measurement. In G. Lindzey & E. Aronson (Eds.), *The handbook of social psychology* (3rd ed., Vol. 1, pp. 509–566). New York: Random House.

Deaux, K., & Lewis, L. L. (1984). Structure of gender stereotypes: Interrelationships among components and gender label. *Journal of Personality and Social Psychology, 46,* 991–1004.

DeFleur, M. L., & Westie, F. R. (1958). Verbal attitudes and overt acts: An experiment on the salience of attitudes. *American Sociological Review, 23,* 667–673.

Depue, R. A., & Monroe, S. M. (1978). Learned helplessness in the perspective of the depressive disorders: Conceptual and definitional issues. *Journal of Abnormal Psychology, 87,* 3–20.

Deutscher, I. (1966). Words and deeds: Social science and social policy. *Social Problems, 13,* 235–254.

Dick and Jane as victims. (1975). Princeton, NJ: Women on Words and Images.

Diener, E., & Wallbom, M. (1976). Effects of self-awareness on antinormative behavior. *Journal of Research on Personality, 10,* 107–111.

Dietz, P. E., Harry, B., & Haselwood, R. R. (1986). Detective magazines: Pornography for the sexual sadist? *Journal of Forensic Sciences, 31,* 197–211.

Dillehay, R. C. (1973). On the irrelevance of the classical negative evidence concerning the effect of attitudes on behavior. *American Psychologist, 28,* 887–891.

Dion, K. K. (1972). Physical attractiveness and evaluation of children's transgressions. *Journal of Personality and Social Psychology, 24,* 207–213.

Dion, K. K., Berscheid, E., & Walster (Hatfield), E. (1972). What is beautiful is good. *Journal of Personality and Social Psychology, 24,* 285–290.

Doherty, W. J., & Baldwin, C. (1985). Shifts and stability in locus of control during the 1970s: Divergence of the sexes. *Journal of Personality and Social Psychology, 48,* 1048–1053.

Dollard, J. (1948). Under what conditions do opinions predict behavior? *Public Opinion Quarterly, 12,* 623–632.

Dominick, J. R., & Rauch, G. E. (1972). The image of women in network TV commercials. *Journal of Broadcasting, 16,* 259–265.

Don't write him off. (1987, February). *World Press Review,* p. 13.

Donnerstein, E. (1984). Pornography: Its effect on violence against women. In N. M. Malamuth & E. Donnerstein (Eds.), *Pornography and sexual aggression* (pp. 53–81). New York: Academic Press.

Donovan, D. M., & O'Leary, M. R. (1978). The drinking-related locus of control scale. Reliability, factor structure and validity. *Journal of Studies on Alcohol, 39,* 759–784.

Donovan, D. M., & O'Leary, M. R. (1983). Control orientation, drinking behavior, and alcoholism. In H. M. Lefcourt (Ed.), *Research with the locus of control construct* (Vol. 2, pp. 107–153). New York: Academic Press.

Doob, L. W. (1947). The behavior of attitudes. *Psychological Review, 54,* 135–156.

Dougan, C., & Weiss, S. (Eds.). (1983). *The Vietnam experience: Nineteen sixty-eight.* Boston: Boston Publishing.

Dovidio, J. F., & Gaertner, S. L. (1986a). Prejudice, discrimination, and racism: Historical trends and contemporary approaches. In J. F. Dovidio & S. L. Gaertner (Eds.), *Prejudice, discrimination, and racism* (pp. 1–34). Orlando, FL: Academic Press.

Dovidio, J. F., & Gaertner, S. L. (Eds.). (1986b). *Prejudice, discrimination, and racism.* Orlando, FL: Academic Press.

Drew, E. (1986, November 24). Letter from Washington. *The New Yorker,* pp. 122, 124, 126–132, 135–138.

Drew, E. (1989, June 12). Letter from Washington. *The New Yorker,* pp. 97–102.

Duke, M. P., & Nowicki, S., Jr. (1972). A new measure and social learning model for interpersonal distance. *Journal of Experimental Research in Personality, 6,* 119–132.

Eagly, A. H., & Himmelfarb, S. (1978). Attitudes and opinions. *Annual Review of Psychology, 29,* 517–554.

Eagly, A. H., & Telaak, K. (1972). Width of latitude of acceptance as a determinant of attitude change. *Journal of Personality and Social Psychology, 23,* 388–397.

Ehrenreich, B. (1987, November). Stand by your flag. *Mother Jones,* p. 12.

Eibl-Eibesfeldt, I. (1977). Evolution of destructive aggression. *Aggressive Behavior, 3,* 127–144.

Elkin, R. A., & Leippe, M. R. (1986). Physiological arousal, dissonance, and attitude change: Evidence for a dissonance–arousal link and a "don't remind me" effect. *Journal of Personality and Social Psychology, 51,* 55–65.

Epstein, S. (1979). The stability of behavior: I. On predicting most of the people much of the time. *Journal of Personality and Social Psychology, 37,* 1097–1126.

Erickson, P. E. (1985). *Reagan speaks.* New York: New York University Press.

Ethnic notions. (1982). Berkeley, CA: Berkeley Art Center Association.

Eysenck, H. J. (1984). Sex, violence, and the media: Where do we stand now. In N. E. Malamuth & E. Donnerstein (Eds.), *Pornography and sexual aggression* (pp. 305–318). New York: Academic Press.

Fall, 1988 prime time network TV monitoring. (1989, February–March). *NCTV* [National Coalition on Television Violence] *News,* p. 8.

Fazio, R. H., Chen, J.-M., McDonel, E. C., & Sherman, S. J. (1982). Attitude accessibility, attitude–behavior consistency, and the strength of the object–evaluation association. *Journal of Experimental Social Psychology, 18,* 339–357.

Fazio, R. H., & Williams, C. J. (1986). Attitude accessibility as a moderator of the attitude–perception and attitude–behavior relations: An investigation of the 1984 presidential election. *Journal of Personality and Social Psychology, 51,* 505–514.

Fazio, R. H., & Zanna, M. P. (1978a). Attitudinal qualities relating to the strength of the attitude–behavior relationship. *Journal of Experimental Social Psychology, 14,* 398–408.

Fazio, R. H., & Zanna, M. P. (1978b). On the predictive validity of attitudes: The roles of direct experience and confidence. *Journal of Personality, 46,* 228–243.

Fazio, R. H., & Zanna, M. P. (1981). Direct experience and attitude–behavior consistency. In L. Berkowitz (Ed.), *Advances in experimental social psychology* (Vol. 14, pp. 162–202). New York: Academic Press.

Fazio, R. H., Zanna, M. P., & Cooper, J. (1977). Dissonance and self-perception: An integrative view of each theory's proper domain of application. *Journal of Experimental Social Psychology, 13,* 464–479.

Feldman, S. (1966). *Cognitive consistency.* New York: Academic Press.

Festinger, L. (1957). *A theory of cognitive dissonance.* Stanford, CA: Stanford University Press.

Festinger, L. (1964). Behavioral support for opinion change. *Public Opinion Quarterly, 28,* 404–417.

Festinger, L., & Carlsmith, J. M. (1959). Cognitive consequences of forced compliance. *Journal of Abnormal and Social Psychology, 58,* 203–210.

Festinger, L., Riecken, H. W., & Schacter, S. (1956). *When prophecy fails.* New York: Harper & Row.

A fiery furor over the flag. (1989, August). *Life,* pp. 106–108, 110.

Finckenauer, J. O. (1982). *Scared straight! and the panacea phenomenon.* Englewood Cliffs, NJ: Prentice Hall.

Fink, A., & Kosecoff, J. (1985). *How to conduct surveys: A step-by-step guide.* Beverly Hills, CA: Sage.

The first four years. (1985, January 28). *Newsweek,* pp. 22–23.

Fishbein, M., & Ajzen, I. (1974). Attitudes toward objects as predictors of single and multiple behavioral criteria. *Psychological Review, 81,* 59–74.

Fishbein, M., & Coombs, F. S. (1974). Basis for decision: An attitudinal analysis of voting behavior. *Journal of Applied Social Psychology, 4,* 95–124.

Fiske, S. T., & Taylor, S. E. (1984). *Social cognition.* Reading, MA: Addison-Wesley.

Forsyth, D. R. (1987). *Social psychology.* Monterey, CA: Brooks/Cole.

Fotheringham, A. (1987, July). Church and state sex scandals. *World Press Review,* pp. 32–33.

Fowler, F. J., Jr. (1984). *Survey research methods.* Beverly Hills, CA: Sage.

Fox, J. A., & Tracy, P. E. (1986). *Randomized response: A method for sensitive surveys.* Beverly Hills, CA: Sage.

Franks, V., & Rothblum, E. D. (Eds.). (1983). *The stereotyping of women: Its effects on mental health.* New York: Springer.

Freund, C. P. (1987, July 6). The zeitgeist checklist. *The New Republic,* p. 8.

Frey, J. H. (1983). *Survey research by telephone.* Beverly Hills, CA: Sage.

Friedan, B. (1963). *The feminine mystique.* New York: Norton.

Gaertner, S., & Bickman, L. (1971). A nonreactive indicator of racial discrimination: The wrong number technique. *Journal of Personality and Social Psychology, 20,* 218–222.

Gallant, M. G. (1986). *More fun with Dick and Jane.* New York: Penguin.

Gallup poll accuracy record. (1985, October). *The Gallup Report,* p. 33.

Gantz, W., Gartenberg, H. M., & Rainbow, C. K. (1980). Approaching invisibility: The portrayal of the elderly in magazine advertisements. *Journal of Communication, 30,* 56–60.

Garland, B. (1987). *War movies.* New York: Facts on File Publications.

Gerard, H. B., Green, D., Hoyt, M. & Conolley, E. S. (1973). Influence of affect on exposure-frequency estimates. *Journal of Personality and Social Psychology, 28,* 151–154.

Gerbner, G., Gross, L., Jackson-Beeck, M., Jeffries-Fox, S., & Signorielli, N. (1978). Cultural indicators: Violence profile No. 9. *Journal of Communication, 28,* 176–207.

Gerbner, G., Gross, L., Signorielli, N., & Morgan, M. (1980). Aging with television:

Images on television drama and conceptions of reality. *Journal of Communication, 30,* 37–47.

Gergen, D. R. (1988, June 13). Now for Reagan's encore. *U. S. News and World Report,* p. 73.

Gibbons, F. X. (1978). Sexual standards and reactions to pornography: Enhancing behavioral consistency through self-focused attention. *Journal of Personality and Social Psychology, 36,* 976–987.

Gilbert, G. M. (1951). Stereotype persistence and change among college students. *Journal of Abnormal and Social Psychology, 46,* 245–254.

Glass, D. P. (1985). Evaluating presidential candidates: Who focuses on their personal attributes? *Public Opinion Quarterly, 49,* 517–534.

Glitches, gaffes, and mud from the campaign. (1989, January). *Life,* p. 24.

Go ahead, make our day. (1988, February 22). *The New Republic,* pp. 7–9.

Goffman, E. (1976). *Gender advertisements.* New York: Harper & Row.

Goldman, P., McAlevey, P., Doherty, S., McCormick, J., & Maier, F. (1985, December 23). Rocky and Rambo. *Newsweek,* pp. 58–62.

Goldstein, M. J. (1959). The relationship between coping and avoiding behavior and response to fear-arousing propaganda. *Journal of Abnormal and Social Psychology, 58,* 247–257.

Gottschalk, L. A., Uliana, R., & Gilbert, R. (1988). Presidential candidates and cognitive impairment measured from behavior in campaign debates. *Public Administration Review, 48,* 613–619.

Greenberg, B. S. (1988). Some uncommon television images and the drench hypothesis. *Applied Social Psychology Annual, 8,* 88–102.

Greenfield, M. (1987, January 26). Thisgate? Or is it Thatscam? *Newsweek,* p. 86.

Greenfield, M. (1987, June 29). Politics and mood swings. *Newsweek,* p. 76.

Greenwald, A. G., & Pratkanis, A. R. (1984). The self. In R. S. Wyer, Jr., & T. K. Srull (Eds.), *Handbook of social cognition* (Vol. 3, pp. 129–178). Hillsdale, NJ: Lawrence Erlbaum Associates.

Greenwald, A. G., Pratkanis, A. R., Leippe, M. R., & Baumgardner, M. H. (1986). Under what conditions does theory obstruct research progress? *Psychological Review, 93,* 216–229.

Gregor, T. (1979). Short people. *Natural History, 88,* 14–23.

Gregory, W. L. (1978). Locus of control for positive and negative outcomes. *Journal of Personality and Social Psychology, 36,* 840–849.

Gruder, C. L., Cook, T. D., Hennigan, K. M., Flay, B. R., Alessis, C., & Halamaj, J. (1978). Empirical tests of the absolute sleeper effect predicted from the discounting cue hypothesis. *Journal of Personality and Social Psychology, 36,* 1061–1074.

Grush, J. E., McKeough, K. L., & Ahlering, R. F. (1978). Extrapolating laboratory exposure research to actual political elections. *Journal of Personality and Social Psychology, 36,* 257–270.

Guenzel, P., Berkmans, T. R., & Cannell, D. F. (1983). *General interviewing techniques.* Ann Arbor, MI: Institute for Social Research.

Guralnick, P. (1986). *Sweet soul music.* New York: Harper & Row.

Gurin, P., Gurin, G., Lao, R. C., & Beattie, M. (1969). Internal–external control in the motivational dynamics of Negro youth. *Journal of Social Issues, 25*, 29–53.

Hackett, G., & Zeman, N. (1988, July 4). From patriots to pariahs. *Newsweek*, p. 21.

Hall, E. T. (1966). *The hidden dimension*. Garden City, NJ: Doubleday.

Hallin, D. C. (1986). *The "uncensored war."* New York: Oxford University Press.

Halliwell, L. (1987). *Halliwell's film and video guide* (6th ed.). New York: Charles Scribner's Sons.

Hamm, N. H., Baum, N. R., & Nikels, K. W. (1975). Effects of race and exposure on judgments of interpersonal favorability. *Journal of Experimental Social Psychology, 11*, 14–24.

Hammer, J. (1989, January 16). Cashing in on Vietnam. *Newsweek*, pp. 38–39.

Hardyck, J. A., & Braden, M. (1962). Prophecy fails again: A report of a failure to replicate. *Journal of Abnormal and Social Psychology, 65*, 136–141.

Harris, M. (1985). *Good to eat*. New York: Simon & Schuster.

Harris, M. J., Mitchell, F., & Schechter, S. (1984). *The homefront*. New York: G. P. Putnam's Sons.

Harrison, A. A. (1968). Response competition, frequency, exploratory behavior and liking. *Journal of Personality and Social Psychology, 9*, 363–368.

Harrison, A. A. (1977). Mere exposure. In L. Berkowitz (Ed.), *Advances in experimental social psychology* (Vol. 10, pp. 39–83). New York: Academic Press.

Harvey, J. H., Ickes, W. J., & Kidd, R. F. (1976–1981). *New directions in attribution research* (Vols. 1–3). Hillsdale, NJ: Lawrence Erlbaum Associates.

Harvey, J. H., & Weary, G. (1981). *Perspectives on attributional processes*. Dubuque, IA: William C. Brown.

Hatfield, E., & Sprecher, S. (1986). *Mirror, mirror... The importance of looks in everyday life*. Albany, NY: State University of New York Press.

Hearold, S. (1986). A synthesis of 1043 effects of television on social behavior. In G. Comstock (Ed.), *Public communication and behavior* (Vol. 1, pp. 65–133). Orlando, FL: Academic Press.

Heberlein, T. A., & Black, J. S. (1976). Attitudinal specificity and the prediction of behavior in a field setting. *Journal of Personality and Social Psychology, 33*, 474–479.

Heider, F. (1958). *The psychology of interpersonal relations*. New York: John Wiley & Sons.

Heingartner, A., & Hall, J. V. (1974). Affective consequences in adults and children of repeated exposure to auditory stimuli. *Journal of Personality and Social Psychology, 29*, 719–723.

Hendrick, C., & Seyfried, B. A. (1974). Assessing the validity of laboratory-produced attitude change. *Journal of Personality and Social Psychology, 29*, 865–870.

Henninger, M., & Wyer, R. S. (1976). The recognition and elimination of inconsistencies among syllogistically related beliefs: Some new light on the Socratic effect. *Journal of Personality and Social Psychology, 34*, 680–693.

Herman, C. P., Zanna, M. P., & Higgins, E. T. (Eds.). (1986). *Physical appearance, stigma, and social behavior.* Hillsdale, NJ: Lawrence Erlbaum Associates.

Hewlett, S. A. (1986). *A lesser life.* New York: William Morrow.

Hewstone, M., & Brown, R. (Eds.). (1986). *Contact and conflict in intergroup encounters.* New York: Basil Blackwell.

Higbee, K. L. (1969). Fifteen years of fear arousal: Research on threat appeals: 1953–1968. *Psychological Bulletin, 72,* 426–444.

The High Court stands 5–4 on a burning issue. (1989, July 3). *U.S. News and World Report,* p. 8.

Hine, T. (1986). *Populuxe.* New York: Knopf.

Hiroto, D. S. (1974). Locus of control and learned helplessness. *Journal of Experimental Psychology, 102,* 187–193.

Hiroto, D. S., & Seligman, M. E. P. (1975). Generality of learned helplessness in man. *Journal of Personality and Social Psychology, 31,* 311–327.

Hoff-Wilson, J. (Ed.). (1986). *Rights of passage.* Bloomington, IN: Indiana University Press.

Hoggart, S. (1988, June). "Lights out in power town." *World Press Review,* p. 64.

Hovland, C. I., Harvey, O. J., & Sherif, M. (1957). Assimilation and contrast effects in reactions to communication and attitude change. *Journal of Abnormal and Social Psychology, 55,* 244–252.

Hovland, C. I., Janis, I. L., & Kelley, H. H. (1953). *Communication and persuasion.* New Haven, CT: Yale University Press.

Hovland, C. I., & Pritzker, H. A. (1957). Extent of opinion change as a function of amount of change advocated. *Journal of Abnormal and Social Psychology, 54,* 257–261.

Hovland, C. I., & Weiss, W. (1951). The influence of source credibility on communication effectiveness. *Public Opinion Quarterly, 15,* 635–650.

Howard, L. (1988, October 24). A blink gap. *Newsweek,* p. 7.

Hoyt, G. C., & Stoner, J. A. F. (1968). Leadership and group decisions involving risk. *Journal of Experimental Social Psychology, 4,* 275–284.

Humphrey, R., & Schuman, H. (1984). The portrayal of blacks in magazine advertisements: 1950–1982. *Public Opinion Quarterly, 48,* 551–563.

Hunter, J. E., Schmidt, F. L., & Jackson, G. B. (1982). *Meta-analysis: Cumulating research findings across studies.* Beverly Hills, CA: Sage.

Hyams, J. (1984). *War movies.* New York: Gallery Books.

Ickes, W., & Barnes, R. D. (1977). The role of sex and self-monitoring in unstructured dyadic situations. *Journal of Personality and Social Psychology, 35,* 315–330.

In the labor camps. (1987, November). *World Press Review,* p. 38.

Insko, C. A., Arkoff, A., & Insko, V. M. (1965). Effects of high and low fear-arousing communications upon attitudes toward smoking. *Journal of Experimental Social Psychology, 1,* 256–266.

Isenberg, D. J. (1986). Group polarization: A critical review and meta-analysis. *Journal of Personality and Social Psychology, 50,* 1141–1151.

Jaccard, J., Knox, R., & Brinberg, D. (1979). Prediction of behavior from beliefs: An extension and test of a subjective probability model. *Journal of Personality and Social Psychology, 37,* 1239–1248.

Janis, I. L., & Feshbach, S. (1953). Effects of fear-arousing communications. *Journal of Abnormal and Social Psychology, 48,* 78–92.

Janis, I. L., & Terwilliger, R. F. (1962). An experimental study of psychological resistances to fear-arousing communications. *Journal of Abnormal and Social Psychology, 65,* 403–410.

Jones, E. E., Davis, K. E., & Gergen, K. J. (1961). Role playing variations and their information value for person perception. *Journal of Abnormal and Social Psychology, 63,* 302–310.

Jones, E. E., & Harris, V. A. (1967). The attribution of attitudes. *Journal of Experimental Social Psychology, 3,* 1–24.

Jowett, G. S., & O'Donnell, V. (1986). *Propaganda and persuasion.* Beverly Hills, CA: Sage.

Jussim, L., Coleman, L. M., & Lerch, L. (1987). The nature of stereotypes: A comparison and integration of three theories. *Journal of Personality and Social Psychology, 52,* 536–546.

Kadushin, C., & Boulanger, G. (1986). Introduction. In G. Boulanger & C. Kadushin (Eds.), *The Vietnam veteran redefined* (pp. 1–12). Hillsdale, NJ: Lawrence Erlbaum Associates.

Kalton, G. (1983). *Introduction to survey sampling.* Beverly Hills, CA: Sage.

Kaplan, M. F., & Miller, C. E. (1987). Group decision making and normative versus informational influence: Effects of type of issue and assigned decision rule. *Journal of Personality and Social Psychology, 53,* 306–313.

Kardes, F. R., Sanbonmatsu, D. M., Voss, R. T., & Fazio, R. H. (1986). Self-monitoring and attitude accessibility. *Personality and Social Psychology Bulletin, 12,* 468–474.

Karlins, M., Coffman, T. L., & Walters, G. (1969). On the fading of social stereotypes: Studies in three generations of college students. *Journal of Personality and Social Psychology, 13,* 1–16.

Karnow, S. (1983). *Vietnam.* New York: Viking.

Katz, D. (1960). The functional approach to the study of attitudes. *Public Opinion Quarterly, 24,* 163–204.

Katz, D., & Braly, K. W. (1933). Racial stereotypes of one hundred college students. *Journal of Abnormal and Social Psychology, 28,* 280–290.

Kaus, M., & Miller, M. (1988, August 29). The political specter of Vietnam. *Newsweek,* pp. 27–28.

Keen, S. (1986). *Faces of the enemy.* New York: Harper & Row.

Kelley, H. H. (1971). Attribution in social interaction. In E. E. Jones, D. E. Kanouse, H. H. Kelley, R. E. Nisbett, Valins, S., & B. Weiner (Eds.), *Attribution: Perceiving the causes of behavior* (pp. 1–26). Morristown, NJ: General Learning Press.

Kelly, S., & Mirer, T. W. (1974). The simple act of voting. *American Political Science Review, 68,* 572–591.

Kelman, H. C. (1974). Attitudes are alive and well and gainfully employed in the sphere of action. *American Psychologist, 29,* 310–324.

Kennedy, D. (1987, October). Still fighting after all these years. *Home Viewer,* pp. 18–19.

Kennett, L. (1985). *For the duration . . .* New York: Charles Scribner's Sons.

Keyes, R. (1980). *The height of your life.* Boston: Little, Brown.

Kiesler, C. A., Collins, B. E., & Miller, N. (1969). *Attitude change.* New York: John Wiley & Sons.

Kiesler, C. A., & Pallak, M. S. (1976). Arousal properties of dissonance manipulations. *Psychological Bulletin, 83,* 1014–1025.

Kish, L. (1965). *Survey sampling.* New York: John Wiley & Sons.

Kitayama, S., & Burnstein, E. (1988). Automaticity in conversations: A reexamination of the mindlessness hypothesis. *Journal of Personality and Social Psychology, 54,* 219–224.

Koop, C. E. (1987). Report of the Surgeon General's Workshop on Pornography and Public Health. *American Psychologist, 42,* 944–945.

Koslowsky, M., Pratt, G. L., & Wintrob, R. M. (1976). The application of Guttman scale analysis to physicians' attitudes regarding abortion. *Journal of Applied Psychology, 61,* 301–304.

Kothandapani, V. (1971). Validation of feeling, belief, and intention to act as three components of attitude and their contribution to prediction of contraceptive behavior. *Journal of Personality and Social Psychology, 19,* 321–333.

Kremer, J., Barry, R., & McNally, A. (1986). The misdirected letter and the quasi-questionnaire: Unobtrusive measures of prejudice in Northern Ireland. *Journal of Applied Social Psychology, 16,* 303–309.

Kriesberg, L., & Klein, R. (1980). Changes in public support for U.S. military spending. *Journal of Conflict Resolution, 24,* 79–111.

Kroll, J. (1989, October 2). The chutzpah of "Miss Saigon." *Newsweek,* p. 68–69.

Kunst-Wilson, W. R., & Zajonc, R. B. (1980). Affective discrimination of stimuli that cannot be recognized. *Science, 207,* 557–558.

Kutner, B., Wilkins, C., & Yarrow, P. R. (1952). Verbal attitudes and overt behavior involving racial prejudice. *Journal of Abnormal and Social Psychology, 47,* 649–652.

Labaw, P. J. (1980). *Advanced questionnaire design.* Cambridge, MA: Abt Books.

Lamm, H., & Myers, D. G. (1978). Group-induced polarization of attitudes and behavior. In L. Berkowitz (Ed.), *Advances in experimental social psychology* (Vol. 11, pp. 147–195). New York: Academic Press.

Langer, E. J. (1983). *The psychology of control.* Beverly Hills, CA: Sage.

Langer, E. J., Blank, A., & Chanowitz, B. (1978). The mindlessness of ostensibly thoughtful action: The role of "placebic" information in interpersonal interaction. *Journal of Personality and Social Psychology, 36,* 635–642.

Langer, E. J., Chanowitz, B., & Blank, A. (1985). Mindlessness–mindfulness in perspective: A reply to Valerie Folkes. *Journal of Personality and Social Psychology, 48,* 605–607.

Langer, E. J., & Piper, A. I. (1987). The prevention of mindlessness. *Journal of Personality and Social Psychology, 53*, 280–287.

Langer, E. J., & Rodin, J. (1976). The effects of choice and enhanced personal responsibility for the aged: A field experiment in an institutional setting. *Journal of Personality and Social Psychology, 24*, 26–32.

Lapham, L. H. (1984, June). The new patriotism. *Harper's*, pp. 7–8.

Lapham, L. H., Pollan, M., & Etheridge, E. (1987). *The Harper's Index book*. New York: Henry Holt.

LaPiere, R. T. (1934). Attitudes vs. actions. *Social Forces, 13*, 230–237.

Lefcourt, H. M. (1973). The function of the illusions of control and freedom. *American Psychologist, 28*, 417–425.

Lefcourt, H. M. (1976). *Locus of control: Current trends in theory and research*. Hillsdale, NJ: Lawrence Erlbaum Associates.

Lefcourt, H. M. (1982). *Locus of control: Current trends in theory and research* (2nd ed.). Hillsdale, NJ: Lawrence Erlbaum Associates.

Lefcourt, H. M., Hogg, E., Struthers, S., & Holmes, C. (1975). Causal attributions as a function of locus of control, initial confidence, and performance outcomes. *Journal of Personality and Social Psychology, 32*, 391–397.

Leo, J. (1989, February 20). A pox on all our houses. *U.S. News and World Report*, p. 65.

Leslie, C. (1988, June 27). Viet memorial: Another battle. *Newsweek*, p. 6.

Leventhal, H. (1970). Findings and theory in the study of fear communication. In L. Berkowitz (Ed.), *Advances in experimental social psychology* (Vol. 5, pp. 119–186). New York: Academic Press.

Leventhal, H., Jones, S., & Trembly, G. (1966). Sex differences in attitude and behavior change under conditions of fear and specific instructions. *Journal of Experimental Social Psychology, 2*, 387–399.

Leventhal, H., & Niles, P. (1964). A field experiment on fear arousal with data on the validity of questionnaire measures. *Journal of Personality, 32*, 459–479.

Leventhal, H., Singer, R., & Jones, S. (1965). Effects of fear and specificity of recommendation upon attitudes and behavior. *Journal of Personality and Social Psychology, 2*, 20–29.

Leventhal, H., & Watts, J. C. (1966). Sources of resistance to fear-arousing communications on smoking and lung cancer. *Journal of Personality, 34*, 155–175.

Leventhal, H., Watts, J. C., & Pagano, F. (1967). Effects of fear and instructions on how to cope with danger. *Journal of Personality and Social Psychology, 6*, 313–321.

Lichty, L. W., & Fouhy, E. (1987, April). Television reporting of the Vietnam war; or did Walter Cronkite really lose the war? *The World and I*, pp. 577–590.

Liebert, R. M. & Sprafkin, J. (1988). *The early window: Effects of television on children and youth*. New York: Pergamon Press.

Likert, R. (1932). A technique for the measurement of attitudes. *Archives of Psychology* (Whole No. 140).

Linville, P. W. (1982a). Affective consequences of complexity regarding the self and others. In M. S. Clark & S. Fiske (Eds.), *Affect and cognition* (pp. 79–109). Hillsdale, NJ: Lawrence Erlbaum Associates.

Linville, P. W. (1982b). The complexity–extremity effect and age-based stereotyping. *Journal of Personality and Social Psychology, 42,* 193–211.

Linville, P. W. (1985). Self-complexity and affective extremity: Don't put all your eggs in one cognitive basket. *Social Cognition, 3,* 94–120.

Linville, P. W. (1987). Self-complexity as a cognitive buffer against stress-related illness and depression. *Journal of Personality and Social Psychology, 52,* 663–676.

Linville, P. W., & Jones, E. E. (1980). Polarized appraisal of out-group members. *Journal of Personality and Social Psychology, 38,* 689–703.

Linz, D., Donnerstein, E., & Penrod, S. (1987). The findings and recommendations of the Attorney General's Commission on Pornography. *American Psychologist, 42,* 946–947.

Liska, A. E. (1975). Preface. In A. E. Liska (Ed.), *The consistency controversy* (pp. vii–viii). New York: John Wiley & Sons.

Locksley, A., Borgida, E., Brekke, N., & Hepburn, C. (1980). Sex stereotypes and social judgment. *Journal of Personality and Social Psychology, 39,* 821–831.

Loder, K. (1985, December 19). Jingo bells. *Rolling Stone,* pp. 107, 172–173.

Lopes, S. (1987). *The wall.* New York: Collins Publishers.

Maddux, J. E., & Rogers, R. W. (1983). Protection motivation and self-efficacy: A revised theory of fear appeals and attitude change. *Journal of Experimental Social Psychology, 19,* 469–479.

Malamuth, N. M., & Donnerstein, E. (Eds.). (1984). *Pornography and sexual aggression.* New York: Academic Press.

Malkis, F. S., Kalle, R. F., & Tedeschi, J. T. (1982). Attitudinal politics in the forced compliance situation. *Journal of Social Psychology, 117,* 79–91.

Maltin, L. (Ed.). (1986). *Leonard Maltin's TV movies and video guide* (1987 edition). New York: Signet.

Manis, M., Paskewitz, J., & Cotler, S. (1986). Stereotypes and social judgment. *Journal of Personality and Social Psychology, 50,* 461–473.

Mansbridge, J. J. (1986). *Why we lost the ERA.* Chicago: University of Chicago Press.

Mansson, H. H. (1969). The relation of dissonance reduction to cognitive, perceptual, consummatory, and learning measures of thirst. In P. G. Zimbardo (Ed.), *The cognitive control of motivation* (pp. 78–97). Glenview, IL: Scott, Foresman.

Manstead, A. S. R., Proffitt, C., & Smart, J. L. (1983). Predicting and understanding mothers' infant-feeding intentions and behavior: Testing the theory of reasoned action. *Journal of Personality and Social Psychology, 44,* 657–671.

Marby, M., & Adams, R. (1989, August 14). A long way from "Aunt Jemima." *Newsweek,* pp. 34–35

Martz, L., Clift, E., & Fineman, H. (1989, March 13). Holier than everyone. *Newsweek,* pp. 22–23.

Matlin, M. W. (1970). Response competition as a mediating factor in the frequency–affect relationship. *Journal of Personality and Social Psychology, 16,* 536–552.

Matlin, M. W. (1971). Response competition, recognition, and affect. *Journal of Personality and Social Psychology, 19,* 295–300.

Mazer, R. A. (1987, April 6). Take a kid to a ball game. *Newsweek*, p. 108.

McCauley, C., & Stitt, C. L. (1978). An individual and quantitative measure of stereotypes. *Journal of Personality and Social Psychology, 36,* 929–940.

McCauley, C., Stitt, C. L., Woods, K., & Lipton, D. (1973). Group shift to caution at the race track. *Journal of Experimental Social Psychology, 9,* 80–86.

McConahay, J. B. (1988). Pornography: The symbolic politics of fantasy. *Law and Contemporary Problems, 51,* 31–69.

McDonough, J. (1985). *San Francisco rock.* San Francisco: Chronicle Books.

McGlaughlin, J. (1984, September 21). The new nationalism. *National Review,* p. 24.

McGlaughlin, S. D., Melber, B. D., Billy, J. O. G., Zimmerle, D. M., Winges, L. D., & Johnson, T. R. (1988). *The changing lives of American women.* Chapel Hill, NC: University of North Carolina Press.

McGuire, W. J. (1964). Inducing resistance to persuasion: Some contemporary approaches. In L. Berkowitz (Ed.), *Advances in experimental social psychology* (Vol. 1, pp. 191–229). New York: Academic Press.

McGuire, W. J. (1969). The nature of attitudes and attitude change. In G. Lindzey & E. Aronson (Eds.), *The handbook of social psychology* (2nd ed., Vol. 3, pp. 136–314). Reading, MA: Addison-Wesley.

McGuire, W. J. (1985). Attitudes and attitude change. In G. Lindzey & E. Aronson (Eds.), *Handbook of social psychology* (3rd ed., Vol. 2, pp. 233–346). New York: Random House.

McGuire, W. J. (1986). The myth of massive media impact: Savagings and salvagings. In G. Comstock (Ed.), *Public communication and behavior* (Vol. 1, pp. 173–257). Orlando, FL: Academic Press.

McLoughlin, M. (1988, October 3). America's new civil war. *U.S. News and World Report,* pp. 23–25, 27–30.

McNeil, J. C. (1975). Feminism, femininity, and the television series: A content analysis. *Journal of Broadcasting, 19,* 259–271.

Milgram, S. (1972). The lost-letter technique. In L. Bickman & T. Henchy (Eds.), *Beyond the laboratory: Field research in social psychology* (pp. 245–250). New York: McGraw-Hill.

Miller, A. (1987, April 20). A sizzling food fight. *Newsweek*, p. 56.

Miller, N. (1978). A questionnaire in search of a theory. In L. Berkowitz (Ed.), *Group processes* (pp. 301–312). New York: Academic Press.

Miller, N., & Brewer, M. B. (Eds.). (1984). *Groups in contact.* Orlando, FL: Academic Press.

Miller, S. H. (1975). The content of news photos: Women's and men's roles. *Journalism Quarterly, 52,* 70–75.

Mischel, W., Zeiss, R., & Zeiss, A. (1974). Internal–external control and persistence: Validation and implications of the Stanford preschool internal–external scale. *Journal of Personality and Social Psychology, 29,* 265–278.

Mita, T. H., Dermer, M., & Knight, J. (1977). Reversed facial images and the mere-exposure hypothesis. *Journal of Personality and Social Psychology, 35,* 597–601.

Moore, P. (1983). *Countdown!* London: Rainbird Publishing Group.

Moreland, R. L., & Zajonc, R. B. (1976). A strong test of exposure effects. *Journal of Experimental Social Psychology, 12,* 170–179.

Moreland, R. L., & Zajonc, R. B. (1977). Is stimulus recognition a necessary condition for the occurrence of mere exposure effects? *Journal of Personality and Social Psychology, 35,* 191–199.

Moreland, R. L., & Zajonc, R. B. (1979). Exposure effects may not depend on stimulus recognition. *Journal of Personality and Social Psychology, 37,* 1085–1089.

Morganthau, T., Warner, M. G., Fineman, H., & Calonius, E. (1987, May 18). The sudden fall of Gary Hart. *Newsweek,* pp. 22–26, 28.

Morganthau, T., Willenson, K., Walcott, J., Horrock, N. M., & Lubenow, G. C. (1985, April 15). We're still prisoners of war. *Newsweek,* pp. 34–37.

Moscovici, S., & Zavalloni, M. (1969). The group as a polarizer of attitudes. *Journal of Personality and Social Psychology, 12,* 125–135.

Movie madness. (1988, August 15). *U. S. News and World Report,* p. 16.

Mueller, J. (1971). Trends in popular support for the wars in Korea and Vietnam. *American Political Science Review, 65,* 358–375.

Mueller, J. (1973). *War, presidents and public opinion.* New York: John Wiley & Sons.

Mueller, J. (1988). Trends in political tolerance. *Public Opinion Quarterly, 52,* 1–25.

Myers, D. G., & Arenson, S. J. (1972). Enhancement of dominant risk tendencies in group discussion. *Psychological Reports, 30,* 615–623.

Myers, D. G., & Bishop, G. D. (1970). Discussion effects on racial attitudes. *Science, 169,* 778–779.

Myers, D. G., & Kaplan, M. F. (1976). Group-induced polarization in simulated juries. *Personality and Social Psychology Bulletin, 2,* 63–66.

Myers, D. G., & Lamm, H. (1975). The polarizing effect of group discussion. *American Scientist, 63,* 297–303.

Myers, D. G., & Lamm, H. (1976). The group polarization phenomenon. *Psychological Bulletin, 83,* 602–627.

A *Newsweek* poll: The voice of the Vietnam generation. (1985, April 15). *Newsweek,* p. 37.

Niedenthal, P. M., & Cantor, N. (1986). Affective responses as guides to category-based inferences. *Motivation and Emotion, 10,* 217–232.

Nisbett, R. E., & Wilson, T. D. (1977). Telling more than we can know: Verbal reports on mental processes. *Psychological Review, 84,* 231–259.

Noone, R. W. (1986). *5/5/2000. Ice: The ultimate disaster.* New York: Harmony Books.

Norman, R. (1975). Affective–cognitive consistency, attitudes, conformity, and behavior. *Journal of Personality and Social Psychology, 32,* 83–91.

Notes and comment. (1976, February 2). *The New Yorker,* p. 25.

NRA's violent crime ads hit home. (1988, January). *American Hunter,* pp. 54–55.

O'Donnell, W. J., & O'Donnell, K. J. (1978). Update: Sex-role messages in TV commercials. *Journal of Communication, 28,* 156–158.

O'Malley, M., & Thistlewaite, D. L. (1980). Inference in inconsistency reduction: New evidence on the "Socratic effect." *Journal of Personality and Social Psychology, 39,* 1064–1071.

Orne, M. T. (1962). On the social psychology of the psychological experiment: With particular reference to demand characteristics and their implications. *American Psychologist, 17,* 776–783.

Ornstein, N., Kohut, A., & McCarthy, L. (1988). *The people, the press, & politics.* New York: Addison-Wesley.

Osgood, C. E., & Luria, Z. (1954). A blind analysis of a case of multiple personality using the semantic differential. *Journal of Abnormal and Social Psychology, 49,* 579–591.

Osgood, C. E., Suci, G. J., & Tannenbaum, P. H. (1957). *The measurement of meaning.* Urbana, IL: University of Illinois Press.

Osgood, C. E., & Tannenbaum, P. H. (1955). The principle of contiguity in the prediction of attitude change. *Psychological Review, 62,* 42–55.

Ostrom, T. M. (1969). The relationship between the affective, behavioral, and cognitive components of attitude. *Journal of Experimental Social Psychology, 5,* 12–30.

Outlook toward nation. (1984, January–February). *The Gallup Report,* p. 4.

Overheard. (1989, May 22). *Newsweek,* p. 33.

Ozick, C. (1988, March 28). A critic at large. *The New Yorker,* pp. 99–108.

Paulhus, D. (1982). Individual differences, self-presentation, and cognitive dissonance: Their concurrent operation in forced compliance. *Journal of Personality and Social Psychology, 45,* 838–852.

Perlman, D., & Oskamp, S. (1971). The effects of picture content and exposure frequency on evaluations of negroes and whites. *Journal of Experimental Social Psychology, 7,* 503–514.

Petersen, K. K., & Dutton, J. E. (1975). Centrality, extremity, intensity. Neglected variables in research on attitude–behavior consistency. *Social Forces, 54,* 393–414.

Petty, R. E., & Cacioppo, J. T. (1981). *Attitudes and persuasion: Classic and contemporary approaches.* Dubuque, IA: William C. Brown.

Petty, R. E., & Cacioppo, J. T. (1986). *Communication and persuasion.* New York: Springer-Verlag.

Pfaff, W. (1986, September 15). Oz. *The New Yorker,* pp. 102–106.

Phares, E. J. (1976). *Locus of control in personality.* Morristown, NJ: General Learning Press.

Phillips, D. P. (1986a). The found experiment: A new technique for assessing the impact of mass media violence on real-world aggressive behavior. In G. Comstock (Ed.), *Public communication and behavior* (Vol. 1, pp. 259–307). Orlando, FL: Academic Press.

Phillips, D. P. (1986b). Natural experiments on the effect of mass media violence on fatal aggression: Strengths and weaknesses of a new approach. In L. Berkowitz (Ed.), *Advances in experimental social psychology* (Vol. 19, pp. 207–250). Orlando, FL: Academic Press.

Pleasants, H. (1974). *The great American popular singers.* New York: Simon & Schuster.

Pliner, P. (1982). The effects of mere exposure on liking for edible substances. *Appetite: Journal for Intake Research, 3,* 283–290.

Pollock, J. C. (1984, June 11). A rebirth of American craftsmanship. *Industry Week,* pp. 36–38.

Pratkanis, A. R., Breckler, S. J., & Greenwald, A. G. (Eds.). (1989). *Attitude structure and function.* Hillsdale, NJ: Lawrence Erlbaum Associates.

Pratkanis, A. R., Greenwald, A. G., Leippe, M. R., & Baumgardner, M. H. (1988). In search of reliable persuasion effects. III. The sleeper effect is dead. Long live the sleeper effect. *Journal of Personality and Social Psychology, 54,* 203–218.

Prentice-Dunn, S., & Rogers, R. W. (1980). Effects of deindividuating situational cues and aggressive models on subjective deindividuation and aggression. *Journal of Personality and Social Psychology, 39,* 104–113.

Press, A., McDaniel, A., DeFrank, T. M., Clift, E., McKillop, P., & Hutchinson, S. (1987, November 16). Pot and politics. *Newsweek,* pp. 46–48, 50–52.

Presser, S., & Converse, J. M. (1977). On Stimson's interpretation of decline in presidential popularity. *Public Opinion Quarterly, 40,* 538–541.

Pruitt, D. G., & Teger, A. I. (1969). The risky shift in group betting. *Journal of Experimental Social Psychology, 5,* 115–126.

Pryor, J. B., Gibbons, F. X., Wicklund, R. A., Fazio, R. H., & Hood, R. (1977). Self-focused attention and self-report validity. *Journal of Personality, 45,* 513–527.

Quattrone, G. A. (1985). On the congruity between internal states and action. *Psychological Bulletin, 98,* 3–40.

Quigley-Fernandez, B., & Tedeschi, J. T. (1978). The bogus pipeline as lie detector: Two validity studies. *Journal of Personality and Social Psychology, 36,* 247–256.

Quotes of the week. (1987, October 26). *U.S. News and World Report,* p. 11.

Rabbie, J. M., & Horwitz, M. (1969). Arousal of ingroup–outgroup bias by a chance win or loss. *Journal of Personality and Social Psychology, 13,* 269–277.

Raden, D. (1985). Strength-related attitude dimensions. *Social Psychology Quarterly, 48,* 312–330.

Rajecki, D. W. (1977). Ethological elements in social psychology. In C. Hendrick (Ed.), *Perspectives on social psychology* (pp. 223–303). Hillsdale, NJ: Lawrence Erlbaum Associates.

Rajecki, D. W. (1982). *Attitudes: Themes and advances.* Sunderland, MA: Sinauer Associates.

Rajecki, D. W. (1983). Animal aggression: Implications for human aggression. In R. G. Geen & E. I. Donnerstein (Eds.), *Aggression: Theoretical and empirical reviews* (Vol. 1, pp. 189–211). New York: Academic Press.

Rajecki, D. W. (1985). Predictability and control in relationships: A perspective from animal behavior. In W. Ickes (Ed.), *Compatible and incompatible relationships* (pp. 11–31). New York: Springer-Verlag.

Rajecki, D. W., Halter, C., Everts, A., & Féghali, C. (1989). *Media reflections of the U.S. "Patriotic Revival" in the 1980s.* Unpublished manuscript.

Rajecki, D. W., Ickes, W., & Tanford, S. (1981). Locus of control and reactions to strangers. *Personality and Social Psychology Bulletin, 7,* 282–289.

Rajecki, D. W., & Wolfson, C. (1973). The rating of materials found in the mailbox: Effects of frequency of receipt. *Public Opinion Quarterly, 37,* 110–114.

Range, P. R., Goode, E. E., Borger, G., Baer, D., & Walsh, K. T. (1988, August 15). The amazing shrinking of presidential politics. *U.S. News and World Report,* p. 22.

Reagan popularity 1981–1984. (1984, December). *The Gallup Report,* p. 10.

Reagan, the man. (1987, July). *The Gallup Report,* p. 4.

Reagan's job performance. (1987, July). *The Gallup Report,* p. 3.

Reagan's job performance—overall. (1987, September). *The Gallup Report,* p. 17.

Red meat and red faces. (1988, June 27). *Newsweek,* p. 44.

Reid, P. T. (1979). Racial stereotyping on television: A comparison of both black and white television characters. *Journal of Applied Psychology, 64,* 465–471.

Rhodes, A. (1983). *Propaganda* (Vols. 1 & 2). New York: Chelsea House.

Rhodewalt, F., & Agustsdottir, S. (1986). Effects of self-presentation on the phenomenal self. *Journal of Personality and Social Psychology, 50,* 47–55.

Riggs, M. (Producer and Director). (1987). *Ethnic notions* [Video]. San Francisco: California Newsreel.

Riordan, T. (1989, March 27). Miller guy life. *The New Republic,* pp. 16–17.

Robertson, I. (1977). *Sociology.* New York: Worth.

Robinson, J. P., Athanasiou, R., & Head, K. B. (1969). *Measures of occupational attitudes and occupational characteristics.* Ann Arbor, MI: Institute for Social Research.

Robinson, J. P., Rusk, J. G., & Head, K. B. (1968). *Measures of political attitudes.* Ann Arbor, MI: Institute for Social Research.

Robinson, J. P., & Shaver, P. R. (1973). *Measures of social psychological attitudes* (Revised edition). Ann Arbor, MI: Institute for Social Research.

Rodin, J., & Langer, E. J. (1977). Long-term effects of a control-relevant intervention with institutionalized aged. *Journal of Personality and Social Psychology, 35,* 897–902.

Rogers, R. W. (1975). A protection motivation theory of fear appeals and attitude change. *Journal of Psychology, 91,* 93–114.

Rogers, R. W., & Mewborn, C. R. (1976). Fear appeals and attitude change: Effects of a threat's noxiousness, probability of occurrence, and the efficacy of coping responses. *Journal of Personality and Social Psychology, 34,* 54–61.

Romer, D. (1983). Effects of own attitude on polarization of judgment. *Journal of Personality and Social Psychology, 44,* 273–284.

Rosellini, L. (1988, March 7). Of Rolexes and repentance. *U.S. News and World Report,* pp. 62–63.

Rosellini, L. (1989, May 29). The exquisite imprisonment of Dan Quayle. *U.S. News and World Report,* pp. 26–27.

Rosenberg, M. J. (1960). Cognitive reorganization in response to hypnotic reversal of attitudinal affect. *Journal of Personality, 28,* 39–63.

Rosenfeld, P., Giacalone, R. A., & Tedeschi, J. T. (1983). Cognitive dissonance vs. impression formation. *Journal of Social Psychology, 120,* 203–211.

Rosenfeld, P., Giacalone, R. A., & Tedeschi, J. T. (1984). Cognitive dissonance and impression management explanations for effort justification. *Personality and Social Psychology Bulletin, 10,* 394–401.

Ross, M., & Fletcher, G. J. O. (1985). Attribution and social perception. In G. Lindzey & E. Aronson (Eds.), *Handbook of social psychology* (Vol. 2, pp. 73–122). New York: Random House.

Rothblum, E. D., & Franks, V. (1983). Introduction: Warning! Sex-role stereotypes may be hazardous to your health. In V. Franks & E. D. Rothblum (Eds.), *The stereotyping of women: Its effects on mental health* (pp. 3–29). New York: Springer.

Rotter, J. B. (1966). Generalized expectancies for internal versus external control of reinforcement. *Psychological Monographs, 80*(Whole No. 609).

Rowland, K. F. (1977). Environmental events predicting death for the elderly. *Psychological Bulletin, 81,* 349–372.

Rozin, P., & Fallon, A. E. (1981). The acquisition of likes and dislikes for foods. In J. Solms & R. L. Hall (Eds.), *Criteria of food acceptance: How man chooses what he eats* (pp. 35–48). Zurich: Foster-Verlag AG.

Rozin, P., & Fallon, A. E. (1987). A perspective on disgust. *Psychological Bulletin, 94,* 23–41.

Rozin, P., Fallon, A., & Augustoni-Ziskind, M. (1985). The child's conception of food: The development of contamination sensitivity to "disgusting" substances. *Developmental Psychology, 21,* 1075–1079.

Rozin, P., & Schiller, D. (1980). The nature and acquisition of a preference for chili pepper by humans. *Motivation and Emotion, 4,* 77–101.

Saegert, S., Swap, W., & Zajonc, R. B. (1973). Exposure, context, and interpersonal attraction. *Journal of Personality and Social Psychology, 25,* 234–242.

Salancik, G. R. (1982). Attitude–behavior consistencies as social logics. In M. P. Zanna, E. T. Higgins, & C. P. Herman (Eds.), *Consistency in social behavior* (pp. 51–73). Hillsdale, NJ: Lawrence Erlbaum Associates.

Salholz, E. (1988, August 29). A media "feeding frenzy?" *Newsweek,* p. 26.

Sample, J., & Warland, R. (1973). Attitude and prediction of behavior. *Social Forces, 51,* 292–304.

Sanoff, A. P., & Thornton, J. (1987, July 13). TV's disappearing color line. *U.S. News and World Report,* pp. 56–57.

Sawyer, A. (1981). Repetition, cognitive responses, and persuasion. In R. E. Petty, T. M. Ostrom, & T. C. Brock (Eds.), *Cognitive responses in persuasion* (pp. 237–261). Hillsdale, NJ: Lawrence Erlbaum Associates.

Scenes from a nightmare. (1985, April 15). *Newsweek,* p. 38.

Schaffner, P. E., Wandersman, A., & Stang, D. (1981). Candidate name exposure and voting: Two field studies. *Basic and Applied Social Psychology, 2,* 195–203.

Schell, J. (1987, January 5). A reporter at large. *The New Yorker,* pp. 35–36, 38–39, 42, 47–57, 60–68.

Schneider, W. (1987, December 21). The harumph of the Will. *The New Republic,* pp. 39–41.

Schulz, R. (1976). Effects of control and predictability on the physical and psychological well-being of the institutionalized aged. *Journal of Personality and Social Psychology, 33,* 563–573.

Schulz, R., & Hanusa, B. H. (1978). Long-term effects of control and predictability-enhancing interventions: Findings and ethical issues. *Journal of Personality and Social Psychology, 36,* 1194–1201.

Schuman, H., & Johnson, M. P. (1976). Attitudes and behavior. *Annual Review of Sociology, 2,* 161–207.

Schuman, H., & Kalton, G. (1985). Survey methods. In G. Lindzey & E. Aronson (Eds.), *The handbook of social psychology* (3rd ed., Vol. 1, pp. 635–697). New York: Random House.

Schuman, H., Steeh, C., & Bobo, L. (1985). *Racial attitudes in America.* Cambridge, MA: Harvard University Press.

Schwartz, S. H. (1978). Temporal instability as a moderator of the attitude–behavior relationship. *Journal of Personality and Social Psychology, 36,* 715–724.

Seamon, J. G., Brody, N., & Kauff, D. M. (1983). Affective discrimination of stimuli that are not recognized: Effects of shadowing, masking, and cerebral laterality. *Journal of Experimental Psychology: Learning, Memory, and Cognition, 9,* 544–555.

Seligman, M. E. P. (1975). *Helplessness: On depression, development, and death.* San Francisco: Freeman.

Seligman, M. E. P. (1978). Comment and integration. *Journal of Abnormal Psychology, 87,* 165–179.

Seligman, M. E. P., & Maier, S. M. (1967). Failure to escape traumatic shock. *Journal of Experimental Psychology, 74,* 1–9.

The selling of the Pope, American style. (1987, June 29). *Newsweek,* p. 49.

Seuss, Dr. (1984). *The butter battle book.* New York: Random House.

The sexism watch. (1989, March 27). *U.S. News and World Report,* p. 12.

Sexton, D. E., & Haberman, P. (1974). Women in magazine advertisements. *Journal of Advertising Research, 14,* 41–46.

Shapiro, W., DeFrank, T. M., Clift, E., Thomas, R., & Greenberg, N. F. (1985, January 28). Four more years. *Newsweek,* pp. 18–20.

Shaver, K. G. (1975). *An introduction to attribution processes.* Cambridge, MA: Winthrop.

Shavitt, S. (1989). Operationalizing functional theories of attitude. In A. R. Pratkanis, S. J. Breckler, & A. G. Greenwald (Eds.), *Attitude structure and function* (pp. 311–337). Hillsdale, NJ: Lawrence Erlbaum Associates.

Sheehy, G. (1987, March 30). Reality? Just say no. *The New Republic,* pp. 16–18.

Sherif, C. W., Sherif, M., & Nebergall, R. E. (1965). *Attitude and attitude change: The social judgment–involvement approach.* Philadelphia: Saunders.

Sherif, M., & Hovland, C. I. (1961). *Social judgment.* New Haven: Yale University Press.

Sherif, M., Taub, D., & Hovland, C. I. (1958). Assimilation and contrast effects of an anchoring stimuli on judgments. *Journal of Experimental Psychology, 55,* 150–155.

Sigall, H., & Page, R. (1971). Current stereotypes: A little fading, a little faking. *Journal of Personality and Social Psychology, 18,* 247–255.

Sigelman, L., & Knight, K. (1983). Why does presidential popularity decline? A test of the expectation/disillusion theory. *Public Opinion Quarterly, 47,* 310–324.

Sigelman, L., & Knight, K. (1985). Expectation/disillusion and presidential popularity: The Reagan experience. *Public Opinion Quarterly, 49,* 209–213.

Simonov, V. (1985, December). The "new patriotism." *World Press Review,* p. 50.

Simons, H. W. (1986). *Persuasion* (2nd ed.). New York: Random House.

Sims, J. H., & Baumann, D. D. (1972). The tornado threat: Coping styles of the north and south. *Science, 176,* 1386–1392.

Sinclair, C. (1985). *Blood libels.* New York: Farrar, Straus & Giroux.

Sistrunk, F., & McDavid, J. (1971). Sex variable in conforming behavior. *Journal of Personality and Social Psychology, 17,* 200–217.

Sivacek, J., & Crano, W. D. (1982). Vested interest as a moderator of attitude–behavior consistency. *Journal of Personality and Social Psychology, 43,* 210–221.

Skinner, B. F. (1957). *Verbal behavior.* New York: Appleton-Century-Crofts.

Smedley, J. W., & Bayton, J. A. (1978). Evaluative race–class stereotypes by race and perceived class of subjects. *Journal of Personality and Social Psychology, 36,* 530–535.

The smoking gun fallacy. (1987, July 6). *The New Republic,* pp. 4, 42.

Snyder, M., & Gangestad, S. (1986). On the nature of self-monitoring: Matters of assessment, matters of validity. *Journal of Personality and Social Psychology, 51,* 125–139.

Snyder, M., & Kendzierski, D. (1982). Acting on one's attitudes: Procedures for linking attitude and behavior. *Journal of Experimental Social Psychology, 18,* 165–183.

Snyder, M., & Monson, T. C. (1975). Persons, situations, and the control of social behavior. *Journal of Personality and Social Psychology, 32,* 637–644.

Snyder, M., Simpson, J. A., & Gangestad, S. (1986). Personality and sexual relations. *Journal of Personality and Social Psychology, 51,* 181–190).

Snyder, M., & Swann, W. B., Jr. (1976). When actions reflect attitudes: The politics of impression management. *Journal of Personality and Social Psychology, 34,* 1034–1042.

Snyder, M., & Tanke, E. D. (1976). Behavior and attitude: Some people are more consistent than others. *Journal of Personality, 44,* 501–517.

Snyder, M., Tanke, E. D., & Berscheid, E. (1977). Social perception and interpersonal behavior: On the self-fulfilling nature of social stereotypes. *Journal of Personality and Social Psychology, 35,* 656–666.

Sommer, R. (1969). *Personal space: The behavioral bases of design.* Englewood Cliffs, NJ: Prentice Hall.

Sparks, G. G., & Fehlner, C. L. (1986). Gender comparisons of magazine photographs. *Journal of Communication, 36,* 70–79.

Staats, A. W., & Staats, C. K. (1958). Attitudes established by classical conditioning. *Journal of Abnormal and Social Psychology, 57,* 37–40.

Stallings, P. (1984). *Rock 'n' roll confidential.* Boston: Little, Brown.

Stang, D. J. (1974a). Intuition as artifact in mere exposure studies. *Journal of Personality and Social Psychology, 30,* 647–653.

Stang, D. J. (1974b). Methodological factors in mere exposure research. *Psychological Bulletin, 81*, 1014–1025.

Steiner, G. (1989, February 6). Books. *The New Yorker,* pp. 103–105.

Sternglanz, S. H., & Serbin, L. A. (1974). Sex role stereotyping in children's television programs. *Developmental Psychology, 10*, 710–715.

Stevens, P. D. (1987). *The Navy Cross.* Forest Ranch, CA: Sharp & Dunnigan.

Stimson, J. A. (1976). Public support for American presidents: A cyclical model. *Public Opinion Quarterly, 40*, 1–21.

Stoner, J. A. F. (1961). *A comparison of individual and group decisions involving risk.* Unpublished master's thesis, Massachusetts Institute of Technology, School of Industrial Management, Cambridge, MA.

Storms, M. D., & Nisbett, R. E. (1970). Insomnia and the attribution process. *Journal of Personality and Social Psychology, 16*, 319–328.

Stults, D. M., Messe, L. A., & Kerr, N. L. (1984). Belief discrepant behavior and the bogus pipeline: Impression management or arousal attribution. *Journal of Experimental Social Psychology, 20*, 47–54.

Suedfeld, P., Epstein, Y. M., Buchanan, E., & Landon, P. B. (1971). Effects of set on the "effects of mere exposure." *Journal of Personality and Social Psychology, 17*, 121–123.

The superstars of rock. (1984). New York: Exeter Books.

Surlin, S. H. (1974). Bigotry on air and in life: The Archie Bunker case. *Public Telecommunications Review, 2*, 34–41.

Sutton, S. R., & Eiser, J. R. (1984). The effect of fear-arousing communications on cigarette smoking: An expectancy-value approach. *Journal of Behavioral Medicine, 7*, 13–33.

Tajfel, H., Billig, M. G., Bundy, R. P., & Flament, C. (1971). Social categorization and intergroup behavior. *European Journal of Social Psychology, 1*, 149–178.

Taylor, D. M., & Moghaddam, F. M. (1987). *Theories of intergroup relations.* New York: Praeger.

Teen-age attitudes. (1987, November). *World Press Review,* p. 39.

Teger, A. I., & Pruitt, D. G. (1967). Components of group risk taking. *Journal of Experimental Social Psychology, 3*, 189–205.

Teger, A. I., Pruitt, D. G., St. Jean, R., & Haaland, G. A. (1970). A reexamination of the familiarization hypothesis in group risk taking. *Journal of Experimental Social Psychology, 6*, 346–350.

"Temptation" tempest. (1988, August 22). *U.S. News and World Report,* p. 7.

Tetlock, P. E., & Manstead, A. S. R. (1985). Impression management versus intrapsychic explanations in social psychology: A useful dichotomy? *Psychological Review, 92*, 59–77.

Thorndike, E. L., & Lorge, I. (1944). *The teacher's wordbook of 30,000 words.* New York: Teachers College, Columbia University.

Thurstone, L. L. (1928). Attitudes can be measured. *American Journal of Sociology, 33*, 529–554.

Trade you a Da Nang for a . . . (1989, August 21). *Newsweek,* p. 42.

Turner, J. C., Hogg, M. A., Oakes, P. J., Reicher, S. D., & Wetherell, M. S. (1987). *Rediscovering the social group.* London: Basil Blackwell.

Uehling, M. D., Underwood, A., King, P., & Burgower, B. (1986, September 1). Clinics of deception. *Newsweek*, p. 20.

Vanaik, A. (1987, February). A White House divided. *World Press Review*, pp. 11–12.

Venkatesan, M. & Losco, J. (1975). Women in magazine ads: 1959–1971. *Journal of Advertising Research, 15*, 49–54.

Vidmar, N. (1970). Group composition and the risky shift. *Journal of Experimental Social Psychology, 6*, 153–166.

Vidmar, N., & Rokeach, M. (1974). Archie Bunker's bigotry: A study of selective perception and exposure. *Journal of Communication, 24*, 36–47.

Vietnam in America. (1985, March 31). *New York Times Magazine*, p. 27.

Vinokur, A., & Burnstein, E. (1978). Depolarization of attitudes in groups. *Journal of Personality and Social Psychology, 36*, 872–885.

Vinokur, A., Burnstein, E., Sechrest, L., & Wortman, P. M. (1985). Group decision making by experts: Field study of panels evaluating medical technologies. *Journal of Personality and Social Psychology, 49*, 70–84.

Wallach, M. A., Kogan, N., & Bem, D. J. (1962). Group influence on individual risk taking. *Journal of Abnormal and Social Psychology, 65*, 75–86.

Waller, D. (1985). *The Motown story*. New York: Charles Scribner's Sons.

Wasserman, I. M. (1984). Imitation and suicide: A reexamination of the Werther effect. *American Sociological Review, 49*, 427–436.

Waters, H. F. (1989, August 14). "Rough, tough and rotten." *Newsweek*, p. 64.

Waters, H. F., McKillop, P., Powell, B., & Huck, J. (1988, November 14). Trash TV. *Newsweek*, pp. 72–76, 78.

Watson, R., Smith, V. E., & Wright, L. (1987, May 11). Fresh out of miracles. *Newsweek*, pp. 70–72.

Weick, K. E., & Penner, D. D. (1969). Discrepant membership as an occasion for effective cooperation. *Sociometry, 32*, 413–424.

Weigel, R. H., Loomis, J. W., & Soja, M. J. (1980). Race relations on prime time television. *Journal of Personality and Social Psychology, 39*, 884–893.

Weigel, R. H., & Newman, L. S. (1976). Increasing attitude–behavior correspondence by broadening the scope of the behavioral measure. *Journal of Personality and Social Psychology, 33*, 793–802.

Weigel, R. H., Vernon, D. T. A., & Tognacci, L. N. (1974). Specificity of the attitude as a determinant of attitude–behavior congruence. *Journal of Personality and Social Psychology, 30*, 724–728.

Weinraub, M., & Brown, L. M. (1983). The development of sex-role stereotypes in children: Crushing realities. In V. Franks & E. D. Rothblum (Eds.), *The stereotyping of women: Its effects on mental health* (pp. 30–58). New York: Springer.

Welch, R. L., Huston-Stein, A., Wright, J. C., & Plehal, R. (1979). Subtle sex-role cues in children's commercials. *Journal of Communication, 29*, 202–209.

Wham! Pow! Bam! (1988, June 13). *U.S. News and World Report*, p. 71.

White, C. B., & Janson, P. (1986). Helplessness in institutional settings: Adaptation or iatrogenic disease? In M. M. Baltes & P. B. Baltes (Eds.), *The psychology of control and aging* (pp. 297–313). Hillsdale, NJ: Lawrence Erlbaum Associates.

Wicker, A. W. (1969). Attitudes versus actions: The relationship of verbal and overt behavioral responses to attitude objects. *Journal of Social Issues, 25*, 41–78.

Wilkins, R. (1987, December). Bringing up the bomb. *Mother Jones*, p. 56.

Wilson, W. R. (1979). Feeling more than we can know: Exposure effects without learning. *Journal of Personality and Social Psychology, 37*, 811–821.

Witkin, G. (1984, July 9). Patriotism is back in style. *U.S. News and World Report*, pp. 58–59.

Wolf, F. M. (1986). *Meta-analysis: Quantitative methods for research synthesis.* Beverly Hills, CA: Sage.

Wood, W. (1982). Retrieval of attitude-relevant information from memory: Effects on susceptibility to persuasion and on intrinsic motivation. *Journal of Personality and Social Psychology, 42*, 798–810.

Word, C. O., Zanna, M. P., & Cooper, J. (1974). The nonverbal mediation of self-fulfilling prophecies in interracial interaction. *Journal of Experimental Social Psychology, 10*, 109–120.

Wrightsman, L. S. (1969). Wallace supporters and adherence to "law and order." *Journal of Personality and Social Psychology, 13*, 17–22.

Wu, C., & Shaffer, D. (1987). Susceptibility to persuasive appeals as a function of source credibility and prior experience with the attitude object. *Journal of Personality and Social Psychology, 52*, 677–688.

Wyer, R. S. (1974). Some implications of the "Socratic effect" for alternative models of cognitive consistency. *Journal of Personality, 42*, 399–419.

Zajonc, R. B. (1968). Attitudinal effects of mere repeated exposure. *Journal of Personality and Social Psychology Monograph Supplement, 9*(2, Part 2), 1–27.

Zajonc, R. B. (1980). Feeling and thinking: Preferences need no inferences. *American Psychologist, 35*, 151–175.

Zajonc, R. B. (1984). On the primacy of affect. *American Psychologist, 39*, 117–123.

Zajonc, R. B., Markus, H., & Wilson, W. R. (1974). Exposure effects and associative learning. *Journal of Experimental Social Psychology, 10*, 248–263.

Zajonc, R. B., & Nieuwenhuyse, B. (1964). Relationship between word frequency and recognition: Perceptual process or response bias? *Journal of Experimental Psychology, 67*, 276–285.

Zajonc, R. B., & Rajecki, D. W. (1969). Exposure and affect: A field experiment. *Psychonomic Science, 17*, 216–217.

Zanna, M. P., & Cooper, J. (1974). Dissonance and the pill: An attribution approach to studying the arousal properties of dissonance. *Journal of Personality and Social Psychology, 29*, 703–709.

Zanna, M. P., & Cooper, J. (1976). Dissonance and the attribution process. In J. H. Harvey, W. J. Ickes, & R. F. Kidd (Eds.), *New directions in attribution research* (Vol. 1, pp. 199–217). Hillsdale, NJ: Lawrence Erlbaum Associates.

Zanna, M. P., & Fazio, R. H. (1982). The attitude–behavior relation: Moving toward a third generation of research. In M. P. Zanna, E. T. Higgins, & C. P. Herman

(Eds.), *Consistency in social behavior* (pp. 283–301). Hillsdale, NJ: Lawrence Erlbaum Associates.

Zanna, M. P., Higgins, E. T., & Herman, C. P. (Eds.). (1982). *Consistency in social behavior.* Hillsdale, NJ: Lawrence Erlbaum Associates.

Zanna, M. P., Olson, J. M., & Fazio, R. H. (1980). Attitude–behavior consistency: An individual difference perspective. *Journal of Personality and Social Psychology, 38,* 432–440.

Zanna, M. P., & Pack, S. J. (1975). On the self-fulfilling nature of apparent sex differences in behavior. *Journal of Experimental Social Psychology, 11,* 583–591.

Zimbardo, P. G., Cohen, A., Weisenberg, M., Dworkin, L., & Firestone, I. (1969). The control of experimental pain. In P. G. Zimbardo (Ed.), *The cognitive control of motivation* (pp. 100–122). Glenview, IL: Scott, Foresman.

Zuckerman, M. (1986). On the meaning and implications of facial prominence. *Journal of Nonverbal Behavior, 10,* 215–229.

Zuckerman, M., & Reis, H. T. (1978). Comparison of three models for predicting altruistic behavior. *Journal of Personality and Social Psychology, 36,* 498–510.

Credits

Sources are identified where the material occurs. Full citations appear in Literature Cited.

Figure 1–1: Courtesy of N. W. Ayer, Inc.

Table 1–IV: From *The Quality of American Life: Perceptions, Evaluations, and Satisfactions* by Angus Campbell, Philip E. Converse, and Willard L. Rodgers. © 1976 by Russell Sage Foundation. By permission of Russell Sage Foundation.

Table 1–V: Courtesy of the Times Mirror Center for the People and the Press.

Figure 2–4: © 1988 by Nick Ut, courtesy of Wide World Photos.

Figure 4–5: Courtesy of Anthony Bannister.

Figure 5–2: Courtesy of the *Michigan Daily*.

Figure 6–1: Redrawn with permission of authors and publisher after: Myers, D. G., & Arenson, S. J. Enhancement of dominant risk tendencies in group discussion. *Psychological Reports*, 1972, 30, 615–623, Figure 1.

Figure 6–3: From Myers & Kaplan, *Personality and Social Psychology Bulletin*, Vol. 2, pp. 63–66. © 1976 by Society for Personality and Social Psychology. Redrawn by permission of Sage Publications, Inc.

Figure 7–4: *Journal of Social Psychology*, Vol. 93, p. 90 (1974). Reprinted with permission of the Helen Dwight Reid Educational Foundation. Published by Heldref Publications, 4000 Albemarle St., N.W., Washington, D.C. 20016. © 1974.

Figures 7–5 and 7–6: From "The control of experimental pain" by P. G. Zimbardo, A. Cohen, M. Weisenberg, L. Dworkin, & I. Firestone. In *The cognitive control of motivation* (pp. 112, 115) edited by P. G. Zimbardo, 1969, Glenview, IL: Scott, Foresman and Company. Reprinted by permission of P. G. Zimbardo.

Figure 8–3: © 1974 by Henry Pleasants. Reprinted by permission of Simon & Schuster, Inc.

Table 8–V: From Brewer & Campbell, *Ethnocentrism and Intergroup Attitudes*. © 1976 by Sage Publications, Inc. Reprinted by permission of Sage Publications, Inc.

Figure 9–1: From Hovland & Weiss, *Public Opinion Quarterly*, Vol. 15, pp. 635–650. © 1951 by Princeton University Press.

Figure 9–11: From *Social Influence* (Figure 2.2) by M. P. Zanna, J. M. Olson, & C. P. Herman, 1987, Hillsdale, NJ: Lawrence Erlbaum Associates. © Lawrence Erlbaum Associates. Adapted by permission.

Figure 9–12: Courtesy of the National Rifle Association of America.

Index

La maison sur la plage

GEORGIA BOCKOVEN

La maison sur la plage

Traduit de l'américain
par Vassoula Galangau

Titre original américain:
THE BEACH HOUSE

PREMIÈRE PARTIE

Mai

1

Julia tira de sa poche la clé du chalet.

Avant d'entrer, elle contempla un instant l'intérieur. La clarté pourpre du couchant pénétrait dans le vestibule par une lamelle manquante du store. La poussière dansait dans le rayon de lumière, alors que tout le reste semblait figé dans une longue expectative.

Elle pensait trouver la maison dans le même état d'abandon que le jardin. Mais ce n'était pas le cas. On eût dit que Ken et elle y avaient passé le week-end précédent. Son sweater traînait sur la chaise où elle l'avait laissé des mois auparavant, le livre de Ken reposait, ouvert, sur la table basse.

Ce soir-là, un doux soir de septembre, lui revint en mémoire. Ils étaient repartis à contrecœur, après un séjour inoubliable sur fond de musique foraine, de promenades romantiques sur la plage, de projets d'avenir mirifiques. Résolus à fonder une famille, ils s'étaient aimés sans aucune protection pour la première fois depuis le début de leur mariage.

Tous les ans, ils revenaient au chalet à partir de septembre, quand la foule des touristes désertait Santa Cruz et que les petites villes des environs étaient rendues à leur population locale, leurs artistes et leurs musiciens.

Et ce fameux soir, en attendant de revenir le vendredi suivant, ils étaient simplement montés en voiture pour prendre la route. Maintenant, certaines nuits, Julia se couchait en se demandant pourquoi le destin en avait décidé autrement. Mais aucune réponse ne jaillissait tandis qu'elle naviguait sur les flots noirs et glacés de la solitude.

Incapable de méditer plus longtemps sur les tristes épaves du passé, elle entra, puis referma la porte. L'absence de Ken lui tomba dessus d'un seul coup. Il lui faudrait du temps pour s'habituer à l'idée que venir ici sans lui ne constituait pas une faute. Ken adorait le chalet. Il était son refuge, son havre de paix, son ermitage de prédilection ; et du coup il semblait en faire partie au même titre que les murs et les fondations. Julia avait tâché de se convaincre qu'elle serait plus forte que les souvenirs mais, en ce lieu, elle ressentait davantage sa faiblesse. À trente-deux ans, elle avait toute la vie devant elle. Une vie entière sans Ken… Et lui, qui était si passionné, aurait été furieux de la voir dans cet état pitoyable à se demander sans cesse si elle parviendrait à lui survivre.

Elle suspendit le sweater dans la penderie de l'entrée, referma le livre et le rangea, avant de passer dans la cuisine pour se servir un grand verre d'eau fraîche. La fenêtre, la seule dont ils n'avaient pas fermé le volet, donnait sur la mer. Ils avaient tant de fois admiré le panorama des vagues déferlantes, les envols d'oiseaux, les ébats d'otaries dans l'écume blanche. D'ailleurs, les jumelles, indispensables à l'observation de l'océan, trônaient à proximité.

Le chalet, qui avait plus d'un siècle, se dressait sur une falaise nichée au cœur d'une large plaine et jouissait d'une vue imprenable de la côte ouest jusqu'à la baie de Monterey. Il appartenait à un îlot de vingt-cinq habitations : un hameau classé, ceint d'une forêt de pins, de séquoias et d'eucalyptus. Le paradis terrestre, selon Ken. Il avait même déclaré un jour qu'il vieillirait ici, avec Julia.

Un rêve de trop !

Peut-être que si, dès la fin de ses études, il n'avait pas connu une fulgurante ascension sociale en tant que fondateur d'une grosse compagnie informatique… Peut-être que s'ils n'avaient pas été aussi amoureux l'un de l'autre… Mais à quoi bon ! Songeuse, Julia porta le verre d'eau à ses lèvres.

Une fourmi solitaire errait sur le lambris de bois. Du coin de l'œil, Julia en aperçut une deuxième. Et puis bientôt, une troisième. Elles avançaient en file indienne avant de disparaître dans une fissure. Des fourmis! Voilà huit ans qu'ils possédaient le chalet et il n'y avait jamais eu le moindre insecte. Julia se mit à ouvrir les placards. Sur le point de conclure que l'invasion venait tout juste de commencer, elle découvrit deux rangées de fourmis autour d'une boîte de sucre entrouverte. Celles aux mandibules pleines montaient, les autres descendaient.

Soudain abattue, Julia regarda l'armée de soldats minuscules poursuivre tranquillement son pillage. Un étrange désespoir la submergea. Pourquoi maintenant? Pourquoi les maudites bestioles avaient-elles choisi ce moment-là pour attaquer? Elle eut envie de tourner les talons, de fuir la maison… Or, fuir ne correspondait pas à sa personnalité. Elle avait toujours fait face. C'était du reste la raison pour laquelle elle était venue préparer le chalet, au lieu de confier cette tâche à quelqu'un d'autre.

Ken aurait été fier d'elle.

Une demi-heure plus tard, elle finit de récurer les placards et le plan de travail, convaincue qu'elle avait gagné la bataille. Armée de l'éponge, elle faisait couler de l'eau dans l'évier rutilant, quand le robinet lui resta entre les doigts. Elle s'efforça de revisser la pièce de chrome pour arrêter le jet. En vain!

Comment s'y prendre? Elle n'en avait pas la moindre idée.

Avec deux frères et un père bricoleurs impénitents, un mari qui s'estimait expert en rafistolages de toutes sortes, elle n'avait jamais eu à mettre la main à la pâte. Pas même à conduire sa voiture chez le garagiste… Comment espérait-elle devenir indépendante si elle était incapable de venir à bout d'un robinet cassé?

L'indépendance, elle ne l'avait jamais cherchée, au contraire. Elle aimait la façon dont Ken la couvait. Et elle se laissait faire, alors qu'elle aurait parfois pu agir autrement. D'ailleurs, elle passait souvent pour une femme gâtée par un mari trop indulgent. Ses amies la jalousaient, et tous s'accordaient à penser qu'elle n'était rien sans Ken. Cependant, maintenant, elle n'avait plus le choix.

Hagarde, elle mesura l'étendue des dégâts. L'eau jaillissait dans l'évier. Eh bien ! elle songerait à la conquête de son indépendance plus tard... Pour l'instant, mieux valait rechercher la solution la plus pratique. Celle-ci avait pour nom Andrew, le propriétaire du chalet voisin.

La porte s'ouvrit sur un homme grand, aux cheveux prématurément gris et aux yeux bleu sombre. Julia ne l'avait jamais vu. Un torchon de cuisine drapait son épaule gauche, et il tenait un verre de vin à la main droite. Une expression de curiosité se peignit sur son visage.

— Oui ?

Un appétissant fumet d'épices, de poivre et d'oignons rappela à Julia qu'elle n'avait rien mangé de la journée.

— Je voudrais voir Andrew, s'il vous plaît.

Un sourire resplendissant transfigura le visage mince de l'homme.

— Andrew n'est pas là. La dernière fois que j'ai reçu de ses nouvelles, il s'apprêtait à quitter Hawaï pour la Nouvelle-Zélande, à bord de son bateau.

— Ah... bon ?

Première nouvelle ! Certes, de temps à autre, il avait la bougeotte : il menaçait alors de tout abandonner et de partir faire le tour du monde. Julia ne l'avait jamais pris au sérieux. Il était trop sédentaire. Et il tenait à son métier.

— Et qui... garde la crèche ?

— La personne qui l'a achetée.

Julia considéra son vis-à-vis, bouche bée. Huit mois seulement s'étaient écoulés, et on eût dit que des années étaient passées !

— Andrew a vendu son affaire ?

— Il a signé la veille de Noël. Le Jour de l'an, aux aurores, il a levé l'ancre.

— Vous êtes un de ses amis ?

— Depuis le collège, oui. Nous appartenions à la même association d'étudiants. Andrew m'a loué son cottage.

— Ah...

Les surprises se succédaient. Julia adressa un sourire perplexe à l'inconnu. Tant pis pour le robinet. On n'importune pas un étranger avec des histoires de plomberie au moment de passer à table.

— Désolée d'avoir interrompu votre dîner. Si vous avez des nouvelles d'Andrew, passez-lui mon bonjour.

— Vous êtes ?

— Julia Huntington.

— C'est vous Julia ?

Il posa le verre et lui tendit la main.

— Enchanté. Andrew m'a recommandé de m'occuper de vous.

— Pourquoi donc ?

— Comme ça… Par amitié.

— Je vois…

Andrew et Ken s'entendaient comme larrons en foire depuis quinze ans. Ken décédé, quoi de plus normal qu'Andrew se sente obligé de veiller sur sa veuve ? Julia accorda un regard circonspect au voisin, qui toussota.

— Bon, d'accord ! Andrew m'a fait un prix, à la condition expresse que je vous vienne en aide si un problème se présente au chalet.

Julia lui serra la main.

— Je n'ai pas saisi votre nom.

— Eric. Eric Lawson.

— Monsieur Lawson, j'ai le regret de vous annoncer que votre logeur a vu juste. J'ai besoin de vos lumières. Avez-vous quelques connaissances en plomberie ?

— Quelques-unes.

Elle sortit le robinet de chrome et le lui remit.

— Qu'en pensez-vous ?

Il ne l'étudia pas plus d'une seconde.

— Poubelle !

— Très bien. Et comment ferme-t-on l'eau ?

— Le robinet d'arrêt ne fonctionne pas ?

— Je n'en sais rien.

— Un instant. Je jette un coup d'œil à ma sauce et j'arrive.

— Cela ne sera pas nécessaire. Dites-moi seulement où se trouve… Monsieur Lawson !

Il avait disparu.

Julia jeta un coup d'œil dans le salon, notant au passage les transformations accomplies par le locataire d'Andrew. Un bureau surmonté d'un ordinateur avait remplacé la vieille chaise longue. Des volumes reliés cuir encombraient les étagères habituellement vides. Quelques livres de poche s'y trouvaient également, preuve que le nouvel occupant du cottage n'était pas un de ces snobs qui se délectent uniquement de littérature intellectuelle. La table basse croulait sous une pile de revues médicales.

— Prête ?

La voix d'Eric la fit se retourner.

— Navrée de vous priver de votre dîner mais…

— Il attendra ! coupa-t-il. Ce ne sera pas long.

Son assurance, sa confiance absolue rappelaient Ken.

— Andrew m'a dit que vous viviez à Atherton, reprit Eric, tandis qu'ils se dirigeaient vers le chalet de Julia. Cette ville vous plaît ?

Il meublait le silence de son mieux. Julia avait envie d'évoquer Atherton comme de se pendre.

— Euh… oui. Beaucoup.

— Mon beau-père a sa clinique là-bas. Quand j'ai terminé mon internat, il voulait que je m'associe avec lui. J'ai refusé. J'aimais mieux le style de Sacramento.

Jusqu'à présent, personne de la connaissance de Julia n'avait crédité Sacramento d'un style quelconque.

— Vous êtes médecin ? demanda-t-elle.

— Oui. Mais je ne pratique pas actuellement.

— Vous êtes en congé d'études ? voulut-elle savoir, sa curiosité piquée au vif.

Il poussa le portail et ils s'engagèrent dans l'allée, qui sinuait dans une anarchique explosion de verdure.

— En quelque sorte. Voudriez-vous que je remonte vos stores demain ?

— Je ne suis pas complètement handicapée, vous savez !

— Bien sûr. N'oubliez pas, toutefois, que j'ai donné ma parole à Andrew en échange d'un rabais du loyer. J'ai toujours pris mes obligations au sérieux.

Elle ouvrit la porte du chalet.

— Andrew est bien gentil, mais il a eu tort de vous coller un tel fardeau sur le dos.

— Je vous en prie, Julia ! Cela ne me dérange pas. D'ailleurs, il n'est pas le seul à m'avoir parlé de vous.

— Ah bon ?

— Vous êtes la chouchoute du village.

— Merci. Ça fait plaisir.

Évidemment, le compliment ne lui était pas adressé directement. Elle bénéficiait de la sympathie que les gens avaient éprouvée pour Ken. Et l'affection qu'ils lui témoignaient représentait une garantie de bonheur sans faille, un merveilleux cadeau puisqu'elle avait été toute sa vie une jeune femme timide.

Arrivé dans la cuisine, Eric se précipita vers l'évier où l'eau jaillissait toujours. Il s'accroupit, ouvrit le placard en dessous et fureta à l'intérieur. L'instant suivant, le jet s'arrêta net.

— Oh… merci ! Comment avez-vous fait ?

— Venez. Je vais vous montrer.

Julia s'accroupit près de lui et pencha la tête.

— Voici le robinet d'arrêt, dit-il en indiquant une petite molette. Il en existe un pour l'évier, les lavabos, la baignoire et les toilettes. Il y a aussi une valve d'arrêt, dehors, qui coupe l'eau dans toute la maison.

Julia se redressa.

— Médecin et expert en plomberie, chapeau !

— Mon oncle était entrepreneur. Quand j'étais petit, je travaillais avec lui chaque été.

Elle eut soudain conscience, de façon incongrue, qu'ils se tenaient tout près l'un de l'autre. En fait, ils se touchaient presque. Elle recula vivement d'un pas, se prit les pieds dans le tapis et trébucha. Il la retint par le coude.

— Holà ! Restez avec moi ! Ça ne va pas ?

— Si… si…

Esquissant un sourire, elle dégagea son bras.

— Ce que je peux être empotée ! Mon second prénom est pourtant Grace.

Il lui rendit son sourire.

— Julia Grace Huntington… Très musical !

Depuis la mort de Ken, elle avait croisé pas mal d'hommes. Certains l'avaient même courtisée. Pourtant, c'était la première fois qu'elle ressentait quelque chose qui ressemblait à un élan. Une sensation tellement inattendue qu'elle en resta sans voix.

— Me… Merci pour la réparation, balbutia-t-elle en battant précipitamment en retraite dans le salon. Quand je reverrai Andrew, je lui dirai que vous avez respecté votre part du marché.

— Je n'ai rien réparé. J'ai opté pour une solution provisoire. Il vous faudra…

— Un plombier, naturellement ! Je m'en occuperai demain matin.

Julia le vit froncer les sourcils. Il se rendait bien compte que son attitude avait changé, qu'elle était pressée de le voir repartir. Heureusement, il en ignorait la raison. Il ne pouvait deviner l'effet qu'il avait produit sur elle, d'autant qu'il n'avait pas agi avec préméditation.

Elle ouvrit la porte.

— Dépêchez-vous. Votre repas va refroidir.

Il s'appuya au chambranle.

— Voulez-vous dîner avec moi ?

D'un revers de main, elle déclina l'offre.

— Je n'ai pas faim. J'ai déjà dîné.

Trop sec ! réalisa-t-elle en même temps. Une reine congédiant un domestique n'aurait pas été plus cassante.

Elle se reprit.

— Merci beaucoup, Eric. Une autre fois, peut-être.

Il la sonda du regard.

— Ce n'est pas facile, n'est-ce pas ? demanda-t-il alors d'une voix douce et compréhensive.

— Quoi donc ? s'étonna Julia.

— De réapprendre à vivre.

Que risquait-elle à se confier ? Elle le reverrait encore une fois, peut-être deux, et ce serait terminé. Elle savait que l'on se livre plus volontiers à des étrangers, car leur jugement a finalement peu d'importance. Pourquoi ne pas dévoiler à cet homme les sentiments qu'elle dissi-

14

mulait soigneusement à ses meilleurs amis ? Elle avala
péniblement la boule qui lui bloquait la gorge, puis
répliqua :

— Non. C'est parfois insoutenable.

— Ça s'améliore petit à petit.

— Quand ?

— Avec le temps. Au début, on se sent mieux pendant
cinq ou dix minutes. Après, ça dure toute une journée.

— Vous avez perdu votre femme ?

— Dans un sens, oui. Elle a trouvé quelqu'un d'autre
et j'ai dû apprendre à ne plus l'aimer.

— Je suis désolée.

— Moi aussi. Mais ça passe.

— Vraiment ?

— Presque ! convint-il. En fait, je me sens encore fau-
tif, mais j'ai bon espoir de vaincre ma culpabilité. J'y travaille.

— L'invitation à dîner est-elle toujours valable ?
demanda-t-elle spontanément.

Le visage d'Eric s'éclaira d'un sourire.

— Vous n'aurez même pas à faire la vaisselle.

— Alors, donnez-moi juste le temps de décharger la
voiture et de me changer.

— Vous aimez l'anguille, j'espère ?

Elle sursauta, incapable de cacher sa répulsion.

— L'anguille ?

Eric pouffa.

— Excusez-moi. Je n'ai pas pu résister. Mais rassurez-
vous, il s'agit d'un simple plat de spaghettis.

Autrefois, elle appréciait les plaisanteries. Elle avait
même de la repartie. À présent, elle n'en était plus si sûre,
mais cela valait le coup d'essayer.

— Je ne sais pas si je peux vous faire confiance. Pourquoi ne pas commander une pizza ?

— À votre guise. Saucisses et poivrons ?

Là-dessus, lui tournant le dos, il redescendit l'allée.

— Eric ! cria-t-elle. Vous renoncez déjà à me faire goûter vos spaghettis ?

Il ralentit l'allure.

— Ma chère amie, je suis l'être le plus facile au monde. Avant, j'étais compliqué. La vie m'a enseigné la simplicité.

— J'aimerais que vous me racontiez comment.

Rester simple constituait une de ses préoccupations principales. Eric se retourna vers elle.

— Je veux bien essayer, dit-il en la fixant un instant.

2

Lorsque Eric fut hors de vue, Julia sortit sa valise du coffre de la voiture. De retour au chalet, elle enfila un ensemble en lin pour le troquer ensuite contre un simple chemisier et un pantalon. Après tout, ce n'était qu'une dînette entre voisins, pas un rendez-vous amoureux !

En traversant le jardin, elle eut envie d'offrir un bouquet à son hôte. Pendant ces huit mois de désolation, le jardinier avait continué à arroser les parterres, mais il n'avait pas taillé les lauriers-roses, les massifs d'hibiscus et les haies d'azalées. Les fleurs proliféraient, leurs tiges ployaient sous les corolles. Tout en marchant, Julia ramassait une fleur de-ci de-là, et ce fut une gerbe rayonnante qu'elle tendit à Eric peu après.

— Pour moi ? s'étonna-t-il. C'est une première.

— Vraiment ? Personne ne vous a jamais offert de fleurs ?

Elle avait souvent envoyé des fleurs à Ken, de simples roses aussi bien que des arrangements plus sophistiqués.

— Non... Si ! Des plantes vertes, quand j'ai ouvert mon cabinet, mais rien de fleuri.

Elle le suivit dans la cuisine, où il remplit un vase d'eau fraîche.

— Mmm ! Ça sent bon ! remarqua Julia, dont l'estomac gargouillait.

— C'est fou ce que l'on peut faire avec de la sauce tomate en conserve et un peu d'imagination.

Il posa le bouquet au milieu de la table, parmi les assiettes garnies d'une serviette en papier bleu, les verres à pied et les bougies rouges et vertes. Il retourna ensuite à la cuisine pour remuer la sauce qui mijotait dans une casserole.

— Puis-je vous aider ? demanda Julia.

— Le pain à l'ail est prêt. Si vous voulez le découper en tranches, vous trouverez le couteau dans le tiroir.

Ils préparèrent le repas en silence, comme deux vieux copains qui auraient dîné ensemble toute leur vie. Lorsque les pâtes, la sauce et le fromage râpé furent sur la table, Eric alluma les chandelles, servit le vin et avança la chaise de son invitée. .

— Merci, dit-elle en prenant place.

Il s'assit en face d'elle et leva son verre.

— Aux robinets cassés et aux nouvelles amitiés.

Julia trinqua avec lui.

— À vos succès dans la périlleuse aventure littéraire.

Les sourcils épais d'Eric, plus foncés que ses cheveux, se joignirent.

— Comment avez-vous deviné ?

— Par déduction. Je me suis demandé ce qu'un médecin en congé sabbatique pouvait fabriquer avec un ordinateur.

— Et… vous avez conclu que j'écrivais un bouquin !

— Exactement. À cause de ceci, également.

Elle se leva pour prendre un livre sur l'étagère ; il s'intitulait *Comment écrire un best-seller en dix leçons.*

— Alors là ! s'écria-t-il. Vous m'en bouchez un coin !

Elle posa le livre et regagna sa place.

— Avez-vous toujours voulu écrire ?

— J'en rêve depuis le lycée. Pourtant, je savais que l'écriture ne fait pas vivre son homme. Moins que la médecine en tout cas !

— Que s'est-il passé ?

Il prit une tranche de pain à l'ail qu'il goûta parcimonieusement.

— J'en ai eu plein le dos de tous les jeunes cadres dynamiques des assurances-maladie, qui voulaient m'expliquer à tout prix quels examens j'étais censé infliger à mes patients.

18

Classique ! Julia hocha la tête. Fille de médecin, elle ne connaissait que trop bien ce refrain.

— Vraiment ? Je croyais que cela s'était arrangé.

— Pas assez à mon goût. Sans parler de mes assistants, qui prescrivaient des traitements aux malades par téléphone.

— Vous avez démissionné ?

— Pas tout de suite. Au début, j'ai persévéré. En vain. Les gens, y compris ma chère et tendre femme, m'ont cruellement déçu. Quand enfin j'ai ouvert les yeux, il était trop tard.

Julia sirota une gorgée de vin.

— Vous ne détestez pas, vous, la sagesse tardive ?

— Plus que vous ne l'imaginez. Je l'exècre.

— Ken a eu sa crise cardiaque sur le chemin de son bureau, dit-elle tranquillement. Il roulait sur la voie de gauche de l'autoroute.

Du bout de sa fourchette, elle écrasa un champignon dans la sauce tomate, comme pour empêcher l'image de Ken derrière le volant de sa voiture d'envahir son esprit.

— Les autres conducteurs ont pilé. Un carambolage monstre a suivi… Le bouchon a duré des heures.

L'accident avait fait la une des journaux télévisés à l'échelle nationale. Le fait divers avait continué à alimenter la presse et les télévisions régionales pendant des semaines. Les magazines avaient ensuite pris le relais. Six mois s'étaient écoulés avant que les feuilles de chou se tournent vers des sujets d'actualité plus brûlants.

Toutefois, une broutille avait échappé aux médias. Un détail que Julia n'avait jamais révélé à personne. Un secret douloureux qu'elle avait relégué dans un coin de son cœur, de sa conscience, et qui la tourmentait sans répit. Il était grand temps de passer aux aveux.

— J'étais sur l'autoroute, ce jour-là, murmura-t-elle. J'ai quitté la maison une demi-heure après Ken. Je me suis trouvée bloquée dans l'embouteillage créé par son accident.

Le reste était plus dur. Elle respira profondément.

— J'étais furieuse. J'avais rendez-vous chez mon coiffeur et j'allais être en retard. Je…

Elle s'interrompit et risqua un regard furtif du côté d'Eric. Il l'écoutait avec attention, sans aucun signe de réprobation. Il ne semblait même pas choqué.

— J'ai dépassé le lieu de l'accident peu après l'arrivée de l'ambulance, mais j'étais trop occupée à regarder ma montre pour remarquer la voiture endommagée. J'ai su plus tard par le médecin des urgences que Ken était vivant quand on l'a tiré de sa Range Rover. Oh, mon Dieu, si seulement je m'étais arrêtée ! Si seulement j'avais été près de lui au moment où…

— Arrêtez de vous culpabiliser, coupa Eric. Ça n'aurait rien changé.

Il posa sa main sur celle de Julia.

— C'est toujours ainsi quand quelqu'un que l'on aime meurt. On a du mal à comprendre que tous les efforts auraient été inutiles.

— J'aurais au moins pu lui dire au revoir.

— Non, Julia ! Vous n'en auriez pas eu le temps. Les sauveteurs étaient sûrement pressés de le sortir de la voiture. Ils ne vous auraient pas laissée vous approcher. Au mieux, vous auriez été assise sur le siège avant de l'ambulance quand il rendait son dernier soupir.

Il avait prononcé exactement les mots qu'elle avait besoin d'entendre. Pas l'absolution. La réalité.

— Vous étiez sûrement un excellent médecin. Je suis sûre que vous manquez à vos patients.

— Je les ai laissés entre de bonnes mains.

— Avez-vous toujours été fataliste ou l'êtes-vous devenu à force de combattre la maladie et la mort ?

— Je l'ai toujours été un peu. Naturellement, je n'irai pas jusqu'à affirmer que votre robinet s'est cassé parce que nous étions destinés à nous rencontrer.

Une lueur amusée alluma le bleu sombre de ses prunelles.

— Les plus belles choses de la vie sont le fruit du hasard, déclara-t-il d'une voix docte.

Lui faisait-il la cour ?

Déconcertée, elle s'empressa de changer de sujet.

— Parlez-moi de vos écrits. Vous apportent-ils des satis-factions ?

— Certains jours.

Elle fit tourner sa fourchette dans sa cuillère pour attraper les spaghettis.

— Et les autres jours ?

— Bah ! C'est un boulot comme un autre.

— Vous êtes-vous fixé des délais ? interrogea-t-elle.

— Pour quoi faire ? Finir le livre ou réussir ?

— Les deux.

— J'aurai terminé à la fin de l'année. Quant à la réus-site, elle ne dépend pas de moi… Et vous ? dit-il en repre-nant du pain. Avez-vous posé des limites ?

— À quoi ?

— Vous savez bien : trois mois pour mettre de l'ordre dans vos finances, six pour faire votre deuil, douze pour recommencer à penser à votre avenir, etc.

Elle secoua la tête.

— Oh, non. Je ne suis pas organisée. Je laisse les évé-nements arriver, puis j'avise.

— J'ai toujours admiré l'insouciance.

Elle lécha la sauce tomate qui maquillait sa lèvre infé-rieure.

— Vous plaisantez ! Je crois que je rendrais les per-sonnes de votre genre folles furieuses.

— Qu'entendez-vous par « les personnes de votre genre » ?

— Tous ceux qui courent après la réussite. Les ambi-tieux.

Le voyant frémir, elle reposa son verre à moitié plein sans le porter à sa bouche.

— Qu'y a-t-il ? Qu'est-ce que j'ai dit ?

— Rien.

— Voyons, Eric ! Soyez honnête.

— Vous parlez… comme ma femme. Pardon ! Mon ex-femme. Elle s'est servie des mêmes mots quand je l'ai priée de m'accorder une seconde chance.

— J'en suis navrée.

— Pas autant que moi.

Il s'accouda à la table et soupira.

— Je ne vois plus mes enfants qu'un week-end sur deux.

— Oh… Comme ça doit être triste.

— Pas tellement. Je déteste l'admettre, mais je passe plus de temps avec eux maintenant que quand nous vivions sous le même toit.

Julia lui adressa un sourire plein de commisération.

— La fameuse sagesse tardive.

— Changeons de sujet, voulez-vous ? Encore un peu de vin ?

— Non, merci. J'ai assez bu.

Le vin la rendait trop bavarde. La preuve ! Eric se servit en revanche une généreuse rasade.

— Avant son départ, Andrew m'a parlé d'un vieux couple qui venait en juillet. Nous avons été interrompus et je n'ai jamais su le fin mot de l'histoire.

Julia eut un sourire attendri.

— Joe et Maggie. Ils ont vendu le chalet à Ken. Et ils ont fini par l'adopter, en quelque sorte.

— D'après Andrew, ils entretenaient des rapports particuliers.

— Au début, ils ne voulaient pas vendre. Puis Joe a eu une hémorragie cérébrale qui a épuisé leur bas de laine. Ils manquaient cruellement d'argent. À l'époque, Ken était locataire, et il leur a fait l'offre suivante : il achetait le chalet, et ils pouvaient en disposer pendant les mois d'été comme bon leur semblait.

— Et ils le louaient pour joindre les deux bouts.

Un nouveau sourire illumina le visage fin de Julia.

— Ils le louaient, oui, mais Joe donnait l'argent à Ken. Il était tellement fier d'aider Ken financièrement à son tour que celui-ci n'a jamais eu le cœur de lui dire qu'il n'en avait pas besoin.

Pendant dix-huit ans, le même rituel réunissait Ken, Maggie et Joe chaque mois de septembre. Ils dînaient ensemble. Joe remettait à Ken le chèque de la location et Ken portait un toast à leur amitié. Quand Ken avait épousé Julia, elle s'était tout naturellement intégrée au groupe.

— Ils ont l'air spéciaux, fit remarquer Eric.

— Ils le sont. Et les locataires aussi. Joe ne choisit pas n'importe qui.

— Il me tarde de voir un jour ce chalet habité. Les volets clos donnent aux maisons un air de mausolée… sinistre.

Il s'interrompit soudain.

— Oh, mon Dieu, Julia, excusez-moi.

— Ça va. La même pensée m'a traversé l'esprit quand je suis arrivée cet après-midi.

— Une tasse de café ? proposa-t-il.

Elle secoua la tête.

— Non, merci. La caféine m'empêche de dormir. Demain, une grande journée m'attend.

— Je vous raccompagne.

N'ayant pas l'énergie de refuser, elle se laissa escorter jusqu'à sa porte.

— Merci pour le dîner. C'était délicieux.

— Comme je vous l'ai déjà dit, le plat s'appelle : « Une conserve et de l'imagination ». Je vous ferai goûter bientôt une autre de mes spécialités. « Un gâteau et de la créativité. » J'ai visité toutes les pâtisseries de la région avant de trouver la base de mon dessert.

— Attention ! Vous marchez sur mes plates-bandes.

— Quoi donc ? Les pâtisseries ?

— Les recettes en général. Mes tiroirs en sont pleins. Je peux cuisiner des plats du monde entier !

Eric lui adressa un regard circonspect.

— Vraiment ? Savez-vous préparer de la charcuterie fine ?

— Casher ou pas ? riposta-t-elle.

Il leva les bras avant de les laisser retomber le long de son corps.

— Vous avez marqué un point.

Julia lui sourit.

— Bonne nuit. Et merci encore pour la leçon de plomberie.

— Tout le plaisir fut pour moi.

Il se pencha, posa un rapide baiser sur la joue de la jeune femme, puis s'éloigna sans un mot de plus.

Julia attendit qu'il traverse la rue pour entrer dans le chalet et refermer la porte. Elle était de nouveau seule.

Seule, mais moins solitaire !

Les choses évoluent d'une drôle de manière, pensa-t-elle. Et le changement ne vient pas toujours quand on l'attend. Ni de la direction que l'on imagine.

3

Le vent déchiquetait la brume, et Eric remonta le zip de son blouson. Une vague roula sur la plage, puis se retira, abandonnant sur le sable des palourdes et des pétoncles vides. Il se pencha pour ramasser une coque. Un *Echinarachnius parma*, communément appelé dollar des sables. Il avait promis à son fils de ramasser ces coquillages. Le petit garçon voulait en faire un collier pour l'anniversaire de sa mère. Dès le lendemain, Eric avait découvert qu'il s'était engagé à la légère. Peu de ces coques fragiles arrivaient intactes du fond de l'océan. En trois jours, il n'en avait rassemblé qu'une demi-douzaine, qu'il avait précieusement conservée dans une boîte en carton.

Quant à sa fille, Susan, du haut de ses cinq ans, elle lui avait commandé une étoile de mer. « Bien orange », avait-elle précisé, comme celles qu'elle avait vues à San Francisco avec Roger, le « nouveau copain de maman ». Eric avait choisi la plus belle dans une boutique de souvenirs de Santa Cruz.

Le divorce remontait à deux ans. Pourtant, la jalousie serrait encore le cœur d'Eric quand il apprenait les rendez-vous galants de Shelly. Elle était fiancée. Bientôt, elle épouserait le dénommé Roger. Eric avait dû se faire à l'idée qu'ils ne vivraient plus jamais ensemble. Il n'arrivait cependant pas à l'imaginer avec quelqu'un d'autre. Comme il ne parvenait pas à se figurer qu'un jour il pourrait tomber amoureux d'une autre femme.

Il retourna le coquillage. Troué ! Il le rejeta dans les flots.

Certains êtres sont destinés l'un à l'autre, songea-t-il. Et pourtant, même quand cela arrive, on est trop aveugle, trop accaparé par son travail ou simplement trop stupide pour comprendre que même prédestiné, l'amour a besoin d'être nourri pour éclore.

Une mouette plongea avec un cri aigu et atterrit sur le bord d'une vague. Elle explora un instant les bulles irisées d'écume, prit son envol, puis disparut dans la brume. Avant de louer la maison d'Andrew, Eric ne s'était jamais considéré comme un homme de la mer. Il avait, jusqu'alors, préféré passer ses vacances à la montagne. Ou en Europe. Pourtant, dès l'instant où il avait marché sur l'étroite bande de sable, bercé par le ressac de l'eau sur les rochers, il avait été ensorcelé.

Égoïstement, il se comportait comme le propriétaire de la plage ; il aimait s'y promener le matin de bonne heure, quand un ou deux pêcheurs s'installaient sur la grève, et tard dans la nuit, sous les étoiles. Il n'avait jamais rencontré personne, à part des couples d'amoureux qui ne s'étaient même pas rendu compte de sa présence. Il savait par les voisins qu'à partir de juin son petit paradis se transformerait en enfer. Des hordes de touristes prendraient d'assaut les hôtels, les auberges et les chambres d'hôtes. De Santa Cruz au paisible hameau, la population décuplerait. Les vacanciers envahiraient les plages et y rôtiraient toute la journée, tandis que leurs radios brailleraient les tubes de l'été et que les surfeurs strieraient les flots bleus.

Oui, Eric était prévenu que sa chère plage regorgerait de corps rouge écrevisse dégoulinants d'huile solaire, qu'il serait privé aussi bien de ses promenades solitaires que de son intimité. Bizarrement, il attendait ce moment. Plus jeune, il avait aimé le bruit, le brouhaha, les rires, tout ce qu'il détestait à présent. Ses enfants seraient bientôt appelés à choisir entre la vie mondaine et l'existence d'ermite qu'il leur offrait. Nul doute qu'ils opteraient pour la première. Là aussi, il allait devoir s'adapter. Mais, pour l'instant, il avait encore le temps… Le temps de revivre ses souvenirs.

Une vague lui lécha les pieds. Se rappelant sa mission, il écarta un écheveau d'algues vertes et brunes, à la recherche de coquillages.

Julia s'arrêta en aval de la ligne humide que la marée haute avait tracée sur le sable la nuit précédente. Elle roula son pantalon kaki sur ses mollets, ôta ses chaussures, puis esquissa un pas sur le sol détrempé et froid. Elle n'était généralement guère matinale. Mais aujourd'hui, elle avait eu envie de sortir, avant même d'avaler sa première tasse de café.

Les mains enfouies dans les poches de son sweat-shirt, elle avança au bord de l'eau. Ses pieds nus s'enfoncèrent dans le sable mouvant, mais elle réussit à garder son équilibre. Exercice quotidien depuis la disparition de Ken : toujours lutter pour rester debout. Chaque fois qu'elle se croyait enfin solide, quelque chose, un événement, un signe, s'était produit, qui l'avait déstabilisée.

À la mi-décembre, par exemple, alors qu'elle commençait à espérer que peut-être elle parviendrait à passer Noël sans Ken, un paquet était arrivé au nom de M. Huntington. Il contenait un bibelot signé Fabergé que son mari avait acheté à une vente aux enchères. Un lis incrusté de perles et de diamants, dans un vase de topaze... La miniature avait dû coûter une fortune et Ken l'avait sans aucun doute choisie pour faire plaisir à Julia.

Elle avait attendu l'anniversaire de leur mariage, en mars, avant de répandre les cendres de Ken en mer, selon les dernières volontés de celui-ci. Geste qui, croyait-elle, symboliserait les adieux qu'elle n'avait pas pu lui adresser lors de la cérémonie funèbre. Erreur ! Elle avait regagné leur appartement convaincue que le lien qui l'unissait à Ken demeurerait à jamais indestructible. La mort qui les avait séparés avait encore renforcé l'image du couple parfait qu'ils incarnaient. Depuis le jour de leur rencontre, ils s'étaient retirés dans une bulle. Un univers qui n'appartenait qu'à eux. Ils se passaient parfois de paroles. Un regard, un sourire remplaçaient aisément les mots.

Après le bonheur, l'heure du malheur avait sonné. Peut-être était-ce le propre de tout grand amour ? Si leurs chemins ne s'étaient pas croisés, si Julia s'était éprise d'un autre homme, elle ne serait pas aussi pitoyable aujourd'hui. Elle comprit que cette passion sublime la condamnait à une perpétuelle solitude.

Souvent, au milieu d'une nuit blanche, la révolte flambait dans son cœur, au détriment du terrible sentiment de perte qui l'habitait. Pourquoi Ken l'avait-il abandonnée ? Comment avait-il osé ? Pourquoi ne lui avait-il jamais dit que son père et son grand-père avaient été terrassés par un infarctus avant cinquante ans ? Elle l'aurait forcé à se surveiller, à passer plus souvent des visites médicales. Ne savait-il donc pas qu'il tenait entre ses mains sa vie et celle de Julia ?

Ses orteils s'enfoncèrent une fois de plus dans le sable ; elle rétablit son équilibre. Le reflux laissa ses pieds exposés. De cet implacable combat intérieur, il y avait sûrement une leçon à tirer. Laquelle ? Elle l'ignorait encore.

Quelque chose s'accrocha à sa cheville : l'emballage en plastique d'un pack de Coca-Cola. Julia le ramassa et l'enfouit dans sa poche. Ken lui avait inculqué le respect de la nature, à moins qu'elle ne l'ait toujours eu sans le savoir. Elle ne savait plus où son esprit s'arrêtait et où commençait celui de Ken.

Le regard perdu vers l'horizon brumeux, elle perçut une voix dans le vent. Quelqu'un l'appelait. Elle se figea, s'efforçant de déterminer la source de la voix. L'appel retentit une seconde fois. Cela ne venait pas du large, mais de la plage. Se retournant, elle vit un homme courir dans sa direction.

L'espace d'une seconde, elle le prit pour Ken.

Mais ce n'était pas lui.

— Bonjour ! lança Eric en se rapprochant. Quelle belle journée !

Il plaisantait.

— Superbe !

S'arrêtant à sa hauteur, il balaya une mèche poivre et sel de son front.

— J'adore ces matins gris! s'exclama-t-il. Presque autant que les orages.

— Vous avez dû vous régaler cet hiver.

— Hélas! non. Le temps s'est amélioré à partir du moment où je me suis installé ici. Dites, j'allais prendre mon petit déjeuner. Voudriez-vous vous joindre à moi?

Julia fit non de la tête. Elle voulait rester seule ce premier matin, sans savoir comment l'annoncer à Eric. Heureusement, il n'insista pas.

— À plus tard, alors.

Bizarrement, maintenant qu'il était sur le point de partir, elle aurait aimé qu'il reste un peu.

— Qu'est-ce que vous avez ramassé?

Il leva la main. Dans sa paume luisait un petit coquillage.

— J'ai promis à mon fils de lui ramasser des dollars des sables, mais je n'ai pas eu de chance.

— Essayez du côté de Sunset State, près de Watsonville, à l'endroit où le Pajaro se jette dans la mer. L'estuaire grouille de mollusques.

— Merci. J'irai dès cet après-midi.

Il fit mine de s'éloigner, puis se retourna.

— Voulez-vous m'y accompagner?

Elle ne se donna pas la peine de considérer l'invitation.

— Non, merci. J'ai mille choses à faire et le temps presse. J'attends le plombier. Je ne sais pas à quelle heure il va venir.

— Vous l'avez appelé?

Il l'avait vue quitter le chalet à six heures du matin, heure à laquelle aucun plombier ne répond au téléphone.

— Non, bien sûr, mais j'ai regardé dans l'annuaire. J'ai noté plusieurs numéros. J'essaierai d'en avoir un qui puisse me dépanner aujourd'hui.

Il lui décocha un sourire plein de mystère.

— Je vous propose un marché. Vous m'aidez à ramasser des coquillages pour Jason, et je répare votre robinet.

— Mais…

Pourquoi résister ? Il lui demandait deux heures de son précieux temps, pas la journée entière. Julia rectifia le tir.

— Je ne me suis même pas brossé les dents.

— Cela veut-il dire que vous viendrez après l'avoir fait, ou est-ce un prétexte pour refuser ?

— Je viens. Mais pas pour longtemps. Vraiment, Eric ! J'ai un millier de choses à faire dans cette maison avant la semaine prochaine.

Un éclat de verre luisait dans le sable ; elle se pencha pour le ramasser.

Eric tapota la poche de son blouson.

— Mettez-le ici, avec le reste.

Lui aussi avait la manie du nettoyage écologique.

— Encore une chose, dit-elle.

— Je vous écoute.

— Du café. Je suis complètement inopérante tant que je n'ai pas eu ma dose.

Il lui entoura les épaules d'un bras amical, l'entraînant vers le chalet.

— Nous nous arrêterons en route. Je connais un troquet…

— Lequel ?

La panique avait assailli Julia, qui s'était arrêtée net. Déconcerté, Eric la scruta, puis une expression compréhensive se peignit sur ses traits.

— Il se trouve à Soquel, en bas de la grand-rue.

— Je ne me rappelle pas…

— Normal. Il a ouvert il y a trois mois.

— Oh…

— Preniez-vous le petit déjeuner dehors, avec Ken ?

— Cela nous arrivait. Il avait un faible pour le moka.

— Et moi, pour le café au lait.

Julia fronça le nez.

— Quel gâchis ! Le vrai café se doit d'être noir et corsé.

— Nous débattrons de ce sujet en route. Mon dernier voyage à Watsonville a frisé la catastrophe. C'était plein de déviations et d'embouteillages à cause d'un tournage dans les parages.

— On tourne des films à Watsonville ? De quel genre ?

— Sérieux. Des ouvriers agricoles immigrés, qui se soulèvent contre leur patron.

— Mon frère est chef de sécurité aux studios Kramer. S'agit-il d'une de leurs productions ?

— Je n'en sais rien. Et, de toute façon, je ne suis pas fichu de citer le nom de trois producteurs.

— Alors, renseignez-vous, si vous ne voulez pas vendre à n'importe qui les droits de votre best-seller.

Ils éclatèrent d'un même rire.

— J'en prends bonne note, dit Eric en s'essuyant les yeux. Et vous, n'oubliez pas votre carnet de chèques. Nous ferons halte à la quincaillerie.

— Vous voulez dire que le robinet ne fait pas partie du marché ?

Depuis quand n'avait-elle pas taquiné quelqu'un ? Elle ne s'en souvenait plus.

Eric sourit.

— Je ne suis qu'un pauvre écrivain, ne l'oubliez pas.

— Qui, néanmoins, boit du vin millésimé tous les jours.

Eric lui plaisait. Il restait lui-même et ne paraissait pas impressionné par l'empire que Ken avait construit et dont Julia avait hérité. D'autres personnes se laissaient prendre à ce piège, et leur attitude créait immédiatement une gêne.

— Je ne vous ai pas tous les jours à ma table, remarqua-t-il.

— Menteur ! Vous aviez débouché la bouteille avant que je vienne sonner à votre porte.

— Oooh ! souffla-t-il, la main sur la poitrine, à l'instar d'un blessé. Touché ! Je passe vous chercher dans cinq minutes ?

— Dix !

— Huit !

En riant pour la seconde fois de la matinée, elle tourna les talons. Les stores baissés ménageaient à l'intérieur du chalet une pénombre oppressante. Hier, la même atmosphère lui avait paru paisible, amicale. Aujourd'hui, la maison semblait hostile à sa subite bonne humeur.

Le soleil perça les nuages dans l'après-midi.

Les chromes de la Mercedes étincelèrent, des reflets mouvants de lumière dansèrent sur les vitres et la surface de l'eau. Le matin gris se mua en une journée magnifique. Julia résistait tant bien que mal au plaisir d'apprécier le beau temps. Elle s'était mise à bêcher rageusement les parterres, alors qu'Eric réparait les stores. En se redressant, elle contempla, perplexe, la terre grasse qui gantait ses mains et s'incrustait sous ses ongles. La maison serait mise en vente en septembre. Pourquoi se donnait-elle tout ce mal, alors qu'elle ne serait plus là pour recueillir les fruits de son labeur? En revenant de Watsonville, elle s'était ruée chez la fleuriste et avait littéralement dévalisé le magasin. Le pick-up d'Eric regorgeait de dahlias, de zinnias, de gueules-de-loup, de giroflées et de capucines.

— Ça va être formidable, s'exclama Eric en sortant du garage.

Assise sur ses talons, Julia leva le regard.

— Voilà des siècles que je voulais replanter l'allée. Demain, je m'occuperai du potager. Dans quelques mois, les tomates, les melons et les pissenlits salueront le printemps.

— Ne s'agit-il pas de pissenlits qui poussent dans l'arrière-cour d'Andrew?

— Oui. Il les aime bien en salade.

— À propos de salade… Je meurs de faim. Pas vous?

— Maintenant que vous le dites, je grignoterais bien un petit quelque chose.

— Sandwichs? Plat cuisiné?

— Sandwichs! dit-elle en se levant et en frottant ses paumes sur son vieux jean. Il y a un excellent traiteur dans la grand-rue. Ken adorait ses sandwichs… C'est moi qui invite!

Eric se contenta de la regarder, les pouces dans son ceinturon.

— Écoutez, Julia, je sais que ce n'est pas mon affaire…

— Mais? coupa-t-elle en lui lançant un coup d'œil acéré.

Elle espérait ainsi lui ôter toute envie de prodiguer ses sages conseils.

Il ne se laissa cependant pas impressionner.

— Mais, reprit-il, implacable, ça ne sert à rien de remuer le couteau dans la plaie. Si j'ai bien compris, vous avez été très heureuse avec Ken. Ruminer vos souvenirs ne fera que vous détruire.

Le visage de Julia se durcit. La fureur lui coupa le souffle. Pour qui se prenait-il ? Qui était-il pour s'autoriser à juger de quelle manière elle devait porter le deuil de son mari ?

— D'accord, murmura-t-il, l'air chagriné. Je suis allé trop loin. Désolé.

— Les conseilleurs ne sont pas les payeurs, Eric.

— On a envie de vous protéger, se justifia-t-il. De vous aider.

— Je ne veux pas de votre aide !

— Et moi, je me passerais bien de vos reproches.

La colère de Julia retomba soudain. Comment en vouloir à quelqu'un qui n'avait même pas connu Ken ? Cet homme ne pouvait deviner le vide que son mari avait laissé derrière lui. Au prix d'un effort surhumain, elle esquissa un sourire.

— Entendu. Je ne vous reprocherai plus rien, sauf de rechercher ma compagnie.

La remarque le prit au dépourvu. En scrutant Julia, il fut frappé par la profondeur de sa solitude. Elle ressemblait à un brave petit soldat laissé pour compte sur un champ de bataille meurtrier. Il brûlait d'envie de voler à son secours. Pourtant, il n'existait aucun moyen pour adoucir sa peine, et il le savait.

— Pickles ? demanda-t-il.

— Pardon ?

— Désirez-vous des pickles avec votre sandwich ? Si vous voulez, je vais y aller tout seul, pendant que vous jardinez.

— Oui.

— Oui, vous voulez des pickles, ou oui, vous préférez rester ici ?

— Les deux. Les pickles à part, s'il vous plaît.

— C'est noté. Quel genre ?

— La marque importe peu.

— Je veux dire : quel genre de sandwich voulez-vous ?

— Jambon-fromage.

— Pain de seigle ?

— Oui. Avec une tonne de mayonnaise. Mais pas de moutarde.

— Frites ?

— Pourquoi pas ? Sauce barbecue.

Il fit une grimace.

— C'est comme si c'était fait. Rien d'autre ?

— Des macaronis en salade.

— Un dessert ?

Elle réfléchit une seconde.

— Gâteau de carottes. Nous pouvons partager, bien sûr.

— Non, merci. Je suis puni et, donc, privé de dessert.

Julia se tut un instant.

— C'était ma faute, avoua-t-elle finalement. Sans le savoir, vous avez touché une corde sensible. Le point faible que j'essaie de soigner depuis des mois. Je n'aurais pas dû me mettre en colère. Je vous demande pardon.

— Ne vous excusez pas. Je me suis mêlé de ce qui ne me regardait pas, vous m'avez remis à ma place, ce n'est que justice.

— Vous avez raison, dit-elle d'une petite voix contrite. Je passe mon temps en pèlerinage. Je retourne partout où je suis déjà allée avec Ken. Pour conjurer le sort. Pour surmonter mon chagrin. Et j'y suis presque parvenue…

La main en visière, elle contempla l'océan.

— Mais depuis que je suis revenue ici, j'ai l'impression de me retrouver à la case départ.

— Parce que vos nombreuses occupations en ville vous avaient fait oublier le chalet ?

— Non, murmura-t-elle. Je ne l'avais pas oublié.

Eric hocha la tête. Il avait compris.

Rien ne pouvait faire oublier le chalet à Julia. Ni le travail, ni la famille, ni les amis. La maison de la plage représentait le seul et unique endroit au monde qu'elle n'arrivait pas à affronter depuis la mort de Ken.

Pourtant, elle était revenue. Elle avait eu ce courage.

À présent, elle fixait l'horizon. Eric en profita pour étudier plus attentivement la jeune femme. Comment était l'ancienne Julia, avant que la tristesse lui dérobe les toutes petites joies qui tissent une journée? Il en avait eu une vision fugitive quand elle l'avait aidé, tout à l'heure, à ramasser des coquillages. Une femme merveilleuse.

Ken avait connu cette femme-là. Existait-elle encore, ou était-elle morte en même temps que lui?

4

Des pas crissèrent sur le gravier. Croyant Eric de retour, Julia s'exclama :

— Enfin ! Il était temps !

— Je serais venu plus tôt, mais je viens seulement de remarquer ta voiture.

Avec un cri de ravissement, la jeune femme laissa tomber son râteau et son plantoir.

— Peter ! Quel plaisir de te revoir !

Le nouveau venu la souleva dans ses bras et la fit tournoyer.

— Je me suis fait un sang d'encre, dit-il en la reposant. Tu ne m'as pas donné signe de vie depuis des lustres.

— Je t'aurais appelé, mais tu sais ce que c'est. J'ai été complètement débordée.

— L'important, c'est que tu sois là, Julia.

Peter Wylie était le plus vieil ami de Ken en Californie. Grand, la mâchoire carrée, les yeux d'un bleu intense, les cheveux noir de jais, il avait plus l'allure d'un maître nageur que d'un artiste peintre. L'hiver précédent, Julia l'avait chargé de dégivrer le réfrigérateur et de fermer le chalet.

Peter, qui était né en Californie, avait enseigné à Ken les rudiments du surf et du bateau à voile. Grâce à lui, Ken s'était parfaitement intégré dans la population locale. Il en était même venu à se comporter et à penser comme un autochtone. Depuis leur folle jeunesse, les deux hommes s'entendaient merveilleusement. Peter avait vendu sa première aquarelle le jour où Ken avait décroché son premier contrat d'ingénieur en informatique. La célébration de leur succès avait duré des jours et des jours.

Aujourd'hui, les aquarelles de Peter Wylie, très prisées par les amateurs d'art, étaient exposées dans la plus grande galerie de la côte ouest. Peter avait les moyens de vivre où bon lui semblait, mais son choix s'était porté sur le petit cottage de cinq pièces qu'il habitait lorsqu'il avait fait la connaissance de Ken. Il y résidait dix mois par an. Il disparaissait généralement en juin et en juillet pour échapper à l'invasion des touristes, faire le tour des galeries et rendre visite à ses amis.

Une fois, Julia lui avait demandé pourquoi il revenait toujours en août, en plein cœur de l'été. Sa seule réponse avait été un mystérieux haussement d'épaules. Dépitée, la jeune femme s'était tournée vers son mari, qui n'avait pas semblé en savoir plus. Elle avait alors finalement cessé de se poser des questions.

— Tu pars bientôt, je présume ? s'enquit-elle.

— C'est exact.

Julia hocha la tête. Une sensation de malaise l'assaillit. Du vivant de Ken, son amitié avec Peter allait de soi ; à présent, ils évoquaient les deux pieds d'un trépied bancal.

— Je vends la maison, déclara-t-elle à brûle-pourpoint.

— Je m'en doutais. Quand ?

— À la fin de l'été. Je voudrais que les locataires en profitent une dernière fois.

Elle ne savait pas encore comment annoncer la nouvelle aux familles qui avaient l'habitude de passer leurs vacances au chalet. Surtout à Joe et à Maggie. Ken leur avait promis qu'ils pourraient venir tant qu'il serait le propriétaire de la maison. Compte tenu de leur âge, ils en avaient déduit qu'ils en auraient pour longtemps, jusqu'à la fin de leurs jours. Qui aurait deviné que Ken partirait le premier ?

— Préviens-moi quand tu mettras officiellement la propriété en vente, dit Peter.

Julia lui lança un regard interrogateur.

— As-tu des projets ?

— Je ne sais pas encore, répondit-il, songeur, en se frottant le menton. Je crois que je ne supporterai pas de voir des étrangers dans la maison de Ken.

— Penses-tu l'acheter, Peter ?

Comme il ne répondait rien, elle reprit :

— Tu ne peux pas peindre ici, la lumière n'est pas bonne. Tu me l'as dit cent fois.

— Mais il est parfaitement possible que je vive ici et que je transforme mon cottage en atelier… J'en ai assez de travailler dans l'espace où j'habite.

L'idée semblait plaisante. Julia se demanda si elle n'avait pas annoncé son intention de vendre à Peter dans l'espoir de l'appâter. Céder le chalet à un ami lui procurerait une sorte de soulagement. Une maigre consolation en vérité.

— Quand t'en vas-tu ? demanda-t-elle.

— Au début de la semaine prochaine. Je laisse le cottage à la belle-fille d'un copain, qui tourne un film à Watsonville.

Julia sourit.

— Il paraît que l'acteur principal a loué la maison de la colline.

— Toute la troupe loge dans les environs. J'en ai aperçu quatre ou cinq l'autre jour. Un comédien et des techniciens. Ils jouaient au volley-ball et sirotaient du Perrier.

— Tu as l'air déçu, observa-t-elle.

— Et comment ! On dit qu'ils sont tous allumés pendant le tournage. Je m'attendais à ce que le whisky coule à flots.

— Comme dans tes vernissages ?

Peter eut un petit rire.

— Absolument ! Mes vernissages assommeraient n'importe quel insomniaque sur-le-champ.

— Et quand reviens-tu ?

— Fin juillet.

C'était toujours pareil.

— Nous reparlerons de la vente du chalet à ce moment-là, dit Julia. À moins que…

Elle s'interrompit. Sans doute ne voudrait-il pas la revoir maintenant que Ken était décédé.

— À moins que quoi ? Je suis toujours partant pour une bonne affaire.

— Mais d'ici là, nous avons le droit de changer d'avis, non ?

De son côté, elle savait qu'elle garderait probablement la même idée, mais elle ne voulait surtout pas acculer Peter à un engagement ferme.

— Excuse-moi, reprit-elle pensivement. Actuellement, je n'arrive pas à suivre une idée jusqu'au bout. Je ne sais plus où j'en suis, Peter.

— Tu as pourtant meilleure mine que quand je t'ai vue la dernière fois.

— Merci, sourit-elle. Je n'ai aucun mérite.

Peter avait sonné à la porte de **sa** villa le jour où elle avait reçu la miniature commandée par Ken. Il avait annulé tous ses rendez-vous d'affaires à San Francisco pour rester avec elle. Elle avait fondu en larmes, et il l'avait écoutée sans lui infliger les platitudes et autres lieux communs de circonstance.

Une portière claqua. Eric descendit du pick-up et avança dans leur direction. À en juger par la taille des sacs qu'il portait à bout de bras, il y avait de quoi nourrir un régiment.

— Salut, Peter, cria-t-il. Où étais-tu passé ?

Le regard de Peter papillonna de Julia à Eric, pour revenir à la jeune femme. La surprise se peignit sur son visage, cédant aussitôt le pas à la confusion et à l'interrogation. La culpabilité tétanisa Julia. Se sentant fautive, elle adressa à Peter un petit sourire penaud.

— Je vois que vous vous connaissez, murmura-t-elle.

Elle aurait souhaité disparaître sous terre.

— Nous nous sommes rencontrés dans des circonstances étranges, confirma Peter. Eric m'a trouvé sur la plage, inanimé. Un pêcheur m'avait tiré dessus, alors que je me promenais en bateau. Plus tard, mon agresseur a prétendu m'avoir pris pour le phoque qui dévorait son saumon.

Julia écarquilla les yeux.

— Seigneur ! Quand est-ce arrivé ?

— Il y a deux mois.

— Et… tu es rétabli ?

— Ce n'était qu'une blessure superficielle, expliqua Peter en agitant son poignet avec désinvolture.

— Il a failli perdre son bras, rectifia Eric.

Se tournant vers Peter, Julia remarqua la cicatrice. Une balafre pâle et luisante, sur le bras gauche, au-dessus du coude.

— Oh, mon Dieu ! s'exclama-t-elle. Mais tu es gaucher. Ta peinture…

— C'est la première chose à laquelle j'ai pensé, moi aussi.

Julia lui toucha le bras, comme pour s'assurer que la blessure avait été réelle.

— Et l'affreux bonhomme ? Qu'est-il devenu ?

Un sourire vengeur éclaira les traits de Peter.

— Je n'ai pas cessé de me répéter le numéro de sa barque, tandis que je regagnais le rivage. Lorsqu'il a accosté à Monterey, la même nuit, les flics l'attendaient sur le quai.

Eric posa les sacs sur le gazon.

— Tu as déjeuné ? demanda-t-il.

Une nouvelle fois, le regard de Peter alla de l'un à l'autre.

— J'ai un rendez-vous, répondit-il finalement.

— Une bière ? proposa Julia.

— Non, merci.

Elle refoula une furieuse envie de crier que, en dépit des apparences, rien ne se passait entre Eric et elle. Et que d'ailleurs, rien ne se passerait plus tard non plus : Julia ne regarderait jamais un autre homme. Elle aimait Ken. Son mari. Son défunt mari.

Oui, Ken était mort. Sa loyauté, son affection planaient dans les limbes du souvenir.

— J'emporte le repas à l'intérieur, déclara Eric.

Elle se retint pour ne pas l'arrêter.

— Pourquoi ne pas déjeuner dehors, sur la table de jardin ? proposa-t-elle.

Il haussa un sourcil.

— Comme vous voulez. Je sors les chaises du garage ?

— Non ! rétorqua-t-elle d'un ton cassant, avec la sensation d'avoir commis une nouvelle gaffe. J'avais oublié que les chaises se trouvaient dans le garage, précisa-t-elle, comme si cela avait une quelconque importance. En fin de compte, on peut déjeuner dans la cuisine.

Elle avait fait en sorte de s'exprimer d'une voix neutre.

— Préférez-vous que nous allions chez moi ? offrit Eric.

Décidément, ça allait de mal en pis. À chaque instant, la faute s'aggravait. Elle articula un « pourquoi pas ? » dépourvu de tonus. Mais que lui arrivait-il ? Elle n'avait de comptes à rendre à personne. Et Eric ne méritait pas d'être traité comme un importun, un vendeur de porte-à-porte. De nouveau, elle se tourna vers Peter.

— Tu es sûr que tu ne veux pas nous rejoindre ?

— Il faut vraiment que je m'en aille.

— Peut-on se voir avant ton départ ?

Il inclina la tête et posa un baiser sur la joue de Julia.

— Bien sûr. Es-tu libre demain soir ?

— Naturellement ! Pourquoi ne serais-je pas libre ?

Eric brisa le silence pesant qui suivit.

— Je vais ranger ces emplettes, dit-il en prenant la direction de son cottage.

Peu de temps après, Julia frappait à sa porte.

— Pas de fleurs aujourd'hui ? demanda-t-il en ouvrant le battant et en s'effaçant pour la laisser passer.

— Désolée.

— Ce n'est pas grave. Celles que vous m'avez apportées hier sont encore magnifiques.

Un soupir gonfla la poitrine de Julia.

— Je ne parlais pas de ça.

Il tendit la main pour ôter une brindille des cheveux de la jeune femme.

— Je sais. Ne vous faites pas de souci. Tout va bien se passer.

— Peter et Ken étaient très amis.

— Peter me l'a dit.

— Vous avez parlé de Ken ?

Eric hocha la tête.

— Oui. Et de vous aussi.

Encore une surprise !

— Vraiment ? Et qu'a-t-il dit ?

— Que vous étiez la plus belle femme qu'il avait jamais vue, et que Ken et vous formiez un couple parfait. Je crois qu'il a même précisé que vous étiez faits l'un pour l'autre.

Belle ! Toute sa vie, les gens l'avaient décrite ainsi. Julia n'accordait aucune importance à cet adjectif. Pour elle, cela n'avait pas plus de sens que de dire « la mer est bleue ». Son image ne présentait aucun intérêt à ses yeux. Et de toute façon, elle aurait volontiers sacrifié sa beauté pour ramener Ken à la vie. Ne serait-ce qu'une heure.

— Je ne sais quoi répondre.

Une lueur d'amusement dansa dans les prunelles d'Eric.

— Rien. Essayez de convaincre vos admirateurs du contraire. S'ils vous comblent de compliments, faites des grimaces, tirez la langue, plissez le nez. Ça devrait marcher.

Un rire involontaire, presque joyeux, échappa à Julia.

— Vous êtes gentil, Eric. Voulez-vous devenir mon ami ?

Il la prit par les épaules et la conduisit dans la cuisine.

— Je le suis déjà. Une grande amitié est née entre le moment où j'ai fermé le robinet d'arrêt, et celui où vous avez fait une tache de sauce tomate sur votre corsage.

— Comment ? Mais je n'ai pas fait de tache…

Il lui adressa un clin d'œil.

— Ah ! Ah ! Je vous ai eue !

Il avait gagné la partie, mais cela avait peu d'importance.

À vrai dire, elle appréciait beaucoup son sens de l'humour.

5

Deux jours s'écoulèrent. Eric était plongé dans l'écriture de son livre, Julia récurait le chalet et recevait les visites des voisins.

Les travaux ménagers la changeaient de son existence citadine. Dans sa résidence en ville, tout resplendissait, chaque pièce d'argenterie brillait de mille feux grâce aux domestiques engagés par Ken.

Lorsqu'ils s'étaient connus, elle venait d'avoir sa maîtrise de lettres et avait commencé à travailler dans une agence de publicité. Ken ne lui avait jamais demandé de quitter son emploi. Il lui avait simplement proposé de l'accompagner à ses réunions à Londres, à Paris ou à Munich, la laissant libre de décider si elle voulait le suivre ou pas.

Ils étaient sortis ensemble pendant un trimestre. Leurs fiançailles avaient duré deux mois. Ken possédait une infaillible capacité de choisir les personnes qui resteraient auprès de lui pour toujours, qu'il s'agisse de son épouse, de ses amis ou de ses employés. Par-delà la mort, leur loyauté subsistait. Les amis continuaient à évoquer Ken comme s'ils l'avaient vu la veille, et aucun de ses collaborateurs n'avait démissionné. Et depuis que Julia avait repris les rênes de la compagnie, tous, du membre du conseil à la stagiaire, lui avaient témoigné le même dévouement qu'à Ken. Toutefois, rien ne pouvait lui faciliter la tâche. Plus elle apprenait et moins elle en savait. Si elle avait eu l'entrain et l'enthousiasme de Ken, elle aurait sûrement mené à bien sa mission. Hélas ! malgré ses bonnes résolutions, malgré ses efforts, elle traînait des pieds. Cependant, par respect pour la mémoire de Ken, elle continuait. Elle lui devait au moins cela.

Elle recula afin d'admirer le salon qui rutilait. Différentes senteurs saturaient l'air. Elle les huma avec satisfaction: parfum citronné de l'encaustique, fragrance de lavande du nettoyant à vitres, arôme fruité du shampoing pour tapis. Elle avait épousseté chaque livre de la bibliothèque. Elle aurait pu convoquer l'équipe de nettoyage habituelle, mais elle avait tenu à effacer elle-même les dernières traces de la présence de Ken. Ses amies l'auraient traitée de folle. Pourtant, ce grand ménage lui avait apporté, outre une saine fatigue, une sensation de catharsis.

Un grattement à la porte attira son attention. Elle alla ouvrir. Eric se tenait sur le perron.

— Vous arrivez juste à temps pour boire le café avec moi, dit-elle.

Il déclina l'offre.

— Je vais au supermarché. Avez-vous besoin de quelque chose?

— De lait. Un quart de litre. Écrémé.

— C'est tout?

— Vous étiez sans doute trop occupé pour remarquer que les voisins m'ont gavée de nourriture ces derniers jours.

— La plupart ont regretté de ne pas avoir pu vous aider lors du décès de votre mari. Alors ils se rattrapent.

— Je ne comprends pas. Après les obsèques, j'ai clairement signifié à tous qu'ils étaient les bienvenus chez moi.

Eric la regarda.

— Franchement, Julia! Avez-vous cru un instant que quelqu'un du village vous rendrait visite à Atherton?

— Pourquoi pas?

Il secoua la tête.

— L'air n'est pas le même en ville qu'à la campagne. Il faut être habitué aux mondanités pour mettre les pieds là-bas.

— Je suis la même partout.

— J'en doute...

44

— Ah oui ? Insinuez-vous, par hasard, qu'avant de venir au chalet, je troque ma garde-robe Armani contre des hardes ?

— Holà ! Je n'ai pas l'intention de me disputer avec vous.

— Je ne suis pas une snob, Eric !

Il eut un sourire.

— Je n'ai jamais dit une chose pareille.

— Ce n'est pas parce que j'ai un peu d'argent…

— Un peu… pour Bill Gates et le Vatican ! Pour le reste de l'humanité, vous êtes richissime.

— Oh, zut ! Pourquoi me persécutez-vous ?

— Parce que vous avez besoin d'un ami qui n'a pas peur de vous dire vos quatre vérités.

Il avait réussi. Pendant un instant, elle resta sans voix.

— Maintenant que nous avons réglé ce problème, reprit-il, voulez-vous autre chose que du lait écrémé ?

— Non. Je pars après-demain.

À son tour, il perdit l'usage de la parole.

— Si… vite ? réussit-il à articuler.

— Les Sadler et les McCormick seront là vendredi prochain.

— Je croyais qu'ils n'arriveraient pas avant juin.

— Je leur ai suggéré d'avancer la date.

— Quand ?

La question semblait singulière. Néanmoins, elle répondit :

— Il y a un mois. Pourquoi me le demandez-vous ?

— Pour rien.

— Eric, insista-t-elle. La vérité !

— Eh bien, je me suis demandé si je n'étais pas pour quelque chose dans ce revirement.

Elle considéra cette déclaration dépourvue de sens.

— Je ne comprends pas ce que vous voulez dire.

— Ma présence vous met-elle mal à l'aise ?

— Pour quelle raison ? Nous avons pris la décision d'être amis, non ?

Les secondes s'égrenèrent, interminables, tandis qu'il la sondait du regard.

— Ça ne fait rien, dit-il enfin. Ce n'est pas grave.

Cette fois-ci, elle ne demanda aucune explication.

— Attendez. Je vais chercher mon porte-monnaie.

— Pour quoi faire ?

— Vous payer le lait.

Il leva la main.

— Je vous en prie. Je peux faire face à cette dépense.

Elle referma la porte.

La situation n'avait pas été clarifiée. L'esprit encombré d'incertitudes, elle se planta devant la fenêtre et le regarda s'éloigner. On devinait à ses longues enjambées assurées qu'il s'adonnait à l'athlétisme, à la course ou à la natation. À un sport non violent, qui exigeait une discipline de fer, un solide engagement. Eric n'avait besoin de personne. Il aimait bien les autres, mais ne s'attachait pas ; une manière d'être qu'elle n'avait pas bien saisie jusqu'à sa rencontre avec Ken.

Sans doute le livre d'Eric en dirait-il davantage sur son caractère, sa personnalité, ses aspirations les plus secrètes, le genre de femme qui lui plaisait. Passant en revue ses amies, Julia s'efforça d'imaginer Eric avec l'une d'elles. Anne, peut-être. Non ! Elle ne supporterait pas qu'un homme la délaisse pour lire un bouquin, encore moins pour l'écrire. Judy refusait de sortir avec quelqu'un dont la fortune n'égalait pas au moins la sienne. Eileen, quant à elle, ne fréquentait que les mâles éblouis par son physique de star.

Eric semblait apprécier la beauté sans toutefois se laisser subjuguer. Apparemment, il avait suffisamment d'argent pour subvenir à ses besoins et à ceux de ses enfants, tout en s'offrant le luxe d'une année sabbatique… Il n'en avait cependant pas assez pour acheter une maison sur la plage. C'était apparemment un homme tout à fait capable d'écouter la pluie aussi bien que de l'opéra… Non, il ne correspondait définitivement pas à l'idéal masculin d'Anne, de Judy ou d'Eileen.

Julia soupira. Elle venait de brosser des portraits peu reluisants de ses amies, tout en ayant abouti à une analyse intéressante de la personnalité d'Eric. Elle eut la conviction que Ken et lui se seraient bien entendus.

Mais qui ne s'entendait pas avec Ken ?

Lorsque, plus tard dans l'après-midi, Eric lui apporta le quart de lait, Julia l'invita à prendre un apéritif. Il déclina l'offre sous prétexte qu'il devait retourner à ses écrits. Il avait suffisamment perdu de temps aujourd'hui, ajouta-t-il. Le lendemain, elle ne le vit pas. Elle commença à suspecter qu'il s'appliquait à l'éviter. Pourtant, le vendredi matin, de bonne heure, il vint lui proposer de se promener.

— Je suis contente que vous soyez venu, dit-elle, tandis qu'ils descendaient les marches de pierre qui menaient à la plage. Je voulais vous parler avant mon départ, mais je n'osais pas vous déranger.

Elle fit une halte à mi-chemin pour remonter la fermeture de son blouson. Eric claqua la langue.

— Vous ne m'auriez pas dérangé. Ce matin, j'ai relu sur écran ce que j'avais écrit hier. Nul ! J'ai tout effacé.

— Ça vous arrive souvent ? voulut savoir Julia en enfouissant ses poings dans ses poches.

— Non, Dieu merci. Même si je trouve toujours un passage à reprendre ou à supprimer, j'ai tout de même parfois de bonnes surprises.

Il posa un pied sur le sable humide, près de l'eau.

— De quoi voulez-vous me parler ? questionna-t-il.

— J'ai un service à vous demander.

— Allez-y.

— Vous avez le droit de refuser. Je ne serai pas vexée.

— Julia, ne vous justifiez pas. Dites-moi ce que vous voulez.

— Andrew a une clé du chalet en cas de besoin. Puis-je compter sur vous pour garder un œil sur ma maison ?

— C'est tout ?

— C'est déjà pas mal ! Alors ?

— Pas de problème.

Une grosse vague roula ; ils s'écartèrent vivement.

— Merci, dit Julia. Je dirai aux locataires que vous avez un double. Ils ont chacun leur clé, mais Margaret s'enferme souvent dehors... Vous aimerez bien Margaret, ainsi que Chris, son fils. J'apprécie moins les McCormick. En fait, je ne peux pas sentir leur fille. Elle est... comment dire...

Elle s'interrompit brutalement.

— Je suis navrée. Je n'ai pas l'habitude des cancans. Je ne sais pas ce qui m'a pris.

— Ooh! s'écria Eric, les yeux plissés, en s'agitant et en pointant le doigt vers le large. Là-bas. Est-ce que vous la voyez?

— Quoi? Où ça?

Il l'attira vers lui, afin qu'elle s'aligne sur son champ de vision.

— Là-bas. Au creux des vagues...

— Je ne vois rien...

Soudain, elle aperçut une loutre de mer qui se laissait flotter sur le dos. Le courant la faisait dériver.

— Ça y est! s'exclama-t-elle. Comme elle est mignonne!

Elle appuya son dos contre la poitrine d'Eric. Ils restèrent ainsi un moment, comme s'ils avaient fait ça toute leur vie, lui, entourant la taille de la jeune femme, elle, riant comme une enfant.

— Quel beau spectacle!

Une lame de fond déferla. Eric se mit à courir, entraînant Julia, tandis que l'eau froide, écumante, partait à l'assaut de la plage. Pendant leur fuite, la jeune femme ne quitta pas la mer des yeux.

— Je l'ai perdue! cria-t-elle soudain. Regardez par là, je regarderai de ce côté.

La petite tête sombre et luisante émergea peu après entre la crête des vagues. Ils suivirent son voyage pendant une demi-heure environ. Enfin, l'animal marin disparut derrière le cap.

— Merci de m'avoir invitée à vous accompagner, dit Julia sur le chemin du retour.

Les pêcheurs et les promeneurs matinaux peuplaient peu à peu le bord de mer. Bientôt, les goélands et les mouettes s'envoleraient vers des endroits plus propices à la quête de leur petit déjeuner.

— De rien, répondit tranquillement Eric.

— J'ai l'impression de me répandre en remerciements depuis une semaine. Puis-je vous inviter à déjeuner avant mon départ? Je connais un excellent restaurant à Aptos.

— En êtes-vous sûre?

Elle saisit le message. « Êtes-vous sûre de vouloir m'emmener quelque part où vous êtes déjà allée avec Ken? »

— Certaine! répliqua-t-elle. Midi et demi vous convient?

— Je serai prêt.

Après le déjeuner, ils firent une halte à la quincaillerie. Elle y acheta un gond pour son portail, et, malgré les protestations d'Eric, se chargea toute seule de remplacer l'ancien.

— Bravo! la félicita-t-il, tandis qu'elle rangeait la pince, la tenaille et le tournevis. Lors de votre prochain passage, je vous montrerai comment fixer la porte du placard de la cuisine.

Il n'y aurait pas de prochain passage, mais elle ne voulut pas relever ce détail, afin de ne pas gâcher la beauté de l'instant présent.

— Il ne me reste plus qu'à ramasser un bouquet pour Margaret et à m'en aller avant que le trafic soit trop dense.

— Margaret, répéta-t-il d'abord sans comprendre. Ah, oui, la locataire de juin. Si j'ai bien compris, les fleurs sont une tradition?

Elle ferma la boîte à outils et commença à ramasser des dahlias roses.

— C'est ma manière de souhaiter la bienvenue à quelqu'un.

Soudain, se redressant, elle lui mit le bouquet entre les mains.

— Et de dire au revoir.

Les doigts d'Eric étreignirent les tiges fragiles.

— Je les mettrai près de l'ordinateur. Peut-être m'apporteront-elles un peu d'inspiration.

— Mon jardin est à votre disposition. Ramassez autant de fleurs que vous voulez. Ça fait du bien aux plantes d'être moins touffues.

Elle se remit à cueillir des fleurs et lui en tendit une de temps à autre. Quand les deux gerbes furent prêtes, elle prit la direction du chalet. Il la retint par le bras.

— Julia ! Prenez soin de vous.

En plongeant ses yeux dans les siens, elle sut qu'il n'avait pas proféré une platitude dépourvue de sens, mais qu'il était sincère.

— Entendu, murmura-t-elle.

Alors, il l'embrassa. Leurs lèvres se touchèrent plus longuement que pour un simple baiser platonique, mais avec tout de même moins d'insistance que s'ils avaient été amants. Au tréfonds de son esprit, ou peut-être de son corps, Julia éprouva le vague frisson d'une réponse.

Eric lui relâcha le bras, puis brandit son bouquet de dahlias.

— Je vais les mettre dans un vase.

Elle inclina la tête.

— Allez-y. Et merci pour tout, Eric.

Il ne dit rien, lui adressa un sourire, puis, après un petit signe de la main, pivota sur ses talons pour s'en aller.

Julia le suivit du regard. À mesure qu'Eric s'éloignait, la solitude lui pesait de nouveau. Cette sensation, elle la connaissait aussi bien que la route d'Atherton qu'elle allait emprunter dans une heure. Le plus drôle, c'était que ces derniers jours, elle ne l'avait que trop souvent oubliée.

DEUXIÈME PARTIE

Juin

1

Margaret Sadler gara sa Volvo poussive dans l'allée et actionna le levier qui commandait l'ouverture du coffre. Se tournant vers son fils, elle demanda :

— Avant de descendre à la plage, peux-tu m'aider à décharger la voiture ?

Poussant la portière, Chris émergea.

— Mmm ! Sens-moi ça !

L'air salin faisait bruire les feuilles longilignes du grand platane et lui ébouriffait les cheveux.

— Un jour, je vivrai au bord de la mer ! affirma-t-il.

Sa mère retint de justesse un commentaire caustique sur les prix exorbitants des résidences dans la région. Depuis le divorce de ses parents, trois ans auparavant, Chris avait assumé un nouveau rôle. Les économies destinées à ses études étant parties en fumée et les revenus de sa mère ayant été réduits de moitié, il n'avait plus évoqué l'université de la Californie du Sud, pas plus que Yale ou Stanford. Il s'était adapté à la nouvelle situation et avait renoncé à l'achat d'une voiture d'occasion. Pour le moment, il poursuivait ses études au lycée. Malgré le règlement qui interdisait aux élèves de travailler, il s'était fait embaucher comme serveur dans le restaurant de son oncle, ce qui lui avait permis de s'offrir ses cours de combat. Il semblait avoir oublié les rêves qui faisaient partie intégrante de sa personne, au même titre que ses cheveux blonds comme les blés ou son corps mince et musclé.

À son tour, Margaret sortit de la voiture. Elle jeta un coup d'œil désolé à la Volvo, que le trajet depuis Fresno avait transformée en un tas de ferraille recouvert de boue et de poussière. Avec un peu de chance, et moyennant un peu d'argent, elle parviendrait à persuader Chris de la laver.

— Rappelle-toi, quand tu achèteras cette maison sur l'océan… commença-t-elle.

— Oui ?

— N'oublie pas de vérifier qu'il y ait une chambre d'amis. Je viendrai te rendre visite… très souvent.

— Pas de problème. Mais tu devras me prévenir à temps afin que je fasse disparaître les traces d'orgies.

Margaret pouffa.

— Comme c'est gentil.

— Je suis un gars prévenant, tu sais.

Il attendait que sa mère ouvre le coffre pour commencer à décharger les bagages.

Dix minutes plus tard, il effectua le dernier voyage.

— Où dois-je mettre la grosse boîte ? cria-t-il en refermant la porte du pied.

— Qu'est-ce qu'il y a écrit dessus ? demanda Margaret, affairée dans la cuisine.

— P.N.

— Produits de nettoyage. Apporte-la ici.

Elle poussa le vase de fleurs, et Chris posa la boîte sur la table de la cuisine.

— Je ne comprends pas pourquoi tu t'encombres de tout ce bazar, dit-il en soulevant le couvercle pour découvrir un nombre incroyable de tubes et de vaporisateurs. La maison est nickel.

— Et c'est ainsi que nous la rendrons, ponctua Margaret.

D'une main prompte, elle écarta son fils de son chemin.

— Je parie que ces produits sont déjà dans l'armoire.

— Tout ce qui est ici appartient à Julia et à…

Elle s'interrompit. Elle ne pouvait songer à la mort prématurée de Ken sans éprouver un sursaut d'indignation. Pourquoi des milliers d'individus oisifs, improductifs, continuaient-ils à vivre, alors que des hommes aussi doués que Ken mouraient en pleine force de l'âge ?

— J'ai peine à croire que Ken nous a laissés, murmura-t-elle. Il était si jeune…

Elle remit à Chris le liquide vaisselle et le paquet de poudre à récurer et lui indiqua du doigt le placard sous l'évier.

— Oui, je sais. Cinq ans de moins que papa et toi. Comment va Julia ?

Il s'accroupit, rangea les deux articles sur l'étagère du dessus et se releva sans effort, avec une grâce féline. Sa mère lui passa le décapant et l'eau de Javel.

— Je n'ai pas osé le lui demander, répondit-elle. C'est une question tellement banale…

— Je ne crois pas.

— Elle a dû l'entendre un million de fois.

— Ça ne la rend pas banale pour autant.

— Chris, il s'agit d'une question purement rhétorique. Comme quand on dit « enchanté » à quelqu'un qui vient de vous être présenté. Je voudrais que Julia sache que je pense beaucoup à elle, mais je ne sais pas comment le lui dire.

— Tu trouvais cela banal quand les gens te deman-daient comment tu allais, après le divorce ?

Margaret regarda son fils, dissimulant de son mieux sa surprise. Son petit garçon était devenu presque adulte, doté d'un solide sens de l'observation. Il avait mûri trop rapidement à son goût… et elle en était la première res-ponsable ! Elle l'avait laissé endosser trop de responsabi-lités par rapport aux autres garçons de son âge.

— Après un grand changement dans sa vie, on a du mal à franchir le cap, dit-elle.

— Tu n'as pas répondu à ma question.

— Ce que j'ai pu éprouver à l'époque est révolu, Chris. À force de trop regarder en arrière…

— … on rate les possibilités qui se trouvent devant soi, acheva-t-il à sa place.

Margaret eut un petit rire.

— Je me répète peut-être ?

— Seulement une petite centaine de fois.

— Cela ne veut pas dire…

— … que ce n'est pas vrai, compléta-t-il.

Elle lui passa les derniers produits ménagers et referma la boîte.

— Range ça et disparais avant que je te frappe !

Il fit semblant d'esquiver des coups.

— Qu'est-ce que tu vas faire ? s'enquit-il en se relevant.

Un soupir de pur plaisir gonfla la poitrine de Margaret à la perspective de s'adonner au doux farniente pendant quelques heures. En ville, entre son travail et la maison, elle était toujours débordée.

— Je voulais laver la voiture mais ça peut attendre. Je vais sûrement bouquiner, et peut-être même m'accorder une petite sieste.

Chris hocha la tête.

— Tu vieillis, maman.

— Jeune homme, surveillez votre langage, sinon vous aurez une fessée !

Il se mit en position de combat, la défiant d'un regard espiègle.

— Essaie ! Avec une main attachée dans le dos, je t'envoie en trente secondes au tapis.

— Oh, tu me sous-estimes ! rétorqua-t-elle. Tu as de la chance que je n'aie pas envie de te corriger.

À l'aide d'un livre de poche, elle lui tapota le derrière.

De tous les sports de combat, Chris avait choisi celui qui déplaisait le plus à sa mère : la lutte. Pendant trois ans, elle l'avait vu se frayer péniblement un chemin dans les différentes étapes du championnat mais n'avait jamais réussi à comprendre comment il pouvait quitter un match avec le sourire, alors qu'il était couvert de bleus.

Il passa un bras autour de ses épaules et la serra gentiment.

— Mère possessive, va !

Elle lui flanqua la boîte vide entre les mains.

— Mets ça au garage avant de sortir.

Il obtempéra mais se retourna sur le seuil de la pièce.

— Au fait, à quelle heure arrivent les McCormick ?

Margaret consulta la pendule murale du regard.

— Leur avion atterrit à San Francisco à trois heures et demie. Le temps qu'ils récupèrent la voiture de location, plus trois heures de route... ils ne seront pas là avant six heures et demie ou sept heures, à condition qu'ils ne décident pas de dîner en route.

Elle s'était exprimée d'une voix naturelle. Chris s'efforçait de lui cacher qu'il était encore amoureux fou de Tracy McCormick. Les deux familles passaient ensemble leurs vacances en juin depuis seize ans, et une décennie plus tôt, Chris avait eu le coup de foudre pour Tracy. Chaque été, il arrivait le cœur en bandoulière, avec le secret espoir, sinon la conviction, que durant les onze mois écoulés, Tracy serait devenue la jeune fille de ses rêves. Il se plaisait à penser qu'elle aurait compris qu'il l'aimait et envisagerait la réciprocité de ce sentiment.

Margaret, quant à elle, caressait l'espoir que Tracy serait suffisamment mûre cette année pour éconduire Chris avec délicatesse. L'amour-propre de son fils, tel un tendre bourgeon, ne demandait qu'à s'épanouir, mais ne manquerait pas de geler au vent froid de l'indifférence. À Fresno, Chris ne se rendait même pas compte que les lycéennes se retournaient sur son passage. Ses muscles, si patiemment travaillés, lui servaient pour le sport, pas pour séduire. Il était poli, généreux, gentil, bien élevé, mais ces qualités qu'une femme recherche chez un homme, les jeunes filles les trouvent ennuyeuses chez un garçon.

— Cette Beverly! maugréa Chris. Je ne sais pas pourquoi elle tient tant à San Francisco. San Jose est plus près.

— Parce que c'est un vol direct de St Louis. Elle déteste les correspondances.

— Beverly déteste un tas de choses.

— Chris!

— Ben quoi? C'est vrai, non?

— Disons qu'elle a des opinions toutes faites, admit Margaret. Et qu'elle n'hésite pas à les exprimer. Tout comme Tracy, d'ailleurs.

Elle se tut, consciente d'aborder un terrain glissant. Chris ne tolérait aucune remarque mettant en doute la perfection de Tracy.

Heureusement, cette fois-ci, il n'opposa aucune objection.

— Peu importe, marmonna-t-il.

— Maintenant, si tu ne sors pas, je peux te trouver une autre corvée.

Il leva son bras libre puis battit en retraite sans demander son reste.

— D'accord, d'accord. À plus tard.

Margaret retourna à la cuisine où elle se mit à déballer les emplettes. Elle avait fait une razzia chez son épicier en attendant d'aller au village le lendemain avec Beverly. Tandis qu'il contournait le chalet en direction de la plage, Chris tapa sur la vitre, et Margaret lui sourit. Elle agita la main et le regarda s'éloigner. Il disparut dans l'escalier menant en bas de la falaise, puis réapparut sur le premier banc de sable. Il mit le cap au nord, à travers le promontoire rocheux qui séparait l'endroit des autres plages privées. Il effectuait de longues enjambées, souples, gracieuses, sans effort.

Lorsque Chris fut hors de vue, Margaret s'éloigna de la fenêtre. Elle remit le vase de fleurs sur la table et ajusta une rose jaune qui s'affaissait. Les différentes fragrances lui rappelèrent le fameux jour où, en arrivant au chalet, huit ans plus tôt, elle avait trouvé un bouquet semblable. Juste avant de partir de Fresno pour rejoindre les McCormick à Santa Cruz, une violente dispute avait éclaté entre Kevin et elle. L'espace d'une seconde, contre toute logique, Margaret s'était laissé bercer par l'illusion que Kevin lui avait envoyé des fleurs pour se faire pardonner.

Elle avait osé lui demander d'où venait le mégot taché de rouge à lèvres carmin qu'elle avait découvert dans le cendrier de sa voiture ; et il était monté sur ses grands chevaux. La discussion avait vite dégénéré quand il l'avait accusée de jeter l'argent du ménage par les fenêtres et qu'elle s'était déclarée prête à reprendre son métier. Il avait alors mis fin à l'entretien en annonçant avec désinvolture qu'il n'irait pas en vacances. Elle était donc partie seule avec Chris.

Elle avait réalisé soudain qu'aucun fleuriste ne lui avait livré le bouquet. Les fleurs avaient été ramassées dans le jardin où elles poussaient à profusion. Depuis, été après été, un splendide bouquet les accueillait au chalet, avec un mot de bienvenue. Bizarrement, cette année, il n'y avait que les fleurs.

Chris emprunta la pente rocailleuse qu'il descendit en zigzag vers la plage. Il faisait exprès d'écraser les coques vides, afin d'entendre leur crissement sous ses semelles. Dans le lointain, un surfeur glissait sur les vagues. En repassant sous le chalet, il leva les yeux dans l'espoir d'apercevoir sa mère sur la terrasse. Il se faisait du souci pour elle. Que deviendrait-elle quand il irait à l'université ? Referait-elle sa vie ? Et la Volvo ne la lâcherait-elle pas avant qu'il ait les moyens de lui offrir une nouvelle voiture ? Telles étaient ses inquiétudes.

Margaret n'aimait pas qu'il l'incite à sortir davantage. En revanche, quand il sortait, elle ne cherchait jamais à savoir avec qui ou jusqu'à quelle heure. Elle était chic pour ça. Même si elle se doutait pour Tracy et lui, elle n'avait jamais posé de questions indiscrètes.

Tracy et lui ! Quelle blague ! Il n'y avait pas plus de Chris et Tracy que de Chris et Stanford ou Yale. Toute sa vie, il avait cru que les études lui seraient offertes sur un plateau. Son père lui avait laissé entendre que le livret d'épargne qu'ils avaient ouvert à sa naissance y pourvoirait.

Après le divorce, sa mère avait insisté pour que l'argent reste au nom de Chris et à celui de son père. Elle avait commis la faute de faire confiance à son ex-mari. Quand celui-ci s'était remarié avec une femme qui avait trois enfants, les fonds avaient commencé à s'envoler. Chris ne s'en était pas aperçu tout de suite. Un jour où il s'était rendu à la banque pour déposer sur son livret les pourboires gagnés au restaurant de son oncle, il avait découvert le pot aux roses : il ne restait plus qu'une somme ridicule.

Le même jour, il s'était rendu au bureau de son père pour lui demander des explications. Kevin avait évoqué sa nouvelle situation familiale. À présent, il avait d'autres priorités, avait-il expliqué. Et d'ailleurs, il n'y avait jamais eu de convention par écrit au sujet du livret.

En quittant la compagnie où son père travaillait, Chris était sorti par le garage. Armé de la clé de la vieille Volvo de sa mère, il avait tracé une éraflure indélébile sur la rutilante carrosserie rouge de la nouvelle BMW de son père.

Il lui avait fallu des mois pour réaliser que l'argent n'avait qu'une importance relative au regard de la trahison de son père. Celui-ci avait créé un rêve pour le détruire par la suite.

Aujourd'hui, un an avant la remise des diplômes au lycée, Chris n'avait pas la moindre idée concernant son avenir. À dix-sept ans, il ignorait toujours quel métier il souhaitait exercer. Absorbé par ces sombres méditations, il ne vit pas la balle de volley-ball arriver dans sa direction. Par pur réflexe, il frappa dans le ballon. Un garçon aux longs cheveux bruns, affublé de lunettes noires, une casquette de base-ball de guingois sur la tête, renvoya la balle d'une volée impeccable au-dessus du filet. La balle revint au serveur. Celui-ci la passa à Chris, qui entra machinalement dans le jeu.

L'équipe adverse perdit un point quand un joueur envoya la balle hors limites. Le jeune homme aux cheveux longs, qui devait à son tour servir, fit signe à Chris de se mettre en position. Il devait avoir vingt ans et était un peu plus jeune que ses compagnons. Il portait un pantalon de jogging défraîchi, un tee-shirt déchiré, de petits anneaux d'or aux oreilles.

— Tu veux jouer ? demanda-t-il.

— Pourquoi pas ?

Il n'avait rien de mieux à faire.

Les deux équipes prirent place. Ils avaient joué jusque-là à deux contre trois. L'arrivée de Chris rétablissait l'égalité.

De nouveau, le match s'engagea. Les équipes jouaient avec entrain. À chaque volée, des cris et des commentaires fusaient. Les joueurs se houspillaient et se taquinaient sans merci. Ils semblaient avoir l'habitude de jouer ensemble.

Quand le service leur revint de nouveau, le garçon aux cheveux longs présenta ses copains au nouvel arrivant, en terminant par lui-même.

— Antonio Gallardo. Tony pour les intimes.

— Chris Sadler.

— À toi, Chris, dit Tony.

Chris effectua un service parfait. La balle atterrit devant le filet, dans le camp adverse. Tony poussa un cri de triomphe en battant l'air de ses poings.

— Génial ! Encore une fois !

Miraculeusement, Chris réitéra l'exploit. Cette fois-ci, tout le monde l'acclama.

Il leur fallut près de quarante-cinq minutes pour gagner la partie. Les adversaires dénoncèrent la tricherie. D'après eux, Chris était un « pro » que Tony avait fait venir à ses frais de Los Angeles. Au début, il crut qu'ils plaisantaient. Mais ils étaient sérieux.

Lorsqu'ils changèrent de côté, Chris en profita pour étudier Tony de plus près. Il n'avait pas l'air assez riche pour assurer les frais de déplacement d'un joueur professionnel, sans parler de son cachet.

Durant la partie, Chris accorda plus d'attention aux rapports des cinq garçons. Il semblait évident que les quatre autres témoignaient à Tony une amitié mitigée de respect. Comme s'il occupait une position sociale légèrement plus élevée que la leur, à l'instar d'un contremaître dans un chantier.

Mais quel que fût leur métier, il devait être temporaire, car la plupart se plaignaient d'avoir laissé leur petite amie qu'ils avaient hâte de retrouver.

Le second match fut plus serré. L'équipe de Tony gagna d'un point, bruyamment controversé. Alors qu'ils s'apprêtaient à changer de côté une nouvelle fois, Chris demanda l'heure. Un grand Afro-Américain tira une montre de sa poche.

— Six heures vingt-cinq.

— Je dois partir, dit Chris.

La balle sous le bras, Tony s'approcha de lui.

— Demain, même heure même endroit ?

Chris enfila son tee-shirt qu'il avait retiré après la première partie.

— Ce n'est pas sûr, répondit-il.

Le troisième membre de l'équipe de Tony, un géant qui semblait sortir tout droit d'un film de gladiateurs, s'avança.

— Hé, mec, lança-t-il, tu ne vas pas nous laisser tomber avec ces trois buses.

— Fous-lui la paix ! intervint l'un de leurs adversaires. Si ce n'est pas sûr, ce n'est pas sûr et voilà tout.

— Va te faire voir, Mason ! riposta Tony en riant. Tu n'as pas envie de perdre encore, c'est ça ?

— J'essaierai, promit Chris.

Il avait apprécié le jeu autant qu'eux. Mais même s'il avait très envie de recommencer, Tracy passait en premier.

Il salua ses nouveaux amis et s'en alla en courant. Un peu plus loin, il rejoignit un chemin parallèle à l'autoroute. Il arriva juste à temps pour apercevoir la tignasse blonde de Tracy, tandis que la voiture de location de sa mère négociait avec grâce le tournant qui menait au chalet.

Il suspendit sa course. Ou il arrivait sur leurs talons, essoufflé, en nage, ou il s'attardait un peu de manière à afficher un air décontracté, voire surpris de les trouver là.

2

— Ce n'est pas Margaret, là-bas ? dit Tracy, alors que la voiture dépassait le cottage voisin.

Beverly jeta un coup d'œil dans le rétroviseur.

— Oui, mais l'homme à qui elle parle n'est pas Andrew.

Margaret agita la main dans leur direction, puis vint au-devant d'elles.

— Tu es superbe ! dit-elle à Beverly en l'embrassant, quand cette dernière fut sortie de voiture.

Elle se tourna vers Tracy.

— Toi aussi, Tracy.

Le bras autour des épaules de Beverly, Margaret sourit à la personne qui accompagnait les nouvelles arrivantes.

— Et à qui avons-nous l'honneur ?

— Janice Carlson, l'amie de Tracy, expliqua Beverly. Clyde ne pouvait pas nous accompagner. Janice a pris sa place. Elle restera avec nous tout le mois.

Margaret surmonta aisément la surprise.

— Ravie de vous connaître, Janice.

— Moi aussi, madame Sadler.

Margaret regarda Beverly.

— Clyde va bien ?

— Il allait très bien, en tout cas, quand il nous a conduites à l'aéroport.

L'expression inquiète de Margaret arracha un sourire à Beverly.

— Ne te fais pas de souci. Tu connais Clyde : quand il est sur un projet, il travaille vingt-quatre heures sur vingt-quatre. Au fait, où est Chris ?

— Il est allé courir sur la plage.

— Dommage ! soupira Beverly. J'espérais qu'il serait là pour nous donner un coup de main avec les bagages. Tu ne peux pas imaginer le nombre de valises que ces demoiselles ont apportées.

Tracy échangea un regard avec Janice.

— Qu'est-ce que je t'avais dit ? chuchota-t-elle, afin que sa mère et Margaret ne l'entendent pas.

— Il n'y a pas de mal à courir sur la plage, observa son amie.

— Sauf quand ça devient une obsession. N'importe qui serait parti voir où ça bouge dans le coin, mais pas cet imbécile de Chris.

— Si ça se trouve, il est en train de draguer.

Tracy haussa les épaules.

— Quand tu le verras, tu comprendras mieux.

Tracy éprouvait quelques réticences au sujet de Janice. Même si elles étaient toutes deux chef des supporters d'équipe, elles n'avaient jamais été très proches. Mais c'était la seule de ses amies qui était libre pendant un mois. En avril, quand sa mère avait commencé à faire des projets de vacances, Tracy, en désespoir de cause, avait fait appel à la compréhension de son père. Il était hors de question, avait-elle déclaré, qu'elle s'embête « comme un rat mort » en Californie. Cette fois-ci, elle refusait de s'y rendre sans une copine.

Son père était allé jusqu'à lui promettre des leçons de golf, mais elle avait tenu bon. Elle aurait été moins obstinée si elle avait su qu'il n'avait pas les moyens de payer un billet d'avion supplémentaire, chose qu'elle avait découverte trop tard : elle avait déjà invité Janice. Et puis tant pis ! Son père ne cessait de se plaindre qu'il manquait de temps pour se consacrer sérieusement à un projet. À présent, il aurait tout un mois devant lui.

Beverly remit une valise à chaque jeune fille.

— Ce que c'est beau, ici ! s'exclama Janice. J'ai hâte d'aller à la plage.

— C'est la première fois que vous venez en Californie ? demanda Margaret.

— Je ne suis jamais allée nulle part, madame Sadler. Nous avons visité Disney World quand j'avais dix ans. J'ai vu la mer pour la première fois quand nous étions dans l'avion.

Tracy poussa un soupir exagérément bruyant.

— Je t'ai déjà dit de ne pas étaler ton ignorance. Les gens vont te prendre pour une arriérée mentale.

Cette Janice ! Elle lui aurait tout fait ! pensait-elle, agacée. Trop conforme à la société du Midwest, elle risquait de passer pour une plouc selon les standards californiens.

— Pas du tout ! objecta Beverly. Moi je trouve la réaction de Janice tout à fait charmante.

Tracy fusilla son amie d'un œil noir.

— Charmante ! répéta-t-elle d'une voix chantante. Tu vois ce que je veux dire ?

Margaret sortit un sac à dos du coffre.

— Écoutez ! Quand vos affaires seront rangées, nous pourrions aller toutes les quatre à la plage ? Le dîner ne sera pas prêt avant une bonne heure.

— Tu n'aurais pas dû préparer le repas ! dit Beverly.

— Oh, ce n'est pas grand-chose : carottes râpées, bœuf bouilli et salade de pommes de terre.

— Je veux un dîner mexicain ! objecta Tracy. Janice n'a encore jamais goûté la cuisine mexicaine.

Elle avait intérêt à poser tout de suite des limites, si elle ne voulait pas que les deux « vieilles biques » lui dictent sa conduite et l'emmènent dans des endroits où elle ne voulait aller pour rien au monde. C'étaient aussi ses vacances, après tout, et elle estimait avoir son mot à dire.

— Demain, répondit Beverly, lui intimant des yeux le silence.

— Désolée, dit Tracy à son invitée. Apparemment, il va falloir que tu attendes.

Mais, soudain, une idée lui traversa l'esprit.

— À moins que nous ne sortions toutes seules ! s'exclama-t-elle.

L'horrible voiture que sa mère avait louée représentait à présent sa seule issue de secours.

— Ça va aller, s'empressa de répondre Janice. Ça m'est égal. De toute façon, je ne tiens pas trop à la cuisine mexicaine.

À la fois furieuse et stupéfaite, Tracy souleva sa valise et se dirigea vers le chalet. Une conversation s'imposait entre Janice et elle. Elle mettrait les choses au point. Avant de venir, elle avait pourtant exposé son plan, mais son amie semblait déjà se désolidariser. Tracy l'avait prévenue que, par exemple, si elles emmenaient Chris avec elles, elles n'auraient pas la moindre chance de connaître d'autres garçons.

— Quand je pense que tu m'as dit que la maison était pourrie ! murmura Janice dans l'entrée. Elle est magnifique.

— Arrête de t'extasier toutes les cinq minutes ! Ça fait ringard !

— Tracy, Janice et toi pourriez vous installer dans la chambre que j'occupe habituellement avec ton père, suggéra Beverly.

— Pourquoi ?

Tracy aimait bien sa chambre ; elle était située à l'arrière de la maison et il y faisait sombre jusque tard dans la matinée. De plus, la fenêtre lui permettait d'aller et venir sans que personne ne le sache.

— Pour que Chris ne soit pas obligé de dormir sur le canapé comme chaque année, lui expliqua sa mère.

— Et où allez-vous dormir, Margaret et toi ?

— Dans ton ancienne chambre… Si cela ne te dérange pas, Margaret.

— Pas du tout. Ce sera comme au bon vieux temps, Beverly. Tu étais une parfaite colocataire.

Tracy n'en croyait pas ses oreilles.

— Vous voulez que je couche dans le même lit que Janice ? s'offusqua-t-elle.

— C'est un lit double, Tracy, remarqua sa mère.

— Je m'en fiche ! Je ne suis pas d'accord.

— Attends, dit Janice, conciliante. Moi, à la maison, je dors avec ma sœur…

— La ferme ! coupa Tracy. Et quant à toi, maman, tu

66

n'as qu'à prendre la chambre au grand lit avec Margaret.

— Ça m'est vraiment égal, déclara cette dernière.

Beverly regarda son ancienne colocataire.

— En es-tu sûre ?

— Certaine.

Tracy eut un sourire victorieux. Enfin, les choses allaient dans son sens.

— Formidable ! Maintenant que ce problème est réglé, allons poser nos valises. Janice et moi irons tout de suite à la plage. Nous rentrerons pour le dîner.

Janice adressa un coup d'œil impuissant à Beverly.

— Vous n'avez besoin de rien, madame McCormick ?

— De rien qui presse, Janice.

— Pourquoi ne venez-vous pas avec nous ? On peut vous attendre, vous savez.

Un gémissement désespéré échappa à Tracy. Si elle avait su que Janice était une telle lèche-bottes, elle l'aurait laissée dans son gourbi.

— Maman ne bougera pas avant d'avoir défait ses bagages, dit-elle. Si tu l'attends, il fera nuit quand tu descendras à la plage et tu ne verras rien.

— Allez-y, les filles. Margaret et moi viendrons plus tard.

Beverly et Margaret retournèrent à la voiture. Lorsqu'elles revinrent, chargées des derniers bagages, les deux jeunes filles s'étaient volatilisées.

— Je suis navrée, murmura Beverly, abattue. Tracy est infernale ces derniers temps. Rien ni personne ne trouvent grâce à ses yeux.

Ce n'est pas nouveau, songea Margaret, s'efforçant néanmoins de consoler son amie.

— L'adolescence est un âge difficile.

— Clyde se demande si ce n'est pas dans la façon dont nous l'avons élevée que nous devons chercher l'origine du mal.

Margaret eut le bon goût de n'émettre aucun commentaire.

— Tu sais, reprit Beverly, les déménagements n'ont pas arrangé les choses. Nous n'avons vécu nulle part plus de deux ans. La pauvre Tracy changeait constamment d'école. C'était toujours la «petite nouvelle», et elle devait fournir des efforts considérables pour prouver sa valeur. Oui, tout ce remue-ménage a dû la traumatiser, tu ne crois pas?

— J'ai vécu la même chose, et c'est vrai que ce n'était pas facile, répliqua Margaret.

Son père, sergent dans l'aviation, avait décidé de faire faire à sa famille le tour du monde aux frais du gouvernement américain.

— Comment t'es-tu débrouillée?

— Je n'avais pas le choix.

Margaret fouilla dans sa mémoire, à la recherche d'un indice qui aurait pu aider Beverly.

— Je pense que c'est pour cette raison que je suis restée à Fresno et que je permets à Kevin, chaque fois que l'on se voit, de m'en mettre plein la vue avec son grand bonheur. Après le divorce, l'envie d'avoir enfin des racines m'a empêchée de changer une nouvelle fois de paysage. Je l'aurais peut-être fait si j'avais su que Kevin ne s'occuperait pas de Chris.

— Je me demande si Tracy sera comme toi, dit Beverly.

Elle ouvrit le sac de voyage, sortit les vêtements de sa fille, les étala sur le lit.

— As-tu des problèmes avec ton fils? s'enquit-elle d'une voix si pleine d'espoir qu'elle en était pathétique.

Margaret ne s'inquiétait que d'une seule chose: elle trouvait Chris trop parfait pour son âge. Il ne rentrait jamais tard, l'appelait toujours pour lui dire où il était et l'aidait à la maison sans qu'elle le lui demande. Le divorce de ses parents lui avait volé une partie de son enfance en lui inculquant une sagesse d'adulte. Un soupir lui échappa. Au moins qu'il soit heureux! pria-t-elle. Qu'il fonde une famille, qu'il ait des enfants.

— Non, pas encore, admit-elle, réalisant qu'elle n'avait pas répondu à la question de son amie. Mais cela ne devrait pas tarder.

Elle prit le sac à dos aux initiales de Tracy et le porta dans la chambre où se trouvaient les lits jumeaux.

— J'ai toujours espéré que Tracy et Chris se mettraient ensemble, dit Beverly. Comme tous les deux iront à l'université l'année prochaine, c'est leur dernière chance de mieux se connaître. Tracy ne le sait pas, mais Clyde a renoncé à son billet pour cette raison. Il avait peur qu'elle ne vienne pas du tout, s'il ne cédait pas.

— Moi, je ne serais pas déçue si cela ne marchait pas, avoua prudemment Margaret. Ils se voient seulement un mois par an. Pour les jeunes de leur âge, les onze mois restants sont une éternité.

Dieu merci ! ajouta-t-elle mentalement, car tout en connaissant les sentiments de Chris à l'égard de Tracy, elle ne pouvait imaginer une union plus terrible.

Beverly rangeait les vêtements de sa fille. Avant de les suspendre sur un cintre, elle fouillait méthodiquement les poches, comme si elle sacrifiait à un rituel. Margaret la suivait du regard, étonnée. Cherchait-elle quelque chose de précis ou était-ce une habitude ? Elle n'aurait jamais eu l'idée de fureter ainsi dans les poches de son fils.

— Clyde estime beaucoup Chris, déclara Beverly.

— Euh… fit Margaret, tirée brutalement de ses méditations. Chris apprécie également Clyde, ajouta-t-elle machinalement.

La porte de l'entrée s'ouvrit.

— Je suis là ! annonça Chris d'une voix forte.

Margaret se rendit dans l'entrée.

— Viens. Nous sommes dans la pièce du fond.

Le sourire radieux du garçon s'effaça quand il ne vit Tracy nulle part. Il regarda par-dessus l'épaule de Beverly, qui lui faisait gentiment la bise, et sa mère pointa le doigt en direction de la plage.

— Regarde-moi toutes ces fringues ! s'exclama-t-il. Elle a vidé ses penderies, ma parole.

— Tracy a invité une de ses amies, lui expliqua sa mère.

— Elle s'appelle Janice Carlson, compléta Beverly. Elle est chef des supporters avec Tracy.

Le garçon haussa les sourcils.

— Tracy est chef des supporters ? Depuis quand ?

Le sourire de Beverly témoignait d'un mélange de satisfaction suprême et d'admiration condescendante.

— Je l'ai pourtant dit à ta mère, j'en suis sûre. Elle a simplement oublié de te le rapporter.

Beverly ne lui avait rien dit du tout, songea Margaret, et elle aurait mieux fait de s'abstenir sur le sujet : Chris n'appréciait pas beaucoup les chefs des supporters de son lycée. Il n'hésitait d'ailleurs pas à les qualifier d'adjectifs peu flatteurs.

— Clyde ne pouvait pas venir, alors nous avons emmené Janice à sa place, poursuivit Beverly. C'est la première fois qu'elle voit la mer.

— Ah, cool, dit le jeune homme sans enthousiasme.

— Je ne t'ai pas encore dit la meilleure, reprit Beverly, intarissable. Cette année, tu auras ta chambre. Fini, le canapé, mon jeune ami.

— Je déménagerai tes affaires ce soir, après le dîner, renchérit Margaret.

— Et où tu dormiras, toi ?

— Avec Beverly.

— Tu n'es pas obligée de faire ça, maman. Le canapé me convient parfaitement.

La réaction de Chris à propos de leurs arrangements nocturnes était trop diamétralement opposée à celle de Tracy pour ne pas susciter une remarque.

— Quelle gentillesse ! s'écria Beverly. Je t'emmène chez moi, si tu veux. C'est peut-être la seule façon d'enseigner les bonnes manières à Tracy.

Chris adressa un regard suppliant à sa mère, qui changea ostensiblement de sujet.

— Où es-tu allé ? Tu as l'air d'avoir fait l'aller-retour entre Santa Cruz et Monterey.

— Je sens le fauve ! dit-il en souriant.

Il leva le bras pour renifler son aisselle.

— Pouah ! Je vais prendre une douche. À quelle heure allons-nous dîner ?

— J'ai dit aux filles dans une heure.

Margaret consulta sa montre.

— Il y a une demi-heure déjà.

Une heure et demie plus tard, Tracy et Janice brillaient toujours par leur absence. Chris partit à leur recherche et les aperçut qui montaient les marches.

— Oh, zut ! marmonna Tracy. Chris ! Il vient nous chercher.

Janice leva les yeux et s'arrêta net.

— C'est lui, Chris Sadler ?

— Oui. Inutile de hurler. Tu vas ameuter le quartier. Ferme la bouche et arrête de le regarder comme une vache amoureuse. Je n'ai jamais dit qu'il était moche.

— Il est superbe, tu veux dire ! murmura Janice.

— Attends qu'il dise un mot, pauvre bécasse.

Elle gratifia Chris du sourire réfrigérant qu'elle adressait aux garçons de son lycée, quand ils la sollicitaient.

— Salut, Chris.

— On s'inquiétait, dit-il.

— J'avais prévenu maman que nous ferions un tour.

Elle attendit qu'il s'efface pour la laisser passer, puis se remit à grimper les marches.

— Le dîner est prêt, ajouta-t-il.

Quand Janice fut à sa hauteur, il la salua.

— Bonjour. Je suis Chris.

Étonnée par une telle marque de politesse, elle serra la main qu'il lui tendait.

— Enchantée. Janice Carlson.

— J'espérais que vous auriez dîné sans nous, lança Tracy. Janice voulait vraiment manger mexicain, ce soir.

Chris se tourna vers Janice, qui confirma mollement :

— C'est vrai. Nous en avons parlé dans l'avion.

— Demain, nous pourrions y aller… commença Chris.

— Après-demain peut-être, coupa Janice. Nous avons tout le mois devant nous.

Les trois jeunes gens poursuivirent ensemble la montée.

— Que penses-tu de la mer, alors ? s'enquit Chris. Beverly a dit que c'était ta première fois.

Les deux filles éclatèrent de rire, amusées par ce sous-entendu involontaire.

— Oh, j'adore, répondit alors Janice en souriant. Mais l'eau est trop froide.

— Le courant de l'Alaska, expliqua Chris. On est très au sud, mais il parvient jusqu'ici. C'est également l'une des raisons pour lesquelles les requins blancs infestent le triangle entre Santa Cruz, San Francisco et les îles Farallon.

— Oh, non ! gémit Tracy. Elle te dit que l'eau est froide et tu te lances dans un cours de biologie marine.

Janice paraissait cependant bien plus intéressée que son amie.

— Et moi qui pensais que les grands blancs apparaissent seulement sur la côte est, comme dans *Les Dents de la mer* !

Chris en savait long sur le film, le tournage et la vie sous-marine dans la baie de Monterey, mais il se tut. Il ne voulait pas que Tracy se méprenne sur ses intentions, ou qu'elle le considère comme un crétin cherchant à impressionner Janice avec ses connaissances.

— Si ça vous dit, nous pourrions visiter l'aquarium de Monterey demain, proposa-t-il. Si vous avez envie d'en savoir plus sur les requins…

— Sans moi ! coupa Tracy. La dernière fois que nous sommes allés dans cet horrible endroit, je me suis juré de ne plus y mettre les pieds. C'est mortel !

— Il y a une nouvelle exposition…

Chris s'interrompit. Tout en prononçant ces mots, il sut qu'il commettait une erreur. Tracy ne changeait jamais d'avis, sur rien.

— Je me fiche pas mal de la nouvelle expo ! Ils peuvent nourrir les requins avec de la chair humaine, ça m'est complètement égal ! Janice et moi sommes venues ici pour nous amuser, pas vrai, Janice ?

3

Le lendemain, alors que les mères étaient parties faire les courses, les filles ne songèrent plus qu'à leur bronzage. Chris, qui les rejoignit sur la plage, ne put tenir plus d'une heure sous les rayons brûlants du soleil.

— Je vais nager, déclara-t-il en se redressant. Je crève de chaud.

Tracy se tourna sur le côté, la tête calée dans sa paume. Ses longs cheveux blonds ruisselèrent et une mèche s'enroula autour de son poignet comme un bracelet d'or. Le petit triangle vermillon de son soutien-gorge glissa un peu plus sur son sein. Encore un centimètre et on en verrait la pointe.

— Avant que tu ne partes, puis-je te demander une faveur ? susurra-t-elle.

Chris attendit les ordres, le regard fixé sur le visage de la jeune fille. S'il regardait plus bas, il risquait de se trahir. Elle allait sûrement le prier de rentrer au chalet afin de leur apporter des boissons.

— Peux-tu m'en mettre sur le dos ? demanda-t-elle finalement en tendant au jeune homme un tube de crème solaire.

Avec un sourire suave, elle se coucha sur le ventre.

— Défais les bretelles, ordonna-t-elle. Je ne veux pas qu'elles deviennent huileuses.

Le garçon se rassit et prit le tube. Il ne respirait plus. Dans ses rêves les plus fous, il dénudait Tracy et passait ses mains sur son corps… Mais pas de cette façon-là. Dans ses rêves, ils étaient seuls. Ils s'embrassaient et elle réagissait à ses caresses par de petits gémissements.

Un voile brûlant recouvrit les joues de Chris, des gouttelettes de sueur perlèrent sur sa poitrine et sur sa nuque.
Bon sang, il avait une érection !

— Qu'est-ce qui ne va pas ?

Tracy voulut rouler sur le côté, mais la main de Chris
sur son épaule la força à rester immobile.

— Le capuchon est collé, bougonna-t-il.

— Appuie dessus. Il ne se dévisse pas.

Il s'exécuta, après quoi, les doigts tremblants, il dénoua
le cordon rouge qui ceignait le dos de Tracy.

— J'enlève aussi celui autour de ton cou ?

— Oui, s'il te plaît.

D'un revers de la main, la jeune fille écarta sa longue
chevelure blonde. Chris tira doucement sur le nœud, qui
se défit tout seul. L'espace d'un instant, il crut que Tracy
se redresserait, les seins nus, les yeux passionnés.

— Dépêche ! se plaignit-elle. On ne va pas y passer la
journée !

Il remplit sa paume avec suffisamment de crème pour
enduire une bonne demi-douzaine de dos. Alors qu'il
essayait d'en remettre une partie dans le tube, il ne réussit qu'à en répandre la moitié sur son bermuda. Janice
détourna la tête, étouffant un rire dans sa main.

Déterminé à mener sa mission à bien, Chris étala le
reste de la lotion sur le dos de Tracy. Le geste ferme, il la
massa jusqu'à la taille. Ensuite, il jeta le tube sur la serviette de bain et annonça, non sans effort :

— Bon, je vais nager.

Dieu merci, son bermuda dissimulait son désir. Il se
mit à courir vers la mer. À mi-chemin, il entendit les deux
filles rire. Elles devaient se moquer de lui, pensa-t-il, hon-
teux. Sans se retourner, il piqua une tête dans l'eau en se
traitant de lâche.

Lorsqu'il émergea des flots, Tracy et Janice n'étaient
plus à leur place. Il les chercha pendant un moment, puis
noua sa serviette autour de ses reins pour remonter au
chalet. Personne. Il se prépara un sandwich au rôti de
bœuf et retourna à l'escalier. Du haut de la falaise, il apercevait toute la plage. Ne les voyant nulle part, il essaya

de se convaincre qu'il les avait ratées. Il redescendit, le cœur lourd.

Il discuta pendant deux heures avec un sauveteur qu'il avait rencontré l'été précédent. L'homme le régala d'anecdotes. Il avait passé l'hiver à voyager à travers le pays et avait été embauché comme artificier. Il avait décidé de quitter cet État « de chômeurs », acheva-t-il. Chris répondit qu'il n'imaginait pas de vivre ailleurs.

Quand un autre sauveteur vint remplacer le premier, il n'y avait toujours aucun signe de Tracy et de Janice. Chris partit voir si le match de volley-ball avait commencé.

La journée suivante fut identique, à ceci près que Tracy demanda à Janice de lui mettre de la crème dans le dos, et que cette dernière vint nager avec Chris. Mais elle ne resta pas plus d'un quart d'heure dans l'eau froide... Cette fois-ci, les jeunes filles disparurent avant que Chris remonte prendre sa douche.

Il resta alors jusqu'à la fin du match de volley-ball. Quand il rentra, le chalet était vide. Un mot de sa mère l'avertit qu'elles étaient parties toutes les quatre dans un restaurant mexicain. Son dîner était dans le réfrigérateur. Margaret finissait ses explications par la promesse de rapporter à son fils des chips et de la sauce mexicaine.

Il réchauffa son repas dans le micro-ondes, et s'installa sur la terrasse où il mangea en regardant le crépuscule. Le vent était tombé, le soleil descendait sur une mer d'huile. La plage, presque déserte à cette heure-ci, s'étirait comme un mince ruban blanc. Durant la nuit, la marée haute effacerait les traces des humains ; elle laisserait le sable vierge aux créatures diurnes qui viendraient chercher leurs proies.

Chris mastiquait lentement, les yeux fixés sur le couchant. Chaque fois qu'il songeait à son avenir, la même conclusion s'imposait invariablement à son esprit. Tout n'était qu'une question d'argent ! Le moindre bungalow à la ronde, même le plus minable, valait plus d'un demi-million de dollars. Il n'osait imaginer les prix dans dix ans, quand il voudrait en acheter un.

Contrairement à Tracy, Chris avait du mal à envisager un été ailleurs. Le plus dur serait quand la jeune fille ne passerait plus ses vacances ici. À ses yeux, elle faisait partie du paysage, comme les vagues ou le sable.

Chaque année, il se disait qu'il était impossible qu'elle soit mieux que dans son souvenir. Et, chaque année, il la découvrait plus belle que jamais. Tracy pouvait s'habiller avec un sac à pommes de terre, elle éclipsait toutes les filles endimanchées au bal de la promo. Tout en elle confinait à la perfection : sa peau, ses cheveux, ses yeux, sa bouche. Même ses seins étaient parfaits, ni trop gros ni trop petits.

Il n'avait pas sa classe. Dans son esprit, c'était clair. Il connaissait ses faiblesses, comme il décelait les défauts de ses adversaires sur le ring. Pourquoi son cœur ne voulait-il pas se rendre à l'évidence ?

Une voix masculine brisa le silence :

— Sublime spectacle, n'est-ce pas ?

Chris se retourna si vivement qu'il renversa son verre de thé glacé.

— Désolé, dit Eric. Je ne voulais pas vous faire peur.

— Je n'attendais personne.

Chris releva son verre et essuya la chaise en fer forgé à l'aide d'une serviette en papier.

— Vous êtes le locataire du cottage voisin ?

— Oui. Je m'appelle Eric Lawson.

— Voulez-vous du thé glacé ? Ou bien une bière ?

— Non, merci. Je revenais d'une promenade quand je vous ai aperçu. Je me suis dit qu'il était temps que je me présente.

— Maman m'a dit que vous êtes écrivain.

Eric cala son épaule contre le poteau de la mangeoire des oiseaux.

— J'essaie.

— Qu'est-ce que vous écrivez ?

— Un roman.

— De quel genre ?

Eric sourit.

— Un thriller médical. C'est du moins l'appellation que mon agent donne à mes écrits. Mon petit doigt me dit que vous êtes un fan de science-fiction.

— Oui, mais j'aime aussi la littérature générale.

Eric ne correspondait pas à l'idée que Chris se faisait des écrivains. Loin d'être « fêlé », il paraissait si normal que c'en était décevant.

— Vous êtes médecin ?

— Félicitations. Vous êtes le premier à faire le rapprochement.

— Ce serait drôlement difficile d'écrire sur un sujet qu'on ne connaît pas à fond.

Mais les médecins ramassaient l'argent à la pelle. Pourquoi celui-ci avait-il abandonné la belle vie pour écrire des bouquins ?

— De toute façon, ce n'est pas facile. Si je n'avais pas quitté mon cabinet, j'y serais sans doute retourné.

Chris sourit. Le dénommé Eric lui plaisait bien. Il semblait sincère et droit, et ne s'adressait pas à lui avec le ton condescendant des adultes, sous prétexte qu'il était adolescent.

— Allez-vous rester tout l'été ? s'enquit-il.

— Je resterai pendant l'absence d'Andrew. Il fait le tour du monde, alors j'en ai sûrement pour un an. Peut-être deux, s'il s'attarde en chemin.

— Quelle chance !

— De partir en bateau ?

— Ah ! Ah ! Non, monsieur ! De rester ici. J'ai toujours rêvé de passer l'hiver au chalet.

— Vous ne reconnaîtriez pas le décor, répondit Eric. La plage est déserte, à l'exception de trois surfeurs dingos et de quelques cinglés comme moi. Nous autres, irréductibles, défions les éléments. Aucun orage, aucune pluie battante ne peuvent nous confiner à la maison. Ce qui explique pourquoi je ne suis pas très avancé dans mon livre.

— Avez-vous des délais pour le finir ?

Eric changea de position.

— Personne ne l'attend, en dehors de mon agent.

— Je parie que vous ne tenez pas en place. Vous voulez savoir coûte que coûte ce que les autres en pensent.

Eric hocha la tête.

— Oui, parfois, admit-il. Mais, la plupart du temps, j'ai sacrément peur.

— Ce sera génial, vous verrez! affirma Chris avec une conviction toute juvénile.

Des phares de voiture éclairèrent soudain l'allée.

— Je crois que votre maman est de retour, fit remarquer Eric.

— Elles sont allées dîner sans moi.

Il considéra un instant sa phrase, puis rectifia :

— Je jouais au volley et je me suis attardé.

— Je vous ai vu.

— Ah, vraiment? s'étonna Chris, à la fois surpris et content.

— Vous êtes sacrément bon. C'est votre sport favori à l'école?

— Je suis inscrit dans l'équipe de lutte. Le volley-ball me sert à conserver la forme, déclara-t-il d'une voix ferme.

— Et vous êtes aussi doué pour le combat?

Chris sentit la fierté le suffoquer. Il avait accumulé de nombreuses médailles mais n'en parlait pour ainsi dire jamais.

— Je me débrouille, répondit-il avec modestie.

— J'ai l'impression que vous faites mieux que vous débrouiller. Est-ce que vous serez là, la semaine prochaine?

— Nous restons jusqu'à la fin du mois. Pourquoi? demanda-t-il avec curiosité.

— Un de mes amis viendra dîner avec moi. Je pense que vous serez content de le connaître. Si vous n'avez rien de mieux à faire, ce soir-là, vous êtes cordialement invité. Il s'appelle Charlie Stephens.

Il fallut à Chris une seconde pour enregistrer le nom.

— Le champion?

Il n'en croyait pas ses oreilles. Charlie Stephens avait ramassé plus de médailles d'or aux Jeux olympiques que n'importe quel lutteur américain.

— Lui-même. Je l'appellerai pour qu'il apporte ses trophées. Il n'aime pas ça, mais il le fera pour me faire plaisir.

La porte vitrée coulissa derrière Chris.

— Ah, te voilà, dit Margaret. Tu as trouvé ton dîner ? Voyant Eric, elle sourit.

— Comment se porte le chef-d'œuvre ?

— Il compte quatre pages de plus qu'hier, à la même heure.

— Sont-elles satisfaisantes ?

— J'ai vu pire.

— Vous ne connaissez pas le reste du groupe. Nous avons rapporté un gâteau du restaurant. Voudriez-vous le goûter avec nous ?

— Non, mais ce n'est que partie remise. Ma pause est terminée pour aujourd'hui.

Margaret prit le plateau de Chris.

— Passez nous voir quand vous voulez. Les filles seront ravies de rencontrer un écrivain.

Eric sourit.

— D'accord, merci. J'en suis flatté.

Il adressa à Chris un signe d'au revoir.

— À bientôt. Je vous ferai savoir quel jour Charlie sera là.

— À un de ces jours, lança Chris, tandis qu'Eric s'éloignait.

Lorsqu'il fut hors de vue, le jeune homme attrapa le bras de sa mère.

— Maman ! Tu ne croiras pas ce qui m'arrive.

Elle le couva d'un regard anxieux.

— Dis-moi que c'est une bonne chose, au moins. J'ai passé la pire soirée de ma vie. Au restaurant, Tracy et Beverly n'ont pas cessé de se chamailler. Tout y est passé, des tacos, pour savoir s'ils sont de la cuisine authentiquement mexicaine, aux bienfaits et aux méfaits du bronzage artificiel.

Chris lui prit l'autre bras et la fit s'asseoir. Quand il eut fini son récit, il eut une fois de plus la preuve qu'il avait la mère la plus cool du monde. Car non seulement Margaret se montra aussi excitée que lui à la perspective d'une rencontre avec Charlie Stephens, mais elle savait qui il était.

4

Le samedi matin, au petit déjeuner, Chris annonça négligemment que le soir même, il était invité à une fête. Il ajouta ensuite deux pancakes dans son assiette et les arrosa abondamment de sirop d'érable. Il restait impassible, mais son cœur battait très fort. Tracy n'avait pas cessé de décliner son ennui sur tous les tons durant la semaine. Il allait enfin lui offrir un divertissement.

— J'ai demandé si vous pouviez venir, Janice et toi, et on m'a dit qu'il n'y avait pas de problème, reprit-il en luttant pour parler d'un ton calme.

Il attendit la réaction, sur des charbons ardents.

Le visage de Tracy s'éclaira.

— Oh, chic ! s'exclama-t-elle. Si tu sors, on ira sur la promenade s...

Elle s'interrompit net et pouffa dans sa main.

— Bonjour le lapsus ! s'esclaffa-t-elle à l'intention de son amie.

Chris se rembrunit. À l'évidence, le mot manquant était « seules ». Il aurait voulu mourir. Là, à table, tout de suite. Tracy lui aurait asséné un coup de couteau, que ç'aurait été un cadeau.

— Une fête, ça pourrait être marrant, remarqua Janice platement. Qui est-ce qui invite ?

— Des copains...

Chris n'eut pas le courage de finir sa phrase. Il coupa un bout de pancake et le laissa intact. Décidément, il n'y avait pas moyen d'impressionner Tracy sans en prendre plein la figure !

Margaret entra dans la salle à manger avec une assiette de bacon supplémentaire, tandis que Beverly, en peignoir, émergeait de sa chambre.

— Bonjour! lança-t-elle en bâillant. Mon Dieu! Je ne me rappelle plus le jour où je me suis réveillée aussi tard.

— Tu es en vacances, dit posément Margaret. Quoi de plus...

— Maman, on a besoin de la voiture! coupa Tracy.

— Que se passe-t-il? demanda sa mère.

— Nous allons sur la promenade, ce soir.

L'adolescente plongea un doigt dans son jus d'orange, puis le fourra dans sa bouche, comme si une seule goutte suffisait à son régime draconien.

— J'aurai besoin d'argent, dit-elle à brûle-pourpoint. Tu es allée au distributeur?

Beverly regarda Chris.

— C'est quoi cette histoire? Tu les accompagnes?

— Il est invité à une fête! lança Tracy à la place de Chris.

Margaret posa l'assiette de bacon sur la table et s'installa face à son fils.

— Où ça? voulut-elle savoir.

— Chez les gens avec qui j'ai joué au volley, expliqua-t-il. Leurs petites amies viennent pour le week-end. Tony reçoit tout le monde chez lui.

Beverly se servit une tasse de café.

— Voilà qui est sympathique. Pourquoi n'iriez-vous pas avec Chris, Tracy?

— Maman!

— Je t'en prie! Je suis sûre que tu peux lui demander cette petite faveur. N'est-ce pas Chris?

Aucun doute ne perçait dans sa voix. Chris respira profondément. Il avait l'impression qu'on le prenait pour un toutou. Un brave bâtard de qui l'on peut tout exiger – «Couché! Assis! Va chercher! Apporte!» – mais qui n'a pas le droit de souiller de sa présence le salon où se prélassent les chiens de race. Écœuré, il repoussa sa chaise et se leva.

— Ça dépend de Tracy, madame McCormick.

— De Tracy ? répéta Beverly. Je ne comprends pas.

— Maman, ça suffit maintenant. Nous avons nos plans !

— Rien d'important, je présume. Écoute, ma petite, tu me feras le plaisir de…

Chris se précipita hors de la pièce. Il n'avait nulle envie d'entendre la suite.

Il prit le chemin de la plage, en faisant une halte sur le pic de la falaise. En bas, c'était noir de monde. Il préféra revenir sur ses pas et coupa à travers le sentier rocailleux en direction de l'autoroute. Il entendit soudain sa mère l'appeler. Sans doute voulait-elle essayer de le consoler ? Il préférait cependant rester seul. En levant la tête, il la vit sur la terrasse et agita la main dans sa direction. Elle lui rendit son geste avec un sourire.

Il s'élança de nouveau dans le sentier, sous l'ombre mouvante des platanes. Il passa devant l'entrée du parking public et déboucha peu après à la croisée des chemins. Le rugissement d'un moteur déchira le silence. Chris regarda par-dessus son épaule. Une Jeep apparut. Avec sa carrosserie noire et ses chromes peints en or, elle semblait sortir d'une revue de mode. Elle le dépassa et suivit le panneau indiquant l'autoroute. Cinquante mètres plus loin, elle s'immobilisa dans un crissement de pneus. Un conducteur paumé, pensa Chris, qui força l'allure, prêt à donner des renseignements. La tête brune de Tony passa par la fenêtre ouverte.

— Hé, mec ! Dépêche-toi.

Chris arriva en courant à sa hauteur.

— Salut, Tony. J'ai cru comprendre que tu travaillais, aujourd'hui.

— Justement, j'y vais. Je t'emmène ?

— À ton boulot ?

L'invitation semblait incongrue.

Tony hocha la tête.

— Monte, on causera après. Tu ne sais pas qui je suis, hein ?

— Non… Je devrais le savoir ?

— C'est mon agent qui va être déçu !

Soudain, Chris fit le rapprochement.

— Ça y est, j'y suis. Tu es acteur. Excuse-moi, tu me disais bien quelque chose, mais je ne te remettais pas.

— On tourne à Watsonville. Et je suis en retard, dit Tony en consultant sa montre. Alors, tu viens ?

Depuis le départ de son père, Chris ne cédait que très rarement à ses impulsions. Les impondérables de la vie, ses nouvelles responsabilités l'avaient rendu prudent. Sa première réaction fut de grimper dans la Jeep, mais il se retint, déchiré par la pensée que sa mère aurait peut-être besoin de lui, même si elle lui avait dit et répété qu'il était libre de s'amuser pendant les vacances. Un second élan fut contrecarré par l'idée désagréable qu'il abandonnait lâchement Tracy et Janice. Toute réflexion faite, les deux adolescentes seraient plutôt satisfaites.

— Oui, d'accord, répondit-il finalement.

Il contourna la Jeep et s'installa à côté de Tony.

Le film fascina Chris à tous points de vue.

Au chaos apparent succédaient des moments d'intense concentration. Les acteurs et les techniciens semblaient à la fois désinvoltes et sérieux. Tout s'orchestrait sur le plateau entouré d'immenses projecteurs, de caméras et d'une multitude de câbles et de fils. Entre deux prises, le maquilleur faisait irruption parmi les comédiens, armé de tubes, de pinceaux et de houppettes.

Pour une raison inconnue, le réalisateur décida de filmer indéfiniment la même séquence. L'unique tâche d'un des assistants consista à remplir de bière le verre d'un acteur et à lui procurer une cigarette consumée aux trois quarts. Chris tomba en admiration devant une femme qui maniait une caméra aussi grosse qu'elle.

Il fut déçu quand le spectacle s'arrêta pour la pause-déjeuner.

Tony déambula sur le plateau vide.

— Ça t'a plu ? demanda-t-il.

Chris esquissa un sourire béat. Tony, dans le rôle d'un jeune ouvrier agricole des années soixante en révolte contre l'idéologie pacifiste de César Chavez, l'avait subjugué.

— Oh, oui, répondit-il, enthousiasmé. J'ai adoré.

Il éprouvait la même excitation qu'à son premier championnat : ses jambes étaient molles, sa tête légère.

— Tant mieux, approuva Tony. Allons avaler un morceau.

À la place des sandwichs et des chips auxquels il s'attendait, Chris découvrit un buffet beaucoup plus somptueux que celui du deuxième mariage de son père.

— Sensas ! dit-il en sifflant. Vous mangez toujours autant ?

Tony s'effaça pour le laisser passer devant lui dans la file.

— Que veux-tu, ça s'impose. On brûle pas mal de calories quand on joue.

Chris attrapa une assiette. Se considérant comme un invité de dernière heure, il choisit de petites quantités dans chaque plat. Lorsqu'il prit deux crevettes du bout de sa fourchette, Tony saisit la grande cuillère de service et en ajouta une bonne douzaine dans l'assiette de Chris, qui se servit ensuite plus librement.

Ils mangèrent dans la roulotte climatisée de Tony, en compagnie de deux autres joueurs de volley-ball. La conversation roula sur différents sujets : la réception de la soirée, le tournage de la veille, les travers d'Untel ou d'Unetelle. Il était question de personnes que Chris ne connaissait absolument pas. Pourtant, il suivit l'échange de propos si religieusement que Tony lui rappela de se nourrir.

Après le déjeuner, ils retournèrent sur le plateau.

— Tu te plais avec nous, on dirait, commenta Tony.

— C'est vrai, admit Chris. Je ne connais rien au cinéma, et je découvre plein de choses. Je n'ai plus tellement les moyens d'y aller et quand ça m'arrivait, avant, j'étais trop jeune pour me demander comment les films étaient fabriqués.

— Aimerais-tu jouer ?

— Qui, moi ?

— Pourquoi pas ?

— Oh, non, Tony, je ne saurais pas faire ce que tu fais. Tu sais, pendant un moment, tu étais vraiment dans la peau de ton personnage. C'était fantastique.

Le comédien lui sourit.

— Merci, mec !

Tandis que Tony allait se faire maquiller, Chris regarda les techniciens. La prochaine séquence exigeait un éclairage différent, et ils s'appliquaient à changer les projecteurs, afin d'obtenir un effet de nuit. Une femme équipée d'un porte-voix pria Chris de déplacer son escabeau. Il obtempéra et, de sa nouvelle place, aperçut Tony. Ce dernier se tenait à la porte du studio, l'air étrangement lointain. Et, sous le regard émerveillé de Chris, l'incroyable transformation s'opéra une fois de plus. Le Tony avec qui il avait joué au volley-ball sur la plage, et qui l'avait emmené ici, disparaissait peu à peu. Bientôt le jeune ouvrier révolté aux yeux farouches se tint à sa place.

Plus tard dans l'après-midi, sur le chemin du retour, Chris bombarda son nouvel ami de questions. Il reçut un cours rapide sur l'art du comédien.

— J'ignorais que l'on pouvait apprendre ce métier. Je pensais qu'on l'avait dans le sang ou pas du tout.

— D'après mon vieux prof de théâtre, la réussite d'un acteur dépend à quatre-vingt-dix pour cent de sa ténacité et à dix pour cent de son talent, dit Tony.

— Mais toi, qu'est-ce que tu en penses ?

Tony fit descendre la vitre, laissant l'air moite du soir se mêler à l'air conditionné.

— La réussite est l'amalgame de plusieurs facteurs. La chance, par exemple, en est un non négligeable.

— Tu te considères comme un chanceux ? interrogea Chris.

— Et comment ! Je ne serais pas ici si je n'étais pas tombé malade, il y a quelques années. Cloué au lit, je rate la croisière que je dois animer. Mais, à peine rétabli, je reçois le coup de fil d'un copain. « Si tu veux gagner trois sous, il y a un type à Malibu qui cherche un barman pour sa réception », me dit-il. Ne faisant ni une ni deux, je me pointe à l'adresse indiquée. Et, une fois sur place, qu'est-ce que je découvre ? Je te le donne en mille. J'étais chez l'agent que j'essayais de joindre depuis des lustres. Le genre de monstre inaccessible, tu saisis ?

Chris hocha la tête.

— Génial ! J'adore ce genre d'histoires.

Tony émit un rire.

— Moi aussi ! Surtout quand elles parlent de moi.

5

Chris trouva la maison vide. La déception noya son enthousiasme. La voiture de location de Mme McCormick n'était pas garée à sa place habituelle. Il avait appelé sa mère du studio pour la prévenir qu'il aurait un léger retard, mais il ne lui avait rien expliqué, préférant tout lui apprendre de vive voix. Et maintenant, elle n'était plus là.

Abominablement frustré, il chercha en vain un indice qui lui révélerait la destination de ces dames, puis fit le tour du jardin afin de s'assurer que sa mère n'arrosait pas les plates-bandes. Personne ! Résolu à attendre, il prit un soda dans le réfrigérateur, sortit sur la terrasse et s'assit. Mais un instant plus tard, il se levait d'un bond. Impossible de tenir en place.

Il lui tardait de raconter sa merveilleuse aventure à sa mère. Et, au fond, la réaction de Tracy lui importait plus encore. Son esprit, à l'instar de celui des enfants, s'attachait à une vengeance puérile. « Un jour, tu verras ! Un jour, tu le regretteras. » Eh bien, le jour tant espéré était survenu plus tôt que prévu. Combien de fois cela arrive-t-il, dans une vie ?

Tracy ne perdait rien pour attendre ! pensa-t-il, avec une délectation rancunière. Quand elle saurait qui l'avait invité, elle le supplierait à genoux de l'emmener à la fête. Les yeux fermés, il laissa son imagination vagabonder. Quand l'image d'une Tracy défaite se dessina derrière ses paupières closes, il ressentit une drôle de sensation, une sorte de grand vide. En proie à la confusion, il battit en retraite vers la cuisine.

Il n'avait pas faim après le déjeuner pantagruélique qu'il avait avalé. Il se mit cependant à fureter dans les placards dans l'espoir d'y découvrir quelque chose qui apaiserait sa nervosité. Il mit la main sur un paquet de chips. Alors qu'il s'apprêtait à l'ouvrir, sa mère poussa la porte d'entrée.

— Ah, tu es là, dit-elle en le voyant surgir de la cuisine.

— Depuis une dizaine de minutes seulement. Où sont-elles passées ?

— Tu penses à quelqu'un en particulier ? le taquina-t-elle gentiment. Elles font du shopping. Tracy voulait acheter une robe neuve pour ce soir. Et quand Tracy veut quelque chose, le Bon Dieu en personne doit se plier à sa volonté.

Margaret avait enfilé un short par-dessus son maillot de bain, signe qu'elle revenait de la plage. Elle s'était exprimée d'un ton réprobateur que Chris ne lui connaissait pas.

— Je suis content qu'elles ne soient pas là, dit-il, surpris de sa propre sincérité. Attends que je te dise où j'étais aujourd'hui. Oh, maman, c'était géant ! Tu ne peux pas savoir.

Son exultation la fit sourire.

— J'ai l'impression que je saurai tout dans une minute.

Chris se lança dans son récit. Margaret ne le décevait jamais. Elle l'écouta attentivement, posa les bonnes questions et fit preuve d'un enthousiasme raisonnable.

— Vraiment ! Tu ne savais pas qui il était ? s'enquit-elle quand il eut terminé.

— Non, franchement. Je les ai pris pour des maçons, tu te rends compte ?

— Eric m'a dit qu'on tournait un film à Watsonville. Mais qui aurait cru que la tête d'affiche jouerait au volley sur la plage, comme n'importe quel quidam ?

— Tu sais, tu ne l'aurais pas reconnu toi non plus. Il a les cheveux longs, il porte des lunettes noires et une casquette.

D'un geste affectueux, Margaret ébouriffa les cheveux de son fils.

— Même si Antonio Gallardo ressemblait trait pour trait au personnage qu'il a joué dans son dernier film, tu ne l'aurais pas reconnu, dit-elle gentiment.

— Ce qui veut dire ?

— Que tu n'es pas ébloui par les vedettes de cinéma.

Sans réfléchir davantage, il demanda :

— Veux-tu venir à la fête, ce soir ?

— Non, merci. J'ai un rendez-vous.

— Avec Eric ?

Surprise, Margaret écarquilla les yeux.

— Pourquoi dis-tu cela ?

— Il est célibataire, toi aussi. Vous avez le même âge. Il a l'air chouette... et tu n'es pas mal non plus.

— C'est vrai, comment pourrait-il résister à mon charme !

— Eh bien ?

— Désolée de te décevoir, mais non, je ne sors pas avec Eric. Beverly m'emmène au cinéma... après avoir déposé les deux péronnelles sur la promenade.

— Tracy sait-elle que vous prenez la voiture ?

— Ça, c'est le problème de sa mère.

Il hocha la tête avec sagesse.

— Je comprends mieux pourquoi tu n'es pas allée faire du shopping cet après-midi.

Un rire échappa à Margaret.

— Tu es trop intelligent, mon garçon, et cela pour ton malheur.

— Hé, maman, fais-moi une faveur.

— Oui ?

— Ne parle à personne du tournage, d'accord ?

— Je suppose que tu veux en mettre plein la vue à tes amies ?

Chris haussa les épaules.

— Justement, je n'en sais rien en définitive. Je n'en ai pas très envie.

— Tracy voudra sûrement aller à la soirée avec toi, quand elle saura.

— Mais moi, je ne suis pas sûr de le vouloir.

— Dis donc! Je suis impressionnée, s'esclaffa Margaret.

— Ne le sois pas. Je peux toujours changer d'avis.

Quand Beverly et Tracy regagnèrent le chalet, la dispute à propos de la voiture battait son plein. Janice se glissa dans le vestibule derrière elles. Tête basse, elle disparut dans la chambre qu'elle partageait avec Tracy, puis réapparut en robe de plage, une serviette sous le bras. Elle déclara qu'elle allait nager, avant de s'éclipser à nouveau.

Margaret regarda son fils.

— Pourquoi ne vas-tu pas avec elle?

Chris alla docilement enfiler son bermuda.

Il sortit peu après. La voix haut perchée de Beverly et celle plus stridente de Tracy le suivirent pendant un moment avant de se fondre dans le silence de la nature.

La plage était bondée. Il fallut plusieurs minutes à Chris pour localiser Janice. La jeune fille était dans l'eau, droite comme un piquet, les bras écartés comme pour arrêter l'incessant va-et-vient des vagues. Elle était aussi bronzée qu'un pain d'épices, ce qui n'avait rien d'extraordinaire vu le nombre d'heures qu'elle passait au soleil avec Tracy. Des mèches mordorées striaient sa chevelure brune.

Chris la trouva jolie. Pas autant que Tracy, naturellement, qui incarnait la beauté parfaite à laquelle celle d'aucune autre fille ne pouvait se comparer.

En général, Chris appréciait les filles qui ne se souciaient pas de leur brushing et qui se maquillaient le soir, mais pas dans la journée. Son regard remonta le long du corps de Janice. Les filles qui nagent sans perdre leur maillot de bain... S'il n'était pas amoureux de Tracy, il aurait cherché quelqu'un comme ça. Quelqu'un qui pourrait aussi le battre à un jeu quelconque, en dehors des jeux télévisés.

Il fendit les flots en direction de Janice.

— Salut! lança-t-il. Est-ce que tu as changé d'avis?

Elle ne montra aucune surprise de le sentir à son côté.

— À propos de l'océan?

— Oui.

— Je l'aime un peu plus chaque jour, dit-elle, campée sur la pointe des pieds pour résister aux vagues. Mais je commence à devenir égoïste. Je déteste tous ces gens qui prennent d'assaut ma plage.

Elle se tourna et adressa un sourire penaud à Chris.

— Je la veux pour moi toute seule.

Les mêmes mots dans la bouche de Tracy auraient été pour Chris un ordre de déguerpir. Dans celle de Janice, ils revêtaient une autre signification.

— Il faudra que tu te lèves très tôt si…

— Je sais, l'interrompit-elle.

Il la scruta plus attentivement.

— Vraiment ?

— Oui. La meilleure heure se situe juste avant le lever du soleil. Il n'y a encore personne. On n'entend pas les radios, ni les gamins. Juste le cri des oiseaux et le bruit des vagues.

Elle prit de l'eau claire dans sa paume et la laissa ruisseler entre ses doigts.

— Tu viens toute seule ? s'étonna-t-il.

Elle émit un rire.

— Sois sérieux, Chris. Tom Cruise en personne n'arriverait pas à tirer Tracy du lit si tôt le matin.

— Fais attention, tout de même. Il ne faut pas nager sans escorte.

— Pourquoi ?

— La mer recèle des dangers insoupçonnés. Il faut toujours nager à deux si l'on veut aller au large.

Il donnait ce conseil à tous ses amis.

— Je refuse de vivre dans la crainte, riposta-t-elle. Ça ne veut pas dire que je suis inconsciente. Il existe un tas d'endroits à St Louis où je ne m'aventurerais pas seule. D'ailleurs, mes frères n'y vont pas non plus.

— Si tu veux, je viendrai avec toi.

— Je n'ai pas besoin d'un garde du corps. Je suis parfaitement capable de prendre soin de moi.

— Je ne voulais pas dire ça. Moi aussi j'aime mieux la plage quand elle est vide.

Elle se tourna pour le dévisager.

— Comment se fait-il, alors, que je ne t'aie jamais rencontré ?

— Je viens la nuit. Quand tout le monde est au lit.

— Ta mère le sait ?

— Non.

— J'en étais sûre !

— Pourquoi dis-tu ça ?

— D'après Tracy, ta mère t'a drôlement serré la bride autour du cou, depuis que ton père est parti.

Chris frissonna. Ainsi, il fournissait un sujet de conversation à Tracy et à son amie.

— Eh bien, elle se trompe ! lâcha-t-il.

— Voyons Chris ! Je l'ai bien vu, moi aussi. Ta mère abuse ; elle te contrôle entièrement. Elle n'a qu'un coup d'œil à te jeter pour que tu fasses la vaisselle ou les courses. Je parie qu'elle t'a dit de me retrouver.

Mais de quel droit jugeait-elle sa mère ?

— Et alors ? Elle se fait du souci pour toi, voilà tout. Où est le problème ?

— Puisqu'elle s'inquiète tellement, pourquoi n'est-elle pas venue elle-même ?

Et dire qu'il avait commencé à apprécier Janice !

— Où veux-tu en venir ? s'enquit-il d'une voix blanche.

— Je pense qu'elle ferait mieux de te lâcher les baskets et de se trouver un homme.

La déclaration laissa Chris sans voix. Lorsqu'il recouvrit l'usage de la parole, il cria :

— Espèce de garce ! Tu peux te noyer, tiens ! Je m'en fiche !

Il rebroussa chemin. Janice le vit courir sur le sable en direction de l'escalier de pierre creusé dans la falaise. Il commença à gravir les marches puis, comme s'il avait changé d'avis, mit le cap vers un autre endroit de la plage.

Janice soupira. Bon sang, qu'est-ce qui lui avait pris ? Elle avait ouvert la bouche, et c'étaient les paroles de Tracy qui en avaient jailli. Elle avait fait de la peine à Chris pour rien. Le pire, c'était qu'elle ne croyait même pas aux âneries qu'elle avait débitées. Elle aurait payé cher pour avoir une mère comme Margaret.

Elle avait subi l'influence de Tracy. Celle-ci n'avait pas cessé de décrire Chris comme un perdant. Visiblement, il avait le béguin pour Tracy ; or celle-ci lui aurait préféré Quasimodo. Au lycée, Tracy adorait être courtisée par les garçons. Ici, elle prenait les égards de Chris comme une insulte.

Janice plongea, sans se soucier de ses cheveux. Ce soir, elle les laverait et tant pis s'il lui fallait des heures pour les coiffer. Au moins, pendant que le sèche-cheveux marcherait, elle n'entendrait pas les plaintes de Tracy contre sa mère et contre Chris.

Chris enfila un jean propre et une chemise blanche. Il se regarda dans la glace et regretta de ne pas avoir une tenue de soirée. Bah ! Ce n'était qu'un barbecue, après tout, pas un dîner mondain. Les paroles venimeuses de Janice avaient terni sa joie, mais il n'était pas d'humeur à les laisser ruiner sa soirée.

La réception avait lieu chez Tony... Ou plutôt dans la propriété que la société de production avait mise à sa disposition. Dès que Tony lui avait donné les premières indications, Chris avait su instantanément de quel endroit il s'agissait. La maison de la colline ! Tout le monde en parlait au village mais personne n'y était jamais allé. Bâtie sur les falaises, du côté méridional, elle jouissait d'une vue panoramique sur toute la baie de Monterey, de Santa Cruz à Pacific Grove. Chris s'était d'ailleurs demandé qui avait les moyens de louer ce petit palais en dehors d'un nabab de Silicon Valley ou des émirats.

Une fois, il avait essayé de l'apercevoir, mais les haies touffues, hautes de trois mètres, et la forêt dense alentour ne permettaient pas la moindre incursion.

Ce soir, en revanche, les grilles du portail en fer forgé s'ouvraient sur le parc. Un garde en uniforme muni d'une liste vérifiait les noms des arrivants. Des limousines garées de part et d'autre de l'allée avertirent Chris que la réception ne correspondait pas au petit rassemblement entre copains qu'il avait imaginé.

Il se gara derrière une Viper bleu cobalt qu'il avait déjà vue sur la couverture d'un magazine. Il l'admira pendant cinq bonnes minutes avant de gravir la colline. Un sourire satisfait flottait sur ses lèvres. Quand ses camarades de lycée sauraient ça! Ils n'en croiraient pas leurs oreilles.

La maison apparut à travers les bosquets. Grande mais pas immense, elle évoquait plutôt les riches demeures de Fresno que les vastes villas de Bel-Air. Mais Chris s'en contenterait! Il n'avait jamais osé rêver d'une maison comme celle-ci et d'ailleurs mieux valait l'oublier tout de suite. La vie n'était pas un conte de fées et rien ne le prédisposait à vivre dans un tel faste. Pourtant, une petite voix intérieure lui murmurait, insidieuse : pourquoi pas? Mais pourquoi pas?

Alors qu'il montait les marches de la terrasse illuminée, une femme vint à sa rencontre. Elle tenait une cigarette dans une main et un verre dans l'autre. Ses talons hauts rendaient sa démarche incertaine, sa robe chatoyait comme le plumage d'un paon au soleil.

— Le même! ordonna-t-elle. Vodka sans glaçons.

Chris lui rendit son sourire.

— Pas de problème, répondit-il. Montrez-moi le bar.

Elle lui adressa un rapide coup d'œil.

— Oh, mon Dieu! Vous êtes un invité. Pardonnez-moi.

Elle jeta sa cigarette par terre et l'écrasa de sa semelle compensée. Ensuite, elle passa son bras sous celui de Chris.

— Venez. Je vais vous présenter à tout le monde. Enfin, à tous ceux que vous n'avez pas déjà rencontrés, ajouta-t-elle dans un rire voilé. Attendez! Quel est votre nom?

— Chris Sadler.

— Enchantée. Je m'appelle Dolorès Langtry.

Elle lui fit signe de pousser la lourde porte d'acajou, puis l'entraîna dans le vestibule de marbre. Chris ne parvenait pas à juger si elle était ivre, excentrique, bizarre ou un mélange des trois. Elle semblait être le genre de personne qui se jette dans le fleuve et entend que les autres suivent son exemple. Chris traversa le séjour derrière elle, jusqu'au patio fleuri, noir de monde.

— Vous tous ! s'écria-t-elle, obtenant un silence satisfaisant. Voici Chris Sadler, un très bon ami à moi.

L'annonce fut accueillie par des rires feutrés et quelques salutations diversement chaleureuses. Tony abandonna le couple avec lequel il conversait et vint au-devant d'eux.

— Salut, mec ! Je vois que tu as rencontré maman.

Le regard de Chris alla de l'un à l'autre. Ils n'avaient rien en commun.

— Dolorès est ta mère ? s'étonna-t-il.

— Oh, cher petit poussin ! s'esclaffa Dolorès en caressant la joue de Chris.

Elle s'était visiblement méprise sur le sens de sa question.

— Un point pour toi, mec ! remarque Tony en souriant.

— Maintenant que ce charmant garçon est entre de bonnes mains, je peux aller chercher mon verre, intervint Dolorès. Qu'est-ce que tu bois, poussin ?

Honnêtement, il ne pouvait pas refuser. Ni laisser la mère de Tony attendre.

— De l'eau, s'il vous plaît.

— Gazeuse ou plate ?

— Gazeuse.

— Avec rondelle ?

— Oui, merci, super !

— Tu lui plais, nota Tony quand sa mère s'éloigna.

— Elle vient juste de me rencontrer.

Un regard alentour le rassura. Il n'était pas le seul à porter un jean.

— Peut-être, mais selon Dolorès, la première impression, si rapide soit-elle, est toujours la bonne.

— Tu appelles ta mère par son prénom ?

Tony le regarda un instant.

— Quel âge as-tu ?

Chris songea d'abord à se vieillir d'un ou deux ans. Mais comme il n'avait pas l'habitude de mentir, cette idée lui lia la langue.

— Ça va, dit Tony. Tu n'es pas obligé de répondre.

— Dix-sept ans.

Le comédien hocha la tête.

— C'est ce que je pensais. Viens, je vais te présenter à mes invités.

Chris se retint pour ne pas demander si son jeune âge lui portait préjudice. *A priori*, il ne voyait pas en quoi mais il supposait que c'était possible.

— J'aurai dix-huit ans en septembre, précisa-t-il.

— Vraiment? Quand, exactement?

— Le vingt-trois.

— Mon anniversaire est le trente.

— Sans blague. Quel âge auras-tu?

— Vingt-sept ans.

Bon sang! se dit Chris. Tony était vieux! Beaucoup plus qu'il ne l'avait imaginé quand il l'avait vu sur la plage ou, plus tard, sur le plateau. En découvrant qu'il s'était pris d'amitié pour un gamin, Tony voudrait-il continuer à le voir?

— La maison est superbe, dit Chris pour meubler le silence.

— Elle appartient à un ami. Je suis en pourparlers pour l'acheter.

Tony fit une halte près d'un groupe assis à une table de verre et de bambou.

— Robert, voici le jeune homme dont je t'ai parlé.

Le dénommé Robert daigna soulever ses paupières lourdes derrière ses lunettes cerclées d'acier. Il portait une chemise de golf avec un requin imprimé sur la poche et une casquette du festival de cinéma de Sundance. Après avoir rapidement examiné Chris, il vissa son cigare au coin de ses lèvres.

— En effet, mon pote. On pourrait le prendre pour David.

— Je suppose que ça te suffit, répondit Tony, satisfait.

Robert eut un petit rire.

— Tu obtiens toujours ce que tu veux, mon salaud!

— Seulement quand j'ai raison.

Chris regarda les autres convives. Visiblement, ils ne savaient pas plus que lui de quoi il retournait.

— Qui est David ? questionna-t-il.

— Je t'expliquerai plus tard, rétorqua Tony.

L'une des femmes, la plus belle que Chris ait jamais vue, tapota une chaise vide près d'elle, l'invitant à s'asseoir.

— Gloria Sinclair, se présenta-t-elle quand Chris fut installé. Quoi qu'ils manigancent, ils ne vous mettront au courant que quand ils seront fixés. Mais ne vous inquiétez pas, mon petit Chris. Ça ne peut être que quelque chose de bon.

Tony se pencha pour embrasser la jeune femme sur la bouche, laissant ses lèvres humides et brillantes.

— Gloria, épouse-moi.

— Je vais y réfléchir.

Un énorme diamant brillait à son annulaire. Avec un sourire, elle fit miroiter sa bague.

— Joli, n'est-ce pas ?

— Je n'en ai jamais vu d'aussi gros, murmura Chris.

Il se retint à temps pour ne pas demander s'il était vrai.

Tony embrassa une nouvelle fois la jeune beauté.

— Il ne reste plus qu'à la persuader de mettre la pédale douce pour m'épouser, déclara-t-il.

— Moi ? Et toi donc !

— Vous êtes comédienne, vous aussi ?

Un silence de mort suivit la question de Chris. La cinquantaine de personnes qui discutaient et riaient autour de Gloria retinrent leur souffle en attendant sa réponse.

Robert fit tomber la cendre de son cigare dans un cendrier en Murano.

— Eh ben dites donc ! s'exclama-t-il. On dirait que vous n'allez pas souvent au cinéma, mon garçon !

Chris sentit peser sur lui les regards de l'assistance.

— Non, admit-il. Pas depuis des années. Je… j'étais très occupé.

— Laissez-le tranquille ! protesta Gloria. J'aime bien savoir qu'il existe des gens qui ne m'ont jamais vue à l'écran. Ça me donne envie de travailler plus durement.

Debout derrière elle, Tony mit ses mains à plat sur ses épaules.

— Oh non ! On se voit déjà à peine.

Elle plaça ses mains sur celles de Tony.

— Patience…

De retour, Dolorès tendit un verre à Chris. Peu à peu, les conversations reprirent. Chris n'en perdait pas un mot. Il apprit que Gloria avait terminé un film qui lui vaudrait sûrement une nomination aux Oscars. Elle était sur le point de devenir l'actrice la plus sexy de la nouvelle génération d'Hollywood.

Plus tard dans la soirée il découvrit qu'elle était une grande comédienne doublée d'une femme de cœur, une personne gentille et agréable.

6

Chris quitta la fête à deux heures un quart du matin. Il s'était amusé comme un fou. Et il avait d'excellentes nouvelles… Des nouvelles épatantes ! Au fond de lui, il espérait que sa mère l'aurait attendu. Des nouvelles comme ça, on a envie de les partager. Il deviendrait dingue s'il devait attendre jusqu'au lendemain matin pour les lui annoncer.

Il allait tourner. Juste une scène de foule mais, d'après Tony, le tournage durerait au moins deux jours. Il allait devoir couper ses cheveux presque à ras mais cela ne le dérangeait pas. De toute façon, il se faisait toujours couper les cheveux à la rentrée, avant de reprendre les cours de combat.

Son cœur bondissait comme un oiseau affolé et, pour la première fois, il trouva que la vie valait la peine d'être vécue. Quel pied !

Si une semaine plus tôt on lui avait parlé du tournage à Watsonville, il ne se serait même pas déplacé, ne serait-ce que par curiosité. Maintenant, après une journée sur le plateau avec Tony, après la fête, il aurait facilement sacrifié une saison de combats pour jouer dans le film. Évidemment, pour le moment, personne ne lui avait demandé de choisir… Le réalisateur l'avait simplement convoqué le lundi suivant.

— Cool ! jubila-t-il en rétrogradant.

La Volvo de sa mère négocia le tournant, avant de s'engager dans le chemin du chalet. Ce fut alors que la grosse voiture de location de Mme McCormick apparut dans le faisceau lumineux des phares. Elle était garée sur le bas-côté de la route. Chris freina et sortit de son véhicule sans éteindre le moteur. Janice, assise au volant, passa la tête par la fenêtre.

— Tracy, c'est toi ? murmura-t-elle.

— C'est Chris.

Elle leva les yeux au ciel.

— Extra ! Il ne manquait plus que toi.

Il s'approcha de la voiture. En se penchant, il jeta un coup d'œil à l'intérieur.

— Qu'est-ce que tu fais ici ? Où est Tracy ?

— Ce n'est pas ton affaire.

— Alors, mille excuses ! riposta-t-il d'un ton las. Je voulais juste t'aider au cas où tu aurais besoin. Ciao.

— Attends ! cria-t-elle.

Chris revint sur ses pas. Janice émergea de la voiture et s'appuya contre la portière. Elle semblait inquiète.

— Tu as raison. J'ai besoin de ton aide mais pas dans le sens où tu l'entends. Oh, Chris, je ne sais pas quoi faire. Tracy m'a donné rendez-vous ici. Je l'attends depuis deux heures.

— Où est-elle ?

— Euh… Avec un garçon que nous avons rencontré sur la promenade.

Il fallut une seconde pour que l'information se fraie un passage jusqu'au cerveau de Chris.

— Et elle t'a plantée ici ?

— J'étais d'accord, dit-elle, sur la défensive.

— Qui est ce type ? Quelqu'un du village ?

— Je ne sais pas. Quelle importance ?

— S'il habite ici, nous pourrions le trouver plus facilement. Quel est son nom ?

— Je n'en sais pas plus.

— Quoi ? Tu la laisses partir avec le premier venu ?

— Que voulais-tu que je fasse ? Je ne suis pas sa mère.

— Non, mais tu es son amie.

— Même pas ! déclara Janice dans une sorte de dénégation passionnée. À l'école, Tracy et moi ne nous fréquentons pas ; on est juste chef des supporters toutes les deux. Elle m'a invitée parce qu'elle n'a trouvé personne d'autre et qu'elle ne voulait pas passer tout le mois de juin seule… avec toi.

La voix de Janice se fêla. Elle avait pressé les doigts sur sa bouche, comme pour empêcher les mots de sortir ; mais il était trop tard ! Elle leva sur Chris des yeux luisants de larmes.

— Elle t'a dit ça ? s'enquit-il doucement.

— Désolée. Je suis méchante. Rien n'est vrai. J'ai tout inventé.

Il aurait pu se contenter de cette réponse, mais à quoi bon ?

— Non, Janice. Tu n'as rien inventé.

— Je suis désolée, répéta-t-elle derrière ses doigts tremblants.

Les larmes jaillirent librement.

— Je t'en prie, murmura Chris. Tu n'as rien fait de mal. Tu as simplement dit la vérité.

— Je ne suis pas une garce, Chris. Mes amis de St Louis te le diront. Je suis même plutôt gentille. Je ne sais pas ce qui m'a pris l'autre jour. J'ai été si mesquine… Ta mère est quelqu'un d'extraordinaire.

Un sanglot la fit hoqueter.

— Je te demande pardon, acheva-t-elle.

Chris soupira. Les larmes l'avaient toujours mis mal à l'aise. Il se fit violence pour rester auprès de la jeune fille.

— Chut… Tu as probablement le mal du pays, murmura-t-il en songeant que sa mère aurait dit quelque chose d'analogue.

Janice essuya ses joues ruisselantes, puis frotta ses paumes humides sur son short.

— Tu crois ? chuchota-t-elle d'une petite voix misérable.

— J'en suis sûr. L'été dernier, j'ai failli avoir une déprime quand j'ai dû rester chez un cousin.

Il mentait, mais la fin justifiait les moyens.

— Tracy n'était pas avec toi ? demanda Janice, étonnée.

L'ombre d'un sourire effleura les lèvres de Chris.

— Pas à ce moment-là. Attends…

Il repartit vers la Volvo, coupa le moteur et revint avec un paquet de Kleenex que sa mère gardait toujours dans la boîte à gants. Janice prit le mouchoir en papier qu'il lui tendait et se moucha… Enfin, levant les yeux, elle eut un pâle sourire.

— Merci. Je me sens mieux.

— Tu es chef des supporters depuis longtemps? demanda-t-il, histoire de dire quelque chose.

— Trois ans.

— Et tu aimes ça?

— Oui, bien sûr. C'est géant…

Elle hésita un instant, comme pour reconsidérer sa réponse.

— Enfin, pas toujours, admit-elle. Parfois, quand, sur un signe du chef, les supporters acclament à tue-tête les joueurs de leur équipe, et que l'équipe adverse en profite pour récupérer le ballon… on a bonne mine.

— J'imagine que personne n'y fait attention.

— Tu parles! Mais des garçons comme toi ne peuvent pas comprendre.

— Qu'entends-tu par « des garçons comme toi »?

— Des mecs qui pensent qu'une fille ne songe qu'à flirter.

Chris sourit.

— Et… j'ai tort?

— Je suis contre les préjugés.

Un rire amusé échappa à Chris.

— Mais encore?

— Eh bien, puisque tu veux tout savoir, je m'intéresse à autre chose qu'aux flirts ou à l'équipe de foot de l'école.

— À quoi par exemple?

— Je ne suis pas obligée de me justifier.

— Alors, restons-en là.

Ils étaient revenus à la case départ. Chris regarda Janice.

— Tu ne veux pas essayer une nouvelle fois?

Elle haussa les épaules.

— Je travaille pour Al-anon, répondit-elle enfin. J'aide d'autres jeunes…

Là aussi, il fallut à Chris une seconde pour enregistrer l'information.

— Les Alcooliques anonymes? Cet endroit…

— Ce n'est pas un endroit mais une organisation… Nous venons en aide aux jeunes dont les parents sont alcooliques.

— Ton père est alcoolique ?

— Ma mère.

Le silence retomba pendant un long moment, puis Janice ajouta :

— Aucune de mes amies n'est au courant.

— Pas même Tracy ?

— Je te l'ai déjà dit : Tracy n'est pas une amie. Je ne suis même pas sûre d'avoir de la sympathie pour elle.

— Ton père est au courant ? Au sujet de ta mère, je veux dire.

Il n'aurait pas pu poser de question plus idiote.

— C'est lui qui m'a emmenée là-bas, avec mes frères.

— Ça doit être drôlement dur…

Le seul alcoolique que Chris connaissait était un collègue de son père. Gris dès le premier verre, il se mettait à raconter des histoires salaces.

— Parfois je la hais, dit Janice. Ensuite, je me sens coupable.

— Parfois je déteste mon père, répondit Chris.

— Parce qu'il a voulu divorcer ?

— Pas tant pour le divorce lui-même que pour la façon dont il s'y est pris. Non content de tromper maman, il s'est fait surprendre par elle au lit. Moins de trois ans plus tard, monsieur était remarié, installé, alors que maman n'avait pas encore eu le moindre rendez-vous.

— Ta mère est sensationnelle, et ton père un salaud.

— Je n'arrête pas de le dire à maman, mais elle n'est pas d'accord. Selon elle, ce qui s'est passé entre eux ne me regarde pas. « Il est ton père, dit-elle, tu lui dois un minimum de respect. »

Il n'avait jamais évoqué ce sujet avec personne. Face à ses camarades d'école, il ne montrait aucune faiblesse.

— Comme si c'était possible ! soupira Janice. Quand je vois comment maman détruit papa, j'ai du mal à le supporter. Elle boit en cachette… Elle se croit maligne alors qu'elle empeste l'alcool. Elle est ivre morte et elle est persuadée que ça ne se voit pas. Mes frères s'en vont quand elle est dans cet état. Moi, je reste. Une fois elle est tombée dans le coma alors qu'elle faisait frire du bacon. Elle a failli mettre le feu à la maison.

— Quel âge ont tes frères?

— Quatorze et quinze ans.

— Où vont-ils, quand ils partent de la maison?

— Chez mamie. Elle habite tout près…

Un nouveau silence se fit.

— Je ne répéterai rien à personne, déclara solennellement Chris.

Il avait envie de gagner sa confiance.

— Merci. Je ne dirai rien en ce qui concerne ton père non plus…

D'une claque, elle écrasa un moustique sur son avant-bras.

— Est-ce que tu crois qu'on peut faire quelque chose pour Tracy? demanda-t-elle.

— Quoi?

— Je ne sais pas mais, franchement, je commence à me faire du souci.

Chris était partagé entre l'inquiétude et l'indifférence. Il connaissait bien Tracy. Si elle s'amusait, Janice pourrait l'attendre toute la nuit.

— Quel genre de voiture a son soupirant?

— Une Mustang bleue, une vraie pièce de collection. Pourquoi?

— Il y a deux ou trois cafés qui restent ouverts tard au village. J'y ferais bien un saut.

— Je viens avec toi.

— Et si elle revient pendant notre absence?

— Elle attendra! Chacun son tour.

Janice prit les clés de la voiture de location, les enfouit dans son sac et claqua la portière.

— Je suis prête.

Ils montèrent dans la Volvo. Après avoir fait demi-tour, Chris emprunta la nationale.

— Ce n'est pas la première fois que Tracy se comporte de la sorte, dit-il. Si elle fait son cinéma habituel, je plains son soupirant.

— Et moi, je plains son petit ami.

Les doigts de Chris se crispèrent sur le volant.

— Quel petit ami ?

— Celui de St Louis. Tu n'as pas remarqué qu'elle est toujours pendue au téléphone ? Et le nombre de cartes postales qu'elle a envoyées ?

— Elle disait qu'elle appelait son père…

Évidemment, il n'y avait aucune raison de mettre en doute les affirmations de Janice. Après un moment, il posa la question qui lui brûlait les lèvres.

— Depuis quand sort-elle avec lui ?

— Depuis l'été dernier.

Une année entière ! Pourtant, Tracy ne lui avait rien dit. Pas plus que Mme McCormick. Il fit la remarque à Janice, qui hocha la tête.

— Beverly ne se risquerait pas à t'avouer que sa fille a un fiancé. Elle espère toujours que vous vous mettrez ensemble !

— Vraiment ? C'est dingue ! Elle ne m'en a jamais parlé.

Peut-être Beverly s'était-elle confiée à sa mère ? songea-t-il, un peu désarçonné par la nouvelle.

— Elle n'a rien dit non plus à Tracy, poursuivit Janice. Elle a trop peur que sa fille fasse exactement le contraire. Tu connais le phénomène !

Chris émit un rire acerbe.

— N'est-ce pas ce qu'elle fait déjà ? Elle me traite comme une saleté sur laquelle elle aurait marché et qu'elle n'arriverait pas à décoller de sa semelle.

— Je ne la comprends pas. Pourquoi t'en veut-elle à ce point ?

— Je ne sais pas. Chaque été, je me rends ridicule dans l'espoir qu'elle me remarque, tandis qu'elle s'évertue à m'éviter.

La phrase avait jailli spontanément. Une sorte de constatation amère qu'il avait jusque-là réussi à refouler au fin fond de son subconscient.

Alors qu'ils dépassaient la maison de la colline, Chris garda les yeux fixés sur le ruban sombre de la route. Peut-être s'était-il trahi ? Peut-être que Janice répéterait tout à Tracy, ainsi il leur fournirait, une fois de plus, l'occasion de se moquer de lui. Bizarrement, il n'y crut pas. Même s'il n'avait aucune raison de se fier à Janice, elle lui inspirait confiance. D'ailleurs, c'était à elle, et pas à sa mère, qu'il aurait voulu parler de la fête et de sa future participation au film.

— Est-ce que tu as entendu parler... commença-t-il. Janice l'interrompit.

— Les voilà ! cria-t-elle en montrant une Mustang bleue qui arrivait en sens inverse.

Elle se retourna afin de mieux observer les passagers.

— Qu'elle aille au diable ! Maintenant que je sais qu'il ne lui est rien arrivé, elle peut se rompre le cou !

Chris fit demi-tour et suivit les feux arrière de la Mustang. Il raconterait la fête à Janice plus tard.

7

Chris freina derrière la Mustang au moment où Tracy émergeait par la portière. La hanche contre la carrosserie, elle attendit que son compagnon coupe le moteur et vienne la rejoindre. Lorsqu'il fut à sa hauteur, elle lui passa les bras derrière la nuque et l'embrassa à pleine bouche en se frottant contre lui.

— Quelle garce! marmonna Janice. Elle se donne en spectacle pour toi, Chris.

Il hocha la tête. Ces démonstrations auraient dû l'affecter. Mais il ne ressentait rien. Rien du tout.

— Pauvre type, murmura-t-il. Je le plains.

— Vraiment?

— Donne-lui les clés et partons d'ici.

— Bonne idée.

Chris redémarra et Janice baissa sa vitre.

— Tiens, Tracy, attrape! cria-t-elle tandis que la Volvo doublait doucement la Mustang arrêtée.

Janice lança les clés sans donner à Tracy le temps de réagir. Le trousseau décrivit un arc de cercle et atteignit les fesses de Tracy.

— Joli coup, la complimenta Chris en accélérant.

Janice eut un large sourire.

— Merci.

En temps normal, Chris se serait garé devant le chalet, de manière à laisser l'allée libre pour Tracy. Mais ce soir-là, il en avait plein le dos de ses caprices.

La pendulette sur sa table de chevet indiquait quatre heures du matin quand il se coucha. Il posa la tête sur l'oreiller, les yeux grands ouverts. Le sommeil le fuyait, il se sentait en pleine forme. Quand les premières lueurs du jour projetèrent l'ombre des persiennes sur le mur, il renonça à dormir et se mit à guetter les bruits familiers qui l'avertiraient que sa mère s'était levée. Son esprit errait d'un sujet à un autre, avec agilité et fièvre.

En moins de vingt-quatre heures, sa vie avait pris un tournant nouveau, inattendu. Le pauvre quidam s'était mué en acteur de cinéma après avoir assisté à une fête chez une star où il s'était gavé de mets succulents. Chris ne se faisait cependant aucune illusion : sa nouvelle existence ne durerait pas plus d'une semaine. Ensuite, les acteurs repartiraient avec armes et bagages, oubliant jusqu'à son nom. Mais Chris, lui, se souviendrait de tout ça. Oh, oui, il s'en souviendrait toujours ! Usant de cette faculté singulière de penser à plusieurs choses en même temps, il évoqua le diamant de Gloria et les cours de comédie. À la rentrée, il s'inscrirait au club de théâtre de l'école. Il ne s'attaquerait pas à un premier rôle, non ! Il commencerait d'abord par des rôles secondaires et, au printemps, il aviserait. Il pourrait peut-être continuer après avoir quitté le lycée. Il allait se renseigner sur les universités qui proposaient des cours d'art dramatique aux étudiants. Non qu'il se prît pour un futur monstre sacré, il n'était pas assez mégalo pour ça. Qui aurait payé sa place pour voir Chris Sadler sur les planches ?

D'ailleurs, devenir vedette ne l'intéressait pas. Il serait content de tourner toute sa vie des scènes de foule. Il ne voulait même pas d'argent, jouer lui suffisait. Tant pis s'il ne pouvait jamais réunir une somme assez conséquente pour acheter un jour un chalet sur la plage.

Il n'arriverait jamais à patienter tout le week-end. Il aurait bien voulu dormir jusqu'à lundi, seulement il était tendu comme un ressort. Une porte s'ouvrit à côté de sa chambre, puis se referma doucement. Sans doute sa mère. Beverly ne se levait jamais avant neuf heures. Chris enfila son pantalon. Il rattrapa Margaret sur le seuil de la cuisine.

— Tu es matinal aujourd'hui, observa-t-elle. Comment s'est passée la fête ?

Il prit sa mère par les épaules et la regarda dans les yeux avec un sourire.

— Merveilleusement !

— Tu t'es bien amusé ?

— Mieux que jamais. Attends un peu que je te raconte.

— Viens. Tu me raconteras pendant que je fais le café.

— Je ne peux pas attendre aussi longtemps.

— Oh ! Ça doit être quelque chose !

Elle le scruta un instant.

— Toi, tu as rencontré une fille !

— J'en ai rencontré des dizaines, mais aucune en particulier.

L'image de Janice lui traversa l'esprit, mais il la balaya de ses pensées embrouillées.

— Maintenant, c'est moi qui ne peux plus attendre ! s'exclama Margaret en souriant. Je t'écoute.

Chris arbora un air décontracté.

— Tout compte fait, je vais d'abord prendre une tasse de café.

— Ah… sale bête !

Elle s'avança vers la cafetière électrique et Chris lui emboîta le pas.

— Maman, je vais jouer dans le film de Tony.

Margaret se retourna vivement, le visage marqué par la surprise. Son absence d'enthousiasme le décontenança et il renifla.

— Rien de mirobolant, rassure-toi. Juste de la figuration.

Comme sa mère ne réagissait toujours pas, il reprit :

— Qu'est-ce qui ne va pas ? Tu n'es pas fière de moi ?

— Si, bien sûr. Tu m'as prise de court…

Elle s'efforça de trouver une réponse plus satisfaisante.

— Je croyais bien te connaître, pourtant je n'ai jamais imaginé que tu t'emballerais autant pour un film.

— Moi non plus, admit-il.

— Veux-tu connaître le fond de ma pensée ? C'est formidable ! Quand le tournage sera terminé, nous arroserons l'événement avec tous tes copains.

Chris regarda sa mère remplir le doseur de café, puis le vider dans le filtre. Ses efforts pour paraître enchantée le décevaient plus encore que son manque d'entrain.

Il décida de taire le reste. Si elle n'avait pas compris son émotion, mieux valait qu'elle ignore son projet de s'inscrire à un cours d'art dramatique.

— Et ta sortie ? demanda-t-il pour changer de sujet. As-tu vu un bon film ?

— Bah… Le temps de lire les sous-titres, j'ai raté l'essentiel.

Elle remplit d'eau le réservoir et brancha la cafetière.

— En revanche, nous avons eu un excellent dîner. Nous sommes allées dans un restaurant indien recommandé par Eric. Beverly a trouvé le curry trop fort, mais…

Chris ne l'écoutait plus. Il se remémora le récit de Janice. Il comprenait parfaitement qu'elle veuille ne pas parler de l'alcoolisme de sa mère. Il existe des secrets que l'on n'a pas envie de divulguer. Chris avait caché à Paul, son meilleur ami, la fameuse histoire de son livret d'épargne. Son entraîneur l'avait aidé à écrire à plusieurs universités pour demander une bourse. Certaines avaient répondu affirmativement, mais aucune ne correspondait à ses souhaits. Certes, il voulait poursuivre les sports de combat. Il était même persuadé qu'il se distinguerait à l'université tout autant qu'au lycée. Pourtant, il ne savait plus à quoi il souhaitait réellement se vouer et…

— Chris ?

Il leva les yeux. Sa mère le regardait.

— Oui, maman ?

— As-tu d'autres projets ?

Il ignorait de quoi elle voulait parler, et pour cause ! Il avait décroché depuis un bon moment.

— Des projets ?

— Pour ce soir.

Elle ne lâcherait pas prise. Chris leva les mains dans un geste résigné.

— D'accord ! Je me rends ! De quoi parles-tu ?

— Eric est passé hier soir. Son ami Charlie vient plus tôt que prévu. Si tu n'as rien de mieux à faire, tu es invité chez lui à huit heures pour le dessert.

— Tu peux venir aussi, tu sais.

— Arrête, Chris. Je ne m'intéresse pas à Eric Lawson. Cesse donc de jouer les entremetteurs.

Elle lui tendit un bol de céréales.

— Ce soir, je sors avec Beverly. Nous allons à un concert à Monterey.

— Qu'est-ce qui te déplaît chez Eric ?

— Rien.

— Alors pourquoi…

— Je te l'ai déjà dit. Je ne suis pas prête pour une relation durable.

— Papa s'est remarié. Je ne vois pas pour quelle raison tu ne t'accorderais pas un peu de bon temps.

— Chéri, assieds-toi.

Elle posa deux tasses de café sur la table et ils s'installèrent face à face.

— Voilà, reprit-elle. Aussi bizarre que cela puisse paraître, j'aime bien être seule. Je suis partie de chez mes parents pour vivre en pension, puis chez mon mari. Pour la première fois de ma vie, je peux disposer de mon temps, de mes loisirs comme bon me semble. Et je n'ai pas l'intention de renoncer à ma liberté.

— Tu ne te sens pas seule ?

— Parfois, si. Mais le prix à payer pour un peu de compagnie est trop élevé… et… j'ai déjà donné !

Elle ajouta un nuage de lait froid dans son café et passa le pot à Chris.

— Un jour, peut-être, je ne dis pas ! Il est possible que je change d'avis. C'est même certain. Mais pas pour l'instant, tu comprends ?

— Maman, regarde la réalité en face. Tu ne rajeunis pas. Les hommes libres de ton âge se font rares. Que feras-tu de ta chère liberté si un jour la solitude devient trop pesante ?

— On ne peut pas tout avoir. Il y a pire dans la vie que vivre seule… Par exemple épouser la mauvaise personne.

— Tu veux dire papa ?

Elle secoua la tête.

— Je ne regrette rien. Si je ne l'avais pas épousé, je ne t'aurais pas eu.

— Maman, bientôt je partirai, moi aussi.

— C'est donc pour cela que tu essaies de me caser ? Parce que tu t'en vas à l'université, tu te fais du souci pour ta pauvre mère ?

— Un peu, admit-il.

— Eh bien, tu as tort, dit-elle en pressant la main de Chris dans la sienne. En fait, j'ai hâte d'avoir la maison pour moi toute seule.

Il n'en crut pas un mot mais feignit le contraire.

— Est-ce une façon comme une autre de me dire de débarrasser le plancher ?

Margaret sourit.

— Je crois que je peux attendre encore un an.

Chris leva les bras et s'étira.

— Je vais courir avant le petit déjeuner. Tu viens avec moi ?

Elle considéra l'invitation.

— Je descendrai à la plage, mais je préfère marcher. Chacun son rythme… Au fait à quelle heure es-tu rentré ?

— Tard.

— Et tu t'es levé aux aurores ? Le tournage te rend nerveux, mon bonhomme.

— Je vais me changer. On se retrouve dehors.

Prenant un magazine, elle se mit à le feuilleter négligemment.

— Trop tard, dit-elle en bâillant. Je n'ai déjà plus le courage. Je serai sur la terrasse si tu as besoin de moi.

Chris hocha la tête en riant.

— Maman, je te le répète : tu vieillis. Il ne te manque plus qu'une canne.

— Je conserve mon énergie, voilà tout.

Lorsque Chris revint de son jogging, une heure plus tard, une violente dispute opposait Tracy à Beverly. La première exigeait la voiture pour l'après-midi, la seconde refusait avec obstination. Au milieu du raffut, Janice, attablée, dégustait des céréales.

— Tu n'as qu'à prendre la voiture de Margaret ! hurla Tracy en tapant du pied. Elle n'en a pas besoin. Elle ne va jamais nulle part.

Beverly ajouta une sucrette dans son café.

— Tracy, ne me pousse pas à bout.

— Je me sers de la Volvo cet après-midi, intervint Chris. Janice et moi allons à Big Sur.

Janice leva le nez. Ses lèvres formulèrent un « merci » muet.

— Ah oui ? Depuis quand ? le défia Tracy.

— Depuis hier soir.

La veille encore, il aurait été incapable de lui tenir tête. À présent, il croisait son regard froid et hostile sans broncher.

— Si tu veux nous accompagner, tu es la bienvenue, proposa-t-il d'un ton ironique.

— J'ai un rendez-vous, articula Tracy avec une supériorité qui frisait le ridicule.

— Alors, où est le problème ? demanda Chris en essuyant de sa manche son front moite. Dis-lui de passer te chercher.

Tracy coula un rapide regard vers sa mère.

— Je ne peux pas. Il ne sait pas où j'habite.

— À quelle heure avez-vous rendez-vous ? Nous te déposerons, répondit-il. Cela ne te dérange pas, Janice ?

La jeune fille secoua vigoureusement la tête.

— Non. Bien sûr que non.

Tracy fusilla son amie d'un regard rageur.

— Comment as-tu pu me faire ça ?

— Assez ! coupa Beverly.

Tracy se tourna vers sa mère, les yeux brillants de larmes.

— Tu m'as promis que cet été, ce serait différent ! vociféra-t-elle. Tu m'as juré que tu ferais tout pour rendre mon séjour agréable.

Beverly essaya d'entourer les épaules de sa fille de son bras, mais cette dernière se dégagea violemment.

— Je veux rentrer à la maison, déclara-t-elle. Tout de suite.

— Tracy, sois raisonnable, plaida Beverly d'une voix chevrotante. Tu sais combien je tiens à ces vacances. C'est le seul moment de l'année où je peux voir Margaret.

— Oh, bien sûr! Il n'y en a que pour toi! Et moi alors? Je ne compte pas?

Chris avait déjà assisté à un millier de disputes entre Tracy et sa mère. Avant, il prenait automatiquement le parti de la jeune fille. Il pensait que sa forte personnalité irritait sa mère, qui aurait préféré avoir quelqu'un de plus malléable sous la main. Aujourd'hui, il voyait les choses sous un autre angle. Comment avait-il pu être aussi aveugle? Aussi stupide?

— Maman, je parle sérieusement! Je veux rentrer! reprit Tracy, implacable.

— Et si je louais une autre voiture pour toi? proposa Beverly. Tu changerais d'avis?

Les larmes de l'adolescente disparurent comme par enchantement.

— Une voiture pour moi seule? demanda-t-elle d'un ton circonspect.

— En rendant le gros véhicule et en en louant deux plus petits, je ne devrais pas payer beaucoup plus cher.

Les yeux de Tracy s'éclairèrent.

— Et ils accepteront de te louer deux voitures?

— Je ne vois pas pourquoi ils refuseraient.

— Si c'était le cas, tu pourrais en mettre une au nom de Margaret, suggéra Tracy, coupant l'herbe sous le pied de sa mère.

— Ça, trésor, il faut que Margaret soit d'accord. Nous allons le lui demander.

— Tu n'as qu'à la mettre devant le fait accompli.

Estimant que la situation ne tarderait pas à s'envenimer, Janice alla rincer son bol sous le robinet.

— Quand veux-tu que je sois prête? chuchota-t-elle à Chris.

— Dans cinq minutes, d'accord?

Une pour prévenir sa mère qu'ils empruntaient la Volvo, et quatre pour se doucher.

— Je préparerai un pique-nique. Nous serons absents toute la journée, je suppose?

Il acquiesça.

— Madame McCormick, dit-il en lui souriant suavement, ne nous attendez pas pour dîner.

Tracy avisa Janice.

— J'allais t'inviter à venir avec nous. Jimmy voulait te présenter un de ses amis. Mais comme tu ne seras pas là de la journée…

Elle exhala un long soupir, mais Janice n'eut pas la réaction escomptée. Au lieu de promettre qu'elle rentrerait à temps, elle ébaucha une grimace.

— Sortir avec un motard? Beurk!

Beverly avala son café de travers et se mit à tousser.

— Parce que tu sors avec un motard?

Tracy fit de gros yeux à Janice.

— Ce n'est pas parce que Jimmy t'a traitée de snobinarde qu'il faut lui casser du sucre sur le dos.

— S'il n'est pas motard, comment expliques-tu ses tatouages de Harley Davidson?

— Comment? Il a des tatouages? s'enquit Beverly d'une voix qui dérapait dans les aigus.

— Tous les jeunes en ont, maman! riposta Tracy. D'ailleurs, j'en aurai un aussi, un de ces jours.

Beverly s'enflamma. Se redressant brusquement, elle pointa un doigt accusateur vers sa fille.

— Tracy, tu es mineure! Et tant que tu seras sous ma responsabilité, je t'interdis de te défigurer avec des tatouages et autres âneries de ce genre.

— Mon corps m'appartient! J'en fais ce que je veux.

— Et moi je refuse de voir ces horreurs sur la peau de mon enfant! N'oublie pas que l'académie St Michael vient d'accepter ta candidature.

— Oh, la ferme! hurla Tracy, les yeux flamboyants. Tu m'avais promis que tu ne dirais rien.

Beverly arbora une expression contrite.

— Ça m'a échappé…

— La bonne excuse! J'en ai marre, tiens!

Tracy partit en courant dans sa chambre et s'y enferma en claquant la porte.

Peu de temps après, Beverly la suivit.

Chris échangea un regard avec Janice.

— Qu'est-ce que c'est, cette histoire d'académie?

Janice haussa les épaules.

— Je n'en suis pas sûre, répondit-elle après une hésitation, mais je présume qu'il y a un rapport entre St Michael et l'institution où ses parents avaient envoyé Tracy du temps où elle se droguait avec son petit copain.

Chris regarda Janice, bouche bée. Il se rendit soudain compte qu'il ne savait rien de la fille dont il était amoureux depuis une éternité.

— Je connais Tracy depuis toujours, murmura-t-il, et j'ignore qui elle est vraiment.

— Ça va aller, Chris?

— Je vais m'habiller et on file au plus vite.

— Je vais préparer des sandwichs.

— Ce n'est pas la peine. Nous nous arrêterons en route.

Il avait hâte d'être loin. Égoïstement, il aurait voulu être seul. Sur la terrasse, il aperçut sa mère, et il sortit afin de la mettre au courant de ses plans.

Tandis qu'il faisait coulisser la porte vitrée, elle leva les yeux de son magazine.

— Inutile de m'expliquer, dit-elle. J'ai tout entendu.

— Étais-tu au courant pour l'école privée?

— Oui... et non. J'aurais pu poser des questions à Beverly et tenter d'approfondir les bribes d'information qu'elle laissait parfois passer dans ses lettres. Mais j'ai préféré la discrétion.

— Ça ne fait rien, si je prends la voiture alors?

Margaret referma le magazine.

— Je n'approuve pas le mensonge mais, après tout, tu n'avais pas le choix. Et puis, c'est difficile d'être à la fois fier et mécontent de quelqu'un.

Comme Chris ne disait rien, elle ajouta:

— Vas-y, mon chéri. Amuse-toi bien avec Janice. N'oublie pas qu'Eric t'attend ce soir.

— À quelle heure t'en vas-tu avec Beverly ?

— Je ne sais pas.

— Où allez-vous ?

— Je n'en ai pas la moindre idée non plus.

Il réfléchit un instant.

— Je vois ce que tu veux dire. Je n'étais pas le seul à mentir.

Sa mère lui sourit.

8

Chris et Janice n'allèrent pas jusqu'à Big Sur. Sur la route de Monterey, elle le pria de s'arrêter au parc aquatique de Cannery Row. La foule bigarrée du dimanche s'étirait en files interminables devant les guichets, mais rien ne semblait pouvoir tempérer l'enthousiasme de Janice. Dans le hall principal, le cou tendu, les yeux écarquillés, elle admira les baleines grandeur nature suspendues au plafond, tandis que le flot des visiteurs continuait d'avancer vers les différentes portes. Chris lui plaqua gentiment la main au creux des reins, la poussant légèrement en avant.

— Mademoiselle, avancez. Nous avons mille choses à voir et seulement six heures devant nous.

— Imagine ! Tu nages, peinard, et pan ! Tu tombes entre deux eaux sur l'un de ces monstres, qui ne fait qu'une bouchée de toi.

— Les cétacés ne mangent pas les humains.

— Tu plaisantes !

Sans donner à Chris le temps de poursuivre, Janice pointa le doigt en direction d'une vaste cuve de Plexiglas à deux étages, entourée d'une cohue remuante.

— Qu'y a-t-il, là-dedans ?

— Des otaries.

— Des vraies ?

Chris eut un rire.

— Pourquoi ? Tu en connais des fausses ?

— Oh, ça va ! Je veux les voir !

Ils se frayèrent péniblement un passage vers le niveau supérieur, d'où ils purent apercevoir les silhouettes souples et ondoyantes des otaries. Une mamie équipée d'un panier se mit à jeter dans l'aquarium des morceaux de poisson cru. Les otaries plongèrent aussitôt parmi les algues et les goémons. De leurs pattes griffues, elles attrapaient le poisson, puis remontaient à la surface et nageaient sur le dos en dévorant leur proie.

Janice s'éloigna de la paroi translucide pour laisser deux jeunes enfants admirer le spectacle. Chris parvint à l'attirer vers la piscine des dauphins.

Elle le bombarda de questions. Lorsqu'il ignorait la réponse, elle s'adressait aux gardiens. Devant la forêt d'algues, elle se lança dans un véritable concours. Chris se prêta au jeu, et tous deux énumérèrent leurs connaissances de la vie marine. Il menait d'un point quand trois poissons émergèrent des fucus : Janice les identifia d'un seul coup.

— J'ai gagné ! exulta-t-elle.

— Bah ! Il n'y a pas de quoi pavoiser.

— Peut-être pas, mais c'est marrant.

Chris la regarda.

— J'ai l'impression d'entendre Tracy.

Janice l'attrapa par la manche.

— Retire ce que tu as dit.

— Sinon ?

— Tu rentres seul à la maison.

Il lui adressa un sourire triomphant.

— Sauf que la voiture est à moi.

Janice répondit à son sourire.

— Bon, je me rends.

Ils poursuivirent la visite, main dans la main. Les cloches transparentes des méduses les retinrent un bon moment. Trois heures plus tard, ils firent leur dernière halte à la boutique des cadeaux. Janice mit une éternité pour choisir un livre et opta enfin pour un petit volume sur les espèces du Pacifique Nord. Lorsqu'elle ouvrit son porte-monnaie pour régler son achat, Chris nota qu'elle dépensait la moitié de son argent de poche.

— Devine ce que je vais faire les trois prochaines semaines, dit-elle, tandis qu'ils ressortaient du bâtiment.

— Je donne ma langue au chat.

— Je vais essayer d'apprendre le maximum sur la flore et la faune sous-marines. C'est passionnant.

Elle avait passé un moment agréable et ne se retenait pas de le proclamer. La plupart des filles du lycée auraient feint de s'ennuyer, qualifiant cette visite de « ringarde ». Mais pas Janice. Elle s'intéressait à tout.

— Et la prochaine fois que je viendrai en Californie, j'aurai mon permis de conduire, déclara-t-elle à brûle-pourpoint, tandis qu'ils s'engageaient dans le parking. Je visiterai le pays en long, en large et en travers.

Chris haussa les sourcils. Après dix jours en compagnie de Tracy, il était étonnant que Janice songe à revenir.

— Et j'irai nager avec les loutres de mer, reprit-elle, passant du coq à l'âne. Ça doit être géant.

— As-tu faim ? demanda Chris alors qu'ils arrivaient à la voiture.

— Oh, oui !

— Hamburger ? proposa-t-il.

— Papa m'étranglera si je ne goûte pas le poisson de la côte au moins une fois.

— Va pour le poisson. Je ne connais aucun restaurant mais on peut toujours se renseigner.

La vieille Volvo démarra. Un peu plus loin, Chris s'arrêta devant une échoppe de tee-shirts. Le vendeur les informa que la meilleure taverne de tacos de poisson se trouvait au nord de Mexico.

— Des tacos de poisson ? s'étonna Janice en ressortant. À mon avis, mon père ne pensait pas à ça. Si nous demandions à quelqu'un d'autre ?

— Ouf… Merci ! J'ai eu peur que tu sois partante.

Elle l'observa à travers ses longs cils noirs et épais.

— Toute réflexion faite… pourquoi ne pas essayer ? demanda-t-elle avec un petit air espiègle.

— Si tu veux y aller, pas de problème, déclara-t-il avec fermeté, sûr qu'elle ferait marche arrière.

— Alors, allons-y.

— La bonne blague !

— Pas du tout. Qu'est-ce qu'on a à perdre ?

— Notre argent.

Elle éclata de rire.

— Allons ! Où est ton sens de l'aventure ?

Sur le chemin du retour, Janice affirma pour la énième fois qu'elle avait adoré les tacos et que, si c'était à refaire, elle n'hésiterait pas. Chris rétorqua que la tarte à la rhubarbe et aux fraises de sa grand-mère, qui lui avait flanqué des crampes d'estomac carabinées, avait été pour lui une meilleure expérience.

Quand, le même soir, Eric proposa à ses invités une tarte à la rhubarbe et aux fraises avec de la glace, Janice eut toutes les peines du monde à garder son sérieux. Elle avait accepté d'accompagner Chris pour rencontrer Charlie Stephens. D'abord légèrement impressionnée, elle s'était peu à peu détendue. Son tempérament exubérant avait ensuite très vite pris le dessus, et elle avait bombardé le champion de questions. Ensuite, elle lui avait avoué en souriant qu'il serait dorénavant son héros préféré.

Elle dévora sa part de tarte avant de s'attaquer à celle de Chris. Celui-ci sourit. Hormis la fête chez Tony, il vivait le plus beau jour de sa vie.

Lorsqu'ils se retrouvèrent tous les deux dehors, sous les étoiles, ils n'eurent qu'à traverser la ruelle qui séparait les deux maisons pour rentrer se coucher.

— Charlie est sympa, dit Janice. Eric aussi, d'ailleurs.

— Merci d'être venue avec moi.

— Il n'y a pas de quoi...

Elle s'immobilisa au milieu de la rue, les bras écartés, comme pour rassembler les souvenirs de cette journée exceptionnelle. Les yeux levés vers le ciel, elle exécuta un cercle lent, semblable à une danse.

— Merci aussi d'avoir menacé de me briser la jambe si je ne venais pas, poursuivit-elle.

— C'était le bras, corrigea Chris en riant.

Elle feignit de perdre l'équilibre.

— Jambe, bras, c'est pareil.

Impulsivement, machinalement, il la souleva dans ses bras pour l'empêcher de tomber et la jeta sur son épaule.

— Si quelqu'un nous voit, il pensera que tu es ivre, dit-il.

— Ou que je me suis évanouie et que tu as eu la bonté de me ramener à la maison.

Elle ne pesait pas plus lourd qu'une plume. Il était arrivé à Chris de soulever des poids plus importants quand il aidait sa mère à faire les courses ou à transporter des valises. Il aurait pu porter Janice jusqu'à la fin des temps… si sa courte jupette n'était pas remontée, dévoilant une petite culotte de dentelle.

Chris se crispa. Ressentant la tension de son compagnon, Janice s'appuya sur ses épaules et se laissa glisser à terre. Ils se tenaient maintenant face à face, les yeux dans les yeux. Et ni l'un ni l'autre ne bougea.

L'air de l'océan, encore chargé de la chaleur du jour, les enveloppa comme une écharpe. Alors, très lentement, sûr de ses gestes, Chris embrassa Janice. Son cœur s'emballa ; il l'entendit battre à ses tempes, estompant l'incessant roulement des vagues. Elle pencha la tête sur le côté, les lèvres entrouvertes. Avec un profond soupir, Chris enlaça Janice, et son baiser se fit plus profond, plus exigeant. Elle se hissa alors sur la pointe des pieds pour mieux le goûter. Quand ils se séparèrent, Chris posa son menton sur le sommet de la tête de Janice.

— Excuse-moi, murmura-t-il. Je ne sais pas ce qui m'a pris.

— Moi non plus…

— Tu m'en veux ?

Elle ne répondit pas tout de suite mais, levant les yeux, elle le sonda du regard.

— Je n'en suis pas sûre, chuchota-t-elle enfin. Si tu recommençais, tu m'aiderais à y voir plus clair.

Une sensation singulière submergea Chris. Un sentiment qu'il avait déjà éprouvé, mais pas dans toute sa plénitude. Un baiser ne lui suffisait pas. Il brûlait d'envie d'aller plus loin.

La bouche de Janice lui parut d'une douceur incroyable; la caresse de sa langue l'enivra. La façon dont elle se soulevait sur ses orteils en lui passant les bras autour du cou fit naître dans son esprit une multitude d'images aussi intimes qu'éblouissantes.

Ce qu'il éprouvait pour Tracy se passait uniquement dans sa tête. Dans son imagination. L'instant présent était bien réel. Et tellement plus excitant!

— Non, murmura-t-elle.

— Non?

Souriante, elle reposa ses talons, les yeux levés vers le visage de Chris.

— Non, je ne t'en veux pas, précisa-t-elle.

Il lui caressa la joue.

— Veux-tu faire un tour?

— Oui.

Elle n'ajouta rien, mais il sut qu'ils partageaient les mêmes pensées, les mêmes sentiments.

Ils descendirent les marches creusées dans la falaise. Sur la plage, Chris prit la main de Janice. Ses jambes bougeaient, mais ses pieds ne touchaient pas terre. On eût dit qu'il marchait dans les airs.

— Je dois partir demain très tôt, dit-il. Je ne sais pas à quelle heure je rentrerai.

— Où ça?

Il lui parla du film. Elle l'écouta, émerveillée.

— Oh, Chris, quelle chance! Promets-moi de tout me raconter demain, dans le moindre détail. Je veux tout savoir.

— Oui, d'accord... Mais ne dis rien à Tracy.

Elle opina, sans demander aucune explication.

Chris s'assit sur une vieille bûche délavée, blanchie, séchée par le sel et le vent marin; il attira Janice à côté de lui. Ils se mirent à parler, à parler vite, sans jamais s'arrêter, comme pour rattraper le temps perdu.

Tout ce qui concernait Janice revêtait pour Chris une extrême importance, de son allergie aux olives à sa passion pour les chants folkloriques irlandais. Ils se découvrirent d'innombrables goûts communs, tels que la politique et la philosophie, et quelques sujets sur lesquels ils n'étaient pas tout à fait d'accord.

La lune brillait dans le ciel nocturne, la marée haute recouvrait la plage, l'air immobile se muait en brise. La fraîcheur du soir s'immisçait dans la chaude atmosphère, mais les deux jeunes gens continuaient à bavarder.

Ce n'était pas facile d'évoquer toute une vie en une seule fois. Ils tentaient pourtant de le faire, en s'efforçant de se donner le plus d'informations possible, de se connaître à fond, de s'assurer que ce qui leur arrivait était vrai et durable.

Le froid finit par les chasser. Janice tremblait malgré le bras de Chris autour de ses épaules.

Il la raccompagna devant la porte de sa chambre. Leurs lèvres s'unirent une dernière fois. Ébloui, il s'aperçut que leurs corps s'épousaient parfaitement. Ils étaient faits l'un pour l'autre. Elle le sentit aussi et se pressa contre lui.

— Tu m'attendras, demain soir ? chuchota-t-il.

— Oui, souffla-t-elle à son oreille.

Il ouvrit la bouche, mais un bruit en provenance de la chambre lui fit garder le silence. Tomber sur Tracy était la dernière chose au monde qu'il souhaitait. Ils échangèrent encore un baiser, plus rapide, avant que Chris longe le couloir menant à sa chambre. Sur le seuil, il se retourna.

— Je rentrerai dès que je pourrai.

— Je serai là, dit-elle doucement.

De la main, des yeux, ils s'adressèrent un au revoir muet. Cette nuit-là, Chris dormit comme un bébé. Et, pour la première fois depuis des années, Tracy ne vint pas hanter ses rêves.

9

Chris roula sur le dos, les mains derrière la nuque, les yeux fixés au plafond. Il n'était pas arrivé à dormir, à faire taire le tumulte de ses pensées.

Depuis deux jours, les changements s'étaient succédé à une allure hallucinante. La figuration avait abouti à un petit rôle de quelques lignes, le tournage avait duré quatre jours. Il commençait aux aurores, terminait tard dans la nuit. Il avait donc peu vu Janice. Ils échangeaient quelques mots le soir, couraient pendant une heure sur la plage le matin. Elle ne cessait de répéter que cela lui était égal, mais peut-être se montrait-elle simplement polie, afin de ne pas ternir sa joie.

Le dernier jour du tournage avait apporté un nouveau changement. Robert, le producteur, s'était montré sur le plateau. Il avait convoqué Chris pour une nouvelle audition. L'adolescent avait oublié la conversation entre Tony et Robert, pendant laquelle ils étaient tombés d'accord sur le fait qu'il ressemblait à un certain David. Il ne s'agissait en fait pas d'un de leurs amis, mais du personnage principal d'un film en cours d'écriture. Le scénario, inspiré d'un roman, était quasiment terminé, mais ils n'avaient encore trouvé aucun comédien pour tenir le rôle. Tous les castings se soldaient par un irréversible refus de l'auteur. Ils s'apprêtaient à abandonner le projet quand Tony avait remarqué Chris.

Et ce soir, l'impossible, l'inimaginable, s'était produit : Robert lui avait offert le rôle-titre. Il ne restait plus à Chris qu'à répondre oui ou non.

Il avait commencé par tergiverser, mettant en avant les exigences de l'auteur, qui ne voulait pas d'un acteur débutant. Robert l'avait alors informé que, dans la semaine, les scénaristes et l'auteur l'avaient regardé tourner. Ils avaient tous accordé leurs violons pour chanter ses louanges : Chris crevait l'écran et incarnait selon eux parfaitement David.

D'abord flatté, Chris n'avait pas tardé à éprouver les premières affres du trac. La bouche sèche, il avait demandé à Robert un délai de réflexion. Abasourdi, le producteur n'avait pu qu'opiner.

Déjà, le plateau tout entier bourdonnait de la nouvelle. Enfin, le prochain film du studio verrait le jour. La société de production apportait les réponses aux questions de Chris. S'il acceptait de travailler avec eux, les meilleurs professeurs seraient mis à sa disposition afin qu'il puisse poursuivre ses études. Le fait qu'il n'avait jamais joué ne posait pas plus de difficultés. Il possédait un talent naturel et, de toute façon, il aurait un coach. De plus, ils loueraient pour lui et sa mère un appartement de fonction. Une voiture avec chauffeur figurait également dans le contrat… Et s'il n'aimait pas jouer, il aurait la possibilité de s'arrêter à la fin de son premier film. Mais cela, personne n'y croyait vraiment.

L'argument majeur, c'était l'argent. Chris gagnerait en une seule fois le financement de ses études à Yale et à Stanford réunis, après quoi il lui resterait une somme suffisante pour s'offrir le chalet de ses rêves à Santa Cruz.

Comment pouvait-il refuser une telle offre ? Et, en même temps, comment pouvait-il accepter ? Pour Chris, devenir acteur signifiait être quelqu'un de spécial ; un ambitieux, un persévérant, voire un acharné. Les collaborateurs de Robert avaient beau affirmer qu'il réussirait, qu'adviendrait-il de lui s'ils se trompaient ? Si, lors du tournage, on se rendait compte qu'il était nul ? Bouger, parler devant une caméra n'avait rien à voir avec une scène de foule. Jouer, c'était s'exposer à la curiosité du public, au jugement des journaux spécialisés.

Et si les critiques le descendaient en flammes ?

Il ne s'agissait pas d'une fiction, d'un film d'action où les effets spéciaux et les cascades l'emportaient sur le jeu des comédiens. L'histoire mettait en scène un jeune homme dont le père avait été accusé à tort d'agression sexuelle sur un mineur. Le livre figurait toujours en tête des best-sellers. Des millions de personnes l'avaient lu et s'étaient forgé une opinion sur David, le héros. Il était difficile de plaire à tout le monde. Chris était lui-même, pas David.

Pourtant, il adorait le cinéma. En tenant son petit rôle auprès de Tony, il s'était pris de passion pour ce métier. Mais comment aurait-il pu imaginer devenir acteur aussi vite, aussi brusquement ? Il se sentait aussi anxieux que s'il avait été qualifié pour les Jeux olympiques.

Se tournant sur le côté, il regarda par la fenêtre les nuages s'effilocher sur le ciel nocturne.

Janice l'avait attendu, comme tous les soirs. Il lui avait aussitôt annoncé la nouvelle et, pendant un long moment, elle était restée muette. Une fois remise de sa surprise, elle avait déclaré qu'il serait idiot de refuser cette chance. Elle comprenait ses appréhensions mais, à sa place, elle n'aurait pas hésité à accepter. Non, pas une seconde. De telles occasions ne se présentent pas tous les jours, avait-elle ajouté.

Chris était attendu dans deux jours aux studios, à Los Angeles, pour des bouts d'essai. C'était une pure formalité, avait précisé Robert, destinée à convaincre ceux qui ne l'avaient pas encore vu jouer.

L'adolescent soupira. Il était la proie d'un dilemme cornélien. Devait-il abandonner le lycée, le championnat de lutte, sa vie entière pour un film qui entraînerait sa consécration ou sa perte ? Il devait prendre une décision avant d'en parler à sa mère. Oui, il était important qu'il ne subisse pas son influence.

Tout en ressassant, il se tourna de nouveau sur le dos en serrant l'oreiller dans ses bras. Au même moment, la porte de sa chambre s'ouvrit. Il releva la tête.

— Qui est-ce ? demanda-t-il, dans l'espoir de voir apparaître Janice.

— Je savais que tu serais réveillé, murmura alors Tracy. Je voudrais te montrer quelque chose.

Confus, surpris, Chris scruta la silhouette au pied du lit.

— À cette heure-ci?

— Tu ne m'as pas laissé le choix. Tu n'es jamais là.

Elle passa les doigts dans ses longs cheveux, les remonta, puis les laissa cascader sur ses épaules.

Il rêvait.

Oui. Il dormait et il faisait un rêve.

Mais pourquoi celui-ci? Pourquoi maintenant? Il n'était plus amoureux de Tracy.

Il faisait sombre dans la chambre mais la jeune fille se déplaça dans la lueur de la fenêtre. Elle portait un court peignoir de soie ouvert sur une nuisette.

Le cœur de Chris fit un bond dans sa poitrine quand elle vint s'asseoir sur le bord du lit. Sa jambe longue et lisse frôla celle de Chris.

— Je m'ennuie sans toi.

Bon sang, ce n'était pas un rêve. Il sentait sa chaleur, son parfum lourd, musqué, trop sucré.

— Qu'est-ce que tu veux, Tracy?

— D'abord, promets-moi que tu ne diras rien à personne.

Il aperçut la blancheur de son sourire dans la semi-obscurité. Elle flirtait avec lui! Les yeux de Chris s'arrondirent. Il n'aurait pas été plus surpris si une lame de fond avait balayé sa chambre.

— Écoute, je suis fatigué et...

Elle posa la main sur sa cuisse, tout près de l'aine.

— Voyons, Chris, je ne te demande qu'une petite promesse.

Elle devait penser qu'elle n'avait qu'à le toucher pour le réduire à sa merci. Furieux, il repoussa sa main avant de rouler au milieu du grand lit.

— Tracy, à d'autres! Dis-moi ce que tu veux au lieu de tourner autour du pot.

Cette fois-ci, elle ne répondit pas tout de suite.

— J'ai peine à l'admettre, commença-t-elle d'une voix traînante, mais Janice m'a fait comprendre que j'avais eu tort de me comporter aussi mal avec toi.

De nouveau, elle secoua ses longs cheveux dorés.

— Nous n'avons plus que deux semaines, reprit-elle. Je voudrais qu'elles soient inoubliables.

Elle mentait. Cela se voyait à son regard fuyant.

— Désolé, répondit-il, gonflé d'une merveilleuse sensation de toute-puissance. Je ne suis pas intéressé.

Tracy eut un sourire suave.

— D'après Janice, tu es fâché à cause de mon soupirant. Mais tes colères ne durent jamais longtemps.

— Je ne sais pas à quoi tu joues, mais je suis fatigué et je dois me lever tôt. Si tu n'as rien d'autre à me dire, va-t'en.

— Te lever tôt ? Mais où vas-tu donc tous les matins ?

Elle avait posé la question avec une innocence feinte. Elle sait ! songea Chris spontanément. Tout s'expliquait à présent. Tracy avait entendu parler du tournage à Watsonville.

— Nulle part, répondit-il.

— Je ne peux pas venir, moi aussi ?

— Pourquoi ?

— Je te l'ai dit, je m'ennuie. Si je ne sors pas d'ici, je vais péter les plombs. Maman me prend la tête et en plus elle aurait une attaque si elle savait ce que j'ai fait.

Elle avait lancé la ligne et il était impossible de ne pas mordre à l'hameçon.

— Qu'as-tu fait ?

— Promets-moi d'abord que tu ne diras rien, insista-t-elle.

Elle se fichait éperdument de ses promesses. Elle tenait seulement à l'amener là où elle voulait. Mais pour la première fois depuis qu'ils se connaissaient, Chris eut la sensation d'avoir le dessus.

— Laisse tomber, lâcha-t-il. Je ne veux pas le savoir.

— Pourquoi es-tu si…

Elle s'interrompit, une lueur malveillante dans les prunelles.

— ... têtu ? Tout ce que je te demande, c'est... oh, et puis zut ! Je te fais confiance, tiens !

Elle alluma la lampe de chevet, écarta les jambes et attendit la réaction de Chris. Un flot de chaleur enflamma le bas-ventre de ce dernier. Son caleçon lui comprima douloureusement le sexe. Tracy rejeta ses longs cheveux en arrière dans un mouvement victorieux. Elle devait penser être arrivée à ses fins.

— Qu'en dis-tu ? demanda-t-elle.

— De quoi ? rétorqua-t-il le plus froidement possible.

— Du tatouage.

Elle plia sa jambe droite. Tout en sachant qu'il commettait une grave erreur, Chris ne put s'empêcher de regarder. À l'intérieur de la cuisse de Tracy, tout près de l'élastique de son minuscule slip bleu ciel, une rose entourée de barbelé ornait la chair soyeuse.

— Génial, non ? s'enquit-elle.

— Si ça te rend heureuse...

— Tu veux toucher ?

Il la regarda, stupéfait. Elle faisait tout ce cirque à cause d'un petit rôle dans un film !

— Non, merci.

Elle se rapprocha, aussi câline qu'une chatte.

— Vas-y, touche. C'est doux comme...

Elle ne finit pas sa phrase. On frappait à la porte. Le battant s'ouvrit sur Janice qui se glissa dans la pièce. Elle portait un short et un sweat-shirt barré de l'inscription « La vie est belle. »

Un sourire vengeur retroussa les lèvres de Tracy.

— Je savais que je te trouverais ici, dit Janice, lui retournant son sourire.

Tracy se blottit contre Chris, la tête appuyée sur le montant sculpté du lit. D'un geste lent, délibérément indolent, elle referma son peignoir.

— La prochaine fois, tu attendras qu'on te dise d'entrer, dit-elle à son amie. Qu'est-ce que tu veux ?

— Il est l'heure de mon jogging avec Chris, rétorqua Janice sans broncher. Nous courons ensemble tous les matins.

— Une minute, dit ce dernier. Je te rejoins.

Janice hocha la tête et sortit.

— Je croyais que tu étais fatigué, remarqua Tracy d'un ton accusateur.

Chris enfila son pantalon de jogging qu'il avait laissé sur le dossier de la chaise.

— Tu n'es pas gênée que Janice nous ait trouvés ensemble ?

— Pourquoi ? Je n'ai rien à cirer de Janice, répondit Tracy avec mépris.

— À ta place, je me méfierais. Elle pourrait tout raconter à ton petit copain.

Furieuse, Tracy s'extirpa du lit.

— Pauvre minable ! Janice et toi vous méritez l'un l'autre.

— Merci, dit-il en passant son tee-shirt. C'est grâce à toi que nous nous sommes rencontrés.

Folle de rage, Tracy ouvrit la porte et faillit entrer en collision avec Margaret, qui sortait de la salle de bains. Elles se regardèrent dans le blanc des yeux.

— Laissez-moi passer ! ordonna finalement Tracy avec fureur.

La mère de Chris fit un pas de côté, et Tracy se fondit dans l'ombre du couloir. Un instant après, la porte de sa chambre claqua avec fracas.

Margaret se tourna vers son fils.

— Que se passe-t-il ?

Chris s'approcha de sa mère, la prit par les épaules et posa un baiser rapide sur sa joue.

— Excuse-moi, maman. Janice m'attend. Nous allons courir.

Après une brève hésitation, il ajouta :

— Attends-moi. Il faut que nous parlions.

Margaret fronça les sourcils, déroutée.

— Oui, en effet, approuva-t-elle. Je pense que c'est nécessaire.

10

Ils ne prononcèrent pas un mot pendant longtemps, tandis qu'ils longeaient à grandes enjambées le bord de mer. Ce fut Chris qui, finalement, brisa le silence :

— Merci d'avoir volé à mon secours. Comment as-tu deviné qu'elle était dans ma chambre ?

Par rapport aux autres matins, Janice était venue le chercher avec une demi-heure d'avance.

— Quand je me suis réveillée, Tracy n'était pas dans son lit ; j'ai tout de suite compris. Et, malheureusement, je ne me trompais pas.

Chris se déporta sur la gauche, afin de pénétrer dans le champ de vision de Janice.

— Tu m'en veux ? cria-t-il contre le vent.

— Je suis déçue.

— Je n'ai pas invité Tracy à venir dans ma chambre.

— Tu ne lui as pas dit non plus de s'en aller.

— Si, mais elle ne voulait rien savoir.

Janice pila brusquement, les poings sur les hanches.

— Ah oui ? Tu n'as pas dû être assez ferme, alors.

L'adolescent sourit. Il aimait la colère de la jeune fille, sa dignité, sa fierté aussi.

— Tu sais que tu es belle ?

— Je sais surtout que tu es amoureux de Tracy.

— Je l'étais, rectifia-t-il.

— On ne cesse pas d'aimer du jour au lendemain.

Elle se mordit la lèvre et détourna le regard.

Chris l'enlaça.

— Janice, murmura-t-il. Tu me fais peur.

— Ouais… Je suis une dure à cuire.

— Je t'aime, dit-il simplement. Je t'aime et je ne sais pas comment m'y prendre.

Il la sentit soudain très calme.

— Tu peux répéter ? demanda-t-elle.

— Je veux te garder ici avec moi, te suivre à St Louis, résoudre les choses pratiques de la vie. Or, je ne peux rien faire pour le moment. Rien du tout. Et c'est très dur.

Sentant fondre sa colère, Janice posa sa tête sur l'épaule de Chris.

— Comment en sommes-nous arrivés là ? Avant nous nous détestions et maintenant…

Il resserra son étreinte.

— Maintenant nous nous aimons. Comment, pourquoi, ça n'a pas d'importance. Tu es la meilleure chose qui me soit jamais arrivée. Et nous allons trouver le moyen de rester ensemble.

— Tu me le promets ?

— Je te le jure.

Janice redressa la tête.

— Nous avons le présent. Nous nous soucierons de l'avenir plus tard.

Ce fut elle qui l'embrassa. Chris n'avait jamais rien goûté de plus exquis que ses lèvres, que sa langue qui explorait sa bouche. Le désir durcit son sexe, envahit ses reins. Mais, cette fois, son désir n'était pas seulement physique, mais aussi mental. Il ressentait la passion de recevoir et de donner, d'aimer et d'être aimé. Il aurait voulu gagner des batailles pour Janice. La tenir dans ses bras. Il n'avait jamais fait l'amour, et jusqu'à présent, sa virginité l'embarrassait. Aujourd'hui, sachant que Janice serait sa première partenaire, il se félicitait d'avoir attendu.

Il la pressa contre lui, sentant son corps s'imprimer dans le sien.

— J'essaierai de remettre mon voyage à Los Angeles à la fin du mois.

— Ainsi, tu as décidé de jouer le rôle de David.

C'était une constatation, pas une question. Le stress quitta Chris d'un seul coup. Libéré d'un fardeau, il poussa un soupir de soulagement. Oui, il avait pris sa décision. Et cela le rendait léger comme l'air.

— Oui, admit-il.

— Est-ce que tu l'as dit à ta mère ?

— Pas encore.

Le ciel virait du gris sombre au pourpre. C'était la dernière journée sur le plateau avec Tony, et Chris ne pouvait se permettre de manquer à l'appel.

— Tony passe me prendre, dit-il. Il faut que je me prépare.

La jeune fille glissa sa main dans celle de Chris, tandis qu'ils avançaient vers l'escalier sculpté dans la falaise.

— Pourrions-nous aller quelque part ce soir, toi et moi ? demanda-t-elle.

Il chercha ses lèvres. La perspective de se retrouver seul avec elle le consuma d'une longue flamme.

— Je rentrerai tôt.

Mais, à son retour, il était déjà presque minuit. Tony allait regagner Los Angeles pour tourner des scènes d'intérieur, et les scriptes avaient organisé un pot d'adieu en son honneur. Chris s'était senti obligé d'assister à la soirée. Il avait vainement tenté d'appeler Janice au chalet ; chaque fois, la ligne était occupée et à son dernier essai, il n'y avait plus personne. Ils sortiraient ensemble le lendemain… Seuls, comme elle l'avait souhaité.

Avant de faire démarrer la Jeep, Tony avait donné ses coordonnées à Chris. Il avait insisté pour que ce dernier le contacte dès qu'il arriverait à Los Angeles. Sur le chemin du retour, ils avaient évoqué le nouveau rôle de Chris, les bouts d'essai. Tony lui avait recommandé de se syndiquer à la Ligue des acteurs de cinéma et de chercher un agent.

Tandis que la Jeep avalait la route, Tony s'était lancé dans une de ses diatribes préférées sur le show-biz. Selon lui, l'art était une chose, mais le business en était une autre. Il fallait toujours avoir en tête qu'une carrière d'acteur pouvait s'achever du jour au lendemain. Un jour, on est porté aux nues, le suivant, jeté aux oubliettes.

« Alors, mec, l'argent que tu gagneras, mets-le de côté. Investis jusqu'au moindre centime. Et n'attrape pas la grosse tête. Les amitiés à Hollywood sont superficielles. On t'apprécie tant que ton étoile brille au firmament du star-système. Ensuite, on te méprise. Et puis, méfie-toi des drogues qui circulent librement dans les soirées mondaines… »

La mère de Chris aurait pu lui tenir le même discours. Mais elle s'en était bien gardée. Margaret avait posé mille questions, bien sûr, après quoi elle avait donné sa bénédiction à son fils avec un calme remarquable.

— Je t'aurai à l'œil ! le prévint Tony, tandis qu'ils empruntaient l'allée du chalet. Si tu te plantes, je serai là. Et si jamais tu as des ennuis, tu me passes un coup de fil, et j'arrive.

Chris hocha la tête. L'émotion l'étreignait. L'amitié de Tony lui était précieuse, et il ferait tout pour ne pas le décevoir.

— Je te tiendrai au courant, dit-il en sortant de la voiture. Au sujet du bout d'essai, je veux dire.

— Entendu. Et nous allons organiser une fête pour arroser la fin de mon film.

Chris referma la portière. Il regarda s'éloigner la Jeep noire aux chromes dorés, puis s'avança vers le chalet. Les lumières étaient allumées mais personne ne l'accueillit.

— Maman ? cria-t-il.

Une seconde s'écoula.

— Janice ?

Pas de réponse. Il prit la direction de la cuisine et trébucha sur une valise posée près du canapé. Sa mère apparut du côté de la terrasse et entra dans le salon par la porte coulissante.

— Il me semblait bien t'avoir entendu, dit-elle.

Chris baissa les yeux sur la valise, puis regarda sa mère.

— Que se passe-t-il ?

Elle posa son index sur ses lèvres et fit signe à son fils de la suivre dans la cuisine. Il s'exécuta. À l'évidence, personne ne pouvait les entendre, pourtant Margaret parlait à mi-voix.

— Beverly ramène les filles ce soir. Elles prendront la navette à San Jose.

Chaque mot résonnait en lui comme un lugubre son de cloche. Les bras ballants, Chris attendit une explication qui ne vint jamais. Janice s'en allait ? Beverly ramenait tout le monde au bercail ? Cela n'avait pas de sens.

— Je ne comprends pas, finit-il par articuler laborieusement.

— Tracy et Beverly ont eu une altercation cet après-midi, quand les deux filles sont revenues de la ville. Tu ne devineras jamais ce que Tracy a fait.

— Oh, si… répondit Chris. Comment Beverly a-t-elle découvert le tatouage ?

Tracy avait très bien pu le montrer à sa mère, rien que pour la provoquer.

— Quel tatouage ? demanda Margaret.

— La rose sur sa…

Il se reprit.

— Si ce n'est pas le tatouage, de quoi s'agit-il ?

— Du piercing. Cette idiote s'est fait poser des anneaux au bout des seins.

— Oh, non ! Et Beverly les a vus ?

— Tracy a saigné. Le docteur a dit…

Janice entra dans la cuisine. Elle avait les paupières bouffies, les yeux rouges.

— Puis-je parler à Chris dehors ? s'enquit-elle poliment.

— Oui, bien sûr, dit Margaret en regardant la pendule murale. Mais n'allez pas trop loin, vous n'avez pas beaucoup de temps.

— Et pourquoi Janice doit-elle partir ? demanda Chris. Pourquoi ne reste-t-elle pas avec nous ?

Margaret soupira.

— Personnellement je n'y vois pas d'inconvénient. Tout dépend de vos parents, Janice.

La jeune fille haussa les épaules. Une lueur d'espoir étincela dans ses yeux noisette.

— Il faudrait que j'appelle papa. Et toi, Chris ? As-tu réussi à repousser la date des bouts d'essai ?

Seigneur! Il avait oublié qu'il partait dans deux jours.

— Non. Ils m'ont dit que le rendez-vous avait été fixé. Trop de personnes sont impliquées pour ajourner la séance. Mais je rentrerai très vite.

Pourvu qu'elle ne s'en aille pas! songea-t-il.

Janice battit des paupières afin de sécher ses larmes.

— C'est très bien comme ça, le rassura-t-elle. Tu dois tenter ta chance dans les meilleures conditions. Si tu t'inquiètes parce que tu dois revenir…

Elle laissa sa phrase en suspens et déglutit péniblement.

— Mais tu ne peux pas partir, murmura Chris en l'attirant dans ses bras. Quand nous reverrons-nous?

La jeune fille blottit sa tête contre la poitrine du garçon, et laissa couler ses larmes.

— Je n'en sais rien. À Noël?

— À Noël? Mais c'est dans cent ans!

— Je t'écrirai tous les jours.

— Je t'appellerai de Los Angeles.

Margaret toucha tendrement le bras de son fils.

— Je vous laisse, les enfants.

Elle se retira discrètement. Avant de refermer la porte de la cuisine, elle entendit Janice s'écrier:

— Ce n'est pas juste!

Margaret consulta sa montre. Mentalement, elle calcula combien de temps Beverly mettrait pour se rendre à l'aéroport. Cela laissait un petit quart d'heure à Chris et à Janice. Quinze minutes pour se dire adieu, ou pour se faire le serment d'un amour éternel. Margaret soupira. Elle comprenait les tourments des deux jeunes gens. Nul ne savait comment évolueraient leurs sentiments dans les mois à venir mais, par expérience, elle savait qu'ils ne seraient plus jamais aussi intenses, aussi douloureux… aussi doux.

Son cœur se brisait à l'idée que la vie les séparerait. Pourtant, un fond d'envie se mêlait à sa tristesse. En les voyant ensemble, enlacés, elle s'était rappelé sa jeunesse qu'elle croyait enfouie à jamais. Margaret avait réussi à se convaincre que l'amour était un luxe. À présent, elle se rendait compte qu'elle avait eu tort.

Elle posa le mot de bienvenue sur les coquillages qu'elle avait ramassés pour Maggie et pour Joe. Elle quittait le chalet cinq jours plus tôt que prévu pour rejoindre Chris à Los Angeles et ne voulait pas accueillir les locataires de juillet avec un bouquet de fleurs fanées. Elle avait passé la maison en revue pour la énième fois, afin de s'assurer que tout était en ordre. Une étrange mélancolie s'immisçait dans son esprit.

Elle sortit sur la terrasse. La brume matinale traînait ses lambeaux sur l'océan, étouffant le roulement des vagues et le cri des mouettes. Les feuilles étroites du grand eucalyptus déversaient un vaporeux nuage de gouttelettes, semblables à des larmes d'adieu.

Les trois semaines et demie qu'elle avait passées ici avaient clos un chapitre de sa vie. Ce chalet avait vu les premiers pas hésitants de Chris lorsqu'il était bébé. Dix-sept ans plus tard, le même décor avait été témoin d'un pas plus décisif, qui mettait fin à son enfance. Ici, Beverly et elle avaient regardé grandir leurs enfants. Ici, Kevin et elle avaient tenté de se réconcilier. Ici encore, elle lui avait demandé le divorce.

Durant ces quelques jours de solitude au chalet, elle avait eu le temps de réfléchir. De faire le point sur sa vie. Un bilan qu'elle n'avait jamais eu le temps ou la volonté d'établir. Margaret avait assisté à la peine de Chris quand Janice était partie, puis à son excitation en vue des bouts d'essai. Il envisageait une carrière cinématographique et elle l'avait encouragé dans cette voie. Sans l'avoir jamais vraiment accepté, elle avait toujours su qu'un jour Chris s'éloignerait d'elle.

Elle ne devait plus être émotionnellement dépendante de son fils. Ce n'était pas sain. Il lui fallait une vie à elle. Grâce à Chris et à Janice, elle en était venue à comprendre qu'une existence partagée recelait des joies que la solitude ne lui procurerait jamais. À partir d'aujourd'hui, elle donnerait une chance à chaque homme qui la courtiserait. Après tout, ils n'étaient pas tous comme Kevin. Quelque part, il existait bien son âme sœur. Un homme qui croyait au miracle de la seconde chance, qui aimait aussi bien l'opéra que les séries télévisées, les cocktails de crevettes que les hamburgers, et qui ne pensait pas qu'à partir d'un certain âge, les femmes ne disposaient plus d'aucune sensualité.

Malgré le brouillard, les vacanciers commençaient à envahir la plage, mais pour Margaret, l'heure du départ avait sonné. Chris lui avait donné rendez-vous l'après-midi même à Beverly Hills, dans les bureaux de l'agence William Morris. Elle avait donc un long chemin à parcourir… Elle monta dans sa vieille Volvo et la fit démarrer. Tout en empruntant l'allée, elle jeta un ultime et bref coup d'œil au chalet dans le rétroviseur. Elle se sentait triste de partir, mais aussi exaltée d'aller vers une nouvelle vie.

TROISIÈME PARTIE

Juillet

1

À quatre-vingt-huit ans et après soixante-cinq ans de vie commune, Joe estimait que Maggie était la plus belle femme qu'il ait jamais connue. Par moments, comme ce matin, il avait la sensation de remonter le temps : il la voyait alors comme au jour de leur mariage, les cheveux dorés, une adorable petite fossette sur sa joue de porcelaine, les yeux brun profond, tout brillants d'amour pour lui.

En retour, elle le considérait comme le plus séduisant, le plus intelligent, le plus prévenant des hommes de la terre.

Les cheveux de Maggie avaient viré au blanc soyeux, et la fossette sur sa joue gauche se creusait à l'occasion d'un rare sourire. Seuls ses yeux restaient les mêmes, pétillants, enjoués, mystérieux et, ces derniers temps, empreints de douleur.

— On a tout ? cria-t-elle de la porte de service du bungalow qu'ils avaient acheté la cinquième année de leur mariage.

Joe ferma le coffre de la voiture.

— Oui, tout ce qu'il y a sur la liste.

— Les médicaments ?

— Dans la boîte à provisions.

— La lettre ?

— Dans ta valise.

— Les jouets de Josi ?

— Dans la mienne.

— Alors, c'est bon.

Adossée au chambranle, elle se figea un instant.

— Un étourdissement ? demanda Joe.

— Un tout petit.

Il lui fallait un maximum de volonté pour ne pas bouger. Quand la tête lui tournait, seule une parfaite immobilité venait à bout du vertige.

— As-tu fermé l'entrée principale ? s'enquit Joe.

Maggie acquiesça.

— Et l'air conditionné ?

— Il est éteint.

— Alors, en route !

Maggie avança d'un pas précautionneux, afin de s'assurer que son équilibre était rétabli, puis descendit les marches du perron.

— Mon sac est sur la table de la cuisine, Joe. Veux-tu aller me le chercher, s'il te plaît ?

Ce dernier contourna la voiture, la main tendue. Maggie s'y appuya. Enchanté, inquiet aussi, comme chaque fois qu'elle acceptait son aide sans protester, il la fit asseoir à la place du passager.

— Les petits vieux ne sont plus bons à rien, dit-elle, une fois installée.

Il ne connaissait que trop bien cette rengaine. Maggie l'avait adoptée depuis qu'un adolescent lui avait demandé sans malice ce qu'une « mamie » faisait au concert de Grateful Dead. Jusqu'alors, elle avait réussi à ignorer la barrière que son âge érigeait dans l'esprit des jeunes.

Joe se pencha et lui frôla la pommette d'un baiser rapide, comme pour lui prouver qu'à ses yeux elle était toujours jeune.

— Je reviens tout de suite.

Il disparut à l'intérieur, pour ressortir presque aussitôt avec Josi sous un bras et le sac de Maggie sous l'autre. Il verrouilla la portière côté passager, puis se glissa derrière le volant. À peine relâchée, la chatte prit son élan et sauta de tout son poids de huit kilos sur les genoux de Maggie. Celle-ci la gratta derrière les oreilles, tandis que Joe faisait tourner le moteur. La grosse Chrysler et Josi émirent de concert un ronronnement continu

144

pendant l'heure et demie que dura le trajet entre San Jose et le chalet.

— Toutes ces nouvelles plantations ! s'écria Maggie quand la voiture prit le dernier virage. Julia s'est surpassée cette année. C'est bon signe, hein, Joe ?

Le jardin déployait ses corolles rayonnantes sous un ciel plombé. La passion du jardinage avait tissé le premier lien d'amitié entre les deux femmes. Par la suite, en dépit d'une différence d'âge d'un demi-siècle, elles s'étaient découvert de nombreux points communs. Maggie avait pleuré l'injuste disparition de Ken mais s'était apitoyée plus encore sur le triste sort de la jeune veuve esseulée.

— Sa voix m'a paru plus ferme la dernière fois que je l'ai eue au téléphone, répondit Joe. Pourtant, venir ici sans Ken a dû lui coûter.

Maggie posa la main sur le genou de son mari.

— Mais elle l'a fait, déclara-t-elle avec un sourire encourageant. La prochaine fois, ce sera plus facile. Ce chalet est un temple au passé… J'ai dit à Julia qu'elle devait revenir. Se fabriquer de nouveaux souvenirs. Ken m'aurait donné raison.

Joe tapota la main de sa femme.

— Eh bien, apparemment, elle t'a écoutée.

— Je sais de quoi je parle, Joe.

Il lui prit la main et pressa ses lèvres sur les doigts déformés par l'arthrite.

— Oui, Maggie. Je sais. Et je n'ai jamais mis en doute ta parole.

Elle eut un petit sourire maussade.

— J'espère que nous pourrons encore passer nos vacances ici l'an prochain.

Joe coupa le moteur. Impatiente d'explorer l'environnement, Josi se redressa et posa ses pattes de devant contre la vitre. Maggie tressaillit. Son mari s'empressa de soulever la chatte, qui lâcha un miaulement indigné.

— Elle n'y est pour rien, dit Maggie.

— Je n'ai pas eu le temps de lui limer les griffes ; elles sont aussi acérées que des poignards, riposta Joe, toujours enclin à récriminer à propos de tout, sauf du cancer qui rongeait Maggie.

— As-tu apporté la pince à ongles ?

Leur conversation dévia vers des sujets anodins, quotidiens, tandis qu'ils sortaient de la voiture. La chatte gambada joyeusement vers la maison, suivie de ses maîtres. Joe insista pour que Maggie se repose sur la terrasse pendant qu'il déchargeait les bagages et, contre toute attente, elle accepta. Elle prit docilement place sur un fauteuil en rotin et laissa Joe lui couvrir les jambes avec un plaid, afin de la protéger de la brise du large. Peu après, le vieil homme ressortit et tendit à sa femme la note qu'il avait trouvée dans la cuisine.

— Un petit mot de Margaret ou de Beverly.

Maggie déplia la feuille de papier parchemin.

— Margaret nous passe le bonjour des deux familles. Elles ont dû partir plus tôt que prévu. Le réfrigérateur et le placard regorgent de nourriture. Le post-scriptum est, ma foi, singulier.

— Raconte !

— Margaret s'apprête à nous annoncer de grandes nouvelles d'ici Noël… Chris et elle sont en passe de changer de vie.

— Je me demande ce que cela signifie.

— Ça ne peut être qu'une bonne chose, affirma Maggie. Son enthousiasme imprègne le papier.

— Veux-tu quelque chose à lire ? proposa Joe.

Maggie secoua la tête.

— Non merci. Je préfère regarder l'océan et écouter les vagues.

Il lui planta un baiser sur le front avant de vaquer à ses occupations.

De sa place, Maggie n'apercevait pas la plage, mais elle jouissait d'une vue plongeante sur l'océan ceint d'eucalyptus. Elle se serait bien assise au bord de la terrasse, de manière à contempler le mouvement incessant des vagues, mais Joe se serait inquiété. Dernièrement, il se faisait tout le temps du souci pour elle, et elle se laissait lâchement dorloter.

146

Contrairement à Joe, qui adorait le calme, Maggie appréciait le bruit, la force, l'activité effrénée de l'été. Les gens en vacances souriaient plus facilement. Ils oubliaient leurs problèmes pendant quinze jours ou trois semaines. Ici, on se saluait, on liait connaissance entre inconnus sans que cela prête à conséquence. Et puis, il y avait les enfants… Des enfants partout !

Elle comprenait parfaitement les raisons qui incitaient les parents de la génération actuelle à distiller la crainte dans l'esprit de leur progéniture. Il y avait eu trop de crimes, trop de petites victimes. On interdisait aux tout-petits comme aux plus grands de s'adresser à des étrangers, si avenants fussent-ils. Maggie avait ressenti cette nouvelle mentalité comme une perte cruelle. Autrefois, c'était différent. Comme elle n'avait pas d'enfants, elle passait pour une tante, puis pour une grand-mère auprès des gamins de son quartier. Tout comme Joe avait été leur oncle, leur grand-père. Leur porte était constamment ouverte, il y avait toujours un gâteau succulent, sorti du four, à partager, des bandes dessinées à feuilleter, des contes illustrés à lire.

Chaque année, un sapin de Noël géant ombrageait une pile de cadeaux chez Maggie et Joe Chapman. Avec leurs petits voisins, ils fabriquaient les décorations au lieu de les acheter dans des magasins.

Deux générations d'enfants avaient grandi dans le quartier avant que les choses commencent subrepticement à changer. Peu à peu, les exigences de la vie avaient poussé les mères de famille à chercher des emplois. Les pavillons demeuraient fermés du matin au soir, et les enfants étaient confiés à des écoles maternelles ou à des crèches. Les rares petits qui restaient à la maison ne sortaient plus mais regardaient la télévision à longueur de journée, barricadés, à l'abri des étrangers et des vieux voisins nostalgiques.

Maggie soupira. Le temps fuyait, le monde changeait à une allure incroyable. Elle aurait payé cher pour se retrouver trente ans en arrière. Soudain, comme si un bon génie avait exaucé son souhait, une petite fille apparut sur le sentier qui menait à la plage. Âgée de cinq ou six ans, elle avait des couettes blondes, un visage en forme de cœur, et de grands yeux chocolat.

Elle sautilla devant la balustrade, afin de mieux observer Maggie.

— Salut !

— Salut, répondit la vieille femme.

— Je m'appelle Susie. Et toi ?

— Maggie.

— Tu habites ici ?

— Parfois.

— Je peux jouer avec tes enfants ?

— Je n'en ai pas, ma chérie.

Susie haussa les épaules comme si, après tout, cela n'avait pas d'importance.

— Ma maman et mon papa ne vivent plus ensemble, dit-elle avec aisance. Ils sont divorcés.

Le cœur de Maggie se serra.

— Es-tu ici avec ta maman ?

— Non, mon papa… Il était docteur, mais maintenant il écrit un roman.

Julia avait bien dit qu'un médecin habitait la maison voisine, mais elle n'avait pas mentionné de petite fille.

— Et où est-il, ton papa ?

— Avec Jason.

— Jason ?

— Mon frère.

— Où sont-ils donc, tous les deux ?

La petite fille pointa le pouce derrière elle.

— Sur la plage. Ils construisent un château de sable.

— Susie !

Une voix masculine dans laquelle vibrait une note de panique retentit. Presque aussitôt, un homme aux cheveux poivre et sel ébouriffés, la lèvre supérieure ombrée d'un début de moustache, émergea du sentier. Il trimbalait un sac débordant de pelles, de seaux et de tours creuses en plastique.

— Je t'ai dit cent fois de ne pas t'en aller toute seule ! gronda-t-il. Jason et moi t'avons cherchée partout.

148

Malgré son ton sévère, on pouvait lire le soulagement sur son visage.

— Je voulais aller aux toilettes, papa. Je te l'ai dit.

— Mais tu ne m'as pas dit que tu remontais.

Il laissa tomber le sac, souleva la petite fille et la flanqua sur ses épaules. En se penchant pour reprendre les jouets, il aperçut Maggie sur la terrasse.

— Désolé... Je ne vous avais pas remarquée.

Susie se mit à gigoter, et il dut la reposer à terre.

— Vous devez être Maggie, dit-il. Je suis Eric Lawson.

Il marqua une pause pour s'assurer que sa voisine avait bien enregistré son nom, puis reprit :

— Le locataire d'Andrew. Julia a dû vous mettre au courant. C'est moi qui ai le double de la clé...

Soudain, un petit garçon apparut. Il avait une tête et demie de plus que Susie et des cheveux châtain doré coupés au bol. En voyant Maggie, il courut se blottir contre la jambe de son père.

Les doigts gourds de Maggie s'empêtrèrent dans le plaid qui lui bordait les jambes.

— Ne vous levez pas, dit Eric. Nous partons.

Susie renversa la tête pour le regarder.

— Je veux rester, moi.

— Non ! Il faut que je fasse le dîner, mademoiselle.

— Qu'est-ce qu'on mange ?

— Des spaghettis.

— Oh non ! gémit-elle. Nous en avons déjà mangé hier soir.

Maggie émit un petit rire.

— Les pâtes réchauffées ne sont pas mon plat préféré non plus. Avec Joe, nous allions commander une pizza... Voudriez-vous vous joindre à nous tous les trois ?

Elle venait d'inventer l'histoire de la pizza, mais la tentation de soudoyer les deux enfants était trop forte.

— Je ne sais pas... commença Eric.

— S'il te plaît, papaaaa ! glapit Susie.

Eric baissa les yeux vers son fils.

— Qu'en penses-tu, Jason ?

Celui-ci se contenta de hausser ses épaules étroites, dans un geste qui ne l'engageait à rien.

— Chez vous ou chez nous ? demanda Eric.

— Ici, si ça ne vous fait rien, répondit Maggie.

Longer l'allée, traverser la rue étroite dépassaient ses forces. Le trajet en voiture l'avait vidée de toute son énergie. Eric mit la main sur la nuque de Jason, qui posa la tête sur la hanche de son père.

— À quelle heure ?

— Six heures ?

Il consulta sa montre.

— Parfait. Cela nous donne le temps de nous débarbouiller.

— Ne vous inquiétez pas, dit Maggie. Venez comme vous êtes.

Jason leva les yeux vers son père.

— J'ai du sable dans mes chaussures, dit-il doucement.

— Alors, enlève-les, suggéra Maggie en souriant. Il ne faut pas mettre du sable partout dans le cottage de ton papa.

Elle s'émerveillait toujours des différences de caractère entre enfants de la même famille. Jason était sérieux, sage, tandis que Susie semblait plus libre, plus exubérante. Les réactions de l'un influaient-elles sur celles de l'autre ?

— Ce n'est pas son cottage, expliqua Susie. Il appartient à son copain. Nous vivons dans l'ancienne maison de papa, et lui, il vit ici tout seul.

Le résumé de Susie affectait son père, se dit Maggie, en notant l'ombre d'un regret dans les yeux d'Eric.

— Quelle sorte de pizza dois-je commander ? demanda-t-elle, changeant intentionnellement de sujet.

— Pas d'ail ! déclara Susie d'un ton sans réplique. Je n'aime pas ça. Et pas de champignons non plus. Jason n'en veut pas.

— Ce n'est pas vrai, objecta Jason.

— Tu ne les aimes pas, insista Susie.

— C'est toi qui ne les manges pas.

Maggie leur adressa un gentil sourire.

150

— Que diriez-vous d'une pizza aux saucisses et poivrons ?

— Extra ! approuva Eric.

— Avec des olives, ajouta Susie. Beaucoup d'olives.

Maggie se tourna vers Eric, qui confirma.

— Je sais que ça ne va pas avec le reste, mais c'est la
vérité. Dites-leur de les livrer à part.

— Je verrai ce que je peux faire.

Eric jeta le sac sur son épaule et tendit sa main libre
à Susie.

— Viens ma puce. Nous allons faire une salade pour
accompagner la pizza.

— On revient ! cria-t-elle à Maggie en attrapant la main
de son père.

— Je vous attends !

Une minute plus tard, Joe fit coulisser la porte vitrée
et sortit sur la terrasse.

— Tu parlais avec quelqu'un ?

— Oui, répliqua-t-elle. Nous avons des invités, ce soir.

— Alors, je cours chez le traiteur.

Joe n'avait jamais posé de questions comme : « Qui vient
dîner ? » Il faisait confiance à Maggie et c'était l'une des
innombrables qualités qu'elle appréciait chez l'homme
qu'elle avait épousé, des décennies auparavant.

— Inutile. Nous commanderons une pizza.

Une fois de plus, elle se débattit pour se libérer du
plaid qui lui enserrait les jambes et, de nouveau, elle dut
renoncer.

— À condition de trouver une pizzeria qui assure les
livraisons, acheva-t-elle.

— Mais tu détestes les pizzas !

— Tu comprendras quand tu verras nos invités.

— Alors j'attends la surprise, dit-il en retirant le plaid.
À quelle heure arrivent-ils ?

— À six heures.

— Excellent. Cela te laisse le temps de faire une petite
sieste.

— Oh, Joe ! Tu m'as promis de me laisser respirer un
peu, protesta-t-elle gentiment.

— Et toi, tu m'as promis de te reposer de temps en temps.

Depuis toujours, Joe prenait soin d'elle. Comment pourrait-il arrêter maintenant ?

— D'accord, mais pas plus d'une demi-heure.

— Marché conclu, convint Joe.

2

Pendant le dîner, le petit Jason ne desserra pas les dents. Il grignotait sa pizza comme s'il subissait une punition. Susie, bavarde comme une pie, ne laissa personne placer un mot, alimentant la conversation de questions, de commentaires et de cancans de famille, qui plongeaient parfois son père dans la perplexité.

À la fin du repas, Susie s'excusa pour aller aux toilettes, tandis que Joe et Eric commencèrent à débarrasser la table. Maggie resta seule avec Jason. Profitant de ce tête-à-tête, la vieille dame pria le garçonnet de l'aider à aller au salon. Elle sentait que le divorce de ses parents l'avait profondément atteint. Dès lors, Jason avait endossé par rapport à sa mère et à sa sœur le rôle protecteur du chef de famille.

Il regarda un instant la main ridée avant de s'en emparer de sa menotte parfaitement lisse. Il conduisit Maggie dans la pièce adjacente et elle le suivit en se déplaçant encore plus lentement que d'habitude. Ce petit parcours, cette infime connivence, elle le savait, contribuerait à abattre la barrière invisible qui les séparait.

— Si on s'asseyait près de Josi ? dit-elle, utilisant sans vergogne son animal domestique comme appât.

La chatte somnolait sur le canapé. Son poil noir, duveteux, soyeux, la faisait paraître plus grosse qu'elle ne l'était réellement.

— Est-ce qu'elle aime les enfants ? demanda Jason.

— Presque autant que moi, répondit Maggie.

Il avança prudemment, aux aguets, tandis que Josi ouvrait à moitié un œil d'agate. Il s'agenouilla sur les coussins du canapé et avança la main. Avant d'effleurer Josi, il jeta un coup d'œil anxieux à Maggie.

— Elle ne va pas me griffer?

— Bien sûr que non.

Du bout des doigts, il toucha la patte de Josi, frôlant le coussinet. La chatte ouvrit l'autre œil. La petite main de Jason remonta vers la fourrure gris sombre du ventre. L'animal releva la tête, les oreilles dressées. Enfin, très doucement, Jason lui caressa le flanc. Josi reposa alors sa tête sur le coussin. Un puissant ronronnement emplit la pièce.

Les yeux écarquillés, le petit garçon écouta un instant le son sourd et continu qui semblait se dérouler à l'infini.

— Qu'est-ce que c'est?

— Ça veut dire qu'elle t'aime bien.

— Vraiment?

Maggie se laissa tomber sur le canapé, près de Jason. La chatte posa une patte possessive sur sa jambe. Mû par une force irrésistible, Jason fit courir sa main dans l'épaisse fourrure de la bête, qui ronronnait de plus belle. Quand ses doigts frôlèrent le bras de Maggie, elle se sentit cajolée, elle aussi.

Susie fit alors irruption dans la pièce.

— Oh! Est-ce que je peux le caresser?

— Ce n'est pas lui, corrigea Jason. C'est elle.

— Je peux?

— Bien sûr, dit Maggie. Vas-y doucement.

Susie se blottit près de Jason et posa sa main à plat sur la tête de Josi.

— C'est quoi, ce bruit?

— Ça veut dire qu'elle m'aime bien, déclara Jason.

Susie regarda Maggie.

— C'est vrai?

Maggie inclina la tête.

— Oui. Et elle t'aime bien aussi.

Susie se pencha pour planter un baiser sur le nez de Josi, qui se frotta le museau avec sa patte.

— Elle a une drôle d'odeur, remarqua la petite fille.

— Parce qu'elle mange beaucoup de poisson.

— Beurk !

Susie se redressa, ayant perdu tout intérêt pour la chatte noire.

— Tu n'as pas de jouets ? demanda-t-elle.

— J'ai des livres, répondit Maggie, se souvenant de sa maigre collection de romans pour enfants rangée dans le placard. Veux-tu que nous en lisions un ensemble ?

— Oh, oui !

Tout en essuyant un verre, Joe passa la tête par la porte du salon avant de se retirer, rassuré. Entourée des deux petits, un illustré sur les genoux, Maggie était dans son élément. La vie s'était montrée cruelle en ne donnant pas d'enfants au couple. Ils avaient fait des pieds et des mains pour en adopter mais, après l'étude de leur dossier, l'assistante sociale n'avait pas donné son feu vert, à cause de l'épilepsie de Maggie. Et quand la médecine avait réussi à contrôler les crises, l'âge était alors devenu une barrière à l'adoption.

— Elle sait s'y prendre avec les gamins, constata Eric, lorsque Joe retourna dans la cuisine.

— Parfois, je me dis que Dieu l'a privée d'enfants parce que beaucoup d'autres avaient besoin d'elle.

Eric se tut. Au bout d'un long moment, il demanda gentiment :

— C'est le cancer, n'est-ce pas ?

Joe le regarda.

— Comment avez-vous deviné ?

— Les signes d'une longue maladie ne trompent pas, même quand le patient les combat farouchement.

— Elle ne se plaint jamais.

Pour se donner une contenance, Joe plongea l'éponge dans l'eau savonneuse et la passa sur le plan de travail.

— Où en est la maladie ?

— Le pronostic n'est pas très bon, murmura Joe d'une voix râpeuse, comme si ces mots lui écorchaient les lèvres.

Il aurait pourtant dû s'habituer, depuis le temps, mais il ne parvenait pas à surmonter son chagrin.

— L'un des médecins prévoit l'issue fatale dans un mois ou deux, reprit-il. Selon un autre, elle vivra jusqu'à Noël.

— Personne ne peut prédire ces choses-là avec certitude, déclara Eric. J'ai eu des patients qui sont décédés juste après le diagnostic, alors qu'ils étaient censés vivre encore un an, et d'autres qui ont défié toutes les lois de la science.

— Mais la plupart meurent plus ou moins à l'échéance fixée par les spécialistes.

— Oui... Joe, si je peux faire quelque chose, n'hésitez pas à me le demander.

— Merci. Julia nous a dit que nous pouvions compter sur vous.

— Julia vous a parlé de moi ?

— Nous lui passons un coup de fil tous les quinze jours. La pauvre petite s'est retrouvée très seule après la mort de son mari. De temps à autre, elle a besoin de parler à quelqu'un. Elle s'est mis dans la tête que vous avez des points communs avec Ken. Que d'une certaine manière, vous êtes faits de la même étoffe...

Eric sortit les couverts en argent du lave-vaisselle.

— Ken était un être hors du commun, n'est-ce pas ? demanda-t-il.

— La crème des hommes.

Joe avait pris l'infarctus de Ken aussi à cœur que le cancer de Maggie.

— Les Huntington formaient le couple idéal, reprit-il avec un soupir. Il faudra un siècle à Julia pour remplacer Ken, si toutefois cela lui arrive.

Muni d'un torchon, il se mit à essuyer les couverts avec une application exagérée. En fait, son esprit vagabondait.

— Julia est jeune. Ce sera dur pour elle de vivre seule toute une vie... Je ne continuerai pas à vivre sans Maggie, ajouta-t-il à mi-voix. Je n'y arriverai pas.

— Êtes-vous mariés depuis longtemps ?

— Nous avons fêté nos soixante-cinq ans de mariage en mars dernier. Maggie avait vingt ans et moi vingt-trois quand nous nous sommes passé la corde au cou… Nous avons beaucoup changé, de l'eau a coulé sous les ponts et, pourtant, j'ai parfois l'impression que c'était hier. Je nous revois encore dans la petite église de Reno…

— Vous vous êtes mariés à Reno ?

— Eh oui. Vous devez croire que cette ville a été inaugurée par la génération de vos parents, mais non ! Cela remonte à la nôtre.

Joe plia le torchon et l'accrocha près de l'évier.

— Avant que j'oublie, dit-il encore. Si jamais vous revoyez Julia, vous ne savez rien au sujet de Maggie. Comme elle venait de perdre Ken, nous ne lui avons rien dit. Elle le saura de toute façon lorsque… vous voyez ce que je veux dire.

— Je comprends.

— Voulez-vous du café ?

— Nous allons partir. Je ne voudrais pas que les enfants abusent de la gentillesse de votre femme.

— Ne dites pas ça, Eric. Ils sont le meilleur remède à ses souffrances. Venez voir.

Il l'entraîna jusqu'à la porte du salon, entrouverte sur une scène charmante : Susie, assise aux pieds de Maggie, jouait avec les coquillages laissés par Margaret ; Jason était pelotonné contre la vieille dame, qui lui lisait *Lassie revient* ; Josi ronronnait, étalée sur les genoux du petit garçon.

— Ils ne rendent pas souvent visite à leurs grands-parents, murmura Eric. Il va falloir remédier à cette lacune.

— En attendant, nous serons heureux de les recevoir.

Il s'agissait d'une prière plutôt que d'une proposition. Joe aurait tout fait pour procurer à Maggie un peu de bonheur, un but dans sa journée, car ils ne vivaient plus qu'au jour le jour.

— C'est une excellente idée et je vous en remercie.

Les yeux bleu sombre d'Eric exprimaient une profonde affection, tandis qu'il observait ses enfants à leur insu.

— Jason a besoin d'attention, de compréhension. Il a très mal vécu notre divorce. Sa mère vient de se remarier. Il refuse d'accepter que nous ne vivrons plus jamais ensemble tous les quatre.

Eric fourra les poings dans ses poches avant de continuer :

— Shelly est en voyage de noces, c'est pourquoi les enfants sont avec moi en juillet au lieu d'août.

— Sans indiscrétion, dit Joe après une hésitation, comment avez-vous vécu, vous-même, ce remariage ?

— C'était inévitable. Shelly est jolie, douce, gentille.

— Papa ! papa ! cria Susie, viens voir ce que j'ai fait.

Eric entra dans le salon, sous le regard ému de Joe. Il s'accroupit près de sa fille et referma sa main autour de la cheville de son fils. Il communiquait par le toucher et cela plaisait au vieil homme.

Maggie leva les yeux. Son regard croisa celui de Joe. Elle lui adressa un sourire satisfait avant de se pencher de nouveau sur le livre. Sa voix claire emplit l'espace.

Quand le cancer s'était déclaré, Joe avait essayé de la persuader de rester tout l'été à San Jose. Il craignait qu'elle ne se fatigue, que son état n'empire. Maggie s'y était opposée. Elle voulait se rendre au chalet et maintenant Joe réalisait qu'elle avait eu raison. Elle avait encore un cadeau à donner et avait trouvé en Jason le parfait destinataire.

Plus tard, ce dernier se rappellerait la vieille dame au chat, qui l'avait gavé de pizza et d'histoires. Et, qui sait, au tréfonds de son âme, peut-être s'efforcerait-il de mériter le précieux don de son temps qu'elle lui avait fait.

3

— Quelle belle journée! s'exclama Maggie.

Sur la terrasse, les pinsons picotaient allègrement les graines dans la mangeoire, tandis que les moineaux, pondérés, patients, nettoyaient sur les dalles les vestiges du festin.

Joe l'enlaça par-derrière et tous deux demeurèrent un instant devant la fenêtre, lui, les yeux encore bouffis d'un sommeil tardif, elle, titubant de fatigue. Mettant son index sous le menton de Maggie, il lui fit relever la tête pour cueillir sur ses lèvres le premier baiser de la journée.

— Ma chérie! Que fais-tu debout aux aurores?

Elle passa son bras autour de la taille de Joe et huma profondément son odeur familière, rassurante, revigorante, aussi indispensable que l'oxygène.

— Je ne pouvais pas dormir.

— Comment vas-tu aujourd'hui?

— Très bien. Je songeais à Jason. Il est extraordinaire. Je ne l'ai vu qu'une fois, mais d'ores et déjà je peux affirmer que je n'ai jamais connu de petit garçon aussi attachant.

— Vous vous entendez bien, tous les deux.

— Il a une belle âme. Par exemple, il n'a pas essayé de tirer la queue de Josi et, quand elle lui a mordillé la main pour qu'il arrête de lui caresser le ventre, il n'a pas paniqué. Ce genre de réaction, ça ne s'invente pas, Joe. Ça fait partie d'un être.

— Sa sœur est très attachante aussi.

Un sourire éclaira les traits tirés de Maggie.

— Si nous avions adopté une petite fille, elle aurait été comme Susie.

Le vieil homme pressa ses lèvres sur la tempe de sa femme.

— Que veux-tu pour ton petit déjeuner ?

— Du thé… Un muffin à la rigueur.

Maggie n'avait plus faim ou alors très rarement. Elle flottait dans ses vêtements. Sa maigreur, même quand parfois elle se sentait mieux, trahissait un départ imminent pour l'ultime voyage.

Mais elle ne regrettait rien. La mort ne l'effrayait pas. Mourir avant Joe l'emplissait de gratitude… et de tristesse. Si le contraire arrivait, elle tiendrait le coup. Ne serait-ce que pour accompagner son mari. Supporter le deuil, la solitude, représentait l'épreuve finale d'un grand amour.

Même le cœur brisé, Joe survivrait. Lors de son dernier check-up, son médecin lui avait annoncé qu'il était parti pour vivre centenaire. C'était supposé être une bonne nouvelle, mais Maggie avait aperçu une lueur désespérée dans les yeux de son mari. Elle avait alors décidé de lui laisser les innombrables souvenirs de leur union heureuse et pas les images affreuses de la maladie.

Quand le diagnostic leur avait été révélé, Maggie avait longuement réfléchi. On se marie pour le meilleur et pour le pire. Eh bien, le pire, elle ne le partagerait pas avec Joe. Depuis soixante-cinq ans, cet homme avait été son meilleur ami et son amant. Il refuserait de la laisser s'en aller, tout simplement. Dans son esprit, il avait peut-être accepté l'inéluctable, mais pas dans son cœur. Il se demanderait sans relâche s'il n'avait pas renoncé trop tôt à se battre. Un jour de plus, une semaine, un mois prendraient alors une importance capitale.

Maggie était résolue à ne pas traîner plus que de raison. Pour rien au monde elle ne voulait que Joe termine sa vie dans le dénuement à cause d'un acharnement thérapeutique aussi ruineux qu'inutile.

Des semaines durant, lors de discussions passionnées, elle était parvenue à le convaincre qu'après tout, elle

avait le droit de choisir. Elle préférait partir lucide, dans la dignité, plutôt que de sombrer dans la déchéance ou de terminer dans une salle de réanimation, branchée à des moniteurs. Ça non, elle ne le voulait pas.

Joe s'était finalement rangé à son opinion. Pas par lâcheté, mais à la suite d'une réflexion sereine, raisonnable.

Maggie avait choisi son anniversaire pour en finir avec la vie. Il s'agissait d'une date hautement symbolique, qui refermerait parfaitement le cercle. Joe l'avait longtemps serrée dans ses bras lorsqu'elle le lui avait dit. Après un interminable silence, il avait simplement répondu qu'il l'accompagnerait jusqu'au bout. Bien sûr, elle avait refusé, mais il avait insisté. Depuis le temps, elle aurait dû savoir qu'il était suffisamment têtu pour ne pas la laisser tout organiser à sa manière.

— Tu es ailleurs, dit-il doucement. À quoi penses-tu? Au petit Jason ou à quelqu'un d'autre?

— À nous. J'ai sûrement eu une vie antérieure exemplaire pour être récompensée par toi dans celle-ci.

— Si c'est le cas, la prochaine sera un tourbillon.

— On verra, murmura-t-elle. Contentons-nous du présent.

— Tu as raison.

— Quel est le programme, aujourd'hui? se renseigna-t-elle.

Autrefois, ils ne faisaient aucun projet. Cette fois-ci, d'un commun accord, ils avaient décidé de préparer leurs journées. Observer les oiseaux-mouches à Carmel Mission, les otaries à Point Lobos, visiter le terrain de golf de Pebble Beach où, jadis, il faisait un parcours pendant qu'elle conduisait la voiture, déguster un pique-nique sur les pentes verdoyantes de Fremont Peak.

— Nous allons déjeuner à Steinbeck House, répondit-il.

Ils étaient des habitués de ce restaurant réputé de la région. Joe y avait sa bouteille de whisky pour l'apéritif.

— As-tu réservé?

Il eut un sourire indulgent.

— Bien sûr. Il y a déjà une semaine.

— Et tu as choisi aujourd'hui…

— Parce que ta quiche préférée figure au menu.

Maggie émit un soupir heureux.

— Tu me gâtes.

Il lui lança un regard empreint d'une feinte surprise.

— C'était ta condition pour que tu acceptes de m'épouser.

Elle se hissa sur la pointe des pieds et l'embrassa.

— J'étais une fille futée. Rappelle-moi tes autres devoirs.

— Faire la vaisselle, laver et repasser mon linge.

— Mmm ! Le règlement se relâche.

— À moins que ce ne soit passer l'aspirateur et astiquer la salle de bains ?

Elle lui décocha un gentil coup de coude dans les côtes.

— Je crois qu'il s'agissait surtout de me convaincre que j'étais la plus belle femme du monde. Sans tricher.

— Oh, si j'avais triché, tu ne m'aurais pas cru.

Pendant soixante-cinq ans, le désir ne s'était pas éteint dans les yeux bleus de Joe.

— À quelle heure as-tu réservé ?

— À une heure.

— Combien de temps nous faut-il pour y aller en voiture ?

Il la scruta un instant.

— Est-ce que tu penses la même chose que moi, chérie ?

— Je crois que oui.

— En es-tu sûre ?

— L'esprit est prompt, donnons une chance à la chair.

Il lui adressa un sourire espiègle.

— Me croiras-tu si je te dis que tu me combles de bonheur ?

— Prouve-le-moi, répondit-elle doucement en lui prenant la main pour l'entraîner vers la chambre.

Quand Joe retira la chemise de nuit de Maggie, il ne remarqua pas sa peau ravagée par le temps et la maladie. Il vit le corps magnifique qu'il avait étreint la nuit

de leurs noces, les seins pleins, haut placés, le ventre plat, les cuisses lisses comme une mer calme, douces comme un murmure.

Ce corps, il le connaissait aussi bien que le sien, il savait où le toucher, quand et comment bouger en elle pour la mener à l'extase. Ses soupirs le guidaient, de petits gémissements l'avertissaient qu'elle était proche de l'orgasme et qu'il devait accentuer la cadence de ses reins.

Il contint sa fougue, afin de ne pas lui faire mal, et cette précaution éveilla en lui la poignante conscience de la peur, refoulée des mois auparavant. Contrairement à Maggie, Joe avait peine à vivre au jour le jour sans songer à la terrible échéance. La vie, leur vie commune, ne représentait plus le cocon sécurisant, à l'abri de tous les dangers. La brèche qui s'y était formée s'élargissait un peu plus chaque jour. À quatre-vingt-huit ans, Joe avait perdu la plupart de ses amis; il aurait dû mieux se préparer à affronter l'inévitable. Mais il n'y avait pas songé. Comme si cela n'arrivait qu'aux autres. Le diagnostic avait mis fin à l'illusion. Les lois de la nature s'appliquaient aussi à lui. Et à Maggie.

Après avoir fait l'amour, la vieille femme se blottit contre son mari avec un sourire de contentement.

— Il n'y a pas de meilleure façon pour commencer la journée.

— Ça va? Je ne t'ai pas fait mal?

Du bout des doigts, elle lui effleura le torse.

— T'ai-je donné l'impression d'avoir mal?

Il eut son sourire espiègle qu'elle aimait tant.

— Je t'ai entendue gémir, à un moment.

— Seulement une fois? demanda-t-elle, taquine.

Il l'attira contre lui.

— Nous avons eu une vie heureuse, Maggie. Je n'aurais pas voulu plus.

— Nous avons été bénis des dieux, mon amour. Nous avons même la chance de pouvoir nous dire adieu.

Elle esquissa une grimace, puis dégagea son bras afin d'apaiser l'élancement dans son épaule. Depuis plusieurs jours, elle avait diminué la dose des antalgiques, préférant l'inconfort à l'anesthésie des sens et de l'esprit. Elle s'efforçait de cacher la douleur lancinante qui la taraudait, mais elle n'y parvenait pas toujours. Tant que Joe pensait qu'elle ne souffrait pas, ils arrivaient à retrouver leur ancienne entente. Et, parfois, les manifestations du mal régressaient au point de se faire oublier.

— J'ai beaucoup pensé à Julia et à Ken, depuis que nous sommes arrivés, dit-elle. Ils étaient tellement heureux. Te souviens-tu de notre dernier dîner à Winslow ? Ken avait porté un toast en émettant le souhait de vivre aussi longtemps et aussi heureux avec Julia que toi avec moi. Je n'ai pas eu alors le moindre doute qu'il en serait autrement.

— Oui, je m'en souviens très bien. Et maintenant, Julia est seule et cela peut-être pour le restant de ses jours ; à moins qu'elle ne tente une seconde chance.

— Cela viendra en temps et en heure. Personne ne prendra la place de Ken, bien sûr, mais un second mari lui procurera un autre bien-être, une relation différente.

Maggie se tourna dans le lit pour regarder Joe dans les yeux.

— Je ne voudrais pas que tu exclues la possibilité de trouver quelqu'un d'autre, mon chéri.

Allongé sur le dos, le vieil homme scruta le plafond d'un air entêté.

— Cela ne risque pas d'arriver. Je t'aime, Maggie. Je t'ai toujours aimée. Il n'y aura personne d'autre.

— Cela ne me dérangera pas, tu sais.

Joe s'assit sur le lit en tournant le dos à sa femme.

— Je ne veux pas parler de ça.

— Je t'en prie, mon chéri. C'est important pour moi. Promets-moi de prendre cette suggestion en considération.

— Mais pourquoi ?

— Parce que te savoir seul me brise le cœur.

Il se tourna brusquement vers elle.

— Me laisser seul, du moins maintenant, c'est ton choix.

Maggie tressaillit.

— Je croyais que tu me comprenais.

La tension quitta soudainement Joe. Se sentant accablé, il ferma les yeux pour contenir un subit flot de larmes.

— Je suis navré. Pardonne-moi.

La vieille dame glissa sa main dans celle de son mari. Elle aurait donné n'importe quoi pour adoucir sa peine, mais elle serra les dents, afin que les mots qu'il souhaitait entendre si désespérément ne jaillissent pas. Elle ne changerait pas d'avis. Plus maintenant.

— Veux-tu prendre une douche ? demanda-t-il, ramenant la conversation sur un terrain neutre.

— Nous avons le temps, non ?

Joe jeta un coup d'œil à la pendulette de chevet, et un petit sourire malicieux fit briller ses prunelles.

— Oui. À condition de prendre notre douche ensemble.

— Monsieur Chapman, je vous aime !

Il porta la main décharnée de Maggie à sa bouche et y pressa ses lèvres.

— Moi aussi, madame Chapman.

4

Le lendemain matin, Maggie cherchait le journal dans la boîte aux lettres, quand Jason traversa à toutes jambes la rue qui séparait les deux propriétés.

— J'ai attendu! cria-t-il en remontant l'allée. Papa m'a permis de venir à condition que tu sois réveillée.

Elle lui sourit.

— Je suis complètement réveillée, vois-tu.

— Tu veux venir voir le feu d'artifice avec nous?

La question la prit de court. Brusquement, elle se souvint qu'ils étaient le quatre juillet, jour de l'Indépendance.

— Oh, oui, avec plaisir. Joe pourra venir aussi?

Jason hocha la tête avec enthousiasme.

— Je dirai à papa de faire quelques sandwichs de plus.

— Et moi? Qu'est-ce que j'apporte?

Le petit garçon fronça les sourcils.

— Tu veux dire des pétards?

— Pourquoi pas... Ou des feux de Bengale.

— Ou alors des cookies aux pépites de chocolat?

— Bonne idée. Je m'en occupe.

Les yeux de Jason s'arrondirent.

— Tu sais les faire?

— Naturellement. Tu les aimes?

Il acquiesça.

— Et Susie?

— Elle les aime aussi, mais moins que moi.

Eric apparut sur le perron de sa maison d'où il agita la main.

— Il vous a trouvée à ce que je vois.

— Oui, et il nous a gentiment invités à fêter avec vous le quatre juillet.

— J'espère que vous serez des nôtres, insista Eric.

— Elle a accepté, exulta Jason.

Susie jaillit alors de la maison.

— Je peux venir, Maggie ? cria-t-elle.

— Bien sûr... Si ton papa est d'accord.

Susie voulut s'élancer, mais Eric la stoppa en plein élan.

— Minute, mademoiselle. Je crains qu'à vous deux, vous ne créiez pas mal de soucis à nos amis.

— Pas du tout, répliqua Maggie. Avec Joe, nous allons faire une promenade sur la plage. Nous serons ravis d'emmener les enfants.

Eric s'accroupit devant Susie, lui susurra quelque chose au creux de l'oreille, et la petite fille hocha vigoureusement la tête. Se redressant, il la prit par la main. Une minute après, ils avaient rejoint Jason et Maggie.

— Je suis enchanté que vous veniez ce soir, déclara Eric. À vrai dire, l'idée était de Jason mais j'y adhère de tout cœur.

— À quelle heure doit-on venir ? Et que désirez-vous que l'on apporte ?

Voyant la déception sur la frimousse de Jason, la vieille dame s'empressa d'ajouter :

— À part les cookies au chocolat, bien sûr.

Eric jeta à son fils un coup d'œil désapprobateur.

— Je suppose que c'est encore une de tes idées ?

— J'ai juste dit à Maggie que je les aimais bien, se défendit le petit garçon.

— Joe en raffole également, dit Maggie. Et moi, j'adore les pique-niques.

Susie enlaça les jambes de Maggie.

— Tu sais, le feu d'artifice, c'est comme des guirlandes de fleurs dans le ciel. C'est papa qui me l'a dit.

Maggie se tourna vers son voisin.

— Quelle métaphore poétique, mon cher.

En riant, il posa la main sur son cœur.

— Je ne suis pas écrivain pour rien. Du moins, je me plais à me le répéter.

— Mon petit doigt me dit que vous n'avez pas beaucoup avancé, ces jours-ci.

— J'écris quand les enfants sont couchés et tôt le matin, avant qu'ils se lèvent.

La porte vitrée coulissa ; Joe apparut sur la terrasse.

— Bonjour, bonjour ! Il me semblait bien entendre des voix.

— Nous sommes invités ce soir à la fête de l'Indépendance, lui annonça Maggie.

Il parut décontenancé un instant, puis s'écria :

— Mon Dieu ! Je perds la notion du temps. J'avais complètement oublié quel jour nous étions.

Il regarda tour à tour les enfants, avec un large sourire.

— Est-ce qu'il y aura un feu d'artifice ? demanda-t-il.

— Oh, oui. Un gros. Comme des fleurs dans le ciel, expliqua Susie.

— S'il n'y a pas de brouillard, lui rappela Eric.

— Un pique-nique et un feu d'artifice, que demande le peuple ! s'exclama Joe, sa large main posée sur l'épaule frêle de Jason. Ça va être une journée mémorable.

Il adressa un clin d'œil complice à Maggie.

— Il ne manque plus que la pêche Melba.

Les papilles gustatives de Maggie réagirent instantanément. L'hémorragie cérébrale de Joe avait mis fin à leur menu traditionnel du quatre juillet : poulet froid, salade de pommes de terre et pêche Melba.

— Je suis sûre qu'il existe au moins un marchand de glaces dans le coin qui vend cette friandise, suggéra Maggie.

— Et même plus d'un, renchérit Joe.

— Je peux venir ? demanda Susie.

— Je ne crois pas que ce soit une bonne idée, coupa Eric avant que ses voisins puissent répondre.

— Mais pourquoi, papa ?

— Soyez tranquille, le rassura Joe. Nous aurons plaisir à nous promener en ville avec nos jeunes amis.

Eric hésita comme pour donner à Joe une chance de changer d'avis.

— Bon, d'accord, dit-il finalement, d'une voix mal assurée.

Jason leva alors ses grands yeux bruns vers Maggie.

— Tu veux venir aussi ? interrogea-t-elle.

— Je peux, papa ?

Eric émit un soupir.

— Je vous préviens, les deux en même temps, ce n'est pas une sinécure.

— Nous nous en sortirons, affirma Maggie avec un sourire.

— Et Josi ? jubila Jason. Elle vient aussi ?

Maggie regarda le petit garçon en riant.

— Les chats sont casaniers, tu sais. Mais elle sera enchantée de te voir quand nous reviendrons.

Jason leva le regard vers son père.

— Papa ?

— Allez-y, concéda Eric. Mais attention ! Si vous n'êtes pas sages, vous serez privés de feu d'artifice.

Ses enfants partis, Eric regagna son bureau. Il se remit au travail, mais en vain. Se concentrer s'avéra impossible. Sans cesse, ses pensées dérivaient vers le charmant vieux couple de voisins. Il n'avait jamais vu Jason et Susie aussi à l'aise avec des adultes qu'avec Joe et Maggie. Ceux-ci attiraient d'emblée la sympathie. Néanmoins, Jason, si réservé d'ordinaire, témoignait à Maggie une sorte d'affection passionnée qui ne lui correspondait pas. Sans doute avait-il besoin de s'attacher à quelqu'un, puisque ses parents ne formaient plus une famille unie. Mais combien de fois le petit garçon supporterait-il de voir basculer son univers par la perte d'un être cher ?

Décidément, la paranoïa te guette, pauvre vieux ! se reprit Eric intérieurement. Maggie n'était pour Jason qu'une amitié de vacances, une connaissance passagère. Il l'oublierait après la rentrée scolaire quand il reprendrait ses habitudes.

Renversé sur sa chaise, Eric contempla le ciel brumeux par la fenêtre. La responsable du feu d'artifice à Monterey l'avait prévenu : en cas de brouillard, les gerbes multicolores ressembleraient à des taches lumineuses dans les nuages. Elle avait ajouté que cela faisait quatre ans que le mauvais temps gâchait le spectacle. Mais les mauvaises prédictions n'avaient jamais effrayé Eric. Sinon, il n'aurait pas fait médecine. À l'époque, personne ne lui accordait la moindre chance de réussir, sous prétexte qu'il sortait d'un lycée réputé moyen pour entrer dans une faculté fréquentée par le gratin. Il avait démenti tous les pronostics et, plus tard, il avait de nouveau étonné son entourage en démissionnant.

Pourquoi se sentait-il attiré par l'écriture ? Il l'ignorait. Sans doute parce qu'il avait quelque chose à dire. Mais qui aurait envie de l'écouter ? De toute façon, la postérité ne l'intéressait pas. Il voulait juste divertir et offrir un peu d'évasion à des gens aussi collet monté que ses anciens patients. Adolescent, il considérait la télévision comme un luxe et la lecture comme une nécessité. Il décelait les mêmes préférences chez Jason et rêvait déjà du jour où tous deux discuteraient de littérature.

Tous les liens sont importants quand on ne vit plus sous le même toit.

La sonnerie du téléphone interrompit ses méditations. Sa première pensée fut que quelque chose était arrivé aux enfants. Il décrocha, au comble de l'anxiété.

— Allô ?

— Eric ?

Il n'avait jamais entendu la voix de Julia au téléphone, mais il sut instantanément que c'était elle. Il eut la sensation qu'elle était partie juste la veille et qu'il attendait son appel.

— Oui, c'est moi. Fidèle au poste, autrement dit à mon ordinateur.

— Je vous dérange en plein travail. Voulez-vous que je vous rappelle plus tard ?

C'était la dernière chose dont il avait envie. Il aurait tout fait pour la garder le plus longtemps possible à l'autre bout de la ligne. Depuis son départ, pas un jour ne s'était écoulé sans qu'il ne pense à elle.

— Justement, je m'apprêtais à faire une pause. Que puis-je pour vous ?

— J'essaie de joindre les Chapman, vous savez, le couple qui occupe le chalet ce mois-ci. Les avez-vous vus, par hasard ?

Il posa les pieds sur le bureau, soudain envahi par un souvenir inattendu : Julia sur la plage, à la recherche de la loutre de mer dans les flots bleus.

— Oui, il y a une heure environ. Ils sont partis faire des courses avec Jason et Susie.

— Jason et Susie ?

— Mes enfants.

— Ah, oui, fit-elle, embarrassée de cet oubli.

La voix de la jeune femme l'imprégnait à l'instar d'une pluie d'été qui donne envie de lécher les gouttelettes brillantes et tièdes au coin de ses lèvres.

— Ils resteront avec moi trois semaines. Leur mère est en voyage de noces.

Elle se tut une seconde, puis murmura avec chaleur :

— Ça va ?

Était-ce la douleur qui l'avait rendue si compréhensive ? Était-elle naturellement sensible aux problèmes des autres ? Eric répondit d'un ton exagérément enjoué :

— Ça va très bien. Je suis heureux pour Shelly. Et pour les enfants.

— Je vous crois.

Il s'aperçut qu'il avait cherché à l'impressionner et se traita mentalement de crétin.

— Avez-vous un message pour Joe et Maggie ?

— Je voulais juste m'assurer qu'ils vont bien. Je les ai appelés deux jours de suite au chalet et une fois chez eux, et je n'ai pas réussi à les avoir. Je commençais à me demander… Oh, ça ne fait rien ! Du moment que je sais qu'ils se portent bien.

Le cœur d'Eric se serra. Sous une apparente désinvolture, on devinait la profonde inquiétude de Julia. Rien d'étonnant que Maggie veuille lui cacher son état.

— Et vous ? Comment allez-vous ? demanda-t-il.

— Mieux.

— Mieux qu'en juin ou mieux que vous n'espériez ?

À l'autre bout du fil, Julia hésita.

— Un peu les deux, je crois. Parfois je déprime mais il y a des jours où j'oublie de me rappeler que je dois faire semblant d'être en forme.

— Les Chapman parlent beaucoup de Ken. Ils l'avaient vraiment adopté.

Il prenait délibérément le risque d'ériger une barrière entre Julia et lui.

— Je sais. Il leur était également très attaché.

— Et maintenant, ce sont mes gamins qui les ont adoptés. Les petits chenapans ne lâchent pas Maggie et Joe d'une semelle. Mon fils, d'habitude si réservé, les tutoie !

Intuitivement, Eric savait que ses enfants se comporteraient de la même manière vis-à-vis de Julia. Elle avait un tas de points communs avec Maggie.

— C'est formidable. Je suis sûre que Joe et Maggie sont aux anges.

— Ce soir, nous allons voir le feu d'artifice à Monterey.

— Et moi je suis invitée à une réception, dit Julia d'une voix morne.

Il aurait voulu lui demander si elle y allait seule mais ne trouva pas le moyen de le glisser dans la conversation.

— Je bougonne toujours avant d'aller à une soirée, compatit-il, et en fin de compte je m'amuse bien.

— J'aurais préféré mille fois me rendre à Monterey avec vous tous.

Ces paroles, somme toute banales, firent à Eric l'effet d'avoir gagné au Loto. Était-ce dû à la solitude, à sa jalousie vis-à-vis de Shelly, à sa volonté de gagner sa part de bonheur, lui aussi ?

— Ne bougez pas. Je viens vous chercher en voiture !

Bon sang, il devenait idiot. Au lieu d'une réponse légère à une déclaration nonchalante, il s'accrochait avec la hargne du missionnaire qui réclame de l'argent. Il plongea les doigts dans sa moustache, qui avait poussé… et qui le démangeait.

— J'aurais sans doute accepté votre offre s'il ne s'agissait pas de la réception annuelle de la compagnie.

Était-elle sérieuse? Diplomate? Il n'aurait su le dire.

— Mais oui. Je suppose que vos activités accaparent une grosse partie de votre temps.

Cette fois-ci, elle garda un long silence avant de répondre:

— Il faut bien que je m'occupe. Mais l'entreprise était le grand amour de Ken, pas le mien.

— Je comprends.

— Je sais.

Une fois de plus, ce lien inexplicable!

— Que comptez-vous faire? s'enquit-il.

— Continuer. Que puis-je faire d'autre?

Une demi-douzaine de poncifs lui vinrent à l'esprit. Il les censura aussitôt. Julia était belle, intelligente, riche, elle n'avait guère besoin de ses conseils.

— Je dirai aux Chapman de vous rappeler, d'accord?

— Ce n'est pas la peine. Je les rappellerai dans quelques jours.

— Savent-ils où vous joindre?

Certain qu'elle était sur le point de raccrocher, il se démenait pour prolonger leur entretien.

— Ils ont mon numéro… Maintenant que j'y pense, je ne vous l'ai pas donné… en cas d'urgence.

— Ça tombe bien, j'ai un crayon et du papier.

Elle lui dicta dix chiffres et les lui fit répéter.

— Avant de finir, comment va votre roman?

— Mon agent a exigé la première moitié. Je la lui ai donc expédiée par la poste.

— Et c'était bon?

Un rire échappa à Eric.

— Je n'en sais rien.

— Que va-t-il se passer maintenant?

— De deux choses l'une. Ou il aime et il m'incite à continuer, ou il déteste, et adieu le best-seller. La troisième solution est qu'il soit alléché par le style mais déçu par le sujet ; dans ce cas-là, il me demandera d'écrire autre chose.

— Quand vous répondra-t-il ?

— J'aimerais bien le savoir.

— Ce qui veut dire que votre cœur bat à cent quarante chaque fois que le téléphone sonne.

— L'attente est une torture, c'est vrai.

— M'appellerez-vous quand vous aurez la réponse ?

Il résista à la tentation de demander à la voir.

— Bien sûr. Et si vous n'êtes pas chez vous, je vous laisserai un message sur votre répondeur.

— Prenez soin de vous, dit-elle.

— Vous aussi.

Il raccrocha. Son regard dériva vers la fenêtre qui surplombait la plage. Aux vacanciers s'était ajoutée la cohue des visiteurs du week-end. L'océan roulait ses vagues couronnées d'écume. Des cerfs-volants de toutes les couleurs striaient le ciel bleu cobalt. Il avait passé toute la matinée à espérer que la journée serait belle… Le résultat avait dépassé ses espérances.

Julia posa son stylo sur le bureau. Dans cinq minutes, elle allait avoir une réunion de travail avec John Sidney et ses assistants. Ils évoqueraient les problèmes de sécurité concernant les conteneurs dans lesquels ils expédiaient le matériel à l'étranger. Sa première réaction avait été de confier à John l'initiative de s'entendre avec le fournisseur mais les choses ne se passaient pas ainsi au sein de la compagnie.

Tout en se réservant le secteur de la production, Ken avait l'œil sur tout. Il contrôlait chaque détail grâce à de brefs meetings avec les directeurs des différents départements, plusieurs fois par jour. Quand Julia avait pris sa place, déchirée entre le deuil et l'apprentissage d'un métier, elle avait réduit ces rencontres à deux par semaine.

Le personnel l'avait soutenue sans la moindre réticence. Chacun s'y était mis pour lui faciliter la tâche. La loyauté, l'enthousiasme de tous l'avaient rassérénée. Et en même temps, ils l'avaient intimidée. Si elle avait rencontré une quelconque résistance, elle aurait pu se convaincre de vendre la société. À la place, les associés et les employés l'avaient entourée de gentillesse, de sympathie et de patience.

Un grattement à la porte lui fit lever la tête.

— Entrez.

Pat Faith, sa secrétaire, se pencha par le battant entrebâillé.

— Je viens d'apprendre que l'épouse de John Sidney a fait une fausse couche hier soir. J'ai pensé que vous voudriez le savoir.

Julia chercha vainement à mettre un visage sur le nom de Mme Sidney. Elles avaient pourtant dû se croiser dans des soirées.

— Je ne me rappelle pas qui elle est.

Pat entra dans la pièce et referma la porte derrière elle.

— Blonde, les cheveux longs, très jolie. Avec un grain de beauté sous l'œil droit…

— Toujours tirée à quatre épingles, même aux piqueniques ?

— C'est elle, confirma Pat.

Avant de partir, elle se retourna.

— Avez-vous pu joindre Joe et Maggie ?

Pendant les seize ans où elle avait été la secrétaire de Ken, et maintenant de Julia, Pat était devenue leur amie et leur confidente.

— Oui… en fait, non. Il semble qu'ils s'amusent bien avec le locataire du cottage voisin.

— L'écrivain ?

Julia ne se souvenait pas de lui avoir parlé d'Eric. Elle inclina la tête.

— Il a un petit garçon et une petite fille. Joe et Maggie adorent les enfants, comme vous savez.

— Ah… Il est marié alors ?

Étrange question !

— Divorcé.

Un sourire illumina le visage de Pat.

— Ravie de l'entendre.

— Attendez… Pourquoi…

— Votre expression quand vous parlez de lui me met sur des charbons ardents. Je redoute de vous voir vous engluer dans une affaire de cœur.

Julia la scruta, bouche bée.

— Votre imagination galope, ma parole. J'ai exactement la même expression, que je parle d'Eric ou de n'importe quel autre ami.

— Mais il n'y a pas de mal à avoir de l'intérêt pour quelqu'un. Cela devait arriver un jour ou l'autre. Cependant, vous devez vous montrer vigilante ; plus que quelqu'un comme moi, par exemple.

Tous les amis de Ken s'étaient donné le mot. Selon eux, non seulement Julia constituait la cible idéale de tous les coureurs de dot de la planète, mais ils refusaient en outre de comprendre qu'elle pourrait un jour remplacer Ken dans sa vie. Après avoir eu le meilleur, pourquoi et comment pourrait-elle se contenter de moins ?

Quelqu'un frappa à la porte.

— John, probablement, dit Julia. Je vais voir si sa femme et lui ont besoin de quelque chose. Entre-temps, faites envoyer à Mme Sidney une gerbe d'orchidées de chez McLellan… Des couleurs claires ; blanches, roses ou jaunes. Rien de sombre. Écrivez un mot simple de la part de nous tous.

— Je m'en occupe, répondit Pat.

Julia se leva et avança vers John Sidney, qui l'attendait à la porte du bureau directorial. La mort de Ken lui avait appris combien un geste de solidarité remonte le moral dans un moment difficile. Et si elle n'accordait pas à John la promotion qu'il désirait le plus au monde, elle pouvait au moins lui donner cela.

5

Ils arrivèrent tous les cinq sur la jetée en fin d'après-midi, équipés de couvertures, de livres, de jeux pour Jason et Susie, d'une chaise longue pliante pour Maggie, de chaises de toile pour Joe et pour Eric. Les lions de mer lançaient des grognements indignés à la marée humaine, tandis qu'Eric observait la nappe de brouillard sur l'océan.

Repus de sandwichs, de salades variées, de viandes froides et de pêches Melba, ils étaient contents d'être enfin installés en attendant le début du spectacle, deux heures plus tard. Joe avait déployé une couverture sur laquelle Jason et Susie s'étaient assis et il leur lisait un conte de fées. Peu à peu, la foule remplissait le port, le môle, la grève, pendant que le soleil plongeait lentement vers les brumes de l'horizon.

— Comment vous sentez-vous, Maggie ? demanda Eric à voix basse, afin que personne d'autre ne puisse l'entendre.

La vieille dame étudia son voisin une seconde avant de répliquer :

— Vous savez, n'est-ce pas ?

— Joe a confirmé ce que j'avais déjà deviné le premier soir.

Elle hocha la tête.

— Je suis un peu fatiguée mais je n'aurais pas troqué une seule minute de cette journée pour un regain d'énergie.

— Essayez de vous reposer davantage… Excusez-moi ! De quoi je me mêle !

— Donniez-vous aussi ce conseil à vos patients qui étaient en train de mourir ?

— C'est possible. Honnêtement, je ne me rappelle plus. J'ai démissionné en partie parce que je croyais être en train de devenir un médecin imbuvable.

— Ma tante disait que la mort est un début. Qu'il s'agit d'un des multiples voyages de la vie. Je pense à elle chaque fois que le fardeau pèse trop lourd.

— J'aime bien cette idée. Puis-je l'utiliser ?

— De quelle.manière ?

— Dans un chapitre, mon héros se pose des questions philosophiques : la vie, l'amour, la mort…

Maggie sourit.

— Ma tante serait très honorée. Et moi aussi.

Eric mit ses mains sur sa nuque, s'étira et croisa ses jambes au niveau des chevilles.

— Julia m'a raconté que le chalet vous appartenait autrefois.

— Nous avons passé notre lune de miel à Santa Cruz. Et nous sommes revenus tous les ans… Soixante-cinq en tout.

— Je comprends votre engouement pour cette région.

— Nous avons acheté le chalet il y a cinquante ans, quand le gynécologue nous a annoncé que nous n'aurions pas besoin de chambres supplémentaires dans notre résidence principale. Juste après sa retraite, Joe a eu une hémorragie cérébrale, nous avons alors vendu la propriété à Ken, en lui demandant de pouvoir y passer l'été, comme avant. Naturellement, Ken a fait en sorte que nous pensions lui rendre service.

Ce souvenir arracha un tendre sourire à Maggie.

— Nous avons fait semblant d'y croire, mais nous avons choisi de rester en juillet seulement. Joe louait le chalet en juin et en août. Ainsi, nous étions persuadés d'aider Ken à payer son emprunt à la banque.

Elle se mit à rire.

— Vous rendez-vous compte ?

— Je crois que j'ai attrapé votre virus, avoua Eric. Je

ne veux plus partir. J'aurai peine à rendre à Andrew son cottage quand il reviendra.

— Si vous aviez vu le paysage à l'époque où nous avons atterri ici pour la première fois! s'exclama Maggie, le visage rêveur. Non que je n'aime pas le modernisme, mais quand même! C'était autre chose.

— Je vous en prie, racontez-moi.

— Seigneur, je ne saurais pas par où commencer.

Elle ne se fit cependant pas prier longtemps. Et pendant qu'ils attendaient le crépuscule, elle narra à Eric l'histoire d'une contrée sauvage, loin de tout, mais très verte et très accueillante.

Cannery Row n'était alors qu'une venelle puante. Les pêcheurs de sardines y vendaient leur marchandise. Il n'y avait que les quais et des bateaux de pêche là où aujourd'hui pullulaient les restaurants et les boutiques de luxe. En ce temps-là, Carmel comptait une poignée de charmantes masures, qui valaient aujourd'hui de l'or, alors que les paysans les avaient bradées pour une bouchée de pain.

À force d'explorer la péninsule de Monterey, les Chapman s'étaient liés d'amitié avec des artistes, des pêcheurs, des fermiers. Tout doucement, le paysage avait changé. Les touristes étaient arrivés, le portefeuille bourré de billets de banque. Le paradis terrestre avait bientôt été vendu, démantelé, morcelé. Les versants jadis recouverts de cyprès, de pins et de chênes arboraient à présent les panneaux « Propriété privée », « Défense d'entrer », accrochés à de solides barreaux.

Afin d'attirer une nouvelle clientèle, l'Ocean Avenue, la principale artère de Carmel, avait vu pousser comme des champignons des échoppes de souvenirs, des boutiques de tee-shirts et d'autres fanfreluches. Des galeries s'étaient installées, exposant des toiles abstraites. Des papiers gras, des canettes de Coca-Cola et de bière jonchaient la chaussée, les poubelles débordaient d'ordures, les rues étaient livrées aux hordes de touristes. Les visiteurs arrivaient par centaines, caméra au poing, dans l'espoir d'apercevoir Clint Eastwood, qui habitait le comté.

Eric posait encore des questions sur Monterey et Carmel quand le crépuscule les enveloppa de ses voiles de cendre. Maggie avait entrepris de lui raconter le tremblement de terre qui avait quasiment détruit Loma Prieta en 1989, quand les premières gerbes du feu d'artifice explosèrent, rouges, blanches, bleues. Jason se blottit contre Maggie, et Susie monta sur les genoux de Joe pendant que des oh! et des ah! fusaient de toutes parts.

— Papa, on dirait vraiment des fleurs! s'exclama Susie. J'aurais aimé que maman les voie.

Le cœur de Maggie bondit. Les gens que l'on aime sont censés s'aimer entre eux. Et l'absence de cet amour attendu constituait une rude épreuve pour un être aussi tendre et aussi jeune que la fillette aux couettes blondes.

— Eh bien, tu lui feras un dessin et nous le lui enverrons demain, proposa Eric.

— Moi aussi je lui ferai un dessin, déclara Jason, les yeux rivés vers le ciel illuminé.

— Et un pour Roger, suggéra Eric avec gentillesse.

— D'accord, dit Susie.

— On verra, ajouta Jason.

Maggie avait deviné combien l'offre avait coûté à Eric. À l'évidence, partager ses enfants avec un autre homme le désespérait, mais il mettait leur bonheur au-dessus de son bien-être.

Les grappes lumineuses déployaient leurs fruits flamboyants et leurs étoiles filantes au firmament quand, sans prévenir, une douleur fulgurante transperça Maggie. Agrippée aux bras de la chaise longue, elle attendit que cela passe. Avait-elle oublié ses médicaments? Impossible. Joe lui présentait à heures fixes un assortiment de cachets sans jamais faillir.

Eric se tourna vers elle pour lui poser une question. Il se figea. Sans attirer l'attention du petit groupe, il lui prit le poignet et tâta son pouls. Peu après, il saisit son sac et en sortit une poche de plastique remplie de flacons orange foncé. Il ne lui fallut pas plus d'une seconde pour déchiffrer les étiquettes. Il extirpa deux cachets et les glissa dans la bouche de Maggie.

— Voulez-vous un verre d'eau ? demanda-t-il en lui prenant la main.

Elle fit signe que non, ferma les yeux, déglutit péniblement, puis attendit l'effet du médicament. Son cancérologue l'avait prévenue : la science n'avait plus les moyens de combattre son mal, elle pouvait seulement améliorer sa vie en phase terminale. Évidemment, le moment viendrait où les puissants antalgiques n'agiraient plus mais, en principe, cela ne devrait pas se produire avant quelques mois.

Peu à peu, comme la vague efface l'empreinte des pas sur le sable, le médicament estompa la douleur. Bientôt, il ne resta plus que le souvenir de la souffrance et la peur qu'elle revienne.

Maggie rouvrit les yeux ; son regard croisa celui d'Eric.

— Je me sens mieux, articula-t-elle, les lèvres blanches, sans émettre aucun son. Merci.

L'incident avait été si fugace que personne, pas même Joe, ne s'en était aperçu. Eric lui serra la main.

— Si jamais vous avez besoin de moi, n'hésitez pas à m'appeler. À n'importe quelle heure du jour ou de la nuit.

— Pourquoi ? demanda Jason en fixant son père.

Eric lui ébouriffa les cheveux.

— Pour n'importe quoi, répondit-il.

— Et pourquoi Maggie aurait-elle besoin de toi ? insista le petit garçon.

Malgré sa conviction que mentir à un enfant équivalait à perdre sa confiance, Maggie jugea que ce n'était pas le moment de révéler sa maladie aux deux petits.

— Pour faire la glace de la pêche Melba, répondit-elle.

L'explication parut satisfaire Jason.

— C'est vrai ? On fera de la glace ?

— Bien sûr. Quand tu veux.

Par chance, le feu d'artifice attira de nouveau l'attention de Jason. Plusieurs explosions illuminèrent le ciel ; ce fut comme un jardin entier de fleurs éphémères.

Le brouillard s'était dissipé ; Maggie suivit du regard l'ultime flamme bleue qui tomba dans l'océan. Une paix singulière se glissa alors en elle. La beauté du spectacle tenait à sa nature passagère. Il en allait de même pour la vie. Celle de Maggie avait été bien remplie. Elle n'avait qu'un seul regret : n'avoir pas lutté suffisamment pour ses convictions. Elle avait participé activement aux mouvements écologistes, avait prononcé des discours sur les espèces en voie de disparition, sur la mort des oiseaux provoquée par des ballons lâchés lors de différentes célébrations, sur les ravages des produits toxiques dans la chaîne alimentaire.

Elle avait reçu des récompenses pour avoir convaincu les gens de ne plus abandonner leurs animaux domestiques pendant les vacances, ainsi que pour son aide aux sans-abri. Et maintenant que sa vie la quittait, elle se disait qu'elle aurait dû lutter davantage contre les injustices.

— On y va ? demanda Joe.

Il lui fallut une fraction de seconde pour comprendre ce qu'il disait. Elle lui offrit un sourire tout en essayant de s'extraire de la chaise longue.

— Mon Dieu, quelle merveille ! remarqua-t-elle en regardant Jason et Susie. Merci de nous avoir invités.

— De rien, répondit Susie.

Dans un élan impromptu, Jason la serra dans ses petits bras.

— Tu viendras avec nous la prochaine fois, d'accord ?

Elle l'enlaça et posa un baiser sur le sommet de sa tête.

— Promis, dit-elle simplement.

Le trajet du retour se déroula dans le calme. Les enfants, puis Joe, s'abandonnèrent dans les bras de Morphée sur la banquette arrière du pick-up d'Eric.

À la vue du portail, Eric se tourna vers Maggie. Elle ne dormait pas.

— Je sais combien c'est ennuyeux d'entendre poser constamment la même question, mais j'en prends le risque, dit-il. Comment vous sentez-vous ?

— Maintenant ou en général ?

— Les deux.

— Aussi bien que possible, vu ma situation.

Elle capta son regard surpris avant d'esquisser un sourire.

— Désolée. J'ai toujours rêvé de répondre cela à un médecin. Frustrant, n'est-ce pas ?

Il ne put s'empêcher de rire.

— Très. En même temps, voilà une excellente façon de me remettre à ma place.

— Mes forces déclinent, Eric. La fin est proche. Vous avez dû souvent assister aux combats perdus d'avance. Je n'ai rien à ajouter, malheureusement.

Elle posa la main sur son bras.

— Mais ne pensez pas que votre sollicitude me pèse, reprit-elle. Je vous ai pris au mot, vous savez. Je vous appellerai en cas de besoin.

— Je voudrais pouvoir vous aider.

— Vous êtes un homme bon, Eric. J'espère que vous trouverez quelqu'un avec qui vous partagerez toutes les choses fantastiques qui vous attendent.

— Lesquelles ? Si vous avez un heureux pressentiment pour mon livre, dites-le-moi. L'attente me porte sur les nerfs.

— Je parlais de la vie, mon ami. Le livre se fera tout seul.

— Rappelez-moi cette phrase tous les jours, voulez-vous ?

Ils ne resteraient pas longtemps ensemble, il le savait, mais Maggie demeurerait sa meilleure amie, tant qu'elle serait de ce monde.

— Entendu, répondit-elle. Avec plaisir.

6

Joe poussa la porte de la chambre avec sa hanche.

Il entra, le plateau du petit déjeuner entre les mains. Josi se frottait contre ses jambes, menaçant de le faire tomber à chaque pas.

— Le brouillard est de retour ! annonça-t-il.

Maggie se cala contre sa pile d'oreillers. La chatte sauta sur le lit, se roula contre sa maîtresse qui lui gratta le menton, et son ronronnement monta, comme un roulement de tambour.

Joe servit deux tasses de thé à l'aide d'un pot qu'ils avaient acheté trente ans plus tôt, lors d'une traversée de l'Atlantique. Il remonta les stores avant de rejoindre Maggie sur le lit.

— As-tu bien dormi, ma chérie ?

Elle n'avait pas fermé l'œil, mais l'avouer n'aurait fait qu'aggraver l'anxiété de Joe.

— Comme un bébé. J'ai fait de beaux rêves.

— Comment désires-tu passer la journée ?

Elle avala avec précaution une toute petite gorgée. Elle n'aurait pas su dire si cela était dû aux médicaments ou à la maladie, mais elle avait perdu la sensibilité au chaud et au froid. À plusieurs reprises, elle s'était brûlée… Le thé était parfait ; elle étreignit la tasse jaune vif dans ses paume et prit une nouvelle gorgée.

— Je pensais bien à quelque chose.

Joe haussa un sourcil. Un sourire conspirateur releva les coins de sa bouche.

— Oui ?

Au lieu de répondre, Maggie l'observa comme si elle le voyait pour la première fois.

— Tu es sans aucun doute le plus bel homme que j'aie jamais vu.

Il émit un rire.

— Je suis tout ouïe.

— Non mais c'est vrai. Et qui devinerait que tu auras bientôt quatre-vingt-dix ans ? Quatre-vingt-dix, Joe ! Qui aurait pensé que tu vivrais aussi longtemps ?

— Sans toi, je serais déjà mort et enterré.

— Faux ! C'est toi et toi seul qui as fait tout le travail. Tu t'es redressé et tu as réappris à marcher, à parler. J'étais simplement là à te regarder.

— Ta modestie te perdra.

Elle dissimula son sourire en avalant une autre gorgée de thé chaud. Le temps avait presque effacé les pénibles réminiscences de ces deux années terribles où Joe avait été si diminué, si faible. Ils avaient été plus forts que la maladie, plus résistants face à l'adversité.

— Dis-moi à quoi tu penses, Maggie.

— Nous avons fait un tas de projets pour cet été, commença-t-elle. Nous nous sommes mis d'accord sur nos déplacements, sur les sites à visiter… Eh bien, je me disais, mais ce n'est qu'une suggestion, bien sûr… C'est juste une idée et je tiens à connaître ton opinion…

— Maggie, cesse de tourner autour du pot.

Josi s'étala sur le dos, les pattes en l'air, les moustaches frémissantes, et Maggie lui caressa distraitement le ventre.

— Que dirais-tu si nous gardions Susie et Jason tous les matins pendant qu'Eric travaille à son livre ? débita-t-elle d'une seule traite. Cela ne sera pas long. Ils ne resteront pas plus d'une semaine… Avec la pêche Melba et tout ce dont nous nous sommes empiffrés hier, je n'ai pas eu l'occasion de faire les cookies au chocolat que j'ai promis à Jason. De plus, je pourrais les aider à dessiner le feu d'artifice pour leur mère et leur beau-père.

— En es-tu sûre, Maggie ? Tu semblais tellement tenir à tes projets…

— Ils n'ont plus aucune importance, Joe.

— Si cela te rend heureuse, ça me convient, ma chérie.

— Je ne pense plus à moi quand je suis avec eux. Je ne m'écoute plus, tu comprends ?

Elle savait que Joe éprouvait la même chose. Le pèlerinage qu'elle avait imaginé pour cette année ne tarderait pas à tourner au cauchemar pour tous les deux. Mieux valait que Joe garde d'elle le souvenir d'une femme enjouée, souriante.

Elle le regarda dans les yeux et y vit le mélange familier d'amour, de regrets et de peine.

— Es-tu d'accord ? s'enquit-elle. Ce sont aussi tes vacances. Je ne veux pas te voler ton plaisir.

— Tant que nous serons ensemble, peu m'importe.

— Il nous faudra convaincre Eric. Sans parler des enfants.

— Eric discutera pour le principe. Quant aux enfants, je sais d'ores et déjà qu'ils seront ravis.

Maggie reposa sa tasse sur le plateau.

— Encore une question. Essaie de me répondre sincèrement.

— Je ne t'ai jamais menti, Maggie.

— Ce n'est pas pareil. Je crois que tu ferais n'importe quoi pour me rendre heureuse.

— Je ne puis te répondre tant que j'ignore ta question.

Elle passa les doigts dans ses cheveux devenus blancs, clairsemés. Autrefois si épais, si blonds et soyeux, ils recouvraient aujourd'hui à peine son crâne.

— Suis-je égoïste ? demanda-t-elle. Serait-ce injuste d'amener Jason et Susie à devenir mes amis ?

Joe posa le plateau par terre pour prendre sa femme dans ses bras.

— Injuste ou pas, mon amour, ils te sont déjà très attachés.

— On était supposés vivre simplement cet été. Et voilà que tout se complique.

Il l'embrassa tendrement sur le bout du nez.

— Peut-être la vie a-t-elle encore une leçon à nous donner ?

Il l'attira contre lui, et elle nicha sa tête au creux de son épaule.

— Veux-tu que j'en parle à Eric ? suggéra-t-il.

— Écoute ! dit-elle en redressant le buste.

— Je n'entends rien.

— L'océan et le ronronnement de Josi ont exactement le même rythme.

Ainsi que le cœur de Joe. Elle en percevait clairement les battements quand elle posait la tête sur sa poitrine. C'étaient les sons de la vie, chacun avec sa cadence, sa signification et sa durée.

Debout sur le perron, Eric suivit du regard Jason et Susie qui s'éloignaient main dans la main avec Joe et Maggie. Le brouillard s'obstinait à brouiller l'éclat du ciel depuis deux jours. Emmitouflés dans des vestes, des écharpes, ils avaient décidé de braver le froid ; ils se dirigeaient vers la plage, avec la ferme intention de construire les plus grandioses châteaux de sable. D'après leur arrangement, Eric devait descendre dans l'après-midi, afin d'inspecter leurs travaux et, éventuellement, décerner un prix aux meilleurs bâtisseurs.

Joe n'avait pas caché sa surprise quand Eric avait accepté la proposition de Maggie de garder les enfants pendant qu'il travaillait. Joe ignorait qu'Eric avait déjà réfléchi à tout cela. Il s'était posé la même question que Maggie : Jason et Susie ne souffriraient-ils pas trop de la perdre ? Or, la joie de faire sa connaissance surpassait, à ses yeux, un deuil trop proche. Eric avait toujours pensé qu'il fallait tirer profit des épreuves de la vie et cet été semblait riche en enseignements. Il avait choisi de laisser ses enfants faire leurs expériences.

Son seul regret, c'était qu'ils n'aient pas rencontré les Chapman plus tôt. Les parents de Shelly n'avaient pas su assumer leur rôle de grands-parents. Jason et Susie leur rappelaient trop leur âge, au sein d'une société où seules la beauté et la jeunesse ont cours. Les visites se limitaient à Noël, de préférence chez Shelly et Eric, loin de leurs amis.

Les parents d'Eric avaient péri dans l'incendie d'un hôtel, quand il était encore étudiant. Le temps que le litige soit résolu, il s'était retrouvé orphelin à vingt-cinq ans.

Joe et Maggie incarnaient le grand-père et la grand-mère que Jason et Susie n'avaient jamais eus. Il n'allait pas refuser à ses enfants ce qui lui avait manqué si cruellement.

En grattant distraitement sa moustache, Eric referma la porte et se dirigea vers son ordinateur.

Maggie remplit de sable mouillé une boîte de conserve de tomate vide, puis la retourna lentement. La forme d'une tour apparut sur la plage, mais Susie déclara qu'il s'agissait du corral pour les chevaux. Couchée sur le ventre, très concentrée, elle planta un petit bâton censé représenter la clôture dans le flanc du cylindre.

— Très joli! la félicita Maggie.

Susie leva les yeux avec un sourire. D'un revers de main, elle balaya les mèches blondes qui barraient son front. Du sable velouta ses sourcils.

— Viens ici, dit Maggie. Ferme les yeux.

Elle essuya le sable à l'aide d'un mouchoir. Au lieu de se remettre au travail, Susie grimpa sur les genoux de sa grande amie.

— Pourquoi on n'a pas emmené Josi?

— J'ai peur qu'elle ne soit pas un chat des sables.

— Tu veux dire qu'elle n'a pas le droit de venir?

— Quelque chose comme ça.

— Comme Jason et moi n'avions pas le droit d'aller avec maman et Roger en voyage de noces?

— Pas exactement. Nous ne laissons pas Josi se rouler dans le sable parce que, quand elle se lèche, elle l'avale et ça lui fait mal au ventre.

Maggie marqua un silence. La seconde partie de la réponse était plus difficile.

— Ta maman et Roger sont partis seuls afin de devenir de très bons copains… Et surtout pour que Jason et toi passiez un moment agréable avec votre père.

Susie passa ses bras autour du cou de la vieille femme.

— Et avec toi.

— Aussi.

— Tu viendras nous voir, quand nous rentrerons à la maison ?

— Je n'aurais pas hésité, Susie, mais je crois que je serai déjà très loin.

— C'est pas grave, puisque tu as une voiture.

— La voiture ne me servira à rien, j'en ai peur.

— Et comment je vais te revoir, moi ?

Maggie effleura la poitrine de la petite fille, à l'endroit du cœur.

— Tu me verras là-dedans.

Les minces sourcils de la fillette se joignirent.

— Où ça ? demanda-t-elle, confuse. Dans mon ventre ?

Maggie éclata de rire. Elle chatouilla Susie, qui se mit à gigoter en riant, elle aussi.

— Oui, exactement là, dans ton petit ventre. Chaque fois que tu te gaveras de pêches Melba ou de cookies au chocolat, je serai là, et je te donnerai un baiser.

Susie roula à terre en riant de plus belle. Sans le faire exprès, elle écrasa le corral de leur château de sable. Au lieu de s'en offusquer, elle redoubla d'hilarité. Retombant en arrière, elle se mit à rouler et à rouler encore jusqu'à ce que leur belle construction fût totalement aplatie.

Maggie riait aussi. Un point sur le côté, qu'elle avait essayé d'ignorer, gagnait du terrain. Mais malgré l'avertissement, elle s'allongea dans le sable près de Susie. Lorsqu'elle se rassit, la douleur l'aveugla. Un puissant regret lui coupa le souffle… Elle n'était pas si prête que ça à renoncer à la vie.

Levant les yeux, elle vit Joe et Jason. Ils venaient vers elle, portant chacun un seau rempli de coques à bout de bras.

— On a construit un vaisseau spatial, déclara Jason, sérieux comme un pape. On va le recouvrir de coquillages.

Joe se pencha vers Maggie.

— Que se passe-t-il ?

Susie riait aux larmes, le visage dans ses mains.

— Rien. Ça ne te regarde pas.

Il l'étudia un instant, avant de demander :

— C'est l'heure du cachet ?

Elle acquiesça.

Joe passa son seau à Jason. Subrepticement, il prit un flacon dans sa poche et tendit le médicament à Maggie. En époussetant le sable de son dos et de ses épaules, il reprit d'une voix circonspecte :

— Je suppose que ça ne me regarde pas non plus ?

— Nous avons écrasé la maison de sable ! cria Susie.

— Je vois.

Joe scruta le visage ravagé de sa femme.

— Pourquoi ?

— C'était amusant, répondit-elle.

— Tu réalises, naturellement, que vous avez un gros handicap, Susie et toi, par rapport à notre vaisseau spatial ?

Maggie hocha la tête, mais il ne bougea pas. Il ne bougerait pas d'un centimètre tant qu'elle ne se sentirait pas mieux. Et il resterait à côté d'elle lorsqu'elle mourrait, à la maison ou à l'hôpital. Il serait là lorsque les hommes en blanc la brancheraient à une machine, qui prolongerait artificiellement sa vie. Et il l'aiderait…

L'esprit de Maggie redevint soudain clair, comme le sable après le déferlement des vagues. Elle tenait à quitter Joe dans de bonnes conditions. Lorsqu'elle le laissa sur la plage, plus aucun doute ne subsistait : elle avait pris la bonne décision.

7

Maggie se trouvait chez Eric lorsqu'il reçut l'appel qui fit tout basculer.

À l'autre bout de la ligne, Shelly avait prié son ex-mari de garder les enfants une semaine de plus, afin qu'elle puisse s'installer avec Roger à leur nouveau domicile. Eric avait accepté, naturellement. Il était ravi de prolonger leur séjour.

Cela signifiait que les deux bambins seraient encore là pour l'anniversaire de Maggie. Par conséquent, son projet si soigneusement préparé de mettre fin à sa vie tombait à l'eau.

Elle informa Joe le soir même, et, sans mots superflus, les deux époux s'assirent sur le canapé, Josi allongée sur leurs jambes, comme si elle aussi allait participer à leur décision.

— Merci de ne pas prendre la présence des enfants pour une providence.

— La providence, Maggie, serait de trouver le remède miracle. La science fait des progrès mais ne guérit pas encore tous les cancers. La victoire viendra mais pas pour nous, malheureusement.

S'il n'avait tenu qu'à lui, il aurait donné sa vie pour sauver Maggie. Il aurait tout sacrifié pour elle.

Josi enfouit son museau sous la main de sa maîtresse; un puissant ronronnement enfla dans la pièce.

— Et maintenant, il faut choisir un autre jour, dit-elle d'une voix morose.

— Pas ce soir. Tu n'es pas capable d'y voir clair.

— Peut-être. Mais si la date est simplement remise aux calendes grecques, j'y penserai davantage.

Ce serait peut-être aussi une raison de découvrir chaque jour une raison d'attendre le lendemain. Elle aimait la pluie comme le soleil, le thé et les toasts tout autant qu'un somptueux dîner. Son cœur bondissait à la vue d'un papillon sur une fleur, les facéties de Josi lui arrachaient invariablement un sourire. Et puis, il y avait Joe. Elle ne respirait que pour lui. Si elle l'avait aimé un peu moins, peut-être serait-elle restée jusqu'au bout.

Jeune fille, sur les bancs du catéchisme, elle croyait au ciel et à l'enfer aussi fermement que l'on croit à l'existence d'autres continents. Avec le temps, des questions sans réponse avaient ébranlé sa foi. Pourquoi Dieu, tout-puissant et miséricordieux, laissait-il mourir des petits enfants dans des conditions atroces ? Ne pouvait-il pas aider les affamés, les pestiférés, les misérables ?

Elle avait fini par comprendre que Dieu n'était pour rien dans les croyances organisées par ses serviteurs. Plus tard, elle sut que Joe, après un parcours analogue, avait tiré les mêmes conclusions.

Leur église était petite : juste Joe, elle, et Dieu. Ils s'étaient voués corps et âme à préserver Sa création, les animaux, la nature. Le seul mot inscrit dans leur Bible avait guidé chaque geste de leur existence. Ce mot était « amour ».

— Tu dors ? demanda doucement Joe.

Elle renversa la tête et le regarda.

— Non. Je réfléchis.

— À quoi ?

Elle hésita une seconde, de crainte qu'il n'interprète son questionnement comme un doute. Sa voix intérieure l'incita cependant à répondre. Elle ne lui avait jamais rien caché, pas même ses pensées les plus intimes.

— Je me demande ce qui se passe quand on meurt.

— Et ?

— Je sais ce que j'aurais voulu.

Il l'embrassa avec une profonde tendresse.

— Moi aussi. Crois-tu qu'on a des chances d'y arriver ?

— Nous serons ensemble, Joe. J'en suis convaincue. Et si le ciel n'existe pas, je serai toujours dans ton cœur.

— Oh, Maggie, notre plus grand bonheur fut de nous rencontrer. On n'a pas le droit de demander plus.

Un drôle de petit sanglot lui serra la gorge ; il déglutit.

— Pourtant, je veux tout, reprit-il. L'éternité avec toi.

— S'il y a un moyen, mon chéri, je le trouverai. Même s'il s'agit d'un petit nuage caché dans l'infini, je le chercherai pour t'attendre là-haut.

Trois jours plus tard, après le déjeuner en compagnie de Jason, de Susie et d'Eric, Maggie alla faire une sieste. Une heure après, Joe la trouva sur le lit en position fœtale, l'œil fixe, le front moite, les traits convulsés par la douleur.

— Le traitement… ne marche plus, parvint-elle à articuler entre ses dents serrées. Appelle Eric.

Joe se rua hors de la pièce, priant pour qu'Eric soit chez lui. Il lui avait semblé que tout à l'heure, pendant le repas, il avait été question qu'il emmène les enfants au cinéma. Il saisit le combiné du téléphone et composa le numéro, tout en jetant un coup d'œil par la fenêtre. Dieu merci, le pick-up était encore là.

Eric arriva aussitôt. Un seul coup d'œil à Maggie lui suffit. Il la souleva et la transporta dans sa voiture. Dix minutes plus tard, ils étaient tous à l'hôpital. Joe resta dans la salle d'attente avec Jason et Susie, tandis qu'Eric poussait Maggie sur un chariot à travers le dédale des urgences.

Pris au piège de sa peur, Joe n'avait pas remarqué l'effet que leur course éperdue avait produit sur Jason. Soudain, il ne le vit plus près de Susie. Le petit garçon, collé au mur, fixait la direction empruntée par son père et Maggie. Joe s'approcha de lui et posa la main sur son épaule.

— J'ai vu un distributeur automatique dans le hall. Tu veux boire quelque chose ?

Les yeux soucieux, Jason le regarda.

— Qu'est-ce qui est arrivé à Maggie ?

— Elle est malade, dit simplement Joe, et les médicaments qu'elle prenait jusqu'à maintenant ne font plus effet. Ton papa va l'aider à obtenir un nouveau traitement.

— Est-ce qu'elle va mourir?

La question méritait une réponse paternelle. Déconcerté, Joe se cantonna dans le silence.

— Elle va mourir, n'est-ce pas, Joe?

Le vieil homme hocha la tête.

— Est-ce que je pourrai lui dire au revoir?

Les yeux clos, Joe sentit le picotement familier des larmes sous ses paupières. Avec son innocence et son affection enfantines, Jason venait de résumer ce qu'il s'efforçait d'admettre depuis des mois... C'était un cadeau du ciel de pouvoir partager les instants ultimes de l'être aimé, de lui dire « je t'aime » une dernière fois avant le grand départ.

— Elle en sera enchantée, dit-il à Jason.

Le petit garçon se pencha vers le vieil homme d'un air conspirateur.

— Je crois qu'il ne faut rien dire à Susie.

Affalée dans un fauteuil, la fillette regardait des dessins animés à la télévision, inconsciente du drame qui se tramait autour d'elle. Joe sourit à son jeune complice.

— Tu es un vrai grand frère, Jason.

De retour au chalet, Maggie dormit le reste de la journée et toute la nuit suivante. Le lendemain matin, assommée par les nouveaux antalgiques, elle demanda à voir Eric et les enfants.

Susie entra dans la chambre la première et bondit sur le lit sans une ombre d'hésitation. Elle se blottit entre Maggie et Josi, qui ronronnait comme un moteur.

— Papa a dit qu'on ne pouvait pas rester longtemps, murmura-t-elle, dans l'espoir que Maggie intercède en sa faveur.

Eric se tenait dans l'embrasure de la porte, Jason à son côté.

— Comment vous sentez-vous? demanda-t-il.

— Très bien... grâce à vous.

Il sourit.

— Merci pour ce compliment qui revient, j'en ai peur, aux gélules jaune et bleu que vous avez rapportées de l'hôpital.

Jason se taisait. Ses grands yeux apeurés brisèrent le cœur de Maggie. Si elle avait su à quoi elle exposait cet enfant, elle n'aurait pas permis à leur amitié de s'épanouir.

— Je suis désolée de t'avoir fait peur, hier, dit-elle. Aujourd'hui, tu peux constater que je vais mieux.

Jason ne bougeait toujours pas.

— Je les ai avertis que la visite serait brève, expliqua Eric. Nous reviendrons cet après-midi, si vous êtes d'accord.

Susie supplia Maggie du regard.

— Bien sûr que je suis d'accord, répondit celle-ci.

Elle prit la menotte de Susie dans sa main flétrie.

— J'ai un travail pour toi, quand tu reviendras.

— Lequel, Maggie ?

— Je ne trouve plus la balle rouge de Josi. Pourras-tu regarder pour moi derrière le canapé ?

— Oh, oui ! s'exclama Susie. Je peux même le faire tout de suite. Je regarderai aussi sous la télé.

Eric fit signe à sa fille de descendre du lit.

— Nous vérifierons en sortant, ma chérie.

Alors qu'Eric entraînait Susie vers le salon, Jason resta un moment à l'entrée de la chambre.

— Je suis triste que tu sois malade, dit-il alors.

— Moi aussi. Je suis navrée de ce qui s'est passé hier.

— Ce n'est pas ta faute. Tu ne l'as pas fait exprès.

— Tu es un brave petit garçon, Jason. Et je suis contente que tu sois mon ami.

Il demeura immobile, déchiré entre la volonté de rester et l'impulsion de prendre la fuite. Finalement, il s'approcha du lit et tomba dans les bras de la malade.

— Joe a dit que je pouvais te dire au revoir, mais je ne peux pas. Pas encore, murmura-t-il.

Maggie leva les yeux. Joe se tenait sur le pas de la porte. Elle l'interrogea du regard et reçut une réponse silencieuse. Elle serra alors Jason et posa un baiser sur ses cheveux fins et parfumés.

— N'aie crainte. Nous avons beaucoup de temps devant nous, assura-t-elle.

— C'est promis ?

— Promis ! Dans combien de jours repars-tu chez toi ?

— Cinq.

— Eh bien, je serai ici chaque jour.

L'instant d'après, Eric réapparut.

— Jason, tu viens ?

— Je te ferai un dessin sur lequel il y aura Susie, papa et moi, déclara Jason.

— Formidable ! Rapporte-le-moi cet après-midi, d'accord ?

— D'accord, papa ?

Eric adressa un sourire à Maggie.

— Si vous vous sentez d'attaque, nous pourrions commander une autre pizza et dîner tous ensemble sur la terrasse.

— Ce sera merveilleux, approuva Maggie. Qu'en penses-tu, Jason ?

Avant qu'il ait le temps de réagir, la voix tonitruante de Susie retentit à travers le chalet.

— Ça y est ! Je l'ai !

La petite fille déboula dans la pièce, brandissant victorieusement la balle rouge.

— Josi ! Attrape !

Elle lança la balle en direction de la chatte, qui la saisit au vol d'un coup de patte. Le jouet rebondit, et Josi suivit ses mouvements avant de se laisser tomber paresseusement sur le matelas.

— C'est l'heure de sa sieste, dit Maggie. Ce soir, elle sera plus alerte.

— Ça ne vous fera pas de mal de dormir un peu avec elle, déclara Eric. En route, les enfants.

Il prit les deux petits par la main et sortit de la pièce.

— Appelez-moi si vous avez besoin de quelque chose, dit-il à Joe. N'hésitez pas.

Le vieil homme revint dans la chambre. Il souleva Josi

pour s'asseoir près de Maggie. La chatte lâcha un feulement indigné, puis sauta de l'autre côté de la malade où
elle se roula en boule.

— Elle a encore grossi, constata Joe.

— Les enfants la gavent de friandises. Ils adorent la
voir quémander.

Joe prit la main de sa femme dans la sienne.

— Comment te sens-tu ?

— Comme quelqu'un qui vient de prendre de la mor-
phine.

— Maggie, réponds-moi.

— La tête me tourne, je suis lessivée, mais je n'ai plus
mal.

— Plus du tout ?

La question concernait sa maladie, alors elle pouvait
donner une réponse honnête. La douleur n'était pas physique. Elle lui étreignait le cœur, l'esprit, l'âme. Refou-
lant ses larmes, Maggie répliqua avec sincérité :

— Non. Plus du tout.

8

La brise du large faisait bruire les platanes. La semaine était terminée. Eric ramenait Susie et Jason chez leur mère. Au milieu de la route, Joe et Maggie regardaient s'éloigner le pick-up. La dernière chose qu'ils virent avant que la voiture disparaisse au tournant fut le petit visage de Jason collé contre la vitre. Ensemble ils lui adressèrent un signe d'au revoir.

— Tu lui manqueras, fit remarquer Joe à Maggie.

Celle-ci lui passa une main dans le dos, dans un geste familier, affectueux.

— Eric a tout expliqué à Shelly. Elle sait que pendant quelque temps son fils aura besoin d'une attention particulière.

— Que veux-tu faire ce soir?

Elle le regarda.

— Il est temps, Joe.

Il crut encaisser un violent coup de poing.

— Mais nous…

— Il le faut, coupa-t-elle sèchement sans lui donner le temps de réagir.

Oh, il aurait tant voulu l'implorer d'attendre encore un peu, une semaine, ou seulement un jour. Or, d'un commun accord, ils avaient décidé que Maggie, seule, avait le droit de choisir l'heure de sa mort.

— Est-ce que tu souffres? demanda-t-il.

— Ça n'a pas d'importance.

— Tu ne veux pas te promener avec moi sur la plage… avant?

Elle secoua la tête, puis lui frôla la joue du bout des doigts.

— Je dois le faire maintenant, Joe.

Il la prit dans ses bras.

— Il y a encore mille choses que j'ai envie de te dire.

— Dis-en une, au hasard, répondit-elle.

Il aspira profondément l'air humide. Le choix ne se posait pas.

— Je t'aime, dit-il simplement.

Main dans la main, ils retournèrent vers le chalet. Près de la grille, Joe cueillit une rose rouge. Après son mariage avec Ken, quand Julia avait commencé à jardiner, elle avait estimé que le parfum des fleurs comptait plus que leur beauté. La rose associait les deux. Joe planta la corolle satinée dans les cheveux de Maggie, puis l'embrassa sur les lèvres.

Une fois à l'intérieur, Maggie se dirigea vers la salle de bains, où elle sortit de leur cachette les pilules soigneusement mises de côté depuis des mois. Avant de les prendre, elle pria Joe de sortir. Cette journée allait suffisamment le traumatiser sans qu'il assiste à cette cérémonie insoutenable. Lorsqu'elle ressortit de la salle de bains, il l'aida à s'allonger, puis s'assit au bord du lit. Il lui prit la main.

Elle lui toucha la joue.

— Va-t'en, maintenant.

Il secoua la tête avec un sourire triste.

— Cette fois-ci je ne t'obéirai pas, mon amour.

Maggie fixa son mari au fond des yeux, dans une communication silencieuse qui lui signifiait qu'elle regrettait de le quitter, mais qu'elle n'avait pas peur.

— Je t'aime, Joe Chapman.

Ce furent ses derniers mots, soufflés tendrement tandis que ses yeux s'embrumaient.

Les paupières de la vieille dame se fermèrent et elle sombra dans le sommeil. Joe resta à côté d'elle jusqu'à son dernier soupir, l'ultime battement de son cœur. Alors il se leva et posa un baiser sur le front pâle. La rose dans les cheveux de Maggie lui emplit les poumons de son parfum suave, lui rappelant la douceur des innombrables étés passés.

— Attends-moi, ma chérie, murmura-t-il. Je ne serai pas long.

Le crépuscule inondait la pièce d'une lueur orange. Joe retira le flacon de pilules qu'il avait dissimulé derrière la pile d'assiettes, dans le placard de la cuisine. Il s'agissait de barbituriques de contrebande qu'il s'était procurés au Mexique, un mois après que Maggie l'eut mis au courant de ses plans. Dès l'instant où le mal s'était déclaré, il avait su que vivre dans un monde sans elle ne le tentait pas. Maggie faisait partie de son existence depuis soixante-cinq ans… Continuer seul n'avait pas de sens. Joe s'était octroyé lui aussi le droit de choisir une meilleure fin à leur histoire.

Il revint dans la chambre, se coucha sur le lit, attira doucement Maggie dans ses bras.

— As-tu vraiment cru que je te laisserais partir sans moi ?

Il ferma les yeux et attendit. Lentement, les cachets qu'il avait ingurgités réduisirent sa conscience à un petit point lumineux. Alors, se sentant libre, léger, il cria à Maggie qu'il arrivait. À son dernier souffle, le point lumineux explosa en un brillant kaléidoscope de couleurs.

Joe reposait en paix.

Et il n'était pas seul.

9

Eric rentra tard cette nuit-là. Il avait caressé le projet de rendre visite à l'ami qui lui avait acheté son cabinet médical à Sacramento, puis il s'était ravisé. Il se sentait si triste, si vide après avoir déposé ses enfants chez Shelly et Roger, qu'il serait sûrement de mauvaise compagnie.

Les lumières étaient éteintes au chalet. Joe et Maggie devaient dormir... Pour la première fois depuis des jours, le temps s'était éclairci. La lune tranchait d'une épée d'argent la surface de la mer. Un sentier magique se dessinait sur le miroir sombre de l'eau. Au lieu d'aller se coucher, Eric fit un tour sur la plage.

Toute la journée, il avait farouchement combattu la jalousie irraisonnée que le bonheur de Shelly avait fait flamber dans son cœur. Un bonheur que, du reste, elle méritait. Pourtant, il avait du mal à s'en accommoder. Entre l'avant et l'après, trop de changements s'étaient produits. Il s'en voulait pour l'échec de leur mariage. Son égoïsme l'avait aveuglé au point de ne pas le laisser voir ses erreurs. Seule la pensée qu'il ne voulait plus vivre avec Shelly l'avait sauvé de la dépression. Il l'avait abandonnée physiquement d'abord, moralement ensuite, mais la séparation semblait réelle depuis seulement un an.

Malgré ses efforts, il n'avait pas réussi à épargner à Jason et à Susie les affres du divorce. Ils semblaient cependant s'en être remis... Il crut les revoir sous le porche, entre Shelly et Roger, le saluant de la main ; une charmante petite famille.

Quelque chose de blanc luisait sur le sable. Eric se pencha. Un dollar des sables, parfaitement constitué, sans la moindre fissure. Le premier coquillage intact qu'il trouvait, alors qu'il en avait cherché tous les jours avec Jason. Il le glissa dans sa poche. Demain, il appellerait son fils pour lui faire part de sa trouvaille. Cette perspective allégea sa tristesse, et il remonta vers son cottage d'un pas plus vif. Les chaussons de Susie, oubliés dans l'entrée, lui arrachèrent un sourire. C'était comme un gage qu'elle allait revenir.

Le lendemain matin, il se mit à son roman. Toutes les demi-heures, il se levait pour regarder par la fenêtre si Joe n'était pas à la boîte aux lettres. À neuf heures et demie, il commença à s'inquiéter. À dix heures, il estima qu'il avait assez attendu.

Il aperçut l'enveloppe sur la porte d'entrée depuis l'allée et força l'allure. Il contempla longuement le carré de papier blanc où son nom avait été tracé d'une écriture nette. La prémonition de ce que l'enveloppe contenait l'assaillit d'un seul coup.

Bon sang, comment avait-il pu négliger les indices ? Peut-être étaient-ils si visibles, si évidents, qu'il n'avait pas voulu y croire.

Une tristesse inouïe le suffoqua. L'air déserta ses poumons. La mort faisait partie de la vie ; c'était ce qu'il avait appris en premier à la faculté de médecine. On a de la compassion pour l'enfant qui meurt sans avoir goûté à la douceur de vivre, pour la jeune mère qui n'aura pas l'occasion de voir grandir ses petits. Mais si l'on tient à faire carrière dans la médecine, il faut se blinder contre le chagrin.

Joe et Maggie avaient eu une existence longue, heureuse. Ils s'étaient aimés avec une force extraordinaire, d'un amour profond, rare. Quoi de plus normal qu'ils meurent comme ils avaient vécu ? Ensemble ?

Sa main, aussi lourde que son cœur, décacheta l'enveloppe. Des larmes inattendues lui mouillèrent les joues lorsqu'il tira la feuille de papier. Sa vue se brouilla, il ne distingua plus les lettres.

Il ne voulait pas qu'ils soient morts!

Du revers de la main, il s'essuya les yeux. Pourquoi était-il aussi sûr de leur message? L'espace d'une seconde, une étincelle d'espoir jaillit, une étoile filante. Sans doute Maggie avait-elle eu des problèmes avec la nouvelle médication. Peut-être étaient-ils retournés à l'hôpital et le priaient-ils d'aller les chercher.

L'étincelle s'éteignit sitôt qu'il lut les premiers mots écrits par Joe.

Cher Eric,

Pardonnez-moi de vous impliquer dans un drame personnel, mais je n'ai pas d'autre solution. Maggie a pris la décision, il y a des mois maintenant, de mettre un terme à sa vie. Je ne m'attarderai pas à vous expliquer pourquoi j'ai choisi de m'en aller avec elle; en tout cas, elle ignorait mes résolutions. J'étais sûr d'avoir pensé à tout et d'avoir seulement à vous demander d'appeler le coroner.

J'avais projeté d'emmener Josi. Je me disais qu'elle serait plus heureuse avec nous. Or, Jason et Susie m'ont fait comprendre que j'avais tort. La pauvre minette a encore de belles années devant elle.

Il serait injuste d'écourter sa vie et, d'ailleurs, Maggie ne me le pardonnerait jamais.

Ce qui m'amène au but de cette note. Pourriez-vous trouver un nouveau foyer à Josi? Excusez-moi du conseil, mais son propriétaire devra se faire à l'idée que cette bête est la meilleure chose qui lui soit jamais arrivée. Si vous réussissez à découvrir l'oiseau rare, le tour est joué.

Il est dur de dire adieu, même dans une lettre. L'amour est un mot trop galvaudé, mais il est le seul apte à décrire mes sentiments et ceux de Maggie à votre égard, et à l'égard de Jason et de Susie.

Navré de rater la sortie de votre livre. Buvez un verre à notre santé quand vous fêterez votre premier contrat de cinéma. Là-haut, nous ferons de même.

Joe.

Eric plia lentement la feuille de papier avant de la glisser dans sa poche de poitrine. Il aurait troqué tout ce qu'il avait, et tout ce qu'il espérait obtenir, contre un amour comme celui de Joe pour Maggie.

Il passa les doigts dans ses cheveux, respira à fond, puis poussa le battant. La porte n'était pas fermée à clé.

Josi miaulait dans le vestibule. Elle se frotta contre les jambes du nouvel arrivant, après quoi elle fila droit vers la chambre du fond. De temps à autre, elle tournait la tête, afin de s'assurer qu'il la suivait. Elle sauta sur le lit, aux pieds de Joe et de Maggie, endormis pour toujours, et laissa échapper un gémissement long et plaintif.

— Moi aussi, Josi, murmura Eric, accablé. Moi aussi.

Il passa la matinée à répondre aux questions d'une femme policier. Lorsque les formulaires furent remplis, il signa sa déposition. La femme lui tendit l'image qu'ils avaient trouvée dans la main de Joe, en demandant si elle avait une signification particulière. Il s'agissait du dessin de Jason. On voyait ce dernier entre son père et sa sœur devant la maison. Eric et Susie souriaient, mais Jason portait des marques sur le visage. On pouvait croire à des taches de rousseur, mais en regardant de plus près, on voyait des larmes.

— Je peux le garder ? demanda Eric.

La femme réfléchit un instant.

— Oui, bien sûr.

La fatigue et l'émotion auxquelles s'ajoutait le désarroi de son fils eurent soudain raison des forces d'Eric.

— Si vous n'avez plus besoin de moi, puis-je vous laisser ?

Voyant la femme hésiter, il ajouta :

— J'habite juste à côté. Le cottage vert et blanc.

— D'accord, mais ne partez pas. Au cas où le coroner voudrait vous poser d'autres questions.

— Je ne bougerai pas.

Josi l'attendait à sa porte. Elle s'enroula si étroitement à ses chevilles, qu'il faillit trébucher. Il se pencha et la souleva, surpris de la facilité avec laquelle elle se laissa faire. Il entra dans la cuisine, puis mit la cafetière électrique en marche. Lorsqu'il voulut poser la chatte par terre, elle enfonça ses griffes dans ses épaules avant de frotter sa tête contre le menton de son hôte. Visiblement, elle voulait quelque chose, mais quoi ? La pâtée et l'eau qu'il lui avait laissées étaient intactes.

Alors il comprit.

— Ils sont partis, Josi, dit-il d'une voix étouffée. Je sais ce que tu éprouves et je n'y peux rien.

Plus tard, quand le coroner vint chercher Joe et Maggie, Eric retourna au chalet. Il n'était pas obligé d'assister à cette cérémonie mais rien n'aurait pu le retenir chez lui. Quelques voisins se tenaient de part et d'autre de l'allée quand la longue voiture noire s'engagea sur la route. Chacun regagna alors son foyer, et seuls les cris et les rires des vacanciers brisèrent la tristesse ambiante.

Un profond silence tomba sur le chalet. Eric prêta l'oreille ne serait-ce que pour capter un piaillement de mouette, un chant d'oiseau. Rien. On eût dit qu'un voile noir, impénétrable, enveloppait le jardin.

Avant de s'en aller, la femme policier lui tendit la liste des personnes à contacter. Il accepta de s'en occuper. Joe mentionnait un avocat pour le testament, un expert-comptable comme exécuteur testamentaire, un médecin, qui était leur voisin à San José. Il y avait également le nom d'une société, Neptune, chargée de s'occuper de l'incinération. Les deux époux souhaitaient que leurs cendres soient mêlées et répandues dans la mer.

En errant dans le chalet, Eric s'aperçut que Joe avait pensé à tout. Le ménage avait été fait dans toutes les pièces, des denrées trônaient sur la table de la cuisine, et les valises, bouclées, étaient alignées dans l'entrée. Là aussi, des instructions écrites demandaient que tout soit envoyé à un foyer de sans-abri.

Joe et Maggie étaient morts comme ils avaient vécu, en donnant tout ce qu'ils avaient aux autres.

10

Eric n'appela pas tout de suite les numéros de la liste de Joe. Il s'accorda une semaine pour recouvrer ses esprits. Il comptait se rendre à Sacramento afin de prévenir Jason et Susie de vive voix. Il aurait voulu attendre pour annoncer la catastrophe à Julia. Mais il trouva le temps long.

Dès le lendemain, alors que Josi, assise sur son manuscrit, le scrutait d'un œil fixe, il essaya de la joindre d'abord chez elle, puis à son travail. Une domestique lui apprit qu'elle était partie une heure plus tôt ; il sut ensuite par sa secrétaire qu'elle serait absente pendant deux jours.

Il émit un soupir, puis raccrocha. L'écran vide de l'ordinateur le narguait. Il repoussa sa chaise et se dirigea vers la cuisine pour se servir sa cinquième tasse de café. Josi sauta à terre. Il la retrouva dressée sur ses pattes arrière contre la porte d'entrée.

— Tu es supposée être un chat d'appartement, minette.

Un miaou dolent lui répondit.

Il ne savait pas ce qu'il allait faire d'elle. Il n'avait jamais eu d'animal, même quand il était petit. Il ne savait absolument pas comment se comporter avec un chat, en dehors de lui donner à manger et à boire. L'idéal serait de confier la chatte aux enfants, mais Shelly souffrant d'asthme et d'allergies, mieux valait ne pas y penser.

Les deux pattes avant sur le panneau de bois, Josi laissa échapper un nouveau miaulement.

Eric ouvrit la porte d'un centimètre. La chatte colla son nez contre la fente étroite. Soudain, sa tête passa, et le reste de son corps suivit.

— Josi ! Reviens !

La chatte s'élança vers le portail. Eric sortit à son tour et vit l'animal bondir à travers la route pour disparaître sous les massifs touffus du jardin voisin. Il n'aurait pas cru qu'un chat aussi gros puisse courir si vite.

Le cœur serré, il monta l'allée. Josi grattait frénétiquement à la porte du chalet. Il essaya de la soulever mais elle lança un feulement furieux suivi d'un petit miaulement plaintif.

Il tira alors de sa poche le double de la clé et lui ouvrit. Josi se précipita à l'intérieur. Ses appels, de plus en plus déchirants, de plus en plus frénétiques, retentirent dans chaque pièce. Enfin, elle déboula dans le salon, le poil hérissé.

— Josi ! Ils ne sont plus là. Je sais que je compte pour des prunes mais je suis tout ce qu'il te reste au monde.

Pour la première fois, il réalisa qu'il l'avait adoptée, et qu'il la garderait, en dépit de ses réticences.

Un bruit de moteur et un grincement de pneus déchirèrent le silence. Il consulta sa montre. Il s'agissait sans doute du bénévole du foyer des sans-abri, chargé de récupérer les vêtements et la nourriture. Eric se dirigea vers la fenêtre. Son cœur fit un bond quand il vit Julia sortir de sa voiture.

Il l'attendit à la porte.

— Que faites-vous ici ? demanda-t-il.

Elle recula d'un pas, surprise de le trouver là.

— La police m'a appelée…

— Oh, mon Dieu, je suis désolé que vous l'ayez appris de cette manière. J'ai essayé de vous joindre, sans succès. Je songeais à vous rappeler mais j'ai eu d'autres priorités.

Elle fureta du regard dans le vestibule.

— Alors c'est vrai ? Ils sont morts ? Tous les deux ?

Sa voix n'était plus qu'un murmure, elle semblait se tasser dans son élégant tailleur Armani.

— J'espérais que c'était une erreur, reprit-elle. Je priais pour que ça le soit.

La croyant sur le point de s'évanouir, il la soutint dans ses bras, elle s'accrocha à lui comme s'ils avaient sauté d'un avion avec un seul parachute. Des sanglots silencieux secouèrent bientôt son corps mince.

Eric l'attira à l'intérieur. Ils s'assirent ensemble sur le canapé où il se mit à la bercer tout doucement. Les sanglots s'estompèrent, et elle fit mine de se redresser. Mais il la retint. Alors elle se détendit, puis ses larmes coulèrent de nouveau.

Il lui tendait des mouchoirs en papier, elle en prenait un, se mouchait, séchait ses larmes qui, inéluctablement, rejaillissaient de la source brûlante de ses yeux.

— Savez-vous pourquoi ils ont… ils se sont… parvint-elle enfin à bredouiller.

— Je crois que Joe ne voulait pas vivre sans Maggie.

— Je ne comprends pas… Que s'est-il passé ?

— Maggie avait un cancer. Elle était en phase terminale. Il lui restait peu de temps à vivre, mais elle avait décidé de mettre fin à son calvaire le jour de sa convenance.

— Elle n'a jamais fait allusion à sa maladie, quand je l'ai vue en mars.

— Elle ignorait en tout cas que Joe avait décidé de l'accompagner dans l'au-delà.

Distraitement, Eric laissa courir sa main sur le bras de la jeune femme, la laine de sa veste glissa sous sa paume comme de la soie.

— Ce que je n'arrive pas à comprendre, poursuivit-il, c'est pourquoi elle a choisi le chalet.

Cent fois, il s'était posé la question. Joe et Maggie chérissaient tendrement Julia. Ils n'auraient pour rien au monde voulu ajouter un chagrin au deuil de Ken en se donnant la mort dans sa maison.

La jeune femme prit un mouchoir de papier et le plia méthodiquement jusqu'à le faire disparaître au creux de sa main.

— Maggie ne savait sûrement pas où aller pour… pour accomplir son acte, articula-t-elle péniblement. Elle comptait sur ma compréhension. Elle devait penser que Joe continuerait à vivre chez eux, à San Jose, et ne voulait pas qu'il se souvienne de sa mort, là-bas.

Durant toute sa carrière de médecin, Eric avait toujours vu les femmes protéger leur mari ou leurs enfants de la même manière. Et cela ne manquait jamais de l'étonner. Il ne douta pas un instant que Julia voyait juste. On eût dit que Maggie elle-même lui avait passé le mot.

— Ils vous aimaient beaucoup tous les deux, dit-il.

Au lieu de lui apporter du réconfort, sa phrase fit jaillir de nouvelles larmes. Julia enfouit son visage dans ses mains.

— Oh, mon Dieu, pourquoi ? Pourquoi ?

Eric jeta un regard aux valises et aux boîtes en carton dans l'entrée. Prostrée sur le rebord de la fenêtre, Josi attendait fidèlement ses maîtres, l'oreille aux aguets. Les marques des civières qui avaient emporté les corps restaient sur le tapis... Il crut que les murs de la pièce se refermaient sur lui. Il se leva d'un mouvement brusque, la main tendue vers Julia, qui continuait à pleurer.

— Venez. Allons-nous-en d'ici.

— Pour aller où ?

— Chez moi. Je vous invite à déjeuner.

— Je n'ai pas faim.

— Vous prendrez bien un peu de café, alors.

Elle promena sur la pièce un regard halluciné.

— Je voudrais...

— Laissez tomber, Julia. Je m'occuperai de tout plus tard. Ne restez pas là, vous vous faites du mal inutilement.

Elle essuya ses larmes du bout de ses doigts, puis se laissa entraîner vers la porte.

— Et Josi ?

— Je reviendrai la chercher plus tard.

La chatte ne bougerait pas tant qu'elle ne comprendrait pas que ses maîtres étaient partis pour toujours. Pendant qu'il refermait la porte à clé, Julia, les bras croisés sur la poitrine, jeta un regard circulaire.

— Les fleurs sont magnifiques, dit-elle à l'instar du patient qui, avant d'entrer dans le bloc opératoire, fait aux infirmières des remarques anodines.

— Joe a appris à Jason à jardiner.

— Jason ?

— Mon fils.

Elle pressa sa paume sur son front.

— Oh, bien sûr. Vos enfants sont-ils encore là ?

— Ils sont retournés chez leur mère il y a deux jours.

Julia fronça les sourcils, s'efforçant de se rappeler.

— Mais avant-hier, Maggie et Joe étaient encore vivants.

Eric hocha la tête.

— Je comprends tout à présent, déclara-t-elle alors. Maggie avait sûrement choisi de mourir le jour de son anniversaire… Et elle a été forcée de retarder son suicide à cause des enfants. Comme cela lui ressemble ! Elle tenait toujours compte des autres avant tout.

Eric passa sa main sur sa nuque raidie par la fatigue. Julia portait des escarpins à talons et des bas noirs.

— J'allais vous suggérer de faire une promenade, mais je suppose que vous n'avez pas apporté de chaussures de marche.

— La police m'a appelée au moment où je partais travailler. J'ai pris l'autoroute directement… L'officier m'a pourtant précisé que ce n'était pas nécessaire…

Elle étouffa un sanglot dans sa main.

— Mais je n'ai pas pu m'en empêcher. J'aurais dû venir pour l'anniversaire de Maggie. Je n'ai pas pu me libérer, à cause de toutes ces maudites réunions… Si j'avais été là, peut-être aurait-elle changé d'avis.

— Je ne crois pas.

— Pourquoi ?

Du regard, elle l'implora de lui donner une réponse crédible.

— Maggie avait un cancer, Julia. Elle se mourait. Et rien n'aurait pu changer le cours des choses.

— Au moins, je l'aurais vue une dernière fois, murmura-t-elle, remâchant son regret.

— Et vous ne lui auriez pas facilité la tâche.

— Je ne suis pas d'accord ! dit-elle avec force. Ils ont eu tort de mourir comme ça. La vie est trop précieuse pour en gâcher un seul instant.

Eric ne répondit pas. Julia n'avait jamais connu quelqu'un atteint d'un cancer des os. La douleur que Maggie

210

essayait d'assoupir à coups d'antalgiques n'était qu'un début. La souffrance aurait augmenté chaque jour, détruisant peu à peu la Maggie que Joe avait tant aimée. La malade aurait échoué dans une salle de réanimation, où son dernier souffle aurait constitué une pure formalité.

Eric poussa la porte de son cottage vert et blanc et s'effaça pour laisser passer Julia. La jeune femme pénétra à l'intérieur et resta debout au milieu de la pièce, l'air perdu.

— Préférez-vous du thé ? s'enquit-il.

Comme elle le regardait sans comprendre, il ajouta :

— À la place du café. Un soda peut-être ?

— Rien, merci, répondit-elle, les yeux rivés sur l'océan à travers la fenêtre. J'ai peine à croire qu'il fut un temps où il me tardait de retrouver ce paysage.

— Vous éprouverez de nouveau ce besoin.

— Non, c'est fini. Je confierai à l'agence immobilière toutes les formalités de la vente et je ne remettrai plus les pieds ici.

Ainsi il ne la reverrait plus ! Une rage inexplicable assaillit Eric, qui en eut l'estomac révulsé.

— Je ne savais pas que vous résolviez vos problèmes en prenant la fuite ! assena-t-il brutalement.

Julia planta les poings sur ses hanches.

— Comment osez-vous débiter une telle ânerie ! se défendit-elle. Vous ne me connaissez pas. Vous ignorez tout de mes problèmes et de ma façon de les résoudre.

Il ne s'était pas attendu à une réaction aussi violente. Il n'eut cependant pas le temps de s'excuser.

— Vous n'avez pas idée de ce qu'est ma vie, poursuivit-elle. Je dirige des centaines de personnes beaucoup plus qualifiées que moi, mais je m'accroche de toutes mes forces. Car si je revends l'entreprise, les associés, les employés, tous ceux qui ont aidé Ken à bâtir son empire se retrouveront à la rue. Pourtant, il m'en coûte de rester.

Elle lui tourna le dos, ferma les paupières et se mordit la lèvre. Trop tard ! Les mots étaient sortis presque à son insu. Quelque chose ne tournait pas rond. Pourquoi avait-elle traité Eric ainsi ? Il ne demandait qu'à l'aider.

Sentant une main sur son avant-bras, elle sursauta. Elle le dévisagea alors de nouveau ; mais à la place de la colère à laquelle elle s'attendait, elle vit quelque chose d'autre, une expression que sur le moment elle ne put déchiffrer.

— Désolée, murmura-t-elle. Il me fallait un bouc émissaire et vous étiez le seul à ma portée.

Dans un mouvement qui parut étonner Eric tout autant qu'elle, il l'embrassa sur les lèvres. Ce baiser ne recelait pas de tendresse, d'amitié ni même de pitié, mais une passion sans mélange. Assaillie par l'appréhension, elle se raidit mais ses sensations furent les plus fortes. Une sorte d'élan primitif la poussait vers cet homme. Elle répondit à son baiser avec toute la fougue de son désespoir.

Depuis près d'un an, la mort, le deuil étaient ses seuls compagnons. Elle vivait avec ses souvenirs, sa solitude, ses visiteurs. Elle n'attendait plus rien de l'existence. Chaque fête, chaque anniversaire, même la plus simple invitation à dîner éveillaient une foule de souvenirs. Le courrier arrivait encore au nom de Ken, sans parler des réunions dans l'entreprise où son absence pesait lourdement sur l'assemblée.

Julia se débattait en pleine traversée du désert quand le coup de fil lui annonçant le décès de Joe et de Maggie l'avait de nouveau expédiée au fin fond du néant. Et maintenant, Eric lui offrait une occasion de goûter à nouveau à la vie... Le pourquoi et le comment importaient peu. La raison ne jouait pas le rôle principal dans ce drame.

Elle lui passa les mains autour du cou et se pressa contre lui. Ses lèvres s'entrouvrirent. Sa langue rechercha celle d'Eric avec une ardeur qui ne dissimulait rien de ses intentions, et qui arracha à l'homme un soupir rauque.

Julia tira sur le tee-shirt d'Eric comme l'on ôte la dernière barrière entre une prison et la liberté. Ses doigts parcoururent le dos musclé, ses ongles s'enfonçant dans la chair ferme. Elle n'avait pas l'habitude des rapports violents mais celui-ci correspondait à un appel au secours.

Eric lui saisit les poignets et renversa la tête pour la regarder dans les yeux.

— C'est ça que tu veux?

— Pas toi?

— Julia, réponds-moi.

— Oui, c'est exactement ça.

— Je n'ai pas de préservatif.

— Je veux bien prendre le risque.

Le sentant hésiter, elle eut l'impression d'être abandonnée, rejetée, comme une naufragée sur son rocher, qui voit le bateau de secours s'éloigner.

— Mais pas toi, apparemment, dit-elle.

Eric se rendit alors compte de la force de son désir.

— Oh que si! grogna-t-il d'une voix enrouée.

Ses doigts s'attaquèrent aux boutons de la veste Armani qui, peu après, glissa à terre. Pourtant, quelque part, dans un recoin de sa conscience, une petite voix lui ordonnait d'arrêter, de considérer les conséquences de son acte, de ne pas profiter de la détresse de cette femme, de se comporter comme l'homme loyal et responsable qu'il avait toujours été. Mais le grondement du désir recouvrit la petite voix et il céda à ses impulsions les plus sauvages.

Son souffle chaud et ses lèvres caressaient Julia. Elle se pressait contre lui, se cambrait, embrasée par la même flamme. Il lui retira son corsage, emprisonna ses seins. Son pouce passa et repassa sur les pointes roses qui se raidirent douloureusement sous la dentelle blanche du soutien-gorge.

— Enlève ça!

Elle obéit. Il se pencha alors pour aspirer la pointe d'un sein, puis l'autre. Elle s'arc-bouta, les yeux clos, retenant un cri de plaisir.

La fermeture de sa jupe s'ouvrit, le tissu satiné glissa sur ses hanches. Elle sentit qu'Eric tirait sur sa petite culotte et baissa les yeux vers sa tête, qui descendait le long de son ventre. Il la débarrassa de ses chaussures avant de remonter vers une cuisse.

— S'il te plaît! supplia-t-elle.

Comment pouvait-elle parler ainsi? De sa vie elle n'avait jamais rien quémandé et, maintenant, elle cherchait avidement des caresses, des baisers. Elle espérait qu'il n'avait pas entendu. Pourtant, bientôt, quelque chose, sa langue, ses lèvres ou ses doigts, frôla le point le plus sensible de son être. Tout son corps en fut irradié. Tremblante, elle s'appuya sur les épaules d'Eric pour ne pas s'affaisser. Ses jambes flageolèrent. Le feu déroula ses flammes dans son bas-ventre. Peu après, un spasme, puis un autre, un autre encore la secoua. Alors Eric la souleva et la porta dans la chambre.

Il se déshabilla, se coucha sur elle et la pénétra. Leurs bouches se cherchaient, se dévoraient. Il accentua ses mouvements, mais elle en voulait plus. Elle lui enlaça la taille de ses jambes, s'ouvrit à lui, cria son nom, comme si c'était la clé du royaume magique.

Les vagues de plaisir l'emportèrent de nouveau. À chaque poussée, il s'enfouissait plus profondément en elle. Elle laissa échapper un cri aigu, puis lui mordit l'épaule. Dans un éblouissement, ils gravirent ensemble les degrés de l'extase.

Eric roula sur le côté, épuisé, en attirant Julia dans le cercle protecteur de ses bras. D'une main douce, il repoussa les cheveux de la jeune femme de son visage pour poser un baiser sur son front moite.

Julia restait immobile. Tout en acceptant ces démonstrations de tendresse, elle luttait contre l'implacable tourbillon des remords. Les minutes s'égrenèrent mais elle ne bougea pas. Alors, se hissant sur le coude, Eric la regarda.

— Julia, qu'y a-t-il?

11

Julia se redressa dans le lit, les bras croisés sur ses seins nus, le dos tourné à Eric comme pour effacer sa présence.

— Oh, mon Dieu! murmura-t-elle d'une voix brisée. Qu'avons-nous fait?

Eric s'assit à côté d'elle. Lui-même se posait des questions. Cependant, il ne comprenait pas cette réaction un peu exagérée.

— Nous avons fait l'amour, dit-il en réponse à une interrogation purement rhétorique.

La jeune femme le foudroya du regard.

— Nous avons eu un rapport sexuel, corrigea-t-elle.

— Tu appelles ça comme tu veux. En tout cas, moi je ne regrette rien.

— Moi, si!

Elle attrapa la chemise d'Eric pour se couvrir.

— Je parie que ce genre de chose ne t'est jamais arrivé, ironisa-t-il.

— C'est exact.

Il se retint pour ne pas la reprendre dans ses bras, sachant qu'elle se défendrait farouchement.

— Comment te sens-tu? s'enquit-il.

Julia passa les doigts dans ses cheveux emmêlés.

— Es-tu devenu fou? Comment veux-tu que je me sente? Vulgaire. Stupide.

À bout de nerfs, elle ramena ses genoux sous son menton et enfouit son visage dans ses paumes. Eric lui écarta les bras, la forçant à le regarder.

— Tu as oublié d'ajouter: rassasiée.

Un voile brûlant colora le visage de Julia.

— En effet, admit-elle à contrecœur.

Il eut un sourire.

— Tu ne me demandes pas comment je me sens ?

— Eric ! Ne plaisante pas avec ça.

— Je ne plaisante pas. Je ne dramatise pas non plus…
La vérité est tout autre.

— C'est-à-dire ?

Eric chercha ses mots un instant, puis déclara :

— Je voulais… J'avais autant besoin que toi d'un peu
de tendresse.

— Je sais que ce n'est pas crédible, mais je n'ai jamais
fait l'amour avec un autre homme que Ken.

Julia se laissa tomber sur l'oreiller, les yeux rivés au
plafond.

— En dehors de toi, acheva-t-elle.

— Pourquoi serait-ce si difficile à croire ?

— À cause de mon comportement.

— Confidence pour confidence, je suppose que je
devrais avouer que tu es la première femme, depuis
Shelly.

Elle se retourna vers lui, oubliant la chemise qui lui
recouvrait les seins.

— Tu plaisantes !

— Pour quelle raison mentirais-je sur un sujet aussi
important ?

— Parce que les hommes…

— Les hommes, Julia ?

Elle haussa les épaules.

— Ils sont plus libres… moins sentimentaux…

— Sans me poser en représentant de la gent masculine, je n'ai jamais considéré les rapports sexuels comme
une agréable aventure d'un soir. Ils font suite à un état
d'esprit. Et j'ai eu envie de faire l'amour avec toi dès que
je t'ai vue, Julia.

— Pourquoi ?

— Je ne peux pas décrire ce que j'ai ressenti.

— Tu es écrivain, pourtant.

— Justement, parfois j'en doute.

Il essaya néanmoins de s'expliquer. La jeune femme l'écouta, redoutant un discours fumeux. À la place, elle entendit l'expression de ses propres sentiments, avec une franchise qu'elle n'avait pas rencontrée depuis la mort de Ken. Ses amis, hommes et femmes, ne la comprenaient pas. Ils ignoraient les doutes et les craintes qui la tourmentaient sans relâche depuis un an. Quand Eric eut terminé, elle lui prit la main.

— Je veux bien une tasse de thé maintenant.

Il lui frôla les lèvres d'un baiser, passa son jean et enfila sa chemise. Avant de sortir, il tira son peignoir de la penderie et le tendit à Julia.

— La salle de bains est là.

Elle glissa ses bras dans les manches de flanelle et serra la ceinture deux fois autour de sa taille.

— Puis-je utiliser ta brosse à dents ?

— Naturellement, répondit-il sans hésiter.

Elle l'avait soumis à un petit test personnel, curieuse de connaître sa réaction. Pour une raison qu'elle ne put analyser, sa réponse lui fit plaisir.

— Et, à propos…

— Oui ?

— J'aime bien ta moustache.

Il porta la main à sa lèvre supérieure.

— Je songeais à la raser.

— Oh, non.

Il lui adressa un sourire.

— D'accord.

Une fois dans la salle de bains, Julia réalisa l'étendue de sa requête. Qu'est-ce que ça pouvait lui faire qu'il garde ou non sa moustache ? Lorsqu'ils se quitteraient cette fois-ci, leur séparation serait sans aucun doute définitive.

Eric posa la bouilloire sur la gazinière. Il prépara une gamelle et un bol d'eau fraîche pour Josi, et alla jusqu'au chalet voisin. Lorsqu'il ouvrit la porte, la chatte débaula dans le vestibule avec un miaulement plein d'espoir. En le voyant, elle arbora un air déçu, presque humain. Il posa la nourriture, s'accroupit et tendit la main pour la caresser. L'animal se laissa tapoter gentiment la tête et toléra sa présence pendant une minute entière, après quoi elle se percha de nouveau sur le rebord de la fenêtre où elle se figea, en attente.

À son retour, la bouilloire sifflait. Il mit des sachets d'earl grey dans deux tasses, versa l'eau frémissante, puis apporta le tout dans la salle de séjour. Il admirait un cerf-volant rouge et jaune sur le ciel gris, quand il sentit Julia à son côté. Elle se tenait elle aussi devant la fenêtre. Son silence semblait plus détendu qu'anxieux.

Le nuage de son parfum enveloppa Eric ; il sut qu'il n'oublierait jamais cette fragrance. Les moments qu'ils avaient passés ensemble, leur étreinte sauvage, le kaléidoscope de leurs émotions s'étaient à jamais gravés dans sa mémoire, aussi intensément qu'un film en couleurs.

Debout près de Julia, il éprouvait un besoin physique d'être touché, cajolé, mais pas forcément avec sensualité. Un peu d'affection lui suffirait amplement. Voilà une éternité que personne ne lui avait planté un baiser sur la joue, qu'aucune main rassurante ne s'était posée sur son épaule, l'air de dire : « Ne t'en fais pas, je suis là ! »

Oui, l'affection lui manquait. La complicité aussi. Une conversation devant un feu de cheminée, une bonne bouteille lors d'un pique-nique, un rire de connivence autour d'une vieille blague que l'on se raconte souvent, un regard échangé lors d'une soirée mondaine…

— Tu peux faire ça ? demanda Julia. Lâcher un cerf-volant ?

— Les yeux bandés et les mains attachées dans le dos.

Soulevant un sourcil, elle le fixa, l'œil pétillant.

— Ah bon ? J'aimerais bien voir ça.

— Moi aussi, dit-il en riant.

— Je devrais m'habiller.

— Pourquoi ?

Elle ne s'attendait pas à cette question.

— Je ne sais pas… Je ne me sens pas très à l'aise dans ton peignoir…

Bizarrement, elle se sentait tout à fait décontractée, au contraire. Le tissu avait la douceur du velours contre sa peau. Mais elle avait simplement formulé ce que lui suggérait sa conscience. L'implacable petite voix pour laquelle il était indécent qu'elle déambule vêtue de la robe de chambre de son amant. Son amant! Ce seul mot lui donnait la chair de poule.

— D'ailleurs, tu es habillé, toi.

Il leva les bras avant de les laisser retomber.

— C'est ça, ou rien!

— Ainsi, tu es l'homme d'une seule robe de chambre, plaisanta-t-elle.

— Je suis aussi l'homme d'une seule femme, renchérit-il d'une voix sérieuse.

La sentant se raidir, il abandonna ce sujet épineux et lui offrit une tasse de thé fumant. Elle la prit et retira le sachet qu'elle posa dans un cendrier vide, sur le bureau d'Eric.

— Parfait, apprécia-t-elle en prenant une gorgée.

Elle serrait la tasse entre ses mains pour se réchauffer.

— Quel sale temps pour un mois de juillet!

— Il fait froid depuis deux jours.

Il posa sa tasse.

— Je reviens tout de suite.

Lorsqu'il réapparut, il lui remit une paire de chaussettes noires en fil d'Écosse.

— Tiens.

Julia les enfila, assise sur le canapé, puis ramena ses jambes sous elle.

— Que vas-tu faire de Josi?

Eric hocha la tête.

— Je n'ai pas encore pris de décision. J'aurais voulu la garder mais je n'ai jamais eu de chat. Je ne sais rien de nos chers félins.

— Moi non plus. J'ai eu un poisson rouge autrefois... Mon petit ami de l'époque l'avait gagné au tir dans une foire. La malheureuse bête n'a pas survécu plus d'une semaine.

Elle le regarda par-dessus le bord de sa tasse.

— Trois jours de plus que le petit ami, précisa-t-elle.

Eric prit place en face d'elle, posant ses pieds nus sur la table basse en noyer. Ne rêve pas ! s'ordonna-t-il. Julia est peut-être entrée dans ta vie sans intention d'y rester.

— Comment as-tu rencontré Ken ?

— Dans un salon d'informatique. Je gardais le stand d'une amie. Ken est arrivé, il s'est mis à me poser des questions et j'ai fait semblant de comprendre ce qu'il disait. Trois mois plus tard, nous étions mariés.

— Maggie m'a dit qu'elle n'avait jamais vu de couple plus amoureux.

— Oui, je sais…

Julia cligna plusieurs fois des paupières, afin de chasser une petite larme qui miroitait sur ses cils.

— Maintenant, je comprends pourquoi Joe s'est suicidé lui aussi, ajouta-t-elle d'une voix chevrotante. Si je n'avais pas été aussi lâche, j'aurais agi de même.

Eric la considéra, horrifié.

— Tu n'es pas sérieuse. Joe avait quatre-vingt-huit ans. Tu en as à peine trente.

— Trente-deux. Les années n'ont rien à voir.

— Tu parles ! Crois-tu vraiment que Joe se serait fichu en l'air à ton âge ?

— Tu ne sais pas ce que c'est que de vivre seul jusqu'à la fin de ses jours.

— Regarde un peu autour de toi, Julia.

La jeune femme fixa le thé sombre au fond de sa tasse.

— Toi, tu as tes enfants.

— Deux fois tous les quinze jours, quand leurs petits copains ne fêtent pas leur anniversaire. Et un jour ils seront grands et préféreront vivre leur vie plutôt que de rendre visite à leur vieux père.

— Oui mais Shelly et toi…

— Quoi ? Nous ne nous aimions pas autant que Ken et toi ? Qu'est-ce que tu en sais ? Dis-toi que j'ai pu détruire le plus grand amour du siècle par pur égoïsme. Ça ne veut pas dire que je ne doive pas espérer une seconde chance.

— Ken était exceptionnel.

— Et pas moi ?

— Pas de la même manière. Nous étions exceptionnels… ensemble.

Eric encaissa le coup.

— Maggie me l'a dit, murmura-t-il.

Quelqu'un frappa à la porte, le dispensant de poursuivre. C'était la remorque municipale pour la voiture de
Joe et de Maggie. Le véhicule serait reconduit à San Jose,
où il serait vendu avec la maison. Eric partit s'occuper
des formalités. À son retour, il trouva Julia habillée et
recoiffée. Les tasses et les sachets de thé avaient disparu.
Il était convaincu que, dans la chambre, le lit avait été
fait, le peignoir rangé dans la penderie. Obscurément, il
se demanda ce qu'elle avait fait des chaussettes.

— Eric, je dois rentrer. Le conseil d'administration se
réunit demain matin. Je ne peux pas manquer la séance.

— Tu n'as pas besoin de te justifier, Julia. Tu es libre.

Elle boutonna sa veste, lissa un pli inexistant.

— J'appellerai l'équipe de nettoyage dont j'ai toujours
utilisé les services. Ils ont la clé et ne te dérangeront pas.

— Cela ne sera pas nécessaire. Il n'y a pas un grain de
poussière dans la maison. Joe a tout briqué avant de tirer
sa révérence.

Elle garda un instant le silence, visiblement boulever-
sée.

— Et… le lit ? s'enquit-elle finalement.

— Ils n'ont pas utilisé ta chambre, Julia… Ils ont préféré la pièce de derrière, celle qui a un lit double, et ils ont
recouvert le matelas de plastique.

Avec un tressaillement, elle se détourna.

Eric avait eu l'intention de lui épargner ces détails
mais, à l'évidence, elle avait besoin de les entendre.

— Et, après le départ du coroner, je me suis occupé de
tout le reste.

Elle leva sur lui un regard brillant de larmes.

— Merci. Il faut que j'y aille.

— Je t'accompagne à ta voiture.

Une fois dans sa Mercedes, Julia baissa la vitre.

— Je ne regrette pas d'être venue, Eric… Et je ne
regrette pas non plus ce qui s'est passé entre nous.

C'était plus qu'il n'attendait, moins qu'il n'espérait.

Mais il ferait preuve de patience. De persévérance. Il accorderait à Julia le temps dont elle avait besoin. Des semaines, des mois, un an. Trois cent soixante-cinq jours de réflexion… Ce n'était pas grand-chose en comparaison d'une vie entière ensemble.

12

Le lendemain, Eric revenait de sa troisième tentative manquée pour ramener Josi quand le téléphone se mit à sonner.

C'était Julia.

— J'ai reçu une lettre de Joe dans le courrier d'aujour-d'hui, annonça-t-elle avec des larmes dans la voix.

— Je me demandais en effet pourquoi il n'avait rien laissé pour toi au chalet.

— Moi aussi.

— Cela t'a-t-il aidée à mieux comprendre son geste?

— J'étais sûre que jamais je ne comprendrais, et pour-tant, c'est arrivé! Il me demande de leur pardonner. Ils ont eu peur que je cesse de venir au chalet à cause de leur suicide. Heureusement que je ne leur avais rien dit à pro-pos de la vente, termina-t-elle après une pause.

— Peut-être devrais-tu reconsidérer tes projets.

— J'ai essayé.

— Résultat?

— Je n'ai pas changé d'avis. Je n'ai plus rien à faire à Santa Cruz. Toutes les personnes que j'ai aimées n'y sont plus.

Eric aurait dû recevoir ces paroles comme une claque. Mais ce fut une image qui lui vint à l'esprit. En Alaska, il avait vu un grizzly sur un rocher en pleine rivière. À un mètre de là, un saumon s'efforçait de remonter le courant, qui l'entraînait inéluctablement vers la gueule ouverte de son prédateur. L'espace de cet instant figé, la vie palpite-rait pour l'éternité dans le poisson frétillant. Ses senti-ments à l'égard de Julia étaient comme cela.

— Alors il ne reste plus qu'à savoir quand tu mettras la propriété en vente.

Il était inutile de discuter. Elle semblait inébranlable. Qu'à cela ne tienne, il la poursuivrait à distance !

— Il se peut que j'évite cette pénible démarche. Peter Wylie m'a fait savoir qu'il était intéressé.

— Peter ? Il ne devrait pas tarder à se montrer, je crois ?

Il se fichait éperdument de la date de retour du vieil ami de Ken. Mais c'était une façon comme une autre de mettre fin à la conversation.

— La semaine prochaine.

— Et la famille qui loue le chalet en août ?

Eric souhaitait savoir combien de temps il avait devant lui avant de prendre une décision définitive concernant Josi.

— Ils arrivent le premier week-end d'août et s'en vont après le Labor Day.

— Julia, excuse-moi, mais j'allais sortir.

Autant qu'elle éprouve, elle aussi, cette sensation de perte qui le torturait.

— Oh, désolée. J'aurais dû te demander si je ne te dérangeais pas.

— Non, mais je suis un peu pressé.

Bon sang ! À quoi rimait cette boule au fond de sa gorge maintenant ?

— Bonne chance, Julia.

La jeune femme répondit avec une seconde de retard.

— Tu as été un ami formidable, Eric. Je te dois beaucoup.

Il ne voulait pas de sa gratitude.

— Tu ne me dois rien.

— Me préviendras-tu quand ton livre sortira ?

— Oui, bien sûr.

— N'oublie pas. Ça m'intéresse vraiment.

— Donne-moi ton adresse. Je t'enverrai un exemplaire.

Il saisit un stylo, et griffonna la rue, le numéro et le code postal au verso d'une page de son manuscrit.

Il ne leur restait plus qu'à se dire au revoir. Eric raccrocha avec la sensation qu'il avait creusé le fossé qui, déjà, les séparait. Mais il avait opté délibérément pour cette tactique. Il fallait que Julia en arrive à se demander pourquoi il lui manquait.

Deux jours plus tard, Josi l'attendait derrière la porte du chalet. Il posa la pâtée et l'eau fraîche, mais la chatte n'y toucha pas. Assise, immobile, elle leva sur lui un regard étrangement circonspect.

— Que se passe-t-il, minette ?

Elle se roula alors à ses pieds, encerclant de sa queue une de ses chevilles. Puis, avec un miaulement énigmatique, elle se rassit et, de nouveau, le scruta.

— Il va falloir que tu m'expliques, dit-il. Je ne parle pas le langage des chats.

Elle ne bougea pas, ne le quitta pas des yeux. Enfin, à titre d'essai, Eric se pencha pour la soulever. Josi s'installa alors dans ses bras, émettant un ronronnement aussi sonore qu'un roulement de tambour.

Le lendemain, avant le déjeuner, Eric travaillait à son ordinateur. Roulée en boule sur le manuscrit, la chatte somnolait, quand la sonnerie du téléphone lui fit dresser une oreille. Eric décrocha.

— Quand peux-tu venir à New York ? claironna dans l'écouteur la voix de Mel, son agent. Je voudrais te présenter à certaines personnes.

— Pour quoi faire ?

— Je me suis permis d'envoyer la première partie de ton œuvre à différentes maisons d'édition.

— Et alors ?

— Si tu tiens à devenir copain avec ton éditeur, il est grand temps que tu saches lequel tu veux. Tu n'as que l'embarras du choix.

— Tu as trouvé un éditeur prêt à publier mon roman ? demanda Eric, incrédule. Il n'est même pas fini.

— Ils sont pourtant nombreux à miser sur toi.

— Tu veux dire qu'ils offrent un contrat, avec une avance à l'appui, avant même que le bouquin soit terminé ?

Il se gratta la moustache, incapable de concevoir le raisonnement des magnats du livre.

— Et si l'intrigue plonge dans la seconde moitié ? Si la fin est mauvaise ? Bref, si je déçois leurs espérances ?

En proie au vieux démon du doute, Eric reprocha à l'agent littéraire son initiative.

— Je t'avais demandé de ne rien tenter avant que j'aie écrit le mot fin, Mel ! Et tu étais d'accord.

— C'était avant que je lise la première partie. Ne te tracasse pas, mon vieux. C'est excellent.

— Pourvu que ça dure !

Ces derniers temps, il avait l'impression d'écrire de la bouillie.

À l'autre bout de la ligne, Mel insista :

— Alors tu viens quand ?

Eric regarda sur le mur le dessin que son fils avait fait pour Joe et Maggie.

— Tu le sauras dans deux ou trois jours. J'ai quelque chose à régler avant.

Il écarta la queue de Josi du téléphone, puis raccrocha.

— Qu'est-ce que je vais faire de toi, mimi ?

Un chat pouvait sans problème survivre pendant plusieurs jours, avec suffisamment de croquettes et la bonne volonté des voisins. Mais après ce que Josi venait d'endurer, il était hors de question de la laisser seule. Se croyant de nouveau abandonnée, elle chercherait à s'échapper.

Le menton dans sa paume, Eric la regarda.

— Je vais peut-être te chercher le foyer que Joe a évoqué dans sa lettre.

Josi bâilla comme un fauve avant de refermer les yeux.

— Tu pourrais au moins avoir la décence de t'inquiéter.

La chatte émit un son, une sorte de gloussement félin. Eric se rappela un article qu'il avait lu à propos de ces animaux étranges que les Égyptiens adoraient comme des divinités. « Un chat ne vous appartient jamais. C'est vous qui lui appartenez. » Josi semblait en connaître long sur ce chapitre.

Sans réfléchir davantage, il composa le numéro de Julia à Atherton.

Elle répondit à la deuxième sonnerie.

— C'est Eric.

— Ah… bonjour…

Comment était-ce possible d'éprouver en même temps de l'excitation et de l'anxiété ? Quelques jours plus tôt, elle avait cru comprendre qu'ils s'étaient fait leurs adieux. Alors, pourquoi cette réaction particulière aujourd'hui ?

— J'ai une faveur à te demander.

— Vas-y. Après tout ce que tu as fait pour moi cet été, je ne peux rien te refuser.

Munie de son téléphone sans fil, la jeune femme émergea sur la terrasse de derrière et se pelotonna sur sa chaise longue préférée. Un faucon décrivit un cercle dans l'azur. Mue par une pulsion absurde, elle faillit lui raconter cette scène, lui décrire sa résidence située en dehors de la ville, parmi les collines vertes et la forêt dense qui lui procuraient un peu de calme dans son existence de plus en plus fiévreuse.

— Je dois m'absenter pendant quelques jours. J'ai besoin de quelqu'un pour garder Josi.

Elle ne l'aurait jamais deviné. Elle marqua une pause imperceptible. Avoir Josi sous les yeux lui rappellerait à chaque instant qu'elle avait perdu Joe et Maggie. Bon sang, elle était devenue tellement lâche !

— Avec plaisir, répondit-elle.

— Je la déposerai chez toi avant d'aller à l'aéroport, si tu n'y vois pas d'inconvénient.

— Entendu. Je te faxerai le plan… Il me semble avoir vu un fax à côté de ton ordinateur. Je me trompe ?

— C'est en effet ainsi que le vendeur a appelé ce machin au magasin où je l'ai acheté. Mais je ne sais pas comment le faire marcher. Tu l'inaugureras.

— Je suis contente que tu aies pensé à moi pour Josi, dit-elle. J'avais peur que, compte tenu de notre dernier entretien…

Elle s'interrompit, la bouche soudain sèche.

— J'essaie simplement de te dire que je ne voulais pas perdre… que je tenais beaucoup à notre amitié.

— Moi aussi.

Eric incarnait pour elle l'ami idéal. C'était le premier qu'elle avait rencontré depuis un an ; il avait le mérite de ne pas avoir connu Ken. En cela, il était un tremplin vers la vie normale. Cette constatation eut le don de l'attrister. Sans souhaiter vivre dans le deuil, la jeune femme répugnait toutefois à avancer vers l'avenir. Son cœur restait attaché au passé. Le temps et les circonstances avaient décidé à sa place.

— Quand viendras-tu ? demanda-t-elle.

— Ça dépend du vol. Et puis, il faut que je me rende...

Il marqua une pause interminable.

— ... à Sacramento, poursuivit-il enfin. Les enfants ne savent pas encore pour Joe et Maggie.

Le cœur de Julia bondit. À l'évidence, Eric adorait ses enfants, et il allait pourtant devoir leur apprendre une nouvelle bouleversante.

— À ton avis, comment vont-ils le prendre ?

— Je ne me fais pas de souci pour Susie. Elle est trop petite pour comprendre le sens de la mort. En revanche, Jason m'inquiète. Il a compris que Maggie était condamnée, le jour où nous l'avons conduite à l'hôpital. Mais j'aurai du mal à lui faire comprendre que Joe est parti aussi.

— C'était donc ça, murmura Julia.

— De quoi parles-tu ?

— Le dessin de Jason que tu as accroché au mur, près de ton ordinateur. Je lui ai longtemps cherché une signification qui me semble claire maintenant. Il leur disait adieu.

— Joe le tenait dans sa main quand il est mort.

— Ne t'inquiète pas pour ton fils, Eric. Il a résolu son problème avec Joe et Maggie avant de partir. Tout est dans le dessin.

— J'espère que tu as raison.

— J'en suis sûre. Fais-moi confiance.

— Je te rappellerai dès que je saurai la date exacte de mon départ.

La main fine de Julia se crispa sur l'écouteur. Eric semblait avoir prononcé cette phrase pour abréger la conversation.

— Sans indiscrétion… où vas-tu ? Non, ça ne fait rien ! coupa-t-elle rapidement. De quoi je me mêle !

Pendant une seconde, elle crut qu'il allait quand même lui répondre. Mais non.

— À très bientôt, dit-il simplement.

— C'est cela, oui.

Mais qu'est-ce qui lui prenait ? Elle terminait des entretiens d'affaires d'une voix plus chaleureuse. À présent, elle n'avait plus qu'à conclure.

— Au revoir, Eric.

— Au revoir, Julia.

Eric reposa l'écouteur sur le combiné, puis regarda distraitement le curseur qui clignotait sur l'écran. C'était étrange de voir comment certains événements tombaient du ciel avec un fracas de fin du monde, tandis que d'autres survenaient si subrepticement, si discrètement, que l'on aurait pu les manquer si l'on n'y avait pas prêté attention.

Il tendit la main et gratta Josi derrière l'oreille. Sans elle, il n'aurait sans doute jamais rappelé Julia. Il n'aurait pas trouvé de raison valable, et il n'aurait pas non plus entendu l'insistante petite voix de sa conscience lui dire que ses sentiments pour elle étaient vrais. Certes, il existait sûrement d'autres moyens en dehors du gros chat noir et gris, mais, pour le moment, Eric n'en voyait aucun.

Plus tard, il appela Shelly, lui expliqua en deux mots le but de son coup de fil et la prévint de son arrivée le lendemain matin.

— C'est étrange, lui dit son ex-femme. Jason parle d'eux comme s'il savait déjà qu'ils sont morts. Je ne l'ai jamais vu comme ça, Eric. On dirait un vieux sage dans le corps d'un enfant.

— Les Chapman étaient des êtres exceptionnels, Shelly.

— En plus, c'est la première fois qu'il perd quelqu'un.

Eric se retint pour ne pas lui rappeler qu'il y avait différents degrés de perte et que Jason en avait déjà gravi quelques-uns, malgré son jeune âge. Il garda le silence. Shelly ne méritait pas de subir sa rancune.

La rencontre se déroula mieux qu'il ne l'avait espéré. Shelly avait raison. Jason avait déjà accepté la mort de ses amis. Il ne voulut pas savoir si Joe était décédé, lui aussi. Dans son esprit, ils formaient une entité. Ce qui arrivait à l'un arrivait fatalement à l'autre. Il avait même deviné que son père avait hérité de Josi.

Eric quitta Sacramento encore sous le choc et s'engagea sur l'autoroute, en direction d'Atherton. Il allait déposer Josi chez Julia pendant son absence. Il ne souhaitait pas la revoir, pas tout de suite. Ses défenses s'amenuisaient, il n'avait pas le moral. Et, au milieu de sa confusion, une partie de son esprit, celle qui savait que Julia n'était pas prête à lui donner ce qu'il souhaitait le plus au monde, demeurait étrangement lucide. D'ailleurs, qu'est-ce qui lui prouvait qu'elle changerait jamais d'opinion à son sujet ? Pourquoi voudrait-elle d'un homme qui avait déjà détruit son premier mariage ?

Cependant, un argument de taille jouait en sa faveur : elle l'aimait, elle aussi. À ceci près qu'elle l'ignorait encore.

QUATRIÈME PARTIE

Août

1

Peter Wylie aperçut Eric à bord de son pick-up. Il sortait du parking longue durée de l'aéroport au moment où lui-même partait avec la navette.

Il appréciait Eric Lawson. Du moins il le pensait. Pourtant, le croiser ici lui procurait une sensation de malaise qu'il ne s'expliquait pas.

Le fait de l'avoir vu au chalet avec Julia l'avait incommodé. Eric n'appartenait pas au même monde que la jeune femme. Bien sûr, on ne pouvait exiger que Julia passe le reste de sa vie seule. Mais de là à se contenter d'un homme moins intéressant que son premier mari… Évidemment, on ne pouvait pas lui en vouloir. Ken était un être hors du commun. À vrai dire, Peter n'en connaissait pas d'autres comme lui.

Ou alors, Eric s'était mis en tête de courtiser Julia. D'où son insistance à faire ses courses, à se rendre indispensable.

Ou bien… nom d'un chien ! Cela ne le regardait pas. Julia ne vivrait pas seule le restant de ses jours pour rester fidèle à Ken.

La navette freina brutalement, mettant fin aux réflexions de Peter. Il prit ses bagages dans le coffre et entra dans l'agence de location de véhicules d'où il ressortit au volant d'une voiture. Peu après, il roulait en direction du sud.

Habituellement, il faisait une halte chez Ken et Julia avant de reprendre la route de Santa Cruz. C'était un rituel qui datait de l'époque où les Huntington s'étaient installés à Atherton. Ils dînaient tous les trois, évoquant les événements qui s'étaient produits pendant les deux mois durant lesquels ils ne s'étaient pas vus. Peter passait la nuit sur place et repartait le lendemain matin.

Il avait envisagé d'appeler Julia, inventant un quelconque prétexte pour briser cette routine. Trois heures de retard à Heathrow, plus le long vol l'avaient épuisé. Il était moulu. Mais quelle que fût l'excuse, la jeune femme ne le croirait pas. Et à juste titre. La vérité était toute simple : Peter ne voulait pas se retrouver dans la villa sans Ken. Chaque fois qu'il avait essayé, il en était reparti abattu. L'absence de son ami était trop pesante, trop évidente.

Même du vivant de Ken, Peter n'avait jamais passé plus d'une nuit à Atherton. L'idée que Katherine était peut-être déjà au chalet l'incitait à repartir au plus vite. À l'instar du boxeur qui se voit accorder une dernière chance de monter sur le ring, il ne tenait pas en place. Au bout de quelques années, ses hôtes avaient cessé de lui demander de rester davantage. Ils avaient fini par accepter son départ, tôt le matin, alors que rien ne pressait. Peter s'en allait, animé par l'espoir que Katherine se trouvait déjà sur place ; chose qui n'était jamais arrivée et qui paraissait aussi insensée que son amour pour elle.

Peter n'avait jamais rien dit à personne à propos de Katherine. Il n'allait pas crier ses sentiments sur les toits. Katherine elle-même les ignorait. Peter vivait d'ailleurs dans la crainte qu'elle ne s'en rende compte un jour. Alors, très certainement, elle ne voudrait plus jamais le revoir. D'un autre côté, en dépit des conséquences, lui déclarer sa flamme le libérerait d'un lourd fardeau. Mais la peur le retenait. Non, il ne ferait rien pour précipiter la confrontation.

D'une certaine manière, au demeurant assez perverse, ce que Peter admirait le plus chez Katherine, c'était son sens du devoir et son dévouement à sa famille. Elle adorait son mari et ses deux fils.

Tous les quatre formaient la famille idéale.

Peter aurait cassé la figure à quiconque aurait essayé de briser leurs liens. Alors pourquoi ne parvenait-il pas à oublier cet amour impossible ?

Il engagea la voiture dans la longue allée de la villa, freina devant la grille et s'annonça à l'interphone. Ken avait installé un système électronique d'ouverture à l'époque où une secte sataniste installée dans les environs avait annoncé la fin du monde. Julia répondit d'une voix vibrante d'excitation, puis les grilles s'ouvrirent. Peter comprit alors qu'il avait eu raison de venir. Julia avait tout perdu, il aurait été injuste de la priver aussi de sa visite. Il avança sur le chemin à trois voies menant au sommet de la colline, où s'érigeait la villa considérée comme la plus belle demeure de la région. L'architecte, d'un commun accord avec Ken, avait tenu compte de l'emplacement de la construction. Chaque fenêtre donnait sur une vue à couper le souffle; il n'y avait d'ailleurs ni rideaux ni volets.

Très spacieuse, la villa était aussi confortable et fonctionnelle que le chalet. Chaque meuble avait été choisi en conséquence; pour sa beauté tout autant que pour son aspect pratique.

Julia l'attendait à la porte, les bras ouverts.

— Peter! Que c'est bon de te revoir! Laisse-moi te regarder. Tu as une mine splendide!… Non! Tu as l'air crevé. Entre! Un bon scotch te remettra sur pied.

Il sourit.

— Je suis content de te revoir en forme, Julia.

Elle le précéda dans le vaste salon.

— Un double?

— Oh, non. Un doigt, noyé de soda. Sinon, tu devras me porter jusqu'à la table pour dîner.

Julia se dirigea vers le bar.

— Où étais-tu cette fois?

— À Londres. Je rendais visite à des amis dans le Connecticut et ils m'ont embarqué. J'ai vu quelques pièces de théâtre, et j'ai assisté à plusieurs réceptions.

La jeune femme lui tendit un verre à whisky en cristal taillé.

— Vraiment? s'étonna-t-elle. Ça ne correspond pas tout à fait à ta conception du divertissement.

— J'ai dû faire appel à toute ma diplomatie. La semaine a été un enfer.

Julia prit place à un bout du canapé d'un blanc satiné, se débarrassa de ses chaussures et fit signe à Peter de s'asseoir près d'elle.

— Je veux tout savoir sur ton voyage. Comment se portent les nababs de l'art ?

Il ôta lui aussi ses chaussures, s'affala sur le canapé et posa ses pieds sur la table basse. Quand Ken et Julia avaient emménagé, Peter avait eu du mal à s'habituer à leurs manières décontractées. Il s'installait sur une chaise à dossier, aussi droit que les conifères autour de la maison. Un jour, Julia lui avait dit de se détendre et, depuis, il faisait comme chez lui.

— Mes tableaux se vendent toujours. Et quant à mon attachée de presse, elle a la trouille que je devienne trop célèbre.

— Mais…

— Si tu la connaissais, tu comprendrais. Elle est du genre anxieux.

Josi traversa allègrement la pièce et s'étendit devant la baie, les yeux fixés sur l'abreuvoir où les oiseaux s'en donnaient à cœur joie.

— Tu as un chat maintenant ? s'étonna Peter.

— Une invitée de passage. Elle est arrivée il y a une heure. Mais visiblement, elle se plaît.

— Tu fais du baby-sitting d'animaux domestiques ?

— C'est un cas spécial. Josi ? appela-t-elle.

La chatte pointa les oreilles mais dédaigna l'appel, trop fascinée par le spectacle des oiseaux.

— Josi ? répéta Peter. N'est-ce pas le nom du chat de Joe et de Maggie ?

Lors du silence qui suivit, une prémonition funeste l'assaillit.

— Il leur est arrivé quelque chose ?

Julia hocha la tête. D'une voix triste, elle lui raconta la fin de ses meilleurs amis.

Dans l'esprit de Peter, les Chapman étaient intimement liés à Ken. Leur rencontre avec ce dernier précédait de plusieurs années ses étés à Santa Cruz, comme ses visites chez les Huntington dans les collines d'Atherton. Peter croisait Maggie et Joe environ une semaine par an mais, en dépit de ce laps de temps trop court, il les avait pris en affection. Leur disparition l'affligea sincèrement. Enclin au romantisme, il saisit néanmoins l'aspect poétique de leur mort simultanée, seule issue possible d'une grande histoire d'amour.

— Et Josi ? Qui s'en occupe en temps normal ?

— Je l'aurais adoptée si elle n'avait pas jeté son dévolu sur Eric. C'est donc lui qui en a hérité.

— Eric Lawson ? Le gars qui a loué le cottage d'Andrew ?

Il avait parfaitement saisi de quel Eric il s'agissait. Eh bien, pour quelqu'un qui s'était retiré au bout du monde pour se consacrer à l'écriture, il semblait se mêler bougrement de la vie de ses voisins !

— Il a été très gentil avec eux, expliqua Julia. Je ne suis pas surprise qu'ils lui aient demandé de garder Josi.

En entendant son nom, la chatte bondit sur le canapé et se roula près de Julia, qui lui caressa la tête.

— Personne n'aura aimé un animal autant que les Chapman, murmura-t-elle.

— Leur as-tu rendu visite pendant qu'ils étaient au chalet ?

— Pourquoi me demandes-tu cela ?

— Je présume que Maggie et Joe t'ont expliqué combien ce type a été formidable, puisque tu sembles ne plus jurer que par lui.

Délaissant Josi, Julia fixa Peter.

— Qu'est-ce que tu me chantes ? As-tu un problème avec Eric ?

— Tu ne trouves pas un peu bizarre sa façon de s'immiscer dans la vie des autres ?

— Comme le jour où il t'a trouvé blessé sur la plage et qu'il t'a secouru avant que tu sois saigné à blanc ?

Peter se redressa et prit la direction du bar, où il ajouta du soda dans son scotch. Une agitation singulière le gagnait. Il paierait cher pour savoir ce qui le dérangeait chez Eric. Ce dernier semblait parfaitement affable en apparence, mais Peter flairait cependant une sorte de mystère en lui.

— Sais-tu quelque chose sur Eric qu'il ne t'ait pas dit lui-même ? interrogea-t-il.

— Peter, où veux-tu en venir ?

— Pardonne-moi, Julia, mais il existe un tas d'escrocs qui courent après les riches veuves.

Au moins, il avait réussi à mettre des mots sur ses soupçons. La jeune femme cligna des paupières.

— Si j'ai bien compris, tu insinues qu'Eric s'est lié d'amitié avec Andrew à l'université, parce qu'il subodorait qu'un jour, son ami deviendrait voisin avec Ken Huntington, et que ce dernier mourrait à trente-neuf ans, laissant sa veuve dans la nature ; une veuve riche et facile à séduire, qui plus est !

— Évidemment, de ce point de vue, ça n'a ni queue ni tête...

— Mais d'un autre point de vue ?

— Je ne prétends pas qu'Eric a tout prévu, concéda-t-il. Je crois qu'il a saisi l'occasion pour te plaire.

— Et sur quoi bases-tu cette brillante déduction ?

— Je ne sais pas. C'est une intuition. Je ne peux pas l'expliquer.

— Mais il a dû faire quelque chose qui a mis ton intuition infaillible en alerte, non ?

Peter prit une gorgée de scotch.

— Il aurait fallu être aveugle pour ne pas comprendre à quoi il pensait quand il te regardait.

— À quoi pensait-il ?

Peter haussa les épaules.

— On aurait dit un gosse qui lorgne les billets de loterie de son meilleur ami. Il aurait dansé la danse du ventre pour t'impressionner.

— Il me semble que tu avais mis Ken en garde de la même manière quand il a commencé à sortir avec moi... Tu craignais que je ne sois pas assez chic pour lui.

L'accusation porta. Peter exhala un soupir. Dès l'instant où Ken avait posé les yeux sur Julia, il avait été convaincu qu'il avait rencontré la femme de sa vie.

— Toute la question est peut-être là, convint-il à contre-cœur. Je crois que je n'accorde désormais à personne le droit de te regarder…

Aux yeux de Peter, Julia serait toujours l'épouse de Ken. Le reste le révoltait tout autant que si l'on rasait le Taj Mahal pour construire un gratte-ciel à la place. Ken ne pouvait pas, ne devait pas être remplacé.

Il tenait sans doute l'explication. Mais de quel droit pouvait-il exiger de Julia une existence entière sans homme?

— Oublie ce que je viens de dire, murmura-t-il. Ça n'a pas de sens.

— Oh, Peter, donne une chance à Eric. Essaie de mieux le connaître quand il reviendra. Fréquente-le. Je suis sûre qu'il te plaira.

Il se servit un deuxième scotch, puis posa les coudes sur le comptoir.

— Est-ce une façon de m'annoncer…

— Je ne t'annonce rien du tout. Eric et moi sommes amis. Je n'oserais pas refaire ma vie de sitôt.

— Pourquoi dis-tu cela?

Au lieu d'une réponse rapide, enlevée, dont Peter avait l'habitude, Julia parut réfléchir avant de déclarer:

— Tu n'es pas le seul à penser que Ken est irrempla-çable. Nos amis, les employés de la firme, ses associés croient la même chose. Je suis en passe de devenir une Jackie Kennedy, c'est-à-dire un symbole dédié au bûcher du veuvage. À la limite, on me pardonnerait une ou deux affaires de cœur, à condition qu'elles soient discrètes. Mais un autre mariage! Jamais! Pour tous ces gens, y compris toi, c'est impensable. Comment convoler en justes noces avec un homme qui ne saurait être qu'infé-rieur à Ken?

Peter la scruta, interloqué. Il n'allait pas nier un rai-sonnement qu'il avait eu lui-même.

— Je n'avais pas idée…

— Personne n'a idée, mon ami, dit-elle en se levant et en allant se planter devant la baie. Le pire, c'est que je me sens coupable. Alors je m'évertue à rentrer dans le moule. Eric ne transgresse pas les règles, ajouta-t-elle en se tournant pour le regarder. Probablement parce qu'il ne les connaît pas.

Avec un sourire maussade, Julia fourra les mains dans les poches de son pantalon de soie blanche.

— Rassure-toi, il n'essaiera plus de m'approcher.

— Aurais-tu envie qu'il le fasse?

La question échappa à Peter, il redouta la réponse.

— Parfois, la nuit, j'essaie de m'imaginer dans vingt, dans trente ans… Alors je prends peur. Le reste du temps, je suis tellement occupée que je ne sais plus comment je m'appelle.

— Tu ne peux pas continuer ainsi.

— Non?

— Ce n'est pas une vie, Julia.

— Quels sont mes choix?

— Ce n'est pas parce qu'Eric n'est pas l'homme qu'il te faut, que tu ne trouveras pas… plus tard…

Mais qu'est-ce qu'il racontait? Trouver égalait s'installer. Se remarier. Remplacer Ken. Cela, Julia le savait. Et la pire des solitudes ne la conduirait pas à cette extrémité.

— Juste par curiosité, Peter, qu'est-ce qui te fait penser qu'Eric n'est pas l'homme qu'il me faut?

— Tu plaisantes?

— Dis toujours.

— Tu as besoin de quelqu'un qui t'aide à diriger l'entreprise. Eric sait à peine compter son argent…

— Pourquoi?

— Pourquoi quoi?

— Pourquoi ai-je besoin de quelqu'un qui m'aide dans l'entreprise? Insinues-tu que je ne peux pas la diriger toute seule?

— Non, pas du tout, dit-il, désarçonné. Mais il te faut un homme qui soit de ton milieu, au moins. Qu'est-ce qu'Eric sait de ta vie? Plus important encore : en quoi peut-elle le concerner?

— Je ne connaissais rien à l'informatique quand j'ai épousé Ken.

— Certes, mais vous n'avanciez pas dans des directions opposées. Eric est un raté, Julia. Il a quitté le cabinet médical qu'il a mis dix ans à bâtir. Ça résume le personnage.

Julia demeura un instant immobile, les épaules tombantes.

— Je n'ai jamais voulu la place de Ken.

— Il aurait été fier de voir que tu as réussi haut la main.

— Oh, non, pitié !

Submergée par une colère inexplicable, la jeune femme leva les yeux au plafond, les dents serrées. Peter vit un camaïeu d'émotions passer sur son visage délicat. Il ne connaissait pas cette femme, torturée et confuse. Jusque-là, il avait vu en elle une veuve digne, une épouse inconsolable qui avait accepté son triste sort avec le fatalisme des êtres qui n'ont eu qu'un seul amour.

— Je ne sais plus quoi dire, murmura-t-il.

— Moi non plus, répliqua-t-elle.

Julia eut alors un sourire qui encouragea Peter à quitter ce sujet épineux. À sa grande honte, il saisit la perche.

— Veux-tu que nous allions dîner dehors ? Dans ce merveilleux petit restaurant où Ken commandait toujours des crevettes au curry…

Il s'interrompit. Nom d'une pipe, fallait-il être crétin !

— Entendu, Peter, répondit son amie, résignée. Va ranger tes bagages. Pendant ce temps, je vais réserver une table pour deux.

Elle était prête à tout lui pardonner. Même ses gaffes et ses maladresses. Il avait été le meilleur ami de Ken. Toutefois, en tant que tel, Peter aurait dû être le premier à comprendre que vivre sans amour équivalait à se condamner à une profonde et perpétuelle solitude.

2

Au milieu de l'allée, Katherine Williams indiquait à grands gestes à Paul, son fils cadet, la direction à suivre. Le jeune homme passa la marche arrière, et sa mère lui fit signe de freiner quand le hayon de la camionnette s'aligna sur la porte du chalet.

— Quel besoin avais-tu d'apporter toute cette camelote! se lamenta Paul en sautant à terre et en contournant la voiture pour aider sa mère à décharger les bagages.

Ils étaient venus plus tôt que prévu cette année et… oui, elle avait emporté trop de choses; mais Katherine garda le silence. Ce n'était pas tellement ça qui agaçait Paul, elle le savait; il craignait plutôt que sa chère mère ne caresse le projet de les convaincre, son frère Michael et lui, de rester tout le mois au lieu du lundi et du mardi convenus.

— On ne sait jamais, répondit-elle. Je pourrais ouvrir un gîte pour sans-abri.

— Les sans-abri ne vivent pas sur les plages de Santa Cruz.

— Paul, mon chéri, ouvre les yeux. Il y en a partout.

S'emparant du panier à provisions bourré à ras bord, Katherine se dirigea vers le chalet. Paul avait grandi dans une petite ville. Cela l'avait préservé des dures réalités de la vie, plus apparentes dans les grandes cités. À trente-cinq kilomètres de Sacramento, et en pleine expansion, Woodland n'en demeurait pas moins une petite ville provinciale.

— Bah! souffla Paul, chargé d'une malle. Ici, devenir sans-abri relève d'un choix philosophique.

Il se sentait concerné malgré tout, cela s'entendait au ton de sa voix ; Katherine n'insista pas. Paul était son ange gardien. Il serait resté s'il appréhendait de la laisser seule au chalet. Son sens de la liberté requérait à la fois l'approbation de sa mère et son exemple. C'était la raison pour laquelle elle avait décidé de passer ses vacances au chalet, comme tous les mois d'août depuis douze ans. Paul avait besoin de cette routine rassurante.

— Ne t'affole pas. Je serai aussi sage que si Michael et toi étiez ici, avec moi.

Elle posa le panier sur la table de la cuisine, cherchant machinalement du regard la carte traditionnelle des Chapman. Cette année, il n'y en aurait pas, Julia l'avait prévenue. La certitude que Joe et Maggie étaient morts ensemble, comme ils avaient vécu, avait tempéré son chagrin. Ses grands-parents, qui avaient exprimé le même souhait, avaient échoué dans des maisons de repos différentes, à des kilomètres de distance l'un de l'autre. Les deux dernières années de leur vie, ils ne s'étaient vus que lors de rares visites… Qui donc avait le droit de juger les Chapman ? Pas elle, non, certainement pas. Dans les mêmes circonstances… Mais ces circonstances ne s'appliqueraient jamais à elle, alors il était inutile de se perdre en vaines méditations.

Paul lui adressa un sourire espiègle.

— Cela veut-il dire que Michael et moi devons rester aussi sages que quand tu es à la maison ?

Katherine sortit un paquet de céréales et le rangea dans le placard au-dessus de l'évier.

— Vous serez si occupés que vous n'aurez pas le temps de vous mettre dans le pétrin.

— Cinq minutes suffisent pour ça, tu sais.

Les poings sur les hanches, elle laissa filtrer un regard lourd de menaces à travers ses paupières mi-closes.

— Attention ! Je peux toujours changer d'avis et rentrer plus tôt que prévu.

Loin de paraître intimidé, Paul éclata de rire.

— Oh, maman ! J'adore quand tu te fâches. Mes copains aussi.

Katherine ne put s'empêcher de sourire.

— Va décharger la voiture au lieu de raconter des bêtises.

En se dirigeant vers la porte, le jeune homme cria par-dessus son épaule :

— Et Michael ? À quelle heure arrive-t-il ?

— Pas avant dix heures ce soir. Il s'arrête en route, chez Allison.

Du haut de ses seize ans, Paul arbora un air de vieux bougon.

— Compris ! Son altesse ne va pas se pointer avant demain. Il va entrer en roulant des mécaniques et annoncer : « J'étais trop fatigué pour conduire. Mieux vaut se reposer que s'endormir au volant. » Tiens, mon œil !

— Qu'il soit là ce soir ou demain, ça n'a pas d'importance, dit Katherine d'un ton posé.

À dix-neuf ans, Michael poursuivait ses études dans une ville universitaire. Il partageait son temps entre la faculté et ses parents et, cet été, Katherine avait lâché du lest.

Son cadet haussa les épaules.

— Non, aucune ! Absolument aucune !

Il sortit sans attendre de réponse.

Sa mère le suivit d'un regard triste. Il lui tardait de repartir, pensa-t-elle, de retrouver son nouveau job, ses amis. Une boule lui noua la gorge. Psychologues, philosophes et autres experts en éducation proclamaient pourtant qu'un parent doit éprouver plénitude et fierté lorsque ses enfants réclament leur indépendance. Eh bien, non, pas elle. Katherine n'était pas prête à franchir le pas. Elle n'était heureuse qu'entourée de ses fils. Elle adorait leurs rires, leurs plaisanteries, les moments privilégiés qu'ils passaient ensemble.

Un an plus tôt, tous les quatre formaient une famille parfaite. Leurs amis, leurs relations, les membres de la congrégation de Brandon, tout le monde les citait en exemple. Ils relevaient le niveau moral de la communauté. Le bon pasteur et sa charmante épouse ne représentaient pas seulement le couple idéal. Ils passaient également pour des parents exceptionnels, qui parvenaient à inculquer des principes sains à leurs enfants sans les étouffer pour autant.

Était-ce possible que ce fût seulement une année auparavant?

Katherine tira du panier un paquet de crackers, ainsi qu'une boîte de conserve de haricots rouges. Elle ignorait pour combien de personnes elle ferait la cuisine et avait fini par prendre un peu de tout. Ses fils lui avaient promis de passer le lundi et le mardi au chalet, comme s'ils craignaient de la décevoir. Et, plus tard, elle les avait entendus tirer des plans sur la comète, donner des rendez-vous qui les retiendraient à Woodland les deux journées en question.

Elle désirait leur compagnie mais ne voulait en aucun cas leur imposer des obligations. Si la solitude lui pesait, c'était son problème.

— Hé! Tu rêves?

Paul entra, un sac au bout de chaque bras.

Katherine se força à sourire.

— L'air iodé prédispose à la rêverie, tu ne savais pas?

Il flanqua les sacs sur le plan de travail.

— Puisque tu adores cet endroit, tu n'as qu'à t'y installer.

L'aisance avec laquelle son fils avait prononcé cette déclaration trahissait ses convictions les plus intimes. Paul savait que ses parents ne se remettraient plus jamais ensemble. Les enfants de la paroisse dont les parents divorçaient n'aspiraient pourtant qu'à être de nouveau réunis sous le même toit.

— Et toi, où habiteras-tu? demanda-t-elle.

— Je voulais dire: quand j'aurai fini mes études, riposta-t-il rapidement.

— Au lycée ou à l'université?

Le jeune homme esquissa un sourire penaud.

— Tout dépendra de l'université dans laquelle je serai accepté.

Paul était affecté par la maladie de tous les adolescents de son âge: l'égocentrisme. Attendre de lui une autre attitude paraissait impensable. Katherine plia le sac de papier brun avant de le ranger dans un tiroir.

— Ne t'inquiète pas. Je n'irai nulle part tant que ton frère et toi…

— Coucou! Où êtes-vous? fit la voix de Michael.

— Dans la cuisine, répondit sa mère.

La figure de Paul s'illumina.

— Salut! s'exclama-t-il. Maman a dit que tu rendrais visite à Allison. Je ne t'attendais pas avant demain matin.

— Je n'y suis pas resté, étant donné que plus rien ne me retenait là-bas.

— Depuis quand? voulut savoir Katherine.

— Depuis que j'ai emmené Allison avec moi.

— Bonsoir, madame Williams, dit la jeune fille. Il n'y a pas de problème, j'espère? Je voulais téléphoner, mais Michael m'en a empêchée.

— Mais il n'y a aucun problème, lui assura Katherine, en s'efforçant de cacher son enthousiasme.

Pour avoir Paul et Michael auprès d'elle, elle aurait volontiers invité tous leurs amis.

— Vous restez jusqu'à quand? interrogea Paul.

— Allison doit rentrer lundi.

La figure étroite de Paul s'éteignit d'un seul coup; une ombre de déception obscurcit ses yeux.

— Génial! feignit-il de jubiler.

— Allison n'est jamais allée sur la promenade, déclara Michael. Nous irons tous demain, si vous êtes d'accord.

Katherine adressa à son aîné un sourire complice. Elle savait pourquoi il agissait ainsi et ne l'en aimait que davantage.

— C'est une merveilleuse idée, approuva-t-elle.

Le week-end fut presque parfait. Chacun fit de son mieux pour le rendre agréable. Cependant, même la pétillante Allison ne suffit pas à masquer l'absence de Brandon. Le moment le plus rude se produisit le dimanche. Michael suggéra de ne pas aller à la messe pour visiter Big Sur. Tous opinèrent, chose impensable du temps de Brandon.

Le lundi matin, les trois jeunes prolongèrent le petit déjeuner autant qu'ils le purent. Ensuite, ils s'en allèrent. Katherine agita le bras en signe d'au revoir jusqu'à ce que les feux arrière de la Honda de Michael aient disparu dans le brouillard. Retourner dans la maison vide augmenterait la sensation de solitude qui l'envahissait peu à peu.

Alors, malgré l'air frais et sa tenue légère, elle prit le chemin de la plage.

Peter arriva une demi-heure plus tard. Sa priorité fut de se rendre au chalet, afin de repérer des signes révélateurs de la présence de la famille Williams. N'en décelant aucun, il regagna son atelier où il défit ses bagages. Après un voyage de deux mois, la chaleureuse atmosphère de son cottage l'enveloppa de manière sécurisante. À chaque retour, il se demandait pourquoi il vivait ici, alors qu'il pouvait s'offrir plus d'espace sous des cieux plus cléments. La réponse s'imposait alors à son esprit : ici, il se sentait chez lui. Dans ce coin perdu, il pouvait travailler sans se laisser distraire par les mondanités et les lumières aveuglantes des galeries d'art.

Et puis un autre avantage le frappa : durant tout le mois d'août, il se trouverait à trois minutes à pied de l'inaccessible rêve qui avait pour nom Katherine Williams.

En remontant les stores de l'atelier, il contempla la nappe de brouillard sur l'océan. Il y avait peu d'espoir que le temps se dégage aujourd'hui. Mais après soixante jours d'ensoleillement perpétuel dans les six États et les deux continents qu'il avait parcourus, la grisaille présentait un contraste agréable. Sur le chevalet trônait encore le croquis d'une loutre de mer et de son petit. Il l'avait réalisé avant son départ et comptait s'en inspirer pour une aquarelle destinée à une vente de charité à San Francisco. Confronté à son œuvre, il pinça les lèvres. Il n'avait pas encore trouvé un équilibre satisfaisant entre les formes.

De Santa Cruz à Monterey, la loutre de mer incarnai la mascotte préférée des touristes. On en trouvait de mu tiples sortes dans toutes les boutiques de souvenirs de région : statuettes de bronze, bibelots de verre, cartes à jouer, cartes postales, peintures. Cependant, depuis des années, Peter rêvait de représenter à sa manière la longue silhouette luisante de cette créature agile. Il souhaitait la définir autrement, créer du jamais-vu.

Il posa une feuille à dessin vierge sur le chevalet, la consolida à l'aide de pinces, puis laissa sa main armée d'un fusain courir sur la surface blanche. Peu après, une loutre surgit sous ses doigts, au milieu d'un fouillis de varechs. Le dessin prit vite une tournure qui lui plaisait.

Un grattement à sa porte lui arracha un juron. Habituellement, il n'ouvrait à personne quand il travaillait, mais cette fois-ci la curiosité eut raison de lui. Le crayon gras à la main, le front plissé par l'effort de concentration, il ouvrit le battant.

Katherine recula d'un pas devant sa physionomie austère.

— Je rentrais chez moi… J'ai vu votre voiture et je me suis arrêtée pour vous dire bonjour… Excusez-moi, je vous dérange, je reviendrai plus tard.

La partie la plus pragmatique du cerveau de Peter refusa d'enregistrer ce qu'il voyait. La fatigue avait dû avoir raison de ses forces, il s'était endormi à son chevalet et rêvait que Katherine était là. Il n'y avait pas d'explication plus raisonnable.

Pourtant, l'apparition se rapprocha pour le regarder sous le nez.

— Peter ? Est-ce que ça va ?

Bon Dieu ! C'était bien elle.

— Euh… oui. Vous m'avez simplement surpris en pleine inspiration… Je ne vous attendais pas avant lundi prochain.

— J'ai décidé de venir plus tôt cette année.

— Comment vont les garçons ? Et Brandon ?

L'ombre d'une hésitation apparut sur les traits de Katherine, qui répondit d'une voix exagérément chaleureuse :

— Ils vont merveilleusement bien. Et ils sont très occupés. Tellement, que je ne sais même pas s'ils descendront au chalet.

Chaque été, Peter se laissait surprendre par la beauté de Katherine. Il aimait ses cheveux auburn, qui ondulaient naturellement, et que le brouillard rendait plus vaporeux. Son regard était doux quand elle souriait, et elle avait une façon charmante de vous observer en penchant la tête sur le côté. Chaque année, le peintre découvrait une nouvelle chose, un nouveau trait, qui lui tenait lieu de souvenir jusqu'à l'été suivant.

— Entrez donc, murmura-t-il, embarrassé.

Il s'effaça pour la laisser passer.

— Voulez-vous boire quelque chose ? Du café ? Il me reste quelques sachets de thé que j'ai conservés depuis la dernière fois que vous êtes venue.

— Non, merci.

Dans le salon, elle s'assit dans le fauteuil Voltaire, devant la cheminée.

— La pièce a changé, remarqua-t-elle.

— Le buffet et le tapis sont nouveaux. J'ai assisté à une vente de charité et, vous savez ce que c'est, j'ai été pris au piège des enchères.

Il voulut s'asseoir dans le fauteuil voisin mais, se ravisant, prit place sur le canapé, un peu plus loin. C'était la première fois que Katherine lui rendait visite sans Brandon ou l'un de ses fils, et il ne voulait pour rien au monde qu'elle surprenne une expression suspecte sur son visage.

— Êtes-vous sûre que vous ne voulez rien boire ?

— En fait, je suis venue vous demander si vous voulez dîner avec moi ce soir. J'ai oublié que je serai seule toute la semaine et j'ai fait un poulet à la cocotte assez gros pour nourrir un régiment.

— Où sont les enfants ?

Elle eut un sourire un peu maussade.

— Les enfants ont grandi. Michael, qui reprend ses études dans deux semaines, préfère maintenant Allison, sa petite amie, à sa mère. Paul a dégoté un job d'été à l'épicerie de Woodland… et il est tombé amoureux fou de la fille de l'épicier. J'aurai de la chance si je le revois de tout mon séjour, celui-là.

— Et Brandon ? s'enquit poliment Peter.

— Il a un jeune pasteur comme assistant et le met au courant de tout.

Elle se tortilla dans le fauteuil, les yeux rivés sur ses mains. Peter se surprit à supposer que quelque chose ne tournait peut-être pas rond chez les Williams. Katherine le regarda soudain avec un sourire désarmant.

— Vous connaissez Brandon. Il aime penser que le Bon Dieu ne peut se passer de ses services.

— Ainsi vous serez seule ici... pendant tout le mois ?

— Il semble bien que oui.

La certitude que le mois à venir serait le meilleur ou le pire de sa vie assaillit Peter.

3

Katherine ferma la porte et s'adossa au battant. Les pas de Peter décrurent dans la nuit. Le dîner avait été une réussite ; exactement ce qu'il lui fallait pour oublier, ne serait-ce que momentanément, que l'an passé, au même endroit, à la même heure, elle se croyait comblée.

La culpabilité la taraudait. Elle avait menti à Peter ; un mensonge par omission. Elle avait pris la décision de passer sous silence sa séparation d'avec Brandon sur une impulsion. Voilà des mois que les gens bien-pensants la bombardaient de questions insidieuses, avec des mines de circonstance et des regards par en dessous. Elle ne voulait pas que Peter se comporte de la sorte. Katherine avait désespérément besoin d'un peu de normalité ; même pour un mois.

Normalité. Une blague ! Elle ignorait à présent la signification de ce mot. Ils avaient été normaux jadis, quand ils formaient une famille, quand Brandon la considérait comme un deuxième don du ciel, après sa vocation. Être la deuxième était égal à Katherine. Comment aurait-elle pu être jalouse de Dieu ?

Issue d'une famille qui consacrait ses dimanches au football, elle avait dû travailler dur pour devenir une parfaite épouse de pasteur. Elle était trop jeune à l'époque pour s'apercevoir que Brandon jouait les Pygmalion. Seule la transformation de la pécheresse en sainte le passionnait. L'accomplissement du défi avait émoussé son intérêt. Ensuite, l'ennui s'était installé entre les deux conjoints.

C'était ainsi qu'il lui avait présenté le sujet de ses préoccupations le soir où il l'avait priée de quitter le loge-ment que l'Église avait mis à leur disposition. Ce n'était pas faute d'avoir combattu sa lassitude, avait-il ajouté, mais rien n'y faisait? Combien de nuits n'avait-il pas passées en prières? Hélas! aucune réponse n'était venue d'en haut. Il se surprenait, parfois, à avoir pour de braves paroissiennes des pensées coupables, des désirs qu'il n'aurait dû ressentir que pour son épouse...

Brandon n'avait pas tardé à mettre sur le dos de sa femme ces désirs innommables. La faute incombait à Katherine, qui avait laissé s'éteindre l'étincelle de leur union. Les rapports sexuels entre les époux étaient devenus pure formalité, le compagnonnage, l'amitié, la complicité, inexistants.

Les fidèles avaient merveilleusement soutenu le couple en péril, et Brandon en particulier. Nul n'avait soufflé mot contre Katherine mais, à l'évidence, tous pensaient qu'elle souhaitait la séparation. Naturellement, Brandon avait essayé de démentir cette rumeur. Il avait même déclaré, lors du sermon dominical, que la décision avait été prise d'un commun accord; mais personne ne l'avait cru. Le révérend Williams, qui n'avait jamais tourné le dos à personne, ne pouvait pas avoir pris l'initiative d'abandonner sa femme.

À la demande de Brandon, Katherine avait cessé de fréquenter les offices à partir du jour où elle avait déménagé dans un trois-pièces en ville : un appartement affreusement étriqué, au loyer modeste. Elle avait repris des études grâce à une bourse et ne pourrait pas payer plus cher tant qu'elle n'aurait pas un emploi.

Cet été, pour la première fois de leur vie, Michael et Paul avaient partagé la même chambre à coucher. Après quelques semaines, n'y tenant plus, Michael était retourné chez son père; Katherine avait ressenti cette décision comme un échec supplémentaire.

Elle jeta un coup d'œil à la pendule qui égrenait son tic-tac monotone sur la cheminée. Il était presque minuit. Elle n'avait pas sommeil. Si elle allait se coucher, elle était bonne pour une nuit blanche.

Elle inspecta les livres sur les étagères. Des thrillers,

dont Ken était friand. Mais pas elle. Margaret Sadler avait laissé plusieurs romans sentimentaux. Katherine en prit un, jeta un coup d'œil au titre et le remit en place. Elle n'allait pas se réjouir du bonheur de l'héroïne ; alors qu'elle-même avait raté l'essentiel !

Elle opta finalement pour une biographie de Doris Duke, une femme qui ne lui ressemblait en rien. Elle ouvrit la porte coulissante pour entendre le bruit des vagues, se pelotonna sur le canapé blanc et se plongea dans sa lecture.

Plusieurs heures plus tard, la nuque raide, grelottant malgré le châle afghan qu'elle avait jeté sur ses épaules, elle alla enfin se coucher.

Bizarrement, juste avant qu'elle sombre dans le sommeil, ses pensées voguèrent vers Peter.

Il représentait exactement l'ami dont elle avait besoin en ce moment. Le compagnon avec lequel on partage un repas, on fait une promenade, sans s'entendre poser mille questions indiscrètes ou prodiguer des conseils. Quelqu'un à qui elle ne penserait plus les onze mois suivants.

Deux jours s'écoulèrent avant que Peter se montre. Il avait tout tenté dans l'espoir de provoquer une rencontre fortuite, sans résultat. Ce n'était pas faute d'avoir surveillé la plage aux jumelles et d'être passé et repassé devant le chalet ! Finalement, il avait fini par venir sonner à sa porte.

Katherine lui ouvrit, vêtue d'un maillot de bain une pièce bleu marine, les cheveux coiffés en une longue natte, des lunettes noires posées sur le haut de la tête, et une serviette éponge sur le bras.

— Bonjour, Peter. J'étais sur le point d'aller à la plage pour une séance de bronzage. Ce n'est pas très bon, je sais, mais j'aime ça.

Elle eut un sourire à faire pâlir de jalousie les modèles de marques de dentifrice.

— Je commençais à craindre que le brouillard ne se lève plus jamais.

Peter se demanda s'il existait un endroit en enfer réservé aux hommes qui convoitent les épouses des pasteurs.

— Je vais en ville aujourd'hui. Voulez-vous venir avec moi, si vous n'avez rien de mieux à faire ? proposa-t-il.

— À quelle heure ?

Elle balaya sur sa joue une frisette qui avait échappé à sa natte. Ce mouvement tendit le tissu du maillot sur son sein, et Peter se fit violence pour regarder ailleurs.

— Vers midi ?

Comme elle ne répondit pas tout de suite, il se hâta d'ajouter :

— Ou plus tard, bien sûr. Mais je me suis dit que nous pourrions nous arrêter quelque part pour déjeuner.

— Midi, c'est parfait.

— Formidable ! dit-il en s'efforçant de bannir l'excitation de sa voix. À tout à l'heure.

Alors qu'il aurait dû tourner les talons, il la fixa malgré lui sans un mot.

— Où nous retrouverons-nous ? demanda-t-elle.

— Pardon ?

— Voulez-vous que nous nous donnions rendez-vous quelque part ?

— Ah ! Je passerai vous chercher.

Elle fit mine de refermer la porte mais la rouvrit aussitôt.

— Et que faites-vous, dans l'immédiat ? se renseigna-t-elle.

Il allait rentrer chez lui et essayer d'ôter de son esprit l'image de cette superbe femme en maillot de bain.

— Rien d'important. Pourquoi ?

— Je sais que pour vous, qui vivez ici toute l'année, cela n'a rien d'excitant mais, comme il fait très beau, pourquoi ne pas venir sur la plage avec moi… exceptionnellement, bien sûr.

Il ne devait absolument pas marcher dans cette combine.

— Oui, pourquoi pas ? Je vais chercher mon maillot.

— Avez-vous une serviette de plage ?

— Je ne crois pas.

— J'apporterai celle de Paul.

Peter longea en courant le chemin de son cottage. Tels le flux et le reflux, ses pensées se répétaient indéfiniment. La voix de sa conscience lui délivrait toujours le même message. Il n'avait pas le droit de prendre des bains de soleil avec une femme mariée, pas plus que de l'inviter à déjeuner en ville. Ce n'était pas sain. Et de surcroît, c'était stupide.

Il revint après avoir enfilé son bermuda.

Katherine eut heureusement le bon goût de ne pas lui demander d'étaler de la crème solaire sur son dos. Ils restèrent un moment côte à côte sur le sable dur et granuleux, ce qui permit à Peter de couler un regard de biais vers Katherine. Il n'avait pas besoin de la toucher pour deviner la douceur de sa peau, ou la façon dont le duvet presque invisible de ses bras lui caresserait les lèvres. Comme tous les artistes, c'était un homme tactile.

Katherine roula sur le côté et se hissa sur un coude.

— Quand avez-vous su que vous vouliez devenir peintre ?

La main en visière, il leva le regard sur elle.

— Très tôt. Depuis toujours, je crois.

— Et quand avez-vous compris que vous gagneriez votre vie grâce à votre art ?

Il sourit.

— Le jour où un amateur a mal lu le prix sur une de mes aquarelles, à l'exposition du foyer des artistes du village, et qu'il a payé sans broncher dix fois le prix d'un paysage, ma foi, très ordinaire.

— Comment décide-t-on de se mettre à peindre ?

C'était la première fois que Katherine le questionnait sur son travail.

— On le sent. C'est indispensable. Et cela constitue aussi un défi.

— J'ai réalisé une peinture, une fois. Une croûte affreuse.

— Vous êtes trop sévère avec vous-même. Ou alors vous vous attendiez à quelque chose de grandiose.

Katherine éclata de rire.

— Non, je vous assure. C'était horrible. Mais je n'ai pas tout perdu. J'ai appris à apprécier ceux qui ont du talent. Comme vous, acheva-t-elle, les yeux étincelants.

— Vous n'avez jamais rien vu de mes œuvres.

— Si ! Dans une galerie de San Francisco, où je me suis d'ailleurs donnée en spectacle. Brandon a failli avoir une attaque quand j'ai commencé à dire à tout le monde que je connaissais l'artiste.

— Et si je vous demandais de poser pour moi ? dit-il aussi tranquillement que s'il s'était agi d'une banalité.

— Parce que je vous intéresse ou parce que vous relevez un nouveau défi ?

— Les deux.

— Je ne sais pas… Poser est tellement narcissique.

— Pas quand c'est moi qui peins.

— Ne me dites pas que vous traversez une période cubiste, comme Picasso.

Un rire échappa à Peter.

— Non, rien d'aussi spectaculaire. Je peins ce que je vois, y compris les comédons.

— Je n'en ai pas… J'ai seulement quelques taches de rousseur.

— Eh bien ?

Il ferma les paupières, afin de dissimuler combien la réponse lui importait.

— Je ne sais pas pourquoi vous voulez peindre quelqu'un comme moi. Mais, si vous êtes sérieux, je suis partante.

Peter rouvrit les yeux.

— Peut-on commencer demain ?

— Sans problème. Paul ne descend pas à Santa Cruz ; il a changé ses horaires à l'épicerie.

— Et Brandon ?

— Il ne vient pas non plus, dit-elle, sans autre explication.

Une incroyable vague de plaisir mêlé de culpabilité inonda Peter à la pensée qu'il aurait Katherine pour lui tout seul jusqu'à la fin de la semaine. S'il achetait le chalet à Julia, il ferait en sorte que les Williams continuent à bénéficier d'un mois de location.

— Ce n'est pas trop difficile? s'enquit-elle. De garder la pose, j'entends.

— Je l'ignore. Je n'ai jamais essayé.

— Et si je bouge?

— Tout sera à refaire.

Elle écarquilla les yeux.

— Oh… Je ne suis pas sûre d'y arriver…

Peter posa la main sur le bras de sa voisine en riant.

— Je plaisante! Je vous promets que vous ne souffrirez pas.

Il n'aurait pas dû la toucher. La brûlure de son bas-ventre irradia dans tout son corps.

— Je vais plonger, annonça-t-il. Vous venez?

Je vous en supplie, dites non! pria-t-il mentalement.

Katherine consulta sa montre.

— Non. Je monte me préparer.

— Alors à plus tard.

D'un pas rigide, Peter se dirigea vers la mer. Sans se donner la peine de s'habituer à la température de l'eau, il fit un plongeon dans la première vague qui déferla. Ensuite, il se mit à nager à contre-courant jusqu'à ce que tous ses membres soient engourdis par le froid. Si seulement son esprit en ébullition pouvait suivre le mouvement!

4

Katherine portait une robe de plage à rayures bleu et jaune, un peu trop grande. Les bretelles glissaient sur ses épaules au moindre mouvement, le décolleté bâillait chaque fois qu'elle se penchait sur son assiette pour piquer une feuille de salade.

Elle surprit Peter en train de l'admirer.

— J'ai perdu du poids sans m'en rendre compte, s'excusa-t-elle. J'espère que mes autres vêtements m'iront mieux.

Elle remonta ses bretelles, redressa les épaules.

— J'ai vécu en jean et en short tout l'été.

— Rien de spécial côté paroisse, je présume ?

Il s'était efforcé de poser une question prudente, voire anodine. Il déplaça sa chaise afin de permettre à son voisin de table d'abriter la sienne du soleil. La brasserie sur Pacific Avenue était noire de monde, mais il l'avait choisie en conséquence. Ici, sa sortie avec Katherine faisait nettement moins « rendez-vous d'amoureux » que dans un des restaurants à l'ambiance feutrée de la ville.

— Je crois bien que c'est la première fois que je mets une robe depuis...

Elle s'interrompit, comme si elle avait perdu le fil de ses pensées. En fait, elle avait eu peur de commettre une gaffe.

— Nous avons battu tous les records de chaleur, cet été, dit-elle finalement.

Peter hocha la tête. Il avait cessé de pratiquer depuis le lycée, mais il lui semblait bizarre que les choses aient évolué au point qu'une épouse de pasteur se promène en jean et en short à Woodland. Il rompit le pain croustillant qui accompagnait sa salade aux fruits de mer et s'appliqua à le beurrer. Au bout d'un moment, il brisa le silence.

— Vous avez bien fait de venir, après tout.

Katherine grimaça un sourire inquiet.

— Pourquoi « après tout » ?

— Je voulais dire seule, sans Brandon et les garçons. Brandon n'avait jamais passé le mois entier à Santa Cruz. Il arrivait le lundi et repartait le vendredi pour préparer son prêche du dimanche. En revanche, les fils Williams restaient avec leur mère au chalet où ils recevaient une ribambelle de copains et de copines.

Katherine pêcha un pépin de tournesol dans sa salade et le lança à un pigeon qui déambulait parmi les tables.

— Je sais que ça ne se fait pas, dit-elle en souriant.

— Mais ?

— J'aime les pigeons. Ce sont des créatures étonnantes. Les derniers survivants urbains se nourrissant de miettes et d'eau renversée…

Peter se cala dans sa chaise.

— Et vous êtes sérieuse !

Une rougeur délicate colora le visage de Katherine.

— Mais pas folle. J'ai de la distance, voyez-vous. C'est du reste la raison pour laquelle je ne parle presque jamais de pigeons.

Au fond de son subconscient, Peter avait formulé l'espoir absurde que mieux connaître Katherine le guérirait de son engouement. Fatalement, le quotidien révélerait des failles, des défauts qu'il n'avait pas remarqués. Elle deviendrait alors une femme comme tant d'autres, et il serait libéré. Hélas ! même au quotidien, Katherine se révélait exceptionnelle.

— Vous n'êtes pas la seule, vous savez. Il existe un tas d'amis des pigeons dans le monde. Des gens dévoués qui vont les nourrir et les abreuver.

Elle sourit.

— Je suis surprise que les adeptes de ces oiseaux extraordinaires n'aient pas encore mis au point des voyages organisés.

— Qu'en savez-vous ?

— Il n'y a pas de cars de tourisme en face de mon appartement.

Tiens donc! Elle vivait dans un appartement! Peter avait pourtant eu l'impression que l'Église de Brandon procurait de meilleurs logements de fonction à ses pasteurs… Il aurait mis sa main au feu qu'il les avait déjà entendus évoquer une maison avec jardin. Il préféra cependant ne pas insister.

— Je me demande où sont partis les pigeons après le tremblement de terre, dit-il, amusé par leur jeu.

— Je me pose la même question, répondit Katherine en jetant un regard circulaire aux tours qui bordaient l'avenue. Ici, on a peine à croire qu'il y a quelques années c'était le chaos.

— Quelle tristesse que d'assister à la destruction de tous les immeubles d'époque!

— Où étiez-vous pendant le dernier tremblement de terre?

C'était une question typiquement californienne, qui donnait à de parfaits étrangers l'illusion d'une expérience commune.

— Je traversais les faubourgs de San Jose en voiture. Je revenais de San Francisco, où j'avais assisté à un de mes vernissages. J'ai écouté pendant cinq heures les bulletins d'information. Aux dires des journalistes, tout avait été rasé dans la région.

— Vous avez mis cinq heures pour parcourir cinquante kilomètres?

— Je m'étais arrêté.

— J'aurais fait la même chose. Y a-t-il eu des dommages chez vous?

— Deux fenêtres brisées, des fissures dans les murs, mais rien de comparable à ce qui s'est passé ici. Toutes les maisons autour de la baie ont été détruites.

— Michael souhaitait s'inscrire à l'université de San Jose, mais je l'ai découragé. Évidemment, je ne lui ai pas donné la véritable raison, sous peine de m'entendre traiter de folle. Il pense qu'un véritable Californien vit avec les tremblements de terre. Alors j'ai triché. Je lui ai suggéré de s'éloigner le plus possible de la maison s'il avait

envie de conquérir son indépendance… Et qu'a-t-il fait ?
Je vous le donne en mille ! Il est parti pour le Kansas, en
plein pays des tornades !

Elle étouffa un petit rire, et Peter lui sourit.

— Est-ce qu'il se plaît à l'université ?

Le visage de Katherine s'éclaira, et la fierté brilla dans
ses yeux, comme toujours lorsqu'elle parlait d'un de ses
fils.

— Au début, il s'est senti un peu perdu. Maintenant, il
adore ses cours. Surtout depuis qu'il a décidé de passer
sa maîtrise.

— Se destine-t-il à l'Église ?

Katherine sirota une gorgée de thé glacé avant de répliquer :

— C'était une idée de Brandon. Dieu merci, Michael a
suffisamment de bon sens pour suivre son propre chemin.

— Ce travail ne lui convient donc pas ?

Elle jeta un autre pépin au pigeon, ce qui suscita un ric-
tus réprobateur au coin de la bouche d'une des clientes
du restaurant.

— Pas plus qu'à moi.

— Ah bon ? Je vous imaginais comme la parfaite candidate à ce poste.

Surprise, elle cligna des paupières.

— Moi ? Et pourquoi ?

Eric devait faire attention à séparer ses sentiments
d'un simple avis amical.

— Vous aimez les gens, vous êtes gentille avec eux…
Vos croyances sont naturelles. Vos paroissiens appren-
draient autant de votre exemple que de vos discours.

— Il y a longtemps que vous n'êtes pas entré dans un
temple, Peter ?

— Très très longtemps, admit-il.

— Ce sont les discours qui plaisent au public. Je n'ai
rien de commun avec une assemblée qui se réunit tous
les dimanches dans le seul but d'écouter de belles paroles.

Si elle avait été prédicatrice, il n'aurait pas manqué l'office un seul dimanche. Il posa ses mains sur ses genoux,
la regarda dans les yeux.

— On y va ?

— Où ça ?

— À la boutique. Il me faut des pinceaux pour attaquer mon chef-d'œuvre.

Elle mit plusieurs secondes à comprendre de quoi il
parlait, puis rougit légèrement.

— Allez-vous aussi utiliser du papier neuf ?

— Oui.

Peter contourna la table mais se ravisa avant de tendre
la main à Katherine. Ne pas toucher ! Pas même par
hasard. Il la désirait avec une telle fougue qu'il n'osait
même pas l'approcher. Il paya l'addition, et ils quittèrent
côte à côte la terrasse de la brasserie.

Dans la rue, elle indiqua une librairie.

— J'y ferais bien un saut, si vous n'êtes pas trop pressé.
Je n'ai plus rien à lire au chalet.

— Allez-y, je vous rejoins. J'ai quelque chose à régler.

Il la trouva dans l'aile concernant la littérature popu-
laire, en train de parcourir la quatrième de couverture
d'un livre de poche. Sitôt qu'il l'aperçut, il se dit qu'il
avait commis une erreur. En la laissant, il s'était préci-
pité chez le fleuriste. Il n'avait pas le droit de lui offrir
des fleurs, et tant pis pour toutes les excuses qu'il avait
imaginées. Il commença à battre en retraite vers la cor-
beille à papier, quand elle leva les yeux.

Refermant le roman, elle le mit sous son coude, avec
un autre récit qu'elle avait choisi.

— Je paie et nous partons.

Il fit semblant de feuilleter un livre d'art pendant
qu'elle se dirigeait vers la caisse. Elle avait vu le bouquet.
Il n'avait plus qu'à le lui donner, en rendant ce présent
le plus anodin possible.

— Je suis en admiration devant les créateurs, dit-elle,
revenant près de lui, et regardant elle aussi le livre d'art.
Dans ma deuxième vie, je serai actrice… non ! Chanteuse.

— Vous croyez à la réincarnation ?

— Pas vraiment… C'est ma façon de me plaindre de
mon manque absolu de talent pour les choses les plus
ordinaires.

— Qu'est-ce que vous racontez ? Vous êtes la femme la
plus extraordinaire que je connaisse.

Croyant qu'il la taquinait, elle ébaucha une révérence.

— Et vous, le plus galant de mes amis.

Était-il possible qu'elle ait une si mauvaise image de sa personne ? Elle qui possédait la capacité de remonter le moral des autres ? Et Brandon ? Ne comprenait-il pas qu'il était l'homme le plus chanceux sur terre ?

Se sentant ridicule avec son bouquet, il le lui tendit.

— Oh ! Elles sont pour moi ?

— Elles vont avec votre robe.

Elle regarda les roses thé, comme si elle s'attendait à les voir disparaître.

— Personne ne m'a jamais offert de fleurs.

— Jamais ?

Elle devait vouloir dire « sans raison particulière ».

— Pas même à l'hôpital, quand j'ai eu mes bébés. Brandon ne croit pas aux démonstrations…

Elle porta le bouquet à son visage pour en humer le parfum.

— Il n'y croit pas du tout. Quand Michael et Paul sont nés, il a demandé aux paroissiens de n'envoyer aucun cadeau, mais seulement des donations aux bonnes œuvres. C'est le genre ni fleurs ni couronnes et il l'a fait savoir à tous dès qu'il est devenu pasteur. Nous avons perdu quelques fleuristes, mais le reste des ouailles a retenu la leçon. Pour Brandon, dépenser de l'argent pour quelque chose d'aussi éphémère, alors qu'on peut avec la même somme nourrir une famille du tiers-monde pendant un mois, confine au péché. On aurait pu penser que les dons à l'assistance publique augmenteraient… mais non.

— Et maintenant, comment vous sentez-vous ?

Elle eut un sourire empreint de plaisir coupable.

— Bien, murmura-t-elle. Très, très heureuse…

C'était si simple.

Il se demanda si Brandon avait une vague idée de ce que lui coûterait peut-être un jour son comportement intraitable.

5

Katherine se regarda dans le miroir de la penderie. Peter lui avait recommandé de s'habiller simplement. Il avait précisé que c'était elle qu'il allait peindre, pas ses vêtements. Elle avait essayé les quatre robes qu'elle avait apportées, mais aucune ne lui allait. Comment avait-elle pu perdre autant de kilos sans même s'en rendre compte ?

Un an plus tôt, Brandon la trouvait trop grosse, empotée et sans attrait.

Elle avait accepté de poser sur une impulsion, sans prêter attention aux conséquences. À présent, y penser l'angoissait terriblement. Peter pourrait juger son portrait inintéressant, invendable. Les modèles étaient supposés être jolis ou, du moins, différents des autres femmes.

Katherine s'estimait ordinaire. À en croire Brandon, elle était même terriblement ennuyeuse. Pour une raison qui lui échappait, Peter ne voyait pas cet aspect de sa personnalité. Probablement parce qu'il ne la connaissait encore pas assez.

En revanche, si le portrait était vendu et que le modèle devenait célèbre… Si cela suscitait le genre de spéculations qui avaient entouré Andrew Wyeth et ses portraits d'Helga ? Eh bien, à la grande satisfaction de Brandon, elle serait incapable d'expliquer un tel succès.

Bon Dieu, elle filait un mauvais coton. La paranoïa la guettait. Avait-elle tellement envie d'un peu d'excitation dans sa vie pour laisser libre cours à une imagination débridée ?

Elle s'assit sur le bord du lit. Quel point commun y avait-il aujourd'hui entre la jeune fille espiègle, invitée à toutes les fêtes, et la femme morose dont les seules amies fréquentaient le temple dont son mari lui avait interdit l'accès ?

Peut-être n'était-elle pas la femme unidimensionnelle que Brandon décrivait. Le sexe avec lui n'avait jamais rien eu à voir avec les étreintes torrides montrées au cinéma ou décrites dans les livres. Chaque fois qu'elle lui avait suggéré de faire l'amour autrement, par exemple ailleurs que dans le lit, ou dans une autre position que celle du missionnaire, elle n'avait récolté que des critiques acerbes. La discussion qui s'ensuivait généralement tuait tout désir en elle. C'était une élève lente. Et elle avait mis longtemps à comprendre que Brandon préférait des rapports sexuels aussi prévisibles et aussi routiniers que sa propre existence.

Du moins l'avait-elle cru.

Si elle avait essayé de découvrir ses véritables besoins, elle n'aurait pas eu à affronter un divorce en rentrant à Woodland. Mais Brandon en avait décidé ainsi. Katherine ne savait plus où elle en était. Elle se sentait aussi abasourdie que si elle avait consulté pour une verrue plantaire et avait appris qu'il ne lui restait pas plus de six mois à vivre.

Elle jeta un coup d'œil à la petite pendule près du lit. Elle avait cinq minutes pour se changer et se rendre à l'atelier de Peter.

Peter savait très exactement comment il allait la peindre. Des années durant, il l'avait représentée dans des croquis qu'il dessinait de mémoire, le plus souvent dans un décor marin. Trois de ces dessins avaient figuré dans des expositions, dans un cadre orné d'une pastille rouge, comme s'ils étaient déjà vendus.

Il avait espéré que ces exercices auraient un effet libérateur et qu'à force de peindre et de repeindre le même sujet, il parviendrait à chasser le modèle de ses pensées. Or, cela ne s'était jamais produit.

Toutes ces années avaient cependant abouti à une résignation qui l'avait apaisé. Il l'aimait. Il l'aimerait jusqu'à la fin de ses jours. Le soleil se lèverait chaque matin, la marée couvrirait la plage et se retirerait, le brouillard tomberait et se dissiperait, et il aimerait toujours Katherine. C'était simple, indiscutable, absolu.

Elle arriva dans une robe bleu céruléen au col arrondi et aux manches courtes, ajustée sous les seins, tombant sur les chevilles. Les bras écartés, elle esquissa un tour sur elle-même.

— Est-ce que cela vous convient ?

— C'est parfait, dit-il, le cœur battant.

— J'ai une faveur à vous demander.

— Tout ce que vous voulez.

— Ne dites pas aux garçons que j'ai posé pour vous. Ils risquent d'être choqués.

— Et Brandon ?

— Je ne… crois pas que le sujet se présentera, répondit-elle après une hésitation.

— Mais s'il se présente ?

— Alors je lui dirai la vérité.

Forcément ! Qu'est-ce qu'il s'imaginait ? Qu'elle allait mentir à son mari ?

— Serait-il fâché de savoir que vous avez posé pour moi ?

Elle enfouit les mains dans les poches de sa robe.

— Ne vous en faites pas, Peter. Brandon ne viendra pas de tout l'été.

Quel sombre crétin ! Il semblait inconcevable à Peter que l'on puisse délaisser pendant un mois entier une épouse comme Katherine.

— Avant de commencer, voulez-vous boire quelque chose ?

— Un verre d'eau. Mais je peux aller le chercher.

Elle pointa un doigt vers l'autre bout de la pièce.

— La cuisine est par là, si je me souviens bien ?

— Je vais vous l'apporter.

— Non, je vous en prie. Je n'aime pas être servie.

Il lui jeta un regard interrogateur auquel elle répondit par un haussement d'épaules, l'air de dire qu'elle n'en savait pas plus.

— Et vous ? Vous ne voulez rien ? proposa-t-elle.

— Non merci. Je viens de prendre une tasse de café.

Elle s'en alla à petits pas rapides, et Peter se fit la réflexion qu'elle avait l'air d'avoir toujours vécu là. Après quoi, il se traita d'idiot. Aimer Katherine avait été un accident. Imaginer des choses inexistantes et qui n'arriveraient jamais semblait aussi insensé que nager les chevilles entravées de poids.

Elle revint avec un verre d'eau.

— Où voulez-vous que je me mette ?

— Sur le parapet de la fenêtre. Nous essaierons plusieurs poses. De profil en regardant la mer, de face, peut-être les yeux fixés sur un interlocuteur invisible.

Elle s'assit sur le coussin et ramena une jambe sous elle.

— Pas mal, approuva-t-il. Oui, c'est très naturel.

Tournée vers la fenêtre, elle laissa son regard errer en contrebas sur les vagues bouillonnantes.

Le soleil éclairait le bas de sa robe. L'ombre et la lumière créeraient différents contrastes suivant les heures de l'après-midi, offrant ainsi à Peter des perspectives changeantes. Il devait dessiner vite pour capter celle qu'il choisirait. Plus tard, il reprendrait les croquis, mais pour le moment seule importait la lumière, la façon dont elle bougerait sur le corps de Katherine, puis illuminerait ses cheveux et donnerait de la texture à sa peau.

Les aquarelles de Peter étaient aussi travaillées que des huiles. Ses mélanges audacieux de peinture à l'eau, de cire, de vernis, d'acrylique ou de gouache avaient choqué les puristes à ses débuts. Mais il ne peignait pas pour plaire aux critiques. Il peignait pour lui-même.

Il commençait toujours par un ou plusieurs croquis et n'utilisait jamais les photos, qui figent le mouvement. Souvent, derrière ses dessins, il griffonnait des notes, afin de mieux se rappeler un détail. Aujourd'hui, il n'en aurait pas besoin.

Katherine se tourna vers lui.

— Oh ! Pardon ! Vous avez déjà commencé.

Elle reprit sa pose initiale.

— Je voulais juste vous parler de l'oiseau sur votre haie.

— Eh bien ?

Elle répondit en s'efforçant de ne pas remuer les lèvres.

— Ça peut attendre.

Il sourit.

— Mettez la main sur votre genou.

Elle s'exécuta.

— Comme ça ?

— La paume vers le haut. Là.

Il étudia l'effet un instant.

— Ne bougez pas. Je reviens.

Il sortit, cueillit une capucine orange, revint en courant et la posa dans la main de son modèle.

— Dorénavant, vous ne poserez pas sans une fleur.

Elle changea d'expression. Ses yeux devinrent songeurs, son regard brumeux ; son esprit voyageait dans un univers qu'elle seule connaissait.

Deux heures s'écoulèrent avant que la lumière vire au jaune. Il fallait attendre l'ambre et l'ocre fluides du crépuscule pour atteindre l'étape suivante.

— On fait une pause ? proposa-t-il.

Katherine s'étira comme un chat trop longtemps endormi devant le feu de cheminée.

— C'était moins dur que je ne le pensais.

— J'en suis ravi. Seriez-vous partante pour une autre séance, ce soir ?

Il posa le dernier dessin sur les croquis précédents, en prenant soin de le retourner. Katherine prit le verre d'eau auquel elle n'avait pas encore touché.

— Que voulez-vous faire maintenant ?

— Des dessins ?

— Non, de vous. Avez-vous faim ? Je prépare un en-cas ?

Elle endossait le rôle auquel elle avait été reléguée toute sa vie, celui de la mère nourricière.

— Je vais m'en occuper, déclara-t-il.

— Oh, non. Détendez-vous. Vous faites tout le travail.

Sans réfléchir davantage, il la prit par la main et la guida vers la cuisine où il la fit asseoir à table. Il ouvrit le réfrigérateur et sortit du gouda, ainsi que deux grappes de raisin. Avec n'importe quelle autre femme, ce geste aurait été tout naturel. Avec Katherine, il revêtait une importance capitale. Il s'était promis de ne jamais la toucher et la seule sensation de sa paume contre la sienne l'avait enflammé. S'il avait osé, il aurait pressé ses lèvres contre sa ligne de vie doucement incurvée où le destin, trop cruel, ne l'avait pas inclus.

Il sortit du tiroir une planche de bois et se mit à découper le fromage en tranches.

— Parlez-moi de cet oiseau.

— Il était tout petit, à peine plus grand qu'un pinson, avec une tête rouge et un corps jaune.

— Les ailes et la queue noires ?

— Je n'ai pas vu la queue, mais les ailes étaient noires, oui.

— C'est peut-être un tangara, mais je ne suis pas expert. Si vous voulez en savoir plus, j'ai un ouvrage sur les oiseaux dans ma bibliothèque : sur l'étagère du bas, à gauche.

Elle se leva mais, au lieu de sortir, prit les grappes de raisin et les rinça soigneusement sous le robinet.

— Excusez-moi. Comme je vous l'ai dit, je n'aime pas être servie.

— Voulez-vous un verre de vin ? demanda-t-il.

— Je préférerais de la bière, si vous en avez.

Il fit mine de se diriger vers le réfrigérateur, puis se ravisa.

— Elles sont là-dedans. Et il y a des verres dans le freezer.

— Très bien, Peter, dit-elle en lui tapotant le bras.

— J'en prendrai une aussi.

Elle sourit.

— Encore mieux.

— Et pendant que vous y êtes, le linge sale se trouve dans la buanderie.

Un rire échappa à Katherine.

— Ne poussez pas !

Elle avait un rire mélodieux, spontané, qu'on avait envie d'entendre de nouveau.

— Vous avez toujours vécu seul ? demanda-t-elle, tandis qu'elle servait la bière dans les verres givrés.

Avant qu'il n'ait saisi le sens de la question, elle reprit :

— Excusez mon indiscrétion. Ce n'est pas mon affaire… Mais comme je ne vous ai jamais vu avec personne… Vous êtes un être exceptionnel, Peter, c'est dommage que vous n'ayez pas quelqu'un pour partager votre vie.

— Je suppose que je n'ai pas encore rencontré la bonne personne, répliqua-t-il prudemment.

Elle posa les grappes sur une serviette propre.

— Il n'y a donc jamais eu…

Elle s'interrompit, réfléchissant pour trouver le terme adéquat.

— … d'alter ego ?

La première réaction de Peter fut de mettre cette phrase incongrue sur le compte de la pudeur de Katherine. Soudain, le sens de ses paroles lui apparut dans toute sa clarté.

Elle le croyait homosexuel !

6

Peter respira profondément. Comme si les nuages s'étaient écartés, il comprit brusquement pourquoi Katherine l'avait si bien accepté dans sa vie, pourquoi elle semblait si à l'aise en sa présence, et pourquoi, en ce moment même, elle était là, chez lui. Ce n'était pas la naïveté qui l'incitait à penser que l'amitié pure était possible entre un homme et une femme. Elle lui vouait une confiance absolue pour la bonne raison qu'elle le croyait incapable de s'intéresser à elle autrement que d'une façon platonique.

La bonne blague !

Mais à qui la faute ?

S'il lui avouait la vérité, partirait-elle en courant ? Mettrait-elle fin à leur amitié ? Pouvait-il prendre le risque de la perdre totalement ?

— J'étais marié autrefois, dit-il, optant pour la franchise. Pendant cinq ans. Ma femme voulait des enfants et un mari susceptible d'apporter la stabilité financière à une famille. À cette époque, je ne vivais pas de ma peinture. Je faisais des petits boulots la nuit, et je peignais le jour. Nous nous voyions les week-ends et encore, pas toujours. Alors ce qui devait arriver arriva... Depuis, j'ai eu quelques liaisons, poursuivit-il, soudain bavard. La dernière a duré plus longtemps que les autres. Il s'agissait d'une jeune femme de San Francisco trop snob pour s'enfermer ici, avec les «ploucs», comme elle disait. Nous sommes restés amis. Je la vois encore, quand je suis de passage en ville.

— Vous ne vous sentez jamais seul ?

Elle avait posé cette question comme si elle se sentait concernée.

— Autrefois, si. J'ai réalisé ensuite que, suivant le vieil adage, mieux vaut être seul que mal accompagné.

Elle tressaillit.

— J'aurais détesté que l'on me dise une chose pareille.

— Mais c'est impossible, Katherine. Vous êtes…

Il dérapait !

— Vous et Brandon êtes faits l'un pour l'autre. Cela se voit comme le nez au milieu de la figure.

— On me l'a déjà dit…

Elle but une longue gorgée de bière glacée.

— Je meurs de soif, soupira-t-elle.

Il sortit une boîte de crackers du placard, les posa dans un plat, puis ajouta le raisin et le fromage.

— Voulez-vous que nous nous installions dans le jardin ?

Elle se dandina d'un pied sur l'autre.

— Je vais rentrer, ça vaut mieux. Vous avez mille choses à faire… Je ne voudrais pas vous déranger.

Peter posa le plat sur la table et fourra les poings dans ses poches pour s'empêcher d'attirer Katherine contre lui. Il avait joué et il avait perdu. Sachant maintenant qu'il n'était pas homosexuel, elle ne se sentait plus en sécurité. Une femme de pasteur ne passe pas ses vacances en compagnie d'un autre homme, si innocentes que soient ses relations avec lui.

— Je n'ai rien à faire. Et vous ne me dérangez pas.

Elle mit son verre vide dans l'évier.

— Vous trouverez bien quelque chose.

La frustration assaillit Peter sous la forme d'une boule au fond de la gorge.

— Reviendrez-vous plus tard, afin que je termine les dessins ?

— Oui, bien sûr. À quelle heure ?

— Un peu après six heures ?

— Entendu. Merci pour la bière.

— De rien.

Il la suivit jusqu'à la porte de devant, puis la regarda longer le chemin qui sinuait dans le sous-bois en direction du chalet. Quelque chose s'était brisé entre eux. Mais il osait espérer qu'elle l'accepterait tel qu'il était.

Katherine sortit la clé de sa poche, la glissa dans la serrure et exécuta plusieurs manœuvres infructueuses avant de débloquer le mécanisme. Elle poussa le battant, puis entra en trombe dans le vestibule.

Quelle idiote !

Comment oserait-elle retourner là-bas et regarder Peter en face ? Elle allait devoir s'inventer une maladie diplomatique, oh, rien de sérieux, juste des maux d'estomac ou une migraine…

Désespérée, elle s'affala sur le canapé. Qu'allait-il penser d'elle ? Il devait mal la juger, vu la facilité avec laquelle elle acceptait ses invitations… sans parler de cette séance de pose ! Encore heureux qu'elle ne lui ait pas annoncé la fin de son union avec Brandon.

Le visage enfoui dans les mains, elle soupira. Le pire, c'était qu'elle prenait plaisir à fréquenter Peter. Or, elle ne pouvait pas se permettre ce genre de libertés. Elle était mariée, du moins encore pendant un certain temps. Elle devait préserver les convenances, sauver les apparences. Brandon aurait été ulcéré d'apprendre que l'on avait vu son épouse en compagnie d'un autre homme.

Elle était d'un pathétique ! On eût dit un chien abandonné sous la pluie, qui attend en vain qu'une âme charitable lui ouvre la porte. Par chance, le téléphone sonna avant qu'elle ne sombre complètement dans des abîmes d'autocritique.

La voix de Michael retentit dans l'écouteur.

— Salut, maman. Ça boume ?

— Super. Un temps magnifique ! Viens donc passer quelques jours avant ton départ pour l'université.

S'il te plaît ! pria-t-elle silencieusement. Elle avait besoin de distractions.

— En fait, je t'appelle pour ça. Je ne descendrai plus à Santa Cruz cet été. Le garçon avec qui je devais partager une chambre sur le campus s'est désisté. Il faut que je cherche un autre colocataire.

Katherine déglutit.

— Quand pars-tu ?

— Demain.

— Si vite ? Mais tu as encore…

Elle respira profondément, compta jusqu'à cinq.

— À quelle heure ? demanda-t-elle finalement.

— Six heures et demie du matin. Je n'ai pas trouvé d'autre vol.

— Depuis quand le sais-tu ?

— Depuis deux jours.

— Dommage que tu ne m'aies pas appelée plus tôt. J'ai promis à Peter de l'aider à faire des rangements ce soir. Je n'aurai pas fini avant neuf heures, peut-être plus tard.

— Ne t'inquiète pas. Papa m'emmènera à l'aéroport.

— Je… je voudrais te voir avant ton départ.

— Voyons, maman ! On s'est dit au revoir la semaine dernière. On ne va pas recommencer !

— Tu n'es pas déçu que je ne sois pas là ?

— Non, au contraire. Je déteste les adieux dans un aéroport. De toute façon, je ne m'en vais pas pour long-temps. Je reviens pour Thanksgiving.

Michael lui servait de la logique là où elle aurait sou-haité un peu d'émotion. Eh bien, pourquoi tendait-elle l'autre joue chaque fois qu'on la frappait, si c'était pour se plaindre ensuite ?

— Je t'aime, murmura-t-elle.

— Je t'aime aussi, maman.

— Tiens-moi au courant de ton installation.

— Promis.

Elle raccrocha avec la sensation désagréable que sa vie se désagrégeait. Les liens qui maintenaient Michael attaché à sa famille cédaient l'un après l'autre. Mais comment pouvait-il en être autrement ? La famille elle-même avait explosé.

Elle avait commis l'erreur de venir seule au chalet cette année. Et ce qui avait commencé comme un besoin de solitude, comme la nécessité d'un temps de réflexion, se terminait comme un rejet, un véritable abandon. Si son fils l'avait un tant soit peu encouragée, elle se serait précipitée à l'aéroport, même si elle avait dû conduire toute la nuit. Il ne l'avait pas fait. Il n'avait pas laissé transparaître le moindre désir.

En regardant la pendule murale, Katherine se demanda si Peter accepterait qu'elle arrive plus tôt. Elle avait besoin d'une présence. De sa présence, plus précisément. Peter était son ami, un ami précieux, surtout en ces moments difficiles.

De nouveau, elle se félicita de ne pas lui avoir appris que Brandon et elle étaient séparés.

7

À mesure qu'il s'approchait de la villa, il tardait à Eric de revoir Julia. À New York, un tourbillon d'occupations l'avait empêché de trop penser à elle. Pourtant, en pleine réunion, l'image de la jeune femme avait jailli dans son esprit. Il avait hâte de lui raconter son séjour, d'avoir son avis sur la décision à prendre. Une sensation d'autant plus remarquable que l'absence de communication avait miné ses rapports avec Shelly.

Mais il avait changé. Secret hier, il appréciait à présent le bonheur d'une véritable intimité. Il ne s'était jamais ouvert à Shelly, n'avait jamais discuté avec elle des tracas ou des petites joies qui tissaient sa journée. Il ne l'avait d'ailleurs pas non plus écoutée lorsqu'elle avait essayé de se confier. Ils avaient commencé leur union comme deux amis et l'avaient terminée comme deux étrangers.

Aujourd'hui, il éprouvait le besoin de se raconter. De s'épancher. De décrire à Julia son voyage, ses nouvelles expériences ; le vertige du succès, de l'argent. L'éditeur qui avait acheté son roman lui offrait un pont d'or : une avance sur ses droits d'auteur supérieure d'un quart de million à celle faite à n'importe quel écrivain débutant. Il lui garantissait aussi que les médias, les télévisions et la presse écrite, s'empareraient du roman dès sa parution. Une publicité dont le prix était beaucoup plus élevé que l'acompte.

La certitude de l'éditeur et de son agent à propos de la réussite du livre effrayait Eric. Selon eux, l'intrigue et le style étaient suffisamment accrocheurs pour séduire le plus récalcitrant des critiques. Eric savait pourtant ce qu'il advenait des romans populaires soumis au jugement des gens de métier. Son ouvrage serait décortiqué, passé au crible et lu à la loupe de manière à ce que le plus infime défaut soit révélé et grossi.

Après tout, mieux valait songer aux lecteurs qui voudraient bien sortir vingt-cinq dollars de leur poche pour acheter le livre. C'était beaucoup d'argent comparé à un litre de lait ou à une baguette de pain… Et pas tant que ça, vu le prix d'une place de cinéma.

Le doute constituait également pour Eric une expérience nouvelle. Une fois le livre remis à l'éditeur, il ne lui appartiendrait plus. Se jeter à l'eau pour un plongeon de haut vol et finir sur le ventre arrivait si fréquemment !

Il n'était même pas sûr qu'il serait capable d'écrire un autre livre…

Il s'engagea dans l'allée et s'arrêta devant le portail où il écrasa le bouton de l'interphone. Il avait d'abord songé à tuer le temps en attendant que le soir tombe, mais il était trop pressé de revoir Julia. Il ressentait une sorte de faim inassouvie, une soif dévorante. Pourvu qu'elle ne soit pas retenue en ville, priait-il tandis qu'il sonnait pour la seconde fois.

Soudain, elle répondit :

— C'est moi, Eric. Je viens chercher Josi.

— J'avais le pressentiment que tu arriverais aujourd'hui. Je t'attends à la porte.

Les grilles s'ouvrirent dans un bourdonnement. Eric redémarra. Était-elle restée volontairement chez elle ? L'attendait-elle ? Cette pensée lui coupa le souffle tout en le réchauffant.

Il l'aperçut juste après le dernier tournant. Elle portait une chemise blanche dont elle avait roulé les manches sur ses coudes et un jean délavé, qui la moulait comme une seconde peau. Elle tenait Josi dans ses bras.

De toutes les belles femmes qu'il avait vue à New York, aucune ne pouvait se comparer à Julia.

La jeune femme s'avança au-devant du pick-up, le visage éclairé d'un sourire.

— Comment ça s'est passé ? Je meurs d'impatience. Pourquoi ne m'as-tu pas appelée ?

Simple curiosité ? Intérêt sincère ? Du moment qu'elle posait la question, il s'estimait satisfait. Il coupa le moteur, puis sortit de sa voiture.

— Désolé. J'ignorais que tu te faisais du souci.

Le sourire de Julia s'effaça, tout comme l'étincelle dans ses prunelles.

— Pourquoi pas ? Nous sommes amis, non ?

Il gratta Josi sous le menton ; la chatte renversa la tête en ronronnant, les yeux mi-clos.

— Tout s'est bien passé, dit-il. Mieux que bien. Le livre est vendu.

— Oh… mais c'est fantastique. Félicitations.

— Merci. Il ne reste plus qu'à finir le morceau.

— Combien de temps cela te prendra-t-il ?

— Trois, quatre mois…

La chatte sauta dans ses bras et s'accrocha à son épaule. Son ronronnement monta, si puissant, qu'il crut devenir sourd d'une oreille.

— Ça s'arrose ! s'écria Julia, les mains dans ses poches, en se balançant sur ses talons. Allons au restaurant ! Oh, non, j'ai une meilleure idée. Restons ici. Je vais préparer à dîner. Aimes-tu le saumon ? Poursuivit-elle sans lui donner une chance de répondre. J'ai une recette extra. Quand tu l'auras goûtée, tu ne pourras plus le manger autrement. Ken disait à ce propos…

Elle s'interrompit, avant de reprendre presque aussitôt :

— Sinon, je réussis fort bien le rôti de porc.

— Que disait donc Ken, Julia ?

Elle fixa le bout de ses souliers.

— Ça n'a pas d'importance.

Naturellement ! Ce qui importait surtout, c'était qu'elle n'arrivait pas à aligner trois phrases sans mentionner son défunt mari.

— Nous célébrerons mon succès une autre fois, répliqua finalement Eric. Je suis resté absent trop longtemps. J'ai envie de rentrer au cottage pour voir s'il n'y a pas de problème.

— Quelle sorte de problème ?

Il la regarda, interloqué. Il ne s'attendait pas à ce qu'elle essaie de le retenir.

— Je ne sais pas… Les problèmes habituels.

— Quelque chose qui ne peut pas attendre ?

— Non.

— Alors il n'y a aucune raison pour que tu ne puisses pas dîner avec moi ce soir.

Il sourit.

— Non. Aucune.

— Parfait. Alors saumon ou rôti de porc ?

— Saumon.

Elle sourit à son tour.

— Je parie que tu aurais préféré le rôti.

Il se demanda comment elle réagirait s'il lui disait ce qu'il aurait vraiment préféré. Un souvenir jaillit : Julia, haletante, se tordant sous lui.

— Cela m'est égal, Julia. Même si nous ne mangeons rien. Être avec toi ce soir me suffit.

Elle choisit de le prendre à la légère.

— Oh là là ! Si tu écris comme tu parles, je comprends que tout le monde saute sur ton livre.

Josi se raidit, prête à bondir. Afin d'éviter de lui courir après comme au chalet, il l'immobilisa sous son bras. La chatte se débattit de plus belle. Il aperçut alors un écureuil qui traversait la cour. De nouveau, Josi contracta tous ses muscles.

— Je ferais mieux de rentrer le fauve, dit-il.

— As-tu peur pour l'écureuil ?

— J'ai un doute.

Il couvrit de sa main les yeux de la chatte, qui lança un feulement indigné.

— Eh bien, dans le doute abstiens-toi, répondit Julia en lui faisant signe de la suivre à l'intérieur de la villa.

Dès qu'ils furent dans la maison, Eric posa Josi. La chatte se mit à se rouler à ses pieds de façon très câline, en poussant de petits miaulements.

— Elle essaie de me dire quelque chose.

— Elle veut prendre sa revanche, remarqua Julia en riant. Toute la semaine dernière, les écureuils se sont payé sa tête. Il suffisait que la pauvre bête soit derrière la baie pour qu'ils organisent une surprise-partie sur la terrasse. Ils ont failli la rendre folle.

— Comment le sais-tu ? Tu n'étais pas à ton bureau ?

— J'ai décidé d'arrêter… un peu, murmura-t-elle d'un ton mystérieux. Moi aussi je fais mes expériences. Qu'est-ce que je te sers à boire ?

Eric aurait aimé un alcool fort. Du whisky de préférence, mais il devait conduire cette nuit-là.

— Un jus de tomate, si tu en as.

— Un bloody mary ?

— Non, un jus de tomate sans vodka.

— Installe-toi. Je reviens tout de suite.

Elle quitta le vestibule et, aussitôt, cessant ses simagrées, Josi la suivit en courant, la queue droite comme un *i*. Eric avança vers le salon. Il n'avait pas encore visité la villa mais le luxe ambiant ne l'étonna pas. Le salon, moins ostentatoire qu'il ne l'avait supposé, déployait des fastes que seuls les millionnaires peuvent s'offrir. La pièce, immense, était agrémentée de tableaux savamment éclairés. Les étagères ne contenaient pas de livres, mais des objets en bronze, en argent, en porcelaine.

Un cadre au-dessus de la cheminée attira l'attention d'Eric. Il traversa la pièce pour contempler les personnages : un homme et une femme immortalisés dans une tendre étreinte.

C'était donc lui, Ken Huntington. Séduisant, souriant, visiblement sous le charme de la femme qu'il tenait dans ses bras. Ken et Julia. Le couple parfait. L'artiste avait su capter un instant magique entre deux êtres profondément amoureux.

Eric étudia la peinture de plus près. Ken, appuyé au tronc d'un aulne, entourait Julia de son bras. Elle l'enlaçait par la taille, la tête posée sur son épaule, et lui se penchait de manière que sa joue touche les cheveux de sa femme. Ils étaient simplement vêtus, comme s'ils revenaient d'une promenade en forêt.

— C'est un cadeau de Peter pour nos huit ans de mariage, déclara Julia en entrant dans la pièce avec un plateau. Quel artiste extraordinaire !

— En effet.

Elle lui tendit son jus de tomate.

— Son atelier mérite le détour. Il te montrera ses œuvres. Je lui ai toujours dit que je fouillerais volontiers dans sa poubelle.

— Et qu'a-t-il répondu ?

— Qu'il brûlait tous les essais ratés.

— Dommage !

— Oui, vraiment.

Elle leva son verre.

— Au succès de ton livre. Que tout soit accompli selon tes désirs.

— Que les lecteurs en aient pour leur argent.

Julia but une gorgée, puis passa sa langue sur ses lèvres.

— Je serai la première à me ruer chez mon libraire. Et je dirai à toutes mes relations d'en faire autant.

Eric hocha la tête. Comment avait-il pu croire qu'il attendrait des mois, voire un an, afin de laisser à Julia le temps de réfléchir ? Il n'y arriverait jamais. Il avait hâte de faire partie de sa vie. Il posa son verre sur le manteau de cheminée, lui prit le sien, le posa à côté.

— Je vais m'en aller, Julia, avant que je dise quelque chose que tu n'es pas prête à entendre.

Il lui toucha la joue puis, lentement, nicha sa main au creux de sa nuque. L'attirant vers lui, il l'embrassa. Les lèvres de la jeune femme étaient incroyablement douces et chaudes. Eric ferma les yeux, s'autorisant pendant une seconde à rêver qu'il n'y avait plus d'obstacle entre eux. Plus de barrière à franchir, plus de fantômes à combattre. Seulement un avenir commun à explorer. Toute l'excitation de la dernière semaine n'était plus qu'une goutte dans l'océan, comparée à cet instant.

Un petit gémissement roula dans la gorge de Julia. Elle répondit à son baiser. Il sentait naître en elle un désir brûlant. Pourtant, elle mit la main contre la poitrine d'Eric pour le repousser gentiment.

Une expression de confusion se peignit sur son visage.

— Excuse-moi, murmura-t-elle.

Elle montra le tableau au-dessus de la cheminée.

— Je ne peux pas… devant lui.

— Je m'en doute.

Il se dirigea vers la baie vitrée et prit Josi sous son bras. Avant de partir, il regarda Julia une dernière fois.

— Tu sais où me trouver, dit-il. La balle est dans ton camp.

Julia dîna seule. Elle prépara le repas avec la même minutie que si Eric était resté. Saumon aux épices. Elle mit une bouteille de chardonnay dans un seau à glace, alluma les chandelles… Elle resta longtemps à table, sans pouvoir avaler une bouchée, puis rangea le tout dans le réfrigérateur pour le déjeuner de Connie, le lendemain.

Elle s'efforça ensuite de chasser Eric de ses pensées en se plongeant dans l'étude d'un rapport sur le marché étranger. Ken avait toujours déclaré qu'il ne comptait pas donner suite et, pourtant, il avait dépensé une petite fortune pour envoyer son équipe de chercheurs dans différents pays. Pour quelle raison? La question hantait Julia depuis qu'elle avait emménagé dans le bureau de son mari.

Cent fois par jour, elle s'efforçait de deviner ce qu'il avait eu en tête en signant tel contrat et pas tel autre. Et malgré l'aide de chacun, elle ne découvrait pas toujours la vérité. Ken était un dieu, et elle était à jamais emprisonnée dans le rôle de sa prêtresse.

Elle se coucha mais ne put fermer l'œil. Deux heures plus tard, lasse de se retourner dans le grand lit, elle se leva et déambula dans le salon. Ses pas la guidèrent devant la cheminée, où elle contempla Ken sur le tableau. Les yeux clos, elle rechercha dans sa mémoire la sensation de ses bras autour de son corps; mais ce fut Eric qui lui vint à l'esprit. Des larmes jaillirent de ses yeux, tandis qu'elle fixait le tableau.

— J'ai essayé, Ken, et une fois de plus, je te laisse tomber. Pardonne-moi, je t'en supplie.

On la secouait, on la remontait de quelque part où elle voulait rester. Elle lutta pour se dégager mais la voix devint plus insistante.

— Madame Huntington! Il est l'heure de vous lever.

Julia ouvrit les yeux.

— Connie? Vous êtes déjà rentrée?

— Il est huit heures et demie, madame.

Julia releva la tête. Elle s'était endormie sur le canapé. Son regard capta la pendule sur la cheminée, et son cœur fit un bond.

— Oh! J'ai une réunion de travail dans cinq minutes.

— Voulez-vous que je prévienne votre bureau que vous serez en retard?

— Non, non. Je me débrouillerai.

Encore ensommeillée, elle se dirigea vers le couloir.

— Il y a autre chose, madame Huntington, dit Connie d'une voix contrite. Josi a disparu.

— Rassurez-vous. Eric est passé la chercher hier soir.

Au lieu de se montrer soulagée, Connie parut déçue.

— J'espérais qu'il allait l'oublier.

— J'ignorais que vous aimiez les chats.

— Ce n'est pas ça. Mais il fallait voir comme elle vous faisait sourire, cette bête.

Connie tapota les coussins du canapé avant de reprendre :

— Pourquoi ne prendriez-vous pas un chat?

Julia se figea un instant. Était-ce ainsi que Connie la voyait finir ses jours? Comme une mémère à chats?

— Je vais y songer, dit-elle.

De sa chambre, elle téléphona au bureau avant de mettre le cap sur la salle de bains attenante. En contournant le lit, elle aperçut du coin de l'œil le monogramme sur la poche de poitrine de son pyjama. Le H stylisé donnait au vêtement l'apparence d'un étendard.

Pat Faith lui emboîta le pas en direction du bureau directorial.

— J'ai remis tous vos rendez-vous, à l'exception de celui avec Adam Boehm, que j'ai dû annuler. Il vous recontactera.

— Et David ? A-t-il rendu les calques ?

— Ce matin, à huit heures.

— Bien.

Julia s'assit à son bureau, saisit le téléphone, puis le remit en place avant de rappeler sa secrétaire.

— Pat ? Avez-vous une minute ?

— Bien sûr, dit la jeune femme en revenant sur ses pas.

Julia lui indiqua le fauteuil devant le grand bureau d'acajou.

— Puis-je vous poser une question personnelle ?

— Oui ?

Sans réfléchir à la faute qu'elle pouvait commettre en s'ouvrant à une employée qu'elle ne connaissait que dans le cadre de l'entreprise, Julia poursuivit :

— Comment vous sentez-vous sans Howard ?

Pat se tassa dans le fauteuil. Son mari était décédé un mois avant Ken. Or, bien qu'elles aient vécu ce drame commun, les deux femmes ne l'avaient jamais évoqué.

— Je pense que cela est moins difficile pour moi que pour vous, admit finalement la secrétaire. Howard était la meilleure chose qui me soit arrivée mais c'était un homme ordinaire pour le reste du monde. Alors que, pour tous ici, Ken est assis à la droite de Dieu le père.

Julia eut la sensation de recevoir un cadeau inestimable. Elle avait enfin trouvé quelqu'un à qui parler, une personne qui pouvait la comprendre.

8

Planté devant la fenêtre de la cuisine, Peter se servit une tasse de café. Les stores de Katherine demeuraient obstinément baissés. Il consulta sa montre. Huit heures moins dix… Elle devait pourtant être réveillée.

Le ciel, resté clair toute la nuit, avait encouragé Peter à mettre son réveil aux aurores. Si le brouillard ne tombait pas, il bénéficierait de la lumière idéale pour achever la peinture commencée la veille.

Il avait longuement étudié ses croquis, jetant son dévolu sur celui où Katherine, assise sur le parapet de chêne, regardait l'océan. Son expression, l'attitude de son corps recelaient une intensité rarement atteinte dans un simple dessin. On eût dit qu'elle contemplait un monde invisible aux autres, un monde qui la fascinait et l'effrayait à la fois.

Au début, il n'avait pas saisi le sens de ce langage secret. Il s'y était repris à trois fois, rassemblant les indices, avant de découvrir l'émotion qu'elle essayait si soigneusement de dissimuler. Une émotion qui, cependant, ne révélait pas la cause profonde qui l'avait générée.

Katherine apercevrait-elle ce détail de sa personnalité lorsqu'elle verrait le portrait terminé? Penserait-elle qu'il avait délibérément violé son intimité?

Leur amitié s'égarait déjà sur un terrain glissant. Leur relation, si facile au départ, avait reçu un coup presque fatal. Il regrettait un peu de ne pas l'avoir laissée croire qu'il était homosexuel.

Un espoir insensé guidait Peter. Une faille de sa personnalité l'incitait à aduler, au fil des ans, une femme qui jamais ne lui retournerait son amour. Un jour, peut-être, parviendrait-il à la conclusion tardive qu'il avait gâché les plus belles années de son existence.

S'il existait un remède contre l'amour, il n'aurait pas hésité à le prendre. Ce n'était pas faute d'avoir essayé de se libérer de l'envoûtement qu'elle exerçait sur lui. Mais toutes ses tentatives avaient échoué. L'amour non partagé constituait un sujet très romantique pour un poème ou une chanson. Dans la vie, c'était autre chose. On pouvait appeler cela de la folie douce ou, plus crûment, de l'obsession.

Il versa le reste du café dans sa tasse, avant de revenir lentement dans l'atelier. Le portrait inachevé de Katherine était posé sur le chevalet. Eh bien, folie ou pas, il l'aimerait à jamais. Essayer de changer ses sentiments paraissait aussi vain que s'acharner à changer les saisons.

Katherine saisit la serviette éponge qu'elle avait laissée sur un rocher et la passa autour de ses épaules. L'eau glacée l'avait frigorifiée et revigorée en même temps. Elle avait nagé contre les vagues avant de se laisser dériver vers la plage et, maintenant, elle se sentait merveilleusement vivante. Elle avait brisé les règles qu'elle avait inculquées à ses enfants : non seulement elle avait plongé dans l'océan après avoir mangé mais elle y était en plus allée toute seule.

Elle frissonna ; elle avait la chair de poule et ses lèvres avaient bleui. Elle claquait des dents. Mais elle ne regrettait pas son audace. Aujourd'hui, elle avait admiré un magnifique lever de soleil, un ciel d'or pur. Au creux d'une vague, elle était tombée nez à nez avec une otarie qui, l'ayant prise pour une autre créature marine, l'avait regardée tranquillement avant de s'éloigner.

Faire quelque chose seule constituait une expérience en soi. Elle n'était jamais allée au restaurant ou au cinéma sans escorte. Toute sa vie, elle avait été dépendante. Il était impensable pour elle de se promener en ville sans son mari ou ses enfants. Maintenant que Brandon avait brutalement rompu le cordon ombilical, elle se découvrait une facette dont elle ignorait l'existence.

Elle s'émerveillait des choses les plus simples. Le fait que la terre ne s'arrêtait pas de tourner si le dîner ne se trouvait pas sur la table à six heures et demie l'emplissait d'une étrange exaltation. Elle mangeait quand elle en avait envie : à cinq heures, à huit, ou pas du tout.

Mieux encore, elle pouvait lire toute la nuit, dormir lorsqu'elle avait sommeil, se lever à huit heures et même à neuf sans être accusée de paresse.

Cette sensation de liberté ne durerait pas, malheureusement. Lorsqu'elle regagnerait Woodland, la routine reprendrait le dessus. Elle devrait se plier aux horaires de Paul et à son propre programme d'enseignement. Cependant, les limites étroites de sa vie antérieure ayant éclaté, elle était bien décidée à ne plus se laisser enfermer dans les structures immuables mises en place par son mari.

Elle avait quarante et un ans. Quarante-deux dans quelques mois. Compte tenu de la longévité de ses parents et de ses grands-parents, elle avait encore plus d'une quarantaine d'années devant elle. Cela voulait dire aussi que la moitié de sa vie s'était écoulée. Brandon aurait certainement vu les choses comme cela.

Elle avait encore quarante ans à vivre.

Elle préférait penser ainsi.

Un sourire étira ses lèvres glacées, tandis qu'elle reprenait le chemin du chalet. Quarante ans. Un tas d'aventures pouvaient lui arriver dans un laps de temps aussi long.

Elle commencerait dès aujourd'hui. Peut-être demanderait-elle à Peter de l'accompagner. Elle avait été décontenancée en comprenant qu'il n'était pas homosexuel, mais la première surprise passée, elle ne voyait pas pourquoi leur amitié ne continuerait pas. La situation ne semblait pas le déranger, lui, pourquoi alors en prendrait-elle ombrage maintenant ? Elle le considérait toujours comme un ami, le seul sans doute qu'elle ait jamais eu. Elle l'aimait bien, Peter. C'était un homme gentil, profond, prévenant… et il la faisait rire.

Si jamais un jour elle décidait de refaire sa vie, elle voudrait trouver un homme qui lui ressemble. Si jamais, se répéta-t-elle, histoire de se remettre les idées en place.

Il avait suffi qu'elle prenne la résolution de s'embarquer pour la seconde rive de sa vie pour qu'un millier d'idées nouvelles se bousculent dans sa tête. Elle avait hâte de commencer. Jusque-là, elle avait passé les hivers à établir la liste de tout ce qu'elle souhaiterait visiter l'été. Le mois d'août arrivait. En dépit de ses promesses, Brandon ne restait pas plus de deux ou trois jours par semaine au chalet ; quant aux enfants, ils étaient plus passionnés par leurs petits copains et leurs jeux sur la plage que par les circuits touristiques auxquels elle rêvait.

L'un des projets qu'elle regrettait le plus consistait à suivre les pas de John Steinbeck à travers la Californie. En traversant cet État, ce grand auteur avait pris des notes sur différents sites et paysages. Katherine estimait qu'il serait drôle et éducatif de les visiter.

Elle gravit les marches creusées dans la falaise, l'esprit obnubilé par le passé… À mi-chemin du chalet, elle remarqua la Taurus vert foncé sous le grand pin centenaire. La voiture de Brandon ?

Hier encore, son cœur aurait bondi dans sa poitrine. Elle aurait pressé le pas, anxieuse de l'accueillir. Aujourd'hui, elle ne savait plus ce qu'elle éprouvait vraiment.

Ce fut lui qui vint vers elle en poussant la porte du jardin.

— C'est un peu tôt pour aller nager, tu ne crois pas ?

Brandon incarnait le beau mâle. C'était l'homme le plus séduisant que Katherine connaissait. Même après vingt ans de mariage, il l'impressionnait, surtout quand il souriait. Les chaussettes de coton blanc, les pantalons de toile et les chemises à carreaux qu'il affectionnait faisaient sur lui le même effet qu'une tenue de soirée.

— Que fais-tu ici ?

Il la regarda, visiblement désarçonné par son air accusateur.

— Je suis venu te voir.

Elle serra la serviette de bain autour de ses épaules.

— Pourquoi ?

— Ai-je besoin d'une raison particulière ?

— Oui.

La voix blanche de Katherine étonna Brandon.

— Entrons, proposa-t-il d'un ton raisonnable. Tu es frigorifiée. Pourvu que les voisins ne nous voient pas dehors comme ça.

Si Brandon n'avait pas opté pour l'Église, il se serait probablement distingué en politique, tant son image le préoccupait.

Katherine chercha la clé épinglée à l'intérieur du soutien-gorge de son maillot de bain, puis ouvrit la porte.

— Qu'est-ce que tu fais ici ? répéta-t-elle, une fois parvenue dans la cuisine.

Brandon évita son regard.

— Il faut que nous parlions, Katherine.

Son assurance n'avait jamais manqué de la séduire. Une sorte d'incroyable pouvoir de persuasion émanait de ses gestes, de ses paroles. Les gens finissaient par se dire qu'il exprimait leurs pensées. Katherine avait mis des années à saisir les méandres de ce procédé. Elle en avait conclu que son mari était un manipulateur. Lorsqu'elle le lui avait fait remarquer, il avait répondu que la fin justifiait les moyens.

À présent, face à lui, elle le regardait droit dans les yeux.

— Tu m'as déjà tout dit.

— J'ai eu tort, Katherine.

Cette déclaration la désarma. Jamais Brandon n'avait admis qu'il se trompait, jamais il ne s'était remis en question. Elle tira sur la serviette qui glissait de ses épaules et attendit la suite.

— Tu me manques, poursuivit-il. Plus que je ne l'aurais imaginé. Ces derniers mois, j'ai vécu un calvaire.

Comme elle restait muette, il laissa échapper un soupir de frustration, puis posa les mains sur les bras nus de sa femme.

— Je ne tournerai pas autour du pot, Katherine. Je veux que tu reviennes à la maison. J'ai eu l'occasion de constater que notre séparation a été une erreur.

Trois jours plus tôt, elle serait tombée dans les pommes, éperdue de reconnaissance… Et une fois remise de ses émotions, elle se serait précipitée dans sa chambre pour faire ses valises.

— Je ne sais que dire, admit-elle enfin.

Il l'attira dans ses bras.

— Ne dis rien. Je vois la réponse dans tes yeux. Tu es aussi heureuse que moi de laisser nos querelles derrière nous.

— La seule chose qui se trouve derrière nous est un mariage brisé, Brandon.

Il ne parut pas l'entendre, à moins qu'il n'ait choisi de l'ignorer. Il l'embrassa, la bouche ouverte. Dans leur code intime, il réservait ce genre de baiser aux préludes amoureux.

Malgré une petite voix intérieure qui la mettait en garde, Katherine se sentit mollir. Des siècles s'étaient passés dans une solitude noire, sans un baiser, sans une caresse. Parfois, le manque d'affection la poussait au désespoir. Finalement, ils étaient encore légalement mariés. Et, après toutes ces années ensemble, quel mal y avait-il à s'aimer une dernière fois avant de se quitter?

— Oui… oui… murmura-t-elle, tandis qu'il promenait ses lèvres sur la peau sensible de son cou, derrière l'oreille.

Une longue flamme jaillit dans son bas-ventre. Il suffisait que Brandon la touche pour qu'elle soit prête à se donner. Mais était-ce vraiment lui qu'elle désirait cette fois-ci? La question venait du plus profond de son être. Elle décida de ne pas l'entendre.

Il la prit par la main et se dirigea vers la chambre.

— Non, dit-elle. Ici.

Il fronça les sourcils.

— Ici? Sur le canapé?

— Sur le canapé, par terre, ça m'est égal.

Cette suggestion aurait dû lui plaire. N'avait-il pas prétendu que leurs étreintes l'assommaient d'ennui?

— Pourquoi faire ça ici, alors que nous avons un lit confortable?

— Nous faisons toujours l'amour dans un lit, dit-elle en l'agrippant par le poignet. Je t'en prie, Brandon. Les enfants ne sont pas là, le téléphone ne sonnera pas, personne ne viendra frapper à la porte.

Il l'enveloppa d'un regard suspicieux.

— Qu'est-ce qui te prend ? Tu ne lis pas des romans pornos, au moins !

La flamme qui consumait Katherine baissa d'intensité ; cependant, l'habitude, le besoin, le manque l'emportèrent. Son estomac se tordit et elle esquissa un sourire implorant.

— D'accord. Sur le lit.

Le triomphe brilla dans les yeux de Brandon.

— Je t'attends dans la chambre.

— Tu… m'attends ? répéta-t-elle sans comprendre.

— Oui. Prends donc une douche ! Le sable et l'eau salée te montent à la tête !

Le froid la submergea, comme s'il l'avait rejetée dans l'océan. Il voulait faire l'amour dans une version aseptisée. Il avait autant envie d'elle que d'aller se faire pendre. Avec une lenteur calculée, elle lui lâcha la main.

— Qu'y a-t-il, Brandon ? Pourquoi es-tu venu aujourd'hui ?

— Je te l'ai dit. J'ai compris que j'avais tort…

— Arrête ton char ! Je ne prends plus des vessies pour des lanternes.

L'attitude du pasteur changea. Une lueur belliqueuse passa dans ses yeux. La colère et l'impatience l'assaillirent.

— Katherine, ça suffit ! Depuis quand mets-tu mes paroles en doute ?

Lui avait-il déjà parlé sur ce ton ?

Comme s'il s'était rendu compte qu'il dépassait les limites, il se radoucit.

— Excuse-moi. Je m'emporte. Mais, ces derniers temps, j'ai souffert de ton absence. La maison est un gourbi. Je n'ai pas eu un repas décent… Mes sermons en pâtissent…

— C'est normal. Je t'ai servi matin, midi et soir, pendant que tu t'occupais de tes chers paroissiens.

— Je ne comprends pas, murmura-t-il. Je croyais que tu voulais sauver notre mariage. J'étais sûr que notre union t'importait autant qu'à moi…

— À d'autres, Brandon. Tu n'as que faire de notre mariage. Si j'ai bonne mémoire, tu m'as flanquée dehors en précisant bien que tout était fini entre nous, que jamais au grand jamais nous ne nous remettrions ensemble.

— Me jeter le blâme ne nous mènera à rien, Katherine, dit-il d'une voix de professeur s'adressant à une élève.

Elle se remit à claquer des dents. Elle avait besoin de temps pour réfléchir.

— Bon, je vais prendre une douche, annonça-t-elle.

— Excellente idée. Tu te sentiras beaucoup mieux après.

Il se pencha et l'embrassa sur la joue tout en lui tapotant la main.

— Je vais faire du café, d'accord ?

— Combien de temps vas-tu rester ?

Visiblement, il s'attendait à tout sauf à cette question.

— Je suppose que cela dépend de toi, Katherine.

Auquel cas, songea-t-elle en empruntant le couloir, il repartirait sitôt qu'elle sortirait de la douche. Elle ralentit, un sourire triste sur le visage… Comment en était-elle arrivée là ? Comment pouvait-elle envisager une vie sans l'homme qu'elle avait considéré pendant vingt ans comme la seule et unique source de son bonheur ?

9

— Je t'en prie, Katherine ! s'écria Brandon. Ne me laisse pas tomber.

La colère flambait en lui, mais il s'efforça de la contrôler.

— Tu as besoin de temps, peut-être ? demanda-t-il. Je te comprends. Je comprends même pourquoi tu voudrais me voir souffrir à mon tour, avant de revenir à la maison. C'est de bonne guerre, Katherine, mais, crois-moi, j'ai déjà souffert énormément, si cela peut te consoler. Autant que toi sinon plus. Combien de nuits n'ai-je pas fermé l'œil ? Combien de fois n'ai-je pas prié pour que tout s'arrange entre nous ? Je pensais à toi constamment, je rêvais de te voir m'accueillir sur le perron, quand je rentrais…

Pour se donner une contenance, Katherine prit sa tasse de café. Ses mains tremblaient comme des feuilles, tant et si bien que la tasse lui échappa. Le liquide chaud éclaboussa ses chaussettes blanches, imprimant une traînée brunâtre en forme de cœur penché. Elle reposa la tasse.

— Je refuse de vivre dans le mensonge, Brandon.

Maintenant qu'elle lui avait arraché la véritable raison de son brusque repentir, elle n'avait plus aucun scrupule.

— Tu aurais dû prévoir qu'une fois divorcé, tu aurais peu de chances de devenir membre du conseil.

Elle prit une serviette en papier et se mit à frotter la tache de café.

— D'ailleurs, c'est grâce à moi que tu es devenu le prédicateur le plus célèbre de la région.

— Tu as raison, admit-il sans conviction. Je n'ai pas prêté attention à tout ce que tu as fait pour moi, Katherine. Mais le passé est le passé. À partir de maintenant, je serai plus indulgent, je te le promets.

Elle ne l'avait jamais vu dans un état aussi pitoyable. De nouveau, elle porta la tasse à ses lèvres et réussit à avaler une gorgée de café sans en renverser. Une petite victoire, songea-t-elle amèrement.

— Dis-moi maintenant, Brandon…

— Te dire quoi ?

— Tout ce que tu reconnais que j'ai fait pour toi.

Il parut désemparé.

— Tu n'es pas juste. Je ne vais pas me mettre à énumérer… laisse-moi le temps de recouvrer mes esprits…

Il lâcha un soupir résigné.

— Trève de plaisanteries ! Que te faut-il pour revenir ? Je ferai ce que tu veux.

— Pour combien de temps ?

— Ai-je jamais trahi mes promesses ?

— En dehors de celle selon laquelle nous devions vivre ensemble jusqu'à ce que la mort nous sépare ?

— Katherine, souviens-toi. Tu as prêté ce même serment devant Dieu. Ça veut dire que chacun des époux doit veiller à la pérennité du mariage. Et même s'il faut mettre ton mouchoir par-dessus ta fierté…

— Tu appelles cela de la fierté, Brandon ?

Pour la première fois, elle haussa le ton de sa voix :

— Comment oses-tu te servir de Dieu pour me manipuler ?

— D'accord, d'accord, j'admets que j'ai eu tort de te demander de partir. Vas-tu me le pardonner ?

Il porta sa tasse vide dans l'évier, puis se retourna pour dévisager sa femme.

— Moi aussi je t'ai pardonné tes fautes.

Les déclarations de son mari la confortaient chaque fois un peu plus dans son opinion : leurs anciens liens semblaient définitivement rompus.

— Formidable, Brandon ! Malgré toutes mes fautes, tu souhaites me donner une seconde chance. Mais mon pauvre chéri, je ne te laisserai pas te sacrifier… Avec ta grande bonté, ta grande vertu, tu mériterais une femme qui te rende vraiment heureux. Je sais que devenir membre du conseil te suffit pour le moment, mais dans deux ou trois ans, quand la nouveauté passera, nous nous retrouverons à la case départ. Je ne veux pas revivre ce drame.

Il hocha lentement la tête ; son visage était empreint de tristesse et de compassion.

— Je ne te savais pas aussi vindicative, Katherine. Si tu ne veux pas revenir pour moi, fais-le pour les enfants. Pense aux souffrances morales que Michael et Paul endurent, en sachant que leurs parents ne vivront plus jamais ensemble.

— Tu n'as pas pensé à eux, toi, quand tu m'as priée de débarrasser le plancher.

Brandon se rassit en soupirant.

— Mais qu'est-ce que tu gagnes à me punir ? Soyons clairs, Katherine. Si tu préfères divorcer, ce sont eux que tu puniras, pas moi.

Un tambourinement à la porte de devant empêcha Katherine de répondre. Peter ! Il ne pouvait pas tomber plus mal. Elle alla ouvrir. C'était bien lui.

— Oh, désolé, dit-il en voyant Brandon, debout au milieu du salon. Je ne savais pas que vous étiez ici… Je n'ai pas remarqué votre voiture.

Il se tut un instant, visiblement gêné.

— Je vais au village, reprit-il alors. Avez-vous besoin de quelque chose ?

— Non, merci, rétorqua Katherine rapidement. J'ai acheté tout ce dont j'avais besoin hier.

— Alors, je vous laisse.

Il salua Brandon d'un petit signe de la main.

— Ça m'a fait plaisir de vous revoir.

Le pasteur de Woodland conserva un silence de bon ton. Il attendit un instant après le départ de Peter, puis il regarda sa femme au fond des yeux.

— Katherine, dis-moi que je me trompe. Dis-moi que Peter et toi…

— Je ne sais pas de quoi tu parles !

Elle fit mine d'avancer ; il lui bloqua le passage.

— Je me demandais aussi… Ton insistance à venir seule au chalet… Est-ce à cause de Peter que tu as renoncé si facilement à notre mariage ?

— Cette question ne mérite aucune réponse.

— Je suis venu dans l'espoir de me réconcilier avec toi, Katherine. À présent, je vois que mes prières ne seront pas exaucées, dit-il en passant les doigts dans ses cheveux. Les voies du Seigneur sont impénétrables. Peut-être a-t-Il jugé que je ne suis pas digne de siéger au conseil.

Il attendit une réplique qui ne vint pas.

— J'espère, Katherine, pour notre bien à tous les deux, qu'Il détient notre sort entre Ses mains.

— Si les desseins du Seigneur prévoient que tu sois membre du conseil, Il te dévoilera un autre chemin.

Brandon se dirigea vers la porte.

— Je demanderai à Roger d'activer la procédure du divorce. Laisser pourrir la situation n'a plus de sens.

— Tu as pris Roger comme avocat ?

Roger et Martha, sa femme, étaient leurs plus vieux amis à Woodland. Katherine se sentait aussi proche d'eux que de sa famille.

— C'est logique, non ?

Naturellement, il ne songeait qu'à lui. Il ne s'était pas donné la peine d'examiner l'effet néfaste que son choix ne manquerait pas de produire sur Katherine. Lui, si attentif au moindre petit problème de ses paroissiens, semblait complètement insensible aux sentiments de son épouse.

— Je t'en prie, dit-elle. Roger est un ami commun. Trouve quelqu'un d'autre.

Il ouvrit la porte et sortit sur le perron.

— J'essaierai.

Elle le suivit dehors.

— Je suis navrée, Brandon. Nous sommes arrivés à un point de non-retour. Je ne peux pas revenir en arrière. Je ne serais pas heureuse.

Pendant deux jours, Katherine ne mit pas le nez dehors. Elle se contentait de prendre le journal dans la boîte aux lettres, puis rentrait vite chez elle. Le brouillard, revenu en force, émoussait toute tentation de sortie. Et quand, par hasard, le soleil perçait la brume, elle fermait les stores.

Il n'y avait jamais eu de divorce dans sa famille. Ses parents, son frère, sa sœur verraient le sien d'un mauvais œil. Ils savaient que Brandon et elle vivaient séparés mais considéraient qu'il s'agissait d'une crise. Une crise qui finirait par se dissiper. Eux aussi portaient Brandon aux nues. Ils étaient aussi fiers de lui que d'autres parents l'étaient de leurs enfants, quand ceux-ci obtenaient un diplôme de médecin ou d'avocat. Existait-il une vocation plus élevée que de se mettre au service du Tout-Puissant?

Katherine ne se perdit pas en conjectures sur la réaction de sa famille. Ils seraient tous probablement du côté de Brandon, surtout lorsqu'ils sauraient que ce dernier lui avait demandé de revenir et qu'elle avait refusé. Il y avait peu de chances qu'ils comprennent qu'entre-temps elle avait découvert sa véritable identité.

Il en serait de même avec les amis. Ils se rangeraient tous dans le camp de Brandon... Mais Katherine ne priait plus pour conserver leur amitié. Elle priait pour son bonheur.

Le troisième jour de son exil, elle fut accueillie au saut du lit par un soleil radieux. Résolue à mettre fin à sa longue introspection, elle passa dans la salle de bains. Elle avait touché le fond. Il était grand temps d'émerger à la vie.

Fraîchement douchée, drapée dans son peignoir jaune, une serviette éponge autour de la tête, elle prit la direction de la cuisine afin de préparer un bon café corsé. Un moteur de voiture retentit dans l'allée.

Elle alla à la fenêtre et écarta deux lamelles du store. Une joyeuse surprise l'assaillit. Elle courut ouvrir la porte.

— Salut, champion! cria-t-elle. Que me vaut l'honneur de ta visite?

Paul lui adressa un large sourire.

— Je suis viré, maman. Le vieux Fielding m'a surpris en train de voler du raisin. La main dans le sac !

Katherine serra son fils cadet dans ses bras plus longuement que de coutume.

— Menteur !

— Tu ne me crois pas capable d'être viré ? Ou de voler ?

— Ni l'un ni l'autre, chenapan !

Elle sourit aux deux meilleurs amis de Paul, qui jaillirent de la Mustang.

— J'espère que vous restez un moment.

Tom, une grande asperge, hocha la tête.

— Si ça ne vous dérange pas !

Elle ajusta la serviette sur ses cheveux.

— Mais non, au contraire. Avez-vous déjeuné ?

— On s'est arrêtés sur la route, expliqua Charlie, petit et trapu.

— C'était il y a deux heures, précisa Paul. Je meurs de faim. Qu'est-ce que la maison peut nous offrir ?

— Pancakes ou toasts grillés, déclara Katherine.

— Pancakes ! répondirent les trois garçons à l'unisson.

— Je vais m'habiller. Ensuite, je trouverai bien un moyen de vous remplir l'estomac. Entrez, cow-boys !

La matinée s'écoula en rires et en plaisanteries. Les pancakes disparurent, tout comme le lait, le miel, le sirop d'érable, les œufs et le bacon. Après le petit déjeuner, Tom et Charlie jetèrent Katherine et Paul dehors, afin de nettoyer la cuisine.

La brise marine soufflait doucement sur la terrasse. Confortablement installée sur le fauteuil en rotin, Katherine se tourna vers son fils.

— Maintenant avoue. Quel est le véritable but de ta visite ?

— J'ai pensé que tu aurais besoin de compagnie.

— Et pourquoi l'as-tu pensé ?

Le garçon haussa les épaules.

— À son retour, papa faisait une drôle de tête.

— Paul, nous en avons déjà discuté. Je ne veux pas que tu te sentes obligé de t'occuper de moi. Mes problèmes avec ton père ne concernent que lui et moi.

298

Elle réfléchit un instant.

— Je retire la dernière phrase. C'est ton problème aussi. Tu avais le droit d'espérer que tes parents se remettraient ensemble pour toujours, surtout maintenant que tu entames la terminale... Je sens que tu as besoin d'un père et d'une mère, mon chéri, mais...

— Maman, si tu continues, tu vas me faire pleurer.

Elle leva sur lui ses yeux pleins d'amour et de larmes.

— Je ne sais pas ce que j'ai fait pour te mériter.

— Rappelle-toi que je suis un garçon hors du commun, la prochaine fois que tu piqueras une colère parce que j'ai oublié de ranger ma chambre.

Avec un rire, elle s'essuya les yeux.

— Quels sont vos projets pour l'après-midi?

— Rien de spécial. Peut-être un tour sur la plage, histoire de repérer les jolies nanas.

— Les nanas? Quel langage!

Paul éclata de rire.

— Oh, maman, ne sois pas vieux jeu, quoi!

— Puisque vous n'avez pas de projet précis, voudriez-vous m'aider à faire une superbe glace? J'ai aperçu un mixer flambant neuf dans le placard de la cuisine.

— Bien sûr, répondit l'adolescent, visiblement pas très excité à la perspective de déguster une glace maison. Veux-tu que nous fassions les courses?

— Non. Tout compte fait, je m'en occupe.

Paul perdrait toute la matinée, si elle l'envoyait au supermarché, muni d'une liste longue comme le bras. Les placards étaient presque vides; elle devrait les remplir à ras bord si elle voulait nourrir trois adolescents pendant une semaine. Cela allait sérieusement écorner son budget de vacances, mais elle ne voyait pas de meilleur moyen de dépenser son argent.

10

Katherine ramassait des gueules-de-loup quand un petit garçon d'une huitaine d'années sortit du sentier ombragé d'eucalyptus.

— Salut! dit-elle avec un sourire.

— Salut.

Il semblait préoccupé. Elle s'accroupit, afin d'être à sa hauteur.

— Tu cherches quelqu'un?

— Mes amis habitaient ici. Mais ils sont morts.

Elle comprit mieux son air sérieux.

— Tu veux dire Joe et Maggie? demanda-t-elle gentiment.

— Oui. C'est vous qui vivez ici maintenant?

— Pendant un certain temps, oui.

— Vous avez des enfants?

— J'ai deux garçons, mais ils sont grands.

Elle ramassa un camélia rouge vif.

— Et toi? Où habites-tu?

— Avec ma sœur, nous sommes chez papa, dit-il en indiquant le cottage d'Andrew.

Katherine savait par Peter qu'Andrew avait loué son cottage à un écrivain, mais elle n'avait encore jamais vu ce dernier.

— Je vais faire de la glace cet après-midi, dit-elle. Tu voudras venir en manger avec ta sœur?

— Quelle sorte de glace?

— Fraise.

— Je préfère la pêche Melba. Maggie en faisait.

Le cœur de Katherine se serra.

— Je veux bien essayer, mais je crains qu'elle ne soit pas aussi bonne que celle de Maggie.

— Ce n'est pas grave. De toute façon, ma sœur et moi devons rentrer chez maman aujourd'hui. Salut !

Le petit garçon agita sa menotte, puis longea l'allée. Elle le regarda s'éloigner. Il avait les yeux graves des enfants du divorce. Encore heureux qu'elle ait préservé l'enfance de Michael et de Paul, se dit-elle.

Songeuse, elle s'approcha du parterre de marguerites géantes, qui proliféraient près de la grille. De là, elle aperçut Peter à sa boîte aux lettres. Elle lui fit signe de la main, et il répondit de même avant de s'approcher. Le cœur de Katherine exécuta un étrange petit bond.

Se redressant, elle épousseta son pantalon, hantée par une pensée incongrue : ses cheveux étaient mal coiffés et elle n'avait pas mis de fond de teint. Tout doucement, durant les deux dernières semaines, elle en était venue à comprendre qu'elle avait toujours associé Peter aux vacances. Il faisait partie du mois d'août ; tout comme les vagues et l'air salin.

— Je ne vous ai pas vue ces jours-ci, vous allez bien ?

— Paul est arrivé avec deux copains. J'étais très occupée.

Elle se sentait toute bizarre, quand elle était avec Peter. Il savait l'écouter. Il semblait concerné par tout ce qu'elle lui racontait, même par les choses les plus banales.

— Et avant cela ?

Elle hésita un instant. Leur amitié n'allait pas jusqu'aux confidences.

— Je ne me sentais pas très bien après le départ de Brandon.

— Vous auriez dû m'appeler. Mon bouillon de poulet est un véritable élixir de consolation.

— Je m'en souviendrai.

De crainte qu'il n'interprète mal ses paroles, elle se retint pour ne pas ajouter qu'elle adorait le bouillon au poulet et qu'elle dégusterait volontiers le sien.

— Où en est le portrait ? demanda-t-elle.

— Il est terminé.

C'était à la fois excitant et un peu effrayant. Les amateurs d'art allaient bientôt la découvrir à travers les yeux de Peter. Katherine posa son bouquet sur le muret.

— Je peux le voir ?

— Quand vous voulez.

— Tout de suite ?

— Venez.

— Je vais me changer et j'arrive.

Il lui tint la grille.

— Vous êtes très bien comme ça.

— Mais…

Il lui prit la main.

— Ce n'est pas un vernissage, Katherine. Ce sera juste vous et moi.

Devant le cottage, elle s'aperçut qu'ils se tenaient encore par la main.

— Je ne peux pas rester longtemps. J'ai promis un bon déjeuner aux garçons quand ils remonteront de la plage.

— Jusqu'à quand restent-ils ?

— Jusqu'à vendredi. Ils m'aideront à fermer la maison.

Peter se recula et regarda Katherine d'un air stupéfait.

— Pourquoi si tôt ? Il reste une semaine et demie avant le Labor Day.

Il avait haussé le ton. Katherine dégagea sa main.

— Je prépare ma rentrée. Je vais prendre quelques cours pédagogiques avant de commencer à enseigner à l'école élémentaire.

— Vous avez trouvé un poste d'institutrice ? Être femme de pasteur n'est plus un job à plein temps ?

Ou elle avouait la vérité, et ils passaient le peu de temps qui leur restait en discussions interminables, ou elle édulcorait, et elle profitait de ces quelques jours de liberté.

— J'ai décidé d'étendre mes activités, répondit-elle simplement.

— Vous savez que Julia mettra bientôt le chalet en vente ?

Il se montrait mesquin mais c'était la seule façon d'inciter Katherine à prolonger un séjour qui risquait d'être le dernier. Il avait pensé qu'ils auraient plus de temps. Et il comptait là-dessus. Il n'était pas prêt à la voir sortir définitivement de sa vie.

— Non, mais ça ne m'étonne pas.

— Et alors ? Comment ferez-vous pour revenir ? L'été prochain, je veux dire.

— Oh, je ne prendrai probablement pas de vacances. Déjà, cette année, j'ai eu du mal à venir... toute seule. Chaque chose a une fin, Peter.

— Et si je vous disais que je suis sur le point de l'acheter ?

— Pourquoi ? Vous avez déjà un...

— C'est un bon investissement. Le mois d'août vous sera alors toujours réservé. Au même prix, naturellement.

— C'est idiot ! Vous pourriez obtenir le double, voire le triple du loyer que nous payons.

Attention ! le prévint la voix de sa conscience. S'il se trahissait, elle saurait la raison pour laquelle il voulait acheter le chalet, et, pour le coup, elle n'y remettrait plus les pieds. Elle était même capable de boucler ses bagages sur-le-champ et de partir en courant.

— Je préfère les locataires qui prennent soin des lieux aux inconnus qui paient davantage et qui laissent une épave.

Ils étaient arrivés devant sa porte.

— J'ai tellement envie de dire oui, murmura-t-elle.

— Dites-moi au moins que vous y réfléchirez.

Il ouvrit la porte et s'effaça pour la laisser entrer. Katherine lui sourit.

— D'accord. Je vous promets d'y réfléchir cet hiver, pendant que je déambulerai sur le campus.

Peter la suivit à l'intérieur.

— Que puis-je vous offrir ? Soda ? Thé glacé ?

— Peter, je vous l'ai dit. Je ne peux pas rester longtemps.

Une étrange nervosité gagnait Peter, qui craignait de montrer le portrait à son modèle. Voilà des années que l'approbation des autres ne le préoccupait plus. Il peignait pour son plaisir. Mais, aujourd'hui, il avait peur. Peur du jugement de Katherine.

— Il est là.

Elle se dirigea vers l'atelier. Ayant recouvré tant bien que mal ses esprits, Peter lui emboîta le pas.

Katherine aperçut la peinture à partir de la porte. Au lieu d'entrer, elle demeura sur place, sans un mot. Enfin, comme attirée par un fil invisible, elle avança jusqu'au milieu de la pièce, puis s'arrêta net devant le chevalet.

— C'est ainsi que vous me voyez? murmura-t-elle.

Il ne pouvait qu'avouer la vérité.

— Oui.

— Mais vous m'avez faite si belle…

— Vous êtes belle.

Elle secoua la tête.

— Pas autant.

— Aimez-vous ce portrait? demanda-t-il, la sondant des yeux.

— Il me fait peur… J'ignore pourquoi… Comment saviez-vous à quoi je pensais? interrogea-t-elle en se rapprochant du tableau.

— J'ai peint ce que j'ai vu.

Soudain elle le scruta.

— Et comment voyez-vous ce que personne d'autre ne peut voir?

— Que voulez-vous savoir exactement?

— Je semble si seule… dit-elle, de nouveau tournée vers le tableau. J'ai l'air de regarder quelque chose… et d'en avoir envie. Mais quoi, Peter?

Il s'aperçut soudain qu'il l'avait imaginée en train de le regarder, lui.

— À vous de me le dire.

— Je ne sais pas.

Il aurait payé cher pour la tirer de sa confusion. Son intuition l'avertissait: il y avait des mots qu'elle avait besoin d'entendre, mais lesquels? Il n'en avait pas la moindre idée.

— Que voulez-vous que je fasse de ce tableau?

— Je ne sais pas.

— Il est peint sur du papier. Il est facile de le déchirer.

— Oh, non ! Ne faites pas ça, s'écria-t-elle, la main sur le bras de Peter. Promettez-moi de ne pas le détruire, implora-t-elle, les larmes aux yeux.

— Je ne voulais pas vous faire de mal, Katherine, dit-il, stupéfait.

— Vous n'y êtes pour rien. C'est moi...

Une larme glissa sur sa joue : elle l'essuya prestement du revers de la main.

— Il faut que je parte.

— Que puis-je faire ?

— Rien.

Il la retint encore un instant.

— Il doit bien y avoir quelque chose...

— C'est mon problème. Je trouverai une solution.

— Laissez-moi vous aider.

Elle lui toucha la joue.

— J'aime ce portrait, dit-elle avec un sourire forcé. J'espère qu'il vous rapportera beaucoup d'argent.

— Il n'est pas à vendre. Le tableau est à moi, Katherine. À vous.

— Je ne... vous ne...

Une fois de plus, elle fixa le visage peint, illuminé par les derniers rayons du couchant. Après un long, un interminable instant, elle réussit à articuler :

— Gardez-le pour moi.

Leurs yeux se rencontrèrent dans une sorte de communion inattendue. Un cadeau. Une promesse. Une cage dorée dans laquelle Peter résiderait désormais.

— Oui, dit-il. Je le garderai. Aussi longtemps que vous le souhaiterez.

Le reste de la semaine passa à une vitesse hallucinante. Paul et ses copains accaparèrent toutes les journées de Katherine. Les trois garçons l'emmenaient partout. Elle fit avec eux le tour de la promenade, goûta à la barbe à papa, dévora des hot dogs brûlants et des pommes caramélisées.

Vendredi arriva trop vite. Dégagé du brouillard, l'océan brillait comme un miroir. Une brise légère tempérait la chaleur, et sur le ciel d'un bleu irréel voguaient des cerfs-volants multicolores. Les trois garçons devaient profiter de cette merveilleuse journée, qui était aussi leur dernière. Katherine insista pour qu'ils aillent nager pendant qu'elle bouclait les valises. Après le déjeuner, ils défirent les lits, nettoyèrent les salles de bains, puis chargèrent les bagages dans le coffre de la voiture.

Paul offrit gentiment à sa mère de faire avec elle le chemin du retour. Elle refusa, sous prétexte qu'elle adorait conduire seule, dans le calme. Les garçons levèrent l'ancre à quatre heures de l'après-midi, car ils étaient invités à une fête le soir même. Debout dans l'allée, elle les regarda s'en aller, puis regagna le chalet.

Elle nettoya méthodiquement chaque pièce, épousseta, passa l'aspirateur. Ses pensées s'envolaient dans tous les sens. Mais inéluctablement, elles revenaient vers Peter. Pendant des jours, elle l'avait cherché des yeux chaque fois qu'elle était sortie. En vain. On eût dit qu'il l'évitait ; ils ne s'étaient pas revus depuis qu'il lui avait montré le portrait.

Le crépuscule lança ses lueurs rouges, tandis qu'elle passait la serpillière dans la cuisine. Après avoir jeté un dernier coup d'œil dans la maison, elle sortit sur la terrasse, d'où elle admira le ciel embrasé. Elle descendit dans le jardin, et son regard chercha la voiture de Peter.

Il était chez lui.

De crainte qu'il ne s'en aille entre-temps, elle ne prit pas le soin d'aller se doucher. Les cheveux épinglés sur le sommet de sa tête, vêtue d'un vieux tee-shirt sur un jean élimé, elle alla frapper à sa porte.

Il ouvrit presque aussitôt, comme s'il attendait de l'autre côté du battant.

— Bonsoir, dit-elle, soudain consciente qu'elle avait l'air d'une souillon.

— Je vous croyais déjà sur la route.

— Les garçons sont partis à quatre heures.

— Voulez-vous entrer ?

— Je ne suis pas là pour vous rendre visite.

— Alors pourquoi venez-vous ? demanda-t-il, après un silence.

Elle avait minutieusement répété la réponse pendant qu'elle faisait le ménage, mais voilà qu'elle avait tout oublié. Spontanément, elle s'approcha du peintre.

— À propos du portrait… je l'aime beaucoup, Peter. Il est important que vous le sachiez.

— Mais vous n'en voulez toujours pas.

Elle avait une bonne centaine de raisons de ne pas emporter le tableau, mais une seule comptait. Il dévoilait une facette de sa personnalité, une partie secrète de son âme que personne d'autre ne devait jamais connaître.

— Un jour peut-être… Pas maintenant.

— Merci d'être passée.

— Il faut que je parte. La route est longue.

Il la regarda sortir, sans un mot.

Chaque pas lui coûtait. Le chemin jusqu'au chalet lui parut incroyablement long. Elle entra, vérifia la fermeture des portes et des fenêtres. Bientôt, l'ultime rayon du couchant disparut dans la mer, et une lumière grise nimba la terrasse. Sa raison lui commandait de s'en aller, mais ses sentiments rendaient ce départ impossible. Ayant déjà tout perdu, elle avait du mal à renoncer à ses dernières illusions.

Le froid la décida enfin à bouger. Résistant à la tentation de passer une nouvelle fois la maison en revue, elle traversa le salon, sortit dans le jardin et donna un tour de clé dans la serrure.

Sa voiture dépassa lentement le cottage de Peter. Elle espérait qu'il serait sur le seuil ou à la fenêtre, afin de lui adresser une dernière salutation de la main… Elle ne l'aperçut nulle part. Une sensation de perte l'envahit. Elle avait prévu de se sentir solitaire, mais la puissance de la sensation la surprit. La certitude d'être passée à côté de quelque chose d'important vint soudain la hanter.

Dix minutes plus tard, elle roulait sur l'autoroute. Le panneau de signalisation indiquait la sortie vers Santa

Cruz. Encore deux kilomètres et elle s'engagerait sur la nationale 17, tournant le dos à l'océan.

Soudain, elle fit demi-tour. Elle ignorait pourquoi, mais elle devait coûte que coûte revoir Peter une dernière fois. Son pied écrasa l'accélérateur, la voiture fila tout droit dans l'obscurité.

Il ne répondit pas, quand elle frappa à sa porte. Elle recommença et attendit. Toujours pas de réponse.

Bizarrement, elle sut où elle devait le chercher. Elle se dirigea vers la falaise. Du haut de l'escalier, elle scruta la plage. Une lune de trois quarts se reflétait dans l'eau et, sur cet écran luminescent, se découpait une silhouette solitaire.

Peter leva les yeux. Quelqu'un venait dans sa direction, foulant le sable fin. Cela ne pouvait pas être Katherine. Elle ne serait pas revenue, non! Et pourtant, elle était maintenant si près qu'il pouvait la toucher.

Elle le regarda au fond des yeux avec intensité.

— Parlez-moi du portrait, dit-elle. Racontez-moi ce que vous y avez mis. Je veux l'entendre de votre bouche.

Le cœur de Peter cessa de battre, puis rebondit contre sa cage thoracique.

— Que voulez-vous savoir?

Les mots se dérobaient, mais elle parvint à reprendre:

— Vous m'avez peinte en train de regarder quelque chose avec une envie extraordinaire. De quoi s'agit-il, Peter?

— De moi, répondit-il.

Ce fut comme s'il avait enfin ouvert la porte d'une prison. Il se sentit libéré du secret qui, depuis tant d'années, lui pesait si lourdement sur le cœur. Il n'y avait plus moyen de faire marche arrière et tant pis si leur vieille amitié en prenait un coup fatal.

— Depuis quand… éprouvez-vous ces sentiments à mon égard? demanda-t-elle doucement.

Il lui adressa un coup d'œil malicieux.

— Je crois bien que tout a commencé la première fois que nous nous sommes rencontrés.

— Je l'ignorais. Je n'ai jamais rien soupçonné. Mais j'aurais dû! dit-elle, les sourcils froncés. Au fond, si vous n'aviez pas été là, je crois que j'aurais cessé de venir ici depuis très longtemps.

Il hocha la tête. Il ne savait pas comment il devait se sentir. Sa confession ne lui avait pas ouvert de portes, pas même une petite fenêtre. Cet aveu ne lui donnait aucun droit, ne résolvait aucun problème.

— C'est drôle comment les choses évoluent, murmura-t-il. Vous avez maintenant une bonne raison de ne plus remettre les pieds ici.

Elle se cantonna dans un très long silence, avant finalement de passer aux aveux.

— Brandon et moi, nous nous sommes quittés. Nous allons divorcer.

Il la regarda, stupéfait.

— Je vais voir un avocat dès que je rentre à Woodland, reprit-elle.

— Est-ce la raison pour laquelle vous êtes revenue? interrogea-t-il prudemment. Pour me le dire?

— Oui.

— Pourquoi maintenant?

— Je n'en sais rien. J'avais probablement peur que la vérité ne brise notre amitié.

— Et maintenant? demanda-t-il après une hésitation.

— Maintenant, je suis sûre que nous serons toujours amis. Quoi qu'il arrive.

Peter prit le visage de Katherine entre ses paumes. Lentement, il l'attira vers lui. Leurs lèvres s'unirent en un baiser incertain. Le second fut plus sûr. Leurs langues, leurs souffles se mêlèrent. Un profond soupir échappa à Katherine quand Peter la souleva dans ses bras, il la fit tournoyer en un cercle lent, une danse sensuelle.

Lorsqu'il la remit sur ses pieds, elle renversa la tête, afin de mieux le scruter.

— Tout arrive si vite! J'ai besoin de temps, Peter.

Il avait l'habitude de la laisser partir mais, à présent, cela exigeait un effort plus pénible.

— Je comprends, articula-t-il laborieusement.

Elle posa la tête sur son épaule.

— Je t'en prie, chuchota-t-elle. Attends-moi.

Il l'enlaça… Les vagues s'écrasaient violemment contre les rochers, un vent humide s'était levé.

— Je t'attendrai, promit-il. Je serai toujours là pour toi.

CINQUIÈME PARTIE

Septembre

1

Roulée en boule sur le manuscrit d'Eric, Josi émettait un ronronnement de bien-être. Soudain elle se leva, s'étirant de tout son long, et avec sa queue touffue fit tomber un stylo par terre. Eric se pencha pour le ramasser et le remit à sa place. Il gratta le menton de Josi, dont le ronronnement monta d'une octave. Ce matin, il n'avait rien fait de mieux, pensa-t-il, dépité.

Le livre prenait une tournure catastrophique. Depuis son retour de New York, il manquait d'inspiration. Les mots lui paraissaient creux ; il n'avait pas réussi à aligner trois phrases satisfaisantes. C'était comme si deux millions d'acompte avaient provoqué la fameuse crampe de l'écrivain. Avant la signature du contrat, il écrivait pour lui-même. Si un paragraphe ne lui plaisait pas, il n'hésitait pas à le supprimer. Désormais, il écrivait pour un éditeur, en s'efforçant de deviner ce qui avait pu le séduire dans la première partie du roman.

Il se renversa dans son fauteuil. Josi passa une patte derrière chaque oreille et, cette fois-ci, sa queue envoya valser la lettre de Charlie Stephens, reçue le matin même. Le champion olympique remerciait Eric de l'avoir mis en contact avec Chris Sadler. Le garçon faisait maintenant partie de l'équipe des lutteurs du Centre d'athlétisme de Los Angeles que Charlie dirigeait. Il venait s'exercer dès que ses obligations vis-à-vis du studio le lui permettaient... Charlie terminait sa missive par un aparté : il avait rencontré Margaret, la mère de Chris... et, depuis quelque temps, ils sortaient souvent ensemble.

Comme toujours quand Eric laissait vagabonder son esprit, ses pensées allèrent vers Julia. Elle n'avait donné aucune nouvelle depuis qu'il avait récupéré Josi, un mois auparavant. Il avait souhaité l'appeler à plusieurs reprises, mais s'était toujours ravisé. La balle était dans son camp ; il le lui avait dit. Il ignorait cependant que ce serait aussi long. L'attente le mettait au supplice.

Il avait appris par Peter qu'elle se portait bien. Elle n'avait pas changé d'avis au sujet du chalet et, d'ailleurs, le peintre voulait l'acheter. Il comptait le louer l'été à différentes familles, du moins pendant un certain temps. La semaine précédente, la locataire du mois d'août était revenue pendant quelques jours. Eric l'avait rencontrée en compagnie de Peter sur la plage.

Abandonnant son ordinateur, il se rendit dans la cuisine où il se servit sa cinquième tasse de café de la matinée. Le breuvage avait un goût amer et brûlé. Eric vida la tasse dans l'évier, prit un soda dans le réfrigérateur, revint dans la salle de séjour en roulant des épaules pour soulager ses trapèzes endoloris, puis se rassit.

Une demi-heure plus tard, il fixait toujours le curseur clignotant en haut d'une page vide, quand Josi dressa une oreille. La chatte resta un instant immobile, la patte en l'air, aux aguets, puis ouvrit les yeux et releva la tête.

Eric attendit. Comme d'habitude, rien ne se produisit.

Lorsque Josi se mit en position assise, il se leva. Au fil des jours, la télépathie entre Josi et la camionnette de livraison du supermarché n'avait cessé de croître. Aussi fallut-il plusieurs secondes au cerveau d'Eric pour enregistrer que la personne sur son perron n'était pas le livreur, mais Julia. Elle portait une robe bleu marine et jaune, à fines bretelles. Ses cheveux flottaient librement sur ses épaules ; ils étaient un peu ébouriffés, comme si elle avait roulé avec la vitre baissée.

Elle n'était pas la Julia Huntington qu'il avait connue, mais il trouva les changements excitants. Et prometteurs.

— Toi ? s'enquit-il.

— Je m'étais imaginé toutes les façons possibles d'être accueillie, sauf celle-ci.

— Alors, je recommence.

Les bras croisés sur la poitrine, il s'appuya contre le chambranle, s'efforçant de masquer ses sentiments. Il enveloppa Julia d'un regard admiratif.

— Tu as l'air… incroyable !

Elle lui sourit, les yeux pétillants.

— Merci. Je me sens assez incroyable, en effet.

— Dois-je en conclure que tu as parcouru tous ces kilomètres uniquement pour me rendre visite ?

— J'espère que cela ne te pose pas de problème.

Il sourit à son tour.

— Je me demande seulement pourquoi tu as mis aussi longtemps.

— J'avais des choses à régler. Si tu me demandes lesquelles, je te raconterai.

Elle passa devant lui et entra dans le cottage. Une fragrance fleurie chatouilla agréablement les narines d'Eric. S'était-elle parfumée pour lui ?

— Comment va ta muse ? fit Julia en grattant affectueusement la tête de Josi.

— Si cette bête est ma muse, il est temps que j'en change.

Il n'en croyait pas ses yeux. Rien ne l'avait préparé à l'arrivée inopinée de Julia. La matinée avait été tout à fait ordinaire. Le soleil n'était pas plus brillant que d'habitude, et l'océan avait toujours le même bleu.

Julia le fixa.

— Le roman n'avance pas ?

— Plus tard. Toi d'abord.

— Je ne sais pas par où commencer.

Il leva la main.

— Attends. Ne commence pas…

Il lui prit les épaules pour la ramener vers lui, étudia un instant son petit visage, ses immenses yeux bleus où dansait allègrement une étincelle espiègle, ses lèvres entrouvertes. En se penchant, il lui donna un chaste baiser ; mais cela ne lui suffit pas. Alors il l'embrassa, encore et encore.

Elle l'enlaça par la taille en soupirant.

— Oh là là ! Exactement comme dans mon souvenir.

— Je t'aime, Julia.

La déclaration avait jailli spontanément. Inutile de la retirer, de la transformer.

— Je sais qu'il est trop tôt, se rattrapa-t-il, je sais aussi que nous ne nous connaissons pas assez, et que les apparences sont contre moi. Mais rien cependant ne pourra changer mes sentiments…

— Tu as raison, Eric. Il est trop tôt; nous avons un tas de détails à apprendre l'un sur l'autre. Mais je crois que je t'aime aussi… Non, je ne crois pas. J'en suis sûre.

Elle le scruta, la tête penchée sur le côté.

— Que dirais-tu si j'emménageais pendant deux ou trois mois à côté? Cela nous aiderait à faire connaissance, non?

— Tu ne vends plus le chalet à Peter?

— Il m'a lâchée en pleine transaction. Il n'en veut plus, figure-toi. Katherine a accepté de vivre chez lui. Alors…

— Et le travail?

— Le mien? dit-elle innocemment.

— Oui, Julia. Le tien.

— C'est arrangé. J'ai mis la compagnie en vente il y a trois semaines. Je l'ai vendue au plus offrant deux jours plus tard. Il me reste une tonne de paperasses à remplir, mais le plus gros est fait.

Il la regarda, stupéfait.

— Julia, je ne comprends pas. Toi qui t'inquiétais tant du sort des employés si jamais tu vendais… Qu'est-ce qui t'a poussée à changer d'avis?

— J'ai fait en sorte que chacun soit à l'abri du besoin, qu'il ait perdu son emploi ou non.

— Et comment?

Un large sourire illumina les traits fins de la jeune femme.

— Je leur ai cédé la moitié de la somme que j'ai touchée. À eux de voir s'ils veulent continuer à travailler pour les nouveaux patrons, s'établir à leur compte ou partir en préretraite. Ils jouissent à peu près de la même liberté que moi.

Eric était bouche bée.

316

— Incroyable ! s'exclama-t-il.

Elle eut un rire.

— C'était pourtant simple. Je ne sais pas pourquoi je n'y ai pas pensé plus tôt.

— As-tu conscience d'avoir démantelé l'empire de Ken ? interrogea Eric, se faisant malgré lui l'avocat du diable.

— Tu ne vas pas t'y mettre, toi aussi ! Tu n'as jamais vu Ken et tu en parles avec la même déférence que tous les autres. Comme s'il était encore en vie. Comme si ma culpabilité n'était pas assez lourde…

— Pardon, Julia ! Je n'avais pas l'intention de te blesser. Je sais comme la perte de Ken t'a coûté… J'ai été maladroit, certes… Je voulais en fait te demander si tu avais vaincu tes vieux démons.

Les beaux yeux bleus se fixèrent sur le col de chemise d'Eric.

— Une partie de moi aimera toujours Ken… Peux-tu le comprendre ? Et vivre avec cette idée ?

— L'amour ne fonctionne pas avec un interrupteur, Julia. On ne peut pas l'allumer et l'éteindre. Tu n'oublieras jamais Ken, je le sais. Et ce n'est que justice.

— Ce n'est pas tout, murmura-t-elle.

Elle parut hésiter, puis prit une profonde inspiration, comme un nageur avant de se jeter à l'eau.

— Te rends-tu vraiment compte de la réaction de mes relations, de tous ceux qui ont connu Ken ?

— Si l'hostilité de Peter à mon endroit, depuis que toi et moi sommes devenus amis, est un indice, oui, je me rends parfaitement compte.

Elle lui adressa un sourire crispé.

— Justement, Peter commence à se montrer plus positif. La dernière fois que je l'ai vu, il a déclaré qu'il ne considérait pas comme impossible que je refasse ma vie avec un homme capable de me rendre heureuse.

— Très gentil de sa part !

— Son attitude témoigne précisément de ce que tu auras à affronter, Eric. Tu vas devenir la cible des anciens amis de Ken… Tous pensent que personne ne lui arrive à la cheville. Ils me pardonneront peut-être d'avoir été victime de ma solitude mais t'en voudront éternellement d'avoir osé te comparer à Ken.

Elle ne cherchait pas à le rassurer. Cela aurait été trop facile. Julia avait toujours prôné la vérité. Les amis de Ken constituaient un sérieux obstacle. Elle n'envisageait pas, cependant, de couper les ponts, car ils avaient été présents pendant la période la plus douloureuse de son existence.

— Je ferai face, Julia. Les gens qui t'aiment, moi y compris, veulent ton bonheur. Quand tes amis s'apercevront que tu es heureuse, ils m'accepteront.

— Je t'aime, dit-elle d'une voix fervente, la paume sur la joue d'Eric. Mon Dieu, je croyais que plus jamais je ne prononcerais ces mots.

— Quand comptes-tu emménager au chalet ?

— Mes bagages sont dans la voiture.

Eric eut le souffle coupé par la confiance que lui témoignait Julia. Il ne put s'empêcher de l'admirer. Elle avait quitté la seule vie qu'elle connaissait, son cocon protecteur, pour tenter sa chance avec lui.

— Oh, Julia, murmura-t-il. Je te promets que tu n'auras pas à revenir sur ta décision.

Elle le regarda longuement.

— Je suis là parce que je veux t'aimer. Pas parce que j'en ai besoin, tu comprends ?

— Oui. Tu m'aimes avec ton esprit et avec ton cœur.

Elle se blottit dans ses bras.

— Bien dit, monsieur l'écrivain ! Et maintenant que nous avons mis les choses au point, nous devrions fêter ça.

— En faisant quoi ? L'amour ?

— Cela aussi, dit-elle en souriant.

— Mais avant ?

— L'amour n'attend pas, murmura-t-elle d'une voix enrouée.

Cette fois-ci, leur étreinte fut tendre. Lentement, Eric explora le corps de Julia, comme pour mémoriser la douceur de sa peau, la souplesse de ses membres.

Lorsqu'il la pénétra, sa chaleur moite l'enveloppa. Elle souleva les hanches afin de mieux l'accueillir, et à chaque poussée, il se plongea plus loin. Les jambes de la jeune femme lui enlacèrent la taille, et il l'entendit crier son nom lorsque l'extase les submergea.

Plus tard, la main sur le ventre de Julia, qui avait niché sa tête au creux de son cou, il demanda :

— Sans vouloir te donner l'impression que nous avons fini de célébrer nos retrouvailles... à quoi d'autre as-tu pensé ?

— Je voudrais rencontrer Jason, Susie... et Shelly. J'espère qu'elle voudra bien nous envoyer les enfants pendant deux ou trois semaines.

Une minute plus tôt, il aurait juré que rien ne pourrait le rendre plus heureux. Il se trompait. Il venait de toucher le summum du bonheur.

— Je suis sûr que Shelly n'y verra aucun inconvénient, à condition que Jason soit en vacances.

— Crois-tu qu'ils vont m'aimer ?

Eric réfléchit un instant. Cette question ne méritait pas non plus une réponse facile.

— Susie n'aura pas de mal. Elle sympathise avec tout le monde et tout le monde l'adore. En revanche, Jason accorde difficilement sa confiance. Il a déjà perdu tellement de gens ! Mais il finira par t'aimer, j'en suis sûr. Et lorsque cela arrivera, vous serez un sacré tandem, tous les deux.

Julia se hissa sur un coude.

— Je veux que nous ayons des enfants, Eric. J'en ai assez des maisons vides.

— Est-ce ce projet que tu souhaites mettre à exécution tout de suite ?

Un rire échappa à Julia.

— Ça peut attendre. Mais pas longtemps.

Il l'attira à lui et l'embrassa tendrement. Il ignorait encore combien de romans il écrirait, mais aucun n'aurait une fin aussi heureuse.

D'ailleurs leur histoire n'était pas finie. Elle venait tout juste de commencer.

6652

Composition Chesteroc International Graphics
Achevé d'imprimer en France (Manchecourt)
par Maury-Eurolivres
le 4 juin 2003.
Dépôt légal juin 2003. ISBN 2-290-33080-9

Éditions J'ai lu
84, rue de Grenelle, 75007 Paris
Diffusion France et étranger : Flammarion